U.S. Cultural History

AMERICAN GOVERNMENT AND HISTORY INFORMATION GUIDE SERIES

Series Editor: Harold Shill, Chief Circulation Librarian, Adjunct Assistant Professor of Political Science, West Virginia University, Morgantown

Also in this series:

AMERICAN EDUCATIONAL HISTORY—*Edited by Timothy Walsh and Michael W. Sedlak**

U.S. RELIGION AND CHURCH HISTORY—*Edited by Garth Rosell**

IMMIGRATION AND ETHNICITY—*Edited by John D. Buenker and Nicholas C. Burckel*

PROGRESSIVE REFORM—*Edited by John D. Buenker and Nicholas C. Burckel**

PUBLIC ADMINISTRATION—*Edited by John E. Rouse, Jr.**

PUBLIC POLICY—*Edited by William J. Murin, Gerald Michael Greenfield, and John D. Buenker**

SOCIAL HISTORY OF THE UNITED STATES—*Edited by Donald F. Tingley*

U.S. CONSTITUTION—*Edited by Earlean McCarrick**

U.S. FOREIGN RELATIONS—*Edited by Elmer Plischke**

U.S. POLITICS AND ELECTIONS—*Edited by David J. Maurer*

U.S. WARS AND MILITARY HISTORY—*Edited by Jack Lane**

URBAN HISTORY AND URBANIZATION—*Edited by John D. Buenker, Gerald Michael Greenfield, and William J. Murin**

WOMEN AND FEMINISM IN AMERICAN HISTORY—*Edited by Donald F. Tingley and Elizabeth Tingley**

*in preparation

The above series is part of the
GALE INFORMATION GUIDE LIBRARY

The Library consists of a number of separate series of guides covering major areas in the social sciences, humanities, and current affairs.

General Editor: Paul Wasserman, Professor and former Dean, School of Library and Information Services, University of Maryland

Managing Editor: Denise Allard Adzigian, Gale Research Company

U.S. Cultural History

A GUIDE TO INFORMATION SOURCES

Volume 5 in the American Government and History Information Guide Series

Philip I. Mitterling

Professor of History and Social Science
and
Chairman of the American Studies Committee
University of Colorado
Boulder

Gale Research Company
Book Tower, Detroit, Michigan 48226

3-12-81   28.00

23963

Library of Congress Cataloging in Publication Data

Mitterling, Philip I
   U. S. cultural history.

   (American Government and history information guide
series ; v. 5) (Gale information guide library)
   Includes indexes.
   1. United States—Civilization—Bibliography.
2. United States—Intellectual life—Bibliography.
I. Title. II. Series.
Z1361.C6M57 [E169.1]   016.973   79-24061
ISBN 0-8103-1369-3

To Doris

VITA

Philip I. Mitterling is professor of history and social science, and chairman of the American Studies Committee at the University of Colorado. He received his B.A. from Muhlenberg College, and his M.A. and Ph.D. degrees from the University of Illinois (Urbana-Champaign). Before joining the faculty of the University of Colorado, he taught at the University of Pittsburgh, Hobart College, and Thiel College, and served as director of the Inter-University Committee on the Superior Student, a national center for honors programs and experimentation in higher education.

Professor Mitterling is the author of AMERICA IN THE ANTARCTIC TO 1840 (University of Illinois Press, 1959) and a number of articles and reviews; co-author of the UNIVERSITY OF COLORADO, 1876-1976 (Harcourt Brace Jovanovich, 1976); and editor of TALENTED WOMEN IN THE AMERICAN COLLEGE (U.S. Office of Education, 1964).

CONTENTS

Contents

PREFACE

In this first annotated guide to American cultural history, it has been my purpose to be inclusive rather than exclusive in order to make this work as useful as possible to scholars, teachers, librarians, college and university students, and other users. Cultural history has always been a broad field. It has included intellectual history and until very recently social history which now is attempting to achieve an identity with distinctive content and several methodologies. Sociocultural topics are included in this guide, but generally I have tried to avoid impinging on the social field.

This coverage of American cultural history focuses on studies produced since 1950, but significant works published earlier also are covered. Chapter headings indicate the obvious subjects which have been arranged chronologically. In the section on general works, I have produced references to works concerning journalism, publishing, philosophical thought, ideas on the country versus the city, women's life-styles and thought concerning them, and other matters. The chapter covering economic, political, and social thought encompasses systematic expositions of ideas as well as attitudes and beliefs concerning racism, nationalism, reform, slavery, foreign relations, and other subjects. Historiography is an important field in intellectual history, and this section should prove useful to librarians and others who are searching for the significant historical interpretations of American epochs and events.

It is important to mention that I have not covered the published papers of such paragons of cultural history as Benjamin Franklin, Thomas Jefferson, Ralph Waldo Emerson, and others because they would require bibliographies in themselves. The published writings of lesser figures have been included, however.

I wish to express appreciation to librarians at the University of Colorado, Denver University, and the Iliff School of Theology (Denver) for facilitating my work. Special thanks are due to Mary Kay, of the University of Colorado, for her assistance. Harold B. Shill, series editor, provided timely editorial suggestions and expedited the preparation of the manuscript.

Philip I. Mitterling
Boulder, Colorado

Chapter 1
REFERENCE MATERIALS

LIBRARY OF CONGRESS AND NATIONAL UNION CATALOGS

U.S. Library of Congress. A CATALOG OF BOOKS REPRESENTED BY LIBRARY OF CONGRESS PRINTED CARDS ISSUED TO JULY 31, 1942. 167 vols. Ann Arbor, Mich.: Edwards, 1942-46.

_____. SUPPLEMENT; CARDS ISSUED AUGUST 1942-DECEMBER 31, 1947. 42 vols. Ann Arbor, Mich.: Edwards, 1948.

_____. LIBRARY OF CONGRESS AUTHOR CATALOG: A CUMULATIVE LIST OF WORKS REPRESENTED BY LIBRARY OF CONGRESS PRINTED CARDS, 1948-52. 24 vols. Ann Arbor, Mich.: Edwards, 1953.

_____. NATIONAL UNION CATALOG: A CUMULATIVE AUTHOR LIST RE-PRESENTING LIBRARY OF CONGRESS PRINTED CARDS AND TITLES REPORTED BY OTHER AMERICAN LIBRARIES, 1953-57. 28 vols. Ann Arbor, Mich.: Edwards, 1958.

_____. NATIONAL UNION CATALOG: A CUMULATIVE AUTHOR LIST RE-PRESENTING LIBRARY OF CONGRESS PRINTED CARDS AND TITLES REPORTED BY OTHER AMERICAN LIBRARIES, 1958-62. 54 vols. New York: Rowan and Littlefield, 1963.

_____. NATIONAL UNION CATALOG: A CUMULATIVE AUTHOR LIST RE-PRESENTING LIBRARY OF CONGRESS PRINTED CARDS AND TITLES REPORTED BY OTHER AMERICAN LIBRARIES, 1963-67. 72 vols. Ann Arbor, Mich.: Edwards, 1968.

_____. NATIONAL UNION CATALOG, PRE-1956 IMPRINTS: A CUMULA-TIVE AUTHOR LIST REPRESENTING LIBRARY OF CONGRESS PRINTED CARDS AND TITLES REPORTED BY OTHER AMERICAN LIBRARIES. Vols. 1-579 in progress. London: Mansell, 1968-- .

_____ . 1952-1955 IMPRINTS: AUTHOR LIST REPRESENTING LIBRARY OF CONGRESS PRINTED CARDS AND TITLES REPORTED BY OTHER AMERICAN LIBRARIES. 30 vols. Ann Arbor, Mich.: Edwards, 1961.

> The Library of Congress catalogs include author cards for which library cards were printed; they list virtually every book related to American cultural history. The NATIONAL UNION CATALOG is a listing of monographs not represented by Library of Congress printed cards; these monographs have been reported by more than 750 North American libraries.

GENERAL REFERENCE SOURCES

AMERICA: HISTORY AND LIFE. Santa Barbara, Calif.: American Bibliographical Center-Clio Press, 1964-- .

> This annual bibliography includes abstracts and short-entry citations of articles from about nineteen hundred serial publications in some thirty languages.

AMERICAN CATALOGUE OF BOOKS, 1876-1910. 9 vols. 1876-1910. Reprint. New York: Peter Smith, 1941.

> As the title of this source indicates, books printed in the United States are listed. There are author, title, and subject headings.

BOOKS IN PRINT. New York: Bowker, 1948-- . Annual.

> This author-title index to PUBLISHERS' TRADE LIST ANNUAL lists books currently available from U.S. publishers. It has been supplemented by a subject guide since 1957.

CUMULATIVE BOOK INDEX: A WORLD LIST OF BOOKS IN THE ENGLISH LANGUAGE. New York: H.W. Wilson, 1928-32-- . 10/year, periodic cumulations.

> The CBI is the most valuable listing of books published in English.

Evans, Charles. AMERICAN BIBLIOGRAPHY: A CHRONOLOGICAL DICTIONARY OF ALL BOOKS, PAMPHLETS AND PERIODICAL PUBLICATIONS PRINTED IN THE UNITED STATES OF AMERICA, 1639-1800. 14 vols. 1903-59. Reprint. New York: Peter Smith, 1941-67.

> Three indexes--author, subject, and printers and publishers--complete each volume. Volume thirteen, completed by Clifford K. Shipton, brings the work through 1800, while volume fourteen, compiled by Roger P. Briston, is a cumulative author-title index to the whole work.

Kelly, James. AMERICAN CATALOGUE OF BOOKS PUBLISHED IN THE UNITED STATES FROM 1861 TO 1871. 2 vols. 1866-71. Reprint. New York: Peter Smith, 1938.

> Kelly follows the format of Roorbach (see entry below) in this trade catalog.

PUBLISHER'S WEEKLY. New York: Bowker, 1872-- .

> This list of books published in the United States is arranged by author and main entry. It also includes forecasts of books to be published.

Roorbach, Orville A. BIBLIOTHECA AMERICANA, 1820-1861. 4 vols. 1852-61. Reprint. New York: Peter Smith, 1939.

> This is the first significant trade bibliography that lists periodicals and reprints. It is arranged by author and title and serves also as a subject bibliography for biography.

Shaw, Ralph R., and Shoemaker, Richard H. AMERICAN BIBLIOGRAPHY: A PRELIMINARY CHECKLIST FOR 1801-1819. 19 vols. New York: Scarecrow Press, 1958-66.

> Shaw and Shoemaker fill the gap between 1800 where Evans stops and 1820 where Roorbach begins. One year is covered in each volume, and the arrangement is by author.

Shipton, Clifford K., and Mooney, James E. NATIONAL INDEX OF AMERICAN IMPRINTS THROUGH 1800: THE SHORT-TITLE EVANS. 2 vols. Worcester, Mass.: American Antiquarian Society and Barre Publishers, 1969.

> This includes the thirty-nine thousand items listed in Evans's AMERICAN BIBLIOGRAPHY and also about ten thousand additional citations. Entries are arranged alphabetically by author where known.

Shoemaker, Richard H. CHECKLIST OF AMERICAN IMPRINTS, 1820-1829. 10 vols. New York: Scarecrow Press, 1964-71.

> A bibliography that represents a continuation of the Shaw and Shoemaker volumes (see entry above) it is designed to supplement the early years of Roorbach.

Tanselle, G. Thomas. GUIDE TO THE STUDY OF UNITED STATES IMPRINTS. 2 vols. Cambridge, Mass.: Belknap Press of Harvard University Press, 1971.

> This is a basic guide to the study of printed matter produced in the United States. It covers bibliographies of imprints of particular localities, bibliographies of works in particular genres, listings of all editions and printings of works by individual authors, and other matters.

Reference Materials

WRITINGS ON AMERICAN HISTORY, 1902-1903. 2 vols. Princeton, N.J.: Library Book Store, 1904; Washington, D.C.: Carnegie Institution, 1905.

> This exhaustive listing of books and articles on American history is arranged by general topics, such as political and cultural history, as well as by geographical sections.

WRITINGS ON AMERICAN HISTORY, 1906-1939/40. 33 vols. Compiled by Grace Gardner Griffin et al. New York, 1908-10; Washington, D.C., 1911-13; New Haven, Conn., 1914-19; Washington, D.C., 1921-44. Publishers vary.

WRITINGS ON AMERICAN HISTORY, 1948-60. 14 vols. Edited by James R. Masterson. Washington, D.C.: Government Printing Office for the National Historical Publications Commission, 1952-72.

WRITINGS ON AMERICAN HISTORY, 1962-73: A SUBJECT BIBLIOGRAPHY OF ARTICLES. 3 vols. Edited by James J. Dougherty, George F. Williss, and Marion Sader. Washington, D.C.: American Historical Association, TKO Press, 1976.

> This new edition of the WRITINGS includes citations of thirty-three thousand articles that are cross-indexed. Volume one is chronological, two is by geographical section, and three is by subject.

WRITINGS ON AMERICAN HISTORY, 1973-74: A SUBJECT BIBLIOGRAPHY OF ARTICLES. Compiled and edited by James J. Dougherty, Robin Byrnes, and Maryann C. Lesso. Washington, D.C.: American Historical Association, 1974. x, 266 p.

> Designed as an annual bibliography, this volume includes thirty-eight hundred articles printed in more than three hundred periodicals. Many are cross-listed and the index is organized by the name of the author.

SPECIALIZED REFERENCE SOURCES

AMERICAN DIARIES IN MANUSCRIPT, 1580-1954: A DESCRIPTIVE BIBLIOGRAPHY. Athens: University of Georgia Press, 1974. xvi, 176 p.

> This list includes five thousand entries covering the time span of the diary, brief discussions of the contents, and a statement as to where the diary is located.

APPLETON'S CYCLOPEDIA OF AMERICAN BIOGRAPHY. Edited by James Grant Wilson and John Fiske. 7 vols. 1888-1901. Reprint. Detroit: Gale Research Co., 1968.

The CYCLOPEDIA was an unprecedented publishing effort since it was designed as a dictionary of biography with articles ranging from a few hundred words to several pages in length. It includes biographies of culture leaders such as clergymen, writers, and educators.

Beach, Mark. A BIBLIOGRAPHIC GUIDE TO AMERICAN COLLEGES AND UNIVERSITIES: FROM COLONIAL TIMES TO THE PRESENT. Westport, Conn.: Greenwood, 1975. vi, 314 p.

This is a collection of fifteen thousand articles and six thousand illustrations from journals dealing with music, opera, dance, and the theater.

Beach lists the major books, articles, and dissertations on the history of institutions of higher learning. Entries are arranged alphabetically by institution.

Belknap, Sara Y. GUIDE TO MUSICAL ARTS: AN ANALYTICAL INDEX OF ARTICLES AND ILLUSTRATIONS. New York: Scarecrow Press, 1957. Unpaged.

This is a collection of fifteen thousand articles and six thousand illustrations from journals dealing with music, opera, dance, and the theater.

Blanck, Jacob. PETER PARLEY TO PENROD: A BIBLIOGRAPHICAL DESCRIPTION OF THE BEST-LOVED AMERICAN JUVENILE BOOKS. Cambridge, Mass.: Research Classics, 1961. vi, 153 p.

This is a listing of more than one hundred juvenile books from an 1827 edition of the TALES OF PETER PARLEY to Will James's SMOKEY, THE COWHORSE, 1926.

Bray, Mayfield. GUIDE TO THE FORD FILM COLLECTION IN THE NATIONAL ARCHIVES. Washington, D.C.: National Archives and Records Service, General Services Administration, 1970. xiii, 118 p.

The Ford Collection covers the period from 1914 to 1940 and includes 1,500,000 feet of motion pictures depicting almost every facet of the American scene.

Brigham, Clarence S. HISTORY AND BIBLIOGRAPHY OF AMERICAN NEWSPAPERS, 1690-1820. 2 vols. Worcester, Mass.: American Antiquarian Society, 1947.

Brigham's bibliography was begun in 1931 and published in a number of different sources. It brings together and shows where 2,120 newspapers were published, most of them being in the Middle Atlantic states.

Burr, Nelson R. A CRITICAL BIBLIOGRAPHY OF RELIGION IN AMERICA. Vol. IV, pts. 1 and 2: RELIGION IN AMERICAN LIFE. Edited by Timothy

Ward Smith and A. Leland Jamison. Princeton, N.J.: Princeton University Press, 1961.

A bibliography that reviews the history of religion in the United States and illustrates the influence of religion on life and thought. It is in the form of an extended bibliographical essay.

Cohen, Hennig, ed. ARTICLES IN AMERICAN STUDIES, 1954-1968: A CUMULATION OF THE ANNUAL BIBLIOGRAPHIES IN THE AMERICAN QUARTERLY. 2 vols. Ann Arbor, Mich.: Pierian Press, 1972.

A classed and annotated bibliography of interdisciplinary periodical literature. It includes an author and main-entry index, an index to names used as subjects, an index of subject categories, and a key to changes in subject categories.

CURRENT BIOGRAPHY. New York: H.W. Wilson, 1940-- . Monthly. Annual cumulation.

This work includes three hundred to 350 biographies each year.

DICTIONARY OF AMERICAN BIOGRAPHY. Edited by Allen Johnson and Dumas Malone. 20 vols. London; Milford, Conn.: Charles Scribner's Sons for the American Council of Learned Societies, 1928-37.

This includes signed biographies of noteworthy people from all periods, each accompanied by a bibliography. Special attention is given to important figures in the sciences, social sciences, and other cultural fields.

DICTIONARY OF AMERICAN BIOGRAPHY, supplements 1-4. Edited by Harvis E. Starr, Robert L. Schuyler, and Edward T. James. New York: Charles Scribner's Sons, 1944-74.

Friedel, Frank, ed., with the assistance of Richard Showman. HARVARD GUIDE TO AMERICAN HISTORY. 2 vols. Rev. ed. Cambridge, Mass.: Belknap Press of Harvard University Press, 1974.

The merit of this bibliography lies in its inclusion of significant topics where the literature is scarce. Volume one is arranged topically and is heavily economic, social, cultural, and biographical; volume two is arranged chronologically with emphasis on political and diplomatic history.

Gephart, Ronald M., comp. PERIODICAL LITERATURE ON THE AMERICAN REVOLUTION: HISTORICAL RESEARCH AND CHANGING INTERPRETATIONS, 1895-1970. Washington, D.C.: Library of Congress, 1971. vi, 94 p.

This selective bibliography of 1,222 entries is arranged by subject and period. Annotations are provided only where additional information seemed necessary to illuminate the historiography.

Gohdes, Clarence. BIBLIOGRAPHICAL GUIDE TO THE STUDY OF THE LIT-
ERATURE OF THE U.S.A. Durham, N.C.: Duke University Press, 1959. xiv,
102 p.

The sections on Library of Congress catalogs, American studies on
American civilization, American history, magazines, newspapers,
selected histories of ideas in the United States, and special topics
in American literature will be particularly valuable to the cultural
historian.

_____. LITERATURE AND THEATER OF THE STATES AND REGIONS OF THE
U.S.A.: AN HISTORICAL BIBLIOGRAPHY. Durham, N.C.: Duke University
Press, 1967. ix, 276 p.

This is a checklist of monographs, anthologies, pamphlets, chapters
in books, and periodical articles on the development of local
belles-lettres and theater in the United States.

Gregory, Winifred, ed. AMERICAN NEWSPAPERS, 1821-1936: A UNION
LIST OF FILES AVAILABLE IN THE UNITED STATES AND CANADA. New
York: H.W. Wilson for the Bibliographical Society of America, 1937. xvi,
791 p.

Newspaper files located in 3,663 repositories are listed in this
bibliography.

Groce, George C., and Wallace, David H. THE NEW-YORK HISTORICAL
SOCIETY'S DICTIONARY OF ARTISTS IN AMERICA, 1564-1860. New Haven,
Conn.: Yale University Press, 1957. xxx, 759 p.

This is a biographical dictionary of more than ten thousand painters,
draftsmen, sculptors, engravers, and lithographers, including both
professionals and amateurs.

Hamer, Philip M., ed. A GUIDE TO ARCHIVES AND MANUSCRIPTS IN THE
UNITED STATES. New Haven, Conn.: Yale University Press, 1961. xxiv,
775 p.

This is a guide that provides information on the manuscript and
archival holdings of eleven thousand three hundred depositories.
For each depository there is a statement concerning its field of
special interest and size and holdings; the papers of individuals
are mentioned when they have appeared in the DICTIONARY OF
AMERICAN BIOGRAPHY.

James, Edward T.; James, Janet Wilson; and Boyer, Paul S., eds. NOTABLE
AMERICAN WOMEN, 1607-1950: A BIOGRAPHICAL DICTIONARY. 3 vols.
Cambridge, Mass.: Harvard University Press, 1971.

Biographies of one thousand three hundred fifty-nine women of the
past 350 years are presented and documented. One section en-

titled "Classified List of Selected Biographies" includes authors, actresses, feminists, suffragettes, philanthropists, and political figures as well as a survey of American women and their activities.

Jones, Howard Mumford. GUIDE TO AMERICAN LITERATURE AND ITS BACK-GROUND SINCE 1890. Cambridge, Mass.: Harvard University Press, 1953. 151 p.

Jones has selected those books he believes were the most influential in shaping the American mind since 1890. He also provides a bibliography for the social, economic, intellectual, and political background of American literature.

Kaplan, Louis, in association with James Tyler Cook, Clinton E. Colby, Jr., and Daniel C. Haskell. A BIBLIOGRAPHY OF AMERICAN AUTOBIOGRAPHIES. Madison: University of Wisconsin Press, 1961. xii, 372 p.

This collection contains notes on 6,377 autobiographies published before 1945 by native or adopted Americans. Entries are arranged alphabetically and by subject.

Keaveney, Sydney Starr. AMERICAN PAINTING: A GUIDE TO INFORMATION SOURCES. Art and Architecture Information Guide Series, vol. 1. Detroit: Gale Research Co., 1974. xiii, 260 p.

An annotated bibliography that contains general sources as well as works on individual artists. Illustrators, cartoonists, and artists who have specialized in a medium other than painting have not been included.

Kehde, Ned, comp. and ed. THE AMERICAN LEFT, 1955-1970: A NATIONAL UNION CATALOG OF PAMPHLETS PUBLISHED IN THE UNITED STATES AND CANADA. Westport, Conn.: Greenwood, 1976. xviii, 515 p.

This work lists 4,018 pamphlets by subject with symbols indicating library holdings. The definition of the American left is quite broad.

Mathews, William, comp., with the assistance of Roy Harvey Pearce. AMERICAN DIARIES: AN ANNOTATED BIBLIOGRAPHY OF AMERICAN DIARIES WRITTEN PRIOR TO THE YEAR 1861. University of California Publications in English, vol. 16. Berkeley and Los Angeles: University of California Press, 1945. xiv, 383 p.

This work is limited to printed diaries, but these for the most part are the most useful. The annotations are full.

Mugridge, Donald H., and McCrum, Blanch P., under the direction of Roy P. Basler. A GUIDE TO THE STUDY OF THE UNITED STATES OF AMERICA:

REPRESENTATIVE BOOKS REFLECTING THE DEVELOPMENT OF AMERICAN LIFE AND THOUGHT. Washington, D.C.: Library of Congress, 1960. xvi, 1,193 p.

This guide contains approximately six thousand five hundred main entries. Each book has been selected as an expression of life in the United States and not because of its reputation.

NATIONAL CYCLOPEDIA OF AMERICAN BIOGRAPHY. New York: White, 1892-- .

This is the most comprehensive American biographical work, with fifty-three volumes published and others in progress. Biographies, which include some living persons, are prepared from questionnaires.

Rubin, Louis D., Jr., ed. A BIBLIOGRAPHICAL GUIDE TO THE STUDY OF SOUTHERN LITERATURE. Baton Rouge: Louisiana State University Press, 1969. xxiv, 368 p.

A bibliography compiled by one hundred scholars that contains checklists of literature on twenty-three general topics and more than two hundred individual writers.

Shadwell, Wendy J. AMERICAN PRINTMAKING: THE FIRST 150 YEARS. Washington, D.C.: Smithsonian Institution Press for the Museum of Graphic Art, 1969. 180 p.

Reproductions of all the most important prints from 1670 through 1820 are included in this catalog.

Shumway, Gary, comp. ORAL HISTORY IN THE UNITED STATES: A DIRECTORY. New York: Oral History Association, 1971. 120 p.

Shumway has compiled descriptions of 230 oral history projects and their holdings in tapes and manuscripts.

Spiller, Robert E., et al. LITERARY HISTORY OF THE UNITED STATES. 2 vols. 4th rev. ed. New York: Macmillan; London: Collier Macmillan Publishers, 1974.

Volume two is an extensive subject-author bibliography that parallels the text in volume one. It is a guide to literary forms, social criticism, cultural history, and the instruments peculiar to various eras.

Walker, Robert H., ed. AMERICAN STUDIES: TOPICS AND SOURCES. Westport, Conn.: Greenwood, 1976. xi, 393 p.

This is a collection of bibliographical essays by leading scholars on topics of current concern.

Wright, Lyle H. AMERICAN FICTION, 1851-1875: A CONTRIBUTION TO-
WARD A BIBLIOGRAPHY. San Marino, Calif.: Huntington Library, 1957.
xx, 413 p.

> Fiction written for adults is included in this bibliography. Almost
> three thousand titles are recorded in serially numbered entries
> arranged by author.

PERIODICAL INDEXES

American Theological Library Association. INDEX TO RELIGIOUS LITERATURE.
Chicago: American Theological Library Association, 1949-1952-- . Annual to
1962, biennial thereafter.

> This includes listings of articles from more than 150 periodicals as
> well as book reviews. It is mainly Protestant in viewpoint.

ART INDEX. New York: H.W. Wilson, 1929-- . Quarterly.

> ART INDEX is a subject and author listing with permanent cumula-
> tions.

BIOGRAPHY INDEX. New York: H.W. Wilson, 1946-- . Quarterly.
Annual and 3-year cumulations.

> It includes biographical materials from magazines and books pub-
> lished in the English language.

CATHOLIC PERIODICAL INDEX. New York: Catholic Library Association,
1930-- . Quarterly. Biennial cumulation.

> This is a subject-author index to selected Catholic periodicals.

EDUCATION INDEX. New York: H.W. Wilson, 1929-- . Monthly, except
July and August. Annual cumulations.

> This is a subject index to some 200 periodicals. Books and pam-
> phlets are included for the years before 1961.

GUIDE TO THE PERFORMING ARTS. New York: Scarecrow Press, 1957-- .
Annual.

> Thirty to forty-five periodicals are indexed in this publication. It
> supersedes Belknap's GUIDE TO MUSICAL ARTS (see p. 5).

HUMANITIES INDEX. New York: H.W. Wilson, 1975-- .

> Along with the SOCIAL SCIENCES INDEX, this supersedes the
> SOCIAL SCIENCES & HUMANITIES INDEX (see p. 11). Sub-
> ject fields are archaeology, folklore, history, literature, political
> criticism, performing arts, philosophy, and religion.

MUSIC INDEX. Detroit: Information Service, 1949-- . Monthly. Annual cumulation.

This index contains listings of articles from more than 180 periodicals and is arranged by author and subject.

NINETEENTH CENTURY READERS' GUIDE TO PERIODICAL LITERATURE, 1890-1899. Edited by Helen Grant Cushing and Adah V. Morris. 2 vols. New York: H.W. Wilson, 1944.

Articles in approximately fifty periodicals are included in this author-subject index.

POOLE'S INDEX TO PERIODICAL LITERATURE, 1802-1881. 2 vols. Rev. ed., 1891. Supplements, January 1882-January 1, 1907. 5 vols. Reprint. New York: Peter Smith, 1938; Gloucester, Mass.: Peter Smith, 1963.

POOLE'S INDEX is a subject list of selective American and English periodicals. Although limited, it is the most comprehensive list of nineteenth-century articles.

READERS' GUIDE TO PERIODICAL LITERATURE. New York: H.W. Wilson, 1900-- . Monthly. Annual and biennial cumulations.

The READERS' GUIDE emphasizes popular magazines and is arranged by author, subject, and title.

SOCIAL SCIENCES AND HUMANITIES INDEX. New York: H.W. Wilson, 1965-74.

This index was formerly the INTERNATIONAL INDEX TO PERIODICALS (1916-65). It was the leading index to scholarly journals in its specialized fields.

SOCIAL SCIENCES INDEX. New York: H.W. Wilson, 1975-- . Quarterly. Annual cumulations.

This consists of author and subject entries to periodicals in anthropology, area studies, economics, environmental science, geography, law, medical science, and other subjects. Along with the HUMANITIES INDEX, it superseded the SOCIAL SCIENCES & HUMANITIES INDEX in 1974.

Chapter 2
GENERAL WORKS

COLONIAL PERIOD TO 1815

Aldridge, Alfred Owen. FRANKLIN AND HIS FRENCH CONTEMPORARIES. New York: New York University Press, 1957. 260 p.

French contemporaries created a Franklin myth that became a Gallic myth of America. Frenchmen believed that the American Revolution was Franklin's handiwork and that his writings were expositions of morality.

Baritz, Loren. CITY ON A HILL: A HISTORY OF IDEAS AND MYTHS IN AMERICA. New York: John Wiley and Sons, 1964. xi, 367 p.

Baritz focuses on formal intellectual systems with their by-products of attitudes and prejudices. He emphasizes the thought of John Winthrop, Jonathan Edwards, John Adams, John Taylor of Caroline, Ralph Waldo Emerson, and Herman Melville.

Boorstin, Daniel J. THE AMERICANS: THE COLONIAL EXPERIENCE. New York: Random House, 1958. xii, 434 p.

This book includes discussions of settlement in Massachusetts, Pennsylvania, Georgia, and Virginia; culture and science, including higher education, the learned professions, and medicine; language and the printed word; and the American practice of war and diplomacy. The author believes the legacy of the colonial period was not great individual thinkers but refreshed community thinking.

Bridenbaugh, Carl. "Philosophy Put to Use: Voluntary Associations for Propagating the Enlightenment in Philadelphia." PENNSYLVANIA MAGAZINE OF HISTORY AND BIOGRAPHY 101 (January 1977): 70-88.

Benjamin Franklin and others put philosophy to use through the overseas facilities and personnel of the Society of Friends. The alliance of meeting house and printing house produced the Library

Company of Philadelphia and a number of voluntary associations to benefit the public.

Buranelli, Vincent. "Colonial Philosophy." WILLIAM AND MARY QUARTERLY 16 (July 1959): 343-62.

Histories of colonial philosophy are curiosities because they are so rare. Buranelli reviews the writings of Woodbridge Riley and others, and urges that the subject deserves recognition because of the intellectual rigor it puts into American studies.

Bushman, Richard L. FROM PURITAN TO YANKEE: CHARACTER AND SOCIAL ORDER IN CONNECTICUT, 1690-1765. Cambridge, Mass.: Harvard University Press, 1967. xiv, 343 p.

Bushman emphasizes that the law and authority which were products of the founders of Connecticut gave way in the eighteenth century because of economic ambitions and the religious impulses of the Great Awakening. He states that the transformation from Puritan to yankee was gradual, but it had a disruptive effect on Connecticut towns.

Cherry, Conrad. "New England as Symbol: Ambiguity in the Puritan Vision." SOUNDINGS: AN INTERDISCIPLINARY JOURNAL 58 (Fall 1975): 348-62.

New England was a symbol of a concrete reality that called up more than one meaning simultaneously. The Puritans tried to resolve this symbolic ambiguity, but church leaders viewed it as an asset and believed that resolution would lead to loss of vision.

Cohen, Hennig. THE SOUTH CAROLINA GAZETTE, 1732-1775. Columbia: University of South Carolina Press, 1953. xv, 273 p.

This study includes a history of the GAZETTE, a description of South Carolina cultural life, and a checklist of names and other matters. Under cultural life, Cohen takes up topics such as "Teachers," "Artists," and "Doctors."

Colbourn, H. Trevor. THE LAMP OF EXPERIENCE: WHIG HISTORY AND THE INTELLECTUAL ORIGINS OF THE AMERICAN REVOLUTION. Chapel Hill: University of North Carolina Press, 1965. viii, 247 p.

The Whig interpretation of history with its myth of Saxon democracy colored colonial explanations of events and furnished Americans with an arsenal of arguments that transformed a rebellion into a revolution. Americans read and used the Whig historians such as Algernon Sidney, Thomas Gordon, Catherine Macaulay, and James Burgh, to mention a few.

Commager, Henry Steele. "The American Enlightenment and the Ancient World: A Study in Paradox." PROCEEDINGS OF THE MASSACHUSETTS HISTORICAL SOCIETY 83 (1971): 3-15.

> History as philosophy teaching by examples was an import from the ancient world and dominated American thinking in the eighteenth century. The purpose of history was to draw from the ancient world all its moral lessons, but Americans did not become prisoners of history.

Cullen, Maurice R., Jr. "Middle-Class Democracy and the Press in Colonial America." JOURNALISM QUARTERLY 46 (Autumn 1969): 531-35.

> This is a critique of the class struggle concept in viewing pre-revolutionary conditions. Colonial journalism moved the people through a newspaper war on Britain, and they spoke clearly for separation.

Cunliffe, Marcus. "Crevecoeur Revisited." JOURNAL OF AMERICAN STUDIES 9 (August 1975): 129-44.

> What is Crevecoeur, the agrarian, optimist, and expounder of the American success story? Cunliffe attempts to answer this question by showing that he was a loyalist during the Revolution and a man who had dual allegiance to the Old World and the New World.

Curti, Merle. "Human Nature in American Thought: The Age of Reason and Morality, 1750-1860." POLITICAL SCIENCE QUARTERLY 68 (September 1953): 354-75.

> Between 1750 and 1860, various branches of Christendom emphasized man's essential baseness and depravity, on the one hand, and his reason and capacity for receiving grace, on the other. This was a century in which people attempted to resolve the basic conflicts between reason and irrationality as well as morality and evil, but failed.

Davis, Harold E. FLEDGLING PROVINCE: SOCIAL AND CULTURAL LIFE IN COLONIAL GEORGIA, 1733-1776. Chapel Hill: University of North Carolina Press, 1976. xi, 306 p.

> Davis covers everyday life, occupations, slavery, class structure, the family, amusements, religion, and education. He argues that Georgia's development was not distinctive but was merely a repetition of what older colonies had experienced.

Davis, Richard Beale. "The Intellectual Golden Age in the Colonial Chesapeake Bay Country." VIRGINIA MAGAZINE OF HISTORY AND BIOGRAPHY 78 (April 1970): 131-43.

Between 1702 and 1789 the Chesapeake Bay region produced such thinking men as Washington, the Lees, Jefferson, and Madison because of a tradition of sustained cerebration and rationally developed good taste. There was a strong expression of discriminating good taste in the arts, a high proportion of literate and educated men, a creativity in belles-lettres, frequent oral discourses on religious doctrine, and reasoned political expression.

_____. INTELLECTUAL LIFE IN JEFFERSON'S VIRGINIA, 1790-1830. Chapel Hill: University of North Carolina Press, 1964. x, 507 p.

Many people, not just the elite economic classes, participated in Virginia's intellectual life. Davis covers many topics from chemistry and medicine to belles-lettres, and shows that old Virginia was an interesting place to live.

Dunlap, Leslie W. AMERICAN HISTORICAL SOCIETIES, 1790-1860. Madison, Wis.: Privately printed, 1944. ix, 238 p.

Dunlap shows that sixty-five historical socities were established by lawyers, preachers, and others before the Civil War. In the east, private societies were the rule, while state-supported organizations had their beginnings in Minnesota and Iowa.

Ellis, Joseph J. THE NEW ENGLAND MIND IN TRANSITION: SAMUEL JOHNSON OF CONNECTICUT, 1696-1772. New Haven, Conn.: Yale University Press, 1973. xii, 292 p.

Ellis portrays Johnson as a sensitive intellectual who was not brilliant but was concerned with the significant religious and moral questions of his day. He read widely, encouraged higher learning, and moved from Puritanism to Anglicanism in the eighteenth century.

_____. "The Puritan Mind in Transition: The Philosophy of Samuel Johnson." WILLIAM AND MARY QUARTERLY 28 (January 1971): 27-45.

This is a study of Johnson's ELEMENTA PHILOSOPHICA (1752). It is argued that this first American textbook in philosophy represents an effort to reconcile the mental categories of William Ames and Peter Ramus with the empirical thought of John Locke, scholasticism with eighteenth-century science, and the philosophical assumptions of New England Puritanism with the English Enlightenment.

Fiering, Norman S. "Will and Intellect in the New England Mind." WILLIAM AND MARY QUARTERLY 29 (October 1972): 515-58.

In the seventeenth century, there were debates at Harvard and other places concerning the nature of will or wherein man's freedom lies. This opposition between head and heart lasted through the Great Awakening and showed that human psychology rather than theology was the central conflict.

Gerbi, Antonello. THE DISPUTE OF THE NEW WORLD: THE HISTORY OF A POLEMIC, 1750–1900. Translated by Jeremy Moyle. Pittsburgh: University of Pittsburgh Press, 1973. xviii, 700 p.

The polemic concerning the conception of a New World goes back to Aristotle. Gerbi discusses the argument in terms of progress, primitivism, the forces of history and geography, the ideas of nature, evolutionism, and other ideas.

Gildrie, Richard P. SALEM, MASSACHUSETTS, 1626–1683: A COVENANT COMMUNITY. Charlottesville: University of Virginia Press, 1975. x, 187 p.

In the 1640s, Salem was a stable Christian community with a status system rooted in church membership, landed wealth, and public service. By the 1680s, commerce changed this and brought into power a vigorous merchant class.

Grabo, Norman S. "The Veiled Vision: The Role of Aesthetics in Early American Intellectual History." WILLIAM AND MARY QUARTERLY 19 (October 1962): 493–510.

The specialized interests of scholars causes them to be blind to historical materials in their own fields, and this applies to intellectual historians of the pre-revolutionary period in the use of literary materials. Grabo examines Susanne Langer's explorations of the nature of art and relates them to the poetry of Edward Taylor.

Gummere, Richard M. THE AMERICAN COLONIAL MIND AND THE CLASSICAL TRADITION: ESSAYS IN COMPARATIVE CULTURE. Cambridge, Mass.: Harvard University Press, 1963. xviii, 228 p.

This is a study of the evidence of classical learning in the colonies. Classical scholars are found everywhere from Virginia to Boston as well as in the Constitutional Convention where Aristotle and Polybius were important sources.

Jennings, Francis. "Virgin Land and Savage People." AMERICAN QUARTERLY 23 (October 1971): 519–41.

Jennings examines the myth that presents European colonization as civilization and Indian subjection as annihilating savagery. He argues that this myth is limited as historical explanation and suggests that the history of Euro-Americans and Amerindians be studied in terms of acculturation or the process of interaction and modification of both English and Indian institutions.

General Works

Jones, Howard Mumford. O STRANGE NEW WORLD: AMERICAN CULTURE, THE FORMATIVE YEARS. New York: Viking Press, 1964. xiv, 464 p.

> Columbus's voyage of 1492 was the beginning of a space age for Europe to a wondrous new world, as an earthly paradise, but one with a dark side that included the terror of nature and cruelty to Indians. Jones emphasizes that English America was part of a larger world.

Koch, Adrienne. "Pragmatic Wisdom and the American Enlightenment." WILLIAM AND MARY QUARTERLY 18 (July 1961): 313-29.

> The American Enlightenment in its thought was characterized by attachment to experimental empiricism and the humanistic ideal of the whole man. Koch calls this pragmatic wisdom and argues that reasonableness rather than dogma was the watchword.

Lockridge, Kenneth A. LITERACY IN COLONIAL NEW ENGLAND: AN INQUIRY INTO THE SOCIAL CONTEXT OF LITERACY IN THE MODERN WEST. New York: W.W. Norton and Co., 1974. xii, 164 p.

> This book is distinguished by methodology rather than conclusions. Studies of literacy have been based on signatures on wills, but Lockridge uses statistical analysis to correct biases arising from the use of will data and the test historical arguments concerning the significance of literacy.

May, Henry F. THE ENLIGHTENMENT IN AMERICA. New York: Oxford University Press, 1976. xix, 419 p.

> May argues that the Enlightenment is essentially a religious phenomenon. He defines four stages--moderate, skeptical, revolutionary, and didactic--that corresponded to developments in Europe.

Meyer, Donald H. THE DEMOCRATIC ENLIGHTENMENT. New York: G.P. Putnam's Sons, 1976. xxvii, 257 p.

> The merger of intellectual and common lives in the eighteenth century is emphasized. The Enlightenment was an age of experiments in religion, politics, and morality.

Miles, Edwin A. "The Young American Nation and the Classical World." JOURNAL OF THE HISTORY OF IDEAS 35 (April-June 1974): 259-74.

> Revolutionary leaders displayed a substantial interest in the history of Greece and Rome, but by the middle of the nineteenth century, Americans viewed Greco-Roman civilization as something to be avoided rather than imitated. This change took place because classical education in the colleges declined, and the people became devoted to anti-intellectualism, materialism, and science.

Nye, Russel Blaine. THE CULTURAL LIFE OF THE NEW NATION, 1776-
1830. New American Nation Series. Edited by Henry Steele Commager and
Richard B. Morris. New York: Harper and Brothers, 1960. xii, 324 p.

Nye emphasizes that political independence freed Americans from
conservative European influences and led to the development of
cultural nationalism. He surveys science, food, dress, manners,
sport, education, religion, literature, the fine arts, and other subjects.

Pochmann, Henry A. GERMAN CULTURE IN AMERICA: PHILOSOPHICAL
AND LITERARY INFLUENCES, 1600-1900. Madison: University of Wisconsin
Press, 1957. xvi, 865 p.

German scientific methodology and philosophic speculations had a
significant impact on American scholarship and literature. This was
more true during the nineteenth century than earlier periods.

Reinhold, Meyer. "Opponents of Classical Learning in America During the
Revolutionary Period." PROCEEDINGS OF THE AMERICAN PHILOSOPHICAL
SOCIETY 112 (15 August 1968): 221-34.

Beginning in the eighteenth century, and mounting in intensity
through the revolutionary period, a campaign was waged to eliminate classical learning from the curriculum or at least subordinate
it. This campaign was initiated or supported by persons of high
standing, including Benjamin Franklin.

_____. "The Quest for 'Useful Knowledge' in Eighteenth-Century America."
PROCEEDINGS OF THE AMERICAN PHILOSOPHICAL SOCIETY 119 (16 April
1975): 108-32.

In eighteenth-century America, the practical value of knowledge
as useful for self-improvement was balanced by the social function
of knowledge. This pragmatism was a national mood but was never
formally articulated in a systematic way.

Schlesinger, Arthur M. PRELUDE TO INDEPENDENCE: THE NEWSPAPER WAR
ON BRITAIN, 1764-1776. New York: Alfred A. Knopf, 1958. x, 318 p.

This is an assessment of the role of the newspaper in undermining
loyalty to Great Britain. After the passage of the Tea Act in
1773, newspapers became more strident and more divided with each
crisis.

Sheehan, Bernard W. "Paradise and the Noble Savage in Jeffersonian Thought."
WILLIAM AND MARY QUARTERLY 26 (July 1969): 327-59.

According to the Jeffersonians, it was axiomatic that the noble
savage lived in paradise and that paradise might be improved. They

took up the Indian and the land and made them into an elaborate ideology of change and the achievement of perfection.

Shipton, Clifford K. NEW ENGLAND LIFE IN THE EIGHTEENTH CENTURY: REPRESENTATIVE BIOGRAPHIES FROM SIBLEY'S HARVARD GRADUATES. Cambridge, Mass.: Belknap Press of Harvard University Press, 1963. xxviii, 626 p.

This is a selection of sixty biographies from the Sibley series. Shipton provides an introduction in which he describes the nature of the enterprise and explains the diversity and liberal faith of those who were graduated from Harvard.

Silver, Rollo G. THE AMERICAN PRINTER, 1787-1825. Charlottesville: University Press of Virginia, 1967. xii, 189 p.

Achievements in the typographical arts are detailed in this study. Of particular interest are the descriptions and plates on the various designs and the problems of the frontier printer in procuring adequate supplies.

Silverman, Kenneth. A CULTURAL HISTORY OF THE AMERICAN REVOLUTION: PAINTING, MUSIC, LITERATURE, AND THE THEATRE IN THE COLONIES AND THE UNITED STATES FROM THE TREATY OF PARIS TO THE INAUGURATION OF GEORGE WASHINGTON, 1763-1789. New York: Thomas Y. Crowell, 1976. xvii, 699 p.

This is a synthesis of the lives and achievements of artists, writers, and cultural entrepreneurs. Silverman explains the impressive amount of cultural activity during the Revolutionary period as being the result of the coming of peace, the effects of classical education, secularization of American life, prosperity, nationalism, and democratic educational theory.

Simpson, Lewis P., ed. THE FEDERALIST LITERARY MIND: SELECTIONS FROM THE MONTHLY ANTHOLOGY AND BOSTON REVIEW, 1803-1811, INCLUDING DOCUMENTS RELATING TO THE BOSTON ATHENAEUM. Baton Rouge: Louisiana State University Press, 1962. xiv, 246 p.

Contributors to the ANTHOLOGY were J.Q. Adams, Fisher Ames, Alexander H. Everett, and others. They were members of the Anthology Society and were bound together by social and scholarly interests.

Stannard, David E. "Death and the Puritan Child." AMERICAN QUARTERLY 26 (December 1974): 456-76.

Stannard argues that distinctions between children and adults existed in Puritan New England, and that these differences can be seen in the child's actual and anticipated confrontation with death. Puritan parents urged on their children an early awareness of sin and death, and children responded with fear and terror.

Stewart, Donald H. THE OPPOSITION PRESS OF THE FEDERALIST PERIOD. Albany: State University of New York Press, 1969. xiii, 957 p.

Stewart has studied the files of approximately five hundred newspapers published in the 1790s. He covers newspaper opinion on the major controversial issues of the period.

Tebbel, John. A HISTORY OF BOOK PUBLISHING IN THE UNITED STATES. Vol. 1: THE CREATION OF AN INDUSTRY, 1630-1865. New York: Bowker, 1972. xvi, 646 p.

This first of a three-volume narrative relates book publishing to the broader history of the United States. The rendition is chronological, but it reviews the economics, specialization, and problems of the book trade.

Tolles, Frederick B. "The Culture of Early Pennsylvania." PENNSYLVANIA MAGAZINE OF HISTORY AND BIOGRAPHY 81 (April 1957): 119-37.

Early Pennsylvania in the period to 1740 is describes by Tolles. William Penn opened the colony to people of every nationality and religion, and established a cultural pluralism that created the conditions for cultural growth.

Wertenbaker, Thomas Jefferson. THE FOUNDING OF AMERICAN CIVILIZATION: THE MIDDLE COLONIES. New York: Charles Scribner's Sons, 1938. xiii, 367 p.

Wertenbaker interprets the transit of culture to the middle colonies and the effect of the environment, the mingling of racial, religious, and regional groups, and the continued intercourse between America and Europe. About one-third of the book is devoted to architecture.

_____. THE GOLDEN AGE OF COLONIAL CULTURE. Anson G. Phelps Lectureship on Early American History. New York: New York University Press, 1942. 171 p.

This is a study of mid-eighteenth-century colonial culture in the urban centers of Boston, New York, Philadelphia, Annapolis, Williamsburg, and Charleston. Wertenbaker evaluates the extent and importance of art and architecture, the artistic crafts, literature, science, music, and the theatre.

_____. THE OLD SOUTH: THE FOUNDING OF AMERICAN CIVILIZATION. New York: Charles Scribner's Sons, 1942. xiv, 364 p.

This is primarily a study of the intellectual life and architecture of the plantation class as it moved into Virginia. The author argues that a new upper class arose on the Chesapeake.

_____. THE PURITAN OLIGARCHY: THE FOUNDING OF AMERICAN CIVILIZATION. New York: Charles Scribner's Sons, 1947. xiv, 359 p.

Wertenbaker theorizes that Massachusetts Bay changed from a Bible state to a liberal, rationalistic one over three generations. He discusses the Puritan planned community rather than theology.

Whitehill, Walter Muir, and Hitchings, Sinclair, eds. BOSTON PRINTS AND PRINTMAKERS, 1670-1775. Boston: Colonial Society of Massachusetts, 1973. xxv, 294 p.

This book is made up of monographs read at a conference hosted by the Colonial Society of Massachusetts. The essays deal with print-makers and prints, the dimension that visual evidence can bring to history, accompanied by 145 illustrations.

Woodward, C. Vann. "The Southern Ethic in a Puritan World." WILLIAM AND MARY QUARTERLY 25 (July 1968): 343-70.

How did southerners manage to escape the Puritan ethic given their exposure to it? Woodward argues that they escaped because of environmental rather than ideological influences.

Wright, Louis B. THE ATLANTIC FRONTIER: COLONIAL AMERICAN CIVILI-ZATION (1607-1763). New York: Alfred A. Knopf, 1947. xi, 354 p.

Wright shows that the Puritans were neither saints nor hypocrites and that their theology was favorable to the accumulation of worldly goods. He argues further that Virginia and Maryland planters were cultured and religious people.

_____. THE CULTURAL LIFE OF THE AMERICAN COLONIES, 1607-1763. New American Nation Series. Edited by Henry Steele Commager and Richard B. Morris. New York: Harper and Brothers, 1957. xvi, 292 p.

This is a balanced account of cultural development in the thirteen colonies. Wright strips plantation life of glamor, treats the Puri-tans with objectivity, and discusses the new aristocracy of trade.

_____. CULTURE ON THE MOVING FRONTIER. Bloomington: Indiana University Press, 1955. 273 p.

The wilderness was challenged by godly and law-abiding pioneers who constructed a relatively homogeneous society. This unity was provided by the English heritage in language, literature, religion, law, and social custom.

_____. THE FIRST GENTLEMEN OF VIRGINIA: INTELLECTUAL QUALITIES OF THE EARLY COLONIAL RULING CLASS. Huntington Library Publication. San Marino, Calif.: Huntington Library, 1940. xi, 373 p.

The basis of a gentleman's status was recognition of an inherent inequality in mankind, an idea brought to the English settlements. Through biographies, Wright shows that eighteenth-century gentlemen valued hard work and intellectual attainments.

_____. "Intellectual History and the Colonial South." WILLIAM AND MARY QUARTERLY 16 (April 1959): 214-27.

The history of the colonial South would be richer if historians attacked problems concerned with ideas and social conditions. They would find that there was not one distinct South and that the same kind of people shaped every colony.

1815-1915

Abbott, Richard H. "The Agricultural Press Views the Yeoman: 1819-1859." AGRICULTURAL HISTORY 42 (January 1968): 35-48.

Abbott argues that the agrarian myth had lost much of its mass appeal even among farmers by the mid-nineteenth century. Agricultural editors defended the dignity of farmers, and they continued to develop the myth as part of this defense even though belief in it was declining.

Ames, William E. A HISTORY OF THE NATIONAL INTELLIGENCER. Chapel Hill: University of North Carolina Press, 1972. xi, 376 p.

The NATIONAL INTELLIGENCER (1800-69) was one of the most durable political newspapers in the nation's capital. It was closely tied to the administrations of Madison, Monroe, and Adams, and then moved into the Whig camp.

Andrews, J. Cutler. THE NORTH REPORTS THE CIVIL WAR. Pittsburgh: University of Pittsburgh Press, 1955. xii, 813 p.

Correspondents are discussed as well as censorship. The gathering of news, relations of reporters with commanding officers, and other matters are detailed.

_____. THE SOUTH REPORTS THE CIVIL WAR. Princeton, N.J.: Princeton University Press, 1970. xiii, 611 p.

Andrews emphasizes military rather than political reporting, and depicts the sometimes haphazard, exaggerated, and inaccurate war coverage. There was always conflict between the press and the military over war coverage, propaganda, and press freedom.

Angle, Paul M. THE CHICAGO HISTORICAL SOCIETY, 1856-1956: AN UNCONVENTIONAL CHRONICLE. Chicago: Rand McNally, 1956. 256 p.

Destruction of the first building and the efforts to save the collection in the great Chicago fire furnish melodrama at its best. The generous bequest of Henry D. Gilpin permitted the society to prosper in the late nineteenth century, and the organization survived the great Depression by erecting its present magnificent headquarters.

Atherton, Lewis A. MAIN STREET ON THE MIDDLE BORDER. Bloomington: Indiana University Press, 1954. xx, 423 p.

This is a study of the small town and its folkways since the Civil War. Towns served adjacent farming areas and represented a classless society, but one that permitted few deviations from a code that excluded dancing, tobacco, movies, and liquor.

Baker, Donald G. "Color, Culture and Power: Indian-White Relations in Canada and America." CANADIAN REVIEW OF AMERICAN STUDIES 3 (Spring 1972): 3-20.

Baker argues against the tendency to attribute the plight of Indians to white racism or the discriminatory practices of whites. He finds instead that white-Indian relations were shaped by a series of encounters or confrontations.

Baker, Thomas Harrison. THE MEMPHIS COMMERCIAL APPEAL: THE HISTORY OF A SOUTHERN NEWSPAPER. Baton Rouge: Louisiana State University Press, 1971. 336 p.

This newspaper has been printed since 1841. The author of this study emphasizes news, advertising, and editorial policies rather than the elements in society to whom the paper spoke.

Ballou, Ellen B. THE BUILDING OF THE HOUSE: HOUGHTON MIFFLIN'S FORMATIVE YEARS. Boston: Houghton Mifflin, 1970. xv, 695 p.

Ballou covers the history of the publishing house to 1920 and includes a chronicle of the ATLANTIC MONTHLY. She focuses on four leaders of the firm and emphasizes how they built a list of authors that included Dickens, Lowell, Longfellow, and Howells.

Barnes, James J. AUTHORS, PUBLISHERS AND POLITICIANS: THE QUEST FOR AN ANGLO-AMERICAN COPYRIGHT AGREEMENT, 1815-1854. Columbus: Ohio State University Press, 1974. xv, 311 p.

The years 1815 through 1854 were a period of failure for those who worked for an Anglo-American copyright treaty. The depression of 1837 caused many publishing firms to fail, and those that stayed solvent pirated the writings of British authors.

Bender, Thomas. "The 'Rural' Cemetery Movement: Urban Travail and the Appeal of Nature." NEW ENGLAND QUARTERLY 47 (June 1974): 196-211.

A rural cemetery was a burial ground located on the outskirts of a city that was designed according to the romantic conventions of English landscape gardening. Americans of the mid-nineteenth century used the cemetery as a counterpoint to the city.

Bestor, Arthur E., Jr. "Patent-Office Models of the Good Society: Some Relationships between Social Reform and Westward Expansion." AMERICAN HISTORICAL REVIEW 58 (April 1953): 505-26.

This is a survey of communitarian convictions as to how social institutions are created. Bestor relates these ideas to the idea of the West as a land of opportunity for the individual.

Bloomfield, Maxwell H. ALARMS AND DIVERSIONS: THE AMERICAN MIND THROUGH AMERICAN MAGAZINES, 1900-1914. The Hague: Mouton and Co., 1967. 174 p.

THE NORTH AMERICAN REVIEW, FORUM, OUTLOOK, COSMO-POLITAN, and AMERICAN, it is argued, mirrored the popular attitudes of the Progressive era. Between 1900 and 1914, a new type of social consciousness emerged that emphasized the primacy of the community rather than the individual.

Boorstin, Daniel J. THE AMERICANS: THE DEMOCRATIC EXPERIENCE. New York: Random House, 1973. xiv, 717 p.

Boorstin's principal actor in this stage of American development is the "go-getter," who is almost always in business. He does not criticize this figure, nor does he emphasize the unpleasant intellectual and cultural aspects of industrialization.

_____. THE AMERICANS: THE NATIONAL EXPERIENCE. New York: Random House, 1965. x, 517 p.

Boorstin maintains that America between the Revolution and the Civil War grew in search of community. Ways were fluid and people constantly believed that something better would show up, all of which produced a new civilization.

Boyer, Paul S. PURITY IN PRINT: THE VICE-SOCIETY MOVEMENT AND BOOK CENSORSHIP IN AMERICA. New York: Charles Scribner's Sons, 1968. xxi, 362 p.

The societies that supported censorship at the beginning of the twentieth century were the same groups that sponsored prison reform, children's aid, and poor relief. Boyer concentrates on New York City and emphasizes that the societies to suppress vice had the support of the establishment concerning censorship until World War I.

Brown, Charles H. THE CORRESPONDENTS WAR: JOURNALISTS IN THE SPANISH-AMERICAN WAR. New York: Charles Scribner's Sons, 1967. xi, 478 p.

The yellow press was irresponsible in fomenting war fever to boost circulation, and papers other than Hearst's JOURNAL and Pulitzer's WORLD were involved. Correspondents were like boys enjoying their own adventure, and they considered the war their own personal affair.

Brown, Dorothy M. "The Quality Magazines in the Progressive Era." MID-AMERICA 53 (July 1971): 139-59.

This is a study of HARPER'S, the ATLANTIC MONTHLY, CENTURY, and SCRIBNER'S. They were not fortresses of the old morality, but raised clear warnings concerning the problems of America and suggested that many old values and goals were no longer viable.

Brown, Francis. RAYMOND OF THE TIMES. New York: W.W. Norton and Co., 1951. ix, 345 p.

Raymond was the NEW YORK TIMES' chief founder. His activities In Journalism and politics are emphasized.

Burns, Rex. SUCCESS IN AMERICA: THE YEOMAN DREAM AND THE IN-DUSTRIAL REVOLUTION. Amherst: University of Massachusetts Press, 1976. x, 212 p.

Success in terms of the yeoman dream was wealth somewhat beyond need, freedom from economic and statutory subservience, and the respect of society for fruitful, honest industry. Burns examines this theme from the standpoints of children's and mechanics' magazines, labor newspapers, and the novels of Nathaniel Hawthorne.

Calhoun, Daniel. THE INTELLIGENCE OF A PEOPLE. Princeton, N.J.: Princeton University Press, 1973. xix, 408 p.

Calhoun attempts to find the intellectual weakness of the American people between the Revolution and the Civil War. He subscribes to the idea that intelligence is a cultural phenomenon, and argues that the national mind narrowed during this time and was degraded.

Cannon, Charles A. "The Awesome Power of Sex: The Polemical Campaign Against Mormon Polygamy." PACIFIC HISTORICAL REVIEW 43 (February 1974): 61-82.

This is a study of the polemical literature directed against Mormon polygamy with the aim of exploring popular attitudes toward sex in America. Sex was viewed as a compelling force that might destroy the moral agency of men to master sexual desire.

Carafiol, Peter C. "James Marsh's AIDS TO REFLECTION: Influence Through Ambiguity." NEW ENGLAND QUARTERLY 49 (March 1976): 27-45.

> This essay concerns Marsh's publication of Samuel Taylor Coleridge's AIDS TO REFLECTION in 1829. In a long preliminary essay, Marsh attempted to revive religious orthodoxy, but he paved the way for transcendentalism.

Cash, W.J. THE MIND OF THE SOUTH. New York: Alfred A. Knopf, 1941. xi, 429 p.

> This is not an intellectual history, but a sociological treatise on southern development from plantation days. It portrays the mind of the average southerner, a romantic mind that displayed hedonism and childlike incapacity for analysis in the antebellum period and a mind of exaggerated individualism and self-consciousness in the period following the Civil War.

Cawelti, John G. APOSTLES OF THE SELF-MADE MAN. Chicago: University of Chicago Press, 1965. xiv, 279 p.

> Cawelti concentrates on individuals such as Franklin, Jefferson, Emerson, and Horatio Alger. He also examines success manuals in different periods and novels having self-made men as their central characters.

Chambers, Lenoir; Shank, Joseph E.; and Sugg, Harold. SALT WATER & PRINTER'S INK: NORFOLK AND ITS NEWSPAPERS, 1865-1965. Chapel Hill: University of North Carolina Press, 1967. viii, 418 p.

> This history shows how eleven Norfolk newspapers founded during the last century came under one ownership in 1933. Even though the city gained a reputation as a wicked place because it was a seaport frequented by sailors on shore leave, newspaper editors supported political reform, slum clearance, and urban redevelopment.

Charvat, William. LITERARY PUBLISHING IN AMERICA, 1790-1850. Philadelphia: University of Pennsylvania Press, 1959. 94 p.

> This book consists of three essays in which the author shows that transportation made New York and Philadelphia distribution centers for books to the South and West. He describes the way books were financed and the manner in which they were packaged for every literary taste.

Clark, Aubert J. THE MOVEMENT FOR INTERNATIONAL COPYRIGHT IN NINETEENTH CENTURY AMERICA. Washington, D.C.: Catholic University of America Press, 1960. x, 215 p.

> Clark describes support for an opposition to the movement for international copyright and also relates the story to economic, politi-

cal, and social change. Pro forces tended to be pure, while the antis emphasized the cultural benefits that came from piracy.

Clark, Thomas D. "Arts and Sciences on the Early Frontier." NEBRASKA HISTORY 37 (December 1956): 247-68.

This is a study of frontier writing and painting, science and medicine. On the frontier, cultural institutions were transported from one layer of settlement to another.

_____. "The Country Newspaper: A Factor in Southern Opinion, 1865-1930." JOURNAL OF SOUTHERN HISTORY 14 (February 1948): 3-33.

Clark argues that the country weekly is a major source of local history, since editors knew what and what not to print according to the attitudes of their subscribers. Rural editors promoted the New South, industrialism, education, and white supremacy.

_____. THE SOUTHERN COUNTRY EDITOR. Indianapolis: Bobbs-Merrill Co., 1948. 365 p.

This study covers the period since the Civil War. The war and Reconstruction altered attitudes toward the North and the Negro, and opened the way for a new kind of editor and a new type of southern newspaper.

Cohn, Jan. "The Civil War in Magazine Fiction of the 1860's." JOURNAL OF POPULAR CULTURE 4 (Fall 1970): 355-82.

For the first half of the Civil War decade, magazine fiction was dominated by women, and their stories were romantic, sentimental, and patriotic. After 1865, however, stories began to appear concerning the experiences of veterans, and with them a realism that was not to become a major ingredient of Civil War fiction until the 1880s.

Colwell, James L. "The Populist Image of Vernon Louis Parrington." MISSISSIPPI VALLEY HISTORICAL REVIEW 49 (June 1962): 52-66.

This study of Parrington's early career on the farm, at the College of Emporia in Kansas, and at Harvard, shows that he was an earnest student preparing for a profession and not a young radical seeking light on social issues.

Commager, Henry Steele. THE AMERICAN MIND: AN INTERPRETATION OF AMERICAN THOUGHT AND CHARACTER SINCE THE 1880'S. New Haven, Conn.: Yale University Press, 1950. ix, 476 p.

Commager covers pragmatism, literature, religious thought, the social sciences, historical literature, the new science of politics, architecture, and other subjects. He views the 1880s and 1890s as a watershed in American history and thought.

Conlin, Joseph R., ed. THE AMERICAN RADICAL PRESS, 1880-1960. 2 vols. Westport, Conn.: Greenwood, 1974. xiv, 368; vii, 352 p.

This is a collection of one hundred essays on 119 periodicals and covers the full range of radicalism--left, right, and independent. The writings include studies of the periodicals of the Knights of Labor, socialists, Wobblies, anarchists, and communists, as well as Eugene Debs, Upton Sinclair, and I.F. Stone.

Conrad, Susan Phinney. PERISH THE THOUGHT: INTELLECTUAL WOMEN IN ROMANTIC AMERICA, 1830-1860. New York: Oxford University Press, 1976. 292 p.

The lives and ideas of Margaret Fuller, Lydia Maria Child, Elizabeth Cady Stanton, and Elizabeth Ellet are discussed. These women are depicted as the first generation of women intellectuals in the United States.

Cramer, C.H. OPEN SHELVES AND OPEN MINDS: A HISTORY OF THE CLEVELAND PUBLIC LIBRARY. Cleveland: Press of Case Western Reserve University, 1972. x, 279 p.

Major events and figures are emphasized in this centennial history. The book draws its title from a decision to open the shelves of circulating volumes to the public.

Curti, Merle. "The American Exploration of Dreams and Dreamers." JOURNAL OF THE HISTORY OF IDEAS 27 (July-September 1966): 391-416.

This is a survey of American speculation concerning dreams from the seventeenth century to the mid-1960s. Curti shows that dreams and dreaming did not become important until the nineteenth century when they were discussed by physicians, described by literary figures, and analyzed empirically by students of William James and others.

_____. AMERICAN PARADOX: THE CONFLICT BETWEEN THOUGHT AND ACTION. New Brunswick, N.J.: Rutgers University Press, 1956. xii, 116 p.

Curti examines American history to determine how far democracy has fulfilled its destiny. The paradox is the failure of democracy to unify thought and action, while condemning those who have practiced thought systematically.

_____. "The American Scholar in Three Wars." JOURNAL OF THE HISTORY OF IDEAS 3 (June 1942): 241-64.

This is an examination of the positions of intellectuals concerning issues in the Revolution, Civil War, and World War I, as well as an analysis of the assumption that wars have forced American thought into new channels. Intellectuals "chose" their places respecting the issues, put their shoulders to the wheel, and engaged in research and writing that promoted the war effort.

_____. THE GROWTH OF AMERICAN THOUGHT. 3d ed. New York: Harper and Row, 1964. xx, 939 p.

Curti surveys the growth of knowledge, thought, values, and the agencies of intellectual life. The book is organized in chronological periods according to the ideas that were characteristic of successive eras of history with emphasis on the nineteenth century.

_____. "Human Nature in American Thought: Retreat from Reason in the Age of Science." POLITICAL SCIENCE QUARTERLY 48 (December 1953): 492-510.

The century following 1860 has been marked by a retreat from reason. The reaction against the intellectual revolution represented distrust of the scientific method as an instrument for guiding men out of chaos and darkness and into peace and light.

_____. "Jane Addams on Human Nature." JOURNAL OF THE HISTORY OF IDEAS 22 (April-June 1961): 240-53.

Addams's conception of human nature was central to her thought. She saw a universal desire in humans to be recognized as unique persons, and she was convinced that the differences separating immigrants and blacks from old stock Americans were not as great as assumed.

_____. "Tradition and Innovation in American Philanthropy." PROCEEDINGS OF THE AMERICAN PHILOSOPHICAL SOCIETY 105 (April 1961): 146-56.

American philanthropy derived its ideology and organization from the Judeo-Christian tradition and English common and statutory law. Tradition and innovation were based on the separation of church and state, the concept of abundance, repudiation of a hereditary class of poor people, immigration, and an emphasis on voluntary associations.

Dain, Phyllis. THE NEW YORK PUBLIC LIBRARY: A HISTORY OF ITS FOUNDING AND EARLY YEARS. New York: New York Public Library, 1972. xix, 466 p.

Dain emphasizes the development of lines of broad policy, physical, and bibliothecal development. She covers the period from the 1890s to 1913.

Davenport, F. Garvin. CULTURAL LIFE IN NASHVILLE ON THE EVE OF THE CIVIL WAR. Chapel Hill: University of North Carolina Press, 1941. x, 232 p.

Nashville's aesthetic and intellectual attainments are detailed. The city was a leader in medical science and education, supported a theater and opera that billed national stars, and developed many amateur cultural activities.

_____. "Culture Versus Frontier in Tennessee, 1825-1850." JOURNAL OF SOUTHERN HISTORY 5 (February 1939): 18-33.

Davenport traces the career of Phillip Lindsley (1786-1855), who left Princeton in 1824 to become president of Cumberland College (later the University of Nashville). He shows that intellectual leaders in frontier Tennessee were "swamped by a wave of ignorance" produced by farmers, who refused to give up land to colleges, and by anti-intellectual and anti-education Methodists and Baptists.

Degler, Carl N. "What Ought To Be and What Was: Women's Sexuality in the Nineteenth Century." AMERICAN HISTORICAL REVIEW 79 (December 1974): 1467-90.

Women of the nineteenth century were not sexless. That they were was a view advanced by sexual advice writers and others, but additional evidence shows that most people did not heed their prescriptions.

Diggins, John P. "Thoreau, Marx, and the 'Riddle' of Alienation." SOCIAL RESEARCH 39 (Winter 1972): 571-98.

Thoreau was a part-time recluse who called for moral regeneration as a prerequisite of moral reform, while Marx was a man of action who saw little value in ethical action. The former suggested contemplation as a means of overcoming alienation, while the latter presented a philosophy of action.

Ditzion, Sidney. ARSENALS OF DEMOCRATIC CULTURE: A SOCIAL HISTORY OF THE AMERICAN PUBLIC LIBRARY MOVEMENT IN NEW ENGLAND AND THE MIDDLE STATES FROM 1859 TO 1900. Foreword by Merle Curti. Chicago: American Library Association, 1947. xiii, 263 p.

This is an analysis of the development of the public library idea. Urbanism provided the setting for the library movement and social interests for multiple reasons accepted it.

Donaldson, Scott. "City and Country: Marriage Proposals." AMERICAN QUARTERLY 20 (Fall 1968): 547-66.

American intellectuals conceived of a middle landscape that would produce a happy marriage between town and country. Historically, the magnet for the middle landscape was the city rather than the country with the suburb becoming the subject of abuse.

Douglas, Ann. THE FEMINIZATION OF AMERICAN CULTURE. New York: Alfred A. Knopf, 1977. x, 403 p.

This is an examination of the impact of literary women and Protestant ministers on nineteenth-century culture and on each other. This interaction corrupted culture, inundated it with sentimentality, and paved the way for the contemporary consumerist mentality.

Duffy, John J., ed. COLERIDGE'S AMERICAN DISCIPLE: THE SELECTED CORRESPONDENCE OF JAMES MARSH. Amherst: University of Massachusetts Press, 1973. xv, 272 p.

James Marsh, professor of moral and intellectual philosophy at the University of Vermont, was Coleridge's principal pre-Civil War editor and spokesman. These letters which deal with post-Kantian idealism cover the period from 1829 to 1842.

Dykhuizen, George. "John Dewey and the University of Michigan." JOURNAL OF THE HISTORY OF IDEAS 23 (October-December 1962): 513-43.

Dewey's years at Michigan began in 1884 and were productive. He became head of the philosophy department, found a wife, and published articles on psychology and philosophy that earned him a reputation as one of the most original thinkers in America.

Eaton, Clement. THE GROWTH OF SOUTHERN CIVILIZATION, 1790-1860. New American Nation Series. Edited by Henry Steele Commager and Richard B. Morris. New York: Harper and Brothers, 1961. xviii, 357 p.

Eaton describes the old Atlantic coastal region, the Cotton Kingdom, and life around the lower Mississippi River. He portrays slavery as being always bad in the abstract, but highly varied as an institution and also depicts town life.

_____. THE MIND OF THE OLD SOUTH. Baton Rouge: Louisiana State University Press, 1964. xiii, 271 p.

In the thirty years before the Civil War, the history of the South was the story of representative men being warped by economic and social forces. Eaton focuses on fifteen men such as James H. Hammond, Cassius M. Clay, Henry A. Wise, William L. Yancey, and others.

_____. THE WANING OF OLD SOUTH CIVILIZATION, 1860-1880'S. Athens: University of Georgia Press, 1968. xii, 195 p.

Eaton argues that southerners in 1860 tended toward individuals with a conservative turn of mind and an intolerance for dissent. Although discouraged and pessimistic, they did not attribute their defeat in the Civil War to the sin of slavery, and they carried their beliefs in states' rights, white supremacy, and the cult of southern womanhood into the New South.

Ewart, Mike. "Cooper and the American Revolution: The Non-Fiction." JOURNAL OF AMERICAN STUDIES 11 (April 1977): 61-79.

Cooper justified the Revolution as a response to tyranny and as a means of replacing irrational and unstable forms of government. He depicted George Washington as a Christian warrior and as a member of the gentry, a stable class that ensured political stability.

Field, James A., Jr. AMERICA AND THE MEDITERRANEAN WORLD, 1776-1882. Princeton, N.J.: Princeton University Press, 1969. xv, 485 p.

This is a blend of intellectual and diplomatic history in which the author examines the role of the new American navy in the Mediterranean. Field emphasizes the fostering of mutually beneficial trade, the peacetime use of the navy as an instrument of foreign policy, Protestant missionary efforts, and other matters.

Flack, J. Kirkpatrick. DESIDERATUM IN WASHINGTON: THE INTELLECTUAL COMMUNITY IN THE CAPITOL CITY, 1870-1900. Cambridge, Mass.: Schenkman, 1975. 192 p.

Intellectuals congregated in Washington even during the Gilded Age. Flack discusses the activities of John Wesley Powell, the scientist; Henry Adams, the social scientist; Edward Gallaudet, the educator; and others.

Ford, Worthington Chauncey, ed. LETTERS OF HENRY ADAMS, 1858-1891. Boston: Houghton Mifflin, 1930. vi, 552 p.

These letters supplement Adams's EDUCATION since they were written during the period when the EDUCATION was being prepared. They reveal the intimate details of the mind of an historian.

_____. LETTERS OF HENRY ADAMS, 1892-1918. Boston: Houghton Mifflin, 1938. x, 672 p.

Adams's comments on people and places are important. In some letters to his brother, Brooks, he forecasts the decline of American civilization.

Frederickson, George M. THE INNER CIVIL WAR: NORTHERN INTELLEC-
TUALS AND THE CRISIS OF THE UNION. New York: Harper and Row,
1965. viii, 277 p.

> Frederickson discusses the pre-Civil War positions of the Emerson-
> ians, the anti-institutional reformers, and their conservative con-
> temporaries, most of whom believed the war was the best means of
> impressing their ideas on the nation. After the war their views
> changed, with many supporting big government and slow change
> directed by an elite.

French, Stanley. "The Cemetery as Cultural Institution: The Establishment of
Mount Auburn and the 'Rural Cemetery' Movement." AMERICAN QUARTERLY
26 (March 1974): 37-59.

> The creation of Mount Auburn in Cambridge, Massachusetts, re-
> presented a change in attitudes concerning death and burial. It
> was to be a cultural institution, a garden, and not a place of
> melancholy.

Gabriel, Ralph Henry. THE COURSE OF AMERICAN DEMOCRATIC THOUGHT.
2d ed. New York: Ronald Press, 1956. xiv, 508 p.

> This is a study of social beliefs that served as guides to action and
> goals for living. Gabriel explores the dignity of human personali-
> ty, the idea that principles of universal validity underlie the lives
> of men in society, and the tenet that the nation exists not only to
> serve its people but also to advance the cause of freedom abroad.

Garrison, Dee. "The Tender Technicians: The Feminization of Public Librarian-
ship, 1876-1905." JOURNAL OF SOCIAL HISTORY 6 (Winter 1972-73):
131-59.

> Women flooded into the library profession because it was low-paid,
> needed plenty of educated workers, and also because there was
> little male opposition. This had the effect of giving the library
> a "homey" atmosphere and the librarian the image of a nonassertive
> "hostess."

Gastil, Raymond D. CULTURAL REGIONS OF THE UNITED STATES. Seattle:
University of Washington Press, 1976. xvi, 366 p.

> Gastil, a historical geographer, divides the United States into thir-
> teen regions and examines each in terms of religious affiliations,
> political behavior, settlement patterns, dialects, folk songs, popu-
> lar music, magazine circulation, and other criteria.

Greene, Theodore P. AMERICA'S HEROES: THE CHANGING MODELS OF
SUCCESS IN AMERICAN MAGAZINES. New York: Oxford University Press,
1970. vi, 387 p.

Greene uses biographical articles in popular magazines to demonstrate that the gentleman was the model of success in the early republic, while the man who gained success through personal achievement was the hero in the 1890s. These late nineteenth-century heroes were creative artists rather than businessmen, but in the progressive period they were replaced by political leaders and eventually by individuals who got things done.

Greenslet, Ferris. THE LOWELLS AND THEIR SEVEN WORLDS. Boston: Houghton Mifflin, 1946. xi, 442 p.

The seven worlds are the historical eras from the colonial period into the twentieth century in which the Lowells played important roles. Of particular interest is the section on the contributions of Percival, Guy, Amy, and Lawrence to science, the arts, and education.

Hage, George S. NEWSPAPERS ON THE MINNESOTA FRONTIER, 1849-1860. St. Paul: Minnesota Historical Society, 1967. ix, 176 p.

In early Minnesota, newspaper history was identified with physical and verbal combat between editors. The content of news stories is emphasized in this study.

Harbert, Earl N. "Charles Francis Adams (1807-1886): A Forgotten Family Man of Letters." JOURNAL OF AMERICAN STUDIES 6 (December 1972): 249-65.

The Adams family began as a political dynasty and ended three generations later as a family literary society. Charles Francis Adams brought about this transition because he was unable to make a place for himself in politics and turned to letters as a family duty.

Heale, M.J. "The Role of the Frontier in Jacksonian Politics: David Crockett and the Myth of the Self-Made Man." WESTERN HISTORICAL QUARTERLY 4 (October 1973): 405-24.

David Crockett was one of the first Americans to make a living as a celebrity. He personified the backwoodsman and his leap to fame enabled his promoters to present him as a truly American creation--the self-made man--and the representative of a cluster of values Americans held dear.

HENRY ADAMS AND HIS FRIENDS. Compiled, with a Biographical Introduction by Harold Dean Cater. Boston: Houghton Mifflin, 1947. cxix, 797 p.

Cater has added some 650 Adams letters to the Ford volumes (1930, 1938), but more important, he has established an oral history of his subject through interviews with the survivors of Adams's circle of intimates. He also sheds important light on Adams's personality.

Herman, Sondra R. "Loving Courtship or the Marriage Market? The Ideal and Its Critics, 1871-1911." AMERICAN QUARTERLY 25 (May 1973): 235-52.

While sexual questions were suppressed during these decades, marriage questions were not avoided since women were leaving home to gain educations and pursue careers. Defenders of traditional marriage focused on the ideals of female domesticity and sexual purity, but critics such as Edward Bellamy, Charlotte Perkins Gilman, and Theodore Dreiser attacked sexual differentiation and argued that female inferiority developed in the marriage market.

Herrnstadt, Richard L., ed. THE LETTERS OF BRONSON ALCOTT. Ames: Iowa State University Press, 1969. xxxvii, 846 p.

This collection includes significant letters to members of Alcott's family, Ralph Waldo Emerson, and others, as well as trivial ones cancelling magazines and accepting speaking engagements. Many shed light on educational and reform movements.

Hofstadter, Richard. ANTI-INTELLECTUALISM IN AMERICAN LIFE. New York: Alfred A. Knopf, 1963. ix, 434 p.

Hofstadter argues that the unpopularity of the life of the mind has been an important phenomenon in American history. He examines manifestations of anti-intellectualism in religion, politics, business, and education.

Hogeland, Ronald W. "'The Female Appendage': Feminine Life-Styles in America, 1820-1860." CIVIL WAR HISTORY 17 (June 1971): 101-14.

Between 1820 and 1860, women were merely appendages to the central drama of male activity. Men made women accountable for the moral welfare of society, but held on to the administrative and intellectual reins of theology and politics.

Hollingsworth, J. Rogers. "American Anti-Intellectualism." SOUTH ATLANTIC QUARTERLY 63 (Summer 1964): 267-74.

Until the twentieth century, the American vocabulary did not include the worlds "intellectual" and "anti-intellectual," and intellectuals did not regard themselves as a separate class. In studying the nineteenth century, historians must distinguish between the nonintellectual and the anti-intellectual, and in the twentieth, they must be cognizant of the image intellectuals had of themselves.

Horowitz, Helen Lefkowitz. CULTURE AND THE CITY: CULTURAL PHILAN-
THROPY IN CHICAGO FROM THE 1880S TO 1917. Lexington: University
Press of Kentucky, 1976. xv, 288 p.

> Horowitz examines philanthropy in music, fine arts, higher educa-
> tion, and research. She is interested in the people who founded
> and supported institutions such as the Chicago Art Institute and the
> John Crerar Library, and their definition of culture.

Howe, Daniel Walker, ed. VICTORIAN AMERICA. Philadelphia: University
of Pennsylvania Press, 1976. 184 p.

> These essays appeared originally in the AMERICAN QUARTERLY.
> They cover political reform, religious thought, prostitution, the
> voluntary hospital, popular sensational fiction, and the intellectual
> attack on Victorianism in the 1920s and thereafter.

Huber, Richard M. THE AMERICAN IDEA OF SUCCESS. New York: McGraw-
Hill, 1971. x, 563 p.

> Using success as the theme, this book ties together religion, moral
> philosophy, psychology, sociology, economics, and politics. The
> author emphasizes the success ideas of middle-class WASPs such as
> Benjamin Franklin, Henry Ward Beecher, Bruce Barton, Dale Car-
> negie, Norman Vincent Peale, and others.

Jackson, Carl T. "The New Thought Movement and the Nineteenth-Century
Discovery of Oriental Philosophy." JOURNAL OF POPULAR CULTURE 9 (Winter 1975): 523-48.

> Jackson examines the discovery of Eastern philosophical and relig-
> ious ideas in the nineteenth century. He focuses on the New
> Thought movement and ancient Indian thought, and suggests that
> neither this movement nor its contemporary counterpart were attrac-
> tive only to intellectuals.

_____. "The Orient in Post-Bellum American Thought: Three American Popu-
larizers." AMERICAN QUARTERLY 22 (Spring 1970): 67-81.

> This is a study of the work of James Freeman Clarke, Samuel John-
> son, and Moncure Conway. These men not only authored treatises
> on Oriental religions but also played active roles in post-Civil
> War movements with interests in the ideas of the Orient.

Jackson, John A. "Sociology and Literary Studies I. The Map of Society:
America in the 1890s." JOURNAL OF AMERICAN STUDIES 3 (July 1969):
103-10.

> Jackson argues that sociology and literary studies have something to
> say to each other in four areas: analysis of the social factors that

surround the writing; the use of literature by sociology to explain
particular periods; the analysis of literary work by a sociologist as
critic; and the appreciation by the sociologist of the weltanshauung
of the writer. He analyzes Crane's MAGGIE as a fictional illus-
tration of one of the problems of the 1890s--the city.

James, Bessie Rowland. ANNE ROYALL'S U.S.A. New Brunswick, N.J.:
Rutgers University Press, 1972. viii, 447 p.

Anne Royall was a contemporary of Frances Trollope and Harriet
Martineau, and a critic of the American people and their society
during the Jacksonian era. She was one of the first female journalists and an antifeminist who opposed suffrage and female abolitionists.

Jones, Robert W. JOURNALISM IN THE UNITED STATES. New York: E.P.
Dutton and Co., 1947. xvi, 728 p.

This book includes materials on rural weeklies, magazines, some
social and economic factors influencing journalism, and academic
instruction for journalists. The social and economic background is
weak and flimsy.

THE JOURNALS OF BRONSON ALCOTT. Selected and edited by Odell
Shepard. Boston: Little, Brown, 1938. xxx, 559 p.

These selections from Alcott's diaries cover his life from 1826 to
1882. They reveal a man who, as a transcendentalist, influenced
Emerson and Thoreau and was associated with most of the important
movements of his time.

Kalisch, Philip Arthur. THE ENOCH PRATT FREE LIBRARY: A SOCIAL HIS-
TORY. Metuchen, N.J.: Scarecrow Press, 1969. 264 p.

Pratt, a wealthy Baltimore merchant, endowed this library because
he believed that books could provide moral edification and social
mobility for the average American. Until 1926, the library's di-
rectors considered it an institution for the continuation of formal
education and made it difficult for the working class to use it.

Kantor, Harvey A. "The City Beautiful in New York." NEW-YORK HISTORI-
CAL SOCIETY QUARTERLY 57 (April 1973): 149-71.

The City Beautiful movement was the aesthetic renaissance that
changed the appearance of many cities in the late nineteenth and
the early twentieth centuries. This is a study of the effort to
bring improvement to New York City.

Kaser, David. MESSRS. CAREY AND LEA OF PHILADELPHIA: A STUDY IN
THE HISTORY OF THE BOOK TRADE. Philadelphia: University of Pennsylvania
Press, 1957. 182 p.

This study covers the period between 1821 and 1838. The development and place of Carey and Lea in the book trade are detailed, including the publication of American authors and reprinting English works.

_____, ed. BOOKS IN AMERICA'S PAST: ESSAYS HONORING RUDOLPH H. GJELSNESS. Charlottesville: University Press of Virginia, 1966. x, 279 p.

Gjelsness was chairman of the Department of Library Science at the University of Michigan. These essays by his students cover early American publishing and printing, college society libraries, French-language printing, children's books before the Civil War, and other subjects.

Kinsley, Philip. THE CHICAGO TRIBUNE: ITS FIRST HUNDRED YEARS. Vol. 1: 1847-1865. New York: Alfred A. Knopf, 1943. xv, 381 p.

From the days of Joseph Medill, who assumed the editorship in the mid-1850s, the TRIBUNE has had flaming personalities governing its editorial policies. Under Medill, it was outspokenly anti-southern, "Know-Nothing," and pro-Republican.

_____. THE CHICAGO TRIBUNE: ITS FIRST HUNDRED YEARS. Vol. 2: 1865-1880. Chicago: Chicago Tribune, 1945. xviii, 349 p.

This volume depicts a period of growth for the TRIBUNE during which the paper's circulation expanded. The paper supported Greeley for President, temperance, tariffs, and recognition of the legal rights of Negroes, but it also expressed the attitudes of big business.

_____. THE CHICAGO TRIBUNE: ITS FIRST HUNDRED YEARS. Vol. 3: 1880-1900. Chicago: Chicago Tribune, 1946. xiv, 359 p.

Joseph Medill was the policymaker during this period. This volume, like the first two in this history, is almost a day-by-day account of what the TRIBUNE reported.

Kligerman, Jack. "'Dress' or 'Incarnation' of Thought: Nineteenth-Century American Attitudes towards Language and Style." PROCEEDINGS OF THE AMERICAN PHILOSOPHICAL SOCIETY 117 (16 February 1973): 51-58.

The "dress" of thought is discursive logic, while the "incarnation" is creative imagination. In the nineteenth century, emphasis was on "incarnation" due to the discovery of metaphor as an organizing principle, with Emerson leading the way.

Knight, Oliver. FOLLOWING THE INDIAN WARS: THE STORY OF THE NEWSPAPER CORRESPONDENTS AMONG THE INDIAN CAMPAIGNERS. Norman: University of Oklahoma Press, 1960. xvi, 348 p.

Newspaper correspondents ate, slept, and fought alongside troops
in the Indian campaigns. They capitalized on interest in the West,
but were limited in performing their duties by commanding officers
who sought and valued publicity.

Kuhn, Anne L. THE MOTHER'S ROLE IN CHILDHOOD EDUCATION: NEW
ENGLAND CONCEPTS, 1830–1860. Yale Studies in Religious Education, no.
19. New Haven, Conn.: Yale University Press, 1947. x, 224 p.

This is an analysis of the flood of books and articles imploring
mothers to take responsibility for their families and offering advice
concerning how to do this during the period of urbanization and
industrialization in New England before the Civil War. Fathers
were abdicating their historical role as the head of the family because of their pursuit of wealth in business.

Lemelin, Robert. PATHWAY TO NATIONAL CHARACTER: 1830–1861. Port
Washington, N.Y.: Kennikat Press, 1974. 154 p.

American character in this study is based on accounts in American
travel books. Lemelin shows the motives for travel as well as the
feelings of insecurity of many Americans.

Lerner, Max. AMERICA AS A CIVILIZATION: LIFE AND THOUGHT IN THE
UNITED STATES TODAY. New York: Simon and Schuster, 1957. xiv, 1,036 p.

Lerner attributes American character to the moving frontier, moving
technology, and the moving democratic idea. Civilization is a
broad term involving the total pattern and total impact of society.

Logan, Rayford W. THE NEGRO IN AMERICAN LIFE AND THOUGHT: THE
NADIR, 1877–1901. New York: Dial Press, 1954. x, 380 p.

The road to reunion following Reconstruction was the road to reaction for the Negro. The period from 1877 to 1901 was one of
exploitation, disfranchisement, discrimination, segregation, and
lynching.

Lord, Clifford L., ed. KEEPERS OF THE PAST. Chapel Hill: University of
North Carolina Press, 1965. 241 p.

This is a collection of vignettes of eighteen pioneers in the growth
of historical societies, museums, archives, and restorations.

Loveland, Anne C. EMBLEM OF LIBERTY: THE IMAGE OF LAFAYETTE IN
THE AMERICAN MIND. Baton Rouge: Louisiana State University Press, 1971.
ix, 196 p.

Loveland concentrates on Lafayette's triumphal tour of the United
States in 1824–25. She finds that the Frenchman did not bulk large

in the American mind, but she argues that his intervention in the Revolution contributed to the American idea of mission.

Lyon, William H. THE PIONEER EDITOR IN MISSOURI, 1808-1860. Columbia: University of Missouri Press, 1965. vi, 202 p.

The pioneer editor was Joseph Charless who first established the GAZETTE in St. Louis. Lyon uses Charless to analyze the relationship between editors and their reading public.

McGovern, James R. "The American Woman's Pre-World War I Freedom in Manners and Morals." JOURNAL OF AMERICAN HISTORY 55 (September 1968): 315-33.

A number of historians have argued that a revolution in manners and morals took place in the 1920s, but McGovern shows that deterioration in controls existed earlier. A shift in morals took place after 1910 that particularly affected women in terms of greater expression of sexuality and diminished femininity.

McVey, Sheila. "Nineteenth Century America: Publishing in a Developing Country." ANNALS OF THE ACADEMY OF POLITICAL AND SOCIAL SCIENCE 421 (September 1975): 67-80.

Nineteenth-century America was almost completely dependent on British books for cultural sustenance. An intellectual neocolonialism existed because of the lack of indigenous authors and the fear of those who did write that books on America would be judged inferior.

Madison, Charles A. BOOK PUBLISHING IN AMERICA. New York: McGraw-Hill, 1966. xiv, 628 p.

The pre-Civil War era was a time of beginnings and piracy, giving way to a golden age in the late nineteenth century. Publishers exercised courtesy and ethics in a period identified by competition, but this atmosphere disappeared under the pressures of commercialism after 1900.

Mead, David. "1914: The Chautauqua and American Innocence." JOURNAL OF POPULAR CULTURE 1 (Spring 1968): 339-56.

It has been argued that World War I marked the end of American innocence and a weakening of the American faith in optimism, progress, and eternal moral values. The Chautauqua idea and the popularity of Chautauqua lectures, however, show that rural America did not reject its faith in American ideals.

Miles, Edwin A. "The Old South and the Classical World." NORTH CAROLINA HISTORICAL REVIEW 48 (July 1971): 258-75.

Many antebellum southerners thought that there was a more genuine appreciation of Greco-Roman civilization in their section than in the North. Some liked to maintain that they possessed a spiritual kinship with the citizens of the slave states of antiquity, and they resisted attacks on the traditional educational curriculum.

Mitterling, Philip I. AMERICA IN THE ANTARCTIC TO 1840. Urbana: University of Illinois Press, 1959. x, 201 p.

This is a study of explorations in the Antarctic region until the conception of a continent was added to geographical knowledge through the discoveries of the Wilkes expedition. It is an analysis of the ideas and arguments that led to the chartering of the first American overseas exploring expedition.

Moore, Arthur K. THE FRONTIER MIND: A CULTURAL ANALYSIS OF THE KENTUCKY FRONTIERSMAN. Lexington: University of Kentucky Press, 1957. xii, 264 p.

Moore argues that the frontier interfered with the development of an original culture of high order, and that the high-minded buckskin hero never existed. There were two types of frontiersmen—the Indian fighter and the "half alligator, half horse" riverman.

Mott, Frank Luther. AMERICAN JOURNALISM: A HISTORY OF NEWSPAPERS IN THE UNITED STATES THROUGH 250 YEARS, 1690 TO 1940. New York: Macmillan, 1941. ix, 772 p.

This study covers the great papers and outstanding editors from Benjamin Franklin to Joseph Pulitzer and William Allen White. Mott highlights news developments in different periods of history.

_____. A HISTORY OF AMERICAN MAGAZINES, 1740-1850. New York: D. Appleton, 1930. xvii, 848 p.

This compendium includes a chronological list of almost six hundred magazines. It is broken down into religious, scientific, and literary periodicals.

_____. A HISTORY OF AMERICAN MAGAZINES. Vol. 2: 1850-1865; Vol. 3: 1865-1885. Cambridge, Mass.: Harvard University Press, 1938. xvi, 608; xiii, 649 p.

The first half of each volume deals with the development of magazines, and the second covers the most important magazines founded during the period. Mott believes that magazines more than newspapers reveal the life of the times during which they were printed.

_____. A HISTORY OF AMERICAN MAGAZINES. Vol. 4: 1885-1905. Cambridge, Mass.: Belknap Press of Harvard University Press, 1957. xxii, 858 p.

This volume covers the golden age of American magazines. It was a time of editors such as Walter Hines Page, S.S. McClure, Albert Shaw, and others, and magazines such as FORUM, ARENA, McCLURE'S, REVIEW OF REVIEWS, and OUTLOOK.

_____. A HISTORY OF AMERICAN MAGAZINES. Vol. 5: 1905-1930. SKETCHES OF 21 MAGAZINES, 1905-1930. Cambridge, Mass.: Belknap Press of Harvard University Press, 1968. xvii, 595 p.

This volume was unfinished at the time of Mott's death in 1964. Of particular importance are his discussions of the AMERICAN MERCURY, NEW REPUBLIC, SMART SET, and TIME.

Muraskin, William A. MIDDLE-CLASS BLACKS IN WHITE SOCIETY: PRINCE HALL FREEMASONRY IN AMERICA. Berkeley and Los Angeles: University of California Press, 1975. xi, 318 p.

Muraskin argues that whites have been too prejudiced to give equal rights to blacks, regardless of their social class, and that the black mass has not been able to identify with the black middle class. Middle-class blacks have not accepted leadership and have attempted to gain white values.

Nash, Roderick. WILDERNESS AND THE AMERICAN MIND. New Haven, Conn.: Yale University Press, 1967. viii, 256 p.

Puritans brought an antiwilderness sentiment to America where primeval forests were a threat to man's survival. Such an idea persisted in the nineteenth century, but in the twentieth century a wilderness cult developed which looked upon wilderness wistfully and led to the Federal Wilderness Act of 1964.

Nye, Russel B. THE ALMOST CHOSEN PEOPLE: ESSAYS IN THE HISTORY OF AMERICAN IDEAS. East Lansing: Michigan State University Press, 1966. x, 374 p.

Nye discusses the idea of progress, nationalism, the tradition of free enterprise, sense of mission, equality, and other matters. He attempts to explain what has been a uniquely American historical experience.

_____. SOCIETY AND CULTURE IN AMERICA, 1830-1860. New American Nation Series. Edited by Henry Steele Commager and Richard B. Morris. New York: Harper and Row, 1974. xiv, 432 p.

This is a study in the ways Americans thought and acted. The author emphasizes transformations but sees change taking place through original institutions and original philosophy.

Ostrander, Gilman M. AMERICAN CIVILIZATION IN THE FIRST MACHINE AGE: 1890-1945. New York: Harper and Row, 1970. vii, 414 p.

> The emergence of an industrial-technological order after 1890 caused a shift in American character from a patriarchal faith in the value of age and experience to a "filiarchal" faith in the promise of youth and technological innovation. Moral absolutism broke down, permissive child-rearing and progressive education spread, ethnic conflict declined, and the United States became an ethnocracy and a pluralist culture with conflict running on generational lines.

Parrington, Vernon Louis, Jr. AMERICAN DREAMS: A STUDY OF AMERICAN UTOPIAS. Brown University Studies, vol. 11; Americana Series, no. 2. Providence, R.I.: Brown University, 1947. 234 p.

> This is a study of utopian literature. The author discusses Hawthorne's BLITHEDALE ROMANCE, some of the muckrakers, James Hilton's LOST HORIZON, and Edward Bellamy's LOOKING BACKWARD, among other works.

Pearce, Roy Harvey. THE SAVAGES OF AMERICA: A STUDY OF THE INDIAN AND THE IDEA OF CIVILIZATION. Baltimore: Johns Hopkins Press, 1953. xv, 252 p.

> Pearce delineates the origins of the idea of the savage in colonial times. He also shows how this important symbol was used in social, historical, and imaginative writings between 1777 and 1851.

Peckham, Howard H. "Books and Reading on the Ohio Valley Frontier." MISSISSIPPI VALLEY HISTORICAL REVIEW 44 (March 1958): 649-53.

> The Ohio Valley frontier was not a bookless wilderness. Settlers brought books with them, storekeepers imported books, printers manufactured them, and books were the inspiration and teacher of the pioneer.

Persons, Stow. AMERICAN MINDS: A HISTORY OF IDEAS. New York: Henry Holt, 1958. xii, 467 p.

> Persons has found five dominant minds in American history: the colonial religious mind, mind of the Enlightenment, mind of nineteenth-century democracy, naturalistic mind, and the contemporary neodemocratic mind. These minds provided intellectuals a common set of assumptions for work and communication.

_____. THE DECLINE OF AMERICAN GENTILITY. New York: Columbia University Press, 1973. viii, 336 p.

Until the Civil War, America was dominated by elites that set standards of gentility. These groups were placed on the defensive during the late nineteenth century and lost their purpose following World War I.

Peterson, Merrill D. THE JEFFERSON IMAGE IN THE AMERICAN MIND. New York: Oxford University Press, 1960. x, 548 p.

Peterson tells the story of the idolatry, distortion, neglect, rediscovery, and ultimate canonization of Jefferson in the memorial in Washington. History from nullification to Franklin Roosevelt based liberalism on Jefferson's creed.

Pierson, George W. TOCQUEVILLE AND BEAUMONT IN AMERICA. New York: Oxford University Press, 1938. xiv, 852 p.

This study combines biographical detail with Tocqueville and Beaumont's developing comprehension of American culture and politics. The setting is in narratives of their travels gleaned from records of conversations, letters, diaries, pamphlets, and other documents.

Porter, Lawrence C. "Transcendentalism: A Self-Portrait." NEW ENGLAND QUARTERLY 35 (March 1962): 27–47.

This self-portrait is taken from the transcendentalists' private statements. They were dedicated to a combination of ideas, but each retained his or her individuality.

Rammelkamp, Julian S. PULITZER'S POST-DISPATCH, 1878–1883. Princeton, N.J.: Princeton University Press, 1967. xiii, 326 p.

This is an institutional history of the St. Louis paper and not a biography of Pulitzer. The paper became the voice of the middle-class merchant and citizen who feared the changes produced by great wealth and monopoly as well as by labor.

Rice, William B. THE LOS ANGELES STAR, 1851–1864: THE BEGINNINGS OF JOURNALISM IN SOUTHERN CALIFORNIA. Edited by John Walton Caughey. Berkeley and Los Angeles: University of California Press, 1947. xvi, 315 p.

The author emphasizes issues in the public mind as reported by this newspaper. The STAR was sympathetic to the South during the Civil War and advocated the establishment of a western republic.

Ross, Margaret. ARKANSAS GAZETTE: THE EARLY YEARS, 1819–1866. Little Rock: Arkansas Gazette Foundation, 1969. xii, 428 p.

This is a study in Arkansas journalistic and political history. The author believes that frontier newspapers were closely bound to politics, but she provides a useful understanding of frontier journalism.

Sanford, Charles L. THE QUEST FOR PARADISE: EUROPE AND THE AMERI-
CAN MORAL IMAGINATION. Urbana: University of Illinois Press, 1961.
x, 282 p.

> The quest for paradise is the myth of return to some lost primal in-
> nocence through self-assertion. The discovery of America rescued
> the Edenic myth from its religious context, and Sanford traces this
> from the Puritans to President Eisenhower and from Henry James to
> Jack Kerouac.

Schlesinger, Arthur M. "'What Then is the American, This New Man?'"
AMERICAN HISTORICAL REVIEW 48 (January 1943): 225-44.

> This is an assessment of American character. Schlesinger argues
> that Americans brought certain traits from Europe, but they also
> acquired such traits as reverence for work, optimism, wasteful
> living, individualism, and others from their New World environ-
> ment.

Schmitt, Peter J. BACK TO NATURE: THE ARCADIAN MYTH IN URBAN
AMERICA. New York: Oxford University Press, 1969. xxiii, 230 p.

> The urge of comfortable Americans to commune with nature was an
> urban desire. It was not a rejection of the city but rather a means
> of strengthening urban life through an easy cooperation between the
> dominant metropolis and a subordinate countryside.

Schneider, Herbert W. A HISTORY OF AMERICAN PHILOSOPHY. New
York: Columbia University Press, 1947. xiv, 646 p.

> Schneider argues that American philosophy represents a number of
> reflections of European philosophy. Only in the twentieth century
> is the United States on the threshold of a new cultural era.

Schroth, Raymond A. THE EAGLE AND BROOKLYN: A COMMUNITY NEWS-
PAPER, 1841-1955. Westport, Conn.: Greenwood, 1974. xv, 304 p.

> The EAGLE was the most widely read evening newspaper in the
> country until the Civil War. Schroth shows that it declined in
> the twentieth century because Brooklyn declined as a haven of the
> Protestant middle class.

Scott, Anne Firor. THE SOUTHERN LADY: FROM PEDESTAL TO POLITICS,
1830-1930. Chicago: University of Chicago Press, 1970. xv, 247 p.

> Scott shows that the antebellum southern lady occupied an ambig-
> uous, often unenviable, position in society, and never was en-
> shrined at the top of the social order. She was resourceful and
> resilient, and she was liberated by the Civil War.

Sheehan, Donald. THIS WAS PUBLISHING: A CHRONICLE OF THE BOOK TRADE IN THE GILDED AGE. Bloomington: Indiana University Press, 1952. xiv, 288 p.

This study covers the period from the end of the Civil War to the beginning of World War I. Chapters are devoted to the philosophy of publishing, business, contracts, the creative aspects of publishing, and the general public as buyer.

Smith, Duane E. "Romanticism in America: The Transcendentalists." REVIEW OF POLITICS 35 (July 1973): 302-25.

Transcendentalism is linked with liberalism. The transcendentalists attempted to use liberal means of a commitment to the uniqueness of individual genius for romantic ends, and they transformed both liberalism and romanticism.

Starr, Louis M. BOHEMIAN BRIGADE: CIVIL WAR NEWSMEN IN ACTION. New York: Alfred A. Knopf, 1954. xx, 368 p.

Starr emphasizes reporting in the NEW YORK TRIBUNE. He also covers the HERALD and the TIMES as well as papers in Boston, Chicago, Philadelphia, and other cities.

Stern, Madeleine B. IMPRINTS ON HISTORY: BOOK PUBLISHING AND AMERICAN FRONTIERS. Bloomington: Indiana University Press, 1956. xii, 492 p.

Frontiers in the land as well as frontiers of the mind are examined. The author emphasizes key figures in publishing who illustrate a particular cultural phenomenon.

Stinson, Robert. "McClure's Road to McCLURE'S: How Revolutionary Were 1890s Magazines." JOURNALISM QUARTERLY 47 (Summer 1970): 256-62.

The rise of cheap monthly magazines in the 1890s did not constitute a journalistic revolution. Stinson demonstrates that McClure's ideas concerning his magazine evolved gradually, and some were imitations of the past.

Stoehr, Taylor. "'Eloquence Needs No Constable'--Alcott, Emerson, and Thoreau on the State." CANADIAN REVIEW OF AMERICAN STUDIES 5 (Fall 1974): 81-100.

Stoehr examines the attitudes toward civic obligations of the three transcendentalists. He shows that they were lured out of their individualism and into partisanship by the antislavery movement, or by the Mexican War and Fugitive Slave Act.

Strout, Cushing. AMERICAN IMAGE OF THE OLD WORLD. New York: Harper and Row, 1963. xvi, 288 p.

> This is the story of the rise, development, and decline of the American tradition of looking toward the Old World which was believed to be alien and inferior. Colonists reluctantly cut Old World ties, the founding fathers were isolationistic, and some writers looked at the Old World nostalgically, while nativists used European images to reenforce their beliefs.

_____. "The Pluralistic Identity of William James: A Psychohistorical Reading of THE VARIETIES OF RELIGIOUS EXPERIENCE." AMERICAN QUARTERLY 23 (May 1971): 135-52.

> In the VARIETIES, James explored all the documentation he could find on wretchedness, fear, spiritual torment, and conversions, and demonstrated the centrality of the twice-born conversion of the sick soul as being the central religious experience. Strout believes that James was expressing his own conversion that was the outcome of a major psyhological crisis in his young life.

Sutton, Walter. THE WESTERN BOOK TRADE: CINCINNATI AS A NINE-TEENTH-CENTURY PUBLISHING AND BOOK-TRADE CENTER. Columbus: Ohio State University Press for the Ohio Historical Society, 1961. xvi, 360 p.

> In the first half of the nineteenth century, Cincinnati was the fourth leading book publishing center in the United States. By the 1830s, presses were issuing three hundred fifty thousand books per year, many of which were McGuffey Readers.

Thomas, John Wesley. JAMES FREEMAN CLARKE, APOSTLE OF GERMAN CULTURE TO AMERICA. Boston: John W. Luce and Co., 1949. 168 p.

> Clarke was a Transcendentalist and Unitarian minister whose philosophy was shaped in opposition to the materialistic atmosphere of Boston. He studied and translated the works of German writers including Goethe.

Thornbrough, Emma Lou. T. THOMAS FORTUNE: MILITANT JOURNALIST. Chicago: University of Chicago Press, 1972. xi, 388 p.

> During the last quarter of the nineteenth century, Fortune made the New York AGE into the most influential black paper and founded the Afro-American League. He enjoyed a close relationship with Booker T. Washington until 1907 when they broke over disfranchisement and segregation.

Thorpe, Earl E. THE MIND OF THE NEGRO: AN INTELLECTUAL HISTORY OF AFRO-AMERICANS. Baton Rouge, La.: Harrington Publications, 1961. xxiv, 562 p.

The central theme of Negro thought has been the quest for freedom and equality. The record indicates that blacks have pursued this objective with modesty, kindness, humility, and faith.

_____. THE OLD SOUTH: A PSYCHOHISTORY. Durham, N.C.: Harrington, 1972. xii, 313 p.

Thorpe's theme is the psychic sickness of a neurotic slaveholding society. He attempts to show the conflict between the slave's idealization of Freud's pleasure principle and the slaveholder's insistence on the reality principle.

Trachtenberg, Alan. BROOKLYN BRIDGE: FACT AND SYMBOL. New York: Oxford University Press, 1965. viii, 182 p.

This is the story of the building of a bridge and its changing role as a cultural symbol. The Brooklyn Bridge was built to realize material gain, promote national unity, and free America from the past, but it evoked many responses.

Trenden, Robert. "The Expurgation of Antislavery Materials by American Presses." JOURNAL OF NEGRO HISTORY 63 (July 1973): 271-90.

The slavepower in the South, as it functioned in the federal government and society, had a great deal of influence in suppressing and expurgating antislavery materials in pieces of American and English literature published by American presses. Its tactics were exposed largely by the abolitionists William Jay and Lewis Tappan.

Tryon, Warren S. "The Publications of Ticknor and Fields in the South, 1840-1865." JOURNAL OF SOUTHERN HISTORY 14 (August 1948): 305-30.

To answer the question as to whether southerners were a bookish people, Tryon examines the records of Ticknor and Fields, publishers of Hawthorne, Holmes, Longfellow, Lowell, Emerson, Thoreau, and others. These records indicate that the sales of this publisher increased year after year in spite of growing sectional differences, but the Cotton Kingdom was not a large purchaser of books compared with other sections.

Tyler, Robert L. "The I.W.W. and the West." AMERICAN QUARTERLY 12 (Summer 1960): 175-87.

This is a study of the Wobblies in popular literature and historiography. They were viewed first as dangerous foreign syndicalists, but later were seen as an organization of manly primitives who were fighting the good fight for freedom.

Vance, James E., Jr. "The Classical Revival and Urban-Rural Conflict in Nineteenth Century North America." CANADIAN REVIEW OF AMERICAN STUDIES 4 (Fall 1973): 149-68.

Vance explores the origin of anti-urban sentiment. He finds it in the Roman conception of citizenship based in the countryside that found expression in the classical revival of the nineteenth century.

Ward, John William. ANDREW JACKSON, SYMBOL FOR AN AGE. New York: Oxford University Press, 1955. xii, 274 p.

Jackson symbolized for the American people all things on which they based their national pride. His victory at New Orleans during the War of 1812 provided a glorious end to that war and made him an important symbol in the American myth structure.

_____. RED, WHITE, AND BLUE: MEN, BOOKS, AND IDEAS IN AMERI-CAN CULTURE. New York: Oxford University Press, 1969. x, 351 p.

These essays cover history and the concept of culture, American culture and the imagination, the culture of freedom, and the intellectual and the university. Ward suggests that man is a symbol-using animal that creates symbols to reflect his social experience, and this has endangered individualism.

Wector, Dixon. THE SAGA OF AMERICAN SOCIETY: A RECORD OF SOCIAL ASPIRATION, 1607-1937. New York: Charles Scribner's Sons, 1937. xiii, 504 p.

This is a history of social prestige in America. Since the settlers did not bring prestige from Europe, they forged it, and this has been going on ever since as witnessed and nourished in newspapers' society pages.

Weigley, Emma Seifrit. "It Might Have Been Euthenics: The Lake Placid Conferences and the Home Economics Movement." AMERICAN QUARTERLY 26 (March 1974): 79-96.

The home economics movement was part of the liberation of women during the years following the Civil War. Pioneers in the movement regarded home economics as family care and worked to bring about its professionalization.

Weiss, Richard. THE AMERICAN MYTH OF SUCCESS: FROM HORATIO ALGER TO NORMAN VINCENT PEALE. New York: Basic Books, 1969. 276 p.

This is a history of the New Thought movement of the early twentieth century that embodied Emersonian idealism and represented an attempt to bring about feelings of mastery. Mastery was to be achieved through material success and also through inner fulfillment and optimism.

Welter, Barbara. "Anti-Intellectualism and the American Woman: 1800-1860." MID-AMERICA 48 (October 1966): 258-70.

Anti-intellectualism emphasized that women used neither logic nor reason, but sought truth through the heart. Women transcended the grossness of the flesh, appeared as the Earth Mother, and were untouched by human intellect.

_____. "The Cult of True Womanhood: 1820-1860." AMERICAN QUARTERLY 18 (Summer 1966): 151-74.

Mid-nineteenth-century writers on women used the phrase "True Womanhood" to symbolize the woman who was a source of stability in an unstable society. She possessed the virtues of piety, purity, submissiveness, and domesticity, and these added up to the role of mother, daughter, sister, and wife.

Welter, Rush. "The Frontier West as Image of American Society: Conservative Attitudes before the Civil War." MISSISSIPPI VALLEY HISTORICAL REVIEW 46 (March 1960): 593-614.

In the middle period, eastern conservative spokesmen reversed a trend to deprecate the influence and prospects of the West. They began to view the region as a place where orthodox, republican, middle-class customs could not only prosper but also triumph in an economic and social utopia.

_____. "The Frontier West as Image of American Society, 1776-1860." PACIFIC NORTHWEST QUARTERLY 52 (January 1961): 1-6.

Between 1776 and 1860 Americans saw the West as a limitless extension of the social, economic, and political values they associated with the country at large. Antebellum commentators on the West emphasized most of the elements that Frederick Jackson Turner developed in his frontier thesis.

_____. "The Idea of Progess in America: An Essay in Ideas and Method." JOURNAL OF THE HISTORY OF IDEAS 16 (June 1955): 401-15.

The European form of the idea of progress matured into a revolutionary dogma that social problems could be eradicated simply by eradicating the society from which they had sprung. This essentially millenarian view was not the meaning of progress in America where it was represented as a continuation of the present.

_____. THE MIND OF AMERICA, 1820-1860. New York: Columbia University Press, 1975. xvi, 603 p.

This is a study of American thought at large, the ideas of the people, rather than systematic thought. It emphasizes the liberal-conservative dichotomy as equated with the Democrats and the Whigs.

Wertheim, Arthur Frank. THE NEW YORK LITTLE RENAISSANCE: ICONO-
CLASM, MODERNISM, AND NATIONALISM IN AMERICAN CULTURE, 1908-
1917. New York: New York University Press, 1976. 276 p.

A new indigenous American art and literature was created between
1908 and 1917. This was the product of radicals who were published in THE MASSES, H.L. Mencken, and contributors to SEVEN
ARTS and THE NEW REPUBLIC.

White, G. Edward. THE EASTERN ESTABLISHMENT AND THE WESTERN EX-
PERIENCE: THE WEST OF FREDERIC REMINGTON, THEODORE ROOSEVELT,
AND OWEN WISTER. New Haven, Conn.: Yale University Press, 1968.
238 p.

How did three easterners respond to the West in the 1880s and
1890s? Discussed here are the circumstances in the backgrounds
of Remington, Roosevelt, and Wister that caused them to need the
masculine experience of life in the cattle country.

White, Morton, and White, Lucia. THE INTELLECTUAL VERSUS THE CITY:
FROM THOMAS JEFFERSON TO FRANK LLOYD WRIGHT. Cambridge: Harvard University Press and M.I.T. Press, 1962. xii, 270 p.

The Whites develop the theme of anti-urbanism beginning with Crevecoeur, Franklin, and Jefferson and concluding with Wright. They
cover the ideas of Melville, Hawthorne, Poe, Henry Adams, William James, Dreiser, Jane Addams, Robert Park, and Dewey, and
conclude that anti-urbanism did not spring from a romanticism inherent in American character.

Whitehill, Walter Muir. BOSTON PUBLIC LIBRARY: A CENTENNIAL HIS-
TORY. Cambridge, Mass.: Harvard University Press, 1956. xii, 274 p.

Whitehill details the activities of such library pioneers as Ticknor,
Everett, and Winsor. He brings the history forward through the
depression years and consolidation.

_____. INDEPENDENT HISTORICAL SOCIETIES: AN ENQUIRY INTO THEIR
RESEARCH AND PUBLICATION FUNCTIONS AND THEIR FINANCIAL FUTURE.
Boston: Boston Athenaeum, 1962. xviii, 593 p.

This is a survey of historical societies, libraries, archival establish-
ments, and museums throughout the United States. Whitehill argues
that these institutions should concentrate on research and publication.

Wiener, Philip P. "The Evolutionism and Pragmatism of Pierce." JOURNAL
OF THE HISTORY OF IDEAS 7 (June 1946): 321-50.

Charles Pierce saw evolutionism as the "cosmic growth of concrete
reasonableness," and he used this conception to construct an evolu-

tionary cosmology. He argued that people cannot grow in reasonableness unless they establish logical procedures in their thought and these procedures become "practical" methods of doing things.

Wild, John. THE RADICAL EMPIRICISM OF WILLIAM JAMES. Garden City, N.Y.: Doubleday, 1969. x, 430 p.

Wild links James with existentialism and phenomenology. James was one of a number of figures in the western world who studied mental phenomena as a means of expressing dissatisfaction with the artificial abstractness of traditional thought.

Williams, Lorraine A. "Northern Intellectual Reaction to Military Rule During the Civil War." HISTORIAN 27 (May 1965): 334-49.

Intellectuals accepted military rule as a wartime necessity. They believed that rigid adherence to the tradition of freedom might end in the destruction of the Union and democratic government should be sufficiently flexible to adapt to emergencies.

_____. "Northern Intellectual Reaction to the Policy of Emancipation." JOURNAL OF NEGRO HISTORY 46 (July 1961): 174-88.

Intellectuals were perturbed with Lincoln's policy of emancipation. They believed, however, that an emancipation policy was the only way to end the war, insure permanent peace, and deter foreign intervention.

Williamson, William Landrum. WILLIAM FREDERICK POOLE AND THE MODERN LIBRARY MOVEMENT. New York: Columbia University Press, 1963. x, 203 p.

Libraries and library development rather than Poole's personality are emphasized. Poole was known as the head of Newberry Library and as the originator of POOLE'S INDEX TO POPULAR LITERATURE.

Wilson, Harold S. McCLURE'S MAGAZINE AND THE MUCKRAKERS. Princeton, N.J.: Princeton University Press, 1970. ix, 347 p.

The objective of this study is to discover the origins of muckraking. McCLURE'S became an instrument of critical journalism after 1900 and developed a coherent social criticism even though an editorial split over muckraking caused a walkout by Ida Tarbell, Ray Stannard Baker, Lincoln Steffens, and others in 1906.

Wish, Harvey. "Aristotle, Plato, and the Mason-Dixon Line." JOURNAL OF THE HISTORY OF IDEAS 10 (April 1949): 254-66.

Wish reviews the ideas of certain proslavery writers in the South and depicts the influence of Aristotle on their thinking. They distorted Aristotle, since he defended only the "natural slave," who was a backward fellow, but he provided them with a feeling of moral superiority over northern radicals who flaunted Plato.

_____. SOCIETY AND THOUGHT IN EARLY AMERICA: A SOCIAL AND INTELLECTUAL HISTORY OF THE AMERICAN PEOPLE THROUGH 1865. SOCIETY AND THOUGHT IN AMERICA, vol. 1. New York: David McKay Co., 1950. xii, 612 p.

Cultural interactions with Europe that resulted in distinctive American institutions are detailed. This study represents a weaving of institutional and intellectual history.

_____. SOCIETY AND THOUGHT IN MODERN AMERICA: A SOCIAL AND INTELLECTUAL HISTORY OF THE AMERICAN PEOPLE FROM 1865. SOCIETY AND THOUGHT IN AMERICA, vol. 2. New York: David McKay Co., 1952. xii, 644 p.

Wish credits the city and the Industrial Revolution with transforming the United States. He also shows how human will and intelligence tended to vary this dominant cultural pattern.

Wishy, Bernard. THE CHILD AND THE REPUBLIC: THE DAWN OF MODERN CHILD NURTURE. Philadelphia: University of Pennsylvania Press, 1968. x, 205 p.

Wishy confines himself to didactic writings on child nurture, the literature of the child-study movement of the 1880s, and children's books. In the period before the Civil War, as doctrines of free grace emerged, parents were taught that tenderness, patience, and love would produce children of integrity, while in the postwar period the emphasis on Darwinism produced a new realism, but preserved the image of the heroically moral child.

Wittke, Carl. THE GERMAN-LANGUAGE PRESS IN AMERICA. Lexington: University of Kentucky Press, 1957. viii, 311 p.

German-language journalism began with the PHILADELPHISCHE ZEITUNG of 1732 and developed through the Forty-eighters and the large groups of immigrants. In the 1890s, some eight hundred German newspapers were being published.

Wyllie, Irvin G. THE SELF-MADE MAN IN AMERICA: THE MYTH OF RAGS TO RICHES. New Brunswick, N.J.: Rutgers University Press, 1954. x, 210 p.

Success in America has meant business success. The central creed of the self-made man has been power within the person rather than outside conditions.

1915 TO THE PRESENT

Bogue, Allan G. "Social Theory and the Pioneer." AGRICULTURAL HISTORY 34 (January 1960): 21-34.

Bogue suggests that the social structure of pioneer communities influenced the personalities of the residents. He examines the work of historians and social scientists to demonstrate this view.

Boorstin, Daniel J. THE IMAGE: OR, WHAT HAPPENED TO THE AMERICAN DREAM. New York: Atheneum, 1962. x, 315 p.

Standards and habits are bad, and Americans fake news, cultivate illusions, and indulge in moral laziness. The author observes television, radio, journalism, and national habits in reading.

Boyer, Paul S. "Boston Book Censorship in the Twenties." AMERICAN QUARTERLY 15 (Spring 1963): 3-24.

This essay shows how "Banned in Boston" became a slogan that was certain to boost sales of books, magazines, and plays. The New England Watch and Ward Society, founded in the late nineteenth century, was devoted to rooting out environmental evils, including reading materials, and it was joined in the 1920s by the Roman Catholic Church in demanding censorship of the new literature.

Buni, Andrew. ROBERT L. VANN OF THE PITTSBURGH COURIER: POLITICS AND BLACK JOURNALISM. Pittsburgh: University of Pittsburgh Press, 1974. xv, 410 p.

Vann was a leading lawyer and editor who made the COURIER into the leading black journal in the nation and served as a key figure for blacks during the New Deal. He served his race vigorously and courageously although he often disagreed with other black leaders.

Capps, Finis Herbert. FROM ISOLATIONISM TO INVOLVEMENT: THE SWEDISH IMMIGRANT PRESS IN AMERICA, 1914-1945. Chicago: Swedish Pioneer Historical Society, 1966. xv, 238 p.

This is a study of the Americanization of Swedish Americans. Their newspapers replaced Swedish with English and their foreign policy views were remarkably constant where they supported the League of Nations and the United Nations, and condemned England and France as profit-loving and power-mad.

Carlisle, Rodney P. "William Randolph Hearst: A Fascist Reputation Reconsidered." JOURNALISM QUARTERLY 50 (Spring 1973): 125-33.

The author examines Hearst by way of contrasting Populist-Progressive ideas and the New Deal. He argues that the publisher broke with Franklin Delano Roosevelt because the administration's actions went beyond his progressivism.

Chenoweth, Lawrence. THE AMERICAN DREAM OF SUCCESS: THE SEARCH FOR SELF IN THE TWENTIETH CENTURY. North Scituate, Mass.: Duxbury Press, 1974. xvi, 237 p.

Modern middle-class Americans have become increasingly frustrated in attempts to find a satisfying life and an understandable society. Chenoweth traces their attitudes by using popular articles, self-help books, and comic strips.

Cohen, Morris. AMERICAN THOUGHT: A CRITICAL SKETCH. Edited by Felix S. Cohen. Glencoe, Ill.: Free Press, 1954. 360 p.

Cohen explicates the thought mainly of Cooley, Pound, Santayana, and Dewey, men whom he knew. This book is a series of intellectual conversations on legal thought, general philosophy, aesthetics, and science.

Conrad, Will C.; Wilson, Kathleen F.; and Wilson, Dale. THE MILWAUKEE JOURNAL: THE FIRST EIGHTY YEARS. Madison: University of Wisconsin Press, 1964. xv, 232 p.

This is a study of the JOURNAL'S editorial policies on national issues and of the individuals who guided the newspaper. The JOURNAL was a voice of moderation, although Democratic in national elections, and a supporter of LaFollette and Milwaukee's Socialists.

Curti, Merle. "American Philanthropy and the National Character." AMERICAN QUARTERLY 10 (Winter 1958): 420-37.

Generosity and mutual helpfulness are traits of American character. Curti traces philanthropy from colonial times to the democratization of giving in the twentieth century, a phenomenon that has added substance and method to democratic faith.

_____. HUMAN NATURE IN AMERICAN THOUGHT. Columbia: University of Missouri Press, 1968. ix, 117 p.

Curti links the Puritans' pessimistic view of human nature with Reinhold Niebuhr, and Jefferson's NOTES ON VIRGINIA with the new history of Beard and Becker. He also examines a third group of historians who, like Henry Adams, tried to find a scientific explanation of human nature and utilized the work of Marx and Freud.

_____. "Intellectuals and Other People." AMERICAN HISTORICAL REVIEW 60 (January 1955): 259-82.

This is a study of the historical bases of American distrust of intellectuals. Curti suggests that intellectuals should examine their own attitudes toward people as thinking citizens and toward themselves.

_____, ed. AMERICAN SCHOLARSHIP IN THE TWENTIETH CENTURY. With essays by Merle Curti et al. Cambridge, Mass.: Harvard University Press, 1953. vii, 252 p.

In this collection of essays, one chapter each is assigned to history, literature, the classics, philosophy, and the social sciences. Of special importance are W. Stull Holt's chapter on history and Rene Welleck's on literature.

Fox, Daniel M. "The Achievement of the Federal Writers' Project." AMERICAN QUARTERLY 13 (Spring 1961): 3-19.

This is essentially a study of the American Guides series that included tourbooks, almanacs, natural history books, state guides, and other publications. The series was affected by the conflict between work relief and culture, as well as by local and regional prejudices.

Graham, Hugh Davis. CRISIS IN PRINT: DESEGREGATION AND THE PRESS IN TENNESSEE. Nashville: Vanderbilt University Press, 1967. viii, 338 p.

During the decade 1954-64, Tennessee's newspapers divided into two groups over desegregation: strict-constructionist defenders of state sovereignty and moderates who supported gradual desegregation. To reinforce the moderate press, Tennessee had a group of moderate politicians, and both worked to maintain a pluralistic rather than a closed society.

Greenleaf, William. FROM THESE BEGINNINGS: THE EARLY PHILANTHROPIES OF HENRY AND EDSEL FORD, 1911-1936. Detroit: Wayne State University Press, 1964. 235 p.

This is a study of Henry Ford's philanthropic activities before the establishment of the Ford Foundation. Ford criticized philanthropy but organized a sociological department in his company and reconstructed the past at Wayside Inn and Greenfield Village.

Hand, Samuel B. "Rosenman, Thucydides, and the New Deal." JOURNAL OF AMERICAN HISTORY 55 (September 1968): 334-48.

Judge Samuel I. Rosenman was drafted by Franklin D. Roosevelt to edit his public papers and addresses for publication. This is a study of Rosenman's editorial endeavors as well as an assessment of the importance of the undertaking.

Hartshorne, Thomas L. THE DISTORTED IMAGE: CHANGING CONCEPTIONS OF THE AMERICAN CHARACTER SINCE TURNER. Cleveland: Press of Case Western Reserve University, 1968. xiv, 226 p.

Hartshorne argues that conceptions of American character have not changed much since the beginning of the twentieth century. Herbert Croly looked to a new urban, collectivist character, nativists feared the impact of immigration, intellectuals criticized Protestant definitions, but in the 1930s social scientists turned away from impressionistic views and attempted to apply culture and personality methods.

Higham, John. "The Schism in American Scholarship." AMERICAN HISTORICAL REVIEW 72 (October 1966): 1-21.

The humanities in America have no meaningful or coherent identity. They should not be considered as distinct from the social sciences because no group of disciplines has a monopoly on values or measurement.

Johnson, Abby Ann Arthur. "The Personal Magazine: Margaret C. Anderson and the LITTLE REVIEW, 1914-1929." SOUTH ATLANTIC QUARTERLY 75 (Summer 1976): 351-64.

The personal magazine is important in literary history because it allows the editor great freedom but also demands much in terms of being provocative. Anderson's magazine was important since she was a colorful personality and recognized quality work in Pound, Joyce, Eliot, Sherwood Anderson, William Carlos Williams, and other writers.

Johnson, Walter. WILLIAM ALLEN WHITE'S AMERICA. New York: Henry Holt, 1947. 621 p.

White was a paradoxical figure, small town, on the one hand, metropolitan, on the other. This is a portrait of a middle-class folk hero, who supported the Republicans and was at his best when fighting demagogues.

Jones, Howard Mumford. IDEAS IN AMERICA. Cambridge, Mass.: Harvard University Press, 1944. xi, 304 p.

This is a collection of Jones's essays and addresses published during the 1930s and early 1940s. The author discusses the needs of literary history and the history of ideas, and presents an Emersonian critique of the society in which he lived.

Juergens, George. JOSEPH PULITZER AND THE NEW YORK WORLD. Princeton, N.J.: Princeton University Press, 1966. xvi, 392 p.

Juergens covers only three years in the life of the WORLD, 1883-85, but these were critical years for the newspaper because Pulitzer rescued it from decline and introduced the new journalism. The publisher and the paper are described in terms of life in New York City during the time.

Keller, Phyllis. "George Sylvester Viereck: The Psychology of a German-American Militant." JOURNAL OF INTERDISCIPLINARY HISTORY 2 (Summer 1971): 59-108.

Keller argues that Viereck's ambivalence concerning America was the result of a conflict between a mother and father fixation. But she also reviews his poetry and other writings in support of Germany, both during World War I and the 1930s, and concludes that in his militancy he sometimes spoke about the psychological, intellectual, and social strivings of German-Americans generally.

Kirkendall, Richard S. "Franklin D. Roosevelt and the Service Intellectual." MISSISSIPPI VALLEY HISTORICAL REVIEW 49 (December 1962): 456-71.

Roosevelt promoted the development of the service intellectual in politics and urged cooperation between politicians and professors. He dominated the New Deal, but he recognized that higher education had been developing a utilitarian emphasis and he employed professors even though he was criticized by both Democrats and Republicans for doing so.

Knoles, George H. "American Intellectuals and World War I." PACIFIC NORTHWEST QUARTERLY 59 (October 1968): 203-15.

World War I evoked a varied response in the United States. Various intellectuals saw it as symptomatic of the disease of mediocrity, an escape from freedom, a death wish, and a bridge of conscience to relieve tension in society.

Kobre, Sidney. FOUNDATIONS OF AMERICAN JOURNALISM. Tallahassee: Florida State University Press, 1958. xi, 362 p.

This is not a history of newspapers and magazines. Kobre covers the evolution of communication and printing, emergence of the editorial page, changes in news-gathering, development of types of reporting, and other matters.

Leary, William M., Jr. "Books, Soldiers and Censorship during the Second World War." AMERICAN QUARTERLY 20 (Summer 1968): 237-45.

The U.S. Army, through the Council on Books in War Time, supplied more than 125 million paperbacks free of charge to members of the armed forces. This program was remarkably free from censorship.

London, Herbert. "American Romantics: Old and New." COLORADO QUARTERLY 18 (Summer 1969): 5-19.

In this essay, hippies are likened to nineteenth-century romantics, particularly the Transcendentalists. London compares Allen Ginsberg with Walt Whitman and Bob Dylan with Theodore Parker.

McDermott, John J. "Nature, Nostalgia, and the City: An American Dilemma." SOUNDINGS: AN INTERDISCIPLINARY JOURNAL 55 (Spring 1972): 1-20.

American urban man functions according to nature metaphors, expectancies, and a nostalgia for a nature experience he never underwent. He does not see the conflict with nature nor does he diagnose the urban conflict in its own terms.

Mackintosh, Barry. "George Washington Carver: The Making of a Myth." JOURNAL OF SOUTHERN HISTORY 42 (November 1976): 509-28.

Mackintosh argues that Carver's accomplishments were undistinguished, yet he attained in his lifetime the image of a genius whose applications for peanuts and sweet potatoes revolutionized the economy of the South. This depiction was a myth perpetuated by blacks who needed a success symbol to stand on equal footing with whites, and by whites who lavished praise on a token black in order to show that the southern social order permitted achievement.

Macleod, David I. CARNEGIE LIBRARIES IN WISCONSIN. Madison: State Historical Society of Wisconsin, 1968. v, 166 p.

Sixty of the seventeen hundred libraries constructed with Andrew Carnegie's $40 million were in Wisconsin. While the philanthropist wanted to provide educational opportunities for disadvantaged youths, he failed because his libraries became temples for the ladies' club culture.

May, Henry F. THE END OF AMERICAN INNOCENCE: A STUDY OF THE FIRST YEARS OF OUR OWN TIME, 1912-1917. New York: Alfred A. Knopf, 1959. xviii, 413 p.

May theorizes that modern American culture represents a repudiation of the values and loyalties of the American past. These features were moralism, a belief in progress, and dedication to a tradition.

Mays, John Bentley. "The Flying Serpent: Contemporary Imaginations of the American Indian." CANADIAN REVIEW OF AMERICAN STUDIES 4 (Spring 1973): 32-47.

> Because men have witnessed the disappearance of nature and the ending of reality, they have rediscovered, since 1965, earlier scripts that related how men played out their anxieties and hopes. This is shown in Carlos Castaneda's TEACHINGS OF DON JUAN and Scott Momaday's HOUSE MADE OF DAWN where assembly lines and freeways are roads to hell and Indian ways are roads to paradise.

Nielson, Waldemar A. THE BIG FOUNDATIONS. New York: Columbia University Press, 1972. xii, 475 p.

> In this study financed by the Twentieth Century Fund, Nielson, a former Ford Foundation administrator, argues that foundations are in trouble because they are viewed as visible examples of special privilege created by an inequitable tax system. He also believes they are vital to democracy because they are independent centers that challenge massive institutions.

Pierson, George W. "The M-Factor in American History." AMERICAN QUARTERLY 14 (Summer 1962): 275-89.

> Pierson does not agree with those who argue that there is not a distinctive American character. He suggests that it is not based on wilderness, empty spaces, or wealth, but on the M-Factor-- movement, migration, and mobility.

Pomfret, John E. THE HENRY E. HUNTINGTON LIBRARY AND ART GALLERY: FROM ITS BEGINNINGS TO 1969. San Marino, Calif.: Huntington Library, 1969, x, 241 p.

> This is a record of a splendid collection, enviable publication record, and enormous endowment. Pomfret, who was director of the library from 1951-66, details an administrative history in which there was conflict between the director and trustees.

Reeves, Thomas C. FREEDOM AND THE FOUNDATION: THE FUND FOR THE REPUBLIC IN THE ERA OF McCARTHYSIM. New York: Alfred A. Knopf, 1969. xi, 355 p.

> Reeves describes the first seven years of the Fund after is incorporation in 1952 and the battles of its president and directors with McCarthyism. Those who attacked the foundation were the House Un-American Activities Committee, American Legion, and Fulton Lewis, Jr.

Salamanca, Lucy. FORTRESS OF FREEDOM: THE STORY OF THE LIBRARY OF CONGRESS. Foreword by Archibald MacLeish. Philadelphia: J.B. Lippincott, 1942. 445 p.

> The Library of Congress was established in 1802, but a century passed before it was regarded as the national library. Salamanca gives considerable attention to the personalities of the librarians and the development of collections.

Schlesinger, Arthur M., Jr., and White, Morton, eds. PATHS OF AMERICAN THOUGHT. Boston: Houghton Mifflin, 1963. viii, 614 p.

> This is a collection of essays on the evolution of the American mind. Except for two essays on European and Asian images of America, ideas that originated in the United States are discussed.

Silverberg, Robert. MOUND BUILDERS OF ANCIENT AMERICA: THE ARCHAE-OLOGY OF A MYTH. Greenwich, N.Y.: New York Graphic Society, 1968. viii, 369 p.

> In many respects, this is a general history of the development of archaeology in the eastern United States. Silverberg examines the myth that the mound builders were a prehistoric master race by describing the controversies concerning the mounds and delineating the current state of archaeological knowledge.

Spiller, Robert E., and Larrabee, Eric, eds. AMERICAN PERSPECTIVES: THE NATIONAL SELF-IMAGE IN THE TWENTIETH CENTURY. Library of Congress Series in American Civilization. Cambridge, Mass.: Harvard University Press, 1961. x, 216 p.

> This is a collection of essays that deal with images of our civilization as a whole, images of parts, such as popular culture, attitudes toward particular aspects of American civilization including business and politics, and the attitudes of particular groups--historians, social scientists, painters, and musicians.

Stott, William. DOCUMENTARY EXPRESSION AND THIRTIES AMERICA. New York: Oxford University Press, 1973. xvi, 361 p.

> Stott argues that documentary literature during the 1930s constituted a movement that characterized the way society was viewed. By means of documentaries, he describes the radio broadcasts of Edward R. Murrow, the dancing of Margaret Graham, the photography of Erskine Caldwell and Margaret Bourke-White, as well as WPA guides to states and regions.

Strong, Bryan. "Images of Nietzsche in America, 1900-1970." SOUTH ATLANTIC QUARTERLY 70 (Autumn 1971): 575-94.

The image of Nietzsche has changed from the prophet of barbarism to the philosopher of existentialism. This change in attitudes reflects a fundamental change in American thinking influenced by the immigration of European intellectuals in the 1930s.

Walters, Ronald G. "The Negro Press and the Image of Success: 1920-1939." AMERICAN STUDIES 11 (Fall 1970): 36-55.

The black press accepted all too uncritically ideas about the nature of success developed in white America. The formula explained success in terms of individual effort and explained failure by blaming it on people who failed, thus increasing black self-contempt.

Yetman, Norman R. "The Background of the Slave Narrative Collection." AMERICAN QUARTERLY 19 (Fall 1967): 534-53.

The Slave Narrative Collection of the Federal Writers' Project was compiled in seventeen states between 1936-38, and consists of more than two thousand interviews with exslaves. Interest in slave narratives originated as a response to U.B. Phillips's interpretation of slave society and to a growing interest in Negro culture.

Young, Mary. "The West and American Cultural Identity: Old Themes and New Variations." WESTERN HISTORICAL QUARTERLY 1 (April 1970): 137-60.

This is a study of writing on the West as an image of American culture. Young criticizes, among other things, those writers such as Henry Nash Smith, who depict the West in terms of the myth of the garden on the basis of land policies and the ideology surrounding them.

Chapter 3

ARCHITECTURE AND THE ARTS

COLONIAL PERIOD TO 1815

Adams, William Howard, ed. JEFFERSON AND THE ARTS: AN EXTENDED VIEW. Charlottesville: University Press of Virginia, National Gallery of Art, 1976. 293 p.

> This is a collection of seven essays in which Jefferson's portraits, efforts at art collecting, work as an architect, and planning of the national capitol are discussed.

Andrews, Wayne. AMERICAN GOTHIC: ITS ORIGINS, ITS TRIALS, ITS TRIUMPHS. New York: Vintage, 1975. 154 p.

> Gothic architecture is not limited to a specific period in American history. It has been part of the landscape from the late eighteenth to the twentieth century.

Archer, John. "Puritan Town Planning in New Haven." JOURNAL OF THE SOCIETY OF ARCHITECTURAL HISTORIANS 34 (May 1975): 140-49.

> The planning of the New Haven colony represented the essence of Puritanism. It merged several strains of European thought with Biblical prototypes.

Burchard, John, and Bush-Brown, Albert. THE ARCHITECTURE OF AMERICA: A SOCIAL AND CULTURAL HISTORY. Boston: Little, Brown, 1961. x, 595 p.

> The authors argue that architecture is a social art. It requires a building to satisfy social needs, the materials and structure must be durable, and it must be art.

Donnelly, Marian Card. THE NEW ENGLAND MEETING HOUSES OF THE SEVENTEENTH CENTURY. Middletown, Conn.: Wesleyan University Press, 1968. x, 165 p.

This is a book on architectural history. Donnelly argues that Puritan meeting houses were not local manifestations of an international Protestant plain style, but were unique structures, without models, which blended religious and civic functions in one building.

Dougherty, J.P. "Baroque and Picturesque Motifs in L'Enfant's Design of the Federal Capitol." AMERICAN QUARTERLY 26 (March 1974): 23-36.

Dougherty argues that L'Enfant's plan was approved because it called for grand buildings but not at the expense of sacrificing vistas of the Potomac. This was a panoramic city, not a baroque street mechanism.

Downer, Alan S., ed. THE MEMOIR OF JOHN DURANG, AMERICAN ACTOR, 1785-1816. Pittsburgh: University of Pittsburgh Press for the Historical Society of York County and the American Society of Theatre Research, 1966. xix, 176 p.

Durang was on the fringes of theater respectability. He was seen in the afterpieces of the legitimate theater, in the circus ring, or at the stage stops that served playhouses between Philadelphia and Harrisburg.

Fitch, James Marston. ARCHITECTURE AND THE ESTHETICS OF PLENTY. New York: Columbia University Press, 1961. xii, 304 p.

American architecture always has been acquisitive, borrowing means. The unique quality of this acquisitiveness has been its scale.

Fleming, E. McClung. "Early American Decorative Arts as Social Documents." MISSISSIPPI VALLEY HISTORICAL REVIEW 45 (September 1958): 276-84.

The decorative arts can throw light on many different aspects of a culture, such as materials available to the artisan and the skills and techniques artisans used at various times. They also yield evidence concerning trade, technology, social patterns and usage, taste, standard of living, and autobiographical data concerning the user.

Flexner, James Thomas. AMERICAN PAINTING: THE LIGHT OF DISTANT SKIES, 1760-1835. New York: Harcourt, Brace, 1954. xiii, 306 p.

Flexner begins with Benjamin West and ends with the approach of the Hudson River School. He also discusses the first schools of American artists that achieved close contact with European painting.

_____. AMERICA'S OLD MASTERS. New York: Viking Press, 1939. Reprint. New York: Dover Publications, 1967. 365 p.

This is a collection of short biographies of Benjamin West, John Singleton Copley, Charles Willson Peale, and Gilbert Stuart. Flexner argues that these painters symbolize the flowering of colonial America.

_____. FIRST FLOWERS OF THE WILDERNESS: AMERICAN PAINTING, THE COLONIAL PERIOD. Boston: Houghton Mifflin, 1947. Reprint. New York: Dover Publications, 1969. xxix, 369 p.

Life in America and the tradition of painting are emphasized. The author shows how portraits provide insight into American mores.

Forman, H. Chandlee. THE ARCHITECTURE OF THE OLD SOUTH: THE MEDIEVAL STYLE, 1585-1850. Foreword by Charles R. Morey. Cambridge, Mass.: Harvard University Press, 1948. xiii, 203 p.

Most southern colonists came from rural England and had little to do with the new Italianate architecture of the cities. They used medieval building methods until the early eighteenth century.

_____. MARYLAND ARCHITECTURE: A SHORT HISTORY FROM 1634 THROUGH THE CIVIL WAR. Cambridge, Md.: Tidewater Publishers, 1968. xvi, 102 p.

This is a study of architectural styles in all types of buildings of seventeenth- and eighteenth-century Maryland.

Glaser, Lynn. ENGRAVED AMERICA: ICONOGRAPHY OF AMERICA THROUGH 1800. Philadelphia: Ancient Orb Press, 1970. 221 p.

This is a collection, classification, and reproduction of the principal engraved works of all major artists between Columbus and the beginning of the nineteenth century.

Gowans, Alan. IMAGES OF AMERICAN LIVING: FOUR CENTURIES OF ARCHITECTURE AND FURNITURE AS CULTURAL EXPRESSION. Philadelphia: J.B. Lippincott, 1964. xv, 498 p.

From the beginning there have been patterns in the development of architecture and furniture that grow from and express the fundamental character of America. There have been basic traditions evolving through the centuries that reflect the relationship between America and Europe.

James, Reese Davis. CRADLE OF CULTURE: THE PHILADELPHIA STAGE, 1800-1810. Philadelphia: University of Pennsylvania Press, 1957. 156 p.

Philadelphia's Chestnut Street Theater is described during a period when American theater was gaining respectability. The study covers actors and actresses, plays, theatrical music, scenery design, and the operations of managers.

Kimball, Fiske. "Architecture in the History of the Colonies and of the Republic." AMERICAN HISTORICAL REVIEW 27 (October 1921): 47-57.

Kimball argues that the arts in America were not of small historical importance. The emphasis on harnessing the frontier in American historiography has obscured the contributions to the arts and architecture.

_____. DOMESTIC ARCHITECTURE OF THE AMERICAN COLONIES AND OF THE EARLY REPUBLIC. New York: Charles Scribner's Sons, 1922. xx, 314 p.

Buildings of the early republic are emphasized in this study. The author develops the history of postcolonial or Greek Revival architecture.

_____. MR. SAMUEL McINTIRE CARVER, THE ARCHITECT OF SALEM. Portland, Maine: Southworth-Anthoenson Press for the Essex Institute of Salem, Massachusetts, 1940. xiii, 373 p.

Carver lived from 1757 to 1811, a time when Salem was a rich and bustling seaport. He built houses for wealthy merchants, as well as churches, public buildings, mastheads, and even submitted a design for the national capitol, all of which were graced by his unique carvings and finely detailed woodwork.

Larkin, Oliver W. ART AND LIFE IN AMERICA. New York: Rinehart and Co., 1949. xviii, 547 p.

Larkin surveys architecture, sculpture, painting, and to some degree, the minor arts. He emphasizes how these arts expressed an American way of living and were related to ideas.

McNamara, Brooks. THE AMERICAN PLAYHOUSE IN THE EIGHTEENTH CENTURY. Cambridge, Mass.: Harvard University Press, 1969. xviii, 174 p.

This study is focused on the design and stage practices of playhouses rather than on scripts and acting. The author surveys theaters in Williamsburg, Charleston, Philadelphia, and other cities.

Pickens, Buford. "Mr. Jefferson as Revolutionary Architect." JOURNAL OF THE SOCIETY OF ARCHITECTURAL HISTORIANS 34 (December 1975): 257-79.

Pickens challenges the interpretation that as an architect Jefferson was a revivalist. He argues that to be radically modern during Jefferson's time was not to invent but to transform.

Quimby, Ian M.G., ed. AMERICAN PAINTING TO 1776. Charlottesville: University Press of Virginia, 1971. x, 384 p.

These papers, presented at the seventeenth annual Winterthur Conference, deal with painting in New England, the Hudson Valley, New York City, and Philadelphia. The work of John Smibert, Robert Feke, and Gustavus Hesselius are emphasized.

Rankin, Hugh F. THE THEATER IN COLONIAL AMERICA. Chapel Hill: University of North Carolina Press, 1965. xiii, 239 p.

Theaters in the colonies were crude replicas of London models, were poorly planned, and hastily constructed. At the same time,

sophisticated colonials enjoyed theatrical productions and helped
pioneer promoters gain recognition for drama-in-performance.

Sellers, Charles Coleman. CHARLES WILLSON PEALE. 2 vols. Vol. 1:
EARLY LIFE (1741-1790); Vol. 2: LATER LIFE (1790-1827). Philadelphia:
American Philosophical Society, 1947. xiv, 293; xii, 468 p.

> Peale was first apprenticed to a saddler, and his work with saddles
> and clocks, experiments with stoves and chimneys, and efforts to
> make false teeth from porcelain provided the background of his
> development as an artist. He became first a portrait painter and
> then a showman whose love of nature caused him to present col-
> lections of paintings and natural history objects in his museum.

_____. PORTRAITS AND MINIATURES BY CHARLES WILLSON PEALE. Ameri-
can Philosophical Society Transactions, vol. 42, pt. 1. Philadelphia: American Philosophical Society, 1952. 369 p.

> Peale gained experience with the American school of Benjamin
> West and was among the first American painters to study in Europe.
> He emphasized draftsmanship and truth in all his portraits.

Waterman, Thomas Tileston. THE MANSIONS OF VIRGINIA, 1706-1776.
Chapel Hill: University of North Carolina Press, 1946. 456 p.

> This study describes pre-revolutionary Virginia homes from the early
> English house of medieval style to Monticello which reflects late
> Georgian building. The author attempts to identify the architec-
> tural inspiration of each designer and assign an English counterpart.

Whitehill, Walter Muir, et al. THE ARTS AND EARLY AMERICAN HISTORY:
NEEDS AND OPPORTUNITIES FOR STUDY. Chapel Hill: University of North
Carolina Press for the Institute of Early American History and Culture, Williams-
burg, Virginia, 1965. xv, 170 p.

> Whitehill discusses the contribution that a study of early arts and
> crafts could make to cultural history, but the major portion of
> this book is devoted to a bibliography that shows English, French,
> and Spanish traditions in art before 1826.

1815-1915

Adams, Richard P. "Architecture and the Romantic Tradition: Coleridge to
Wright." AMERICAN QUARTERLY 9 (Spring 1957): 46-62.

> In aesthetic theory, romantic means organic. Horatio Greenough
> was the first American to apply the theories of Coleridge and
> others to architecture and to argue that in building form should be
> determined by needs and not by prior assumptions as to what is cor-
> rect or beautiful.

Alexander, Robert L. THE ARCHITECTURE OF MAXIMILLIAN GODEFROY. Baltimore: Johns Hopkins University Press, 1974. xiii, 246 p.

> Godefroy spent fourteen years in the United States and designed buildings in Baltimore, such as St. Mary's Chapel and the Unitarian Church, that have been designated as national historical landmarks. His work shows the compromise between European styles and American preferences.

Allen, William Francis; Ware, Charles Pickard; and Garrison, Lucy McKim, comps. SLAVE SONGS OF THE UNITED STATES. New York: Oak Publications, 1965. 175 p.

> These songs were collected during the period of the Port Royal experiment after the Civil War. They are chiefly from South Carolina and Georgia, and include spirituals, "shouts," and rowing songs.

Appleton, Le Roy H. INDIAN ART IN AMERICA. New York: Charles Scribner's Sons, 1950. xvi, 279 p.

> Appleton covers the symbolism of Indian artists, records their stories, and reproduces examples of art work from every area and tribe. Indian art shows awe of power.

Baigell, Matthew. A HISTORY OF AMERICAN PAINTING. New York: Praeger, 1971. 288 p.

> This survey emphasizes the gradual development of American painting away from European art. Realism and a concern for the specific characterize American painting, and this has been reflected in the perspectives and judgments of both painting and literature.

Barker, Virgil. AMERICAN PAINTING: HISTORY AND INTERPRETATION. New York: Macmillan, 1950. xxvii, 717 p.

> Barker concentrates on the art of painting. Technique is emphasized, and biographical data on the painters is restricted to those facts that illuminate their art.

Beal, Rebecca J. JACOB EICHOLTZ 1776-1842: PORTRAIT PAINTER OF PENNSYLVANIA. Philadelphia: Historical Society of Pennsylvania, 1969. xxxiii, 401 p.

> Eicholtz, a folk painter, produced more than nine hundred likenesses of his Lancaster, Pennsylvania, neighbors. He was largely self-taught, but his representations of plain, rural faces were careful, exact, and bright in color.

Bernard, Kenneth A. LINCOLN AND THE MUSIC OF THE CIVIL WAR. Caldwell, Idaho: Caxton Printers, 1966. xix, 333 p.

> Lincoln could not carry a tune, but he was fond of music, especially popular music. This study covers the role music played in the Civil War.

Blodgett, Geoffrey. "Frederick Law Olmsted: Landscape Architecture as Conservative Reform." JOURNAL OF AMERICAN HISTORY 62 (March 1976): 869-89.

> This is an effort to place Olmsted in the group structure of Gilded Age reform. He was a genteel reformer who developed the idea of the public park and attempted to enrich the quality of urban life.

Bloomfield, Maxwell. "Muckraking and the American Stage: The Emergence of Realism, 1905-1917." SOUTH ATLANTIC QUARTERLY 66 (Spring 1967): 165-78.

> The muckrakers had a lasting impact on twentieth-century theater. American dramatists wrote on American themes and exposed the uglier aspects of American life.

Bonner, James C. "Plantation Architecture of the Lower South on the Eve of the Civil War." JOURNAL OF SOUTHERN HISTORY 11 (August 1945): 370-88.

> Greek Revival architecture was the prevailing form on plantations until the 1840s when Gothic Revival surpassed it. Actually, southerners who expressed themselves on architecture felt that both styles were out of harmony with the southern landscape.

Briggs, Harold E., and Briggs, Ernestine Bennett. "The Early Theatre on the Northern Plains." MISSISSIPPI VALLEY HISTORICAL REVIEW 37 (September 1950): 231-64.

> Travelling companies brought theater in the nineteenth century to Sioux City, Iowa; Yankton, Fargo, and Grand Forks, Dakota Territory; Cheyenne, Wyoming, and other places. They followed the settlers and made acting a worthy profession.

Brockett, Oscar G., and Findlay, Robert R. CENTURY OF INNOVATION: A HISTORY OF EUROPEAN AND AMERICAN THEATRE AND DRAMA SINCE 1870. Englewood Cliffs, N.J.: Prentice-Hall, 1973. xiv, 826 p.

> The authors of this study mention every director and designer of importance as well as a few actors. Drama is placed in the focus of the social, political, psychological, and artistic settings of each period.

Bryant, William Cullen II. "Painting and Poetry: A Love Affair of Long Ago." AMERICAN QUARTERLY 22 (Winter 1970): 859-82.

Bryant explores the relationship between William Cullen Bryant, the poet, and the young painters of the Hudson River School. The poet performed many services for the artists, both managerial and aesthetic, and this association was illustrated by Asher B. Durand in his painting, "Kindred Spirits," depicting Bryant and Thomas Cole standing on a Catskill mountain ledge.

Bunting, Bainbridge. HOUSES OF BOSTON'S BACK BAY: AN ARCHITEC-TURAL HISTORY, 1840-1917. Cambridge, Mass.: Belknap Press of Harvard University Press, 1967. xvii, 494 p.

It is argued that Back Bay homes charted the course of architectural development for the United States. Styles changed from French Academic before the Civil War to Brownstone Gothic, Richardson Romanesque, and Queen Anne in the 1870s and 1880s, and even-tually to the so-called McKim Classical, Late-Georgian, and High-Georgian early in the twentieth century.

Burg, David F. "The Aesthetics of Bigness in Late Nineteenth Century Ameri-can Architecture." JOURNAL OF POPULAR CULTURE 7 (Fall 1973): 484-92.

Bigness and simplicity became a goal of American architects in the 1880s. It began with residences, spread to public buildings, and reflected the American infatuation with bigness that has not abated since that time.

Condit, Carl W. THE CHICAGO SCHOOL OF ARCHITECTURE: A HISTORY OF COMMERCIAL AND PUBLIC BUILDING IN THE CHICAGO AREA, 1875-1925. Chicago: University of Chicago Press, 1964. xviii, 238 p.

Condit emphasizes commercial building as well as designer-engineer partnerships such as Burnham and Root, and Adler and Sullivan. He shows how Chicago rose from the fire of 1871 through the con-struction first of elevator buildings and later skyscrapers.

Cone, John Frederick. OSCAR HAMMERSTEIN'S MANHATTAN OPERA COM-PANY. Norman: University of Oklahoma Press, 1966. xvi, 399 p.

Opera in New York and Philadelphia was revitalized between 1906 and 1910 because of Hammerstein's rivalry with the Metropolitan Opera Company. He made money from cigar manufacturing and poured it into opera, which he democratized.

Crane, Sylvia E. WHITE SILENCE: GREENOUGH, POWERS, AND CRAW-FORD, AMERICAN SCULPTORS IN NINETEENTH-CENTURY ITALY. Coral Gables, Fla.: University of Miami Press, 1972. xviii, 499 p.

Italy in the nineteenth century offered an atmosphere of appreciation of art, models, a good supply of white marble, skilled work-
men to fashion the sculptors' designs, a low cost of living, and
customers. Life in Florence and Rome, where Greenough, Powers,
and Crawford lived and worked, is portrayed, as is the trouble
they experienced in transcending the neoclassical Italian aesthetics
in their work.

Davis, Ronald L. A HISTORY OF OPERA IN THE AMERICAN WEST. Englewood Cliffs, N.J.: Prentice-Hall, 1965. xii, 178 p.

The author covers the development of opera in New Orleans,
Chicago, San Francisco, Dallas, Central City, Santa Fe, and
other cities. He also provides details about conductors and performers.

_____. OPERA IN CHICAGO. New York: Appleton-Century-Crofts, 1966.
xi, 393 p.

Chicago supported opera as early as 1850 as westerners sought to
bring culture with them from the East. This book contains vignettes
of performers and audiences as well as commentary on the quality
of productions.

Demos, John. "George Caleb Bingham: The Artist as Social Historian."
AMERICAN QUARTERLY 17 (Summer 1965): 218-28.

Bingham's nineteenth-century paintings fall into two categories:
town society and river society. He emphasized the political aspects of town life and showed the relationship between the river
town and the boatmen, and fur traders.

Dickson, Harold E. ARTS OF THE YOUNG REPUBLIC: THE AGE OF WILLIAM
DUNLAP. Chapel Hill: University of North Carolina Press, 1968. vi, 234 p.

William Dunlap published his HISTORY OF THE RISE AND PROG-
RESS OF THE ARTS OF DESIGN in 1834. In order to honor him,
Dickson compiled this collection of almost two hundred illustrations
of art in his time.

Duncan, Hugh Dalziel. CULTURE AND DEMOCRACY: THE STRUGGLE FOR
FORM IN SOCIETY AND ARCHITECTURE IN CHICAGO AND THE MIDDLE
WEST DURING THE LIFE AND TIMES OF LOUIS H. SULLIVAN. Totowa, N.J.:
Bedminster Press, 1965. xxii, 616 p.

This study deals with the rise of the Chicago School and its defeat
at the Columbian Exposition and the architectural philosophy of
Sullivan. Duncan relates Sullivan's thought to the ideas of social
function of John Dewey and George Herbert Mead.

Eaton, Leonard K. AMERICAN ARCHITECTURE COMES OF AGE: EUROPEAN REACTION TO H.H. RICHARDSON AND LOUIS SULLIVAN. Cambridge: M.I.T. Press, 1972. xiii, 256 p.

> Eaton shows that American architectural influence expanded beyond national borders during the time of Richardson and Sullivan. An aspect of the dialogue between Europe and America is depicted.

_____. TWO CHICAGO ARCHITECTS AND THEIR CLIENTS: FRANK LLOYD WRIGHT AND HOWARD VAN DOREN SHAW. Cambridge: M.I.T. Press, 1969. ix, 259 p.

> Eaton selected important Chicago houses at the turn of the twentieth century as his field of study. Wright's clients were self-made small businessmen, while those of Shaw were wealthier and more powerful.

Ernst, Alice Henson. TROUPING IN THE OREGON COUNTRY: A HISTORY OF FRONTIER THEATRE. Portland: Oregon Historical Society, 1961. xx, 197 p.

> This study covers the period from the first performance at Fort Vancouver in 1846 to the days of resident stock companies at the turn of the twentieth century. Connections with San Francisco are shown as is the relationship between the theater in Portland and Seattle.

Felheim, Marvin. THE THEATER OF AUGUSTIN DALY: AN ACCOUNT OF THE LATE NINETEENTH CENTURY AMERICAN STAGE. Cambridge, Mass.: Harvard University Press, 1956. xiv, 329 p.

> Although not an actual playwright, Daly was an important impresario. He was devoted to Shakespeare and also to natural acting in an ensemble.

Fine, Richard A. "Albert Bierstadt, Fitz Hugh Ludlow and the American Western Landscape." AMERICAN STUDIES 15 (Fall 1974): 91-99.

> The collaboration between Bierstadt, the artist, and Ludlow, the journalist, is detailed in this essay. Fine contends that Bierstadt's paintings captured the imagination of the public because of his concern with bigness and the ideal of the American West.

Flexner, James Thomas. NINETEENTH CENTURY AMERICAN PAINTING. New York: G.P. Putnam's Sons, 1970. 256 p.

> Flexner discusses American painting in its own terms. This is a chronicle of aesthetic development that could not have taken place in the nations of Europe.

_____. THAT WILDER IMAGE: THE PAINTINGS OF AMERICA'S NATIVE SCHOOL FROM THOMAS COLE TO WINSLOW HOMER. Boston: Little, Brown, 1962. xxii, 407 p.

Flexner evaluates American painters of the nineteenth century as nationalists and tilts at European strawmen. He emphasizes what they said about themselves and what critics said as true assessments of their works.

Forman, H. Chandlee. OLD BUILDINGS, GARDENS, AND FURNITURE IN TIDEWATER MARYLAND. Cambridge, Md.: Tidewater Publishers, 1967. xi, 326 p.

Forman covers the things in history that communicate the feeling, mood, style, and values of society. This book is a record of primary materials that is similar to a museum display.

Fowble, E. McSherry. "Without a Blush: The Movement toward Acceptance of the Nude as an Art Form in America, 1800-1825." WINTERTHUR PORTFOLIO 9 (1974): 103-22.

The use of the nude represented an effort on the part of artists to educate the public. In a limited way, by 1825, they had encouraged the public to view the nude without a blush, but they were far from the goal they had set for themselves and many turned to nature as a subject.

Freeman, Martha Doty. "New Mexico in the Nineteenth Century: The Creation of an Artistic Tradition." NEW MEXICO HISTORICAL REVIEW 49 (January 1974): 5-26.

In the twentieth century, New Mexico was full of artists and writers such as Willa Cather and D.H. Lawrence who perpetuated sublime and mysterious images of the land. This is a study of this artistic tradition begun in the nineteenth century by topographical engineers.

Friedlaender, Marc. "Henry Hobson Richardson, Henry Adams, and John Hay." JOURNAL OF THE SOCIETY OF ARCHITECTURAL HISTORIANS 29 (October 1970): 231-46.

Richardson designed homes for Adams and Hay on Lafayette Square in Washington, D.C., in the 1880s. This essay mainly concerns Richardson's ideas and the architect-client relationship.

Gardner, Albert TenEyck. YANKEE STONECUTTERS: THE FIRST AMERICAN SCHOOL OF SCULPTURE, 1800-1850. New York: Columbia University Press for the Metropolitan Museum of Art, 1945. 84 p.

This is a study of the classico-Jacksonian school of art that thrived on patronage. It shows the relationship of the sculptors to their political, social, and cultural background.

Garrett, Wendell D.; Norton, Paul F.; Gowans, Alan; and Butler, Joseph T. THE ARTS IN AMERICA: THE NINETEENTH CENTURY. New York: Charles Scribner's Sons, 1969. xix, 412 p.

> These essays cover public and commercial architecture, sculpture, painting, and the decorative arts. The familiar idea that Americans wavered between adopting European values and seeking a unique art is emphasized.

Geselbracht, Raymond H. "Transcendental Renaissance in the Arts, 1890-1920." NEW ENGLAND QUARTERLY 48 (December 1975): 463-86.

> Frank Lloyd Wright, Charles Ives, and Isadora Duncan produced a second outburst of transcendentalism in the arts in the 1890s. There was a feeling that the spirit of man, not material evolution, was the primary creative force.

Handlin, David P. "New England Architects in New York, 1820-1840." AMERICAN QUARTERLY 19 (Winter 1967): 681-95.

> As New York became the commercial center of the nation after the War of 1812, many New Englanders migrated there, principally from Connecticut. Some carried with them a desire to influence the values of the community by providing ethical and moral lessons in architecture, through orderly structures symbolizing a rationally ordered society.

Harbert, Earl, and Harbert, Ellen. "Art Criticism in America, 1865-1880: The Early Voices of Dissent." JOURNAL OF AMERICAN STUDIES 8 (August 1974): 203-10.

> Art criticism in the late nineteenth century aided the creative forces of Impressionism and experiment, and prepared the way for the famous Armory Show of 1913. Critics criticized other critics who demanded accurate representation in art, and suggested a new and liberal aesthetic philosophy in judging contemporary art.

Harris, Neil. THE ARTIST IN AMERICAN SOCIETY: THE FORMATIVE YEARS, 1790-1860. New York: Simon and Schuster, 1966. xvi, 432 p.

> This is a study of changing American attitudes toward art and the legitimization of the artistic enterprise. Art was justified as an instrument of social improvement, and patrons caused artists to make their work serve conservative social goals.

_____. "The Gilded Age Revisited: Boston and the Museum Movement." AMERICAN QUARTERLY 14 (Winter 1962): 545-66.

> Harris believes that the decade of the 1890s was a great cultural watershed and he criticizes those who depict the Gilded Age as a

cultural wasteland. He looks at the development of the Boston
Museum of Art and shows that this institution was devoted to popular culture and dedicated to the education of the people from its
inception.

Harwell, Richard Barksdale. "Brief Candle: The Confederate Theater." PRO-
CEEDINGS OF THE AMERICAN ANTIQUARIAN SOCIETY 81 (21 April 1971):
41-160.

Soldiers and other patrons of the Confederate theater desired to be
amused as a means of escaping the war. They wanted glitter, and
they cared not that this was paste and tinsel and the shows mas-
querade.

Hatch, Christopher. "Music for America: A Critical Controversy of the 1850s."
AMERICAN QUARTERLY 14 (Winter 1962): 578-86.

The controversy centered on whether American musical achievement should be measured against Europe. William Henry Fry,
music critic of the NEW YORK TRIBUNE, argued that American
musical institutions should be reformed in an effort to bring about
America's artistic independence through innovation.

Hayden, Dolores. SEVEN AMERICAN UTOPIAS: THE ARCHITECTURE OF
COMMUNITARIAN SOCIALISM, 1790-1975. Cambridge: M.I.T. Press, 1976.
ix, 401 p.

This study combines cultural history, design analysis, and political
theory. Hayden considers communitarians from the Shakers to the
Llano del Rio community in California (1914-17) and examines the
design process in terms of authority and participation, and community and society.

Hills, Patricia. THE PAINTERS' AMERICA: RURAL AND URBAN LIFE, 1810-
1910. New York: Praeger, 1974. vii, 160 p.

The painters' America of the nineteenth and twentieth centuries
was highly selective and revealing of dreams and ideals. Art was
humorous, nostalgic, and nationalistic, but rarely socially critical.

Hines, Thomas S. "The Paradox of 'Progressive' Architecture: Urban Planning
and Public Buildings in Tom Johnson's Cleveland." AMERICAN QUARTERLY
24 (October 1973): 426-48.

Influenced by the World's Columbian Exposition (1893), Cleveland
planners under Johnson worked on the city's facelifting. Interestingly, they fastened on neoclassical architecture, instead of the
designs of Louis Sullivan and Frank Lloyd Wright.

Holden, Wheaton A. "The Peabody Touch: Peabody and Stearns of Boston, 1870–1917." JOURNAL OF THE SOCIETY OF ARCHITECTURAL HISTORIANS 32 (May 1973): 114–31.

> Peabody and Stearns have been called the most important arbiters of building taste after H.H. Richardson. One of the characteristics of their basic forms was the tower, but they showed eclecticism in their residential architecture.

Homer, William Innes, with the assitance of Violet Organ. ROBERT HENRI AND HIS CIRCLE. Ithaca, N.Y.: Cornell University Press, 1969. xvii, 308 p.

> Henri (1865–1910) was one of America's most influential art teachers. He was involved with every major art movement during the late nineteenth and early twentieth centuries when aesthetic provincialism was collapsing.

Hunter, Doreen. "America's First Romantics: Richard Henry Dana, Sr. and Washington Allston." NEW ENGLAND QUARTERLY 45 (March 1972): 3–30.

> This is a study of the reasons artists in the second decade of the nineteenth century lapsed into despair and mediocrity after showing promise. The careers of Dana and Allston indicate that this condition resulted from the intellectual difficulty of reconciling romantic ideas with the traditional requirement of a public philosophy.

Karlowicz, Titus M. "D.H. Burnham's Role in the Selection of Architects for the World's Columbian Exposition." JOURNAL OF THE SOCIETY OF ARCHITECTURAL HISTORIANS 29 (October 1970): 247–54.

> A controversy existed over the selection of architects for the exposition. Burnham, who was chief of construction, chose eastern architects and was accused of selling out Chicago firms.

Kendall, John S. THE GOLDEN AGE OF THE NEW ORLEANS THEATER. Baton Rouge: Louisiana State University Press, 1952. viii, 624 p.

> This study covers New Orleans theater from the 1790s until after the Civil War when touring companies replaced stock companies. The city was a theater center with almost every actor and actress of any importance filling engagements there.

Kirker, Harold. CALIFORNIA'S ARCHITECTURAL FRONTIER: STYLE AND TRADITION IN THE NINETEENTH CENTURY. San Marino, Calif.: Huntington Library, 1960. xiv, 224 p.

> The colonial nature of California's frontier is explained in terms of its architecture. The book covers California history from pioneer beginnings to the native mission movement of the 1890s.

Kmen, Henry A. MUSIC IN NEW ORLEANS: THE FORMATIVE YEARS, 1791-1841. Baton Rouge: Louisiana State University Press, 1966. xiv, 314 p.

Kmen covers gala balls, brass bands, Negro music, and concert life, but he concentrates on opera. He argues that New Orleans was a cultural center of the first magnitude populated by diverse cultural groups that fused their cultures into something new, something American.

Kwiat, Joseph J. "The 'Ash-Can' School: The Magazine as Matrix." CANADIAN REVIEW OF AMERICAN STUDIES 7 (Fall 1976): 163-75.

American realist painters of the period before World War I began their careers as newspaper artists, but graduated to magazines where they revolted against the quality of life. Like their literary counterparts, such as Theodore Dreiser, Stephen Crane, and Frank Norris, they found that graphic art provided a freer medium of expression than did newspaper art.

Landy, Jacob. THE ARCHITECTURE OF MINARD LAFEVER. New York: Columbia University Press, 1970. xii, 313 p.

LaFever (1798-1854) was a New York architect. He was an adapter of current modes from English Regency to Greek Revival and Gothic, and gave these forms new meaning without introducing innovations.

Maass, John. THE GLORIOUS ENTERPRISE: THE CENTENNIAL EXHIBITION OF 1876 AND H.J. SCHWARZMANN, ARCHITECT-IN-CHIEF. Watkins Glen, N.Y.: American Life Foundation, 1973. 156 p.

This book is filled with plates and engravings and shows the impact of American life and the exhibition on European visitors. The author also weaves in a biography of Schwarzmann.

Miller, Lillian B. "Paintings, Sculpture, and the National Character, 1815-1860." JOURNAL OF AMERICAN HISTORY 53 (March 1967): 696-707.

Americans did not dispute their national character based on the new land with its unique institutions, but some members of the middle and upper classes observed the crudity of business activities and amusements. They set out to reform national character and make it more susceptible to intellectual influences by encouraging the fine arts.

_____. PATRONS AND PATRIOTISM: THE ENCOURAGEMENT OF THE FINE ARTS IN THE UNITED STATES, 1790-1860. Chicago: University of Chicago Press, 1966. xv, 335 p.

Miller treats apologias for support of art ranging from Alexander Everett to Charles Eliot Norton, the commissions granted to decorate the U.S. capitol, and the formation of academies and athenaeums in the nineteenth century. She also explores the links between art and nationality.

Miller, Ross L. "The Landscaper's Utopia Versus the City: A Mismatch." NEW ENGLAND QUARTERLY 49 (June 1976): 179-93.

Landscape architects were in a unique position in the mid-nineteenth century to influence city planning. They failed, however, because they were committed to an agrarian ideology that was not hospitable to urbanization.

Novak, Barbara. AMERICAN PAINTING OF THE NINETEENTH CENTURY: REALISM, IDEALISM, AND THE AMERICAN EXPERIENCE. New York: Praeger, 1969. 350 p.

Novak argues that there are characteristics of American art that can be denoted as American. She emphasizes key figures from John Singleton Copley to William Harnett.

Perrin, Richard W.E. THE ARCHITECTURE OF WISCONSIN. Madison: State Historical Society of Wisconsin, 1967. vii, 175 p.

Wisconsin's architectural styles emerged from its various national and ethnic settlers. Scandinavians built long houses, West Germans half-timber structures, and New Yorkers cobblestone homes.

Pickens, Buford. "Wyatt's Pantheon, the State House in Boston, and a New View of Bulfinch." JOURNAL OF THE SOCIETY OF ARCHITECTURAL HISTORIANS 29 (May 1970): 124-31.

This is a study of how architectural forms move slowly in time. Charles Bulfinch's work is examined and he is characterized as a provincial urban designer who became an architect.

Randel, William. "Frederick Delius in America." VIRGINIA MAGAZINE OF HISTORY AND BIOGRAPHY 79 (July 1971): 349-66.

The American experience and the impact on Delius and his music are discussed. He spent a two-year residence between 1884-86 in Florida and Virginia where he was exposed to lush tropical sights and sounds as well as Afro-American melodies.

Rhoads, William B. "The Colonial Revival and American Nationalism." JOURNAL OF THE SOCIETY OF ARCHITECTURAL HISTORIANS 35 (December 1976): 239-54.

Much of the popularity of colonial architecture in the 1880s was based on patriotism. Buildings were preserved and restored, and models were created in a movement that lasted into the twentieth century.

Rich, Arthur Lowndes. LOWELL MASON: THE FATHER OF SINGING AMONG CHILDREN. Chapel Hill: University of North Carolina Press, 1946. vii, 224 p.

Mason (1792-1872) was a musical missionary who pioneered the teaching of music in the public schools. He democratized music, organized conventions for training teachers, and compiled tune books for children.

Ringe, Donald A. "Painting and Poem in the Hudson River Aesthetic." AMERICAN QUARTERLY 12 (Spring 1960): 71-83.

The Hudson River painters tried to compose their works so as to present a dominant idea that would strike the mind of the beholder and release a train of associations. This aesthetic theory came about in response to criticism that painting was secondary to poetry in speaking to the imagination.

Ross, Marvin C., ed. GEORGE CATLIN: EPISODES FROM LIFE AMONG THE INDIANS AND LAST RAMBLES. Civilization of the American Indian Series, vol. 55. Norman: University of Oklahoma Press, 1959. xxvi, 357 p.

Catlin is known for his paintings of American Indians done in the 1830s. This collection also includes his work of the 1850s as well as excerpts from his diaries.

Rudisill, Richard. MIRROR IMAGE: THE INFLUENCE OF THE DAGUERRO-TYPE ON AMERICAN SOCIETY. Albuquerque: University of New Mexico Press, 1971. ix, 342 p.

Rudisill advances the idea that daguerrotypes revealed American attitudes toward nationalism, the world, and reality. These pictures, produced mainly in the 1840s and 1850s, promoted a sense of national identity by depicting the varied as well as unifying qualities in American life.

Schwab, Arnold T. JAMES GIBBONS HUNEKER: CRITIC OF THE SEVEN ARTS. Stanford, Calif.: Stanford University Press, 1963. xii, 384 p.

Huneker represented the avant-garde among American critics from 1880 to 1920. He trumpeted the American debut of Flaubert, Anatole France, Nietzsche, and Dostoevsky, and was intimately involved with music, the theater, and literature.

Scully, Arthur, Jr. JAMES DAKIN, ARCHITECT: HIS CAREER IN NEW YORK AND THE SOUTH. Baton Rouge: Louisiana State University Press, 1973. xiv, 209 p.

> Scully maintains that Dakin, who has been neglected, was an important figure in nineteenth-century architecture. His most significant structures were in Mobile, New Orleans, and even Havana, Cuba.

Scully, Vincent J., Jr. THE SHINGLE STYLE: ARCHITECTURAL THEORY AND DESIGN FROM RICHARDSON TO THE ORIGINS OF WRIGHT. New Haven, Conn.: Yale University Press, 1955. 181 p.

> This study covers the wooden, suburban building from 1872 to about 1889. The thoughts of architects as they were expressed in professional journals are discussed.

Stein, Roger B. JOHN RUSKIN AND AESTHETIC THOUGHT IN AMERICA, 1840-1900. Cambridge, Mass.: Harvard University Press, 1967. xviii, 321 p.

> Stein begins with a survey of American intellectual premises in the nineteenth century. Ruskin's influence as well as doubts about his ideas are discussed from the standpoint of scientists, novelists, philosophers, and preachers.

_____. SEASCAPE AND THE AMERICAN IMAGINATION. New York: Clarkson N. Potter, 1975. xiii, 144 p.

> This is a catalog of American seascapes exhibited in the Whitney Museum in 1975. It focuses on eighteenth- and nineteenth-century painters and regards seascapes, such as those by Washington Allston, Thomas Cole, and others, as an important genre.

Sturges, Walter Knight. "Arthur Little and the Colonial Revival." JOURNAL OF THE SOCIETY OF ARCHITECTURAL HISTORIANS 32 (May 1973): 147-63.

> No revival has been more truly a revival in American architectural history than the colonial revival. It began in the mid-1870s, and Arthur Little was one of its most notable practitioners.

Townsend, J. Benjamin. THIS NEW MAN: A DISCOURSE IN PORTRAITS. Washington, D.C.: Smithsonian Institution Press, 1968. 217 p.

> Taking its title from Crevecoeur, this collection attempts to portray American restlessness and mobility, rebelliousness and conformity, individualism and altruism, and practicality and idealism through portraits and brief biographies.

Van Zandt, Roland. THE CATSKILL MOUNTAIN HOUSE. New Brunswick, N.J.: Rutgers University Press, 1966. xxii, 416 p.

The Catskill Mountain House was a resort rising high above the Hudson River. The Hudson River School found inspiration in this region, and during the Gilded Age this Greek-revival building represented America's search for the sublime.

_____. "The Catskills and the Rise of American Landscape Painting." NEW-YORK HISTORICAL SOCIETY QUARTERLY 49 (July 1965): 257-82.

This is a study of the discovery of the Catskills in 1825 as a source for landscape painting. The shaping of the Hudson River School of artists also is discussed.

Wainwright, Nicholas B. PHILADELPHIA IN THE ROMANTIC AGE OF LITHOG-RAPHY: AN ILLUSTRATED HISTORY OF EARLY LITHOGRAPHY IN PHILA-DELPHIA WITH A DESCRIPTIVE LIST OF PHILADELPHIA SCENES MADE BY PHILADELPHIA LITHOGRAPHERS BEFORE 1866. Philadelphia: Historical Society of Pennsylvania, 1958. vi, 261 p.

This study includes a list of 480 lithographs of Philadelphia made between 1828-66, reproductions of 110 of them, and a short history of lithography in Philadelphia.

Wall, James T. "The Ashcan School: Transition in American Art." SOUTH ATLANTIC QUARTERLY 69 (Summer 1970): 317-26.

The Ashcan School of the early years of the twentieth century roused the gallery-going public out of romanticism and introduced a new realism. The exhibition of their work in 1908 was a victory for liberty of expression and a herald of new concepts in subject and technique.

Weisman, Winston. "The Commercial Architecture of George B. Post." JOUR-NAL OF THE SOCIETY OF ARCHITECTURAL HISTORIANS 31 (October 1972): 176-203.

Post, one of the architects for the Columbian Exposition of 1893, participated in the conception of the first skyscraper or elevator building. He also is credited with having introduced and popularized the use of terra-cotta.

Welsh, John R. "An Anglo-American Friendship: Allston and Coleridge." JOURNAL OF AMERICAN STUDIES 5 (April 1971): 81-91.

Welsh traces the relationship of the painter Washington Allston with Samuel Taylor Coleridge. They were close friends between 1806-18, and Welsh suggests that this provided a connection between American and English romanticism.

Wilkins, Thurman. THOMAS MORAN: ARTIST OF THE MOUNTAINS. Norman: University of Oklahoma Press, 1966. xvi, 315 p.

Moran was a romantic painter who got his start when he was hired by the Hayden surveying expedition in Yellowstone during the 1870s. He depicted the grandeur of the Grand Canyon, Yosemite, Zion Canyon, and the Tetons to easterners.

Wilson, Garff B. A HISTORY OF AMERICAN ACTING. Bloomington: Indiana University Press, 1966. x, 310 p.

This is a series of sketches of the careers of forty-four major nineteenth-century actors. Edwin Forrest, Lawrence Barrett, James Rees, W.R. Alger, Gabriel Harrison, and Richard Moody are among those included.

_____. THREE HUNDRED YEARS OF AMERICAN DRAMA AND THEATRE: FROM YE BEAR AND YE CUBB TO HAIR. Englewood Cliffs, N.J.: Prentice-Hall, 1973. viii, 536 p.

This study combines a history of theater with a history of drama. The author summarizes different periods by explaining what it was like to buy tickets and even to enter and leave a theater.

Winter, Robert. "Architecture on the Frontier: The Mormon Experiment." PACIFIC HISTORICAL REVIEW 43 (February 1974): 50-60.

Winter discusses the Mormon temples at Kirtland, Ohio; Nauvoo, Illinois; and Salt Lake City with attention also to town planning. The mixing of classical and Gothic details as well as the influence of freemasonry are shown.

Wodehouse, Lawrence. "Alfred B. Mullett and His French Style Government Buildings." JOURNAL OF THE SOCIETY OF ARCHITECTURAL HISTORIANS 31 (March 1972): 22-37.

Mullett became supervising architect for the U.S. Treasury Department and designed many buildings in the Second Empire style. These were ornate buildings of which Mullett was a major developer.

1915 TO THE PRESENT

Cox, Richard. "Coney Island, Urban Symbol in American Art." NEW-YORK HISTORICAL SOCIETY QUARTERLY 60 (January-April 1976): 35-52.

Coney Island was a symbol of basic social and art issues. Artists between 1910-40 saw the amusement park as a mirror that reflected key sociopolitical problems facing a fast-changing America and as a microcosm of frenetic machine-age New York City.

Davidson, Aubrey. "Transcendental Unity in the Works of Charles Ives." AMERICAN QUARTERLY 22 (Spring 1970): 35-44.

> When Ives discussed unity in music, he was revolting strongly against conventional forms. He chose his own symbol of unity from nature, whether it was a church bell or more importantly the unity of a day.

Echols, Paul Clinton. "The Development of Shell Architecture in the United States, 1932-1962: An Examination of the Transfer of a Structural Idea." SOUTH ATLANTIC QUARTERLY 67 (Spring 1968): 203-42.

> Shell architecture is a method of building with a thin shell of reinforced concrete. This is a study of an idea from a technique in the hands of civil engineers to a broadly based form of architectural expression.

Engel, Martin. "Frank Lloyd Wright and Cubism: A Study in Ambiguity." AMERICAN QUARTERLY 19 (Spring 1967): 24-38.

> Engel believes that Wright's work represents an effort to resolve the rational and geometric with the irrational and the organic. His plans for houses were not unlike cubist paintings since they expressed nature by showing many different aspects of it.

Finley, David Edward. A STANDARD OF EXCELLENCE: ANDREW W. MELLON FOUNDS THE NATIONAL GALLERY OF ART AT WASHINGTON. Washington, D.C.: Smithsonian Institution Press, 1973. xii, 193 p.

> Finley was the first director of the National Gallery (1938-56), but he does not show the prices or the criteria of the art works purchased. The gallery has not played a major role in American art because it was founded too late.

Geselbracht, Raymond H. "Evolution and the New World Vision in the Music of Charles Ives." JOURNAL OF AMERICAN STUDIES 8 (August 1974): 211-27.

> This is a study of Ives's vision of America. His technique of composition was modern, but his message was old, since he expressed the New World vision of America.

_____. "The Ghosts of Andrew Wyeth: The Meaning of Death in the Transcendental Myth of America." NEW ENGLAND QUARTERLY 47 (March 1974): 13-29.

> Wyeth has gained the stature almost of a culture hero, but not because his paintings bear a resemblance to what Americans know as everyday life. On a profound level, his paintings have contributed to the transcendental myth of America--the idea that America

is the New World that has escaped the Old World's history—and he
has done this by the presence of time past.

Goldstein, Malcolm. THE POLITICAL STAGE: AMERICAN DRAMA AND
THEATER OF THE GREAT DEPRESSION. New York: Oxford University Press,
1974. x, 482 p.

Goldstein deals with the realistic social-message work of the 1930s
such as was produced in the Workers' Laboratory Theater of the
Communist Party, the Theater Union, and the Group Theater that
produced a number of the plays of Clifford Odetts. He emphasizes that playwriting changed after 1935 when radicals became
more sophisticated and exploited the individual's search for a better life rather than unions and unemployment.

Hoffman, Donald. THE ARCHITECTURE OF JOHN WELLBORN ROOT. Baltimore: Johns Hopkins University Press, 1973. xviii, 263 p.

Root practiced his profession in Chicago, Cleveland, Kansas City,
and San Francisco. He contributed to utilitarian architecture by
emphasizing a building's purpose.

Howard, John Tasker, with the assistance of Arthur Mendell. OUR CONTEM-
PORARY COMPOSERS: AMERICAN MUSIC IN THE TWENTIETH CENTURY.
New York: Thomas Y. Crowell, 1941. xv, 447 p.

This provides biographical data on composers, lists of works, and
even reviews of first performances. The best chapters are those
on the experimenters such as Ives, Riegger, and Cowell, and folk
song and racial expressions.

Kirker, Harold. "California Architecture and Its Relation to Contemporary
Trends in Europe and America." CALIFORNIA HISTORICAL QUARTERLY 51
(Winter 1972): 289-305.

Successive waves of immigrants have made colonialism the chief
characteristic of California architecture. An immigrant culture
usually represents the interaction between imported ideas and the
challenge of a new environment, but in California the influence
of the environment has been blunted by diversity.

McDonald, William F. FEDERAL RELIEF ADMINISTRATION AND THE ARTS.
Columbus: Ohio State University Press, 1969. xiv, 869 p.

This is a study of the New Deal's five professional programs: federal art, theater, music, and writers' projects, and the historical
records survey. It is mainly an administrative history of the projects seen from the perspective of the Washington office.

McKinzie, Richard D. THE NEW DEAL FOR ARTISTS. Princeton, N.J.: Princeton University Press, 1973. xii, 203 p.

The social and political forces that inspired the patronage of artists from 1939–42 are discussed. The New Deal employed about eleven thousand artists in an effort to make art a larger part of American life.

Mathews, Jane De Hart. "Arts and the People: The New Deal Quest for a Cultural Democracy." JOURNAL OF AMERICAN HISTORY 62 (September 1975): 316–39.

Franklin Roosevelt believed that the American people were entitled to cultural enrichment as well as economic betterment and social justice. New Deal cultural enthusiasts brought the arts to the people, but in the long run most Americans refused to believe that the arts were a public right and a personal necessity.

Neil, J. Meredith. "American Indifference to Art: An Anachronistic Ideal." AMERICAN STUDIES 13 (Fall 1972): 93–106.

Neil argues that Americans have not been indifferent to art. Where the myth of indifference has persisted in educated circles, he believes this is evidence of the persistence of the myth of the American Adam.

Perrin, Richard W.E. "Frank Lloyd Wright in Wisconsin: Prophet in His Own Country." WISCONSIN MAGAZINE OF HISTORY 48 (Autumn 1964): 32–47.

This is a survey of Wright's architectural ideas and his buildings in Wisconsin. His different periods of architecture are depicted in the text and photographs.

Perry, Rosalie Sandra. CHARLES IVES AND THE AMERICAN MIND. Kent, Ohio: Kent State University Press, 1974. xx, 137 p.

Perry maintains that while Ives was an innovator, much of his music was program music about the American past. The composer was influenced by transcendentalism, realism, the Social Gospel, and pragmatism.

Purcell, Ralph. GOVERNMENT AND ART: A STUDY OF AMERICAN EXPERIENCE. Washington, D.C.: Public Affairs Press, 1956. x, 129 p.

This is a narrative of the niggardly patronage by federal, state, and local governments for the arts. Until the twentieth century, government patronage was limited to the commissioning of artistic works for public buildings, but since then the federal government has become an art collector of considerable prominence.

Remley, Mary Lou. "The Wisconsin Idea of Dance: A Decade of Progress, 1917-1926." WISCONSIN MAGAZINE OF HISTORY 58 (Spring 1975): 179-95.

> Margaret N. H'Doubler developed the Wisconsin Idea of Dance which eventually culminated in the introduction of dance into physical education curricula throughout the United States. This approach emphasized that dance should evolve from the experiences of the individual and serve as a means of self-realization for the student.

Ross, Ronald. "The Role of Blacks in the Federal Theatre, 1935-1939." JOURNAL OF NEGRO HISTORY 59 (January 1974): 38-50.

> The Federal Theatre Project was designed to make drama available to the masses. It provided blacks with their first extended opportunity in the professional theater and they demonstrated that they were proficient in playwriting, directing, staging, and acting.

Rossiter, Frank R. CHARLES IVES AND HIS AMERICA. New York: Liveright, 1975. 420 p.

> This is a study in cultural history and psychological analysis. Ives's isolation as an artist and a human being is delineated.

Schroeder, Fred E.H. "Andrew Wyeth and the Transcendental Tradition." AMERICAN QUARTERLY 17 (Fall 1965): 559-67.

> The transcendental tradition is an honest and continuous unity and continuity between the wild and the domestic and this became the "organic principle" in design, architecture, city planning, poetry, and art. Through Robert Frost, Emily Dickinson, and Thoreau, Wyeth has devised an artistic theory based on transcendental origins.

Vitz, Robert C. "Clubs, Congresses, and Unions: American Artists Confront the Thirties." NEW YORK HISTORY 54 (October 1973): 424-47.

> Artists, suffering from the economic debacle, turned to professional and political activism to redefine their role. They reacted against capitalism and totalitarianism, and found it impossible to paint nudes and landscapes.

_____. "Struggle and Response: American Artists and the Great Depression." NEW YORK HISTORY 57 (January 1976): 81-98.

> The Depression brought suffering to artists, but they were stimulated to seek answers to aesthetic questions. They combated their traditional isolation, and gained a new sense of community as well as a new role in society through artist organizations and government programs.

Wittke, Carl. THE FIRST FIFTY YEARS: THE CLEVELAND MUSEUM OF ART, 1916-1966. Cleveland: Press of Case Western Reserve University, 1966. xi, 161 p.

> Wittke emphasizes the museum's educational achievements in bringing cultural experiences to Cleveland's children, ethnic groups, and social classes. This was an institution that did much for the community, but retained its private character through the munificence of wealthy individuals.

Chapter 4

BIOGRAPHY

COLONIAL PERIOD TO 1815

Akers, Charles W. CALLED UNTO LIBERTY: A LIFE OF JONATHAN MAY-
HEW, 1720-1766. Cambridge, Mass.: Harvard University Press, 1964. xii,
285 p.

> Akers emphasizes Mayhew's religious positions and does not exag-
> gerate his political influence. Mayhew approached religious and
> political disputes with a missionary zeal and was a clerical ration-
> alist who has been called the father of Unitarianism.

Berkeley, Edmund, and Berkeley, Dorothy Smith. DR. ALEXANDER GARDEN
OF CHARLES TOWN. Chapel Hill: University of North Carolina Press,
1969. xiv, 379 p.

> Garden, a Scottish physician, who migrated to Charles Town in
> 1752, was a major naturalist. He not only knew leading Ameri-
> can scientists such as John Bartram, but also developed correspon-
> dence with leading English and European taxonomists.

Chinard, Gilbert. THOMAS JEFFERSON, THE APOSTLE OF AMERICANISM.
Boston: Little, Brown, 1929. xviii, 548 p.

> In this biography, Chinard emphasizes Jefferson's mental processes
> and philosophy. He argues that his subject was an original thinker.

Covey, Cyclone. THE GENTLE RADICAL: A BIOGRAPHY OF ROGER WIL-
LIAMS. New York: Macmillan, 1966. viii, 273 p.

> Williams is presented as a seventeenth-century Puritan preacher
> whose independence of thought in matters relating to church and
> state came from his early associations with Separatists, Anabaptists,
> and other Reformation sources. He believed in responsible democ-
> racy and liberty under authority.

Biography

Cuningham, Charles E. TIMOTHY DWIGHT, 1752-1817: A BIOGRAPHY. New York: Macmillan, 1942. viii, 403 p.

This biography of Dwight is important because it describes Puritan orthodoxy in the late eighteenth century and yet depicts a man who was also open-minded and a forerunner of a new age. Dwight became president of Yale in 1795 when the school was little more than an academy and laid the foundations of the university.

Green, Constance McL. ELI WHITNEY AND THE BIRTH OF AMERICAN TECH-NOLOGY. Library of American Biography. Edited by Oscar Handlin. Boston: Little, Brown, 1956. viii, 215 p.

Whitney not only invented the cotton gin but also pioneered in the manufacture of arms by developing a system based on interchangable parts. His inventions contributed importantly to the rise of an industrialized North.

Hamlin, Talbot. BENJAMIN HENRY LATROBE. New York: Oxford University Press, 1955. xxxvi, 633 p.

Latrobe is known as the father of American architecture, but he was also an engineer, linguist, historian, painter, dramatist, poet, musician, and industrialist. He came to the United States from London in 1796 and became noted for his U.S. capitol drawings.

Hindle, Brooke. DAVID RITTENHOUSE. Princeton, N.J.: Princeton University Press, 1964. ix, 394 p.

Rittenhouse was a member of the enlightened circle that brought the American Philosophical Society into being. He conducted experiments in basic science, but also served as a technical adviser on a large number of subjects.

Morgan, Edmund S. THE GENTLE PURITAN: A LIFE OF EZRA STILES, 1727-1795. New Haven, Conn.: Yale University Press for the Institute of Early American History and Culture, Williamsburg, Virginia, 1962. xiv, 490 p.

Morgan depicts Stiles as a religious liberal who greatly influenced change in America. Stiles lived at the time when the transition from Reformation to Enlightenment came to New England.

_____. THE PURITAN DILEMMA: THE STORY OF JOHN WINTHROP. Library of American Biography. Edited by Oscar Handlin. Boston: Little, Brown, 1958. xiv, 224 p.

The Puritan dilemma was how to apply a rigorous ethic without endangering the structure of the community. Winthrop learned to keep his mind on God without withdrawing from the world and to march in company with other sinners because perfection was unattainable.

Peterson, Merrill D. THOMAS JEFFERSON AND THE NEW NATION. New York: Oxford University Press, 1970. ix, 1,072 p.

Peterson presents the world as Jefferson saw it. He argues that Jefferson's scientific, architectural, and anthropological contributions are evidence of Jefferson's goal of providing enlightenment for America.

Pilcher, George William. SAMUEL DAVIES: APOSTLE OF DISSENT IN COLONIAL VIRGINIA. Knoxville: University of Tennessee Press, 1971. xi, 229 p.

Davies is depicted as a great pulpit orator and a champion of the New Light movement that extended pietism and religious dissent into the South. He was a major figure in the Great Awakening in Virginia.

Schlenther, Boyd S., ed. THE LIFE AND WRITINGS OF FRANCIS MAKEMIE. Philadelphia: Presbyterian Historical Society, 1971. 287 p.

Makemie was the father of American Presbyterianism and a strong defender of religious dissent in the colonies. He was important in preventing the establishment of Anglicanism in the middle colonies.

Thompson, Mack. MOSES BROWN: RELUCTANT REFORMER. Chapel Hill: University of North Carolina Press for the Institute of Early American History and Culture, Williamsburg, Virginia, 1962. xii, 316 p.

Brown was one of the brothers of Providence, Rhode Island, who made a fortune in commerce. He turned to Quakerism in response to his wife's death in 1773 and became an abolitionist, pacifist, educator, welfare economist, expert in preventive medicine, and civic reformer.

Van Doren, Carl. BENJAMIN FRANKLIN. New York: Viking Press, 1938. xix, 845 p.

This study not only portrays Franklin as a scientist, diplomat, politician, and literary figure, but also as a man who preached thrift but did not practice it, emphasized homely virtues but devoted himself to pleasant graces, and expounded conservatism but became a revolutionary in his old age.

Van Dyken, Seymour. SAMUEL WILLARD, 1640-1707: PREACHER OF ORTHODOXY IN AN ERA OF CHANGE. Grand Rapids, Mich.: William B. Eerdmans, 1972. 224 p.

Willard was an important defender of orthodoxy during a period when religious zeal waned in Puritan New England. He used the

pulpit to discuss matters of church and state, and even became
acting president of Harvard for six years.

Wildes, Harry Emerson. WILLIAM PENN. New York: Macmillan, 1974. ix,
469 p.

This is a straightforward, chronological account of Penn's life.
Wildes concludes that the Quaker leader was a man of paradox
who gradually lost his optimistic faith in men and democratic
government and became a defender of aristocratic privilege.

Winslow, Ola Elizabeth. MASTER ROGER WILLIAMS: A BIOGRAPHY. New
York: Macmillan, 1957. xiv, 328 p.

"Soul-liberty," separation of church and state, and conversion of
the Indians governed Williams's thoughts and actions. Winslow
argues that Providence, Rhode Island, was not the democracy it
had been asserted as being.

Ziff, Larzer. THE CAREER OF JOHN COTTON: PURITANISM AND AMERI-
CAN EXPERIENCE. Princeton, N.J.: Princeton University Press, 1962. xii,
280 p.

Cotton is depicted as being the most influential clergyman in molding Massachusetts Bay and New England Congregationalism. Ziff
elucidates Cotton's views on church and state and his disputes with
Roger Williams.

1815-1915

Allen, Gay W. THE SOLITARY SINGER: A CRITICAL BIOGRAPHY OF WALT
WHITMAN. New York: Macmillan, 1955. xii, 618 p.

This is a study of the growth of Whitman's mind and the development of his art. The poet tried to express national life through
his poems.

Baer, Helene G. THE HEART IS LIKE HEAVEN: THE LIFE OF LYDIA MARIA
CHILD. Philadelphia: University of Pennsylvania Press, 1964. 339 p.

Child was a writer and reformer of the pre-Civil War period. She
published the first of her novels in 1824, pioneered in the production of juvenilia, and became a leading antislavery propagandist
and editor.

Bailey, Hugh C. EDGAR GARDNER MURPHY: GENTLE PROGRESSIVE. Coral
Gables, Fla.: University of Miami Press, 1968. 274 p.

This High Church Episcopalian rector, who served in the South, spoke out against lynchings, the disfranchisement of Negroes, and child labor. His most significant contribution was serving as executive secretary of the southern education board between 1901-09, which accomplished something of a renaissance in southern education, but also convinced northern promoters that they should shift their concern from blacks to whites.

Barker, Charles Albro. HENRY GEORGE. New York: Oxford University Press, 1955. xvii, 696 p.

George is depicted as a man driven by an inner spirit, who combined love of God with love of man and a desire for fame. He was a liberal reformer and a man of consistent purpose.

Beringause, Arthur F. BROOKS ADAMS: A BIOGRAPHY. New York: Alfred A. Knopf, 1955. xiv, 404 p.

Beringause sees Adams as more than a scholar and a prophet of doom. Adams wanted to save civilization through rule by an elite made up of qualified individuals, but he also fell prey to racism and jingoism.

Bloch, E. Maurice. GEORGE CALEB BINGHAM: THE EVOLUTION OF AN ARTIST. Berkeley and Los Angeles: University of California Press, 1967. xxiv, 339 p.

This study embraces Bingham's biographical, social, and political background. He was a Missouri frontier artist and primarily a painter of genre, elevating everyday scenes to artistic significance.

Blumberg, Dorothy Rose. FLORENCE KELLEY: THE MAKING OF A SOCIAL REFORMER. New York: Augustus M. Kelley, 1966. xii, 194 p.

This study of the first forty years of Kelley's life emphasizes her role in socialism, social reform, and the women's rights movement. The overriding factor in her drive to reform was the senseless discrimination against women.

Breeden, James O. JOSEPH JONES, M.D.: SCIENTIST OF THE OLD SOUTH. Lexington: University of Kentucky Press, 1975. xiii, 295 p.

Jones was one of the few nineteenth-century scientists to investigate southern diseases. After the Civil War, he settled in New Orleans and became an authority on medicine and public health.

Brodie, Fawn M. NO MAN KNOWS MY HISTORY: THE LIFE OF JOSEPH SMITH, THE MORMON PROPHET. New York: Alfred A. Knopf, 1945. ix, 476 p.

This is an objective history of Smith and the early Mormon Church.
As a boy, Smith was a seeker of treasure and a product of frontier
evangelical Protestantism, while the BOOK OF MORMON was a
literary work and one of the earliest examples of frontier fiction.

Brooks, Juanita. JOHN DOYLE LEE: ZEALOT--PIONEER BUILDER--SCAPE-
GOAT. Glendale, Calif.: Arthur H. Clark, 1961. 404 p.

Lee was a Mormon leader and officeholder who lived through the
expulsion from Missouri, the fall of Nauvoo in 1845-46, and the
trek to Utah. This biography shows the strength of the Mormon's
faith and the authoritarian nature of the church.

Brown, Arthur W. ALWAYS YOUNG FOR LIBERTY: A BIOGRAPHY OF
WILLIAM ELLERY CHANNING. Syracuse, N.Y.: Syracuse University Press,
1956. xii, 268 p.

Channing is depicted mainly as a participant in the beginnings of
Unitarianism in New England. To a lesser extent his role as a
social theorist and reformer is shown.

Brown, Charles H. WILLIAM CULLEN BRYANT. New York: Charles Scribner's Sons, 1971. 576 p.

This study, based mainly on published sources, traces the transition
in Bryant's career from poet to editor and politician. Brown tells
what Bryant's editorials said, but he does not analyze his political
thought or his influence on politics.

Buckler, Helen. DANIEL DALE WILLIAMS, NEGRO SURGEON. New York:
Pitman, 1968. xvi, 381 p.

Williams was a gifted Chicago surgeon who founded Provident Hospital in 1891, the first hospital run by blacks where blacks were
accepted on an equal basis. He also served as chief surgeon at
Freedman's Hospital in Washington and performed the first successful operation on a human heart.

Byrne, Frank L. PROPHET OF PROHIBITION: NEAL DOW AND HIS CRU-
SADE. Madison: State Historical Society of Wisconsin for the Department of
History, University of Wisconsin, 1961. viii, 184 p.

Dow was the champion of the Maine Law of 1851, who carried the
cause of prohibition to other states, England, and Canada. He
was an impetuous man who revealed little evidence of affection
toward the individuals with whom he associated.

Canby, Henry Seidel. THOREAU. Boston: Houghton Mifflin, 1939. xx,
508 p.

Canby traces Thoreau's life in terms of a writer in search of a theme, an audience, and a way of life. The sources of Thoreau's thought are delineated as well as is Emerson's influence on the young men of his time.

_____. WALT WHITMAN: AN AMERICAN: A STUDY IN BIOGRAPHY. Boston: Houghton Mifflin, 1943. viii, 381 p.

This is a life and society portrayal in which Whitman the individualist is merged with Whitman the product of a collective social consciousness. The author shows that Whitman's poetic form resulted from intense emotional experiences he could not understand and the capacity to draw inspiration from daily routine.

Caughey, John Walton. HUBERT HOWE BANCROFT, HISTORIAN OF THE WEST. Berkeley and Los Angeles: University of California Press, 1946. ix, 422 p.

Bancroft was an energetic businessman and a publisher who developed a penchant for history. His collection of materials on the West has not been surpassed and he sold six thousand sets of his thirty-nine-volume history of the Pacific states.

Chisholm, Lawrence W. FENOLLOSA: THE FAR EAST AND AMERICAN CULTURE. New Haven, Conn.: Yale University Press, 1963. xiv, 297 p.

Ernest Francisco Fenollosa (1853-1908) was known for his translations of Oriental poetry and his aesthetic theories based on the nature of the Chinese written character. He influenced literary and artistic rebels through emphasizing the psychology of individual liberation, as well as the belief that art should be an expression of democratic vitality.

Clark, Robert D. THE LIFE OF MATTHEW SIMPSON. New York: Macmillan, 1956. xiv, 344 p.

Simpson (1811-84) became a preacher, professor, and Methodist bishop at the age of forty. He tried to adjust Methodism to changing conditions and called for college-educated preachers, Gothic architecture, and the acceptance of Darwinian evolution as another example of God's grand design.

Commager, Henry Steele. THEODORE PARKER. Boston: Little, Brown, 1936. ix, 339 p.

Parker was a preacher and crusader who, with others, kept Boston in a state of agitation during the thirty years before the Civil War. This antislavery reformer was distinguished for his hard-hitting eloquence.

Coughlan, Neil. YOUNG JOHN DEWEY: AN ESSAY IN AMERICAN IN-
TELLECTUAL HISTORY. Chicago: University of Chicago Press, 1975. xii,
187 p.

> This psychobiography is subtle. It shows how Dewey grew out of
> liberal Congregationalism through neo-Hegelianism to instrumental-
> ism.

Coulson, Thomas. JOSEPH HENRY: HIS LIFE AND WORK. Princeton, N.J.:
Princeton University Press, 1950. vii, 352 p.

> Henry's scientific career and accomplishments are evaluated. He
> is depicted as a great experimental scientist whose conceptions
> were limited by a qualitative approach.

Cramer, Clarence H. ROYAL BOB: THE LIFE OF ROBERT G. INGERSOLL.
Indianapolis: Bobbs-Merrill Co., 1952. 314 p.

> Ingersoll is best known as a champion of unorthodox religious views
> and as the "great agnostic." He was also a successful lawyer and
> orator who supported a variety of humanitarian causes.

Cromwell, Otelia. LUCRETIA MOTT. Cambridge, Mass.: Harvard University
Press, 1958. xiv, 241 p.

> Cromwell shows that Mott was a leading women's rights advocate,
> liberal religious thinker, and abolitionist. She subscribed to the
> program of the New England Non-Resistance Society, helped split
> the Anti-Slavery Society by her insistence on women's rights, and
> helped call the Anti-Sabbath Convention.

Cross, Barbara M. HORACE BUSHNELL: MINISTER TO A CHANGING
AMERICA. Chicago: University of Chicago Press, 1958. xvi, 201 p.

> Bushnell's mission was fitting Calvinism to scientific, transcenden-
> tal America. This biography depicts his orthodoxy and his han-
> dling of his congregation during a time of change.

Crouthamel, James L. JAMES WATSON WEBB: A BIOGRAPHY. Middletown,
Conn.: Wesleyan University Press, 1969. x, 262 p.

> Webb was editor of the New York COURIER & ENQUIRER, a mer-
> cantile newspaper, from the age of Jackson to the Civil War. He
> gave voice to rationalizations and conservative caution to the com-
> mercial classes concerning the veto of the Bank of the United
> States' charter and the expansion of slavery.

Crowe, Charles. GEORGE RIPLEY: TRANSCENDENTALIST AND UTOPIAN
SOCIALIST. Athens: University of Georgia Press, 1967. x, 316 p.

This is a study of a leading figure in transcendentalism, president of the Brook Farm community, and later, literary critic of Greeley's NEW YORK TRIBUNE. Especially valuable in this study is the treatment of Brook Farm and the Fourierist movement.

Cruden, Robert. JAMES FORD RHODES: THE MAN, THE HISTORIAN, AND HIS WORKS. Cleveland: Press of Case Western Reserve University, 1961. xiv, 290 p.

Rhodes is depicted as a Calvinist who made oversimplified moral judgments, an advocate of the economics of Herbert Spencer, and an anti-Semite and believer in Anglo-Saxonism and white supremacy. His work was popular because he told Americans what they wanted to hear, particularly that the values of the middle class were founded on eternal verities.

Destler, Chester McArthur. HENRY DEMAREST LLOYD AND THE EMPIRE OF REFORM. Philadelphia: University of Pennsylvania Press, 1963. 657 p.

In this biography of Lloyd, Destler maintains that progressivism did not burst upon America, but emerged after a gestation period that began in the late 1870s. Lloyd is shown as both a prophet and product of this development.

Dillon, Merton L. BENJAMIN LUNDY AND THE STRUGGLE FOR NEGRO FREEDOM. Urbana: University of Illinois Press, 1966. vi, 285 p.

Lundy, a Quaker, was the most continuous opponent of slavery in the 1820s and converted Garrison to abolitionism. He supported voluntary emigration by some free Negroes as a means of lessening prejudice, furnished evidence on the slave power in Texas, and encouraged abolitionists to use the ballot.

_____. ELIJAH P. LOVEJOY: ABOLITIONIST EDITOR. Urbana: University of Illinois Press, 1961. xii, 190 p.

Lovejoy was born and raised in Maine, but he migrated to St. Louis where he became a liberal Presbyterian minister and editor of religious newspapers. He was drawn to abolitionism and became a martyr defending his press in 1838.

Dorn, Jacob Henry. WASHINGTON GLADDEN: PROPHET OF THE SOCIAL GOSPEL. Columbus: Ohio State University Press, 1967. x, 489 p.

Liberal theology and the social gospel were Gladden's response to late nineteenth-century science, scholarship, industrialization, and urbanization. He was a prolific writer who popularized the liberal Protestant position for laymen and led the victory of liberalism over orthodoxy at the beginning of the twentieth century.

Drinnon, Richard. REBEL IN PARADISE: A BIOGRAPHY OF EMMA GOLD-
MAN. Chicago: University of Chicago Press, 1961. xvi, 349 p.

Goldman was a Jewish immigrant from Russia who became one of
America's foremost radicals in the twentieth century. Finding
sweatshops and Jewish communities in America little better than in
Europe, she became an anarchist who was involved in the Haymar-
ket Affair and an advocate of free love, before her deportation in
1919.

Drury, Clifford Merrill. WILLIAM ANDERSON SCOTT: "NO ORDINARY
MAN." Glendale, Calif.: Arthur H. Clark, 1967. 352 p.

Scott rose to positions of influence and prestige in the Presbyterian
church in the South and California before the Civil War. He was
elected moderator of the Old School General Assembly and also
became involved in controversies concerning slavery, Bible reading
in the public schools, and vigilantism in San Francisco.

Duberman, Martin. JAMES RUSSELL LOWELL. Boston: Houghton Mifflin,
1966. xxii, 516 p.

Duberman covers Lowell the editor, teacher, diplomat, public commentator, and writer. He attempts to show Lowell's human side
as a man of warmth, geniality, and tolerance.

Dupree, A. Hunter. ASA GRAY, 1810-1888. Cambridge, Mass.: Belknap
Press of Harvard University Press, 1959. xvi, 505 p.

Gray was the patriarch of American botany and a confidant of
Charles Darwin. He contradicted a view that affirmed a Divine
Will in nature and achieved a modern insight into organic creation.

Earhart, Mary. FRANCES WILLARD: FROM PRAYER TO POLITICS. Chicago:
University of Chicago Press, 1944. x, 418 p.

This biography portrays Willard as a masterful politician, as exemplified by her conversion of southern women to temperance at a
time northerners were opposed. She was born into a tyrannical
Puritan household, invented "For God and Home and Native Land"
as her slogan and contributed to the advancement of women's suffrage, labor unionism, and socialism, besides temperance.

Eby, Cecil D., Jr. "PORTE CRAYON": THE LIFE OF DAVID HUNTER
STROTHER. Chapel Hill: University of North Carolina Press, 1960. xiv,
258 p.

Strother was a Virginia gentleman, who became a popular writer
and illustrator, a military aide to Union generals, and consul
general to Mexico. As "Porte Crayon," he wrote popular serials
and articles for HARPER'S WEEKLY.

Edelstein, Tilden G. STRANGE ENTHUSIASM: A LIFE OF THOMAS WENT-
WORTH HIGGINSON. New Haven, Conn.: Yale University Press, 1968.
ix, 425 p.

> In this study, the mentality of a nineteenth-century reformer is
> probed. Higginson was a liberal minister, antislavery and women's
> rights advocate, conspirator in John Brown's raid, leader of black
> troops during the Civil War, and a postwar litterateur.

Ellis, Elmer. MR. DOOLEY'S AMERICA: A LIFE OF FINLEY PETER DUNNE.
New York: Alfred A. Knopf, 1941. x, 310 p.

> Dunne was a humorist whose characters, Mr. Dooley and his audi-
> ence Hennessey, were national figures in the late nineteenth and
> early twentieth centuries. Ellis displays Dunne's sharp satire and
> shows that he was not a man who expected the public to follow
> his preachments.

Ellis, John Tracy. THE LIFE OF JAMES CARDINAL GIBBONS, ARCHBISHOP
OF BALTIMORE, 1834-1921. 2 vols. Milwaukee: Bruce Publishing Co.,
1952.

> Between the Civil War and World War I, Cardinal Gibbons was
> the leading Catholic prelate in the United States. He was the
> center of public discussion of controversial issues such as immigra-
> tion, the relationship of church and state, religious prejudice, and
> the rights of organized labor.

Farrison, William Edward. WILLIAM WELLS BROWN: AUTHOR AND PER-
FORMER. Chicago: University of Chicago Press, 1969. xii, 482 p.

> Brown was a fugitive slave during most of his adult life. After his
> flight to freedom in 1835, he lectured for the American Anti-
> Slavery Society, wrote a celebrated sentimental novel, CLOTEL,
> and prepared Negro histories, but he was always beholden to the
> white world of reform.

Fatout, Paul. AMBROSE BIERCE: THE DEVIL'S LEXICOGRAPHER. Norman:
University of Oklahoma Press, 1951. xv, 349 p.

> Fatout depicts Bierce as a secondary literary figure whose DEVIL'S
> DICTIONARY is his only work that deserves to live. He was one
> of America's great newspaper columnists.

Fein, Albert. FREDERICK LAW OLMSTED AND THE AMERICAN ENVIRON-
MENTAL TRADITION. New York: George Braziller, 1972. xi, 180 p.

> Olmsted's career falls into two periods--the first as a public plan-
> ner who created Central Park in New York among other large city
> parks; the second as a planner in the private sector who designed

Stanford University's campus and the great White City built for the Chicago Exposition of 1893.

Filler, Louis. RANDOLPH BOURNE. Introduction by Max Lerner. Washington, D.C.: American Council on Public Affairs, 1943. xi, 158 p.

Bourne was an important social critic and writer of the pre-World War I generation. He was a disciple of John Dewey, a critic of the melting-pot theory, a crusader for peace, and a fighter against injustice.

Findlay, James F., Jr. DWIGHT L. MOODY: AMERICAN EVANGELIST, 1837-1899. Chicago: University of Chicago Press, 1969. ix, 440 p.

Moody was a link between early nineteenth-century scriptural Protestantism with its Arminian leanings and the demands of an urban age. He also was an entrepreneur in religion whose qualities were mirrored by the businessmen with whom he associated.

Fladeland, Betty. JAMES GILLESPIE BIRNEY: SLAVEHOLDER TO ABOLITIONIST. Ithaca, N.Y.: Cornell University Press, 1955. xii, 323 p.

This candidate for president of the Liberty Party in 1840 and 1844 was a Princeton-educated slaveholder. He was a moderate, southern aristocrat who was uncomfortable both in reform and politics.

Flanagan, John T. JAMES HALL, LITERARY PIONEER OF THE OHIO VALLEY. Minneapolis: University of Minnesota Press, 1941. vii, 218 p.

Hall was a prosecuting attorney, circuit judge, state treasurer, editor and publisher, historian, and educator. Most of his important work was done in Illinois between 1820-33 where he established the ILLINOIS MONTHLY MAGAZINE, first literary magazine west of the Ohio.

Fleming, Donald. JOHN WILLIAM DRAPER AND THE RELIGION OF SCIENCE. Philadelphia: University of Pennsylvania Press, 1950. ix, 205 p.

This chemist and physicist came to the United States from England in 1832. He is portrayed as a man who tried to find meaning in science, history, and society, and who fought the forces that opposed science.

Forbush, Bliss. ELIAS HICKS: QUAKER LIBERAL. New York: Columbia University Press, 1956. xxii, 355 p.

Hicks's teachings enabled nineteenth-century Quaker liberals to remain in the sect. He fought for separation of church and state

and the emancipation of slaves, while opposing the entry of
Quakers into political life.

_____. MOSES SHEPPARD: QUAKER PHILANTHROPIST OF BALTIMORE.
Philadelphia: J.B. Lippincott, 1968. 317 p.

A self-made Baltimore merchant and investor, Sheppard retired in
middle age to devote himself to humanitarian causes. He sponsored developments in the biological and physical sciences, worked
for the protection of the Iroquois Indians, supported African colonization, and left the bulk of his estate to an experimental mental
hospital.

Ford, Alice. EDWARD HICKS, PAINTER OF THE PEACEABLE KINGDOM.
Philadelphia: University of Pennsylvania Press, 1952. xvi, 161 p.

This primitive graphic artist's painting sometimes included views of
the Delaware Water Gap in Pennsylvania, a variety of animals,
and a vignette of William Penn's treaty with the Indians. He was
also preoccupied with Quaker doctrine and controversy.

_____. JOHN JAMES AUDUBON. Norman: University of Oklahoma Press,
1964. xiv, 488 p.

Audubon's life is described more than is his art. His travels and
efforts to sell his paintings are chronicled.

Fornell, Earl Wesley. THE UNHAPPY MEDIUM: SPIRITUALISM AND THE LIFE
OF MARGARET FOX. Austin: University of Texas Press, 1964. x, 204 p.

Spiritualism was an important religious, social, and intellectual
system in the mid-nineteenth century. This study covers a few episodes in the cult mainly associated with the life of Margaret Fox.

Fox, Stephen R. THE GUARDIAN OF BOSTON: WILLIAM MONROE TROTTER.
New York: Atheneum, 1970. ix, 307 p.

Along with Booker Washington and W.E.B. DuBois, Trotter was a
leading black spokesman during the first decade of the twentieth
century. He founded the Boston GUARDIAN, opposed Washington's accommodationist policies, and demanded full equality for
blacks in American life.

Fuller, Paul E. LAURA CLAY AND THE WOMAN'S RIGHTS MOVEMENT.
Lexington: University Press of Kentucky, 1975. x, 217 p.

Clay was the daughter of Cassius M. Clay and stood as a moderate
in the suffrage movement. She was a leader in the formation of
the Equal Rights Association in Kentucky and opposed the centralization of the suffrage movement.

Harlan, Louis R. BOOKER T. WASHINGTON: THE MAKING OF A BLACK LEADER, 1856-1901. New York: Oxford University Press, 1972. xi, 379 p.

> Harlan emphasizes the forces that shaped Washington's personality and philosophy. His early thought was shaped by white leaders, and it was not until the founding of Tuskegee Institute that he was influenced by blacks.

Harlow, Ralph Volney. GERRIT SMITH, PHILANTHROPIST AND REFORMER. New York: Henry Holt, 1939. vi, 501 p.

> Smith was not a leader among pre-Civil War reformers because he was a dabbler. His zeal drew him to temperance, abolition, peace, prison reform, women's rights, and education.

Harrison, John M. THE MAN WHO MADE NASBY, DAVID ROSS LOCKE. Chapel Hill: University of North Carolina Press, 1969. ix, 335 p.

> This Gilded Age journalist, publisher, lecturer, and satirist created the fictional character, Petroleum V. Nasby. As publisher of the Toledo WEEKLY BLADE, he crusaded for temperance, sound money, popular education, women's suffrage, and civil rights, and left a legacy with his wit, satire, and caricature.

Hirshson, Stanley P. THE LION OF THE LORD: A BIOGRAPHY OF BRIGHAM YOUNG. New York: Alfred A. Knopf, 1969. xx, 391 p.

> Young is portrayed as a courageous, determined, bloodthirsty, dictatorial, lustful, generous, and devout man possessed of organizational skills and a capacity to lead. This balanced study makes use of sources little used by Mormon historians.

Horine, Emmet Field. DANIEL DRAKE (1785-1852): PIONEER PHYSICIAN OF THE MIDWEST. Philadelphia: University of Pennsylvania Press, 1961. 425 p.

> This doctor struggled to raise the standards of medical education and engaged in various social activities in Cincinnati. His PRINCIPAL DISEASES OF THE INTERIOR VALLEY OF NORTH AMERICA was a landmark in human geography and environmental medicine.

Joyce, Davis D. EDWARD CHANNING AND THE GREAT WORK. The Hague: Martinus Nijhoff, 1974. xi, 231 p.

> This is a biography of Channing and of his work, A HISTORY OF THE UNITED STATES, in six volumes. Channing is viewed as a transitional figure in American history between George Bancroft and the new professional historians.

Kuklich, Bruce. JOSIAH ROYCE: AN INTELLECTUAL BIOGRAPHY. Indianapolis: Bobbs-Merrill, 1972. ix, 270 p.

This is not a biography in the traditional sense. Kuklich traces Royce's epistemology and metaphysics as systems of ideas and virtually ignores his relationships with colleagues.

Larkin, Oliver W. SAMUEL F.B. MORSE AND AMERICAN DEMOCRATIC ART. Library of American Biography. Edited by Oscar Handlin. Boston: Little, Brown, 1954. viii, 215 p.

Painting was not merely to delight and amuse persons of leisure, it was to enlighten the masses it served. Morse's career in art, invention, and politics is delineated.

Leidecker, Kurt F. YANKEE TEACHER: THE LIFE OF WILLIAM TORREY HARRIS. New York: Philosophical Library, 1946. xx, 648 p.

Harris was a disciple of Hegelian idealism and Spencerian individualism, who founded the JOURNAL OF SPECULATIVE PHILOSOPHY and published five hundred titles in the nineteenth century.

Leopold, Richard William. ROBERT DALE OWEN: A BIOGRAPHY. Harvard Historical Studies. Cambridge, Mass.: Harvard University Press, 1940. xii, 470 p.

Owen came to America in 1825 with his father, Robert Owen, and helped to found the community of New Harmony, Indiana. After the failure of that enterprise, he moved to New York where he conducted a freethought and anticlerical journal, published the pioneer American tract on birth control, advocated political action in the labor movement, and served in the U.S. Congress as a Democrat during the 1840s.

Lerner, Gerda. THE GRIMKE SISTERS OF SOUTH CAROLINA: REBELS AGAINST SLAVERY. Boston: Houghton Mifflin, 1967. xiv, 479 p.

The Grimkes escaped patriarchal southern society, suffered discrimination as women in the antislavery movement, and campaigned against all forms of racial discrimination. Angelina married Theodore Weld, but the sisters stayed together, although family life impeded their reform activities.

Lowenthal, David. GEORGE PERKINS MARSH: VERSATILE VERMONTER. New York: Columbia University Press, 1958. xii, 442 p.

Marsh's MAN AND NATURE (1864) was the most original geographical work of the nineteenth century. He turned from books to nature because of poor eyesight, witnessed the depletion of forests, knew the nation's best scientific minds through the Smithsonian Institution, and served as minister to both Turkey and Italy.

Lumpkin, Katharine Du Pre. THE EMANCIPATION OF ANGELINA GRIMKE. Chapel Hill: University of North Carolina Press, 1974. xv, 265 p.

This is a study of Grimke's inner life as related to her public career. The tensions in her slaveholder family, relations with her sister, and her marriage to Theodore Weld are emphasized, but little is said about her role as a feminist and public speaker.

Lurie, Edward. LOUIS AGASSIZ: A LIFE IN SCIENCE. Chicago: University of Chicago Press, 1960. xiv, 449 p.

Lurie shows that Agassiz's best work was done before he came to America. The opportunities for science in America drained him, left him unprepared for the ORIGIN OF THE SPECIES, and brought a decline in his influence on American naturalists.

Lutz, Alma. SUSAN B. ANTHONY: REBEL, CRUSADER, HUMANITARIAN. Boston: Beacon Press, 1959. xii, 340 p.

Anthony was a strong believer in freedom, equality, and the intrinsic worth of human beings. She was disillusioned because other reformers did not see that freedom for the Negro was also essential to women, and she tried to make the Fourteenth and Fifteenth Amendments applicable to members of her sex.

Lyon, Peter. SUCCESS STORY: THE LIFE AND TIMES OF S.S. McCLURE. Deland, Fla.: Everett, Edwards, 1967. xv, 433 p.

McClure is depicted in his own terms, but not without faults. As an editor, he was proud of the industry of Irish immigrants, his victories in a hostile environment, and of muckraking, but he was also a womanizer, junketeer, and visionary, who drove associates to distraction and died broke.

Mabee, Carleton. THE AMERICAN LEONARDO: A LIFE OF SAMUEL F.B. MORSE. Introduction by Allan Nevins. New York: Alfred A. Knopf, 1943. xix, 420 p.

This biography presents rich details concerning the status of art in the early nineteenth century. Mabee illuminates the controversies concerning Morse's invention of the telegraph.

McAllister, Ethel M. AMOS EATON, SCIENTIST AND EDUCATOR, 1776-1842. Philadelphia: University of Pennsylvania Press, 1941. xiii, 587 p.

Eaton was a distinguished agricultural chemist and geologist, who pioneered in geological studies for the improvement of agriculture. He also helped found Rensselaer Polytechnic Institute in 1824 where learning by doing was emphasized and women were admitted.

McGloin, John Bernard. CALIFORNIA'S FIRST ARCHBISHOP: THE LIFE OF JOSEPH SADOC ALEMANY, O.P., 1814-1888. New York: Herder and Herder, 1966. 412 p.

> This priest reached California during the gold rush. He was a Dominican who spent his life spreading Catholic doctrine and teaching in frontier areas that now comprise northern California, Utah, and Nevada.

McLean, Robert Colin. GEORGE TUCKER: MORAL PHILOSOPHER AND MAN OF LETTERS. Chapel Hill: University of North Carolina Press, 1961. xiv, 265 p.

> A novelist, historian, philosopher, and political economist, Tucker embraced Scottish common sense philosophy. He was optimistic about the prospects for American literature because he believed civilization would progress as population grew, and he criticized both Malthusian pessimists and Jeffersonian idealists.

Mann, Harold W. ATTICUS GREENE HAYGOOD, METHODIST BISHOP, EDITOR, AND EDUCATOR. Athens: University of Georgia Press, 1965. viii, 254 p.

> Haygood was a minister, college president, and supporter of Negro education in the South during the post-Civil War years. In his economic and political attitudes, he was a Bourbon and a Redeemer dedicated to restoring white supremacy, which did not reflect his liberal racial and theological views.

Marshall, Helen E. MARY ADELAIDE NUTTING: PIONEER OF MODERN NURSING. Baltimore: Johns Hopkins University Press, 1972. v, 396 p.

> Nutting served as superintendent of nursing at Johns Hopkins and Teachers College, Columbia University, from 1894 to 1925. She prepared programs, drafted curriculum guides, wrote a four-volume HISTORY OF NURSING, and put together proposed legislation.

Mead, Sidney Earl. NATHANIEL WILLIAM TAYLOR, 1786-1858: A CONNECTICUT LIBERAL. Chicago: University of Chicago Press, 1942. xi, 259 p.

> This professor of theology at Yale was a protege of Timothy Dwight. He and his associates, notably Lyman Beecher, were practical theologians who stimulated revivals to save souls and for further social and political ends such as stemming the rise of republicanism and Unitarianism.

Merrill, Walter M. AGAINST WIND AND TIDE: A BIOGRAPHY OF WM. LLOYD GARRISON. Cambridge, Mass.: Harvard University Press, 1963. xviii, 391 p.

Garrison is viewed as a universal reformer who did more than any
other abolitionist to give publicity to the slavery question and create abolition sentiment. He expressed humility but was egotisti-
cal, espoused nonresistance but was sympathetic to the use of violence, and did not always adhere to his no-government idea.

Messerli, Jonathan. HORACE MANN: A BIOGRAPHY. New York: Alfred
A. Knopf, 1972. xviii, 604 p.

Mann was a temperance reformer, Whig politician, antislavery
leader, and an educational reformer. He is portrayed as an in-
flexible and unimaginative moralist who produced simplistic educational solutions for every national problem.

Morgan, Arthur E. EDWARD BELLAMY. Columbia Studies in American Culture, no. 15. New York: Columbia University Press, 1944. xvii, 468 p.

As a thinker, the author places Bellamy with Freud, Emerson, Whitman, and George. He also criticizes the faulty reasoning in
LOOKING BACKWARD.

Nye, Russel B. GEORGE BANCROFT, BRAHMIN REBEL. New York: Alfred
A. Knopf, 1944. x, 300 p.

Bancroft was one of a few Americans who combined successfully
public life with scholarship. As a politician, he did not go with
the crowd, and hence was a rebel, and in his histories he exalted
the common man as the instrument of the Almighty.

_____. WILLIAM LLOYD GARRISON AND THE HUMANITARIAN REFORMERS.
Library of American Biography. Edited by Oscar Handlin. Boston: Little,
Brown, 1955. viii, 215 p.

Nye places Garrison in the mainstream of reform between 1800 and
the Civil War. He shows that the reformer favored pacifism, perfectionism, and women's rights, and opposed slavery, war, civil
government, liquor, and tobacco.

Odgers, Merle M. ALEXANDER DALLAS BACHE: SCIENTIST AND EDUCA-
TOR, 1806-1867. Pennsylvania Lives. Philadelphia: University of Pennsylvania Press, 1947. vii, 223 p.

Bache was the grandson of Benjamin Franklin and an influential
leader in the development of science. As an educator, he served
as president of Girard College, and as a scientist, among many
things, he directed the U.S. coast survey from 1843 until his death
in 1861.

Ofari, Earl. "LET YOUR MOTTO BE RESISTANCE": THE LIFE AND THOUGHT OF HENRY HIGHLAND GARNET. Boston: Beacon Press, 1972. xi, 221 p.

The author attempts to examine the "roots" of the black liberation movement. Garnet was a preacher, abolitionist, and emigrationist who wanted to restructure American society and who called upon the slaves to revolt.

Overmyer, Grace. AMERICA'S FIRST HAMLET. New York: New York University Press, 1957. 439 p.

John Howard Payne is best known for composing "Home Sweet Home," but he was also an important actor and playwright in both America and England. In the United States after 1832, he became a champion of the rights of the Cherokees and was even imprisoned by the Georgia militia for championing the cause of these Indians.

Parker, Franklin. GEORGE PEABODY: A BIOGRAPHY. Nashville: Vanderbilt University Press, 1971. x, 233 p.

This is principally a study of Peabody's philanthropy. He founded the firm that became the House of Morgan and distributed his accumulated wealth to various projects, such as libraries, science education, education in the South, housing for the industrious poor in London, and Arctic exploration.

Perry, Ralph Barton. THE THOUGHT AND CHARACTER OF WILLIAM JAMES. 2 vols. Boston: Little, Brown, 1935.

Perry develops James's biography as well as his thought. He also includes the philosopher's correspondence and published writings.

Randel, William Pierce. EDWARD EGGLESTON, AUTHOR OF THE HOOSIER SCHOOL-MASTER. New York: King's Crown Press, 1946. vi, 319 p.

The HOOSIER SCHOOL-MASTER, published in 1871, became a minor classic by the 1880s. In this biography, Randel assesses Eggleston's writings and also shows the environmental influences that enabled him to produce interesting social history.

Resek, Carl. LEWIS HENRY MORGAN: AMERICAN SCHOLAR. Chicago: University of Chicago Press, 1960. xii, 184 p.

Morgan studied the Iroquois Indians, kinship systems of primitive people, and social evolution. He also was a lawyer for railroad and mining interests and a part-time legislator.

Rice, Madeleine Hooke. FEDERAL STREET PASTOR: THE LIFE OF WILLIAM ELLERY CHANNING. New York: Bookman Associates, 1961. 360 p.

Channing was the main formulator of Unitarianism, a leading social reformer, and a man of letters. This biography shows his religious development and personal life.

Rodgers, Andrew Denny III. JOHN MERLE COULTER: MISSIONARY IN
SCIENCE. Princeton, N.J.: Princeton University Press, 1944. viii, 321 p.

Coulter was a middle westerner who served as president of Indiana
University and Lake Forest College. He attained international
status as a plant physiologist.

_____. JOHN TORREY: A STORY OF NORTH AMERICAN BOTANY.
Princeton, N.J.: Princeton University Press, 1942. 352 p.

The author depicts Torrey as a pioneer taxonomist in nineteenth-
century America. This scientist was noted for his botanical explorations of the southwestern and western United States.

Roper, Laura Wood. FLO: A BIOGRAPHY OF FREDERICK LAW OLMSTED.
Baltimore: Johns Hopkins Press, 1973. xvii, 555 p.

In this biography, Olmsted is depicted as a leading nineteenth-
century intellectual and man of affairs. He developed an idea of
civilization in the United States from which his social theories and
environmental designs came.

Roselle, Daniel. SAMUEL GRISWOLD GOODRICH, CREATER OF PETER PAR-
LEY: A STUDY OF HIS LIFE AND WORK. Albany: State University of New
York Press, 1968. 181 p.

Goodrich was an author and editor of children's books in the era
before the Civil War. His stories were didactic rather than fanci-
ful in which aspersions frequently were cast on non-Protestants.

Rosenstine, Robert A. ROMANTIC REVOLUTIONARY: A BIOGRAPHY OF
JOHN REED. New York: Alfred A. Knopf, 1975. xxvii, 430 p.

This apostle of Lincoln Steffens was a member of the pre-World
War I Left. This study portrays him as a radical willing to join
almost any cause and as a man whose life was a struggle between
social status and conscience.

Ross, Dorothy. G. STANLEY HALL: THE PSYCHOLOGIST AS PROPHET.
Chicago: University of Chicago Press, 1972. xix, 482 p.

Hall is presented as a representative type. He was graduated from
Williams College, studied under William James, went to Germany,
taught at Johns Hopkins, served a stormy presidency at Clark University, and created a friendly base for Freudian ideas.

Rusk, Ralph L. THE LIFE OF RALPH WALDO EMERSON. New York: Charles Scribner's Sons, 1949. xi, 592 p.

> Rusk emphasizes how Emerson and his contemporaries spoke for themselves and acted during their lives. The growth of Emerson's ideas is explicated.

Samuels, Ernest. HENRY ADAMS: THE MAJOR PHASE. Cambridge, Mass.: Belknap Press of Harvard University Press, 1964. xv, 687 p.

> This covers the period in Adams's life of CHARTRES and the EDU-CATION. It shows his engagement with intellectual experiments during his later years.

_____. HENRY ADAMS: THE MIDDLE YEARS. Cambridge, Mass.: Belknap Press of Harvard University Press, 1958. xiv, 514 p.

> This is the second of a three-volume biography. It depicts the life of Adams, his wife, and their circle and argues that the HIS-TORY more than any of his works justifies Adams as an intellectual and historian.

_____. THE YOUNG HENRY ADAMS. Cambridge, Mass.: Belknap Press of Harvard University Press, 1965. xvi, 378 p.

> Adams' life from 1838-77 is covered. This is the period when he polished the tools of his trade as a historian and also dabbled in politics.

Schlesinger, Arthur M., Jr. ORESTES BROWNSON: A PILGRIM'S PROGRESS. Boston: Little, Brown, 1939. 320 p.

> Brownson's life during the turbulent period before and after the Civil War represented a search for intellectual and spiritual cer-tainty. Born a Calvinist, he converted to Catholicism; associated with various radicalisms, he became an extreme conservative.

Schor, Joel. HENRY HIGHLAND GARNET: A VOICE OF BLACK RADICAL-ISM IN THE NINETEENTH CENTURY. Westport, Conn.: Greenwood, 1977. xii, 250 p.

> Garnet is known for his radical call for slave resistance. He was more important as the leader of those blacks who abandoned Gar-rison's nonpolitical stance and of emigrationists.

Schwartz, Harold. SAMUEL GRIDLEY HOWE: SOCIAL REFORMER, 1801-1876. Cambridge, Mass.: Harvard University Press, 1956. xii, 348 p.

> Howe pioneered in the establishment of schools for the blind, deaf, and dumb, and participated in the antislavery movement. His pub-lic career rather than his personal life and personality is emphasized.

Scott, Clifford H. LESTER FRANK WARD. Boston: Twayne, 1976. 192 p.

Scott argues that Ward's importance was in attempting to reconcile mid-nineteenth-century democratic assumptions with late nineteenth-century change. He analyzes Ward's ideas on education, natural science, government, and sociology.

Shepard, Odell. PEDLAR'S PROGRESS: THE LIFE OF BRONSON ALCOTT. Boston: Little, Brown, 1937. xvi, 546 p.

This biography places Alcott in the context of his times. The men and women he worked with, such as Theodore Parker, William Lloyd Garrison, and Margaret Fuller, are portrayed sympathetically in terms of their values.

Sherwin, Oscar. PROPHET OF LIBERTY: THE LIFE AND TIMES OF WENDELL PHILLIPS. New York: Bookman Associates, 1958. 814 p.

Phillips's life, personality, and ideas are covered within the context of contemporary history. The emotional, political, and moral milieu in which Phillips functioned is detailed.

Skipper, Ottis Clark. J.D.B. DE BOW: MAGAZINIST OF THE OLD SOUTH. Athens: University of Georgia Press, 1958. x, 269 p.

De Bow was a leader in the movement for southern nationalism. In his magazine, he advocated states' rights and slavery, and he looked forward to the economic independence of his section.

Sklar, Kathryn Kish. CATHARINE BEECHER: A STUDY IN AMERICAN DO-MESTICITY. New Haven, Conn.: Yale University Press, 1973. xv, 356 p.

Beecher, who devoted herself to schools and teachers, was not a first-rank intellectual organizer, but a woman sensitive to the religious, social, and economic changes of her time. She struggled to adapt nineteenth-century evangelical Calvinism to the needs of Victorian women and emphasized in her writings the dilemma of people who were displaced between Calvin and Freud.

Spalding, Thomas W. MARTIN JOHN SPALDING: AMERICAN CHURCHMAN. Washington, D.C.: Consortium, 1974. xi, 373 p.

Next to Archbishop John Hughes, Spalding was probably the most significant Catholic cleric in America during the mid-nineteenth century. Emphasis in this biography is concentrated on his activities.

Spencer, Samuel R., Jr. BOOKER T. WASHINGTON AND THE NEGRO'S PLACE IN AMERICAN LIFE. Library of American Biography. Edited by Oscar Handlin. Boston: Little, Brown, 1955. xii, 212 p.

Spencer sympathizes with Washington's conciliatory approach to the black problem in the South. Washington believed in inevitable progress which would gain for the Negro everything that was his due.

Sveino, Per. ORESTES BROWNSON'S ROAD TO CATHOLICISM. New York: Humanities, 1971. 339 p.

Sveino is a Norwegian scholar who believes there was an intellectual consistency in Brownson's road to Catholicism. Through his progress from the ideas of the Enlightenment, to transcendentalism, and finally to romanticism, Brownson displayed a sense of the worth of God and religion that climaxed in his conversion to Catholicism in 1844.

Thomas, Benjamin P. THEODORE WELD, CRUSADER FOR FREEDOM. New Brunswick, N.J.: Rutgers University Press, 1950. xii, 307 p.

Weld is given a position of prime importance in the antislavery movement. His activities in the manual labor school movement and temperance also are detailed.

Thomas, John L. THE LIBERATOR: WILLIAM LLOYD GARRISON, A BIOGRAPHY. Boston: Little, Brown, 1963. viii, 502 p.

Thomas sees Garrison as being irascible, irresponsible, vindictive, single-minded, and courageous. His moral values were real and compelling, and he was largely responsible for creating the moral absolutism that caused the Civil War and freed the slave.

Thompson, Lawrance. ROBERT FROST: THE EARLY YEARS, 1874-1915. New York: Holt, Rinehart and Winston, 1966. xxvi, 641 p.

This is the first of a projected three-volume authorized biography of Frost and covers the years before he became famous. Frost's personality grew erratically under harsh self-teaching.

Tolis, Peter. ELIHU BURRITT: CRUSADER FOR BROTHERHOOD. Hamden, Conn.: Archon Books, 1968. ix, 309 p.

A blacksmith by trade, Burritt learned fifty foreign languages, served as a lyceum lecturer, and became an important reformer in antebellum America. He worked for free trade, abolition of capital punishment, cheap postage, antislavery, and especially world peace.

Tryon, W.S. PARNASSUS CORNER: A LIFE OF JAMES T. FIELDS, PUBLISHER TO THE VICTORIANS. Boston: Houghton Mifflin; Cambridge, Mass.: Riverside Press, 1963. xvi, 445 p.

Fields was a nineteenth-century publisher, discoverer of literary talents, molder of literary careers, publicist, critic, and reviewer. He was one of the first to seek out American writers, encourage them, and pay them well.

Vance, Maurice M. CHARLES RICHARD VAN HISE: SCIENTIST-PROGRES-SIVE. Madison: State Historical Society of Wisconsin, 1960. 246 p.

Van Hise, a Wisconsin native, became president of the University of Wisconsin. He was a geologist who became interested in conservation, the university extension service, progressive movement, and the League to Enforce Peace.

Wade, Louise C. GRAHAM TAYLOR: PIONEER FOR SOCIAL JUSTICE, 1851-1938. Chicago: University of Chicago Press, 1964. 268 p.

From 1892 to 1938, Taylor's activities earned him the title of the "Conscience of Chicago." He founded settlement houses, promoted the movement through the publication of articles, championed good government, crusaded against crime and vice, and founded the Chicago School of Civics and Philanthropy.

Wade, Mason. MARGARET FULLER, WHETSTONE OF GENIUS. New York: Viking Press, 1940. xvi, 304 p.

The author describes Fuller's transition from an unhappy and narrow preoccupation with self-culture and feminism to her satisfaction in the love of an Italian revolutionist and follower of Mazzini. She is portrayed as a barometer of the intellectual currents of her time.

Wagenknecht, Edward. JOHN GREENLEAF WHITTIER: A PORTRAIT IN PARA-DOX. New York: Oxford University Press, 1967. viii, 262 p.

Whittier's views on art and ideas, politics, labor, pacifism, and religion are the focuses of this study. He is depicted as neither a Quaker sectarian nor a social extremist.

_____. WILLIAM DEAN HOWELLS: THE FRIENDLY EYE. New York: Oxford University Press, 1969. x, 340 p.

As an author, editor, and critic, Howells attempted to adapt small-town ideals to an urban civilization. His realism brought commentary on divorce, spiritualism, capital punishment, labor, and materialism, as well as socialist doctrines.

Walsh, Justin E. TO PRINT THE NEWS AND RAISE HELL! A BIOGRAPHY OF WILBUR F. STOREY. Chapel Hill: University of North Carolina Press, 1968. ix, 303 p.

Storey was a Detroit and Chicago editor of the mid-nineteenth century noted for his lurid style and slashing editorials. He was a Democrat in the 1850s and a virulent Copperhead in the 1860s, who bridged the gap in journalism between prewar partisanship and the "new journalism" of Joseph Pulitzer and William Randolph Hearst.

Wells, Anna Mary. DEAR PRECEPTOR: THE LIFE AND TIMES OF THOMAS WENTWORTH HIGGINSON. Boston: Houghton Mifflin, 1963. xiv, 363 p.

Higginson was a minister, writer, and reformer known chiefly for his interests in abolition and women's rights. He supported John Brown, led a black regiment during the Civil War, and was active in the affairs of the WOMAN'S JOURNAL.

West, William Garrett. BARTON WARREN STONE: EARLY AMERICAN ADVOCATE OF RELIGIOUS UNITY. Nashville: Disciples of Christ Historical Society, 1954. xvi, 245 p.

This Presbyterian minister formed a group called "the Christians," met Alexander Campbell in 1824, and united with his sect. Stone was a left-wing Protestant in the early nineteenth century.

Wisby, Herbert A., Jr. PIONEER PROPHETESS: JEMIMA WILKINSON, THE PUBLICK UNIVERSAL FRIEND. Ithaca, N.Y.: Cornell University Press, 1964. xiv, 232 p.

Wilkinson was an important communitarian leader of the early national period who founded Jerusalem, New York. Wisby shows the pattern of similarities between her, Mother Ann Lee, Joseph Smith, and similar religious leaders.

Wish, Harvey. GEORGE FITZHUGH: PROPAGANDIST OF THE OLD SOUTH. Southern Biography Series. Baton Rouge: Louisiana State University Press, 1943. ix, 360 p.

This proslavery propagandist became popular because he followed the dominant class and adjusted his arguments to shifts in public opinion. Wish does not criticize Fitzhugh's ideas nor does he place him in the context of his times.

Wyatt-Brown, Bertram. LEWIS TAPPAN AND THE EVANGELICAL WAR AGAINST SLAVERY. Cleveland: Press of Case Western Reserve University, 1969. xxi, 376 p.

Lewis Tappan was always evangelical and religious, and these concerns led him into various reform activities. He and his brother, Arthur, first worked with Garrison, but later broke with him and founded a rival antislavery society as well as the NATIONAL ERA, an antislavery journal in Washington.

1915 TO THE PRESENT

Billington, Ray Allen. FREDERICK JACKSON TURNER: HISTORIAN, SCHOLAR, TEACHER. New York: Oxford University Press, 1973. x, 599 p.

> Billington pictures Turner as a theorist of multiple causation. Of signal importance in this study is the portrayal of academic life from the perspective of a professor rather than an institution.

Dalleck, Robert. DEMOCRAT AND DIPLOMAT: THE LIFE OF WILLIAM E. DODD. New York: Oxford University Press, 1968. ix, 415 p.

> This study is valuable in intellectual history for its discussion of Dodd's career as a historian at the University of Chicago. He was a scholar who defended academic freedom, supported educational reform, and pioneered in the development of the "New History."

Dykhuizen, George. THE LIFE AND MIND OF JOHN DEWEY. Carbondale, Ill.: Southern Illinois University Press, 1973. xxv, 429 p.

> This is the first comprehensive life of Dewey. His existence is chronicled in detail and his approaches to teaching, learning, and other social concerns are discussed.

Furman, Necah Stewart. WALTER PRESCOTT WEBB: HIS LIFE AND IMPACT. Albuquerque: University of New Mexico Press, 1976. xiv, 222 p.

> Webb's life reads like an academic Horatio Alger story. He was rescued from poverty by a benefactor, received an education, and became a historian who wrote to be read.

Garwood, Darrell. ARTIST IN IOWA: A LIFE OF GRANT WOOD. New York: W.W. Norton and Co., 1944. 259 p.

> This artist was a satirist who portrayed bigoted and self-righteous farmers and small townspeople. He contributed to the development of an indigenous American art.

Hesseltine, William B. PIONEER'S MISSION: THE STORY OF LYMAN COPELAND DRAPER. Madison: State Historical Society of Wisconsin, 1954. ix, 384 p.

> Draper contributed greatly to Wisconsin's State Historical Society. He not only traveled widely to record the reminiscences of pioneers, but also collected books and manuscripts.

Holley, Edward G. CHARLES EVANS: AMERICAN BIBLIOGRAPHER. Urbana: University of Illinois Press, 1963. xiv, 343 p.

Evans was a hot-tempered and irascible librarian who found himself without employment at age fifty-one, and announced his intention of preparing a bibliography of American printing through 1800. Although discouraged from every quarter, Evans published his work in twelve volumes before his death in 1935.

Hoopes, James. VAN WYCK BROOKS: IN SEARCH OF AMERICAN CULTURE. Amherst: University of Massachusetts Press, 1977. xviii, 346 p.

This is an intellectual biography based on Brooks's criticism. His intellectual life, broken by bouts of mental illness and depression, was based on his quest for an organic American literature.

Hovey, Richard B. JOHN JAY CHAPMAN: AN AMERICAN MIND. New York: Columbia University Press, 1959. xvi, 391 p.

Chapman was a wealthy lawyer who wrote more than a hundred essays on literature, higher education, religion, and the politics of reform. But he also produced tasteless articles in which he expressed fear of the Germans during World War I, dread of the Catholic Church, and dislike for international Jewry.

Hudson, Wilson M. ANDY ADAMS: HIS LIFE AND WRITINGS. Dallas: Southern Methodist University Press, 1964. xv, 274 p.

Adams was a popular writer who made a significant contribution to the life and literature of the cow country. He deplored depictions of ranching by writers of fiction and tried to set the record straight by describing the cowboy as a working man rather than as a gunslinger.

Johnson, Diane. EDWIN BROUN FRED: SCIENTIST, ADMINISTRATOR, GENTLEMAN. Madison: University of Wisconsin Press, 1974. x, 179 p.

This biography emphasizes Fred's scientific achievements. From 1913-34, he built a reputation as a bacteriologist whose discoveries were useful to farmers and brought support for the University of Wisconsin from the state.

Johnson, Niel M. GEORGE SYLVESTER VIERECK: GERMAN-AMERICAN PROPAGANDIST. Urbana: University of Illinois Press, 1972. x, 282 p.

This is a study of Viereck's efforts to interpret Germany to America between the two World Wars. He was never a spokesman for German-Americans, but he propagandized for Germany to ensure fair play.

Kreuter, Kent, and Kreuter, Gretchen. AN AMERICAN DISSENTER: THE LIFE OF ALGIE MARTIN SIMONS, 1870-1950. Lexington: University of Kentucky Press, 1969. 236 p.

Simons was a student of Turner who became a socialist and wrote one of the first Marxist interpretations of American history. After World War I, he switched to popularizing Frederick W. Taylor's scientific management ideas and then ended his life as a researcher for the American Medical Association.

Landsberg, Melvin. DOS PASSOS' PATH TO U.S.A.: A POLITICAL BIOG-RAPHY, 1912-1936. Boulder: Colorado Associated University Press, 1972. xi, 292 p.

In this biography, the author shows the connections between Dos Passos' early career and his later literary works. Landsberg analyzes the forces that influenced his personality and his interest in politics.

Levy, Eugene. JAMES WELDON JOHNSON: BLACK LEADER, BLACK VOICE. Chicago: University of Chicago Press, 1973. xiii, 380 p.

Born of professional parents in Jacksonville, Florida, Johnson became an editor, lawyer, diplomat, and literary figure. His novel, THE AUTOBIOGRAPHY OF AN EX-COLORED MAN (1912) may have signaled the beginning of the Harlem renaissance and he pushed for congressional legislation against lynching as chief executive of the NAACP during the 1920s.

McGrath, Sylvia Wallace. CHARLES KENNETH LEITH, SCIENTIFIC ADVISER. Madison: University of Wisconsin Press, 1971. xii, 255 p.

Leith was appointed full professor of geology at the University of Wisconsin at the age of twenty-eight and taught there the rest of his life. He served as an important adviser on mineral policy and accumulated a small fortune investing in mining securities.

McLoughlin, William G., Jr. BILLY SUNDAY WAS HIS REAL NAME. Chicago: University of Chicago Press, 1955. xxx, 325 p.

Sunday abandoned professional baseball to become a "gymnast for Jesus." He carefully planned and organized the sensational and commercial elements in his revivals and utilized assembly-line techniques.

Mathews, Marcia M. HENRY OSSAWA TANNER: AMERICAN ARTIST. Chicago: University of Chicago Press, 1969. xvii, 261 p.

This member of one of Philadelphia's most distinguished black families was an artist who became an expatriate and lived most of his life in France. As a painter, he was a romantic, who specialized in painting Biblical scenes.

Mathias, Frank Furlong. ALBERT D. KIRWAN. Lexington: University Press of Kentucky, 1975. xiv, 190 p.

> This is an informal biography of a distinguished University of Kentucky historian whose work helped shape southern history. Known chiefly for his biography of John J. Crittenden, Kirwan also served as dean of students, graduate dean, and interim president of the university.

Mead, Margaret. RUTH BENEDICT. New York: Columbia University Press, 1974. viii, 180 p.

> This volume, includes a biographical essay, seven of Benedicts papers, and a selected bibliography of her writings. Mead depicts a humane, reflective person who contributed much to modern anthropology.

Moore, Ruth. NEILS BOHR: THE MAN, HIS SCIENCE, AND THE WORLD THEY CHANGED. New York: Alfred A. Knopf, 1966. xvi, 436 p.

> Bohr was a successful scientist who understood the political impact of science. He changed the concept of nature with his theory of the structure of the atom, and he turned scientists to politics in his efforts to control atomic energy.

Nevins, Allan. JAMES TRUSLOW ADAMS: HISTORIAN OF THE AMERICAN DREAM. Urbana: University of Illinois Press, 1968. 315 p.

> Adams worked as a Wall Street broker only long enough to earn the money he needed to become a writer of history. Much of this book consists of his letters that illustrate the work and concerns of a free-lance historian during the 1920s and 1930s.

Rodgers, Andrew Denny III. ERWIN FRINK SMITH: A STORY OF NORTH AMERICAN PLANT PATHOLOGY. Philadelphia: America Philosophical Society, 1952. x, 675 p.

> Smith was a government scientist who worked mainly with the U.S. Department of Argiculture. He became an international authority on plant diseases, and his researches and discoveries are detailed in this biography.

_____. LIBERTY HYDE BAILEY: A STORY OF AMERICAN PLANT SCIENCES. Princeton, N.J.: Princeton University Press, 1949. 506 p.

> This scientist was the dean of horticulturists and an important agricultural educator. He studied under Asa Gray and served most of his professional life at Cornell University.

Rosenstock, Morton. LOUIS MARSHALL, DEFENDER OF JEWISH RIGHTS. Detroit: Wayne State University Press, 1965. 334 p.

> The first three decades of the twentieth century, when nationalism coincided with anti-Semitism, were critical in the adjustment of Jews to American life. Marshall, who was president of the American Jewish Committee from 1912-29, combatted attempts to denigrate and isolate the Jewish community.

Ross, B. Joyce. J.E. SPINGARN AND THE RISE OF THE NAACP, 1911-1939. New York: Atheneum, 1972. xii, 305 p.

> Spingarn was a German-American Jew and professor of comparative literature at Columbia University, who was dismissed in 1911 for boldly advocating academic due process. He abandoned academe and published a reformist paper, managed Harcourt, Brace Publishing Company, and presided over the NAACP.

Rudwick, Elliott M. W.E.B. DUBOIS: A STUDY IN MINORITY GROUP LEADERSHIP. Philadelphia: University of Pennsylvania Press, 1960. 382 p.

> DuBois is depicted as a man who believed that Negroes were capable of developing their own superior culture. He argued that blacks should organize themselves to prepare for integration, but he felt safe emotionally only among Negroes.

Schorer, Mark. SINCLAIR LEWIS: AN AMERICAN LIFE. New York: McGraw-Hill, 1961. xxiii, 867 p.

> Lewis was an artist who was temperamentally unable to objectify his anxieties or draw upon them except in a most superficial way. He was a man of many selves, who claimed Thoreau as his major influence.

Schwarz, Richard W. JOHN HARVEY KELLOGG, M.D. Nashville: Southern Publishing Association, 1970. 256 p.

> This physician is known for his sanitarium in Battle Creek, Michigan, and for his development of flaked cereals. Schwarz portrays him as a man who promoted an awareness of common and simple habits and physical well-being, as well as a pioneer in preventive medicine.

Stegner, Wallace. THE UNEASY CHAIR: A BIOGRAPHY OF BERNARD DE VOTO. Garden City, N.Y.: Doubleday, 1974. xiii, 464 p.

> Stegner discusses De Voto, the iconoclast, idealist, and historian, with adoration. At the same time, he criticizes the winner of the Pulitzer Prize and the National Book Award for history as a man who posed as an expert on everything.

Steward, Julian H. ALFRED KROEBER. New York: Columbia University Press, 1973. xii, 137 p.

> To many scholars, Kroeber was the dean of anthropology in the twentieth century. This book consists of a biographical essay, an interpretation of Kroeber's writings, and excerpts from his works.

Thompson, Lawrance. ROBERT FROST: THE YEARS OF TRIUMPH, 1915-1938. New York: Holt, Rinehart and Winston, 1970. xxii, 744 p.

> Frost was a man of unusual hopes, fears, and depression. He triumphed not only as a poet but also over inner chaos.

Thompson, Lawrance, and Winnick, R.H. ROBERT FROST: THE LATER YEARS, 1938-1963. New York: Holt, Rinehart and Winston, 1976. xxiii, 468 p.

> In his later years, Frost gained great pleasure in the power he possessed of appearing as a unity of opposites. He was always a rebel and attacked some of the prevailing tendencies of society in his poetry.

Tomkins, Mary E. IDA M. TARBELL. New York: Twayne, 1974. 182 p.

> Tarbell was an effective magazine journalist, but her studies of Lincoln, Napoleon, Elbert Gary, and others were not distinguished. She is depicted as the defender of New England "WASP" values.

Townsend, Charles R. SAN ANTONIO ROSE: THE LIFE AND MUSIC OF BOB WILLS. Urbana: University of Illinois Press, 1976. xv, 395 p.

> This popular fiddler from Texas led his band from the mid-1930s to the late 1960s. He helped create a style of music known as western swing and he borrowed heavily from jazz, blues, pop music, and the ethnic styles of Texas.

Wigdor, David. ROSCOE POUND: PHILOSOPHER OF THE LAW. Westport, Conn.: Greenwood, 1974. xi, 356 p.

> Pound sought to form a union of the law with the social sciences, but when New Dealers attempted to employ his ideas in reform, he criticized their work as illegitimate. This anomaly resulted from Pound's conservatism.

Wilkins, Burleigh Taylor. CARL BECKER: A BIOGRAPHICAL STUDY IN AMERICAN INTELLECTUAL HISTORY. Cambridge: M.I.T. Press and Harvard University Press, 1961. x, 246 p.

> This Iowa farm boy became a great professor and an influential historian, who was primarily interested in explaining the present in

terms of the past. He argued in his works that there were four histories: history as it happened; the history of Everyman; history as a result of the historian; and history as it proved to be useful because Everyman liked it.

Wreszin, Michael. OSWALD GARRISON VILLARD: PACIFIST AT WAR. Bloomington: Indiana University Press, 1965. ix, 342 p.

Villard was a writer, businessman, reformer, and sometime publisher of the New York EVENING POST and the NATION. He was a liberal man with a social conscience who found it difficult to align himself as a pacifist with reactionary isolationists before Pearl Harbor.

_____. THE SUPERFLUOUS ANARCHIST: ALBERT JAY NOCK. Providence, R.I.: Brown University Press, 1972. xi, 196 p.

In this biography, Nock is depicted as a philosophical anarchist who believed in the perfectibility of man. A voluminous writer, he gained his reputation as editor of the FREEMAN in the 1920s.

Wright, Helen. EXPLORER OF THE UNIVERSE: A BIOGRAPHY OF GEORGE ELLERY HALE. New York: E.P. Dutton, 1966. 480 p.

Hale was a skilled astronomer and promoter, who influenced science as much as any scientist born in America. Besides inventing the spectroheliograph and founding the ASTROPHYSICAL JOURNAL, he promoted the construction of the Yerkes Laboratory in Williams Bay, Wisconsin; Mount Wilson Observatory near Pasadena, California; and the Palomar Observatory in southern California.

Chapter 5

ECONOMIC, POLITICAL, AND SOCIAL THOUGHT

COLONIAL PERIOD TO 1815

Adams, W. Paul. "Republicanism in Political Rhetoric Before 1776." POLITI-
CAL SCIENCE QUARTERLY 85 (September 1970): 397-421.

> The first phase of the American Revolution cannot be viewed as a
> struggle for republican government. Until 1776, the words "repub-
> lic", and "republican" were used only cautiously as smear words by
> supporters of the colonial cause.

Appleby, Joyce. "The New Republican Synthesis and the Changing Political
Ideas of John Adams." AMERICAN QUARTERLY 25 (December 1973): 578-95.

> The new republican synthesis is more than a reconstruction of past
> thought, it is a description of a socially ordered consciousness ex-
> pressed in belief and behavior. Appleby argues that Adams's politi-
> cal views were conditioned by his eight-year residency in Europe.

Arieli, Yehoshua. INDIVIDUALISM AND NATIONALISM IN AMERICAN
IDEOLOGY. Cambridge, Mass.: Harvard University Press, 1964. xiii, 442 p.

> The thesis of this book is that American nationalism rests on ideo-
> logical consensus based on the values of democracy and individual-
> ism. The first Americans did not make up a true nationality, but
> through their desires for citizenship and national self-determination
> they fashioned a nation.

Autican, Chester J. RIGHTS OF OUR FATHERS. Vienna, Va.: Coiner Publications, 1968. v, 296 p.

> The author argues that the doctrine of natural rights was the most
> popular political philosophy in America during the late eighteenth
> century. He organizes his discourse in terms of conscience and
> religion, association and assembly, freedom from physical restraint,
> property rights, and other topics.

Bailyn, Bernard. THE IDEOLOGICAL ORIGINS OF THE AMERICAN REVOLU-
TION. Cambridge, Mass.: Belknap Press of Harvard University Press, 1967.
xiii, 335 p.

> Bailyn concludes that the Revolution was ideological rather than a
> struggle between social groups. He makes it clear that colonial
> constitutional and political ideas owed much to Whig thinkers.

_____. "Political Experience and Enlightenment Ideas in Eighteenth-Century
America." AMERICAN HISTORICAL REVIEW 67 (January 1962): 339-51.

> The political and social ideas of the European Enlightenment were
> more universally accepted in America than in Europe. The Ameri-
> can Revolution completed, formalized, systematized, and symbolized
> Enlightenment liberalism.

Bailyn, Bernard, ed., with assistance of Jane H. Garrett. PAMPHLETS OF
THE AMERICAN REVOLUTION, 1750-1776. Vol. I: 1750-1765. Cambridge,
Mass.: Belknap Press of Harvard University Press, 1965. xvi, 771 p.

> Bailyn provides a 200-page introduction that covers the sources
> and traditions of the pamphleteers. He clarifies the ramifications
> of English Whig concepts in the colonies.

Banning, Lance. "Republican Ideology and the Triumph of the Constitution,
1789 to 1793." WILLIAM AND MARY QUARTERLY 31 (April 1974): 167-88.

> The constitution was accepted because Americans lived in a world
> of classical constitutionalism that prevented them from harboring
> anticonstitutional feelings. Men opposed an energetic government,
> but they attacked the administration rather than the government
> itself.

Barker, Charles W. AMERICAN CONVICTIONS: CYCLES OF PUBLIC
THOUGHT, 1600-1850. Philadelphia: J.B. Lippincott, 1970. xix, 632 p.

> Barker elucidates major interpretations in the history of education,
> religion, political thought, and law. He follows the theory of
> Bertrand Russell in which he argues that defiances against organi-
> zation have produced compromises and agreements yielding not free-
> dom but organization and institutionalization.

Beatty, Edward Corbyn Obert. WILLIAM PENN AS SOCIAL PHILOSOPHER.
Foreword by Marcus W. Jernegan. New York: Columbia University Press,
1939. xiii, 338 p.

> This is a study of Penn's social and political theories, as well as
> his attitudes on war and peace, religion, racial equality, educa-
> tion, and other matters. Of particular importance is the presenta-
> tion of the transit of European ideas to America and their modifi-
> cation in the New World.

Beitzinger, A.J. A HISTORY OF AMERICAN POLITICAL THOUGHT. New York: Dodd, Mead, 1972. xii, 628 p.

This is a survey of political ideas from Locke and Hobbes to Lippmann and Niebuhr. Reitzinger believes American political thought has been grounded on the concepts of a higher moral law, democracy, and the balanced state.

Bercovitch, Sacvan. "Colonial Puritan Rhetoric and the Discovery of American Identity." CANADIAN REVIEW OF AMERICAN STUDIES 6 (Fall 1975): 131-50.

Puritan rhetoric gave the title "the New Israel" an individual, historical, and prophetic meaning to transform secular into sacred identity. It was used to prove the Old World was a second Babylon and to show that the New World was sacred space.

_____. THE PURITAN ORIGINS OF THE AMERICAN SELF. New Haven, Conn.: Yale University Press, 1975. x, 250 p.

Bercovitch emphasizes the Puritan imagination of the seventeenth century, especially the rhetoric of American identity. He looks at a comparative European context in terms of language, myth, and society.

Blassingame, John W. "American Nationalism and Other Loyalties in the Southern Colonies, 1763-1775." JOURNAL OF SOUTHERN HISTORY 34 (February 1968): 50-75.

As their ties with Britain weakened after 1763, southern colonists acquired an American identity. They acted as if they were living under a sovereign government and they accepted the Continental Congress as the supreme legislature.

Boorstin, Daniel J. THE LOST WORLD OF THOMAS JEFFERSON. New York: Henry Holt, 1948. xi, 306 p.

Boorstin examines the heritage of Jefferson through his writings, and those of David Rittenhouse, Benjamin Rush, Benjamin S. Barton, Joseph Priestley, Charles Willson Peale, and Thomas Paine. He emphasizes that their ideas represented an integrated pattern of thought concerning God and man, and nature and society.

Breen, T.H. THE CHARACTER OF THE GOOD RULER: A STUDY OF PURITAN POLITICAL IDEAS IN NEW ENGLAND, 1630-1730. New Haven, Conn.: Yale University Press, 1970. xx, 301 p.

Political theory during New England's first century changed from Puritan consensus on the covenant between ruler and ruled and the responsibility of the magistrates for the promotion of religion and orthodoxy to the Whig tradition of upholding the rights of Englishmen. After the Glorious Revolution there were ideological splits between those who favored rule by an elite of the wealthy and educated and others who promoted the revolutionary belief that government should protect the liberty and property of citizens.

Bridenbaugh, Carl. THE SPIRIT OF '76: THE GROWTH OF AMERICAN PATRIOTISM BEFORE INDEPENDENCE. New York: Oxford University Press, 1975. xii, 162 p.

The spirit that caused Americans to rebel in 1776 began as a love of land and then became a more abstract affection for their new country. Protestantism was a unifying influence.

Brockunier, Samuel Hugh. THE IRREPRESSIBLE DEMOCRAT: ROGER WILLIAMS. Ronald Series in History. Edited by Ralph H. Gabriel. New York: Ronald Press, 1940. xii, 305 p.

This is not a biography but a study of Williams's public life and ideas in their social environment. It deals with the establishment of democracy and economic equalitarianism in Rhode Island in the 1640s.

Buell, Richard, Jr. SECURING THE REVOLUTION: IDEOLOGY IN AMERICAN POLITICS, 1789-1815. Ithaca, N.Y.: Cornell University Press, 1972. xii, 391 p.

This is a study of the influence of public opinion on political issues and protagonists. Buell emphasizes the debates over power, federalism, and foreign affairs in the 1790s.

Bumsted, J.M. "'Things in the Womb of Time': Ideas of American Independence, 1633 to 1763." WILLIAM AND MARY QUARTERLY 31 (October 1974): 533-64.

Men who wrote on the American question between 1633 and 1763 did not consciously intend to promote independence, but they did discuss the possibility of a break with Britain. They explained British policy as part of a consistent program to keep America dependent.

Carroll, Peter N. PURITANISM AND THE WILDERNESS: THE INTELLECTUAL SIGNIFICANCE OF THE NEW ENGLAND FRONTIER, 1629-1700. New York: Columbia University Press, 1969. xi, 243 p.

Carroll examines the impact of the frontier on social thought. The Puritans compared their hardships with those of the ancient Jews, and developed a self-image as a chosen people protected by the Lord, who would transform their area into a wilderness Zion.

Cohen, William. "Thomas Jefferson and the Problem of Slavery." JOURNAL OF AMERICAN HISTORY 56 (December 1969): 503-26.

Cohen attacks the view that Jefferson was a proto-abolitionist, lenient slaveholder. He argues that the author of the Declaration of Independence bought and sold men as he saw fit, tracked down runaways, wrote a slave code for Virginia, believed Negroes were innately inferior to whites, and created a way of life at Monticello based on forced labor.

Conkin, Paul K. PURITANS AND PRAGMATISTS: EIGHT EMINENT AMERICAN THINKERS. New York: Dodd, Mead, 1968. viii, 495 p.

Examined in this work are the perennial issues of philosophy, such as nature, mind, reality, values, and consciousness. The author shows how the riddles of human thought have taken on various formulations in the ideas of Edwards, Franklin, John Adams, Emerson, William James, Pierce, Dewey, and Santayana.

_____. SELF-EVIDENT TRUTHS: BEING A DISCOURSE ON THE ORIGINS AND DEVELOPMENT OF THE FIRST PRINCIPLES OF AMERICAN GOVERNMENT--POPULAR SOVEREIGNTY, NATURAL RIGHTS, AND BALANCE AND SEPARATION OF POWERS. Bloomington: Indiana University Press, 1974. xii, 211 p.

Conkin shows the evolution of the concepts of popular sovereignty, natural rights, and balanced separation, and then relates how they were handled in the political arena by leaders such as Adams and Jefferson.

Connor, Paul W. POOR RICHARD'S POLITICKS: BENJAMIN FRANKLIN AND HIS NEW AMERICAN ORDER. New York: Oxford University Press, 1965. xiv, 285 p.

This book emphasizes the consistency of Franklin's thought. The author argues that Franklin's political ideal emphasized a "virtuous order" in which mutual concern overcame self-interest; an "evolving order" that included a growing political achievement; and a "harmonious order" that ensured political stability through equality and cohesion.

Craven, Wesley Frank. THE LEGEND OF THE FOUNDING FATHERS. New York: New York University Press, 1956. viii, 191 p.

This is a study in the history of American nationalism. In looking at historians and other writers over the broad range of history, Craven concludes that the United States had difficulty finding a unified view of its origins.

Crowley, J.E. THIS SHEBA SELF: THE CONCEPTUALIZATION OF ECO-NOMIC LIFE IN EIGHTEENTH-CENTURY AMERICA. Baltimore: Johns Hopkins University Press, 1974. xi, 161 p.

Sheba symbolized sin and great wealth. This book develops the colonists' attitudes concerning work and luxury as well as the relationship between self and society.

Dunn, Mary Maples. WILLIAM PENN: POLITICS AND CONSCIENCE. Princeton, N.J.: Princeton University Press, 1967. x, 206 p.

Dunn explains the interaction between Penn the active politician, and Penn the political thinker. Pennsylvania became a demonstration of his governmental theories and of his conviction that religious liberty would bring harmony.

Gilbert, Felix. TO THE FAREWELL ADDRESS: IDEAS OF EARLY AMERICAN FOREIGN POLICY. Princeton, N.J.: Princeton University Press, 1961. viii, 173 p.

George Washington's Farewell Address stands alone in the long and important influence it exerted over American foreign policy. Gilbert depicts how European concepts and American assumptions were brought together to form the ideas of foreign policy.

Greenberg, Kenneth S. "Revolutionary Ideology and the Proslavery Argument: The Abolition of Slavery in Antebellum South Carolina." JOURNAL OF SOUTHERN HISTORY 42 (August 1976): 365-84.

Greenberg shows that revolutionary South Carolinians, like their northern compatriots, condemned colonial status as a form of "slavery," but in using this term they were not referring to the condition of their slaves. They believed that their own liberty rested on the ownership of slave property, and in their defenses of slavery after 1820, they went to great pains to prove that masters were neither abusive nor possessed of complete power over their chattels.

Handler, Edward. AMERICA AND EUROPE IN THE POLITICAL THOUGHT OF JOHN ADAMS. Cambridge, Mass.: Harvard University Press, 1964. xiv, 248 p.

Adams is presented as an American Whig. He was both a universalist, imputing a common nature to men and societies, and a relativist, who attributed a unique character to nations.

Howe, John R., Jr. "Republican Thought and Political Violence of the 1790s." AMERICAN QUARTERLY 19 (Summer 1967): 147-65.

Political writings and rhetoric of the 1790s were loaded with ferocity, passion, and venomous satire. This was not the result of political and social differences between political parties but rather a product of republicanism which was a crisis-ridden ideology with virtually no tradition of success behind it.

Jones, Howard Mumford. THE PURSUIT OF HAPPINESS. Cambridge, Mass.: Harvard University Press, 1953. xi, 168 p.

Jones discusses theories of happiness in the eighteenth century, definitions in the law, literary and psychological expressions, and invitations to easy happiness offered by advertisers in the twentieth century. He reconstructs the history of happiness before 1900 in terms of important individuals.

Jordan, Winthrop D. WHITE OVER BLACK: AMERICAN ATTITUDES TOWARD THE NEGRO, 1550-1812. Chapel Hill: University of North Carolina Press, 1968. xx, 651 p.

The history of blacks and the larger society is developed in the perspective of European responses to Africans. Jordan shows that Englishmen were prejudiced before they condemned blacks to slavery in the colonies, and he assesses the importance of sexual impulses, inhibitions, fears, and jealousies in shaping white attitudes.

Kates, Don B., Jr. "Abolition, Deportation, Integration: Attitudes Toward Slavery in the Early Republic." JOURNAL OF NEGRO HISTORY 53 (January 1968): 33-47.

The great statesmen of the period from 1770 to 1810 abhorred slavery, but the prospect of abolition placed them in a severe dilemma. They searched for alternatives to integration, rejected deportation, and generally preferred slavery to a free black population.

Kenyon, Cecelia M. "Republicanism and Radicalism in the American Revolution: An Old-Fashioned Interpretation." WILLIAM AND MARY QUARTERLY 19 (April 1962): 153-82.

Kenyon examines the intellectual forces that have contributed to the confusion over whether the Revolution was radical or conservative. She concludes that it was both because some of the men who made it wanted to preserve the past while others wished to abandon it.

Kerber, Linda K. FEDERALIST IN DISSENT: IMAGERY AND IDEOLOGY IN JEFFERSONIAN AMERICA. Ithaca, N.Y.: Cornell University Press, 1970. xii, 233 p.

This is a study of the rhetoric and ideology of articulate Federalists as expressed essays, orations, and satirical literature. In the arts, science, education, law, and the social order, Federalists saw degeneration, and blamed it on Jefferson's dedication to the crude, novel, and superficial.

Ketcham, Ralph. FROM COLONY TO COUNTRY: THE REVOLUTION IN AMERICAN THOUGHT, 1750-1820. New York: Macmillan, 1974. xiv, 318 p.

This is a survey of political thought in the era of the Revolution. Ketcham maintains that colonial protest began as a means of finding a place in the British Empire and that the Constitution was an answer to the question of how the majority could be prevented from trampling on the rights of individuals.

_____. "James Madison and the Nature of Man." JOURNAL OF THE HISTORY OF IDEAS 19 (January 1958): 62-76.

In letters, speeches, and notes, Madison showed an unwavering faith in the will of the majority, and in man's virtue and intelligence. There was also a skepticism, even a pessimism, concerning human nature and an admonition not to depend on the wisdom of a single individual.

Leder, Lawrence H. "Constitutionalism in American Thought, 1689-1763." PENNSYLVANIA HISTORY 36 (October 1969): 411-18.

Colonial Americans were fascinated by the nature of constitutions as a theoretical issue. They viewed the British constitution as a fixed body of laws, but they also held that Parliament was the constitution and subject to change.

_____. LIBERTY AND AUTHORITY: EARLY AMERICAN POLITICAL IDEOLOGY, 1689-1763. Chicago: Quadrangle, 1968. 167 p.

The author attempts to discover whether the political theory developed by Americans was latently revolutionary. He uses the press to discover beliefs and concludes that American ideology was not revolutionary and that the concept of empire did not challenge British authority.

Lokken, Roy N. "The Political Theory of the American Revolution: Changing Interpretations." HISTORY TEACHER 8 (November 1974): 81-95.

Lokken reviews interpretations of political theory and concludes that historians have made them according to their own contemporary frames of reference. This has been obstructive to any real understanding of what the revolutionary generation thought.

_____. "The Social Thought of James Logan." WILLIAM AND MARY QUARTERLY 27 (January 1970): 68-89.

Logan was a proprietary agent and Philadelphia merchant in the eighteenth century who attempted a technical and systematic philosophy of man and his relations with the world. His social thought was in tune with the intellectual ethos in which he lived-- a Newtonian universe of harmony and rational order and a quest for a corresponding orderliness in human affairs.

Marks, Frederick W. III. "American Pride, European Prejudice, and the Constitution." HISTORIAN 34 (August 1972): 579-97.

Americans emerged from the Revolution with a great sense of patriotic pride. Thus, national honor played an important role in motivating the friends of the constitution.

Merritt, Richard L. "The Emergence of American Nationalism: A Quantitative Approach." AMERICAN QUARTERLY 17 (Summer 1965): 319-35.

Merritt's approach to nationalism is through content analysis because words symbolize attitudes. He tabulated the use of self-referent symbols in eighteenth-century newspapers and found that in the years after 1764 the distinction between "British colonists" and "Americans" became a real one.

Morgan, Edmund S. THE MEANING OF INDEPENDENCE: JOHN ADAMS, GEORGE WASHINGTON, THOMAS JEFFERSON. Charlottesville: University Press of Virginia, 1976. 85 p.

Morgan discusses the personal qualities of Adams, Washington, and Jefferson, as well as the interaction between these qualities and the movement for independence. He sees in Washington and Jefferson a connection between privatism, personal independence, and American independence.

Mudge, Eugene TenBroeck. THE SOCIAL PHILOSOPHY OF JOHN TAYLOR OF CAROLINE: A STUDY IN JEFFERSONIAN DEMOCRACY. Columbia Studies in American Culture, no. 4. New York: Columbia University Press, 1939. xii, 227 p.

Taylor spent his life crusading for a democracy based on agrarian foundations. He created a literature of protest against the alien and sedition laws, judicial review, and protective tariffs.

Nash, Gary B. "The Image of the Indian in the Southern Colonial Mind." WILLIAM AND MARY QUARTERLY 29 (April 1972): 197-230.

The English image of the Indian revealed conscious and unconscious strivings as well as efforts to control, civilize, or exterminate. Eighteenth-century observers took Indian culture on its own terms, but by that time native Americans were slipping into a state of dependency that eroded white respect for them.

Rossiter, Clinton. SEEDTIME OF THE REPUBLIC: THE ORIGIN OF THE AMERICAN TRADITION OF POLITICAL LIBERTY. New York: Harcourt, Brace, 1953. xiv, 558 p.

This is a study of the American colonial ideas of freedom and liberty. Rossiter begins with 1765 and covers political thought that emphasized liberty as freedom from alien control and natural rights.

Ruchames, Louis. "The Sources of Racial Thought in Colonial America." JOURNAL OF NEGRO HISTORY 52 (October 1967): 251-72.

Ruchames argues that the attitudes of Englishmen during the sixteenth, seventeenth, and eighteenth centuries were formed through their experience with the slave trade. The Negro as a slave, torn from Africa, and transported to the New World determined the English image of the Negro.

Savelle, Max. "Nationalism and Other Loyalties in the American Revolution." AMERICAN HISTORICAL REVIEW 67 (July 1962): 901-23.

A feeling of affection for the mother country persisted into the years of revolution, even to the eve of independence. At the same time, Americans thought themselves to be different from Britons, but this was the product of a slow intellectual and social growth.

_____. SEEDS OF LIBERTY: THE GENESIS OF THE AMERICAN MIND. New York: Alfred A. Knopf, 1948. xix, 587 p.

Savelle covers the economic thought and practice, social mores and beliefs, science and applications, and religion and philosophy of the pre-Revolution generation. He also discusses literature, art, architecture, and music, and shows how a consciousness of an American national character developed.

Schutz, John A., and Adair, Douglas, eds. THE SPUR OF FAME: DIALOGUES OF JOHN ADAMS AND BENJAMIN RUSH, 1805-1815. San Marino, Calif.: Huntington Library, 1966. viii, 301 p.

This collection of letters is valuable principally for its exposition of Adams's political ideas. He believed that a few rule the many in all forms of government, aristocracy must be chained, and ameliorating the condition of man is an intelligible idea.

Stourzh, Gerald. ALEXANDER HAMILTON AND THE IDEA OF REPUBLICAN GOVERNMENT. Stanford, Calif.: Stanford University Press, 1970. viii, 278 p.

Stourzh virtually ignores Hamilton's writings on political economy and concludes that his subject was a faithful servant of the American people and a devoted defender of independence, freedom, and security. On the other hand, he shows Hamilton as a seeker of fame and glory who refused to serve under any chief and burned for distinction.

_____. "Reason and Power in Benjamin Franklin's Political Thought." AMERI-CAN POLITICAL SCIENCE REVIEW 47 (December 1953): 1092-1115.

There are two outstanding and sometimes contradictory factors in Franklin's political thought. He understood the power factor in human nature and he revolted in the name of equality against the imperfections in the existing order.

Tate, Thad W. "The Social Contract in America, 1774-1787: Revolutionary Theory as a Conservative Instrument." WILLIAM AND MARY QUARTERLY 22 (July 1965): 375-91.

Americans used contract theory to explain the process of separation from Great Britain and the establishment of new governments. They practiced two basic precepts: the right of revolution and the origin of government in consent.

Varg, Paul A. "The Advent of Nationalism, 1758-1776." AMERICAN QUARTERLY 16 (Summer 1964): 169-81.

The term "America" as a nationalistic expression, found frequent employment and meaning after 1759 because colonists developed strong convictions of their importance in the world. Not only were they being fought over by the British and the French, but their society was also maturing.

Weyant, Robert. "Helvetius and Jefferson: Studies of Human Nature and Government in the Eighteenth Century." JOURNAL OF THE HISTORY OF THE BEHAVIORAL SCIENCES 9 (January 1973): 29-41.

Weyant argues that two theories of human nature that had a bearing on government policy emerged in the eighteenth century. One held that man is egocentric or motivated by personal pleasure and pain, while the other postulated that man is sociocentric through a social sense.

Wood, Gordon S. THE CREATION OF THE AMERICAN REPUBLIC, 1776-1787. Chapel Hill: University of North Carolina Press, 1969. xiv, 653 p.

In this study of political thought in the revolutionary era, Wood argues that the anti-Federalists forced the Federalists to accept democracy. This received expression in the ideas of dual sovereignty and the ultimate power of the people.

Zimmer, Anne Young, and Kelly, Alfred H. "Jonathan Boucher: Constitutional Conservative." JOURNAL OF AMERICAN HISTORY 58 (March 1972): 897-923.

> Boucher, a colonial cleric and Maryland loyalist, has been characterized as a reactionary political theorist and a high Tory. Zimmer and Kelly argue that he was not an extreme reactionary but a conservative in the mold of Edmund Burke and a thinker whose views were not unlike those of the conservatives in the Constitutional Convention.

1815-1915

Abzug, Robert B. "The Influence of Garrisonian Abolitionists' Fears of Slave Violence on the Antislavery Argument, 1829-1840." JOURNAL OF NEGRO HISTORY 55 (January 1970): 15-28.

> The fear of slave violence played a major role in the emergence of immediatism in the antislavery movement. Abolitionists tried to show that emancipation would be safe, based on the West Indian example, and they tried to reach those most endangered.

Bannister, Robert C., Jr. RAY STANNARD BAKER: THE MIND AND THOUGHT OF A PROGRESSIVE. New Haven, Conn.: Yale University Press, 1966. xiv, 335 p.

> Baker was important as a muckraker, progressive, and Wilsonian aide and biographer. His path was from conventional values to social awareness and finally to self-delusion and withdrawal.

Beisner, Robert. TWELVE AGAINST EMPIRE: THE ANTI-IMPERIALISTS, 1898-1900. New York: McGraw-Hill, 1968. xvi, 310 p.

> Beisner examines the ideas and personalities of Carl Schurz, William James, E.L. Godkin, Charles Eliot Norton, Andrew Carnegie, Benjamin Harrison, John Sherman, and others. These men believed that by imposing rule on others, the United States was deserting the Declaration of Independence and the Monroe Doctrine.

Bender, Thomas. TOWARD AN URBAN VISION: IDEAS AND INSTITUTIONS IN NINETEENTH-CENTURY AMERICA. Lexington: University of Kentucky Press, 1975. xv, 277 p.

> This is a study of the image of the city in the American mind. Bender argues that by the middle of the nineteenth century, Americans had abandoned agrarianism for a new understanding of the city and country, art and nature.

Bernard, L.L., and Bernard, Jessie. ORIGINS OF AMERICAN SOCIOLOGY: THE SOCIAL SCIENCE MOVEMENT IN THE UNITED STATES. New York: Thomas Y. Crowell, 1943. xiv, 866 p.

> The social science movement preceeded the birth of academic sociology. In this study, the authors show that the movement was dedicated to improving mankind through social reconstruction.

Bertelson, David. THE LAZY SOUTH. New York: Oxford University Press, 1967. ix, 284 p.

> Bertelson deals with the concept of southerners as pursuers of unlimited freedom and economic opportunity. He argues that southerners took pride in their independent ways and their liberty to enjoy a comparatively easy existence which made them lazy.

Berthoff, Rowland T. "Southern Attitudes Toward Immigration, 1865-1914." JOURNAL OF SOUTHERN HISTORY 17 (August 1951): 328-60.

> Between 1865 and 1907, southern planters, railroaders, and industrialists sought to encourage foreign immigration for the cheap labor, but generally southern people were hostile to immigrants. The South was ethnically more homogeneous than the North and many individuals rallied to protect their culture.

Bestor, Arthur Eugene, Jr. BACKWOODS UTOPIAS: THE SECTARIAN AND OWENITE PHASES OF COMMUNITARIAN SOCIALISM IN AMERICA: 1663-1829. Philadelphia: University of Pennsylvania Press, 1950. xi, 288 p.

> Bestor maintains that the religious socialism of the seventeenth century evolved into the secular socialism of the nineteenth century. He sees Robert Owen as a theorist interested in the moral state of man.

Billington, Ray Allen. THE PROTESTANT CRUSADE, 1800-1860: A STUDY OF THE ORIGINS OF AMERICAN NATIVISM. New York: Macmillan, 1938. viii, 514 p.

> The hatred of Catholics and foreigners was growing steadily for more than two centuries before it took political form in the Know-Nothing movement. Political nativism of the 1850s was supported by lower-class whites whereas earlier nativism had been a manifestation of the middle class.

Blau, Joseph L., ed. AMERICAN PHILOSOPHIC ADDRESSES, 1700-1900. Columbia Studies in American Culture, no. 17. New York: Columbia University Press, 1946. xxi, 762 p.

> This is a companion to Schneider's HISTORY OF AMERICAN PHILOSOPHY (see p. 46). The addresses deal with the philosophy of

American culture and include expressions from Emerson, Phillips, Edwards, Brownson, Parker, and others.

Blodgett, Geoffrey T. "The Mind of the Boston Mugwump." MISSISSIPPI VALLEY HISTORICAL REVIEW 48 (March 1962): 614-34.

Mugwumps tried to escape the status given them by indulgent families and they became rebels against their own experiences. Boston Mugwumps were more genial than their New York counterparts, but they cherished their view of themselves as a minority, and they attempted to break fixed rules of political behavior.

Boller, Paul F., Jr. AMERICAN THOUGHT IN TRANSITION: THE IMPACT OF EVOLUTIONARY NATURALISM, 1865-1900. Chicago: Rand McNally, 1969. xiii, 271 p.

Boller reviews the impact of Darwinism on religion, social theory, economics, social reform, and race. James, Holmes, and Veblen are emphasized, but James clearly was the central figure in this era.

THE BOOKER T. WASHINGTON PAPERS. Edited by Louis R. Harlan et al. 2 vols. Vol. 1: THE AUTOBIOGRAPHICAL WRITINGS. Vol. 2: 1860-89. Urbana: University of Illinois Press, 1972. xi, 469 p.; xl, 557 p.

The first volume includes UP FROM SLAVERY, THE STORY OF MY LIFE AND WORK, and other shorter autobiographical pieces. The second volume deals largely with Washington's life at Hampton Institute and Tuskegee Institute.

_____. Edited by Louis R. Harlan et al. Vol. 3: 1889-95. Urbana: University of Illinois Press, 1974. xxx, 618 p.

Washington's life and ideas from 1889 through the famous "Atlanta Compromise" speech are covered. His papers show him as the strong-willed, often tyrannical, principal of Tuskegee Institute.

_____. Edited by Louis R. Harlan et al. Vol. 4: 1895-98. Urbana: University of Illinois Press, 1975. xxx, 593 p.

In this volume, Washington assumes national leadership and places Tuskegee Institute on a sound financial footing. After the "Atlanta Compromise," however, conditions for blacks deteriorated.

Bourke, Paul F. "The Social Critics and the End of American Innocence: 1907-1921." JOURNAL OF AMERICAN STUDIES 3 (July 1969): 57-72.

Social critics writing before America's involvement in World War I, such as Herbert Croly, Walter Lippmann, and Randolph Bourne, have been identified as the theoretical wing of progressivism be-

cause they asked questions common to theoreticians of political
movements. Bourke argues that the self-consciousness of performing a novel function by criticizing an entire culture made these
writers unique.

_____. "The Status of Politics 1909-1919: THE NEW REPUBLIC, Randolph
Bourne and Van Wyck Brooks." JOURNAL OF AMERICAN STUDIES 8 (August
1974): 171-202.

This is an essay concerning crisis and its effects on political rhetoric in the United States. During World War I, writers in the
NEW REPUBLIC expressed the hope that the crisis might produce
"political-mindedness" that could lead to collectivism, but both
Bourne and Brooks used the way to mount a radical critique of
liberal or progressive politics.

Bremner, Robert H. FROM THE DEPTHS: THE DISCOVERY OF POVERTY IN
THE UNITED STATES. New York: New York University Press, 1956. xiv,
364 p.

Bremner describes the awakening of America to a new concept of
poverty and the rise of social work. Between 1897 and 1917,
poverty was redefined in terms of insufficiency and insecurity rather
than dependency, and scientific philanthropy replaced almsgiving.

Brock, Peter. PACIFISM IN THE UNITED STATES: FROM THE COLONIAL
ERA TO THE FIRST WORLD WAR. Princeton, N.J.: Princeton University
Press, 1968. xii, 1,005 p.

In this study, Brock embraces not only the peace movement, but
also institutions and ideologies of religious and nonsectarian organizations. He believes that the American context and conditions
gave pacifism distinguishing characteristics.

Brock, William. "The Image of England and American Nationalism." JOUR-
NAL OF AMERICAN STUDIES 5 (December 1971): 225-45.

Americans looked to a future of greatness in the early nineteenth
century, but they were divided between those who emphasized that
American identity rested on not being English and others who believed that American interests demanded the cultivation of English
associations. Northern politicians expressed Anglophobia, those in
the South, Anglophilia.

Burns, Edward McNall. THE AMERICAN IDEA OF MISSION: CONCEPTS OF
NATIONAL PURPOSE AND DESTINY. New Brunswick, N.J.: Rutgers University Press, 1957. xii, 385 p.

The idea of mission has been ethical and religious in character and
designed to show the rest of the world the pathway to liberty,

justice, and democracy. Burns discusses the influence of God on
American destiny, the meaning of democracy, free enterprise, the
problems of war and pacifism, and the welfare state.

Burton, David H. "Theodore Roosevelt's Social Darwinism and Views on Imperialism." JOURNAL OF THE HISTORY OF IDEAS 26 (January–March 1965):
103–18.

Examining Roosevelt's ideas concerning imperialism, Burton argues
that he was not a thoroughgoing Social Darwinist. He expressed
Darwinist views, to be sure, but he believed that human consciousness lay outside evolutionary law and he also based his imperialism
on the welfare of mankind.

Capers, Gerald M. "A Reconsideration of John C. Calhoun's Transition from
Nationalism to Nullification." JOURNAL OF SOUTHERN HISTORY 14 (February 1948): 34–48.

Calhoun has been depicted as the symbol of the purity of southern
motives and as a man motivated by only the loftiest incentives.
Capers argues contrarily that he was a politician consumed by a
desire to become president and his political positions were created
with this ambition in mind.

Carneiro, Robert L. "Herbert Spencer's THE STUDY OF SOCIOLOGY and the
Rise of Social Science in America." PROCEEDINGS OF THE AMERICAN
PHILOSOPHICAL SOCIETY 118 (27 December 1974): 540–54.

The STUDY OF SOCIOLOGY grew out of the friendship of Spencer and Edward L. Youmans. It was serialized in the POPULAR
SCIENCE MONTHLY and had a profound effect on American social
thought and teaching.

Cave, Alfred A. "The Case of Calvin Colton: White Racism in Northern
Antislavery Thought." NEW-YORK HISTORICAL SOCIETY QUARTERLY 53
(July 1969): 215–29.

Colton, an active supporter of the Whig Party and a biographer of
Henry Clay, is depicted as a northern moderate. He believed
slavery was morally defensible and that the Negro was innately inferior.

Chamberlin, J.E. THE HARROWING OF EDEN: WHITE ATTITUDES TOWARD
NATIVE AMERICANS. New York: Seabury, 1975. 248 p.

In this study, white attitudes toward Indians in both the United
States and Canada are compared and contrasted. The author shows
the deterioration of the concept of the noble savage in the face
of progress and evolutionary determinism.

Chatfield, Charles. "World War I and the Liberal Pacifist in the United States." AMERICAN HISTORICAL REVIEW 75 (December 1970): 1920-37.

The meaning of the word "pacifist" changed under the pressure of patriotic conformity to mean those who opposed the way to end war. Pacifism had been oriented to liberal values, and pacifists saw that these were being threatened by violence and authoritarianism.

Connor, Paul. "Patriarchy: Old World and New." AMERICAN QUARTERLY 17 (Spring 1965): 48-62.

This is a study of southerners' use of the "father" metaphor to defend their plantation society. Connor examines the origins of George Fitzhugh's patriarchal thought.

Conway, Jill. "Women Reformers and American Culture, 1870-1930." JOURNAL OF SOCIAL HISTORY 5 (Winter 1971-72): 164-77.

Conway attempts to answer the question of why female reformers found social activism unattractive after gaining the franchise and a liberal view of marriage ties. She argues that while some women were wielding national power, the old stereotype concerning female personality had not disappeared.

Cooke, Jacob E. "Tench Coxe, American Economist: The Limitations of Economic Thought in the Early Nationalist Era." PENNSYLVANIA HISTORY 42 (October 1975): 267-90.

Coxe, as an economist, was an activist and a man of practical mind. What was useful was good and what was good could be described by statistical data.

Cooper, Frederick. "Elevating the Race: The Social Thought of Black Leaders, 1827-50." AMERICAN QUARTERLY 24 (December 1972): 604-25.

Black social thought emphasized self-help, although this could not be characterized as black nationalism. Leaders emphasized education and moral reform or adherence to conventional American morality, especially temperance.

Cord, Steven B. HENRY GEORGE: DREAMER OR REALIST? Philadelphia: University of Pennsylvania Press, 1965. 272 p.

This is a review of George's ideas as expressed by historians and economists who have written about them. Cord covers such writings from the Progressive era to the 1960s.

Crowe, Charles R. "'This Unnatural Union of Phalansteries and Transcendentalists.'" JOURNAL OF THE HISTORY OF IDEAS 20 (October-December 1959): 495-502.

This is an essay on the effort of the leaders of Brook Farm to reconcile transcendental individualism with Fourierist socialism. George
Ripley believed that socialist organization was the key to freedom
because it harmonized and balanced human passions.

Curti, Merle. THE AMERICAN PEACE CRUSADE, 1815-1860. Durham, N.C.:
Duke University Press, 1929. viii, 250 p.

Curti covers the organized peace movement from the end of the
War of 1812 to the Civil War. The activities of the Massachusetts Peace Society, American Peace Society, William Ladd, and
the Quakers are detailed.

_____. THE LEARNED BLACKSMITH: THE LETTERS AND JOURNALS OF
ELIHU BURRITT. New York: Wilson-Erickson, 1937. ix, 241 p.

Burritt is known as a crusader for peace who won recognition on
both sides of the Atlantic. Most of the letters are to coworkers,
but the collection also includes correspondence with Charles Sumner and Gerrit Smith.

_____. THE ROOTS OF AMERICAN LOYALTY. New York: Columbia Uni-
versity Press, 1946. x, 267 p.

The development of patriotism among a heterogeneous people is
described. Curti shows that first there was a devotion to the land
and the concept of a unique people, then in the pre-Civil War
period to the development of an organic theory of the nation, and
finally to the growth of nationalism and loyalty in the wars.

Curtis, Bruce. "William Graham Sumner 'On the Concentration of Wealth.'"
JOURNAL OF AMERICAN HISTORY 55 (March 1969): 823-32.

Curtis focuses on Sumner's 1909 essay to dispel the image of the
sociologist as an unrelenting social Darwinist. In this piece of
writing, Sumner analyzed industrialism and monopoly in terms of
their impact on democracy and found that inequalities in property
would lead to class war.

Davis, Allen F. SPEARHEADS OF REFORM: THE SOCIAL SETTLEMENTS AND
THE PROGRESSIVE MOVEMENT, 1890-1914. New York: Oxford University
Press, 1967. xviii, 322 p.

Leaders in the movement to plant settlement houses in slum neigh-
borhoods were relatively well-off collegiate idealists who wanted
to help immigrants. Davis delineates the contributions of these
reformers to urban planning and to the expansion of curricula in
public schools.

Davis, David Brion. "The Emergence of Immediatism in British and American Antislavery Thought." MISSISSIPPI VALLEY HISTORICAL REVIEW 49 (September 1962): 209-30.

"Immediate emancipation" meant more than the immediate abolition of slavery without preparation. It was present as a doctrine in eighteenth-century British antislavery thought in opposition to gradualism which was represented by the type of mind that emphasized self-interest, expediency, moderation, and planning in accord with economic and social laws.

_____. THE PROBLEM OF SLAVERY IN THE AGE OF THE REVOLUTION. 1770-1823. Ithaca, N.Y.: Cornell University Press, 1975. 576 p.

Davis discusses the historical contexts and consequences of change in moral perception within the white enslaving culture and the ways in which black responses impinged on and altered white attitudes concerning the problem of slavery. This is a comparative study of antislavery activity mainly in Britain and America.

_____. THE PROBLEM OF SLAVERY IN WESTERN CULTURE. Ithaca, N.Y.: Cornell University Press, 1966. xiv, 505 p.

This is a survey of the different ways men responded to slavery in order to show the uniqueness of abolitionist concerns. Slavery was always a latent source of tension in Western culture, but it did not become a potent source until new experiences were produced by European expansion, general intellectual discussion, and the persistence of those who had fought for their freedom.

_____. THE SLAVE POWER CONSPIRACY AND THE PARANOID STYLE. Baton Rouge: Louisiana State University Press, 1969. ix, 97 p.

The paranoid style, according to Davis, represents a general social climate in which visions of subversive forces were used to explain political frustrations. As change took place in Jacksonian America, the threat of evil was a means of expressing individual and communal anxieties.

_____. "Some Ideological Functions of Prejudice in Ante-Bellum America." AMERICA QUARTERLY 15 (Summer 1963): 115-25.

Davis argues that the prejudice exhibited toward Masons, Mormons, and Catholics between 1825 and 1860 was the result of perceived threats to liberty and equality. The literature of these counter-subversive movements reveals a preoccupation with the problem of intellectual and moral diversity in a free society.

_____. "Some Themes of Counter-Subversion: An Analysis of Anti-Masonic, Anti-Catholic, and Anti-Mormon Literature." MISSISSIPPI VALLEY HISTORICAL REVIEW 47 (September 1960): 205-24.

Movements of counter-subversion during the second quarter of the nineteenth century differed as to historical origin but they were alike as to pattern. The nativist saw evil groups conspiring against the nation's welfare, and in this he found an outlet for irrational tendencies while paying lip-service to American values and ideals.

Degler, Carl N. "Charlotte Perkins Gilman on the Theory and Practice of Feminism." AMERICAN QUARTERLY 8 (Spring 1956): 21-39.

When Gilman published WOMEN AND ECONOMICS in 1898, she became the idol of radical feminists. Degler portrays her as a rationalist radical who refused to allow tradition or sentiment to inhibit her thinking.

Destler, Chester McArthur. AMERICAN RADICALISM, 1865-1901: ESSAYS AND DOCUMENTS. Connecticut College Monograph, no. 3. New London: Connecticut College, 1946. xii, 276 p.

Destler attempts to distinguish between American and European radicalism. Radicals in the post-Civil War period were "collectivists" such as the populists, voluntarists of the Samuel Gompers group, socialists, and anarchists.

Detweiler, Philip F. "The Changing Reputation of the Declaration of Independence: The First Fifty Years." WILLIAM AND MARY QUARTERLY 19 (October 1962): 557-74.

To Americans of the 1770s and 1780s, the Declaration was merely a statement of independence. In the 1790s, men of opposing politics held opposing views, but in the nineteenth century nationalism gave the Declaration prestige.

Dick, Robert C. BLACK PROTEST: ISSUES AND TACTICS. Westport, Conn.: Greenwood, 1974. xiii, 338 p.

This is an intellectual history of blacks in the pre-Civil War period beginning with 1827 when the first black newspaper was published. Black men and women speak for themselves on colonization, participation in white organizations, militant resistance, the nature of the Constitution, and politics.

Doherty, Herbert J., Jr. "Voices of Protest from the New South, 1875-1910." MISSISSIPPI VALLEY HISTORICAL REVIEW 42 (June 1955): 45-66.

Southern social and economic critics such as Timothy Thomas Fortune, George W. Cable, Walter Hines Page, Thomas E. Watson, and others are described. They criticized the plight of Negroes, child labor, the prison system, railroads, and other matters.

Donald, David. "The Proslavery Argument Reconsidered." JOURNAL OF SOUTHERN HISTORY 37 (February 1971): 3-18.

Donald believes the substance of proslavery thought is well known but the reasons for the argument are not. He maintains that pro-slavery writers were less interested in defending slavery than in defending a bygone age.

Dorfman, Joseph. THE ECONOMIC MIND IN AMERICAN CIVILIZATION. Vols. 1-2: 1606-1865. New York: Viking Press, 1946. xii, 502 p.; vii, 494 p.

This is a mine of information organized in the form of short biog-raphies and summaries of economic writings. Long continuities and the interrelationship of economic ideas are stressed.

_____. THE ECONOMIC MIND IN AMERICAN CIVILIZATION. Vol. 3: 1865-1918. New York: Viking Press, 1949. vii, 494 p.

Dorfman covers issues such as the money problem, the elimination of depression and unemployment, and the proper methods of run-ning the economy. He demonstrates how a vast domestic economy rose and proliferated.

Duberman, Martin, ed. THE ANTISLAVERY VANGUARD: NEW ESSAYS ON THE ABOLITIONISTS. Princeton, N.J.: Princeton University Press, 1965. x, 508 p.

Essay titles include "Slavery and Sin," and "The Psychology of Commitment." Orange Scott, Wendell Phillips, and Frederick Douglass are given attention.

Dumond, Dwight Lowell. ANTISLAVERY: THE CRUSADE FOR FREEDOM IN AMERICA. Ann Arbor: University of Michigan Press, 1961. x, 422 p.

Dumond argues that antislavery forces were not attacking slave-holders as individuals, they were attacking an organized system. They cited instances of cruelty, but they did this to depict the unjustifiable character of the system itself.

Durden, Robert F. "J.D.B. De Bow: Convolutions of a Slavery Expansionist." JOURNAL OF SOUTHERN HISTORY 17 (November 1951): 441-61.

DE BOW'S REVIEW is used to trace the shifting southern ideas con-cerning slavery expansion. De Bow deplored arguments for and against slavery, because the issue had been settled and expansion was the question.

Easton, Loyd D. HEGEL'S FIRST AMERICAN FOLLOWERS. THE OHIO HE-GELIANS: JOHN B. STALLO, PETER KAUFMANN, MONCURE CONWAY, AND AUGUST WILLICH, WITH KEY WRITINGS. Athens: Ohio University Press, 1966. ix, 353 p.

These Ohioans publicized and defended Hegel's philosophy in Cincinnati during the 1850s. They saw Hegel as a phenomenalist who devised a concept of the state based on individual freedom that could only be found in a democratic republic.

Eaton, Clement. THE FREEDOM-OF-THOUGHT STRUGGLE IN THE OLD SOUTH. Rev. ed. New York: Harper and Row, 1964. xiii, 418 p.

The author calls this study "a case history in the record of human liberty and intolerance." He shows that the two great taboos in southern culture were criticism of slavery and heterodoxy in religion.

Ekirch, Arthur A., Jr. THE DECLINE OF AMERICAN LIBERALISM. New York: Longmans, Green and Co., 1955. xiv, 401 p.

Liberalism has been in decline since the founding of the republic. By liberalism, the author means limited representative government and the widest possible freedom of the individual.

_____. THE IDEA OF PROGRESS IN AMERICA, 1815-1860. Studies in History, Economics, and Public Law, no. 511. Edited by the Faculty of Political Science of Columbia University. New York: Columbia University Press, 1944. 305 p.

Public officials and plain people in the early republic proclaimed their faith in a glorious future. They believed it was America's destiny to spread religious and political liberty, safeguard democratic progress through education, and advance reform, notably antislavery.

Elkins, Stanley M. SLAVERY: A PROBLEM IN AMERICAN INSTITUTIONAL AND INTELLECTUAL LIFE. Chicago: University of Chicago Press, 1959. viii, 248 p.

Elkins argues that the slave was childlike, a "Sambo," because the slave system was not unlike Nazi concentration camps where severe repression reduced prisoners to childlike behavior. He also points out that slavery was less harsh in Latin America than in the United States because the church served as a mediating institution, and that American abolitionists lacked institutions to help them formulate policy.

Farrell, John C. BELOVED LADY: A HISTORY OF JANE ADDAMS' IDEAS ON REFORM AND PEACE. Baltimore: Johns Hopkins Press, 1967. 272 p.

Addams's early life was dominated by a desire to find a satisfying intellectual and emotional basis for vocational duty. She gained satisfaction in her work with Chicago's immigrant poor and in her undogmatic efforts to promote peace.

Faulkner, Robert Kenneth. THE JURISPRUDENCE OF JOHN MARSHALL. Princeton, N.J.: Princeton University Press, 1968. xxi, 307 p.

This is an analysis of Marshall's political theory. The foundation of his jurisprudence was the Lockean view of natural law as applied to individual rights of life, liberty, and property.

Feldman, Egal. "Prostitution, the Alien Woman, and the Progressive Imagination, 1910-1915." AMERICAN QUARTERLY 19 (Summer 1967): 192-206.

Many Americans believed that commercialized prostitution was a product of urban living and that foreigners were responsible for the white slave traffic. Female reformers led the assult on this form of vice and they attempted to convince the public that alien girls had to be protected.

Fellman, Michael. "Theodore Parker and the Abolitionist Role in the 1850s." JOURNAL OF AMERICAN HISTORY 61 (December 1974): 666-84.

Parker became an abolitionist following the passage of the Fugitive Slave Law in 1850. His message was that slavery would destroy the North if nothing was done concerning it.

_____. THE UNBOUNDED FRAME: FREEDOM AND COMMUNITY IN NINE-TEENTH CENTURY AMERICAN UTOPIANISM. Westport, Conn.: Greenwood, 1973. xx, 203 p.

In analyzing the concepts of freedom and community, Fellman concentrates on the ideas of Albert Brisbane, John Humphrey Noyes, Horace Mann, Margaret Fuller, Ignatius Donnelly, and others. He considers individual development and autonomy, group coercion and cohesion, optimism and pessimism, and alienation.

Feuer, Lewis. "John Dewey and the Back to the People Movement in American Thought." JOURNAL OF THE HISTORY OF IDEAS 20 (October-December 1959): 545-68.

Feuer argues that Dewey's thought cannot be subsumed under expressions such as "the revolt against formalism," because he was caught up in the back to the people movement beginning in the 1880s. This movement, spearheaded by Jane Addams and others, caused Dewey to infuse his ideas with a spirit of democratic Socialist reform.

Filler, Louis. THE CRUSADE AGAINST SLAVERY, 1830-1860. New American Nation Series. Edited by Henry Steele Commager and Richard B. Morris. New York: Harper and Brothers, 1960. xviii, 318 p.

New England reformers and particularly Garrison were the main leaders in the antislavery movement, and the denial of human freedom, rather than sin, was central in antislavery arguments. Other reform movements, such as communitarian socialism and phrenology, are discussed.

_____. CRUSADERS FOR AMERICAN LIBERALISM. New York: Harcourt, Brace, 1939. viii, 422 p.

The crusaders for American liberalism are the muckrakers. These writers exposed political corruption, the exploitation of natural resources, oppression of ethnic groups, and the avarice of corporations.

Fine, Sidney. LAISSEZ FAIRE AND THE GENERAL-WELFARE STATE: A STUDY OF CONFLICT IN AMERICAN THOUGHT, 1865-1901. Ann Arbor: University of Michigan Press, 1956. x, 468 p.

Fine discusses laissez-faire thinking and criticisms of it such as the social gospel, greenbackism, socialism, populism, and others. He focuses less on outstanding spokesmen and more on popular currents of thought.

Fladeland, Betty. MEN AND BROTHERS: ANGLO-AMERICAN ANTISLAVERY COOPERATION. Urbana: University of Illinois Press, 1972. xiv, 478 p.

This is a study of letters, speeches, pamphlets, newspapers, and lobbying. Fladeland attempts to show how antislavery activities influenced public policy.

Flexner, Eleanor. CENTURY OF STRUGGLE: THE WOMAN'S RIGHTS MOVEMENT IN THE UNITED STATES. Cambridge, Mass.: Belknap Press of Harvard University Press, 1959. xiv, 384 p.

This study covers more than the suffrage movement. Flexner discusses Negro women, the labor movement, industrial employment, and educational opportunities.

Fogarty, Robert S. "American Communes, 1865-1914." JOURNAL OF AMERICAN STUDIES 9 (August 1975): 145-62.

Communal societies in the United States did not die with the Civil War. There were cooperative colonizers based on the Owenite model, charismatic perfectionists who joined one another for the sanctity of membership, and political pragmatists who wanted to prove that socialism worked.

Forcey, Charles. THE CROSSROADS OF LIBERALISM: CROLY, WEYL, LIPPMANN, AND THE PROGRESSIVE ERA, 1900-1925. New York: Oxford University Press, 1961. xxx, 358 p.

This is a study of the "New Republic" and its leading lights. Croly, Weyl, and Lippmann transformed the old liberalism of economic individualism, minimal government, and isolation into a new liberalism of regulated capitalism, the welfare state, and internationalism.

Fox, Daniel M. THE DISCOVERY OF ABUNDANCE: SIMON N. PATTEN AND THE TRANSFORMATION OF SOCIAL THEORY. Ithaca, N.Y.: Cornell University Press, 1967. xiii, 259 p.

Patten made a name for himself as an economist in 1885 by theorizing that modern technology and productivity had made poverty unnecessary and that an economy of abundance had replaced an economy of scarcity. In his career, he tried to relate his ideas to Freudian psychology, Jamesian pragmatism, and other concepts.

Fox, Richard W. "The Paradox of 'Progressive' Socialism: The Case of Morris Hillquit, 1901-1914." AMERICAN QUARTERLY 26 (May 1974): 127-40.

From the founding of the Socialist Party in 1901, Hillquit was the organization's principal writer and he was responsible for strict adherence to contemporary Marxist or social democratic doctrine. He believed that when industrial concentration was advanced, workers would respond to Socialist propaganda.

Frederickson, George M. THE BLACK IMAGE IN THE WHITE MIND: THE DEBATE ON AFRO-AMERICAN CHARACTER AND DESTINY, 1817-1914. New York: Harper and Row, 1971. xiii, 343 p.

Frederickson discusses white racist thought in the nineteenth century from the standpoint of democratization, romantic thought, nationalism, statism, and evolutionary thought. Equalitarianism reached its height in 1830 and slid downward after that time.

_____. "A Man but Not a Brother: Abraham Lincoln and Racial Equality." JOURNAL OF SOUTHERN HISTORY 41 (February 1975): 39-58.

To create a usable Lincoln, some writers have depicted the Civil War president as one of the heroes of egalitarianism, while others have condemned him as a typical white racist. Frederickson believes that Lincoln was morally opposed to slavery and accepted the humanity of blacks, but also favored colonization because white prejudice made racial equality impossible.

Friedman, Lawrence J. INVENTORS OF THE PROMISED LAND. New York: Alfred A. Knopf, 1975. xxxi, 344 p.

This is a book of essays on nationalism and patriotism. Friedman contrasts the national goal of perfectability with the individual desire for rootedness.

_____. THE WHITE SAVAGE: RACIAL FANTASIES IN THE POSTBELLUM SOUTH. Englewood Cliffs, N.J.: Prentice-Hall, 1970. vii, 184 p.

Friedman focuses on postbellum southerners such as Thomas Nelson Page, Tom Watson, George Washington Cable, and Woodrow Wilson by way of concluding that southerners fantasized about blacks as well as themselves. They slandered uppity Negroes as savages as a means of blinding themselves to their own aggressions and fears.

Fries, Sylvia D. "Staatstheorie and the New American Science of Politics." JOURNAL OF THE HISTORY OF IDEAS 34 (July-September 1973): 391-404.

Until World War I, political science was dominated by the German idea of the state, a state whose nature was organic, unified, sovereign, and devoted to the moral perfection of mankind. It was found, however, that German concepts and American experience were different.

Furner, Mary O. ADVOCACY AND OBJECTIVITY: A CRISIS IN THE PROFESSIONALIZATION OF AMERICAN SOCIAL SCIENCE, 1865-1905. Lexington: University Press of Kentucky, 1975. xv, 357 p.

Furner shows the process by which academic economists, sociologists, and political scientists developed ideas of separate disciplines. She emphasizes the connection of these efforts at professionalization with Gilded Age reform.

Gaston, Paul M. THE NEW SOUTH CREED: A STUDY IN SOUTHERN MYTH-MAKING. New York: Alfred A. Knopf, 1970. viii, 298 p.

The South after Appomattox was poor, despised, ridiculed, and saddled with many burdens. To find a way out of this condition, optimistic young southerners talked hopefully about a new scheme of things that they called the New South, a new myth embodying racial peace and a social order based on industry.

Gatewood, Willard B., Jr. BLACK AMERICANS AND THE WHITE MAN'S BURDEN. Urbana: University of Illinois Press, 1975. xi, 352 p.

Gatewood shows that blacks assessed American imperialism in terms of their own status and the status of other people. They viewed the Cuban war for independence and the war in the Philippines as black men's conflicts.

Gettleman, Marvin E. "Philanthropy as Social Control in Late Nineteenth-Century America: Some Hypotheses and Data on the Rise of Social Work." SOCIETAS 5 (Winter 1975): 49-59.

Americans have discovered the poor at different times in history and have made wars on poverty. One such time was the late nineteenth century when the Charity Organization Society of New York mounted a crusade that led to the professionalization of social work and operated as a brake on social radicalism.

Gilbert, James. DESIGNING THE INDUSTRIAL STATE: THE INTELLECTUAL PURSUIT OF COLLECTIVISM IN AMERICA, 1880-1940. Chicago: Quadrangle, 1972. ix, 335 p.

Gilbert argues that American intellectuals must accept a large share of the responsibility for designing the industrial state, because their ideas led to collectivist solutions. His intellectuals are a curious group since they include the inventor of the safety razor blade, "King" Gillette; the General Electric inventor, Charles Steinmetz; James Burnham; and Reinhold Niebuhr.

Gilhooley, Leonard. CONTRADICTION AND DILEMMA: ORESTES BROWNSON AND THE AMERICAN IDEA. New York: Fordham University Press, 1972. xv, 231 p.

The American idea is the sum of the American dream, the American experiment, and the American mission. Gilhooley attempts to show Brownson's consistency from his radical labor period to his conversion to Catholicism.

Gillespie, Neal C. THE COLLAPSE OF ORTHODOXY: THE INTELLECTUAL ORDEAL OF GEORGE FREDERICK HOLMES. Charlottesville: University Press of Virginia, 1972. x, 273 p.

Holmes was a significant nineteenth-century literary and historical scholar who spent most of his career at the University of Virginia. He is portrayed as a critic of civilization who defended slavery, a Christian faced by science, and a historian who attempted to discover laws of human development.

_____. "The Spiritual Odyssey of George Frederick Holmes: A Study of Religious Conservatism in the Old South." JOURNAL OF SOUTHERN HISTORY 32 (August 1966): 291-307.

In the nineteenth century, innovations in science and scholarship created troubling doubts concerning traditional ideas about man. Holmes moved intellectually from a liberal theology to conservative views concerning the implications of science.

Ginger, Ray. ALTGELD'S AMERICA: THE LINCOLN IDEAL VERSUS CHANGING REALITIES. New York: Funk and Wagnalls, 1958. viii, 376 p.

The Lincoln ideal included deep understanding with a sense of responsibility for social welfare and equal opportunity for all in a competitive society. Many business leaders forgot all but the last part, the struggle for success, and reformers such as John P. Altgeld tried to revive the humanitarian aspects.

_____. "The Idea of Process in American Social Thought." AMERICAN QUARTERLY 4 (Fall 1952): 253-65.

The idea of process means that everything is changing, changes are cumulative, and these cumulative changes do not eventuate in any final term. Ginger examines the thought of Dewey, Veblen, Wesley C. Mitchell, Theodore Dreiser, and Clarence Darrow, and argues that social development should be studied as the interaction of all spheres of culture.

Glaser, William A. "Algie Martin Simons and Marxism in America." MISSISSIPPI VALLEY HISTORICAL REVIEW 41 (December 1954): 419-34.

Simons's career provides a picture of the dilemma and failure of Marxism in America. He became a Socialist not because he was an alienated industrial worker, but because he was a middle-class intellectual who wanted to express his concern for rural and urban problems in a militant manner.

Gleason, Philip. "The Melting Pot: Symbol of Fusion or Confusion?" AMERICAN QUARTERLY 16 (Summer 1964): 20-46.

As a symbol, the term "melting pot" means the process by which immigrants are absorbed into American society and are somehow changed. The term as a symbol has been much more important than as a social theory because of the difficulty in framing an adequate theory of immigrant adjustment.

Gossett, Thomas F. RACE: THE HISTORY OF AN IDEA IN AMERICA. Dallas: Southern Methodist University Press, 1963. ix, 512 p.

Racism toward Negroes, Indians, and southern and eastern Europeans is emphasized. The story is told in terms of the ideas of writers, ministers, and scholars; scientific theories of race; status of minorities; nativism and immigration restrictions; and the theories of historians and literary critics.

Graybar, Lloyd J. ALBERT SHAW OF THE REVIEW OF REVIEWS: AN INTELLECTUAL BIOGRAPHY. Lexington: University of Kentucky Press, 1974. xiii, 229 p.

Shaw was a progressive from the Middle West who came East and helped to shape reform ideas in the late nineteenth and early twentieth centuries. He became an activist Bull Moose progressive and later was condemned as an anachronism during the New Deal.

Griffin, Clifford S. THEIR BROTHER'S KEEPERS: MORAL STEWARDSHIP IN THE UNITED STATES, 1800-1865. New Brunswick, N.J.: Rutgers University Press, 1960. xvi, 332 p.

This is a study of the major national benevolent societies. Griffin deals with a category of individuals he calls "trustees" or "stewards of the Lord" who watched over the moral behavior of their fellow men.

Grimes, Alan P. THE PURITAN ETHIC AND WOMAN'S SUFFRAGE. New York: Oxford University Press, 1967. xiii, 159 p.

Woman suffrage in the West is emphasized. The author argues that the movement was as much conservative as progressive and that it was a regional phenomenon.

Haber, Samuel. EFFICIENCY AND UPLIFT: SCIENTIFIC MANAGEMENT IN THE PROGRESSIVE ERA, 1890-1920. Chicago: University of Chicago Press, 1964. xiii, 181 p.

Haber discusses the spread and influence of scientific management and describes the impact of ideas of efficiency on progressive thinkers such as Louis Brandeis, Herbert Croly, and Walter Lippmann. These men used themes of scientific management to advocate expertness and elitism without appearing to violate democratic ideals.

Hansen, Klaus J. "The Millenium, the West, and Race in the Antebellum American Mind." WESTERN HISTORICAL QUARTERLY 3 (October 1972): 373-90.

The symbolic significance of the American West, the pursuit of the millenium, and the racial self-image of whites influenced the canons and assumptions of American romanticism. The millenial image of a racially pure West offered the possibility of escape from a society beset by the ills of industrialization, immigration, and modernization.

Harlan, Louis R. "Booker T. Washington and the White Man's Burden." AMERICAN HISTORICAL REVIEW 71 (January 1966): 441-67.

Washington was substantially involved in African affairs. This did not require a readjustment in his outlook because he subscribed to the "White Man's Burden" of leadership and authority whether in America or Africa.

Harrison, J.F.C. QUEST FOR THE NEW MORAL WORLD: ROBERT OWEN AND THE OWENITIES IN BRITAIN AND AMERICA. New York: Charles Scribner's Sons, 1969. xi, 392 p.

In this comparative intellectual and social history, Harrison examines Owen's conceptions of society and socialism, as well as what was comparable in industrial England and frontier America that caused these societies to respond to Owenism. He argues that

Owenism was not an ideology of a particular class but a response to social change.

Hartz, Louis. THE LIBERAL TRADITION IN AMERICA: AN INTERPRETATION OF AMERICAN POLITICAL THOUGHT SINCE THE REVOLUTION. New York: Harcourt, Brace, 1955. x, 329 p.

Hartz argues that the absence of a feudal past has been at the center of the American intellectual tradition. He believes that Lockean ideology has ruled without an opposition faith.

Heale, M.J. "From City Fathers to Social Critics: Humanitarianism and Government in New York, 1790-1860." JOURNAL OF AMERICAN HISTORY 63 (June 1976): 21-41.

This essay deals with humanitarian reform efforts in response to the restless New York City population of the early industrial era. It shows the development of humanitarian societies supported by philanthropists that often became critics of city government.

Herman, Sondra R. ELEVEN AGAINST WAR: STUDIES IN AMERICAN INTERNATIONALIST THOUGHT, 1898-1921. Stanford, Calif.: Hoover Institution Press, 1969. xiv, 264 p.

By examining the thought of Elihu Root, Jane Addams, Thorstein Veblen, and others, Herman tries to demonstrate that the ground for internationalism in America was prepared before Wilson. She depicts Wilson as a nationalist who advocated American interests in search of international machinery.

Herreshoff, David. AMERICAN DISCIPLES OF MARX: FROM THE AGE OF JACKSON TO THE PROGRESSIVE ERA. Detroit: Wayne State University Press, 1967. 215 p.

Marxism has always meant different things to different people. As a consequence, Herreshoff sees Daniel De Leon, Eugene Debs, Ralph Waldo Emerson, Henry David Thoreau, and Orestes Brownson as American proponents of Marxist philosophy.

Higham, John. STRANGERS IN THE LAND: PATTERNS OF AMERICAN NATIVISM, 1860-1925. New Brunswick, N.J.: Rutgers University Press, 1955. xiv, 431 p.

This is a study of the impact of political, social, economic, and organizational pressures upon nativist thought and action. It is held together by a focus on the narrative of immigration restriction.

Hinkle, Roscoe C. "Basic Orientation of the Founding Fathers of American Sociology." JOURNAL OF THE HISTORY OF THE BEHAVIORAL SCIENCES 11 (April 1975): 107-22.

Hinkle examines the thought of Lester Ward, William Graham Sumner, Charles Horton Cooley, and others for common elements. He argues that the founders of sociology were evolutionary naturalists as well as social materialists and idealists.

Hirschfeld, Charles. "Brooks Adams and American Nationalism." AMERICAN HISTORICAL REVIEW 69 (January 1964): 371-92.

Adams's mature views were neither conservative nor liberal. From the turn of the twentieth century, Adams was a nationalist of a new variety who advocated American expansion in the world and radical reform in American society and politics.

Hite, James C., and Hall, Ellen J. "The Reactionary Evolution of Economic Thought in Antebellum Virginia." VIRGINIA MAGAZINE OF HISTORY AND BIOGRAPHY 80 (October 1972): 476-88.

Virginians led the way in formulating a rationale for the antebellum South's economic organization. The authors of this essay examine the thought of John Taylor of Caroline, George Tucker, Thomas Dew, and George Fitzhugh.

Hofstadter, Richard. THE AGE OF REFORM: FROM BRYAN TO F.D.R. New York: Alfred A. Knopf, 1955. vii, 328 p.

This is a study of the political thinking and psychology of reform groups. Reform is urban-centered and Progressives were largely urban people who were motivated toward reform by a desire to regain status.

_____. THE AMERICAN POLITICAL TRADITION AND THE MEN WHO MADE IT. New York: Alfred A. Knopf, 1959. ix, 378 p.

Hofstadter is interested in the consequences of political thought. He examines consequences by discussing the thinking of political leaders from the founding fathers to Franklin Roosevelt.

_____. THE PARANOID STYLE IN AMERICAN POLITICS AND OTHER ESSAYS. New York: Alfred A. Knopf, 1965. xiv, 314 p.

This is an examination of a trend of thought in which some people evaluate the motives of their opponents in terms of good and evil. Opposition is more than error; it is evidence of malignant disposition and conspiracy.

_____. SOCIAL DARWINISM IN AMERICAN THOUGHT, 1860-1915. Philadelphia: University of Pennsylvania Press for the American Historical Association under sponsorship of the Albert J. Beveridge Memorial Fund, 1944. viii, 191 p.

Hofstadter shows how social theories from biology were accepted in the social environment of the late nineteenth century. These theories were advanced by William Graham Sumner, Lester Ward, and others.

Horowitz, Daniel. "Genteel Observers: New England Economic Writers and Industrialization." NEW ENGLAND QUARTERLY 48 (March 1975): 65–83.

The ideas of Edward Atkinson, David A. Wells, Carroll D. Wright, and Francis A. Walker are delineated. Horowitz argues that in spite of anachronistic yearnings, these thinkers used historical and statistical materials to develop a comprehensive view of economic development in the late nineteenth century.

Jaher, Frederic Cople. DOUBTERS AND DISSENTERS: CATACLYSMIC THOUGHT IN AMERICA, 1885–1918. New York: Free Press of Glencoe, 1964. 275 p.

This is a study of prophets of doom such as Ignatius Donnelly, Henry Adams, Brooks Adams, and Jack London. Personality and social background contributed to the difference between those who prophesied catastrophe and other social critics.

Jenkins, William Sumner. PRO-SLAVERY THOUGHT IN THE OLD SOUTH. Chapel Hill: University of North Carolina Press, 1935. xi, 381 p.

Jenkins describes the complexity of proslavery thought. Among the theories discussed are the origin of slavery and its legal basis, status under the constitution, and the institution's moral and religious background.

Johnson, Guion Griffis. "Southern Paternalism toward Negroes after Emancipation." JOURNAL OF SOUTHERN HISTORY 23 (November 1957): 483–509.

Southern paternalistic thought concerning the Negro had been formulated before Plessy v. Ferguson (1896). This thought developed from a moderate equalitarianism to a permanently unequal status under paternal supervision, a group of ideas in which the black was permanently inferior and only capable of unskilled labor when supervised by whites.

Kasson, John F. CIVILIZING THE MACHINE: TECHNOLOGY AND REPUBLICAN VALUES IN AMERICA, 1776–1900. New York: Grossman, 1976. xiv, 274 p.

This is a collection of five essays. They cover the introduction of domestic manufacturers in the revolutionary period; response to the model factory town of Lowell, Massachusetts; Emerson's internal dialogue with technology; aesthetic responses to machinery; and utopian novels of the 1880s and 1890s.

Kearns, Francis E. "Margaret Fuller and the Abolition Movement." JOURNAL OF THE HISTORY OF IDEAS 25 (January-March 1964): 120-27.

Fuller made notable contributions to the women's rights movement, but she never embraced abolitionism. She was cautious because her desire to liberate both blacks and women was more radical than the conservative reformers in the abolition group.

Kelley, Robert. THE TRANSATLANTIC PERSUASION: THE LIBERAL-DEMO-CRATIC MIND IN THE AGE OF GLADSTONE. New York: Alfred A. Knopf, 1969. xiii, 433 p.

Through essays on Adam Smith, Edmund Burke, and Thomas Jefferson, Kelley describes the Liberal-Democrat. In the nineteenth century, this type existed in British, Canadian, and American politics in the persons of William Gladstone, Alexander Mackenzie, and Grover Cleveland.

Kerber, Linda K. "The Abolitionist Perception of the Indian." JOURNAL OF AMERICAN HISTORY 62 (September 1955): 271-95.

Radical abolitionists perceived the problem of the United States as being the definition of men by race and they were sensitive to the white man's extermination of the Indian. They believed the Indian wanted to be civilized and assimilated, and they did not see the conflict of cultures.

Kirby, Jack Temple. DARKNESS AT THE DAWNING: RACE AND REFORM IN THE PROGRESSIVE SOUTH. Philadelphia: J.B. Lippincott, 1972. vii, 210 p.

Progressivism in the South was not a single party or movement. It developed from agrarian reform and from professional, business, and urban groups that wanted to create a new social order.

Kirkland, Edward C. "Rhetoric and Rage Over the Division of Wealth in the Eighteen Nineties." PROCEEDINGS OF THE AMERICAN ANTIQUARIAN SO-CIETY 79 (15 October 1969): 227-44.

With the breakdown of agrarian beliefs in the late nineteenth century, wealth acquired a new face. This is a study of men and movements that argued for the redistribution of wealth but failed because of the popularity of prosperity and the prospect of getting rich.

Kohn, Hans. AMERICAN NATIONALISM: AN INTERPRETIVE ESSAY. New York: Macmillan, 1957. xii, 272 p.

Kohn argues that American nationalism has been based on the idea of liberty in diversity. An immense and thinly populated land made diversity possible, and millions of immigrants provided talents and potentialities.

Kraditor, Aileen. THE IDEAS OF THE WOMAN SUFFRAGE MOVEMENT, 1890-1920. New York: Columbia University Press, 1965. xii, 313 p.

The woman suffrage movement was devoted to one idea—the enfranchisement of women. Women argued that they should have the right to vote because they were people, citizens, and taxpayers, and also because they would benefit society by championing worthy causes.

_____. MEANS AND ENDS IN AMERICAN ABOLITIONISM: GARRISON AND HIS CRITICS ON STRATEGY AND TACTICS, 1834-1860. New York: Pantheon, 1969. xvi, 296 p.

Kraditor argues that the splits in abolitionism were not the result of factionalism, but of basic differences in social philosophies. She is friendly to Garrison and shows that disputes centered on religious beliefs and questions of political action.

Lasch, Christopher. "The Anti-Imperialists, the Philippines, and the Inequality of Man." JOURNAL OF SOUTHERN HISTORY 24 (August 1958): 319-31.

In the debate concerning the cession of the Philippines, southern Democrats condemned imperialism on the grounds that Asiatics, like blacks, were inferior to white people. That northern liberals did not respond is an indication of the extent to which they had retreated from their earlier idealism and also of the nationalization of racism.

Leiman, Melvin M. JACOB N. CARDOZO: ECONOMIC THOUGHT IN THE ANTEBELLUM SOUTH. New York: Columbia University Press, 1966. 263 p.

Cardozo was a Charleston newspaper editor and political economist whose active career covered the years 1817-73. He wrote on rent, wages, profits, banking, the tariff, business cycles, and slavery, and generally assumed a conservative stance.

THE LETTERS OF WILLIAM LLOYD GARRISON. Vol. 1: I WILL BE HEARD! 1822-1835. Edited by Walter M. Merrill. Cambridge, Mass.: Belknap Press of Harvard University Press, 1971. xxx, 616 p.

These letters cover the founding of the LIBERATOR, the establishment of the New England and American antislavery societies, Garrison's trip to England for abolition, and the Boston mob scene that nearly cost him his life in 1835.

_____. Vol. 2: A HOUSE DIVIDING AGAINST ITSELF: 1836-1840. Edited by Louis Ruchames. Cambridge, Mass.: Belknap Press of Harvard University Press, 1971. xxxi, 770 p.

This collection shows Garrison as a complex and controversial aboli-tionist. He sought to make abolitionism part of a universal reform movement, for he was a reformer who cared about Indians and about Christians who practiced their religion one day a week.

_____. Vol. 3: NO UNION WITH SLAVEHOLDERS, 1841-1849. Edited by Walter M. Merrill. Cambridge, Mass.: Belknap Press of Harvard University Press, 1973. xxiii, 719 p.

Garrison's ideas after the schism in the antislavery movement in 1839-40 are developed. The letters record his tribulations with political abolition and his answer in disunion.

_____. Vol. 4: FROM DISUNION TO THE BRINK OF WAR, 1850-1860. Edited by Louis Ruchames. Cambridge, Mass.: Belknap Press of Harvard University Press, 1975. xxv, 737 p.

These letters cover Garrison's increasing radicalism and isolation in the antislavery movement. They also show division among the Garrisonians in the late 1850s.

Levine, Daniel. JANE ADDAMS AND THE LIBERAL TRADITION. Madison: State Historical Society of Wisconsin, 1971. xviii, 277 p.

Addams influenced the transition from laissez-faire to the welfare state. Levine argues that American reform sought to broaden partici-pation in decision making, while Addams fought for fundamental changes in institutions and ethics that would improve the quality of life.

_____. VARIETIES OF REFORM THOUGHT. Madison: State Historical So-ciety of Wisconsin, 1964. xiii, 149 p.

This study focuses on the period from 1890 to 1912. The Civic Federation of Chicago was the right wing of reform thought that sought social stability and order, while Jane Addams, Samuel Gom-pers, Albert Beveridge, Edgar Gardner Murphy, and Robert M. La Follette each sought to change the social environment.

Le Warne, Charles Pierce. UTOPIAS OF PUGET SOUND, 1885-1915. Seattle: University of Washington Press, 1975. xiv, 325 p.

Socialists in the late nineteenth century chose the state of Wash-ington for transformation, and they organized a number of utopian, cooperative communities. This study covers five of these experi-ments.

Lewis, Elsie M. "The Political Mind of the Negro, 1865-1900." JOURNAL OF SOUTHERN HISTORY 21 (May 1955): 189-202.

> Black leaders during the Civil War evolved a political ideology for the betterment of their people based on the Declaration of Independence and supporting ideas. They formed the Equal Rights League and admitted the failure of the Republican Party to guarantee full citizenship.

Lubove, Roy. THE PROFESSIONAL ALTRUIST: THE EMERGENCE OF SOCIAL WORK AS A CAREER, 1880-1930. Cambridge, Mass.: Harvard University Press, 1965. viii, 291 p.

> Lubove begins with the Charity Organization Society movement of the 1880s and traces the professionalization of social work. Urbanization made private charity organizations outmoded and social work provided insights into the psychological, physical, and social needs of people.

Lutzker, Michael A. "The Pacifist as Militarist: A Critique of the American Peace Movement." SOCIETAS 5 (Spring 1975): 87-104.

> During 1898-1914, a prerequisite for the directorship of a peace movement was having served as secretary of war. As a result, a consensus existed between peace leaders and those having a more military orientation on America's mission of world leadership.

McClellan, James. JOSEPH STORY AND THE AMERICAN CONSTITUTION: A STUDY IN POLITICAL AND LEGAL THOUGHT. Norman: University of Oklahoma Press, 1971. xvii, 413 p.

> This study is devoted mostly to Story's views on natural law, Christianity and the common law, property, and the Union. McClellan identifies Story with conservative natural-law teaching and with a Christian-classical tradition that he learned from reading Blackstone and Burke.

McCloskey, Robert Green. AMERICAN CONSERVATISM IN THE AGE OF ENTERPRISE: A STUDY OF WILLIAM GRAHAM SUMNER, STEPHEN J. FIELD, AND ANDREW CARNEGIE. Cambridge, Mass.: Harvard University Press, 1951. xi, 193 p.

> McCloskey shows how neoconservatism turned American democracy and ethnics upside down. Materialism, elitism, and laissez-faire benefitted business leaders.

McWilliams, Wilson Carey. THE IDEA OF FRATERNITY IN AMERICA. Berkeley: University of California Press, 1974. xiv, 695 p.

> This is, at once, a survey of political ideas from the Puritans to the pluralists, a study of moral and social tensions in writers from

Emerson to James Baldwin, and an attack on American liberalism. After the seventeenth-century Puritans, fraternity survived only fitfully.

Madden, Edward H. CIVIL DISOBEDIENCE AND MORAL LAW IN NINE-TEENTH-CENTURY AMERICAN PHILOSOPHY. Seattle: University of Washington Press, 1968. vii, 214 p.

> Academic orthodoxy in early nineteenth-century colleges was a potent source for civil disobedience. College presidents abandoned determinism for free will and believed that the individual was free to choose his course of action.

Madison, Charles A. "Anarchism in America." JOURNAL OF THE HISTORY OF IDEAS 6 (January 1945): 46-66.

> In Europe, anarchism was a reaction against oppressive regimes, but in the United States the frontier made it a practical necessity long before it was used against British tyranny. Thoreau, Garrison, and Wendell Phillips espoused an anarchism based on the love of freedom.

_____. CRITICS AND CRUSADERS: A CENTURY OF AMERICAN PROTEST. New York: Henry Holt, 1946. xii, 572 p.

> This is a study of eighteen prime movers in forging American social progress in the nineteenth and early twentieth centuries. They include Garrison, Phillips, Margaret Fuller, Thoreau, Emma Goldman, Henry George, Thorstein Veblen, Lincoln Steffens, and Eugene Debs.

Mann, Arthur. "British Social Thought and American Reformers of the Progressive Era." MISSISSIPPI VALLEY HISTORICAL REVIEW 42 (March 1956): 672-92.

> Britain appeared as a social clinic to American reformers. British social thought influenced Americans broadly through literature, criticism, and theory.

_____. YANKEE REFORMERS IN THE URBAN AGE. Cambridge, Mass.: Harvard University Press, 1954. xiv, 314 p.

> This is a study of how Boston adjusted to modern industrial life during the last two decades of the nineteenth century. Mann examines the thought of social gospelers, Catholic reformers, Socialists, liberal editors, labor leaders, academicians, and others.

Marcell, David. "John Fiske, Chauncey Wright, and William James: A Dialogue on Progress." JOURNAL OF AMERICAN HISTORY 56 (March 1970): 802-18.

Marcell argues that the demarcation between the nineteenth and twentieth century, as seen by people in the years following, was not abrupt, but rather a shift in emphasis and style. He examines the ideas of Fiske, Wright, and James and shows that faith in progress did not end in the years following the turn of the twentieth century.

Marchand, C. Roland. THE AMERICAN PEACE MOVEMENT AND SOCIAL REFORM, 1898-1918. Princeton, N.J.: Princeton University Press, 1973. xix, 441 p.

This is an examination of the diverse efforts for peace. Marchand shows how international lawyers, business leaders, suffragists, social workers, and labor and religious leaders, as well as socialists, organized separately for peace.

Martin, James J. MEN AGAINST THE STATE: THE EXPOSITIORS OF INDIVIDUALIST ANARCHISM IN AMERICA, 1827-1908. Foreword by Harry Elmer Barnes. DeKalb, Ill.: Adrian Allen Associates, 1953. ix, 306 p.

Individualist anarchists viewed America as a place where human beings might live as they pleased, free from conformity or coercion from people or government. Leading spokesmen were Josiah Warren, Ezra Heywood, and Stephen Pearl Andrews.

Mathews, Donald G. "The Abolitionists and Slavery: The Critique Behind the Social Movement." JOURNAL OF SOUTHERN HISTORY 33 (May 1967): 163-82.

Scholars have argued that abolitionists did not understand slavery, but Mathews insists that behind their inflated rhetoric was astute insight and wide knowledge. They not only portrayed absolute power and its effect on people, but also demanded that reform produce social change.

Meier, August. NEGRO THOUGHT IN AMERICA, 1880-1915: RACIAL IDEOLOGIES IN THE AGE OF BOOKER T. WASHINGTON. Ann Arbor: University of Michigan Press, 1963. xii, 336 p.

Negroes struggled for desegregation and integration, but in forming civil rights organizations they appeared to be creating a segregated movement. Meier deals with Booker T. Washington's ideology which he argues accorded with the prevailing climate of opinion and was devoted both to accommodation and racial equality.

Merk, Frederick. MANIFEST DESTINY AND MISSION IN AMERICAN HISTORY: A REINTERPRETATION. New York: Alfred A. Knopf, 1963. xii, 266 p.

Merk maintains that the American people did not accept the program of a few publicists that the United States should take over the continent of North America with force if necessary. Continental expansion was not an expression of the national spirit.

Meyers, Marvin. THE JACKSONIAN PERSUASION: POLITICS AND BELIEF. Stanford, Calif.: Stanford University Press, 1957. vi, 231 p.

Meyers develops what he calls the "expressive role of politics." The Jacksonian appeal was to recall agrarian republican innocence to a society drawn to the main chance and the long chance.

Mohl, Raymond A. "Humanitarianism in the Preindustrial City: The New York Society for the Prevention of Pauperism, 1817-1823." JOURNAL OF AMERICAN HISTORY 57 (December 1970): 576-99.

Humanitarianism in the early nineteenth century was influenced by social transformations occasioned by immigration, urbanization, and industrialization. In urban centers such as New York City, voluntary organizations responded to demands for social control of social evils such as pauperism, which was regarded as an unnecessary and an eradicable evil.

Moore, Edward C. WILLIAM JAMES. New York: Washington Square Press, 1966. 194 p.

Pragmatism is placed in the developing context of James's intellectual system, and empiricism is depicted not as a reorientation of the past but as anticipation of future experience. The organizing theme of this study is James's concern for the relationship between science and man.

Moore, R. Laurence. EUROPEAN SOCIALISTS AND THE AMERICAN PROMISED LAND. New York: Oxford University Press, 1970. xxiii, 257 p.

European Socialists used America as an example to prove or disprove their contentions concerning Europe. In America, on the other hand, Socialists employed European predictions concerning the coming of socialism in this country to advance their cause, particularly between 1895 and 1905.

Moreau, John Adam. RANDOLPH BOURNE: LEGEND AND REALITY. Washington, D.C.: Public Affairs Press, 1966. viii, 227 p.

Bourne supported progressive education, pacifism, social, cultural criticism, and youth. This study indicates that the social critics of the 1910s and 1920s had talent and creativity, but their work was not based on reality because they held grassroots America in contempt.

Morrow, Ralph E. "The Proslavery Argument Revisited." MISSISSIPPI VALLEY HISTORICAL REVIEW 48 (June 1961): 79-94.

Morrow argues that proslavery supporters did not merely emphasize the South's conviction of the justice of slavery and the belief that her course would be vindicated. Proslavery writers looked at the South itself and attempted to reinforce the region's own psychological commitment to the institution.

Mosier, Richard D. MAKING THE AMERICAN MIND: SOCIAL AND MORAL IDEAS IN THE McGUFFEY READERS. New York: King's Crown Press, 1947. vi, 207 p.

McGuffey imposed a pattern of moral and social ideas on white men and Indians without really proving his point. The author of this study measures behavior patterns with sociological definitions.

Muller, Dorothea R. "Josiah Strong and American Nationalism: A Reevaluation." JOURNAL OF AMERICAN HISTORY 53 (December 1966): 487-503.

Strong has been portrayed mainly as an advocate of Anglo-Saxon imperialism based on the Darwinist idea of competition among nations and races. Muller sees him as a proponent of social Christianity who believed an Anglo-Saxon nation had an obligation to hasten the coming of the kingdom through evangelizing the world.

_____. "The Social Philosophy of Josiah Strong." CHURCH HISTORY 28 (June 1959): 183-201.

Strong's social philosophy indicates the harmony that existed between social Christianity and progressive reform. He emphasized the concepts stressed by both movements, such as faith in science, social use of evolution, an organic concept of society, and optimism concerning human nature and progress.

Murphree, Idus L. "The Evolutionary Anthropologists: The Progress of Mankind. The Concepts of Progress and Culture in the Thought of John Lubbock, Edward B. Tylor, and Lewis H. Morgan." PROCEEDINGS OF THE AMERICAN PHILO-SOPHICAL SOCIETY 105 (June 1961): 265-300.

The evolution of Lubbock, Tylor, and Morgan was the evolution of development and not the newer Darwinian mode of evolution through ordeal. Their concept of cumulative experience and the idea of progress almost seemed to duplicate the philosophical program of the Enlightenment.

Nagel, Paul C. ONE NATION INDIVISIBLE: THE UNION IN AMERICAN THOUGHT, 1776-1861. New York: Oxford University Press, 1964. viii, 328 p.

Nagel examines the meanings of the label "Union." He describes the shift from an early emphasis on Union as an experiment to one in which Union was viewed as a spirit or voluntary bond and finally as the idea that Union was an absolute.

_____. THE SACRED TRUST: AMERICAN NATIONALITY, 1798-1898. New York: Oxford University Press, 1971. xvi, 376 p.

Nationality is explicated in terms of an American "trust" and the obligation of being a "steward." The ideas, hopes, and fears as well as anxieties and doubts during different periods are described.

Nicklason, Fred. "Henry George: Social Gospeller." AMERICAN QUARTERLY 22 (Fall 1970): 649-64.

George believed that if his plan for a single tax was carried out, it would create a Christian society on earth. His writings both stimulated and reflected the social gospel movement and his weekly newspaper, THE STANDARD, drew clergymen and laymen to his side.

Noble, David W. THE PARADOX OF PROGRESSIVE THOUGHT. Minneapolis: University of Minnesota Press, 1958. x, 272 p.

This is a study of the climate of opinion of progressive-minded social philosophers such as Herbert Croly, Richard T. Ely, Charles Horton Cooley, and Thorstein Veblen. The paradox of progressive thought is viewing civilization as a mechanism and also including the innocence of the Garden on the wilderness in the American Empire.

Nolen, Claude H. THE NEGRO'S IMAGE IN THE SOUTH: THE ANATOMY OF WHITE SUPREMACY. Lexington: University of Kentucky Press, 1967. xix, 232 p.

Nolen shows the effects of prejudice on the white man's belief structure and the consequences for public policy and action. He traces the conceptual background of southern white racial attitudes and the forms they took in public policy.

O'Neill, William L. DIVORCE IN THE PROGRESSIVE ERA. New Haven, Conn.: Yale University Press, 1967. xii, 295 p.

Divorce was an essential part of the family system, because it served as a safety valve in the Victorian family when intimacy became suffocating. O'Neill examines the divorce controversy of the Progressive era, including the "New Morality," whose spokesmen exalted physical love and equated sexual fulfillment with happiness.

_____. EVERYONE WAS BRAVE: THE RISE AND FALL OF FEMINISM IN AMERICA. Chicago: Quadrangle, 1969. xi, 369 p.

O'Neill argues that the feminist movement was a failure. Women gained the right to vote but they remained second-class citizens and by the 1940s feminism was dead.

_____, ed. ECHOES OF REVOLT: THE MASSES, 1911-1917. Chicago: Quadrangle, 1966. 303 p.

The writers and artists of THE MASSES were Max Eastman, Floyd Dell, Sherwood Anderson, Amy Lowell, and William Rose Benet, to mention a few. This was a magazine devoted to fun and the class struggle that deflated stuffed shirts and attacked capitalism and oppression.

Osterweis, Rollin G. ROMANTICISM AND NATIONALISM IN THE OLD SOUTH. New Haven, Conn.: Yale University Press, 1949. x, 275 p.

The southern cult of chivalry is examined in this volume. It is argued that chivalry and romanticism made the Confederacy.

Paulson, Ross E. RADICALISM AND REFORM: THE VROOMAN FAMILY AND AMERICAN SOCIAL THOUGHT, 1836-1937. Lexington: University of Kentucky Press, 1968. xxiii, 299 p.

Hiram Perkins Vrooman fathered five sons who protested against the status quo in America. One was a social gospeller, another a functionary of the Socialist Labor Party, and still another a professional agitator, but all were distinguished by their rejection not only of the performance of society but of its professions.

Pease, William H., and Pease, Jane H. "Antislavery Ambivalence: Immediatism, Expediency, Race." AMERICAN QUARTERLY 17 (Winter 1965): 682-95.

Antislavery crusaders were ambivalent over the meaning of immediatism and also concerning the Negro himself. They seemed to agree only that immediate abolition meant immediate repentance from the sin of slavery, but they were undecided as to whether the Negro was equal or inferior to whites.

_____. BOUND WITH THEM IN CHAINS: A BIOGRAPHICAL HISTORY OF THE ANTISLAVERY MOVEMENT. Westport, Conn.: Greenwood, 1972. xvii, 334 p.

This volume includes short biographies of Maria Weston Chapman, Cassius Clay, Benjamin Lundy, Samuel May, Samuel Cornish, Joshua Giddings, and others. The authors show the diversity of the movement.

_____. THEY WHO WOULD BE FREE: BLACKS' SEARCH FOR FREEDOM, 1830-1861. New York: Atheneum, 1974. xi, 331 p.

This is an assessment of the goals and strategies of black leaders from 1830 to 1861. The Peases emphasize these blacks' powerlessness, factionalism, and inability to mobilize the black masses.

Perry, Lewis. RADICAL ABOLITIONISM: ANARCHY AND THE GOVERNMENT OF GOD IN ANTISLAVERY THOUGHT. Ithaca, N.Y.: Cornell University Press, 1973. xvi, 328 p.

Perry shows the inner dynamics and interconnections of radical religious ideas. He analyzes Garrison, Henry Wright, Bronson Alcott, Adin Ballou, Nathaniel Rogers, and others who espoused immediatism, nonresistance, communitarianism, "come-outerism," and anarchism.

_____. "'We Have Had Conversation in the World': The Abolitionists and Spontaneity." CANADIAN REVIEW OF AMERICAN STUDIES 6 (Spring 1975): 3-26.

Abolitionists and other antebellum reformers may be on their way to being stereotyped as resisters of change and middle-class citizens who wanted to display their virtues in a society that was losing sight of standards. Perry argues that seeing nothing but repression is a mistake and he suggests that they should be viewed as persons with faith in the ability of men and women to escape from sin and enter a new life.

Pfeifer, Edward J. "The Scientific Source of Henry George's Evolutionary Theories." PACIFIC HISTORICAL REVIEW 36 (November 1967): 397-404.

George's source was not reform Darwinism but the neo-Lamarkian theory of evolution. The neo-Lamarkians believed the environment overshadowed natural selection in channeling evolutionary changes and George used this to challenge Spencer and Sumner.

Pivar, David J. PURITY CRUSADE: SEXUAL MORALITY AND SOCIAL CONTROL, 1868-1900. Westport, Conn.: Greenwood, 1973. x, 308 p.

The social purity crusade began before the Civil War as a quest for social perfection led by antislavery reformers, feminists, and Quakers. Purity reform included attacks on liquor, prostitution, and white slavery that were spearheaded by the American Purity Alliance.

Pollack, Norman. THE POPULIST RESPONSE TO INDUSTRIAL AMERICA: MIDWESTERN POPULIST THOUGHT. Cambridge, Mass.: Harvard University Press, 1962. 166 p.

Pollack argues that populism was a progressive and radical social force that accepted industrialization and sought an alliance with labor. Populists looked forward rather than backward, and were neither anti-Semitic, isolationist, nor proto-Fascist.

Post, Albert. POPULAR FREETHOUGHT IN AMERICA, 1825-1860. Studies in History, Economics, and Public Law, no. 497. New York: Columbia University Press, 1943. 258 p.

Robert Owen, his son Robert Dale, and Frances Wright were intellectual leaders of the freethinkers who devised rationalist alternatives to religion. In this volume their propaganda, organization, and scope are discussed.

Qualey, Carlton C., ed. THORSTEIN VEBLEN: THE CARLETON COLLEGE VEBLEN SEMINAR ESSAYS. New York: Columbia University Press, 1968. ix, 170 p.

Two essays in this collection stand out. Charles B. Friday shows that Veblen's ideas were relevant in the 1960s because he foresaw to some extent the welfare state and wasteful consumption, while David Noble argues that Veblen was a Puritan whose criticisms of business were based on a belief in a mythical Eden which business had destroyed.

Quandt, Jean B. FROM SMALL TOWN TO GREAT COMMUNITY: THE SOCIAL THOUGHT OF PROGRESSIVE INTELLECTUALS. New Brunswick, N.J.: Rutgers University Press, 1970. vii, 260 p.

This is a study of the concept of community held by Jane Addams, Frederic Howe, William Allen White, John Dewey, Charles Horton Cooley, and other intellectuals. Each was born in a small town, but each sought a larger type of solidarity based on the assumptions that society is organic and people must unite through communication.

Quarles, Benjamin. BLACK ABOLITIONISTS. New York: Oxford University Press, 1969. x, 310 p.

Quarles charts the cooperation that existed between black and white antislavery leaders. He also emphasizes that blacks wanted integration and equality, and that pride in blackness was part of their search for dignity.

Quint, Howard H. THE FORGING OF AMERICAN SOCIALISM: ORIGINS OF THE MODERN MOVEMENT. Columbia: University of South Carolina Press, 1953. ix, 409 p.

Bellamy's nationalism, Christian socialism, populism, Marxism, and anarchism were all part of the same stream. This study is based on left-wing periodicals from 1886 to 1901.

Rader, Benjamin G. THE ACADEMIC MIND AND REFORM: THE INFLUENCE OF RICHARD T. ELY IN AMERICAN LIFE. Lexington: University of Kentucky Press, 1966. vi, 276 p.

Ely was a Christian Socialist reformer from 1884-94, but this impulse conflicted with his scholarly ambitions. He and the economics department at the University of Wisconsin influenced Wisconsin progressivism.

_____. "Richard T. Ely: Lay Spokesman for the Social Gospel." JOURNAL OF AMERICAN HISTORY 53 (June 1966): 61-74.

Ely, the economist, was as influential as any clergyman in advancing the social gospel. His writings influenced reform ministers and as a distinguished academician he commanded a high aura of authority on social problems.

Ratner, Lorman. POWDER KEG: NORTHERN OPPOSITION TO THE ANTI-SLAVERY MOVEMENT, 1831-1840. New York: Basic Books, 1968. xii, 172 p.

This is a study of antiabolition thought in New England and the Middle States in the 1830s. Ratner shows that abolitionism came under attack because of antiblack prejudice, the belief that foreigners were directing American antislavery, the contention that slavery was guaranteed by the constitution, and the fear that abolition agitation would lead to violence.

Redkey, Edwin S. "Bishop Turner's African Dream." JOURNAL OF AMERICAN HISTORY 54 (September 1967): 271-90.

Henry McNeal Turner (1834-1915) pushed his way into the upper levels of Negro leadership although he lacked formal education and was disdained by Negro intellectuals. He was always hostile to the United States and developed an infatuation with Africa.

Riegel, Robert E. AMERICAN FEMINISTS. Lawrence: University of Kansas Press, 1963. xii, 223 p.

Riegel presents women who played roles in the evolution of feminism and the reasons they did so. He believes that feminists overemphasized legal disabilities and that the division of functions between men and women was reasonable in terms of existing conditions.

Ringenbach, Paul T. TRAMPS AND REFORMERS, 1873-1916: THE DISCOVERY OF UNEMPLOYMENT IN NEW YORK. Westport, Conn.: Greenwood, 1973. xv, 224 p.

Attitudes concerning unemployment changed after 1893 from blaming laziness or inherited deficiencies to emphasizing social and economic conditions over which people had little control. This was shown in the abandonment of the workhouse and the call for farm colonies and vacant-lot gardening.

Rosenberg, Carol Smith. "Beauty, the Beast and Militant Woman: A Case Study in Sex Roles and Social Stress in Jacksonian America." AMERICAN QUARTERLY 23 (October 1971): 562-84.

This is an essay on the New York Female Moral Reform Society, assembled in 1834, that crusaded against the city's brothels and attempted to convert prostitutes to evangelical Protestantism. This work to reform sexual mores reflected an underlying resentment of the male-dominated society and an effort to create a less-constricted image of female identity.

Rosenberg, Charles E. "Sexuality, Class and Role in 19th-Century America." AMERICAN QUARTERLY 25 (May 1973): 131-53.

Beginning in the 1830s, medical and biological attitudes toward sex tended toward repression and control since these were important building blocks of personality. At the same time, these attitudes emphasized gender roles which implied conflict between the sexes.

Rossiter, Clinton. CONSERVATISM IN AMERICA. New York: Alfred A. Knopf, 1955. 328 p.

Rossiter defines the conservative tradition, traces its historical development, and proposes a conservative theory and program for American democracy. His program comes close to the liberalism of Adlai Stevenson, Reinhold Niebuhr, Arthur Schlesinger, Jr., and others.

Rucker, Darnell. THE CHICAGO PRAGMATISTS. Minneapolis: University of Minnesota Press, 1969. ix, 200 p.

The Chicago school was a rare thing in American thought because it consisted of a group of scholars in separate disciplines united by common presuppositions and a concern for relating scholarship to society. John Dewey was the leader, but George Herbert Mead, James H. Tufts, and James Rowland Angel played important roles.

Sancton, Thomas A. "Looking Inward: Edward Bellamy's Spiritual Crisis." AMERICAN QUARTERLY 26 (December 1973): 538-57.

Writers have argued that LOOKING BACKWARD was the product of Bellamy's religious philosophy. Sancton attempts to prove that the novel grew out of severe depression in the early 1870s and represented the substitution of the military, among other things, for the self and individuality.

Schlossman, Steven L. "The 'Culture of Poverty' in Ante-Bellum Social Thought." SCIENCE AND SOCIETY 38 (Summer 1974): 150-66.

The culture of poverty is not a twentieth-century idea. It was articulated by urban, middle-class citizens in antebellum America, who warned that the public must intervene in the lives of the youth of the foreign born in order to preserve the cities.

Schultz, Stanley K. "The Morality of Politics: The Muckrakers' Vision of Democracy." JOURNAL OF AMERICAN HISTORY 52 (December 1965): 527-47.

Democracy in muckraker thought was a moral force. The muckrakers exposed evil because it was the nature of man as a moral creature that held hope for America.

Semonche, John E. RAY STANNARD BAKER: A QUEST FOR DEMOCRACY IN MODERN AMERICA, 1870-1918. Chapel Hill: University of North Carolina Press, 1969. ix, 350 p.

Baker is depicted as a reformer and Progressive. This side of his work is emphasized rather than his role as a journalist during a period when journalism was burgeoning.

Shalhope, Robert E. "Race, Class, Slavery, and the Antebellum Southern Mind." JOURNAL OF SOUTHERN HISTORY 37 (November 1971): 557-76.

Shalhope examines the theories of Eugene Genovese and Wilbur Cash-Charles Sellers concerning slavery as a cause of the Civil War and suggests that both class consciousness and race were significant in the southern mind. He demonstrates that the objectives of the few thousand Confederates who fled to Mexico following the war included maintaining a planter society.

_____. "Thomas Jefferson's Republicanism and Antebellum Southern Thought." JOURNAL OF SOUTHERN HISTORY 42 (November 1976): 529-56.

Using cognitive theory, Shalhope criticizes both traditional and revisionist interpretations of Jefferson's liberalism. He argues that Jefferson's thought suggests the republican consensus of the Revolution broke apart with the South retaining agrarian republicanism and that Jefferson held to a pastoral ideology resting on slavery.

Smiley, David L. "Cassius M. Clay and John G. Fee: A Study in Southern Anti-Slavery Thought." JOURNAL OF NEGRO HISTORY 42 (July 1957): 201-13.

Although from the same county in Kentucky, Clay and Fee differed in their antislavery views. Clay saw slavery as harmful to white laborers and to a diversified economy in the South, while Fee emphasized religion and condemned slavery because of a "higher law."

Smith, Wilson. PROFESSORS AND PUBLIC ETHICS: STUDIES OF NORTHERN MORAL PHILOSOPHERS BEFORE THE CIVIL WAR. Ithaca, N.Y.: Cornell University Press for the American Historical Association, 1956. viii, 244 p.

Smith traces moral philosophy out of its European backgrounds and identifies his philosophers with Whig ethics. These ethics were a combination of Christian principles and social responsibilities, but they tended to be conservative.

Solomon, Barbara Miller. ANCESTORS AND IMMIGRANTS: A CHANGING NEW ENGLAND TRADITION. Cambridge, Mass.: Harvard University Press, 1956. xii, 276 p.

This is a study of the changing attitudes of upper-class Bostonians toward immigrants from before the Civil War to the 1930s. These attitudes changed from sympathy to immigration restriction.

_____. "The Intellectual Background of Immigration Restriction in New England." NEW ENGLAND QUARTERLY 25 (March 1952): 47-59.

With the death of Brahmin life in the 1890s came a movement for immigration restriction. The idealization of the New England heritage hardened into idolatry which destroyed the creative experimental quality of the past and repudiated a free America.

Somkin, Fred. UNQUIET EAGLE: MEMORY AND DESIRE IN THE IDEA OF AMERICAN FREEDOM, 1815-1860. Ithaca, N.Y.: Cornell University Press, 1967. xi, 233 p.

Somkin examines the social attitudes of clergymen, Fourth-of-July orators, and literary figures. All in all, these moralists of the Jacksonian generation attempted to reinforce social and political values they imputed to the founding fathers.

Southern, David W. THE MALIGNANT HERITAGE: YANKEE PROGRESSIVES AND THE NEGRO QUESTION, 1901-1914. Chicago: Loyola University Press, 1968. x, 116 p.

Southern depicts the racism of northern Progressives as being more subtle than that of their southern contemporaries. He also argues that their prejudice hastened the triumph of racism in America.

Spain, August O. THE POLITICAL THEORY OF JOHN C. CALHOUN. New York: Bookman Associates, 1951. 306 p.

As a political thinker, Calhoun argued first from principles and rarely from experience and observation. Spain summarizes his ideas.

Spann, Edward K. IDEALS AND POLITICS: NEW YORK INTELLECTUALS AND LIBERAL DEMOCRACY, 1820-1880. Albany: State University of New York Press, 1972. xii, 269 p.

This book purports to be "a historian's version of the novels of C.P. Snow, studies of the interplay of human personalities and the clash of attitudes within a group devoted to a common enterprise." The group includes William Cullen Bryant, James Fenimore Cooper, William Leggett, Parke Godwin, and others, and the common enterprise is the liberal democratic tradition.

Sproat, John G. "THE BEST MEN": LIBERAL REFORMERS IN THE GILDED AGE. New York: Oxford University Press, 1968. ix, 356 p.

Social ideas and politics of college-educated men in post-Civil War America are analyzed. These people looked to Carl Schurz, in politics, and E.L. Godkin, in journalism, as model reformers, and they created a brand of liberalism that failed with the Mug-wump revolt of 1884.

Stewart, James Brewer. "Peaceful Hopes and Violent Experiences; The Evolution of Reforming and Radical Abolitionism, 1831-1837." CIVIL WAR HISTORY 17 (December 1971): 293-309.

Stewart contends that negative reactions to moral suasion caused the immediatists to alter their beliefs and strategies. Garrison's perfectionism evolved from his own ideas and experiences.

Stoller, Leo. AFTER WALDEN: THOREAU'S CHANGING VIEWS ON ECONOMIC MAN. Stanford, Calif.: Stanford University Press, 1957. viii, 163 p.

Thoreau rejected the individualism, primitivism, and irresponsibility of the Walden period and no longer advised man to resign from industrial society. Thoreau's thoughts on conservation are delineated.

Tager, Jack. THE INTELLECTUAL AS URBAN REFORMER: BRAND WHITLOCK AND THE PROGRESSIVE MOVEMENT. Cleveland: Press of Case Western Reserve University, 1968. 198 p.

Whitlock is portrayed as an intellectual and novelist who made his name as the reform mayor of Toledo, Ohio. Tager examines his efforts to adapt Jeffersonian ideals of freedom for all men in the new urban-industrial America.

Thomas, John L. "Romantic Reform in America, 1815-1865." AMERICAN QUARTERLY 17 (Winter 1965): 656-81.

Reform in the antebellum era was based on the romantic faith in human perfectability. Abolitionists and other reformers practiced the faith that if society could be rearranged to remove oppressive features then the individual could flourish as a reservoir of possibilities.

_____. "Utopia for an Urban Age: Henry George, Henry Demarest Lloyd, Edward Bellamy." PERSPECTIVES IN AMERICAN HISTORY 6 (1972): 135-66.

Thomas examines the identical concerns of George, Lloyd, and Bellamy in adjusting the older agrarian realities to a new, urban, industrial America. Each held a liberal faith composed of natural law and evangelical attitudes.

Thorpe, Earl E. EROS AND FREEDOM IN SOUTHERN LIFE AND THOUGHT. Durham, N.C.: Seeman Printery, Harrington Publications, 1967. xii, 210 p.

The violent and hateful side of race relations in the Old South has obscured the intimacy and affection that existed between Negroes and whites. Freedom or nonrepression was the central theme of southern history and most blacks benefitted from it.

Timberlake, James H. PROHIBITION AND THE PROGRESSIVE MOVEMENT, 1900-1920. Cambridge, Mass.: Harvard University Press, 1963. 238 p.

This is an examination of the religious, scientific, economic, and political arguments of the dry crusade. It also briefly covers the Anti-Saloon League and the campaign for the Eighteenth Amendment.

Tomsich, John. A GENTEEL ENDEAVOR: AMERICAN CULTURE AND POLITICS IN THE GILDED AGE. Stanford, Calif.: Stanford University Press, 1971. 236 p.

This is a study of eight Gilded Age writers including Charles Eliot Norton, George W. Curtis, and Thomas Bailey Aldrich. Known as "Mugwumps," these men spoke for a humanistic high culture designed to promote social stability in an age of change and technology.

Tyack, David. GEORGE TICKNOR AND THE BOSTON BRAHMINS. Cambridge, Mass.: Harvard University Press, 1967. x, 289 p. ·

Tyack concentrates on the intellectual framework in which Ticknor functioned as a teacher, scholar, critic, and Brahmin leader. He pictures the Bostonian as a man eager to create a conservative persuasion and fashion standards of tastes and propriety.

Tyler, Robert L. "The I.W.W. and the Brainworkers." AMERICAN QUARTERLY 15 (Spring 1963): 41-51.

Technology and applied science made the Marxist projection of
class struggle and poverty virtually meaningless, and some socialists
in America recognized this historical fact. The Industrial Workers
of the World made the most explicit theoretical connection between
the scientist and the old proletarian and tried to adapt Marxist
orthodoxy to technology.

Van Deusen, Glyndon G. "Some Aspects of Whig Thought and Theory in the
Jacksonian Period." AMERICAN HISTORICAL REVIEW 63 (January 1958):
305-22.

One of the most important aspects of Whig thought was optimism
concerning the future of the country. Whigs stood with the Jacksonians as one people who believed that the success of a part was
the success of the whole.

Walters, Ronald G. THE ANTISLAVERY APPEAL: AMERICAN ABOLITIONISM
AFTER 1830. Baltimore: Johns Hopkins University Press, 1976. xvii, 196 p.

Walters emphasizes the cultural and social situation that gave abolition its style. Abolitionists reflected a desire to impose order on
a rapidly changing society and their in-fighting helped to unify
them by setting limits for self-definition.

_____. "The Erotic South: Civilization and Sexuality in American Abolition-
ism." AMERICAN QUARTERLY 25 (May 1973): 175-201.

Immediatist antislavery after 1830 was the product of changing attitudes toward sex. Abolitionists symbolized an erotic South as
something negative and regressive because they wanted to control
man's animal nature.

_____. "The Family and Ante-Bellum Reform: An Interpretation." SOCIETAS
3 (Summer 1973): 221-32.

The forty years before the Civil War have been characterized as
an age of individualism, but writings on the family belie this assumption. Many writers focused on the redeeming value of the
family and prominent among their ideas was a desire to guide sexual proclivities and thus bring about social control.

Warren, Sidney. AMERICAN FREETHOUGHT, 1860-1914. Studies in History,
Economics, and Public Law, no. 504. New York: Columbia University Press,
1943. 257 p.

Freethought includes deism, atheism, agnosticism, and other positions opposed to religious orthodoxy. Warren discusses the liberating influence of Darwinian theories and portrays the changes in
freethought in response to the social conditions of the late nineteenth century.

Weinberg, Albert K. MANIFEST DESTINY: A STUDY OF NATIONALIST EXPANSIONISM IN AMERICAN HISTORY. Baltimore: Johns Hopkins University Press, 1935. xiii, 559 p.

This is a study of the evolving attitudes concerning manifest destiny from the Revolution to the 1930s. Expansionists justified their accomplishments under an ideology that included natural rights, extension of the area of freedom, self-defense, and world leadership.

Weinberg, Julius. "E.A. Ross: The Progressive as Nativist." WISCONSIN MAGAZINE OF HISTORY 50 (Spring 1967): 242-53.

Ross was a Populist and Progressive, but he was also a nativist who opposed southern and eastern European immigrants. He was deeply committed to the men and women of rural America and ambivalent toward the city, its inhabitants, and their ways.

_____. EDWARD ALSWORTH ROSS AND THE SOCIOLOGY OF PROGRESSIVISM. Madison: State Historical Society of Wisconsin, 1972. xii, 260 p.

Weinberg argues that Ross's boyhood as an orphan in Iowa determined his reformist and sociological views. This experience caused him to reject determinism and emphasize free will.

White, G. Edward. "The Social Values of the Progressives: Some New Perspectives." SOUTH ATLANTIC QUARTERLY 65 (Winter 1971): 62-76.

White stresses common views and shared persuasions. He indicates that progressivism had four sets of values--Anglo-Saxonism, moral righteousness, popular elitism, and progress.

Wilson, Major L. "The Concept of Time and the Political Dialogue in the United States, 1828-1848." AMERICAN QUARTERLY 19 (Winter 1967): 619-44.

Americans between 1828 and 1848 were avowedly liberal, but a dialogue existed on the kind of liberal society that should be built. At the core of this debate was the question as to whether freedom was complete at the beginning or the end of the process.

_____. "The Free Soil Concept of Progress and the Irrepressible Conflict." AMERICAN QUARTERLY 22 (Winter 1970): 769-90.

Free-Soilers expressed an idea of progress based on the belief that the nation had begun its career with a perfect and complete design. Slavery expansion represented a regression from this idea.

_____. "'Liberty and Union': An Analysis of Three Concepts Involved in the Nullification Controversy." JOURNAL OF SOUTHERN HISTORY 33 (August 1967): 331-55.

Arguments on the past of those who wanted to save the Union in the nullification crisis involved also a presentation of ideas concerning the form of the liberal society yet to be created. Wilson examines the thinking of Daniel Webster, John Quincy Adams, and Andrew Jackson.

_____. "The Repressible Conflict: Seward's Concept of Progress and the Free-Soil Movement." JOURNAL OF SOUTHERN HISTORY 37 (November 1971): 533-56.

Historians have explained the course of William Seward's thought from his radicalism in 1850 to his disposition to conciliate the South during the secession crisis in various ways. Wilson argues that Seward was consistent if his concept of progress is examined.

_____. SPACE, TIME, AND FREEDOM: THE QUEST FOR NATIONALITY AND THE IRRESPRESSIBLE CONFLICT, 1815-1861. Westport, Conn.: Greenwood, 1974. x, 309 p.

A history of nationalism, this study identifies the concept with space, time, and freedom. From a corporate concept of freedom, such as Henry Clay's American system, the idea advanced to liberty for individuals under the Jacksonians.

Wilson R. Jackson. "Experience and Utopia: The Making of Edward Bellamy's LOOKING BACKWARD." JOURNAL OF AMERICAN STUDIES 11 (April 1977): 45-60.

In LOOKING BACKWARD and other works, the industrial city was a thing of the past. Instead of forecasting a futuristic, technological utopia, Ballamy was unwilling to confront the industrial city with its factories and proletarian labor force.

_____. IN QUEST OF COMMUNITY: SOCIAL PHILOSOPHY IN THE UNITED STATES, 1860-1920. New York: John Wiley and Sons, 1968. viii, 177 p.

Wilson examines the idea of community in the thought of Charles S. Pierce, James M. Baldwin, Edward A. Ross, G. Stanley Hall, and Josiah Royce. These intellectuals were part of a revolution that occurred after 1860 in which Americans came to believe that the individual was part of and dependent on his society.

Wood, Forrest G. BLACK SCARE: THE RACIST RESPONSE TO EMANCIPATION AND RECONSTRUCTION. Berkeley and Los Angeles: University of California Press, 1968. ix, 219 p.

This study is principally valuable for the insights it provides on the sexual aspects of racism during the Civil War and Reconstruction. It deals with psychosexual pathology in analyzing human behavior.

Woodward, C. Vann. AMERICAN COUNTERPOINT: SLAVERY AND RACISM IN THE NORTH-SOUTH DIALOGUE. Boston: Little, Brown, 1971. 301 p.

> The South's emphasis on leisure represented an attachment to the life-style condemned by the Protestant ethic. Southern life generally was flawed by a high commitment to white supremacy based on a paternalistic concept of race relations.

_____. THE STRANGE CAREER OF JIM CROW. New York: Oxford University Press, 1955. xii, 155 p.

> Woodward explodes the myth that segregation was established by the "redeemers" in the South who regained control from Reconstruction governments. Except for schools, segregation came later and benefitted from the passive leadership of Booker T. Washington.

Zetterbaum, Marvin. TOCQUEVILLE AND THE PROBLEM OF DEMOCRACY. Stanford, Calif.: Stanford University Press, 1967. ix, 185 p.

> The central questions of Tocqueville's commitment to democracy-equality as the principle of a naturally just regime are analyzed. Zetterbaum also indicates that the principle of material interest is Tocqueville's panacea for the decay of civic virtue and human excellence in democratic times.

1915 TO THE PRESENT

Alexander, Charles C. NATIONALISM IN AMERICAN THOUGHT, 1930-1945. Chicago: Rand McNally, 1969. xiii, 272 p.

> Nationalism and the New Deal are the key subjects in this study. The internationalist flourishes of Franklin Roosevelt's foreign policy did not counter the basic nationalism of American life.

Anderson, Clifford B. "The Metamorphosis of American Agrarian Idealism in the 1920's and 1930's." AGRICULTURAL HISTORY 35 (October 1961): 182-88.

> Agrarianism was very much alive in the 1920s and 1930s, but the emphasis was shifting from moral to economic terms. The moral belief that agriculture was basic because it fed and clothed America gave way to the economic conviction that agriculture was important because of its purchasing power.

Auerbach, M. Morton. THE CONSERVATIVE ILLUSION. New York: Columbia University Press, 1959. xiv, 359 p.

> Auerbach analyzes the writings of Allen Tate, Russell Kirk, Clinton Rossiter, Peter Drucker, Daniel Boorstin, and others. He tests their ideas for viability against the movement of events.

Bacciocco, Edward T. THE NEW LEFT IN AMERICA: REFORM TO REVOLU-
TION, 1956-1970. Stanford, Calif.: Hoover Institution Press, 1974. xvi,
300 p.

This is a narrative of the history of the New Left from the 1950s
to the demise of the Students for a Democratic Society (SDS).
Lunch counter sit-ins, the election of John F. Kennedy, advent of
Castro, and the influence of C. Wright Mills brought the New
Left into existence.

Beitzinger, A.J. "The Idea of Freedom in Contemporary American Political
Thought." REVIEW OF POLITICS 35 (October 1973): 475-88.

The idea of freedom in the thought of B.F. Skinner, Erich Fromm,
Herbert Marcuse, Walter Lippmann, and others is discussed. Each
thinker has been concerned with the aimlessness, conformist anonym-
ity, and destructive aspects of American life.

Belz, Herman. "Changing Conceptions of Constitutionalism in the Era of World
War II and the Cold War." JOURNAL OF AMERICAN HISTORY 59 (December
1972): 640-69.

Constitutionalism is a major theme of political thought that emphasizes the role of written constitutions in defining the framework,
purposes, and values of the polity. The threat of totalitarianism
caused neoconstitutionalists to argue that the constitution be used
to organize power in the presidency, but it also made them ask
that the power of the state be checked.

Bennion, Sherilyn Cox. "Reform Agitation in the American Periodical Press,
1920-29." JOURNALISM QUARTERLY 48 (Winter 1971): 652-59, 713.

During the twenties, most popular magazines showed pride in America, respect for business, and a lack of concern for social problems. But crusading was not over, particularly among intellectuals
who expressed discontent in spite of the small audiences they attracted.

Bordeau, Edward J. "John Dewey's Ideas about the Great Depression." JOUR-
NAL OF THE HISTORY OF IDEAS 32 (January-March 1971): 67-84.

Dewey's political theory justifiably has been criticized as "metho-
dolatry" and "intellectualism." During the Depression, however,
he supported the League for Independent Political Action, an organization that served as a clearinghouse for independent radical
groups to work for the creation of a third party.

Borning, Bernard C. THE POLITICAL AND SOCIAL THOUGHT OF CHARLES
A. BEARD. Seattle: University of Washington Press, 1962. xxvi, 315 p.

Borning shows that Beard was dedicated to social ideas and civil liberties, but he was philosophically inconsistent. He traces Beard's thought from early economic materialism to ethical ideas concerning social direction and historical meaning.

Broderick, Francis L. W.E.B. DUBOIS: NEGRO LEADER IN A TIME OF CRISIS. Stanford, Calif.: Stanford University Press, 1959. xvi, 259 p.

This is an analysis of the development of DuBois's ideas. Broderick covers his long career from boyhood to his flirtation with the extreme left in the 1950s and presents his changing thought in the context of time and place.

Butler, Johnnella, and Marable, Manning. "The New Negro and the Ideological Origins of the Integrationist Movement." JOURNAL OF ETHNIC STUDIES 2 (Winter 1975): 47-55.

Negro intellectuals in literature and politics during the 1920s were proud of being Negroes, but they also sought assimilation. The Negro renaissance lacked a cultural philosophy autonomous from white America, but it expressed the reality of the psychological mulatto.

Chadwin, Mark Lincoln. THE HAWKS OF WORLD WAR II. Chapel Hill: University of North Carolina Press, 1968. ix, 310 p.

Chadwin analyzes the ideas and activities of the Century Group and the Fight for Freedom Committee that attempted to convince Americans in 1940-41 to join the fight against Hitler. Their militancy gave the Roosevelt administration room to maneuver in coping with isolationist critics.

Chambers, Clarke A. "The Belief in Progress in Twentieth-Century America." JOURNAL OF THE HISTORY OF IDEAS 19 (April 1958): 197-224.

Americans have had an absolute faith in progress as a rule of life in spite of critics such as Reinhold Niebuhr, Frederic C. Howe, Lewis Mumford, and others. Despite depression and war, Henry Luce, Robert Sherwood, and David Sarnoff sounded progress themes in the 1950s.

_____. PAUL U. KELLOGG AND THE SURVEY: VOICES FOR SOCIAL WELFARE AND SOCIAL JUSTICE. Minneapolis: University of Minnesota Press, 1971. xii, 283 p.

Kellogg was editor of the SURVEY MIDMONTHLY and SURVEY GRAPHIC following 1912 and helped shape liberal reform-social work ideology. He was committed to the ideal of democratic social engineering and to the benevolent potential of government under the aegis of professionals, experts, and social technicians.

_____. SEEDTIME OF REFORM: AMERICAN SOCIAL SERVICE AND SOCIAL ACTION, 1918-1933. Minneapolis: University of Minnesota Press, 1963. xx, 326 p.

Chambers shows that private social welfare organizations grew in sophistication during the 1920s. Progressivism remained viable by absorbing new techniques from psychology and psychiatry, and through movements to eliminate child labor, protect working women, and ameliorate slums.

Chatfield, Charles. FOR PEACE AND JUSTICE: PACIFISM IN AMERICA, 1914-1941. Knoxville: University of Tennessee Press, 1971. xiii, 447 p.

This study is an analysis of the ideas, programs, and tactics of pacifists in which the author emphasizes fundamental values. Pacifists crusaded for disarmament, opposed compulsory ROTC, attacked munitions makers, and often worked in the Socialist Party.

Clark, Norman H. DELIVER US FROM EVIL: AN INTERPRETATION OF AMERICAN PROHIBITION. New York: W.W. Norton and Co., 1976. 246 p.

Prohibition became a social movement when public drunkenness became a social problem. As a movement, it must be examined in terms of the motive and tradition behind it, and it should not be regarded as the antithesis of reform.

Clecak, Peter. RADICAL PARADOXES: DILEMMAS OF THE AMERICAN LEFT, 1945-1970. New York: Harper and Row, 1973. x, 358 p.

This is a study of the contradictions in the thought principally of C. Wright Mills, Paul Baran, Paul Sweezy, and Herbert Marcuse, whom the author calls "plain Marxists" to differentiate them from other thinkers on the Left. Among the paradoxes Clecak examines are powerlessness and the contradiction between democracy and revolutionary socialism.

Cohen, Bronwen J. "Nativism and Western Myth: The Influence of Nativist Ideas on the American Self-Image." JOURNAL OF AMERICAN STUDIES 8 (April 1974): 23-39.

Cohen shows that interest in the West grew at the time a scientific racial rationale for restricting immigration grew in the 1920s. He believes these developments were related since Western writers portrayed blonde, blue-eyed cowboys and emphasized the power of Saxon Americans over Mexicans.

Cooper, John Milton, Jr. THE VANITY OF POWER: AMERICAN ISOLATIONISM AND THE FIRST WORLD WAR, 1914-1917. Westport, Conn.: Greenwood, 1969. xii, 271 p.

The isolationist position was not completed until Wilson opted for war and called for a future world organization. Among foreign policy idealists, agrarian-minded Democrats followed Wilson, while Progressive Republicans developed neoisolationism.

Coser, Lewis A., and Howe, Irving, eds. THE NEW CONSERVATIVES: A CRITIQUE FROM THE LEFT. New York: Quadrangle, 1974. viii, 343 p.

The new conservatism of the 1960s represented a response from social scientists and editors to New Left activists and counterculturists. In publications such as COMMENTARY and PUBLIC INTEREST, intellectuals such as Patrick Moynihan, Irving Kristol, and Seymour Martin Lipset regailed against the New Leftists.

Crockatt, Richard. "American Liberalism and the Atlantic World, 1916-17." JOURNAL OF AMERICAN STUDIES 11 (April 1977): 123-43.

Contemporary historians speak of "Jacksonian liberalism" and Lincoln's "liberal nationalism," but the term "liberal" was not used in the United States in a political sense before the twentieth century. It entered the political vocabulary during 1916 in the pages of the NEW REPUBLIC.

Cross, Whitney R. "Ideas in Politics: The Conservation Policies of the Two Roosevelts." JOURNAL OF THE HISTORY OF IDEAS 14 (June 1953): 421-38.

Cross argues against the assumption that there has been little distinction between liberal and conservative statesmen. Using the conservation policies of the Roosevelts, he shows that both introduced collectivist solutions, but also steadfastly believed in individualism, an individualism that yielded to social responsibility.

Cywar, Alan. "John Dewey: Toward Domestic Reconstruction, 1915-1920." JOURNAL OF THE HISTORY OF IDEAS 30 (July-September 1969): 385-400.

Dewey pursued domestic reconstruction throughout World War I, as he had before. He emphasized education in the remaking of society and he subsumed the voluntary association as a reform technique into a decentralized system of worker unions.

Deleon, David. "The American as Anarchist: Social Criticism." AMERICAN QUARTERLY 25 (December 1973): 516-37.

Social critics of the 1960s did not direct their attacks on any particular institution. Criticism was directed against the egalitarian, pacifist mythology of the federal government.

De Maio, Gerald. "Richard Weaver, Southerner: The Paradox of American Conservatism." CANADIAN REVIEW OF AMERICAN STUDIES 7 (Fall 1976): 176-86.

Weaver was a rhetorician who taught at the University of Chicago, but he was also one of the originators of the new conservatism of the 1950s and 1960s. In his studies of the nature of regimes, particularly the South, he celebrated classical liberalism in the constitution and the FEDERALIST.

DiClerico, Robert. "The New Left: An Alternative Vision." SOUTH ATLANTIC QUARTERLY 75 (Summer 1976): 339-50.

DiClerico focuses on one aspect of New Left thought--a proposed alternative to the current U.S. political system. New Leftists emphasized that individuals would be self-fulfilled and self-actualized if only they had control over their own lives through participatory democracy.

Diggins, John P. THE AMERICAN LEFT IN THE TWENTIETH CENTURY. New York: Harcourt Brace Jovanovich, 1973. xii, 210 p.

Diggins is interested in three American Lefts--the "Lyrical Left" of World War I, the Old Left of the Depression, and the New Left of the 1960s. He uses generational rebellion as the unifying concept.

_____. "Flirtation with Fascism: American Pragmatic Liberals and Mussolini's Italy." AMERICAN HISTORICAL REVIEW 71 (January 1966): 487-506.

Mussolini's Fascist dictatorship gained more admiration from democratic America than any other Western nation. Fascism's appeal to liberals in the 1920s was found in its experimental nature, antidogmatic temper, and moral elan.

_____. "The Italo-American Anti-Fascist Opposition." JOURNAL OF AMERICAN HISTORY 54 (December 1967): 579-98.

Italo-American labor leaders, radical partisans, and a few liberal intellectuals produced one of the first anti-fascist campaigns in the 1920s. They were unable to convince the U.S. government to take a strong stand against dictatorship, however, and they did not cause the Italian masses to rally against Mussolini.

_____. "Mussolini and America: Hero-Worship, Charisma, and the 'Vulgar Talent.'" HISTORIAN 28 (August 1966): 559-85.

Many Americans in all walks of life eulogized Mussolini in the 1920s and 1930s. Activistic values such as experimentation and efficiency were seen in the Italian dictator and Americans made him into the image of their own domestic heroes.

Dorfman, Joseph. THE ECONOMIC MIND IN AMERICAN CIVILIZATION. Vols. 4-5: 1918-1933. New York: Viking Press, 1959. x, 398 p.; vii, 377 p.

Dorfman divides this period into the era of adjustment and progress (1918-29), and the Depression (1929-33). He covers monetary thinking in currency and banking, foreign trade policy, business cycle theory, unemployment and social insurance, and agricultural economics.

Douglass, Paul F. SIX UPON THE WORLD: TOWARD AN AMERICAN CULTURE FOR AN INDUSTRIAL AGE. Boston: Little, Brown, 1954. 443 p.

The ideas of Paul G. Hoffman, William Z. Foster, Alfred P. Sloan, Walter Reuther, Francis Cardinal Spellman, and James B. Conant are summarized. The author is confident that technology will produce a better social and economic order.

Duram, James C. NORMAN THOMAS. New York: Twayne, 1974. 176 p.

Thomas's voluminous writings are emphasized. The discussion of Thomas's respect by Americans while he presided over the demise of the Socialist Party is provocative.

Ekirch, Arthur A., Jr. IDEAS, IDEALS, AND AMERICAN DIPLOMACY: A HISTORY OF THEIR GROWTH AND INTERACTION. New York: Appleton-Century-Crofts, 1966. xiii, 205 p.

Ekirch surveys isolationism, the idea of mission, manifest destiny, overseas expansion, and other subjects up through the Cold War and Vietnam. There is difficulty relating the Cold War to earlier ideas because policies have undergone revolutionary changes.

_____. IDEOLOGIES AND UTOPIAS: THE IMPACT OF THE NEW DEAL ON AMERICAN THOUGHT. Chicago: Quadrangle, 1969. ix, 307 p.

This is a study of intellectual opinion concerning the New Deal. Ekirch covers the intellectual response to the Depression and the evolution of New Deal ideologies and policies.

Elias, Robert H. "ENTANGLING ALLIANCES WITH NONE": AN ESSAY ON THE INDIVIDUAL IN THE AMERICAN TWENTIES. New York: W.W. Norton, 1973. xvi, 228 p.

In this "climate-of-opinion" study, the author argues that when a number of ideas converge they present a historical experience. He discusses the importance of the thought of John B. Watson, Abraham Flexner, John Dewey, Henry Ford, Herbert Hoover, Al Capone, Marcus Garvey, and others.

Elsner, Henry, Jr. THE TECHNOCRATS: PROPHETS OF AUTOMATION. Syracuse: Syracuse University Press, 1967. vi, 252 p.

Technology was a craze of the 1930s when a group of engineers and publicists called for an end of the price system and the substitution of an economy based on the utilization of America's technology and natural resources. Led by an engineer named Howard Scott, the technocrats promised but did not deliver studies on comprehensive energy that would validate their notions.

Feuer, Lewis S. "American Travelers to the Soviet Union, 1917-1932: The Formation of a Component of New Deal Ideology." AMERICAN QUARTERLY 14 (Summer 1962): 119-49.

The New Deal was described from its earliest days as being pragmatic and experimental. Feuer shows that among the Americans who influenced New Deal policy and practice were those who traveled in the Soviet Union and were impressed by social experiments.

Finkle, Lee. "The Conservative Aims of Militant Rhetoric: Black Protest during World War II." JOURNAL OF AMERICAN HISTORY 60 (December 1973): 692-713.

As contrasted with the "Close Ranks" slogan of World War I where blacks were urged not to protest, the "Double V" protest of World War II has been viewed as the beginning of militant black protest. Black leaders and black newspapers actually took a conservative stance and tried to restrain militant elements.

Freedman, Estelle B. "The New Woman: Changing Views of Women in the 1920s." JOURNAL OF AMERICAN HISTORY 61 (September 1974): 372-93.

Freedman surveyed the scholarly literature, historical and otherwise, concerning women. She discovered that women were characterized as emancipated in terms of work and sex, although they did not vote as a bloc following the passage of the nineteenth amendment.

Fullenwider, S.P. THE MIND AND MOOD OF BLACK AMERICA: 20TH CENTURY THOUGHT. Homewood, Ill.: Dorsey Press, 1969. xi, 255 p.

The mind and mood of twentieth-century black Americans were filled with tensions. On the one hand, they were committed to the image of the "Christ-like" Negro who would be a living example of democratic and Christian potential, while, on the other, they harbored a deep hatred of white men because of oppression.

Fusfeld, Daniel R. THE ECONOMIC THOUGHT OF FRANKLIN D. ROOSEVELT AND THE ORIGINS OF THE NEW DEAL. New York: Columbia University Press, 1956. 337 p.

Roosevelt developed an economic philosophy between the time of his entrance to Harvard and his election to the presidency. As governor of New York, he did little to solve agricultural problems, but he developed a reforming attitude toward agriculture and business, and developed social welfare legislation.

Gardner, Lloyd C. ARCHITECTS OF ILLUSION: MEN AND IDEAS IN AMERICAN FOREIGN POLICY, 1941-1949. Chicago: Quadrangle, 1970. xi, 365 p.

Gardner blames the Cold War on American policymakers. He believes the United States failed to capitalize on opportunities for accommodation with the USSR, because of dedication to liberal objectives such as an end to spheres of influence and the maintenance of an open world.

Gatewood, Willard B., Jr. "Embattled Scholar: Howard W. Odum and the Fundamentalists, 1925-1927." JOURNAL OF SOUTHERN HISTORY 31 (November 1965): 375-92.

As a scholar in the University of North Carolina, Odum probed race, religion, and mill conditions, subjects that prompted criticism. This article covers the outbursts of evolutionists over two articles Odum permitted to be published in his JOURNAL OF SOCIAL FORCES.

_____. PREACHERS, PEDAGOGUES, AND POLITICIANS: THE EVOLUTION CONTROVERSY IN NORTH CAROLINA, 1920-1927. Chapel Hill: University of North Carolina Press, 1966. viii, 268 p.

North Carolina was one of a number of southern states where proscriptive legislation concerning Darwinism was defeated. A small group of journalists, academicians, politicians, and clergymen, and especially members of the university, spoke out against such a law.

Geselbracht, Raymond. "Recovering the New World Dream: Organic Evolution in the Work of Lewis Mumford." AMERICAN STUDIES 15 (Fall 1974): 5-20.

Geselbracht places Mumford in the intellectual stream of Emerson, Whitman, Thoreau, Charles Ives, and Frank Lloyd Wright. He shows that Mumford rethought the consequences of civilization and nature for each other and reevaluated the meaning of the former and inspiration of the latter for twentieth-century man.

Glazer, Penina Migdol. "From the Old Left to the New: Radical Criticism in the 1940s." AMERICAN QUARTERLY 24 (December 1972): 584-603.

The New Left had antecedents in the 1940s. The decline of communism and the rise of radical peace groups are charted.

Gordon, Linda. WOMAN'S BODY, WOMAN'S RIGHT: A SOCIAL HISTORY‌ OF BIRTH CONTROL IN AMERICA. New York: Grossman, 1976. xviii, 479 p.

This is more intellectual than social history, since the author emphasizes the ideas of Victoria Woodhull, Ezra Heywood, William J. Robinson, and others. There were three stages in the birth-control movement: "voluntary motherhood" (late nineteenth century), "birth control" (1910-20), and "planned parenthood" (after 1920).

Grantham, Dewey W., Jr. "The Regional Imagination: Social Scientists and the American South." JOURNAL OF SOUTHERN HISTORY 34 (February 1968): 3-32.

As the social sciences began to establish their separate identities by 1920, regional awareness developed. Charles S. Johnson, of Fisk University and Howard W. Odum, of the University of North Carolina, spearheaded the study of regional patterns and the identification of social problems.

Greer, Thomas H. WHAT ROOSEVELT THOUGHT: THE SOCIAL AND POLITICAL IDEAS OF FRANKLIN D. ROOSEVELT. East Lansing: Michigan State University Press, 1958. xvi, 244 p.

Greer depicts Roosevelt as a moral person who believed in divine guidance which afforded man considerable freedom in achieving the abundant life. He saw the state as an institution for fitting people for survival rather than as an instrument for presiding over the survival of the fittest.

Grimes, Alan P. EQUALITY IN AMERICA: RELIGION, RACE, AND THE URBAN MAJORITY. New York: Oxford University Press, 1964. x, 136 p.

Democracy in America resulted in an unequal division of freedom, placing superior power in the hands of the rural, white, Protestant majority. Urban centers challenged this unequal distribution, and equality became the standard for settling the dispute.

Hamby, Alonzo L. "The Liberals, Truman, and FDR as Symbol and Myth." JOURNAL OF AMERICAN HISTORY 56 (March 1970): 859-67.

Liberals, who were mainly middle-class reformers, but often described as intellectuals, were held together by beliefs in equal opportunity, economic security, racial equality, and other matters. They were demoralized after the death of Roosevelt because he symbolized their persuasion and gave them an identity Harry Truman could not provide.

Hitchcock, James. "The McCarthyism of the Left." SOUTH ATLANTIC QUARTERLY 69 (Spring 1970): 171-85.

Liberals have been under fire from the New Left as they had been during the McCarthy era. The inability of liberals to satisfy their critics as to their integrity and trustworthiness has much to do with the fact that the conspiratorial beliefs of the Right and Left go far beyond politics.

Hixson, William B. "The Negro Revolution and the Intellectuals." AMERICAN SCHOLAR 33 (Autumn 1964): 581-93.

American intellectuals have not reinforced the educated public's race prejudice, but they have reinforced its conservatism. Conservative theories such as consensus, pluralism, and human fallibility have placed a barrier between the "revolutionary" Negro and the intellectuals.

Hughes, H. Stuart. THE SEA CHANGE: THE MIGRATION OF SOCIAL THOUGHT, 1930-1965. New York: Harper and Row, 1975. x, 283 p.

Hughes describes the flight of intellectuals from fascism to England and America. He analyzes the impact of Franz Neumann, Gaetano Salvemini, Hannah Arendt, Max Horkheimer, Herbert Marcuse, and Erik Erikson, among others.

Jay, Martin. "The Frankfurt School in Exile." PERSPECTIVES IN AMERICAN HISTORY 6 (1972): 339-88.

This is a study of the Frankfurt Institute for Social Research's sixteen-year exile in the United States. These scholars saw changes of such magnitide as to render obsolete the Marxism they brought with them from Germany.

Johnpoll, Bernard K. PACIFIST'S PROGRESS: NORMAN THOMAS AND THE DECLINE OF AMERICAN SOCIALISM. Chicago: Quadrangle, 1970. xi, 336 p.

Johnpoll pictures Thomas as a middle-class intellectual and social gospel preacher who did not understand the aspirations of the working class. The morality he drew from Christianity proved fatal to American socialism.

Jonas, Manfred. ISOLATIONISM IN AMERICA, 1935-1941. Ithaca, N.Y.: Cornell University Press, 1966. xi, 315 p.

In the 1930s, radical isolationists believed a war would threaten New Deal goals, while conservatives thought global involvement would wreck free enterprise. The author argues that isolationists did not favor the neutrality legislation of the period and refused to assume the task of world leadership.

_____. "Pro-Axis Sentiment and American Isolationism." HISTORIAN 29 (February 1967): 221-37.

Isolationism in the 1930s was the direct result of the threat of a major war pitting Great Britain and France against Germany. American involvement was conceivable only if this country joined the side of the European democracies and for this reason isolationists supported Germany.

Jones, Alfred Haworth. "The Search for a Usable Past in the New Deal Era." AMERICAN QUARTERLY 23 (December 1971): 710-24.

The great crash discredited the symbols of an era of prosperity. In a time of insecurity, intellectuals dared not repudiate their forebears, and they rediscovered a heroic past embodied in the lives of nineteenth-century spokesmen for democracy.

Josephson, Harold. JAMES T. SHOTWELL AND THE RISE OF INTERNATIONALISM IN AMERICA. Rutherford, N.J.: Fairleigh Dickinson University Press, 1975. 330 p.

This study emphasizes the interwar period when Shotwell was most active as a peace worker. The Columbia historian articulated the present in his research and sought alternatives to war.

Kaplan, Sidney. "Social Engineers as Saviors: Effects of World War I on Some Americans." JOURNAL OF THE HISTORY OF IDEAS 17 (June 1956): 347-69.

This is an essay on the effect of World War I on Dewey, Croly, Lippmann, and Bourne. The war affected these men in different ways and they moved in different directions.

Karl, Barry D. CHARLES E. MERRIAM AND THE STUDY OF POLITICS. Chicago: University of Chicago Press, 1974. xiv, 337 p.

The academician in modern America is portrayed. The importance of practical experience on the theoretician, the behavioral revolution in political science, and Merriam's efforts to create a new science of politics are emphasized.

King, Richard. THE PARTY OF EROS: RADICAL SOCIAL THOUGHT AND THE REALM OF FREEDOM. Chapel Hill: University of North Carolina Press, 1972. 227 p.

The cultural or sexual radicalism of the 1950s and 1960s that made the release of private tensions and the achievement of personal happiness a political objective are discussed. King details the thought of Wilhelm Reich, Herbert Marcuse, Paul Goodman, Norman O. Brown, Theodore Roszak, Philip Slater, and Charles Reich.

Kirby, John B. "Ralph J. Bunche and Black Radical Thought in the 1930's." PHYLON 34 (Summer 1974): 129-41.

Bunche saw that black people needed to free themselves from racial determinism. He attacked New Deal planning, the NAACP, Urban League, and black separatism, and urged that poor people, both black and white, form a new movement to gain a voice in the welfare state system.

Kirkendall, Richard S. SOCIAL SCIENTISTS AND FARM POLITICS IN THE AGE OF ROOSEVELT. Columbia: University of Missouri Press, 1966. ix, 358 p.

This is a study of a well-trained group the author calls "service intellectuals," who tried to bring about farm prosperity. These individuals came from the grassroots and came to power with Henry A. Wallace in 1933.

Lasch, Christopher. THE AGONY OF THE AMERICAN LEFT. New York: Alfred A. Knopf, 1969. ix, 212 p.

This book is a collection of essays on the decline of Populism, American Socialists, the Congress for Cultural Freedom, black power, and political controversy in the sixties. Lasch is a historian and Socialist who is critical of the revolutionary rhetoric and romantic posture of contemporary radicals.

_____. THE NEW RADICALISM IN AMERICA: THE INTELLECTUALS AS A SOCIAL TYPE. New York: Alfred A. Knopf, 1965. xviii, 349 p.

Lasch argues that radicals constituted a class around 1900 and that they wanted to reform culture as well as politics. Many of these radicals were radicalized because of severe social problems.

Lawson, [R.] Alan. "John Dewey and the Hope for Reform." HISTORY OF EDUCATION QUARTERLY 15 (Spring 1975): 31-66.

Lawson discusses Dewey's remoteness from social action in the 1930s and from both Freudianism and Marxism. He suggests that the state of limbo Dewey perceived in social reform in the New Deal and the Left denied him public favor to test his philosophy.

_____. THE FAILURE OF INDEPENDENT LIBERALISM, 1930-1941. New York: G.P. Putnam's Sons, 1971. 322 p.

Independent liberals rejected both Marxian radicalism and New Deal reformism, and favored centralized national planning or regionalism. Lawson discusses the thought of George Soule, Stuart Chase, Horace Kallen, Lewis Mumford, and Howard Odum.

Liebman, Arthur. "The Ties That Bind: The Jewish Support for the Left in the United States." AMERICAN JEWISH HISTORICAL QUARTERLY 66 (December 1976): 285-321.

>The Left in the United States from the pre-World War I years through post-World War II was largely dependent on the support of Jews. This support has eroded since the second World War, because Jews no longer need the support of leftist groups.

Link, Michael. THE SOCIAL PHILOSOPHY OF REINHOLD NIEBUHR: AN HISTORICAL INTRODUCTION. Chicago: Adams, 1975. iii, 143 p.

>This is a summary of Niebuhr's analyses of communism, fascism, and liberalism. It shows his transformation from the social gospel through sympathy for Marxism to liberal democracy.

Lora, Ronald. CONSERVATIVE MINDS IN AMERICA. Chicago: Rand McNally, 1971. xiii, 274 p.

>This study focuses on Burkean conservatism and on the twentieth century. Lora develops the conservative critique of both materialism and egalitarianism.

Lynd, Staughton. INTELLECTUAL ORIGINS OF AMERICAN RADICALISM. New York: Pantheon Books, 1968. vii, 184 p.

>Lynd addressed his book to the actors of the 1960s. Radicalism began early in American history as an expression of obedience to conscience, and indeed a devotion to freedom has been the base of radicalism.

Marcell, David W. PROGRESS AND PRAGMATISM: JAMES, DEWEY, BEARD, AND THE AMERICAN IDEA OF PROGRESS. Westport, Conn.: Greenwood, 1974. xiv, 402 p.

>James, Dewey, and Beard are placed in the context of the revolt against formalism and as critics of the use of determinism in relation to human beings. Each emphasized freedom and pragmatism in looking at progress.

Matthews, F[red]. H. "The Revolt Against Americanism: Cultural Pluralism and Cultural Relativism as an Ideology of Liberation." CANADIAN REVIEW OF AMERICAN STUDIES 1 (Spring 1970): 4-31.

>The revolt against Americanism that was begun in the 1920s by dissident intellectuals was a revolt against Lockean individualism as majority coercion. It gained expression in the ideas of Horace Kallen, Randolph Bourne, John Collier and, most particularly, Ruth Benedict.

_____. "White Community and 'Yellow Peril.'" MISSISSIPPI VALLEY HIS-
TORICAL REVIEW 50 (March 1964): 612-33.

> This is a study of the responses, mainly of scholars, to the so-called
> "Yellow Peril" in California during the first quarter of the twentieth
> century. Some spoke for a homogeneous community without unassim-
> ilable groups, while others argued that prejudice was invulnerable
> to change and prevented Asiatics from becoming part of the com-
> munity.

Meier, August, and Rudwick, Elliott. CORE: A STUDY IN THE CIVIL
RIGHTS MOVEMENT, 1942-1968. New York: Oxford University Press, 1973.
xii, 563 p.

> The Congress on Racial Equality (CORE) was established by the
> Christian student movement in the 1930s. The dominant mood of
> the organization remained "black and white together" until 1968,
> when it became black nationalist and excluded whites from member-
> ship.

Metz, Joseph G. "Democracy and the Scientific Method in John Dewey."
REVIEW OF POLITICS 31 (April 1969): 242-62.

> Through instrumentalism, Dewey resolved the potential antithesis
> between philosophy and experimental science. Only the scientific
> method could do justice to the integrity of experience and through
> its application to political democracy it was the link connecting
> instrumentalism and democracy.

Nash, George H. THE CONSERVATIVE INTELLECTUAL MOVEMENT IN
AMERICA: SINCE 1945. New York: Basic Books, 1976. 463 p.

> The nature of conservatism, its place in a liberal society, and con-
> troversies within the conservative camp are emphasized. The author
> discusses the Foundation for Economic Education, Henry Regnery's
> publishing firm, the NATIONAL REVIEW, and the Young Americans
> for Freedom.

Nelson, John K. THE PEACE PROPHETS: AMERICAN PACIFIST THOUGHT,
1919-1941. James Sprunt Studies in History and Political Science, vol. 49.
Chapel Hill: University of North Carolina Press, 1967. viii, 153 p.

> Nelson describes pacifist responses to immediate concerns that ap-
> peared in periodical literature. These were responses to war and
> conflict, the relevance of pacifism, economic and social justice,
> and the formulation of a program for a stable international order.

Newby, I.A. CHALLENGE TO THE COURT: SOCIAL SCIENTISTS AND THE
DEFENSE OF SEGREGATION, 1954-1966. Baton Rouge: Louisiana State University Press, 1967. xii, 239 p.

This is a study of the development of scientific racism following the Brown decision of 1954. Such racism is defined as the use of science and social science to defend segregation, and it has taken the form of tests for intelligence and other matters.

Noble, David W. "The NEW REPUBLIC and the Idea of Progress." MISSISSIPPI VALLEY HISTORICAL REVIEW 38 (December 1951): 387-402.

Noble analyzes the NEW REPUBLIC from 1914 to 1920 to show how one group of pre-1920 liberals passed from the Progressive period into the twenties. The war years undermined the faith of Herbert Croly, Walter Weyl, and Walter Lippmann in a better America.

Paterson, Thomas G., ed. COLD WAR CRITICS: ALTERNATIVES TO AMERICAN FOREIGN POLICY IN THE TRUMAN YEARS. Chicago: Quadrangle, 1971. 313 p.

This book contains essays on Walter Lippmann, James Warburg, Henry Wallace, Glen Taylor, I.F. Stone, Robert A. Taft, and others. The authors argue that the Cold War was a post-World War II phenomenon.

Pells, Richard H. RADICAL VISIONS AND AMERICAN DREAMS: CULTURE AND SOCIAL THOUGHT IN THE DEPRESSION YEARS. New York: Harper and Row, 1973. xv, 424 p.

Pells describes how American intellectuals attempted to construct an alternative society and culture during the 1930s. That they were unsuccessful, he believes, hurt intellectual life after 1945.

Potter, David M. PEOPLE OF PLENTY: ECONOMIC ABUNDANCE AND THE AMERICAN CHARACTER. Chicago: University of Chicago Press, 1954. xxviii, 219 p.

Abundance has been the key to American character. It explains the mobility and status of the American people, the actual role of the frontier, the growth of democracy, and the American mission.

Purcell, Edward A., Jr. "American Jurisprudence Between the Wars: Legal Realism and the Crisis of Democratic Theory." AMERICAN HISTORICAL REVIEW 75 (December 1969): 424-46.

In attempting a scientific study of the law, some scholars during the 1930s developed a sweeping critique of American jurisprudence and initiated intellectual debates. Their attacks on legal conceptions raised questions about democratic theory and the nature of the law.

_____. THE CRISIS OF DEMOCRATIC THEORY: SCIENTIFIC NATURALISM AND THE PROBLEM OF VALUE. Lexington: University Press of Kentucky, 1973. xii, 331 p.

Purcell describes the tensions between abolutism and relativism in American thought since the beginning of the twentieth century. Scientific naturalism had its ascendancy in law faculties and social science departments, and many academics abandoned democratic theory during the 1920s and 1930s.

Radosh, Ronald. PROPHETS OF THE RIGHT: PROFILES OF CONSERVATIVE CRITICS OF AMERICAN GLOBALISM. New York: Simon and Schuster, 1975. 351 p.

The views of Charles Beard, O.G. Villard, John Flynn, Lawrence Dennis, and Robert A. Taft are discussed. The author attempts to show the similarity of their work with that of New Left historians.

Resek, Carl, ed. WAR AND THE INTELLECTUALS: ESSAYS BY RANDOLPH S. BOURNE, 1915-1919. New York: Harper and Row, 1964. xvi, 197 p.

This collection includes Bourne's writings on World War I, as well as those in which he searched for a culture that would be more democratic than the one invoked during the war. His essays were directed more against intellectuals than against the government.

Ricci, David M. "Democracy Attenuated: Schumpeter, the Process Theory, and American Democratic Thought." JOURNAL OF POLITICS 32 (May 1970): 239-67.

This is a study of the theory that democracy is desirable and is a political system guaranteeing civil rights, maintaining equal balances of economic and social forces, and employing competitive procedures. It has been criticized because it acclaims the enormous influence of elites and defends the present distribution of power.

Rosenof, Theodore. "Freedom, Planning, and Totalitarianism: The Reception of F.A. Hayek's ROAD TO SERFDOM." CANADIAN REVIEW OF AMERICAN STUDIES 5 (Fall 1974): 149-65.

Hayek's book appeared at a time when radical thinkers were disillusioned by the New Deal's moderate position concerning the economy. They criticized his unitary view that political and economic freedom were inseparable and that the New Deal was the road to central planning and socialism.

Rumble, Wilfred E., Jr. AMERICAN LEGAL REALISM: SKEPTICISM, REFORM, AND THE JUDICIAL PROCESS. Ithaca, N.Y.: Cornell University Press, 1968. xiv, 245 p.

This is an analysis of the thought of those legal theorists who emerged in the 1920s and 1930s and termed themselves "Realists." They were influenced by pragmatism and sociological jurisprudence, and attacked established rules as valid bases for decision making.

Ryan, Henry Butterfield, Jr. "The American Intellectual Tradition Reflected in the Truman Doctrine." AMERICAN SCHOLAR 42 (Spring 1973): 294-306.

The Truman Doctrine of 1947 represented a lofty promise to help free people maintain their institutions from the aggressive movements of totalitarian regimes. Ryan maintains that this pronouncement was part of the intellectual tradition of viewing the world in terms of virtue and vice, desiring to spread Americanism, and stressing individualism.

Scott, Ann Firor. "After Suffrage: Southern Women in the Twenties." JOURNAL OF SOUTHERN HISTORY 30 (August 1964): 298-318.

Before suffrage, the South adopted a more rigid definition of the role of women than the North, a definition that gained the position of a myth. Leaders among women hoped to modify this role, but they did not succeed in creating an image of a new woman to replace the southern lady.

Shapiro, Edward S. "Decentralist Intellectuals and the New Deal." JOURNAL OF AMERICAN HISTORY 58 (March 1972): 938-57.

Emphasis in the intellectual history of the 1930s has been on John Dewey, Reinhold Niebuhr, and magazines such as the NEW REPUBLIC and NATION. Intellectuals, who called themselves decentralists and included Herbert Agar and Allen Tate, urged a quiet revolution leading to widespread distribution and decentralization of property, and criticized liberalism as being interested only in ameliorating the worst aspects of capitalism.

_____. "The Southern Agrarians, H.L. Mencken, and the Quest for Southern Identity." AMERICAN STUDIES 13 (Fall 1972): 75-92.

The most prominent characteristic of southern intellectual history during the 1920s and 1930s was regionalism based partly on the image of the benighted South. Southern agrarians defended the South and specifically attacked Mencken, the major propagator of the benighted image.

Smith, William H. "William Jennings Bryan and Racism." JOURNAL OF NEGRO HISTORY 54 (April 1969): 127-49.

Bryan, like many Progressives, spoke for rule by the people and human brotherhood, but his attitudes toward Negroes were segregationist. He was not anti-Semitic or anti-Indian.

Sochen, June. MOVERS AND SHAKERS: AMERICAN WOMEN THINKERS AND ACTIVISTS, 1900-1970. New York: Quadrangle, 1973. xi, 320 p.

This is a collection of sketches of twentieth-century feminists such as Emma Goldman, Grace Abbott, Alice Paul, Eleanor Roosevelt, and Lady Bird Johnson. In the sketches, the author emphasizes public activity.

_____. THE NEW WOMAN: FEMINISM IN GREENWICH VILLAGE, 1910-1920. New York: Quadrangle, 1972. xi, 175 p.

The new women were Crystal Eastman, Henrietta Rodman, Ida Rauh, Neith Boyce, and Susan Gaspell. They were new because they advocated the communization of the family and an unrestricted professional life for women.

_____. THE UNBRIDGEABLE GAP: BLACKS AND THEIR QUEST FOR THE AMERICAN DREAM, 1900-1930. Chicago: Rand McNally, 1972. xii, 136 p.

The American dream is what Gunnar Myrdal called the American creed of freedom, equality, and opportunity in his AMERICAN DILEMMA (1944). Except for a few whites, Sochen argues that the American dream was a myth.

Stein, Harry H. "The Muckraking Book in America, 1946-1973." JOURNALISM QUARTERLY 52 (Summer 1975): 297-303.

Muckraking has not ceased in the United States and has experienced a resurgence in the 1960s. Stein examines muckraking books published since the end of World War II and argues that contemporary muckrakers express beliefs shared by the muckrakers of the Progressive era.

Steinkraus, Warren E. "Martin Luther King's Personalism and Non-Violence." JOURNAL OF THE HISTORY OF IDEAS 34 (January-March 1973): 97-112.

Steinkraus describes the connection between King's personal idealism and political tactics. As a philosopher, the black leader believed that only personality is ultimately real when it provided him with a philosophical grounding for the idea of a personal God as well as a basis for the worth and dignity of all human personality.

Stember, Charles Herbert, el al. JEWS IN THE MIND OF AMERICA. New York: Basic Books, 1966. xiv, 413 p.

This is an analysis of the American Jewish Committee's studies of anti-Semitism and a collection of essays by representatives of various disciplines. John Higham shows that anti-Semitism has not been regarded as a subject of great significance by American historians nor has it been an important political issue.

Tindall, George B. "The Significance of Howard Odum to Southern History: A Preliminary Estimate." JOURNAL OF SOUTHERN HISTORY 24 (August 1958): 285-307.

Odum was a sociologist. He contributed to southern history through his depiction of southern folk, both black and white, and through his integration of the social sciences into a regional framework.

Tucker, Robert W. THE RADICAL LEFT AND AMERICAN FOREIGN POLICY. Baltimore: Johns Hopkins University Press, 1971. ix, 156 p.

Tucker criticizes radical critics such as Noam Chomsky, Lloyd C. Gardner, Gabriel Kolko, and others, who have argued that foreign policy was expansionist and imperialist because of institutional necessity. He finds that their work is weak in logic and evidence.

Tytell, John. "The Beat Generation and the Continuing American Revolution." AMERICAN SCHOLAR 42 (Spring 1973): 308-17.

In the silence of the 1950s, the "Beats" proclaimed a humanistic philosophy and the beginnings of a new life-style. Tytell reviews some of their writings and concludes that what they said has become prophecy even though they have been scorned in official circles and by the media.

Urofsky, Melvin I. A MIND OF ONE PIECE: BRANDEIS AND AMERICAN REFORM. New York: Charles Scribner's Sons, 1971. xiii, 210 p.

Brandeis attempted to formulate new modes by which old principles of liberty, justice, and democracy could be applied in a transitional society. He did not halt trends toward bigness, but he was successful in humanizing government, making business accountable to people, and insisting that the law serve public rather than private needs.

Veysey, Laurence. THE COMMUNAL EXPERIENCE: ANARCHIST AND MYSTICAL COUNTER-CULTURES IN AMERICA. New York: Harper and Row, 1973. xi, 495 p.

This study considers twentieth-century communes, notably the Modern School of Stelton, New Jersey, which was anarchist; the Vedanta monastery; La Crescente of Boston; and the New Age Commune in New Mexico. The author shows the differences in attitudes that separate the early anarchist movement from modern utopias.

Warren, Frank A. III. LIBERALS AND COMMUNISM: THE "RED DECADE" REVISITED. Bloomington: Indiana University Press, 1966. ix, 276 p.

Warren reassesses the involvement of left-liberal intellectuals in the 1930s with communism. He analyzes the writings of Charles Beard, Carl Becker, John Chamberlain, Bruce Bliven, Stuart Chase, Elmer Davis, and others.

Weinstein, Allen. "The Symbolism of Subversion: Notes on Some Cold War Icons." JOURNAL OF AMERICAN STUDIES 6 (August 1972): 165-79.

> Historians and others have reduced the Hiss, Rosenberg, and Oppenheimer security cases from problems of evidence to images of an event. In the three are continuities of appraisal that made them simple morality tales.

White, Morton G. SOCIAL THOUGHT IN AMERICA: THE REVOLT AGAINST FORMALISM. New York: Viking Press, 1949. viii, 260 p.

> This is an analysis of the thought of Dewey, Beard, Veblen, Holmes, and Robinson, who are depicted as pragmatists. It covers the course of liberal social thought from the end of the nineteenth century to the 1930s.

Wittner, Lawrence S. REBELS AGAINST WAR: THE AMERICAN PEACE MOVEMENT, 1941-1960. New York: Columbia University Press, 1969. xi, 339 p.

> Wittner argues that the peace movement declined in the 1940s because it did not offer an alternative to Nazi aggression. The threat of nuclear annihilation brought it a resurgence after the war, however.

Wyatt-Brown, Bertram. "The New Left and the Abolitionists: Romantic Radicalism in America." SOUNDINGS: AN INTERDISCIPLINARY JOURNAL 54 (Summer 1971): 147-63.

> Parallels are drawn between the abolitionists and the New Left. Wyatt-Brown suggests that the radical vision came from the style of upbringing, problems of adolescent adjustment, and an introspective disillusionment with a society unsure of itself.

Yates, Gayle Graham. WHAT WOMEN WANT: THE IDEAS OF THE MOVEMENT. Cambridge, Mass.: Harvard University Press, 1975. xi, 230 p.

> This is a study of the ideas of the contemporary women's movement. Yates defines ideas in terms of feminist, women's liberationist, and androgynous ideologies.

Young, James O. BLACK WRITERS OF THE THIRTIES. Baton Rouge: Louisiana State University Press, 1973. xiii, 257 p.

> One group of writers viewed the Negro problem in racial terms, while another saw it in terms of economic and class theories. The author argues that a third group composed of novelists and poets, such as Margaret Walker and Richard Wright, saw the problem realistically and synthesized racial and economic themes.

Chapter 6

EDUCATION

COLONIAL PERIOD TO 1815

Axtell, James. "The Scholastic Philosophy of the Wilderness." WILLIAM AND MARY QUARTERLY 29 (July 1972): 335-66.

> Although New Englanders failed to remake the Indian in their own image, they learned from the Indian as a neighbor, warrior, and as a model of a different way of life. Indians were remarkably successful in converting Englishmen, especially the young, to their way of living.

_____. THE SCHOOL UPON A HILL: EDUCATION AND SOCIETY IN CO-LONIAL NEW ENGLAND. New Haven, Conn.: Yale University Press, 1974. xxi, 298 p.

> This is a study of the socialization of children. Education is de-fined as a self-conscious pursuit of certain intellectual, social, and moral ideals by a society in order to perserve and transmit its dis-tinctive character.

Bailyn, Bernard. EDUCATION IN THE FORMING OF AMERICAN SOCIETY: NEEDS AND OPPORTUNITIES FOR STUDY. Chapel Hill: University of North Carolina Press for the Institute of Early American History and Culture, Williams-burg, Virginia, 1960. xvi, 147 p.

> Bailyn criticizes educational historians for using their subject to communicate an ideology for the teaching profession rather than to describe a significant part of American history. He tries to break through this parochialism by urging that education be considered as part of a process by which culture transforms itself.

Burr, Nelson R. EDUCATION IN NEW JERSEY, 1630-1871. Princeton, N.J.: Princeton University Press, 1942. 355 p.

This volume covers the education concerns and activities of religious denominations as well as the development of public education. The growth of public education in New Jersey was stimulated by democracy and industrialization.

Carrell, William D. "American College Professors: 1750-1800." HISTORY OF EDUCATION QUARTERLY 8 (Fall 1968): 289-305.

Using biographical and statistical data, Carrell shows that college teaching was an esteemed occupation, although not a profession. Professors were men of intellectual accomplishment who were members of the best intellectual societies of their day, and clergymen who stressed rationality in religion and stability in society.

Cheyney, Edward Potts. HISTORY OF THE UNIVERSITY OF PENNSYLVANIA, 1740-1940. Philadelphia: University of Pennsylvania Press, 1940. x, 461 p.

Cheyney describes the relationship between the university and revolutionary leaders such as Franklin, Dickinson, Rush, and Wilson. He also illuminates the history of professional education.

Conway, Jill K. "Perspectives on the History of Women's Education in the United States." HISTORY OF EDUCATION QUARTERLY 14 (Spring 1974): 1-12.

The Puritans placed high value on literacy for their women, but only to ensure salvation, while revolutionary leaders such as Franklin argued that female instruction should be directed toward happiness in marriage. As female roles changed in the nineteenth century, women first became the moral guardians of children and then service professionals, which was not a liberating experience.

Cremin, Lawrence A. AMERICAN EDUCATION: THE COLONIAL EXPERIENCE, 1607-1783. New York: Harper and Row, 1970. xiv, 688 p.

Cremin defines education broadly and considers not only schooling but also the family, churches, politics, newspapers, and other subjects. He sees colonial culture as English, and education as utilitarian and expressive of the American culture of the preacher and businessman.

Curti, Merle, and Nash, Roderick. PHILANTHROPY IN THE SHAPING OF AMERICAN HIGHER EDUCATION. New Brunswick, N.J.: Rutgers University Press, 1965. vi, 340 p.

Without donations from England and local communities, higher education would not have developed in the colonies. In the nineteenth century, philanthropists directed the course of higher education, while in the twentieth, foundations and corporations shaped its destiny.

Herbst, Jurgen. "The First Three American Colleges; Schools of the Reformation." PERSPECTIVES IN AMERICAN HISTORY 8 (1974): 7-54.

>This is a study of three schools: Harvard, William and Mary, and Yale. Herbst argues that these schools were created as unincorporated Latin grammar schools governed by trustees and were closely related to contemporary academic institutions in reformed Europe.

Hiner, N. Ray. "The Cry of Sodom Enquired Into: Educational Analysis in Seventeenth-Century New England." HISTORY OF EDUCATION QUARTERLY 13 (Spring 1973): 3-22.

>Seventeenth-century Puritans inquired into their educational system because they became convinced that it was failing to produce children who duplicated their own intense, personal religious experience. Conversion was the aim of Puritan education which was carried on in the family, church, and, secondarily, the school.

Hornick, Nancy Slocum. "Anthony Benezet and the Africans' School: Toward a Theory of Full Equality." PENNSYLVANIA MAGAZINE OF HISTORY AND BIOGRAPHY 99 (October 1975): 399-421.

>Benezet was a Quaker educator and humanitarian who saw the inherent equality of blacks and whites. He applied his radical Protestant theories of human brotherhood during the eighteenth century in his classes for black children and proved that the belief in black mental and moral inferiority was founded on the fears and prejudices of ruling whites.

Humphrey, David C. FROM KING'S COLLEGE TO COLUMBIA, 1746-1800. New York: Columbia University Press, 1976. 413 p.

>Humphrey emphasizes the battles over Anglican control of King's College as well as government, curriculum, students, and finances. Of special importance is his discussion of the college's intellectual and political legacy.

_____. "The Struggle for Sectarian Control of Princeton, 1745-1760." NEW JERSEY HISTORY 91 (Summer 1973): 77-90.

>Princeton founders emphasized that the school was not narrowly sectarian. At the same time, they undermined this point of view by engaging in a series of maneuvers to insure Presbyterian control.

Kaestle, Carl F. THE EVOLUTION OF AN URBAN SCHOOL SYSTEM: NEW YORK CITY, 1750-1850. Cambridge, Mass.: Harvard University Press, 1973. xiv, 205 p.

>During the century covered in this study, New York's education institutions evolved from informal and private ones to a full-fledged

public school system. The most important organization was the Free School Society, founded in 1805, that established a network of elementary schools that eventually became the public school system.

McAnear, Beverly. "College Founding in the American Colonies, 1754-1775." MISSISSIPPI VALLEY HISTORICAL REVIEW 42 (June 1955): 24-44.

College founding was stimulated by a spirit of rationalism in the colonies, sectarian conflict, and prosperity after 1748. Promoters of colleges were interested in promoting higher education through affiliation either with a library company or a church.

_____. "The Raising of Funds by Colonial Colleges." MISSISSIPPI VALLEY HISTORICAL REVIEW 38 (March 1952): 591-612.

Early in their history, colonial colleges such as Harvard, William and Mary, and Yale were publicly supported. Because of the popular interest in higher education, they gained private support, but they were in dire financial straits before the Revolution.

Marietta, Jack D. "Quaker Family Education in Historical Perspective." QUAKER HISTORY 63 (Spring 1974): 3-16.

Quakers did not believe that formal, liberal education served religious ends. Schools were inadequate for the transmission of culture and the family was the most obvious and constant influence on children's lives.

Middlekauff, Robert. ANCIENTS AND AXIOMS: SECONDARY EDUCATION IN EIGHTEENTH-CENTURY NEW ENGLAND. Yale Historical Publications, Miscellany 77. New Haven, Conn.: Yale University Press, 1963. xii, 218 p.

Middlekauff argues that new educational ideas, social and economic changes, and the opportunity for experimentation in the post-revolutionary era had little effect on secondary education. Classics were deeply embedded in the curriculum.

_____. "A Persistent Tradition: The Classical Tradition in Eighteenth-Century New England." WILLIAM AND MARY QUARTERLY 18 (January 1961): 54-67.

A student's knowledge of Latin and Greek, not his mastery of navigation, surveying, or history, interested colleges. Colonial boys were tested in these languages before they entered college, and they had to be content with a classical education.

Miller, Harold. THE REVOLUTIONARY COLLEGE: AMERICAN PRESBYTERIAN HIGHER EDUCATION, 1707-1837. New York: New York University Press, 1976. xxiii, 381 p.

This is a study of religious and educational history. Presbyterian colleges were shaped by positions concerning the nature of social union that came out of the Great Awakening, Revolution, and the Second Great Awakening.

Morrison, Samuel Eliot. THREE CENTURIES OF HARVARD, 1636-1936. Cambridge, Mass.: Harvard University Press, 1936. viii, 512 p.

This is the story of Harvard's struggles to ward off theological and political control during the more than two centuries before President Eliot. Curriculum development is explicated and the personalities of leaders are described.

Novak, Steven J. THE RIGHTS OF YOUTH: AMERICAN COLLEGES AND STUDENT REVOLT, 1798-1815. Cambridge, Mass.: Harvard University Press, 1977. vii, 218 p.

Between 1798 and 1815, American colleges were characterized by student rebellions, gross disorder, and insubordination. Novak argues that students were attempting to establish their identity in an environment shaped by republican principles and were responding to an academic tradition poorly equipped to concede their rights.

Peckham, Howard H. "Collegia Ante Bellum: Attitudes of College Professors and Students Toward the American Revolution." PENNSYLVANIA MAGAZINE OF HISTORY AND BIOGRAPHY 95 (January 1971): 50-72.

Tories and neutralists had little influence on students for the vast majority turned out to be rebels. Professors also had little influence because they were few in number and political arguments were beyond their province.

Robinson, W. Stitt, Jr. "Indian Education and Missions in Colonial Virginia." JOURNAL OF SOUTHERN HISTORY 18 (May 1952): 152-68.

Robinson argues that the efforts of colonial Virginians to civilize and Christianize the Indians represented more than pious intentions. Their plans included private instruction for Indian boys, bringing families into the settlements to live, and educating boys at the College of William and Mary.

Rudolph, Frederick. THE AMERICAN COLLEGE AND UNIVERSITY: A HISTORY. New York: Alfred A. Knopf, 1962. xii, 516 p.

The theme of this book is the development of the English-inspired, classically oriented college of the colonial and pre-Civil War periods to the modern, partly German-inspired university of the late nineteenth and twentieth centuries. Rudolph covers the curriculum, extracurriculum, religion, finance, government relations, the professoriate, education of women, and football, among many things.

Sloan, Douglas. THE GREAT AWAKENING AND AMERICAN EDUCATION: A DOCUMENTARY HISTORY. New York: Teachers College Press, 1973. x, 270 p.

> This collection of documents presents the argument that the Great Awakening was fundamentally a large-scale educational movement. Conflicts in ministerial education, the purposes of colleges, self-education, and philosophy are described.

_____. THE SCOTTISH ENLIGHTENMENT AND THE AMERICAN COLLEGE IDEAL. New York: Teachers College Press, 1971. xi, 298 p.

> This study is limited to influences of the Scottish Enlightenment on men in Presbyterian academies and Princeton. Educators, John Witherspoon, Samuel Stanhope Smith, and Benjamin Rush are emphasized.

Teaford, Jon. "The Transformation of Massachusetts Education, 1670-1780." HISTORY OF EDUCATION QUARTERLY 10 (Fall 1970): 287-307.

> Teaford maintains that there was a decline in Puritan education in the eighteenth century, but this was a decline in emphasis on classical learning as opposed to vocational and English learning. The grammar school that stressed the study of Latin was replaced by the English school that taught writing and cyphering.

Thomson, Robert Polk. "Colleges in the Revolutionary South: The Shaping of a Tradition." HISTORY OF EDUCATION QUARTERLY 10 (Winter 1970): 399-412.

> William and Mary was the only college in the South when the Revolution began, but by 1800 seventeen colleges had been chartered. Legislatures began a tradition of failing to provide financial support or standards for curricula for the colleges they founded.

Tucker, Louis Leonard. PURITAN PROTAGONIST: PRESIDENT THOMAS CLAP OF YALE COLLEGE. Chapel Hill: University of North Carolina Press for the Institute of Early American History and Culture, Williamsburg, Virginia, 1962. xviii, 283 p.

> Clap was the personification of Old Puritanism. He represented an orthodox reaction against liberal and democratic elements inherent in Puritanism and he tried to make eighteenth-century Yale in this mold.

Tyack, David. "Education as Artifact: Benjamin Franklin and Instruction of 'A Rising People.'" HISTORY OF EDUCATION QUARTERLY 6 (Spring 1966): 3-15.

Franklin cast aside both academic custom and religious orthodoxy
in his education and tried to relate instruction and social roles.
In describing his academy, he said he wanted schooling to be de-
lightful and entertaining as well as useful, and he called for flexi-
bility that would give students a choice in what they learned.

Vine, Phyllis. "The Social Function of Eighteenth-Century Higher Education."
HISTORY OF EDUCATION QUARTERLY 16 (Winter 1976): 409-24.

Vine focuses on three colleges founded in the 1740s and 1750s--
the College of New Jersey, College of Philadelphia, and King's
College. In each instance, educators perceived a moral crisis in
society and they pinned their hopes for social stability on an orderly
generation of youth trained in colleges.

Warch, Richard. SCHOOL OF THE PROPHETS: YALE COLLEGE, 1701-1740.
New Haven, Conn.: Yale University Press, 1973. xii, 339 p.

Yale's commitment during the college's first thirty-nine years reflected the purposes of Connecticut's Congregational leaders. The
school was unstable until Elihu Yale's gift in 1718, and was upset
again in the 1720s when several faculty defected to the Anglican
Church.

Wechsler, Louis K. BENJAMIN FRANKLIN: AMERICAN AND WORLD EDUCA-
TOR. Boston: Twayne, 1976. 206 p.

Franklin is depicted as constantly striving to teach. His short-
range goal was teaching man to meet immediate problems and his
long-range objective was raising the level of knowledge and morality.

Wertenbaker, Thomas Jefferson. PRINCETON, 1746-1896. Princeton, N.J.:
Princeton University Press, 1946. 424 p.

Wertenbaker follows Princeton's history through a number of periods
that reflected the aims of the college. He relates this development
to colonial history and national life.

Wright, Louis B. "The Prestige of Learning in Early America." PROCEEDINGS
OF THE AMERICAN ANTIQUARIAN SOCIETY 83 (18 April 1973): 15-28.

Colonial Americans brought with them an ideal of learning inherited
from the Renaissance. In the colonial period, in both the North
and South, learning was expected to help men improve their social
status and be gentlemen.

Education

Allen, Frederick S., et al. THE UNIVERSITY OF COLORADO, 1876-1976.
New York: Harcourt Brace Jovanovich, 1976. xii, 319 p.

> The University of Colorado has reached a position of prominence
> among state universities in spite of being starved financially, from
> its inception, by the state legislature. This study is organized by
> presidential administrations.

Allmendinger, David F., Jr. "The Dangers of Ante-bellum Student Life."
JOURNAL OF SOCIAL HISTORY 7 (Fall 1973): 75-85.

> Disorder in antebellum colleges represented disruption of institutional
> order and a form of anarchy in personal life. Colleges experienced
> an infiltration of the poor and this changed the old institutional
> order of a residential community sustained by a "parental" system
> of ordering students' lives.

_____. PAUPERS AND SCHOLARS: THE TRANSFORMATION OF STUDENT
LIFE IN NINETEENTH-CENTURY NEW ENGLAND. New York: St. Martin's
Press, 1975. 160 p.

> This book draws heavily on evidence from Amherst, Williams, Har-
> vard, and Yale. Allmendinger indicates that the regional colleges
> attracted students from the rural areas, many of whom were poor.

_____. "The Strangeness of the American Education Society: Indigent Stu-
dents and the New Charity, 1815-1840." HISTORY OF EDUCATION QUAR-
TERLY 11 (Spring 1971): 3-22.

> The American Education Society was founded to provide financial
> backing for indigent youth to study for the ministry. By providing
> loans rather than financial grants, it freed these young men from
> the control of individuals and local institutions, and allowed them
> to make important decisions concerning themselves.

Barnard, John. FROM EVANGELICALISM TO PROGRESSIVISM AT OBERLIN
COLLEGE, 1866-1917. Columbus: Ohio State University Press, 1969. 171 p.

> This is a study of the way students in Oberlin thought about social
> issues. From its founding, Oberlin was devoted to racial equality,
> women's rights, and Christianity, but after 1900 it became a leader
> in general social reform.

Barnes, Sherman B. "Learning and Piety in Ohio Colleges, 1865-1900." OHIO
HISTORICAL QUARTERLY 69 (October 1960): 327-53.

> New knowledge entered the curriculum during the Gilded Age and
> piety played a constructive role in nourishing this new learning.
> Colleges professed themselves to be Christian but undenominational.

Becker, Carl. CORNELL UNIVERSITY: ITS FOUNDERS AND THE FOUND-
ING. SIX LECTURES DELIVERED AT CORNELL UNIVERSITY ON THE MESSEN-
GER FOUNDATION IN THE YEAR 1943. Ithaca, N.Y.: Cornell University
Press, 1943. viii, 240 p.

> Becker argues that the founding of Cornell represented the overthrow
> of the old order in higher education. This book is particularly
> valuable for its discussions of the Morrill Land Act, Ezra Cornell,
> and his extraordinary collaborator, Andrew D. White.

Berrol, Selma C. "Education and Social Mobility: The Jewish Experience in
New York City, 1880-1920." AMERICAN JEWISH HISTORICAL QUARTERLY
65 (March 1976): 257-71.

> This essay argues against the interpretation that most New York City
> Jews leaped from poverty to the middle class because of education.
> Berrol contends that widespread use of secondary and higher educa-
> tion followed improvements in economic status and was a result of
> social mobility.

Betterworth, John K. PEOPLE'S COLLEGE: A HISTORY OF MISSISSIPPI
STATE. University: University of Alabama Press, 1953. xii, 471 p.

> Mississippi State was unique as a land-grant college. It had a
> manual labor system for boys, coeducation because of the need for
> training in home economics, anachronistic paternal control, and
> political pillaging that discredited academic standing.

Bledstein, Burton J. THE CULTURE OF PROFESSIONALISM: THE MIDDLE
CLASS AND THE DEVELOPMENT OF HIGHER EDUCATION IN AMERICA.
New York: W.W. Norton and Co., 1976. xii, 354 p.

> Ambitious middle-class people succeeded in structuring society to-
> ward careers. With the establishment of the university, the middle
> class found a matrix for its evolving types of behavior.

Bode, Carl. THE AMERICAN LYCEUM: TOWN MEETING OF THE MIND.
New York: Oxford University Press, 1956. x, 275 p.

> Lyceums collected books, specimens, and scientific instruments in
> order to improve American education. They spread across the na-
> tion and featured talks by people such as Henry Ward Beecher,
> Wendell Phillips, Ralph Waldo Emerson, and others.

Bowers, C.A. "The Ideologies of Progressive Education." HISTORY OF EDU-
CATION QUARTERLY 7 (Winter 1967): 452-73.

> During the early years of the twentieth century, progressive educa-
> tors were dedicated to individualism and extracting meaning in edu-
> cation from experience. In the 1930s and 1940s, however, pro-
> gressivism took on a radically different meaning when educators

began arguing that schools should direct the course of social change and promote a collectivist democracy.

Bragdon, Henry Wilkinson. WOODROW WILSON: THE ACADEMIC YEARS. Cambridge, Mass.: Belknap Press of Harvard University Press, 1967. xiii, 519 p.

Bragdon finds Wilson a southern Bourbon, racial conservative, Jefferson-style Cleveland Democrat, and an impractical, inconsistent man. At the same time, he admires Wilson's work as a political theorist, especially his CONGRESSIONAL GOVERNMENT, where he described a strong president who would not hesitate to offer strong leadership to an amorphous Congress.

Buck, Paul, ed. SOCIAL SCIENCES AT HARVARD, 1860-1920: FROM INCULCATION TO THE OPEN MIND. Cambridge, Mass.: Harvard University Press, 1965. xiv, 320 p.

The period covered in these essays was one in which great changes occurred in curricula, approaches to learning, and the nature of truth. Developments in economics, psychology, education, social ethics, and history are described.

Bullock, Henry Allen. A HISTORY OF NEGRO EDUCATION IN THE SOUTH: FROM 1619 TO THE PRESENT. Cambridge, Mass.: Harvard University Press, 1967. xi, 339 p.

This study is focused on the separate system of education for Negroes that existed from the late nineteenth century until the 1950s. The contributions of the Southern Education Board and the Slater, Jeanes, and Rosenwald funds to the development of a Negro school that emphasized agricultural and vocational training are delineated.

Bullough, William A. "'It Is Better To Be a Country Boy': The Lure of the Country in Urban Education in the Gilded Age." HISTORIAN 35 (February 1973): 183-95.

Bullough maintains that the lure of the country was an important intellectual trend in the late nineteenth century. This was advanced by educators who were hostile or ambivalent toward the city.

Carlson, Robert A. "Americanization as an Early Twentieth-Century Adult Education Movement." HISTORY OF EDUCATION QUARTERLY 10 (Winter 1970): 440-64.

Americanization became a consensus in the United States as a counter to the humanitarians who wanted to preserve the immigrants' own culture and the restrictionists who wanted to limit immigration. Because it became a little crusade for democracy during World War I, Americanization was criticized by liberals and eventually discredited by large segments of American society.

Cavallo, Dom. "From Perfection to Habit: Moral Training in the American Kindergarten, 1860-1920." HISTORY OF EDUCATION QUARTERLY 16 (Summer 1976): 147-62.

> This is a study of the controversy concerning the methods and mo-tives of kindergarten education that was spearheaded by the fol-lowers of the German educator Friedrich Froebel, and the psycholo-gists G. Stanley Hall, John Dewey, and Edward Thorndike. All agreed that the kindergarten should be used for moral training and after 1900 this training meant bureaucratizing the child's moral faculties.

Clark, Thomas D. INDIANA UNIVERSITY: MIDWESTERN PIONEER. Vol. 1: THE EARLY YEARS. Bloomington: Indiana University Press, 1970. xvii, 371 p.

> Indiana made a provision in its constitution for a university in 1816, but one in name did not come into being until 1838. This institu-tion confronted adversity from the beginning in terms of niggardly financial support as well as conflict over programs, and it was not until the administration of David Starr Jordan (1885-91) that these problems were partially solved.

_____. INDIANA UNIVERSITY: MIDWESTERN PIONEER. Vol. 2: IN MID-PASSAGE. Bloomington: Indiana University Press, 1973. xviii, 429 p.

> This volume covers the period from 1902 to the late 1930s and em-braces the presidency of William L. Bryan. This was a time of improving conditions, but Indiana did not match the universities of Michigan and Wisconsin or the University of Chicago.

Cohen, Sol. "The Industrial Education Movement, 1906-17." AMERICAN QUARTERLY 20 (Spring 1968): 95-110.

> At the beginning of the twentieth century, when the United States had become the foremost industrial nation, educational reformers perceived the appearance of the masses in the public schools. The Industrial Education Movement was conceived as a means of sorting out children as to their probable destinies and also to thwart the upward mobility of the new immigrants.

Craig, Hardin. WOODROW WILSON AT PRINCETON. Norman: University of Oklahoma Press, 1960. xii, 175 p.

> Craig attempts to show the philosophy underlying Wilson's efforts to enliven teaching methods by introducing preceptorials, reorganizing the departmental structure, and strengthening curricular requirements. He was a preceptor at Princeton during Wilson's tenure.

Cremin, Lawrence A. THE AMERICAN COMMON SCHOOL: AN HISTORIC CONCEPTION. Foreword by George S. Counts. New York: Bureau of Publi-cations, Teachers College, Columbia University, 1951. xi, 248 p.

This is an analysis of American public schools to 1850. Cremin emphasizes the importance of the development of democratization on the public schools, the liberalizing of religion, the rise of reforms, and other subjects.

_____. TRADITIONS OF AMERICAN EDUCATION. New York: Basic Books, 1977. ix, 172 p.

American educational tradition is complex, being Protestant, culturally diverse, and individualized in purposes. Education in the nineteenth and twentieth centuries, although it had a seamy side, was liberating.

_____. THE TRANSFORMATION OF THE SCHOOL: PROGRESSIVISM IN AMERICAN EDUCATION, 1876-1957. New York: Alfred A. Knopf, 1961. xiv, 387 p.

Progressive educational reform is delineated. John Dewey and others saw the school as an instrument for improving a changing society, and education changed in the 1920s and 1930s as a part of larger social and intellectual developments.

Crofts, Daniel W. "The Black Response to the Blair Education Bill." JOURNAL OF SOUTHERN HISTORY 37 (February 1971): 41-65.

The education bill advanced by Sen. Henry W. Blair of New Hampshire during the 1880s would have permitted segregated education, but it also would have required minimum standards of fair treatment for blacks. Most blacks, both the elite and the inarticulate, supported this piece of legislation, because they thought it would ensure equitable treatment for black schools.

Curran, Francis X. THE CHURCHES AND THE SCHOOLS: AMERICAN PROTESTANTISM AND POPULAR EDUCATION. Chicago: Loyola University Press, 1954. viii, 152 p.

Curran explains how Protestantism surrendered to the state the traditional claim of Christianity to the control of popular elementary education. The principal motive for the acceptance of state schools was the hate and fear of Catholicism.

Curti, Merle. THE SOCIAL IDEAS OF AMERICAN EDUCATORS. American Historical Association, Report of the Commission on the Social Sciences, part 10. New York: Charles Scribner's Sons, 1935. xxii, 613 p.

American education is discussed as part of the emerging social order. The study is limited to the elementary and secondary schools and their relationship to movements in business and industry.

Curti, Merle, and Carstensen, Vernon. THE UNIVERSITY OF WISCONSIN: A HISTORY, 1848-1925. 2 vols. Madison: University of Wisconsin Press, 1949. xviii, 739 p.; x, 668 p.

This history relates the university to the social and intellectual progress of the region. Volume one covers academic controversies, student life, and administrative problems. Volume two focuses on the years 1900-1925, a period viewed by many as the golden age of the institution, and it emphasizes the presidencies of Charles R. Van Hise and Edward A. Birge.

Cutler, William W. III, "Status, Values, and the Education of the Poor: The Trustees of the New York Public School Society, 1805-1853." AMERICAN QUARTERLY 24 (March 1972): 69-85.

The Public School Society attracted many social activists as trustees. At the same time, these men were of high economic status and were active in politics.

Dunbar, Willis F. THE MICHIGAN RECORD IN HIGHER EDUCATION. Detroit: Wayne State University Press, 1963. 463 p.

Michigan has emphasized public higher education because the University of Michigan was founded in 1817 when elsewhere churches were establishing schools. It was not until 1855 that church-related colleges were founded in the state.

Durkin, Joseph T. GEORGETOWN UNIVERSITY: THE MIDDLE YEARS. (1840-1900). Washington, D.C.: Georgetown University Press, 1963. viii, 333 p.

Georgetown's college department had forty-three students in 1840, and the campus had an air of a southern plantation where a permanent house party for the neighbors' children was going on. After establishing a medical department and a school of law, the institution opted in the 1870s for the development of a real university.

Earnest, Ernest. ACADEMIC PROCESSION: AN INFORMAL HISTORY OF THE AMERICAN COLLEGE, 1636 TO 1953. Indianapolis: Bobbs-Merrill, 1953. 368 p.

Earnest is concerned with the mission of colleges and how it was fulfilled during different historical periods. He considers the quarter century following the Civil War as "miraculous years in American higher education."

Eaton, Clement. "Professor James Woodrow and the Freedom of Teaching in the South." JOURNAL OF SOUTHERN HISTORY 28 (February 1962): 3-17.

Woodrow was the uncle of Woodrow Wilson, and a professor in the Columbia Theological Seminary and the University of South Carolina. He fought for the right to teach evolution in the seminary in the 1880s.

Ellis, John Tracy. THE FORMATIVE YEARS OF THE CATHOLIC UNIVERSITY OF AMERICA. Washington, D.C.: American Catholic Historical Association, 1946. 415 p.

The Catholic University was founded in 1889 for the postgraduate training of religious brotherhoods and sisterhoods, as well as diocesan clergy. It represented a new era of scholarship because Catholic universities such as Georgetown and Notre Dame did not have graduate training worthy of the name.

Elson, Ruth Miller. "American Schoolbooks and 'Culture' in the Nineteenth Century." MISSISSIPPI VALLEY HISTORICAL REVIEW 46 (December 1959): 411-34.

Schoolbooks were written by printers, journalists, future lawyers, teachers, and ministers. These authors were committed to useful knowledge, and children were guided by their books to be honest, industrious, religious, and moral citizens.

_____. GUARDIANS OF TRADITION: AMERICAN SCHOOLBOOKS OF THE NINETEENTH CENTURY. Lincoln: University of Nebraska Press, 1964. xiii, 424 p.

The schoolbook taught children that America was great and the best possible place to live. Children also learned from these volumes that the nineteenth century was created for man, and man for God, and that the white race was the typical race.

Ezell, John S. "A Southern Education for Southrons." JOURNAL OF SOUTHERN HISTORY 17 (August 1951): 303-27.

As slavery and sectional pride pushed North and South farther apart after 1830, there were increasing efforts to control the minds of southern youth. These efforts were centered on upgrading southern education to keep young men at home.

Finkelstein, Barbara. "The Moral Dimensions of Pedagogy: Teaching Behavior in Popular Primary Schools in Nineteenth-Century America." AMERICAN STUDIES 15 (Fall 1974): 79-90.

In the relatively low-cost popular schools of the nineteenth century, teachers saw their role as channeling youthful energies into a highly controlled series of intellectual exercises. They assumed that literacy was the basis of right conduct.

_____. "Pedagogy as Intrusion: Teaching Values in Popular Primary Schools in Nineteenth-Century America." HISTORY OF CHILDHOOD QUARTERLY 2 (Winter 1975): 349-78.

Teachers were responsible for overcontrolling children and this was an important aspect of child-rearing in the nineteenth century. They inculcated values and morals in a rigid and highly controlling manner and thus extended the intrusive mode of child-rearing common in the home.

Fletcher, Robert Samuel. A HISTORY OF OBERLIN COLLEGE FROM ITS FOUNDATION THROUGH THE CIVIL WAR. 2 vols. Oberlin, Ohio: Oberlin College, 1943. xvii, 502; xi, 507-1004 p.

Fletcher details the forces such as learning and revivalism, abolitionism, an antislavery church, and coeducation that shaped Oberlin's traditions. He depicts student life, the village community, extracurricular activities, and the college's part in the Civil War.

Flexner, Abraham. DANIEL COIT GILMAN: CREATOR OF THE AMERICAN TYPE OF UNIVERSITY. New York: Harcourt Brace, 1946. ix, 173 p.

Flexner portrays Gilman as a radical who adapted his educational and political ideas to a time of rapid social change. He borrowed from Europe, but he was foremost a functionalist who believed American schools had to serve American people.

Flynt, Wayne L. "Southern Higher Education and the Civil War." CIVIL WAR HISTORY 14 (September 1968): 211-25.

The Civil War decimated southern higher education. Only a few schools remained open when the war was over and they accomplished this feat by offering grammar school work or by converting to military academies.

French, John C. A HISTORY OF THE UNIVERSITY FOUNDED BY JOHNS HOPKINS. Baltimore: Johns Hopkins University Press, 1946. xii, 492 p.

Johns Hopkins, founded in the 1870s, was meant to be a different institution. French focuses on the first four presidents in a topical manner and mentions many of the outstanding figures of the university's life and work.

Fries, Sylvia Doughty. "The Slavery Issue in Northern School Readers, Geographies and Histories, 1850-1875." JOURNAL OF POPULAR CULTURE 4 (Winter 1971): 718-31.

Northern schoolbooks presented a picture of the American Negro that made him little different from the African savage. In a nation created by white Christians, the Negro did not belong because he was ignorant, brutish, pagan, and savage.

Education

Gerber, David A. "Education, Expediency, and Ideology: Race and Politics in the Desegregation of Ohio Public Schools in the Late Nineteenth Century." JOURNAL OF ETHNIC STUDIES 1 (Fall 1973): 1-33.

Gerber shows that blacks in Ohio were divided on the question of whether integrated or segregated schools provided the best setting for the education of black children. Integration was supported by black upper classes, while the masses may have regarded it as a racial panacea.

Godbold, Albea. THE CHURCH COLLEGE OF THE OLD SOUTH. Duke University Publications. Durham, N.C.: Duke University Press, 1944. xi, 221 p.

From the establishment of William and Mary by the Episcopalians, other denominations founded colleges in the southern states. They were motivated by the need for a trained ministry, fear of state-controlled schools, commitment to strengthen denominational loyalty, and the desire to spread Christian doctrines.

Going, Allen J. "The South and the Blair Education Bill." MISSISSIPPI VALLEY HISTORICAL REVIEW 44 (September 1957): 267-90.

The Blair Bill of the 1880s provided for the distribution of funds to the states in proportion to the illiteracy rate. This proposal was acceptable to the dominant leadership of the lower South, where Negroes were concentrated, but it was opposed by agrarian and states' rights southerners.

Harding, Thomas S. COLLEGE LITERARY SOCIETIES: THEIR CONTRIBUTION TO HIGHER EDUCATION IN THE UNITED STATES, 1815-1876. New York: Pageant, 1971. xv, 537 p.

Literary societies were of significance because they were controlled by students and countered the theological and philosophical bases of college studies. They were social and fraternal clubs dedicated to studying history, fiction, and contemporary European thought.

Harlan, Louis R. SEPARATE AND UNEQUAL: PUBLIC SCHOOL CAMPAIGNS AND RACISM IN THE SOUTHERN SEABOARD STATES, 1901-1915. Chapel Hill: University of North Carolina Press, 1958. xiv, 290 p.

This is a study of the extent to which Negro schools, teachers, and children did not share in educational progress. Harlan emphasizes the role of the Southern Education Board, a joint effort of northern philanthropists and southern educators, in urging northerners to make concesions toward white supremacy.

_____. "The Southern Education Board and the Race Issue in Public Education." JOURNAL OF SOUTHERN HISTORY 23 (May 1957): 189-202.

The Southern Education Board, created in 1901, was made up of
northerners who were moderate on racial and sectional issues, and
southerners who believed education was a key to regional progress.
This board was to direct a public school crusade, but northern progressives early capitulated to southern white supremacists and black
schools suffered as a result of their efforts.

Hawkins, Hugh. BETWEEN HARVARD AND AMERICA: THE EDUCATIONAL
LEADERSHIP OF CHARLES W. ELIOT. New York: Oxford University Press,
1972. xi, 404 p.

This is an examination of Eliot's role in America's only academic
revolution. The paradox of his career is that he was a laissez-
faire individualist but fashioned a large-scale organization common
in the late nineteenth century.

_____. "Charles W. Eliot, Daniel C. Gilman and the Nurture of American
Scholarship." NEW ENGLAND QUARTERLY 39 (September 1966): 291-308.

American institutions of higher learning began to encourage rather
than repel scholarship because of transformations in the scientific
schools at Harvard and Yale that were led by Eliot and Gilman.
Both taught at these schools and both, as university presidents, emphasized free institutions and fostered research.

_____. "Charles W. Eliot, University Reform, and Religious Faith in America,
1869-1909." JOURNAL OF AMERICAN HISTORY 51 (September 1964): 191-
213.

In order to provide freedom in the emerging university, Eliot made
Harvard unsectarian, but he also tried to demonstrate that loyalties
to scientific truth need not be harmful to religion. By maintaining
theology as a respected discipline in the Divinity School, the fears
of religionists were answered and freedom for scientific inquiry was
gained.

_____. PIONEER: A HISTORY OF THE JOHNS HOPKINS UNIVERSITY,
1874-1889. Ithaca, N.Y.: Cornell University Press, 1960. xiv, 368 p.

Hawkins emphasizes the contributions of Daniel Coit Gilman, the
trustees of the Hopkins's fortune, professors, and students. These
people are depicted as intelligent and critical individuals who
sought truth, science, religion, applied knowledge, and reform.

_____. "Three University Presidents Testify." AMERICAN QUARTERLY 11
(Summer 1959): 99-119.

When Johns Hopkins died in 1873, he left a $7 million fortune to
establish a university and a hospital. The trustees called upon the

the presidents of other institutions for advice, and Eliot of Harvard, Angell of Michigan, and White of Cornell responded with searching commentaries.

———. "The University-Builders Observe the Colleges." HISTORY OF EDUCATION QUARTERLY 11 (Winter 1971): 353-62.

Some university-builders pointed to the colleges as examples of what universities would not be and even urged their abolition. In the 1890s, they sought to standardize the colleges and fit them into an ordered educational system.

Hiner, N. Ray. "Professions in Process: Changing Relations Between Historians and Educators, 1896-1911." HISTORY OF EDUCATION QUARTERLY 12 (Spring 1972): 34-56.

This is a study of the collaboration of leading educators and professional historians in preparing a history program for the public schools. Both groups agreed on the value of historical-mindedness in creating good citizenship, but the historians disagreed as to the relative importance of ancient and modern history in accomplishing this goal.

Hofstadter, Richard, and Metzger, Walter P. THE DEVELOPMENT OF ACADEMIC FREEDOM IN THE UNITED STATES. New York: Columbia University Press, 1955. xvi, 527 p.

This work covers both European and American practices. The authors develop the changing attitudes of scholars toward the academic enterprise, and show that academic freedom had little connection with freedom of speech or press.

Hogeland, Ronald W. "Coeducation of the Sexes at Oberlin College: A Study of Social Ideas in Mid-Nineteenth-Century America." JOURNAL OF SOCIAL HISTORY 6 (Winter 1972-73): 160-76.

Hogeland argues that the introduction of coeducation at Oberlin was conceived with masculine priorities in mind. Charles G. Finney and his followers recognized that the years of college and theological education fostered autocratic habits, and they admitted women to reduce sexual energy and promote constructive relationships.

Horlick, Allan S. "Phrenology and the Social Education of Young Men." HISTORY OF EDUCATION QUARTERLY 11 (Spring 1971): 23-38.

When large numbers of young men migrated to the cities in the 1840s and 1850s, employers and employees were worried about finding the right job. Phrenology was used as a technique in vocational guidance.

Issel, William H. "Modernization in Philadelphia School Reform, 1882-1905."
PENNSYLVANIA MAGAZINE OF HISTORY AND BIOGRAPHY 94 (July 1970):
358-83.

The Philadelphia Public School Reorganization Act of 1905 was a
precedent-breaking measure that radically transformed old ways. It
symbolized the establishment of a centralized, standardized, and
bureaucratic educational system which tells much about the nature
of progressive educational reform.

Jackson, Sidney L. AMERICA'S STRUGGLE FOR FREE SCHOOLS: SOCIAL
TENSION AND EDUCATION IN NEW ENGLAND AND NEW YORK, 1827-42.
Introduction by Merle Curti. Washington, D.C.: American Council on Public
Affairs, 1941. viii, 276 p.

Jackson is interested in the emergence of the free school idea.
Many public leaders held conflicting beliefs and opposed the common school because they wanted to maintain the status quo.

Johnson, Henry C., Jr., and Johanningmeier, Erwin V. TEACHERS FOR THE
PRAIRIE: THE UNIVERSITY OF ILLINOIS AND THE SCHOOLS, 1868-1945.
Urbana: University of Illinois Press, 1972. xx, 508 p.

The College of Education in the University of Illinois was not able
to reconcile the ambuiguity between the tasks of training teachers
and teaching education. As a consequence, educators lost touch
with the schools of the state.

Johnson, William R. "Education and Professional Life Styles: Law and Medicine in the Nineteenth Century." HISTORY OF EDUCATION QUARTERLY 14
(Summer 1974): 185-207.

Johnson discusses the medical and legal professions in Wisconsin to
show how professional life affected medical and legal education.
It was easy to gain admission to the bar and legal practice was isolated and competing medical theories led to the establishment of
medical societies to define orthodoxy and competence.

Katz, Michael B. "The Emergence of Bureaucracy in Urban Education: The
Boston Case, 1850-1884." HISTORY OF EDUCATION QUARTERLY 8 (Summer,
Fall 1968): 155-88, 319-57.

Katz indicates that urban school systems became full-fledged bu-
reaucracies during the third quarter of the nineteenth century. In
Boston, schoolmen implemented the organizational plan, but the
financial crisis of the early 1870s brought attacks by laymen who
wanted responsiveness from the system to public demands.

_____. THE IRONY OF EARLY SCHOOL REFORM: EDUCATIONAL INNO-
VATION IN MID-NINETEENTH CENTURY MASSACHUSETTS. Cambridge, Mass.:
Harvard University Press, 1968. xii, 325 p.

This is a study of the controversy over public high schools in New England towns, the conflict between liberal pedagogues and those who espoused more orthodox instructional techniques, and the development of a state-operated reform which was to be devoted to individual betterment and social purposes. Katz tries to show Massachusetts's educational reform as it was, and he depicts the reasons many people rejected educational innovation.

_____. "The 'New Departure' in Quincy, 1873-1881; The Nature of Nineteenth-Century Educational Reform." NEW ENGLAND QUARTERLY 40 (March 1967): 3-30.

Reform in Quincy, Massachusetts, was begun in the 1870s when the school committee discovered the students could not write with facility nor read fluently. They hired a new superintendent and embarked on reform only to be stymied by their efforts to reduce costs.

_____. "The Origins of Public Education: A Reassessment." HISTORY OF EDUCATION QUARTERLY 16 (Winter 1976): 381-408.

Katz suggests that public education was established in response to industrialization, urbanization, and immigration and represented a faith in the power of formal institutions to alleviate personal and social distress. Public education should deal with the problems of crime and poverty, cultural heterogeneity, the need to train and discipline an industrial work force, and the anxiety of the middle class concerning their adolescent children.

Kersey, Harry A. JOHN MILTON GREGORY AND THE UNIVERSITY OF ILLINOIS. Urbana: University of Illinois Press, 1968. ix, 252 p.

Gregory was the first president of Illinois Industrial University, established in 1867. He is depicted as striking a balance between the humanities and technical education, showing a warm concern for students, defending academic freedom, and promoting scholarly activities.

Krug, Edward A. THE SHAPING OF THE AMERICAN HIGH SCHOOL. New York: Harper and Row, 1964. xvii, 486 p.

The high school assumed its familiar shape and characteristics between 1880 and 1920. Krug emphasizes clashing doctrines and points of view which reflected an antiacademic bias.

Lannie, Vincent P. "Alienation in America: The Immigrant Catholic and Public Education in Pre-Civil War America." REVIEW OF POLITICS 32 (October 1970): 503-21.

In mid-nineteenth-century America, the public schools were given the responsibility of socializing Irish and German Roman Catholic immigrants. Since the schools reflected the pervasive Protestantism of American culture and were unresponsive to the religious sensibilities of these people, Catholics withdrew support from public education and formed their own separate school systems.

⸱

_____. PUBLIC MONEY AND PAROCHIAL EDUCATION: BISHOP HUGHES, GOVERNOR SEWARD, AND THE NEW YORK SCHOOL CONTROVERSY. Cleveland: Press of Case Western Reserve University, 1968. xii, 282 p.

This is a study of attempts of the New York Catholic community to gain public funds for its schools in the years 1840-42. New York public schools were sectarian (anti-Catholic), and Seward supported the Catholics because of his dedication to the principal of free education.

_____. "William Seward and the New York School Controversy, 1840-1842: A Problem in Historical Motivation." HISTORY OF EDUCATION QUARTERLY 6 (Spring 1966): 52-73.

Lannie argues that Governor Seward did not propose publicly-supported schools in which Catholic children would be instructed by Catholic teachers in order to gain Catholic votes. His motivation was a commitment to universal education based on beliefs in the unity of mankind and natural rights.

Lazerson, Marvin. "F.A.P. Barnard and Columbia College: Prologue to a University." HISTORY OF EDUCATION QUARTERLY 6 (Winter 1966): 49-64.

When Barnard arrived in 1864, Columbia was a conservative, classical college. Lazerson pictures him as a reformer-agitator par excellence who changed minds and laid the foundation for the work of Nicholas Murray Butler.

_____. ORIGINS OF THE URBAN SCHOOL: PUBLIC EDUCATION IN MASSACHUSETTS, 1870-1915. Cambridge, Mass.: Harvard University Press, 1971. xix, 278 p.

Lazerson elucidates the shift in attitudes of educators from modest hope to cynicism as the children of non-English-speaking immigrants inundated the schools. He depicts urban education by way of contrasts with rural education.

_____. "Urban Reform and the Schools: Kindergarten in Massachusetts, 1870-1915." HISTORY OF EDUCATION QUARTERLY 11 (Summer 1971): 115-42.

The evolution of the kindergarten in Massachusetts from an agency mainly for the socialization of affluent children to its institutionalization in urban schools is discussed. At first, it was used to care for and control the unfortunate in slum districts, but by the first World War it had become a means of aiding immigrant children so that they could move into the work force more quickly.

Le Duc, Thomas. PIETY AND INTELLECT AT AMHERST COLLEGE, 1865-1912. Columbia Studies in American Culture, no. 16. New York: Columbia University Press, 1946. ix, 165 p.

In the post-Civil War period, Amherst's sense of mission, its religious orthodoxy, was shattered by German scholarship and science. It shifted from religious authority to intellectual freedom, from a quest for individual salvation to social idealism.

McBride, Paul W. "The Co-Op Industrial Education Experiment, 1900-1917." HISTORY OF EDUCATION QUARTERLY 14 (Summer 1970): 209-21.

The National Society for the Promotion of Industrial Education, founded in Boston in 1907, was the lobby of the alliance between educators and industrialists to promote industrial education. McBride shows that co-op schools exploited apprentices by requiring four years of training and paying as little as seven cents an hour in wages.

McGiffert, Michael. THE HIGHER LEARNING IN COLORADO: AN HISTORICAL STUDY, 1860-1940. Denver: Sage Books, 1964. xiii, 307 p.

This is a survey of the histories of all the public and private institutions in the state. It depicts the controversies over the location of colleges and the competition for students.

McLachlan, James. AMERICAN BOARDING SCHOOLS: A HISTORICAL STUDY. New York: Charles Scribner's Sons, 1970. x, 381 p.

McLachlan shows that boarding schools were not an English importation nor aristocratic. These institutions were products of the Federalist period when people sought rural education for their sons to escape urban influences.

McPherson, James M. "White Liberals and Black Power in Education, 1865-1915." AMERICAN HISTORICAL REVIEW 75 (June 1970): 1357-86.

Black power means greater control by Negroes themselves over their institutions. In this period following the Civil War, blacks did not want to restructure schools founded by northern liberals and abolitionists, they desired a greater role in managing these institutions and they gained it.

Madsen, David. THE NATIONAL UNIVERSITY: ENDURING DREAM OF THE USA. Detroit: Wayne State University Press, 1966. 178 p.

The idea of a national university can be traced back to 1775. It was promoted most actively in the first two decades of the republic, in the 1870s, 1890s, and around 1914, but it was forestalled by states' rights thinking.

Manley, Robert N. CENTENNIAL HISTORY OF THE UNIVERSITY OF NE-
BRASKA. Vol. 1: FRONTIER UNIVERSITY (1869-1919). Lincoln: University
of Nebraska Press, 1969. xii, 331 p.

This is the story of a land-grant institution feeling its way toward
accomplishing its role. Chancellors and professors wanted to emphasize the liberal arts, legislators and citizens urged a practical
curriculum, and students, wisely, wanted both.

Mattingly, Paul H. THE CLASSLESS PROFESSION: AMERICAN SCHOOLMEN
IN THE NINETEENTH CENTURY. New York: New York University Press,
1975. xxiii, 235 p.

This is an effort in collective biography of educational leaders in
the nineteenth century. Mattingly provides an understanding of
professionalization, changes in normal schools, and shifts in career
choices.

_____. "Educational Revivals in Ante-Bellum New England." HISTORY OF
EDUCATION QUARTERLY 11 (Spring 1971): 39-71.

The teacher's institute changed the conception of the teacher from
something close to an evangelical minister to a professional with
technical training. Originated in the 1840s, institutes functioned
first as quasi-religious institutions, but later they were transformed
into professional conventions and summer schools.

Melder, Keith. "Mask of Oppression: The Female Seminary Movement in the
United States." NEW YORK HISTORY 55 (July 1974): 260-79.

Seminaries were not institutions offering women new opportunities
and freedoms. They were new schools designed to mold their students academically and emotionally to become ideal women according to contemporary definitions.

_____. "Woman's High Calling: The Teaching Profession in America, 1830-
1860." AMERICAN STUDIES 13 (Fall 1972): 19-32.

By their willingness to answer the demand for teachers and their
belief in the capacity of the schools to bring about cultural progress, young women made a comprehensive public school system
possible. Victorian attitudes toward women as natural guardians
of the young assumed that they had special capacities to teach.

Moore, James T. "The University and the Readjusters." VIRGINIA MAGA-
ZINE OF HISTORY AND BIOGRAPHY 78 (January 1970): 87-101.

Readjusters, who wanted to reform social conditions, drew support
from agrarian masses and attacked the entrenched forces of tradition and were swept into power in Virginia for a few years follow-

ing 1879. Although the University of Virginia was a bastion of the Bourbon order, readjuster officials won the cooperation of faculty and students because they attempted to modernize the institution.

Morris, Stuart. "The Wisconsin Idea and Business Progressivism." JOURNAL OF AMERICAN STUDIES 4 (July 1970): 39-60.

From 1900 onward, the commitment of state universities to community service and the devotion of progressive intellectuals to efficiency brought about a vast expansion of business education at the university level. This program became a substitute for social Darwinism in business since it made business leaders "professional" and gave them claims to leadership.

Morrison, Theodore. CHAUTAUQUA: A CENTER FOR EDUCATION, RELIGION, AND THE ARTS IN AMERICA. Chicago: University of Chicago Press, 1974. viii, 351 p.

This is a sympathetic history that does not emphasize debate over purposes. Chautauqua began as a Sunday-school university and progressed to a music, artistic, and lecturing center. It maintained an open platform for differing views.

Nevins, Allan. THE STATE UNIVERSITIES AND DEMOCRACY. Urbana: University of Illinois Press, 1962. x, 171 p.

Nevins examines the four periods of state university growth. The ideas of the founders, the gap between aspirations and attainments in the early years, the period of growth and achievement, and expectations for the future are covered.

Newby, Robert G., and Tyack, David B. "Victims Without 'Crimes': Some Educational Perspectives on Black Education." JOURNAL OF NEGRO EDUCATION 40 (Summer 1971): 192-206.

This is a survey of black education since Reconstruction. The authors argue that a quest for power has been the common theme.

O'Connor, Michael J.L. ORIGINS OF ACADEMIC ECONOMICS IN THE UNITED STATES. New York: Columbia University Press, 1944. x, 367 p.

Political-economy textbooks published in the 1820s and 1830s are analyzed. O'Connor argues that the clerical school of economists dominated colleges in the Northeast, backed religious and mercantile interests, and opposed universal democracy.

Olneck, Michael R., and Lazerson, Marvin. "The School Achievement of Immigrant Children: 1900-1930." HISTORY OF EDUCATION QUARTERLY 14 (Winter 1974): 453-82.

The authors take issue with those interpretations that see the schools as being either an immense success in providing opportunities for immigrants or as reactionary institutions designed to perpetuate the existing order. They show that different nationality groups adapted to public education at different rates.

Peterson, George E. THE NEW ENGLAND COLLEGE IN THE AGE OF THE UNIVERSITY. Amherst, Mass.: Amherst College Press, 1964. viii, 260 p.

Peterson argues that the college always maintained an existence apart from the university, and it is wrong to view the history of higher education as a transition from one institution to the other. The college was transformed in the late nineteenth century but in its own terms and in those of its Protestant middle-class constituency.

Phillips, J.O.C. "The Education of Jane Addams." HISTORY OF EDUCATION QUARTERLY 14 (Spring 1974): 49-67.

Although her father provided a role model for activism and Rockford College showed her that education and especially science might win new respect for the female spirit, Jane Addams clung to the belief that a woman's character was spiritual and her obligations were to home and family. Hull House fulfilled her spiritual and intellectual needs because it was a home for immigrants and she was mother superior.

Pierson, George Wilson. YALE COLLEGE, AN EDUCATIONAL HISTORY, 1871-1937. Vol. 1: YALE: COLLEGE AND UNIVERSITY, 1871-1921. New Haven, Conn.: Yale University Press, 1952. xv, 773 p.

Pierson emphasizes the evolution of the course of study, the politics of control, and the personalities of faculty and administration. The Yale faculty's search for a perfect curriculum was political rather than educational, especially the issue of the elective system.

_____. YALE COLLEGE, AN EDUCATIONAL HISTORY, 1871-1937. Vol. 2: YALE: THE UNIVERSITY COLLEGE, 1921-37. New Haven, Conn.: Yale University Press, 1955. xviii, 740 p.

The college between the wars grew in numbers, departments, and general resources. It became a university college with creative decisions being made above and from the outside.

Porter, Earl W. TRINITY AND DUKE UNIVERSITY, 1892-1924: FOUNDA-TIONS OF DUKE UNIVERSITY. Durham, N.C.: Duke University Press, 1964. ix, 274 p.

The growth and resources of Trinity College, location of institutional power, relationships with the Methodist Church, and academic policies are discussed. The author also deals with personalities and controversies such as the John Spencer Bassett academic freedom case.

Potts, David B. "American Colleges in the Nineteenth Century; From Localism to Denominationalism." HISTORY OF EDUCATION QUARTERLY 11 (Winter 1971): 363-80.

Instead of a trend from sectarianism to secularism in nineteenth-century colleges, Potts sees a movement from localism to denominationalism. These schools were not narrowly sectarian, however, and they helped disperse the nation's cultural resources and popularize higher education.

Rabinowitz, Howard N. "Half a Loaf: The Shift from White to Black Teachers in Negro Schools of the Urban South, 1865-1890." JOURNAL OF SOUTHERN HISTORY 40 (November 1974): 565-94.

At the same time black education was becoming separate and unequal, a shift from white to black teachers took place in Negro public schools. This resulted from black protest, but not without a considerable cost, since blacks thus accommodated themselves to segregated school systems.

Rainsford, George N. CONGRESS AND HIGHER EDUCATION IN THE NINETEENTH CENTURY. Knoxville: University of Tennessee Press, 1972. xi, 156 p.

This is an analysis of the use of public land to support education. Rainsford discusses the ordinances of 1785 and 1787, the Ohio Enabling Act (1802), Deposit Act of 1836, Distribution Act of 1841, the Morrill Act of 1862, and others.

Reinders, Robert C. "New England Influences on the Formation of Public Schools in New Orleans." JOURNAL OF SOUTHERN HISTORY 30 (May 1964): 181-95.

Jacksonian reform in the South meant an expanded franchise, but not demand for a public school system. A notable exception was New Orleans which was populated by northerners and led politically by Whigs rather than Democrats.

Ringenberg, William C. "Church Colleges vs. State University." MICHIGAN HISTORY 55 (Winter 1971): 305-20.

In the pre-Civil War period, the University of Michigan was as much a Protestant school as the state's five denominational colleges. The university and the colleges opposed each other on religious grounds which often took the form of arguments concerning the centralization of education in the state.

Robarts, Jason R. "The Quest for a Science of Education in the Nineteenth Century." HISTORY OF EDUCATION QUARTERLY 8 (Winter 1968): 431–45.

Seeking a science of education was an effort to professionalize teaching and provide an intellectual context for normal schools. Efforts to create a science failed because fundamental issues defied permanent solutions.

Ross, Earle D. DEMOCRACY'S COLLEGE: THE LAND-GRANT MOVEMENT IN THE FORMATIVE STAGE. Ames: Iowa State College Press, 1942. 267 p.

Ross traces the development of the land-grant movement down to the "Second Morrill Act" of 1890. He indicates that the movement was at least in part an expression of dissatisfaction with the limited opportunities and content of American education.

_____. "Religious Influences in the Development of State Colleges and Universities." INDIANA MAGAZINE OF HISTORY 46 (December 1950): 343–62.

This is a survey of attitudes and tendencies in education and religion. Sectarian influences on state colleges waned during the past generation and conflict subsided, but the need for religious ministration and instruction did not end.

Rudolph, Frederick. MARK HOPKINS AND THE LOG: WILLIAMS COLLEGE, 1836–1872. New Haven, Conn.: Yale University Press, 1956. xiv, 267 p.

In the middle of the nineteenth century, students at Williams exerted a force for institutional change. They introduced fraternities, developed libraries, and improvised voluntary activities.

Sack, Saul. HISTORY OF HIGHER EDUCATION IN PENNSYLVANIA. 2 vols. Harrisburg: Pennsylvania Historical and Museum Commission, 1963. xii, 817 p.

Sack tells the story of Pennsylvania higher education by discussing Protestant denominationalism, the Catholic contribution, the movement toward secular higher education, women in higher education, growth of the graduate school, social life on the campus, and other topics.

Schlabach, Theron F. "An Aristocrat on Trial: The Case of Richard T. Ely." WISCONSIN MAGAZINE OF HISTORY 47 (Winter 1963–64): 146–59.

This is a study of the trial of Ely instigated by the state superintendent of education in Wisconsin with the assistance of the NATION magazine in the depression year of 1894. His social views were under attack.

Schlossman, Steven L. "G. Stanley Hall and the Boys' Club: Conservative Applications of Recapitulation Theory." JOURNAL OF THE HISTORY OF THE BEHAVIORAL SCIENCES 9 (April 1973): 140–47.

Recapitulation theory covers the pedagogical uses of play and the persistence of primeval energies in children. Boys' clubs were an important urban institution of the Progressive era and Hall's ideas had an important bearing on their development as instruments for social control.

Schmidt, George Paul. "Colleges in Ferment." AMERICAN HISTORICAL RE-VIEW 59 (October 1953): 19-42.

Colleges were complacent and tradition-ruled during the century between the founding of Dartmouth and the accession of President Eliot at Harvard. The impact of Darwinism and the development of the university placed them in a state of ferment with speciali-zation being the watchword.

_____. THE LIBERAL ARTS COLLEGE: A CHAPTER IN AMERICAN CUL-TURAL HISTORY. New Brunswick, N.J.: Rutgers University Press, 1957. x, 310 p.

This study is oriented toward administration and curriculum. Schmidt delineates the development of the college before 1875 and details the process by which the classical college either became submerged in or competed with the university.

Schudson, Michael. "The Flexner Report and the Reed Report: Notes on the History of Professional Education in the United States." SOCIAL SCIENCE QUARTERLY 55 (September 1974): 347-61.

The present pattern of medical and legal education emerged from the Flexner study (1910) and the Reed report (1921). The Flexner recommendations were endorsed by the American Medical Associa-tion, but the Reed Document was condemned by the American Bar Association because it advocated two different types of legal train-ing.

Schultz, Stanley K. THE CULTURE FACTORY: BOSTON PUBLIC SCHOOLS, 1789-1860. New York: Oxford University Press, 1973. xvi, 394 p.

The principal themes of this volume are that public schools were established by Boston's political and social elite to maintain social control and that these people inhibited reform by applying tech-niques of factory management and mass production. Reform efforts are examined in their complexity, including those to integrate the schools racially.

Scott, Roy V. THE RELUCTANT FARMER: THE RISE OF AGRICULTURAL EX-TENSION TO 1914. Urbana: University of Illinois Press, 1970. xi, 362 p.

The rise of agricultural extension work represented the search for a teaching device effective with rural adults. This is a state-by-state survey of agricultural education through fairs, farmers' institutes, college-directed short courses, and demonstrations.

Servin, Manuel P., and Wilson, Iris Higbie. SOUTHERN CALIFORNIA AND ITS UNIVERSITY: A HISTORY OF USC, 1880-1964. Los Angeles: Ward Ritchie Press, 1969. xix, 319 p.

The University of Southern California was an undistinguished Methodist school until 1920 when a new president cut the Methodist ties, expanded academic offerings, and emphasized athletics. Although USC was the first complete university in the region, it was not fully committed to academic excellence until the 1960s.

Shade, William G. "The 'Working Class' and Educational Reform in Early America: The Case of Providence, Rhode Island." HISTORIAN 39 (November 1976): 1-23.

Shade examines the Providence Association of Mechanics and Manufacturers and indicates that this organization supported educational reform. He criticizes historical revisionists who argue that the working class opposed educational and other reforms.

Silcox, Harry C. "Delay and Neglect: Negro Public Education in Antebellum Philadelphia, 1800-1860." PENNSYLVANIA MAGAZINE OF HISTORY AND BIOGRAPHY 97 (October 1973): 444-64.

Negroes faced delays in efforts to gain admission to Philadelphia's public schools. After the intense racism of the 1830s, blacks turned to their own schools for help.

Sizer, Theodore R. SECONDARY SCHOOLS AT THE TURN OF THE CENTURY. New Haven, Conn.: Yale University Press, 1964. xiv, 304 p.

This is a study of the committee of ten, chaired by Charles W. Eliot, that reported to the National Council of Education in 1894. This group, in assessing the needs of the schools, advocated a middle ground between the classics and new subjects.

Smith, Timothy L. "Immigrant Social Aspirations and American Education, 1880-1930." AMERICAN QUARTERLY 21 (Fall 1969): 523-43.

Immigrants from central and southeastern Europe displayed a concern for learning that was motivated by a desire to earn a better living, shape a family and community, and forge a national identity to fulfill the duty to homeland and not contradict allegiance to America. The presence of large numbers of immigrants promoted experiments and reform in education.

_____. "Native Blacks and Foreign Whites: Varying Responses to Educational Opportunity in America, 1880-1950." PERSPECTIVES IN AMERICAN HISTORY 6 (1972): 309-38.

Larger numbers of black youngsters were enrolled in schools in major cities than foreign whites, according to the census of 1910. Smith examines changing patterns of response to educational opportunity.

_____. "Protestant Schooling and American Nationality, 1800-1850." JOURNAL OF AMERICAN HISTORY 53 (March 1967): 679-95.

With the conviction that general education under religious auspices was vital to the republic and that there was a connection between law and piety, Americans in the nineteenth century founded public schools. These schools were not simply religious, they were distinctly Protestant with a vision of the Christian millenium.

Solberg, Winton U. "The Conflict Between Religion and Secularism at the University of Illinois, 1867-1894." AMERICAN QUARTERLY 18 (Summer 1966): 183-99.

The founding of state colleges and universities provided a new context for religion in institutions of higher learning. The University of Illinois was avowedly Christian at the outset, with compulsory chapel.

_____. THE UNIVERSITY OF ILLINOIS: AN INTELLECTUAL AND CULTURAL HISTORY. Urbana: University of Illinois Press, 1968. x, 494 p.

Illinois Industrial University was a new idea in 1867, but it did not prosper. The school suffered from limited vision, stingy legislatures, and reactionary presidents who lacked understanding of state universities and had trouble with students.

_____. "The University of Illinois Struggles for Public Recognition, 1867-1894." JOURNAL OF THE ILLINOIS STATE HISTORICAL SOCIETY 59 (Spring 1966): 5-29.

The University of Illinois sought the public eye during the first quarter century of its existence because of a dearth of students, hunger for funds, need to disarm critics, and the desire to overcome a sense of inferiority. This advertising was effective within narrow limits but the growth of the institution was shaped by social forces.

Spring, Joel. "Education and Progressivism." HISTORY OF EDUCATION QUARTERLY 10 (Spring 1970): 53-71.

Spring argues that progressive social and educational thought was based on the vision of a corporate society dependent on specialization and cooperation. Progressive thinkers sought to change human motivation from desire for economic gain to unselfish interest in working for the good of society.

Stevens, Edward W., Jr. "Social Centers, Politics, and Social Efficiency in the Progressive Era." HISTORY OF EDUCATION QUARTERLY 12 (Spring 1972): 16-33.

> The social center movement was an effort to boost community efficiency and expand the social functions of schools by using them as art galleries, debating clubs, polling places, etc. Social centers would enable citizens to use leisure time more efficiently by promoting personal growth, individual efficiency, and social usefulness.

Storr, Richard J. THE BEGINNINGS OF GRADUATE EDUCATION IN AMERICA Chicago: University of Chicago Press, 1953. ix, 195 p.

> Colleges were founded to impart an orthodoxy and little was done for more than a century and a half to advance knowledge. The beginnings of graduate education coincided with the growth of scientific knowledge.

_____. HARPER'S UNIVERSITY: THE BEGINNINGS. A HISTORY OF THE UNIVERSITY OF CHICAGO. Chicago: University of Chicago Press, 1966. xvi, 411 p.

> This is a history of the university from its birth in 1880 to the death of William Rainey Harper in 1906. The emphasis is on the university as an intellectual endeavor and on Harper's role in its administration.

Story, Ronald. "Harvard Students, the Boston Elite, and the New England Preparatory System, 1800-1870." HISTORY OF EDUCATION QUARTERLY 15 (Fall 1975): 281-98.

> Harvard became aristocratically exclusive after 1820. As Boston lawyers and businessmen gained administrative power at the institution, they also supervised many of the private academies, and in both they raised costs and requirements in order to create an elite.

Strickland, Charles E. "The Child, the Community, and Clio: The Uses of Cultural History in Elementary School Experiments of the Eighteen-Nineties." HISTORY OF EDUCATION QUARTERLY 7 (Winter 1967): 474-92.

> Cultural history was introduced into elementary education to relieve the drudgery of learning the three R's and to give relevance to the curriculum. Some educators adopted a culture-epoch approach to the past while others used a sociological method, but both were dedicated to showing children what was worthy, lovely, and harmonious.

Strong, Bryan. "Ideas of the Early Sex Education Movement in America, 1890-1920." HISTORY OF EDUCATION QUARTERLY 12 (Summer 1972): 129-61.

By the beginning of the twentieth century, sex as pleasure was replacing sex as procreation as a dominant idea. Defenders of the
older morality used sex education to teach a sexual morality that
proclaimed sex pure only when it took place between man and
wife.

Trecker, Janice Law. "Sex, Science, and Education." AMERICAN QUAR-
TERLY 26 (October 1974): 352-66.

This is a survey of sex bias in education in the late nineteenth
century when the woman's movement was gaining momentum. Scientists attacked women's education on the grounds that menstruation
was the dominating fact of female life and that in women the conservation of energy should be observed.

Troen, Selwyn K. THE PUBLIC AND THE SCHOOLS: SHAPING THE ST.
LOUIS SYSTEM, 1838-1920. Columbia: University of Missouri Press, 1975.
xi, 248 p.

The relationship of educational thought and institutions to urbanization is described. Education was the product of conflicting interests and socioeconomic classes.

Tyack, David. "Bureaucracy and the Common School: The Example of Portland, Oregon, 1851-1913." AMERICAN QUARTERLY 19 (Fall 1967): 475-98.

A team of educational experts from Stanford University studied the
Portland schools in 1913 and concluded that the fundamental principle upon which they were organized was a rigid, mechanical
system poorly adapted to the needs of the children and the community. In this city, and elsewhere, education had succumbed to
bureaucracy which earlier had been viewed as reform.

_____. THE ONE BEST SYSTEM: A HISTORY OF AMERICAN URBAN EDU-
CATION. Cambridge, Mass.: Harvard University Press, 1974. xii, 353 p.

Tyack covers the period from 1870 to 1940 and examines power relationships and the ethnic blocs behind them. Cities were slow to
spend money to educate all students and bureaucratization quickly
set in.

_____. "Pilgrim's Progress: Toward a Social History of the School Superin-
tendency, 1860-1960." HISTORY OF EDUCATION QUARTERLY 16 (Fall 1976):
257-300.

School superintendents in the nineteenth century conceived of themselves as aristocrats of character who were engaged in an evangelical enterprise of high moral purpose. In the twentieth century,
they began seeing themselves as a distinct occupational group in
quest of new sources of authority.

_____. "The Tribe and the Common School: Community Control in Rural Education." AMERICAN QUARTERLY 24 (March 1972): 3-19.

The rural school belonged to the community in more than a legal sense in the nineteenth century, and relations with teachers depended on personalities rather than formal status. Beginning in the 1890s, reformers attempted to improve the curriculum as well as discipline, and they tried to take control of these schools away from communities and give it to professionals.

Urban, Wayne. "Organized Teachers and Educational Reform During the Progressive Era: 1890-1920." HISTORY OF EDUCATION QUARTERLY 16 (Spring 1976): 35-52.

Teachers in some urban schools opposed progressive education because it was directed toward the centralization of school boards and the institutionalization of the pedagogical ideas of John Dewey. They saw reform as a threat to their economic well-being and job security.

Veysey, Laurence R. "The Academic Mind of Woodrow Wilson." MISSISSIPPI VALLEY HISTORICAL REVIEW 49 (March 1963): 613-34.

This is a study of Wilson's academic aims, theories, and attitudes. As an academic, he opposed vocational utility in undergraduate education, urged that the university be a community standing apart from particular concerns, and emphasized mental discipline.

_____. THE EMERGENCE OF THE AMERICAN UNIVERSITY. Chicago: University of Chicago Press, 1965. xiv, 505 p.

Veysey discusses both the academic philosophies that competed for control of higher education between 1865 and 1910 and developments in the academic structure. He describes university leaders in the 1890s as being creative and influential, but they gradually became bland and weak in their convictions.

Weber, Evelyn. THE KINDERGARTEN: ITS ENCOUNTER WITH EDUCATIONAL THOUGHT IN AMERICA. New York: Teachers College Press, 1969. xi, 282 p.

The kindergarten was established in the 1850s, but it did not become an object of conflict among educators until the days of John Dewey. The conflict was between progressives and conservatives with the former dominating and making the kindergarten a center for social training.

Wein, Roberta. "Women's Colleges and Domesticity, 1875-1918." HISTORY OF EDUCATION QUARTERLY 14 (Spring 1974): 31-47.

This is a study of Bryn Mawr and Wellesley colleges. During its first twenty years, Bryn Mawr exalted the intellectual life with sixty-two percent of its graduates pursuing graduate education and independent careers, while Wellesley was dedicated to the cultivation of domestic life.

Welter, Rush. POPULAR EDUCATION AND DEMOCRATIC THOUGHT IN AMERICA. New York: Columbia University Press, 1962. xvi, 473 p.

Welter argues that the central goal of democratic theory and practice in education is that education has been advanced to fulfill democracy, and that twentieth-century Americans are losing sight of this fact. Democratic and educational thought merged in the nineteenth century.

West, Earl H. "The Peabody Fund and Negro Education, 1867-1880." HISTORY OF EDUCATION QUARTERLY 6 (Summer 1966): 3-21.

West traces the history of the Peabody Fund, established in 1867, and shows that more than a million dollars was spent on education in the South before 1880, of which little more than $75,000 was given to Negro schools. He concludes, however, that this should not be interpreted as discrimination, because leaders of the fund hoped to prepare enlightened white leaders who would eventually become committed to social progress through universal education.

Wiebe, Robert H. "The Social Functions of Public Education." AMERICAN QUARTERLY 21 (Summer 1969): 147-64.

The role of public education has always been defined by the leading members of a locality. Since 1900, schools have only had leeway in the means of achieving goals, not in setting the goals themselves.

Woytanowitz, George M. UNIVERSITY EXTENSION: THE EARLY YEARS IN THE UNITED STATES, 1885-1915. Iowa City, Iowa: American College Testing Publications, 1974. xi, 171 p.

This is a study of the Chautauqua type of extension system rather than the agricultural type. This system of cultural education was introduced into the United States by Herbert Baxter Adams in 1885 and included lectures and classes.

1915 TO THE PRESENT

Altbach, Philip G., and Peterson, Patti. "Before Berkeley: Historical Perspectives on American Student Activism." ANNALS OF THE AMERICAN ACADEMY OF POLITICAL AND SOCIAL SCIENCE 395 (May 1971): 1-14.

Student activism in the twentieth century is surveyed. The authors argue that student political groups provided a political education for many who later became active in intellectual life, the labor movement, and other areas.

Beale, Howard K. A HISTORY OF THE FREEDOM OF TEACHING IN AMERI-
CAN SCHOOLS. Report of the Commission on Social Studies, American Historical Association, part 16. New York: Charles Scribner's Sons, 1941. xviii,
343 p.

> Beale finds that inadequate training, inferior social status, insuffi-
> cient appropriations for the schools, and the belief of the public
> that education should reflect the views of the majority have re-
> stricted freedom in the classroom. Teachers generally have been
> allowed freedom in discussing matters of little importance and denied
> freedom concerning ideas about which people cared.

Belles, A. Gilbert. "The College Faculty, the Negro Scholar, and the Julius
Rosenwald Fund." JOURNAL OF NEGRO HISTORY 54 (October 1969): 383-
92.

> This is a study of the efforts of the Rosenwald Fund in the mid-
> 1940s to encourage the appointment of Negro professors to other-
> wise all-white college and university faculties. The fund exhorted
> administrators to employ Negroes, and it achieved a fair amount of
> success.

Biebel, Charles D. "Private Foundations and Public Policy: The Case of
Secondary Education during the Depression." HISTORY OF EDUCATION QUAR-
TERLY 16 (Spring 1976): 3-34.

> The Rockefeller Foundation's General Education Board attempted to
> reform secondary education during the 1930s so that young people
> could adjust to the realities of American society. The board used
> its financial power to manipulate education organizations to foster
> an emphasis on vocational training.

Bodnar, John. "Materialism and Morality: Slavic-American Immigrants and
Education, 1890-1940." JOURNAL OF ETHNIC STUDIES 3 (Winter 1976):
1-20.

> Bodnar takes issue with the interpretation that immigrants were com-
> mitted to the idea of free public education and the promise it of-
> fered for social success. He shows that cultural continuity rather
> than Americanization was an overriding concern of Slavic Ameri-
> cans and they were critical of the schools because they did not of-
> fer instruction in blast furnaces, open hearths, or mines.

Bogue, Allan G., and Taylor, Robert, eds. THE UNIVERSITY OF WISCONSIN:
ONE HUNDRED AND TWENTY-FIVE YEARS. Madison: University of Wisconsin Press, 1975. x, 289 p.

> This carries forward the history of the university from 1925. It con-
> sists of a collection of essays on governance, students, courses, re-
> search, and the arts.

Education

Bowers, C.A. "Social Reconstructionism: Views from the Left and the Right--1932-1942." HISTORY OF EDUCATION QUARTERLY 10 (Spring 1970): 22-52.

Social reconstructionists, who wanted to use education to regenerate society, were challenged by Communists and American Legion Rightist types. Leftists perceived social reconstruction as a threat to the orthodox Marxist position on education, while those on the right feared that the minds of the young were being filled with un-American ideas.

Butts, R. Freeman. "Public Education and Political Community." HISTORY OF EDUCATION QUARTERLY 14 (Summer 1974): 165-84.

Butts is critical of the revisionist moods in the history of American education because they argue that the schools played only a minor role in the education process and that the schools miseducated the American people by enforcing the ideals and values of the dominant economic classes. He calls for another revisionism that emphasizes the concept of modernization, the role of the organized school in social change, and a comparative perspective.

Callahan, Raymond E. EDUCATION AND THE CULT OF EFFICIENCY: A STUDY OF THE SOCIAL FORCES THAT HAVE SHAPED THE ADMINISTRATION OF THE PUBLIC SCHOOLS. Chicago: University of Chicago Press, 1962. xii, 273 p.

Businessmen placed economic efficiency above human dignity, school administrators acting under business pressure put economic efficiency above educational values, and professors of administration produced superintendents who subordinated educational questions to business considerations.

Carbone, Peter F., Jr. "The Other Side of Harold Rugg." HISTORY OF EDUCATION QUARTERLY 11 (Fall 1971): 265-78.

Rugg was a professor at Teachers College, Columbia University, who believed that the school should be in the vanguard of social change. In this essay, Carbone indicates that he was influenced by Van Wyck Brooks and the SEVEN ARTS magazine group, and dedicated himself to integrating self and society, science and art, intellect and imagination.

Clark, Burton R. THE DISTINCTIVE COLLEGE: ANTIOCH, REED AND SWARTHMORE. Chicago: Aldine, 1970. vi, 280 p.

Antioch, Reed, and Swarthmore were deviant academic subcultures that blossomed and then sustained themselves. Their success is attributed to powerful presidents who launched innovation and were supported by loyal senior faculty, students, and alumni.

Cummins, Cedric. THE UNIVERSITY OF SOUTH DAKOTA, 1862-1966. Vermilion, S.D.: Dakota Press, 1975. v, 334 p.

The University of South Dakota is one of many institutions in which a majority of young Americans receive their education. South Dakota has been a pluralistic university that offered something special to the people of the state.

Drost, Walter H. DAVID SNEDDEN AND EDUCATION FOR SOCIAL EFFICIENCY. Madison: University of Wisconsin Press, 1967. ix, 242 p.

Snedden was a pioneer educational sociologist who taught at Stanford and the Columbia Teachers College, and served as commissioner of education in Massachusetts. He believed the social and vocational destination of each child could be determined scientifically and education should lead to the achievement of efficiency with Latin, history, and mathematics being replaced by civics, hygiene, and courses in work skills.

Eisen, Jonathan, and Steinberg, David. "The Student Revolt against Liberalism." ANNALS OF THE AMERICAN ACADEMY OF POLITICAL AND SOCIAL SCIENCE 382 (March 1969): 83-94.

Students rebelled against the establishment philosophy of "corporate liberalism" as exemplified by the idea of the university delineated in Clark Kerr's USES OF THE UNIVERSITY. They counterposed their own concept of "participatory democracy."

Fisher, Berenice M. INDUSTRIAL EDUCATION: AMERICAN IDEALS AND INSTITUTIONS. Madison: University of Wisconsin Press, 1967. xiii, 267 p.

Industrial education is depicted in terms of the philanthropic ideal, success or engineering ideal, and the skilled worker or trade-training ideal. Fisher focuses on the South; Burbank, California; and the Job Corps.

Gatewood, Willard B., Jr. EUGENE CLYDE BROOKS: EDUCATOR AND PUBLIC SERVANT. Durham, N.C.: Duke University Press, 1960. xiv, 279 p.

Brooks was one of the leaders in establishing a graded public-school movement in North Carolina in the twentieth century. As state superintendent of public instruction, he reorganized the schools along lines advocated by professional educators.

Goodenow, Ronald. "The Progressive Educator, Race and Ethnicity in the Depression Years: An Overview." HISTORY OF EDUCATION QUARTERLY 15 (Winter 1975): 365-94.

The progressive education movement became cognizant of race and ethnicity problems during the 1930s when there was little actual interest in race relations or racism in American society. Progressives called for tolerance but skirted racial integration and politics in order to avoid conflict.

Graham, Patricia Albjerg. PROGRESSIVE EDUCATION: FROM ARCADY TO ACADEME. A HISTORY OF THE PROGRESSIVE EDUCATION ASSOCIATION, 1919-1955. New York: Teachers College Press, 1967. x, 193 p.

The Progressive Education Association was formed in 1919 and had as its objective carrying the gospel of progressive education to every school. Graham emphasizes the child-centeredness, freedom, creativity side of progressivism rather than group activity and social adjustment.

Griffin, Clifford S. THE UNIVERSITY OF KANSAS: A HISTORY. Lawrence: University of Kansas Press, 1974. xiv, 808 p.

In this detailed study, few names are omitted. Griffin is at his best when discussing the politics of administrative organization and state control in the twentieth century.

Harris, Michael R. FIVE COUNTERREVOLUTIONISTS IN HIGHER EDUCATION: IRVING BABBITT, ALBERT JAY NOCK, ABRAHAM FLEXNER, ROBERT MAYNARD HUTCHINS, ALEXANDER MEIKLEJOHN. Corvallis: Oregon State University Press, 1970. 224 p.

All of these men believed that the goals of the university should be intellectual and cultural rather than utilitarian. To Harris, they were romantic counterrevolutionists who tried to reverse the tide in higher education toward vocationalism and social utility.

Hofstadter, Richard, and Hardy, C. DeWitt. THE DEVELOPMENT AND SCOPE OF HIGHER EDUCATION IN THE UNITED STATES. New York: Columbia University Press, 1952. x, 254 p.

Hofstadter emphasizes the secularization of higher education, curriculum content, graduate education, mass education, and anti-intellectualism. Hardy argues that education must enlist American energies for creative purpose in an age of doubt and insecurity.

Karier, Clarence J. "Liberalism and the Quest for Orderly Change." HISTORY OF EDUCATION QUARTERLY 12 (Spring 1972): 57-80.

Karier examines the philosophy and action mainly of John Dewey and argues that American liberals always have been bent on using the power of the political state to make the corporate system work more efficiently and effectively. For Dewey and other liberals, freedom meant control through science and technology, and they placed their faith in a mass education system dedicated to adjusting individuals to the industrial state.

Krug, Edward A. THE SHAPING OF THE AMERICAN HIGH SCHOOL. Vol. 2: 1920-1941. Madison: University of Wisconsin Press, 1972. xv, 375 p.

Between the world wars, the high school not only gained a universally accepted place in American public education, but social efficiency as a goal triumphed as well. The individual was subordinated to the group and an emphasis on conformity grew.

Ladd, Everett Carll, Jr., and Lipset, Seymour Martin. THE DIVIDED ACADEMY: PROFESSORS AND POLITICS. New York: McGraw-Hill, 1975. xv, 407 p.

This study is based on a 1969 Carnegie Commission on Higher Education survey of faculty attitudes and opinions. The authors found that professors were divided on political and academic issues, with those in the social sciences and humanities being left-leaning, and those in business, engineering, and agriculture being most conservative.

Lipset, Seymour Martin, and Riesman, David. EDUCATION AND POLITICS AT HARVARD. New York: McGraw-Hill, 1975. xi, 440 p.

Lipset and Riesman try to show why Harvard is the best university in the United States. Lipset writes on political controversies both intra- and extramural, while Riesman examines educational reform.

Morison, Robert S., ed. THE CONTEMPORARY UNIVERSITY: U.S.A. Boston: Houghton Mifflin, 1966. xvi, 364 p.

When this collection of essays was published, the country was reaching the point where about half of the population of college age was enrolled in an institution of higher learning. Specialists were important and education was becoming more vocational and technical.

Nicholas, William E. "World War I and Academic Dissent in Texas." ARIZONA AND THE WEST 14 (Autumn 1972): 215-30.

Between 1917 and 1919 both the University of Texas and Rice Institute were swept by loyalty crises. Academic dissent concerning pacifism, pro-Germanism, and political radicalism resulted in faculty dismissals.

Nowak, Marion. "'How To Be a Woman': Theories of Female Education in the 1950s." JOURNAL OF POPULAR CULTURE 9 (Summer 1975): 77-83.

In the 1950s, a new domesticity was entrenching itself in American life. This was seen in women's education where girls were prepared for future slots in life, notably those of the wife, homemaker, and mother.

Education

Olson, Keith W. THE G.I. BILL, THE VETERANS, AND THE COLLEGES. Lexington: University Press of Kentucky, 1974. x, 139 p.

> When the G.I. Bill was passed many believed it would not be used extensively by veterans. Not only did a wave of veterans attend college, they also out-performed nonveterans and raised the level of work in most schools.

_____. "The G.I. Bill and Higher Education: Success and Surprise." AMERICAN QUARTERLY 25 (December 1973): 596-610.

> The G.I. Bill was a success because it provided for the education of more than two million veterans. It was a surprise since proponents regarded it as an antidepression measure, while veterans and the public saw it as a veterans bonus.

Orfield, Gary. THE RECONSTRUCTION OF SOUTHERN EDUCATION: THE SCHOOLS AND THE 1964 CIVIL RIGHTS ACT. New York: John Wiley and Sons, 1969. xi, 376 p.

> In Title VI of the Civil Rights Act, the federal government was required to eliminate segregation in programs receiving government financial support. This is a study of the legislative history of Title VI guidelines in the U.S. Department of Health, Education, and Welfare.

Rudy, Willis. SCHOOLS IN AN AGE OF MASS CULTURE: AN EXPLORATION OF SELECTED THEMES IN THE HISTORY OF TWENTIETH-CENTURY EDUCATION. Englewood Cliffs, N.J.: Prentice-Hall, 1965. viii, 374 p.

> Rudy ranges widely in these essays. He deals with the child study movement, PTAs, foundations, pressure groups, extracurricular activities, church and state, segregation, and the Cold War.

Sawyer, R. McLaran. CENTENNIAL HISTORY OF THE UNIVERSITY OF NEBRASKA. Vol. 2: THE MODERN UNIVERSITY, 1920-1969. Lincoln, Neb.: Centennial, 1973. x, 292 p.

> Nebraska, like other state universities, faced the question of university function in this period. Should a state institution seek truth and knowledge or should it provide vocational training.

Spring, Joel. THE SORTING MACHINE: NATIONAL EDUCATIONAL POLICY SINCE 1945. New York: McKay, 1976. vi, 309 p.

> Educational policy is divided into two categories: schooling for individual liberty and education that sorts individuals according to social service needs. Spring shows how the cold war has been the major coercive force in prodding different educational postures and how presidents used education to forestall domestic upheaval and social disruption.

Szasz, Margaret. EDUCATION AND THE AMERICAN INDIAN: THE ROAD TO SELF-DETERMINATION, 1928-1973. Albuquerque: University of New Mexico Press, 1974. xviii, 251 p.

This study focuses on government schools, their administration, and the Bureau of Indian Affairs. It deals with bureaucratic politics rather than what went on in the classroom, and maintains that the government regarded Indian education as a means of cultural conquest.

Thorp, Margaret Farrand. NIELSON OF SMITH. New York: Oxford University Press, 1956. viii, 363 p.

Smith became one of the nation's great colleges during William Allan Nielson's presidency (1917-39). He built up the plant and funds, and recognized the central role of the faculty.

Tyack, David B. "The Perils of Pluralism: .The Background of the Pierce Case." AMERICAN HISTORICAL REVIEW 74 (October 1968): 74-98.

This essay covers the background of the Supreme Court decision in Sisters v. Pierce (1925), which ruled unconstitutional an Oregon law that required public schooling and essentially outlawed private elementary schools. This law expressed the outlook of Fundamentalists, such as members of the Ku Klux Klan, concerning parochial schools and elite academies.

Wiggins, Sam P. THE DESEGREGATION ERA IN HIGHER EDUCATION. Berkeley, Calif.: McCutchan, 1966. xiii, 106 p.

Wiggins shows that quantitative desegregation was just beginning in the mid-sixties. Advancement was directly related to political leadership, but organizations, such as the Southern Regional Council, played important roles.

_____. HIGHER EDUCATION IN THE SOUTH. Berkeley, Calif.: McCutchan, 1966. xix, 358 p.

This is a survey of the collegiate scene in the 1960s from community colleges to state universities. Wiggins maintains that there was much respect for authority, faculty-student solidarity, and a belief in paternalism that permitted presidents to run the institutions.

Wilson, Louis R. THE UNIVERSITY OF NORTH CAROLINA, 1900-1930: THE MAKING OF A MODERN UNIVERSITY. Chapel Hill: University of North Carolina Press, 1957. xxii, 633 p.

During this period, North Carolina emerged from a college of five hundred students to a fully developed university. A highly qualified faculty was recruited and a spirit of democracy, idealism, and learning manifested itself.

Wolters, Raymond. THE NEGRO ON CAMPUS: BLACK COLLEGE REBEL-LIONS OF THE 1920s. Princeton, N.J.: Princeton University Press, 1975. viii, 370 p.

The black colleges studied are Fisk, Tuskegee, Hampton, Howard, Florida A.&M., Lincoln (Missouri), Wilberforce, and Lincoln (Pennsylvania). Rebels demanded a respectable liberal arts curriculum, more black faculty members, administrators, and trustees, rather than a patronizing, subservient style, and their cause prevailed.

Chapter 7

HISTORIOGRAPHY

COLONIAL PERIOD TO 1815

Brown, Robert E. CARL BECKER ON HISTORY AND THE AMERICAN REVO-
LUTION. East Lansing, Mich.: Spartan Press, 1970. vi, 285 p.

Brown argues that Becker was a darling of the Old Left and now
of the New Left because he developed a class conflict interpretation of American history. His anticapitalist bias provided a lesson
that Progressive historians used to turn history into propaganda.

_____. CHARLES BEARD AND THE CONSTITUTION: A CRITICAL ANALYSIS
OF "AN ECONOMIC INTERPRETATION OF THE CONSTITUTION." Princeton,
N.J.: Princeton University Press, 1956. viii, 219 p.

This is an examination of Beard's ECONOMIC INTERPRETATION
from the standpoint of historical method. Brown challenges Beard's
sources and contends that the connections between economic interests and political behavior are simplified.

Cappon, Lester J. "American Historical Editors before Jared Sparks." WILLIAM
AND MARY QUARTERLY 30 (July 1973): 375–400.

Sparks was well acquainted with the work of predecessors, but in
his own editing he was his own man. Early compilations of documents were in the form of annals, but Ebenezer Hazard, Jeremy
Belknap, and William Waller Hening held larger concepts of historical presentation.

Colbourn, H. Trevor. "The Debate on the American Revolution as an Intellectual Movement." NORTH DAKOTA QUARTERLY 42 (Summer 1974): 7–17.

This is a survey of the movement away from interpreting the Revolution as an economic movement. Emphasis has been on ideology,
but Colbourn believes there should be greater effort at correlation
of the economic, social, and political context in which the Revolution took place.

Eisenstadt, A.S. CHARLES MCLEAN ANDREWS: A STUDY IN AMERICAN HISTORICAL WRITING. New York: Columbia University Press, 1956. xx, 273 p.

> Andrews was trained to believe that the history of institutions came first. He emphasized the colonial in American colonial history and depicted the colonies as part of an empire.

Ernst, Joseph. "Ideology and the Political Economy of Revolution." CANADIAN REVIEW OF AMERICAN STUDIES 4 (Fall 1973): 137-48.

> There has been a move away from political economy interpretations of the American Revolution such as those of the Progressive historians. This is a critique of Bernard Bailyn's interpretation of the Revolution in which ideology rather than social discontent or economic distress was paramount.

_____. "Political Economy and Reality: Problems in the Interpretation of the American Revolution." CANADIAN REVIEW OF AMERICAN STUDIES 7 (Fall 1976): 109-17.

> Ernst argues that the theories of the "ideological school" concerning the Revolution are false. These historians ignore the fact that economic thinking in revolutionary America was ideological since it was expressed by interests and the spokesmen of interests.

Fischer, David Hackett. "John Beale Bordley, Daniel Boorstin, and the American Enlightenment." JOURNAL OF SOUTHERN HISTORY 28 (August 1962): 327-342.

> Fischer takes issue with Boorstin's assumption that America was uniquely different from Europe during the seventeenth and eighteenth centuries and that Americans were relatively untouched by European ideas. He displays the career of Bordley, a Maryland planter, to qualify Boorstin's sweeping generalizations and to suggest that he overhomogenizes American culture.

Gay, Peter. A LOSS OF MASTERY: PURITAN HISTORIANS IN COLONIAL AMERICA. Berkeley and Los Angeles: University of California Press, 1966. viii, 164 p.

> This is an examination of William Bradford, Cotton Mather, and Jonathan Edwards. They are described as modernized, Protestant, Anglicized theologians of history who were concerned with the glorification of God and the denunciation of religious opponents.

Greene, Jack P. "The Flight from Determinism: A Review of Recent Literature on the Coming of the American Revolution." SOUTH ATLANTIC QUARTERLY 61 (Spring 1962): 235-59.

Since World War II, American scholars have interpreted the Revolution in a style that may be called neo-Whig. They have emphasized immediate issues and individuals, and while they have been cautious about using formal psychology, they have asked psychological questions.

_____. "Search for Identity: An Interpretation of the Meaning of Selected Patterns of Social Response in Eighteenth-Century America." JOURNAL OF SOCIAL HISTORY 3 (Spring 1970): 189-219.

Greene argues against the interpretation that Americans in the late eighteenth century adjusted to reality and assumed an easy pragmatism and a compulsive pursuit of wealth. He believes that these traits were counterbalanced by a tension characterized by fear of failure, and that instead of assuming an American identity, they depended for their normative values on the colonial past and an idealized image of English society and culture.

_____. "The Social Origins of the American Revolution: An Evaluation and an Interpretation." POLITICAL SCIENCE QUARTERLY 88 (March 1973): 1-22.

Two hypotheses have been advanced concerning colonial social life in the late seventeenth and eighteenth centuries. One is that there was an erosion of internal social cohesion between 1690 and 1760, while the other is that the social structure of the colonies was becoming more rigid and social strain more intense.

Hoffer, Peter C. "The Constitutional Crisis and the Rise of a Nationalistic View of History in America, 1716-1788." NEW YORK HISTORY 52 (July 1971): 305-23.

In the controversy over the constitution, politicians discovered a nationalistic view of history as a popular argument. The new constitution was appraised in terms of America's unique past.

Kammen, Michael. EMPIRE AND INTEREST: THE AMERICAN COLONIES AND THE POLITICS OF MERCANTILISM. New York: J.B. Lippincott, 1970. x, 186 p.

This is an important historiographical study in intellectual and comparative history. Using the concepts concerning interest groups developed by political scientists, Kammen argues that eighteenth-century British political culture was made unstable by interest groups that matched the political instability of the American colonies.

_____. "The Meaning of Colonization in American Revolutionary Thought." JOURNAL OF THE HISTORY OF IDEAS 31 (July-September 1970): 337-58.

While historians have been correct in depicting the intellectual history of the Revolution as being in a state of flux, Kammen shows that the one important constant in this thinking was the historical meaning of colonization. Revolutionists focused on colonial origins and argued that the first Americans had emigrated to seek and preserve civil and religious liberty.

_____. PEOPLE OF PARADOX: AN INQUIRY CONCERNING THE ORIGINS OF AMERICAN CIVILIZATION. New York: Alfred A. Knopf, 1972. xvii, 316 p.

This is a criticism of consensus theories in American history. Kammen sees American history as contradictions—love and hate, peace and war.

Kraus, Michael. A HISTORY OF AMERICAN HISTORY. New York: Farrar and Rinehart, 1937. x, 607 p.

Kraus surveys the work of those historians who "contributed most to the writing of American history in a comprehensive manner." He begins with the Icelandic sagas and concludes with the cooperative histories of the twentieth century.

Leder, Lawrence H., ed. THE COLONIAL LEGACY. 2 vols. Vol. 1: LOYALIST HISTORIANS. Vol. 2: SOME EIGHTEENTH CENTURY COMMENTATORS. New York: Harper and Row, 1971. 206; 228 p.

The essays in these volumes examine the writings and lives of sixteen historians, including George Chalmers, William Douglass, Alexander Hewat, Jonathan Boucher, Joseph Galloway, Robert Proud, and others.

_____. THE COLONIAL LEGACY. 2 vols. in one. Vol. 3: HISTORIANS OF NATURE AND MAN'S NATURE; vol. 4: EARLY NATIONALIST HISTORIANS. New York: Harper and Row, 1973. vi, 344 p.

In this work, familiar names as well as obscure writers of state and local histories are covered. John Marshall, Cadwallader Colden, and Jeremy Belknap, as well as Thomas Jones, Francois-Xavier Martin, and Le Page du Pratz, receive attention.

McGiffert, Michael. "American Puritan Studies in the 1960s." WILLIAM AND MARY QUARTERLY 27 (January 1970): 36-67.

This article covers trends in the study of seventeenth-century New England Puritanism, with particular attention to the works published since the death of Perry Miller in 1963. One can speak of Puritan studies because Miller provided a model that gives the subject definition and discipline.

Mason, Bernard. "The Heritage of Carl Becker: The Historiography of the Revolution in New York." NEW-YORK HISTORICAL SOCIETY QUARTERLY 53 (April 1969): 127–47.

This is a study of Becker's conceptualization of the Revolution in New York and the controversy that has surrounded this subject. Today's scholarship has found flaws in Becker's history, but it has not offered wholly satisfactory equivalents.

Morgan, Edmund S. "The American Revolution: Revisions in Need of Revising." WILLIAM AND MARY QUARTERLY 14 (January 1957): 3–15.

The imperial, social-economic, and Namierist interpretations of British politics have made important contributions to eighteenth-century American and English history. These ideas must be re-examined in light of the Revolution and the Revolution needs to be re-examined in light of these ideas.

Pole, J.R. "The American Past: Is it Still Usable?" JOURNAL OF AMERICAN STUDIES 1 (April 1967): 63–78.

Historians who have been educated entirely in the tradition and environment of the United States cannot gain freedom from the American version of space and time. This has partly resulted from the American version of the Whig interpretation of history or the belief that the United States was responsible for the preservation and advancement of certain ideals.

_____. "Historians and the Problem of Early American Democracy." AMERICAN HISTORICAL REVIEW 67 (April 1962): 626–46.

The earliest national period of U.S. history was a period of revolution and constitution making. To use the term "democracy" in this era is to raise a problem of definition since there is so little agreement on what "democracy" means, especially since early constitutions were conservative and excluded the common people from decision making.

Shaffer, Arthur H. THE POLITICS OF HISTORY: WRITING THE HISTORY OF THE AMERICAN REVOLUTION, 1783-1815. Chicago: Precedent, 1975. 228 p.

This study brings together the literary materials of early historians of the Revolution. These historians--Ramsay, Belknap, and others-- regarded themselves as gentlemen of public affairs who viewed history as a patriotic duty.

Shalhope, Robert E. "Toward a Republican Synthesis: The Emergence of an Understanding of Republicanism in American Historiography." WILLIAM AND MARY QUARTERLY 29 (January 1972): 49–80.

This is a historiography of the evolution of republicanism between 1760 and 1789. Shalhope argues that a republican synthesis in intellectual history would contribute to an understanding of the emergence of political institutions, social dynamics, and the polarization of American society.

Smith, William Raymond. HISTORY AS ARGUMENT: THREE PATRIOT HISTORIANS OF THE AMERICAN REVOLUTION. The Hague: Mouton, 1966. 207 p.

History should be read from the perspective that historians are trying to demonstrate their own positions concerning things. This method is applied to David Ramsay, Mercy Warren, and John Marshall, who controlled their treatment of events by being a moderate Federalist, extreme Republican, and an extreme nationalist.

Van Tassel, David D. RECORDING AMERICA'S PAST: AN INTERPRETATION OF THE DEVELOPMENT OF HISTORICAL STUDIES IN AMERICA, 1607-1884. Chicago: University of Chicago Press, 1960. xii, 223 p.

Van Tassel is more concerned with state and local rather than national history, and with the development of historical societies. In indicating the character of historical activity before scientific history, he emphasizes the attempts of writers to justify the Revolution as a rights-of-man movement, the dominance of New England in textbook writing, the trumpeting of New England virtues as the American heritage, and other matters.

Wood, Gordon S. "Rhetoric and Reality in the American Revolution." WILLIAM AND MARY QUARTERLY 23 (January 1966): 3-32.

Historians have stressed the intellectual character of the Revolution. Wood discusses historiography and suggests that while the social and economic approach of the Progressives has been rejected, we may be approaching a period of writing where idealism and behaviorism will meet.

1815-1915

Bannister, Robert C. "'The Survival of the Fittest is Our Doctrine': History or Histrionics." JOURNAL OF THE HISTORY OF IDEAS 31 (July-September 1970): 377-98.

Reformers in the late nineteenth century, such as Henry George, Edward Bellamy, and Henry Demarest Lloyd, charged that classical economics had become wedded to Darwinism, a view supported by the historians Richard Hofstadter, Merle Curti, Eric Goldman, and others in the twentieth century. Bannister argues that the nineteenth-century reformers used Darsinism to provide a basis for their reform proposals and this was passed on until they were made forerunners of the New Deal.

Billington, Ray Allen. THE GENESIS OF THE FRONTIER THESIS: A STUDY IN HISTORICAL CREATIVITY. San Marino, Calif.: Huntington Library, 1971. xi, 315 p.

Billington examines Turner's experience and psyche, and describes the influences of Herbert Baxter Adams and the University of Wisconsin in the formulation of the frontier hypothesis. He also discusses Turner's behavior as a scholar, his procrastination, inattention to details, and performance under pressure.

Bonner, Thomas W. "Civil War Historians and the 'Needless War' Doctrine." JOURNAL OF THE HISTORY OF IDEAS 17 (April 1956): 193-216.

This is an essay on historical causation in which Bonner examines the ideas of Avery Craven, J.G. Randall, and others. He argues that causation is meaningless as portrayed by these revisionist historians who maintained that the Civil War was avoidable and therefore needless.

Bowden, Henry Warner. CHURCH HISTORY IN THE AGE OF SCIENCE: HISTORIOGRAPHICAL PATTERNS IN THE UNITED STATES, 1876-1918. Chapel Hill: University of North Carolina Press, 1971. xvi, 269 p.

With the rise of "scientific history," church historians faced the dilemma of maintaining Christian assumptions and facing criticisms from their colleagues. Bowden's approach is biographical and he discusses the evolution of church history as a theological discipline.

_____. "Science and the Idea of Church History: An American Debate." CHURCH HISTORY 36 (September 1967): 308-26.

The rise of scientific history in the late nineteenth century had an important bearing on church history. The climate of opinion in that period made it increasingly difficult to base church history on a confession of faith and at the same time command respect in the scholarly world.

Buenker, John D. "The Progressive Era: A Search for a Synthesis." MID-AMERICA 51 (July 1969): 175-93.

This is a brief survey of Progressive historiography. Buenker suggests that historians will not achieve a comprehensive explanation of Progressive reform until they understand that the movement was caused by the interaction of industrialization, immigration, and urbanization.

Campbell, A.E. "An Excess of Isolation: Isolation and the American Civil War." JOURNAL OF SOUTHERN HISTORY 29 (May 1963): 161-74.

This is a critique of David Donald's thesis that the Civil War came about because the decline of governments in the United States was accompanied by an increase in popular participation that led to the failure of conservative efforts to solve problems. Campbell maintains that there was an excess of isolation since Americans carried on their debates in isolation from other nations and were thrown back on their own resources, thereby magnifying dissensions.

Caughey, John Walton. "Hubert Howe Bancroft, Historian of Western America." AMERICAN HISTORICAL REVIEW 50 (April 1945): 461-70.

This is a sketch of Bancroft, showing the development of his collecting activities and historical writing. Bancroft was a child of the West--a successful businessman whose collecting illustrated the region's cultural aspirations, and a historian whose histories revealed intellectual maturity.

Cooke, Jacob E. FREDERICK BANCROFT, HISTORIAN. Introduction by Allan Nevins. Norman: University of Oklahoma Press, 1957. xiv, 282 p.

Bancroft was not a central figure in American scholarship, but he was one of the historians of the late 1890s who attempted to make history a profession. He was a financially independent gentleman scholar who functioned outside the academic world. This book also includes three hitherto unpublished essays on "The Colonization of American Negroes from 1801 to 1865," by Bancroft.

Cox, La Wanda, and Cox, John H. "Negro Suffrage and Republican Politics: The Problem of Motivation in Reconstruction Politics." JOURNAL OF SOUTHERN HISTORY 33 (August 1967): 303-30.

The Coxes examine the historiography of the Fifteenth Amendment which gave Negro citizens the right to vote. They believe that Republican motivation needs to be examined and suggest that politicians acted out of principle rather than expediency since Negro votes did not give an advantage to the Republican Party.

Craven, Avery. AN HISTORIAN AND THE CIVIL WAR. Chicago: University of Chicago Press, 1964. v, 233 p.

In these essays, Craven attempts to depict his struggle in unravelling the coming of the Civil War. He pays little attention to the 1850s and argues that the roots of the war lay in the 1830s.

Crowe, Charles. "The Emergence of Progressive History." JOURNAL OF THE HISTORY OF IDEAS 27 (January-March 1966): 109-24.

Progressive history was a framework of related pragmatic and progressive assumptions. Crowe briefly reviews progressive historiography and describes the reaction against it in the 1950s and 1960s.

Curry, Richard O. "The Abolitionists and Reconstruction: A Critical Appraisal." JOURNAL OF SOUTHERN HISTORY 34 (November 1968): 527-45.

In response to the racial tensions of the 1960s, a number of historians have argued that emancipation failed to create social planning for racial democracy because the Radicals abandoned the Negro during Reconstruction for political and social reasons. Abolitionists, on the other hand, were dedicated to social equality, but Curry suggests that they were not prototypes of twentieth-century social planners.

_____. "The Civil War and Reconstruction, 1861-1877: A Critical Overview of Recent Trends and Interpretations." CIVIL WAR HISTORY 20 (September 1974): 215-38.

The politics of the Civil War and Reconstruction should be considered as a unit. The issue of Reconstruction was the central theme in Civil War party struggles in the loyal states.

De Graaf, Lawrence B. "Recognition, Racism, and Reflections on the Writing of Western Black History." PACIFIC HISTORICAL REVIEW 44 (February 1975): 22-51.

This is a study of the history of blacks in the westward movement. Generally, the black has been invisible in frontier history, but an important literature concerning the denial of rights to blacks on the frontier has come into being.

Dillon, Merton L. "The Abolitionists: A Decade of Historiography, 1959-1969." JOURNAL OF SOUTHERN HISTORY 35 (November 1969): 500-22.

Writings on the abolitionists in this decade brought about their rehabilitation and even made them objects of admiration and respect. Dillon reviews the literature, playing off new interpretations against those of Gilbert Barnes, Dwight Dumond, and David Donald.

Donovan, Timothy Paul. HENRY ADAMS AND BROOKS ADAMS: THE EDUCATION OF TWO AMERICAN HISTORIANS. Norman: University of Oklahoma Press, 1961. xii, 220 p.

Donovan shows that both Adamses were devoted to theorizing concerning force and energy in history and to achieving scientific certitude. They sensed that they lived in an era of collisions of power and the degradations of standards.

Doughty, Howard N. FRANCIS PARKMAN. New York: Macmillan, 1962. x, 414 p.

Parkman's histories had fundamental relevance to nineteenth-century American problems. They challenged democratic leadership and dramatized the conflict between civilized man and nature.

Historiography

Dudden, Arthur P. "Nostalgia and the American." JOURNAL OF THE HISTORY OF IDEAS 22 (October–December 1961): 515–30.

Dudden regards the idea of progress in America as an ideological dogma that has had its day, but nostalgia still remains. He examines some of the materials that lie beneath the surface of American history, such as the effects of the rampant capitalism of the Jacksonian era, and concludes that both progress and nostalgia are oversimplifications of history and recurrent forms of cultural lag.

Filene, Peter G. "An Obituary for 'The Progressive Movement.'" AMERICAN QUARTERLY 22 (Spring 1970): 20–34.

This is a review of the historiography of the Progressive movement in which the author concludes that historians should give up their search for conceptual order in history. An obituary should be delivered for the Progressive movement as a frame of reference because it was ambiguous and incoherent.

Foner, Eric. "The Causes of the Civil War: Recent Interpretations and New Directions." CIVIL WAR HISTORY 20 (September 1974): 197–214.

The 1960s saw new interpretations of slavery, the abolitionists, and racism, but this did not bring historians closer to a generally accepted interpretation of the causes of the Civil War. Foner suggests that the war was a struggle for the future of the nation with both North and South fighting to preserve a society.

Genovese, Eugene D. "Rebelliousness and Docility in the Negro Slave: A Critique of the Elkins Thesis." CIVIL WAR HISTORY 13 (December 1967): 293–314.

The Sambo-like figure of the Negro was not the product of the slave system but goes back to the fourteenth century. Elkins has not described the slave personality, but demonstrated the limiting case of the slavish personality.

Harper, Alan D. "William A. Dunning: The Historian as Nemesis." CIVIL WAR HISTORY 10 (March 1964): 54–66.

Dunning's view that Negro incapacity caused the failure of Reconstruction has fed the fires of hate. His prejudice has been a far more important force than his scholarship.

Higham, John. "Anti-Semitism in the Gilded Age: A Reinterpretation." MISSISSIPPI VALLEY HISTORICAL REVIEW 43 (March 1957): 559–78.

Interpretations of anti-Semitism have shifted from linking it with conservatism and privilege to associating it with agrarian radicalism in the late nineteenth century. Higham argues that not only patricians and agrarians but also immigrants in the cities energized anti-Semitic ideology.

Holt, W. Stull. "The Idea of Scientific History in America." JOURNAL OF THE HISTORY OF IDEAS 1 (June 1940): 352-62.

Historians of the late nineteenth and early twentieth centuries expressed the belief that history was scientific with one group arguing that the discipline was scientific because it was based on natural laws and another emphasizing the ideal of complete objectivity. The first assumption, which Henry Adams championed, did not gain many supporters.

Jacobs, Wilbur R., ed. LETTERS OF FRANCIS PARKMAN. 2 vols. Norman: University of Oklahoma Press, 1960. lxvi, 204; xl, 286 p.

This collection contains four hundred letters arranged chronologically. Biographical rather than historical information is emphasized.

Jordy, William H. HENRY ADAMS: SCIENTIFIC HISTORIAN. New Haven, Conn.: Yale University Press, 1952. xv, 327 p.

This study consists of an analysis of Adams's HISTORY OF THE UNITED STATES and a discussion of his attempt to mire history in the natural sciences. Jordy argues that Adams embraced scientific history after he became pessimistic and lost the zest for life.

Kreuter, Kent, and Kreuter, Gretchen. "The Vernacular History of A.M. Simons." JOURNAL OF AMERICAN STUDIES 2 (April 1968): 65-81.

Simons' SOCIAL FORCES IN AMERICAN HISTORY is more than a Marxist curiosity for he used it to delineate a new American hero who protested against the cult of gentility in American life. The collective hero in all of Simons's writings was the farmer and worker, the true democrats, who were subjected to plunder and greed.

Levin, David. HISTORY AS ROMANTIC ART: BANCROFT, PRESCOTT, MOTLEY, AND PARKMAN. Stanford, Calif.: Stanford University Press, 1959. 260 p.

Levin shows that the four historians not only approached history from a common cultural position but also used similar literary techniques. They displayed a romantic attitude toward the past and used the literary methods of other romantic writers.

Loewenberg, Bert James. AMERICAN HISTORY IN AMERICAN THOUGHT: CHRISTOPHER COLUMBUS TO HENRY ADAMS. New York: Simon and Schuster, 1972. 731 p.

Loewenberg portrays historians as events since they show the preconceptions of their times and thus record the changing processes of the national mind. Historians of the national period propagandized for national power, but after the Civil War history became technical, and new methods prepared the way for less narrow interpretations of the past.

_____. "John William Burgess, The Scientific Method, and the Hegelian Philosophy of History." MISSISSIPPI VALLEY HISTORICAL REVIEW 42 (December 1955): 490-509.

Burgess developed a scientific method based on Hegelian philosophy. He defined history as "spirit," by which he meant mind or reason, with causal explanation being dependent on the intent of creative power.

Lynd, Staughton. "On Turner, Beard and Slavery." JOURNAL OF NEGRO HISTORY 48 (October 1963): 235-50.

The significance of slavery in American history has been obscured because the twin giants of American historiography, Turner and Beard, minimized its importance. Turner shifted attention from slavery to the frontier, while Beard portrayed the institution as a form of agrarianism.

McNaught, Kenneth. "American Progressives and the Great Society." JOURNAL OF AMERICAN HISTORY 53 (December 1966): 504-20.

Historians such as Samuel P. Hays, George E. Mowry, Robert H. Wiebe, Gabriel Kolko, and others have portrayed progressivism as a movement to achieve the rationalization of business through government regulation. McNaught argues that Socialist-Progressives, a group that included Walter Lippmann and Felix Frankfurter, were a viable political force that patterned their thinking on Graham Wallas's GREAT SOCIETY.

Marshall, Lynn L., and Drescher, Seymour. "American Historians and Tocqueville's DEMOCRACY." JOURNAL OF AMERICAN HISTORY 55 (December 1968): 512-32.

Historians need to recognize that central to Tocqueville's concerns was the structure and administration of organizations in their formal and informal, public and private operations. He recognized that the democratic individual in society was defined by the roles he played in organizations.

Mindel, Joseph. "The Uses of Metaphor: Henry Adams and the Symbols of Science." JOURNAL OF THE HISTORY OF IDEAS 26 (January-March 1965): 89-102.

Mindel concludes that Adams's use of science as method in history late in his life was based on limited knowledge and productive of far-fetched conclusions. Nevertheless, his use of science as a metaphor was significant in deepening his historical understanding, since metaphors do not need to be true to be useful.

Muller, Philip R. "Look Back Without Anger: A Reappraisal of William A. Dunning." JOURNAL OF AMERICAN HISTORY 61 (September 1974): 325-38.

This is a study mainly of Dunning's writings on Reconstruction and his seminar at Columbia. RECONSTRUCTION, POLITICAL AND ECONOMIC, 1865-1877, was racist, partisan, and based on filmsy research, but it has occupied a revered place in American historiography.

Noble, David W. HISTORIANS AGAINST HISTORY: THE FRONTIER THESIS AND THE NATIONAL CONVENANT IN AMERICAN HISTORICAL WRITING SINCE 1830. Minneapolis: University of Minnesota Press, 1965. 197 p.

Noble argues that English Puritans came to Massachusetts Bay and created a community sustained by a covenant with God which delivered them and their children from the vicissitudes of history so long as they kept their society pure and simple. He regards this as a national covenant in historical writing and examines the work of Bancroft, Beard, Becker, Boorstin, and others in this context.

Pease, Otis A. PARKMAN'S HISTORY: THE HISTORIAN AS LITERARY ARTIST. New Haven, Conn.: Yale University Press, 1953. xi, 86 p.

This is a study of Parkman's literary development and of his history of France and England in America. Pease indicates what made Parkman's narrative style so attractive to readers.

Pollack, Norman. "Fear of Man: Populism, Authoritarianism, and the Historian." AGRICULTURAL HISTORY 39 (April 1965): 59-67.

Populism is the conscience of modern America. It sought the establishment of a social order founded on a democratized industrial system and a transformation of social values with greater concern for the welfare of all.

_____. "Hofstadter on Populism: A Critique of 'The Age of Reform.'" JOURNAL OF SOUTHERN HISTORY 26 (November 1960): 478-500.

Pollack is critical, on a methodological basis principally, of Hofstadter's identification of five dominant themes in Populist ideology. He maintains that Populists were not retrogressive utopians who held outdated producers values, nor were they anti-Semitic.

Potter, David M. "The Historian's Use of Nationalism and Vice Versa." AMERICAN HISTORICAL REVIEW 67 (July 1962): 924-50.

The historian deals with human beings as people in groups. Nationality has been a criterion for organizing much of modern history, but the pattern of loyalties between 1820 and 1860 was more intricate than the antithesis between nationalism and sectionalism.

Historiography

Pressly, Thomas J. AMERICANS INTERPRET THEIR CIVIL WAR. Princeton, N.J.: Princeton University Press, 1954. xvi, 347 p.

This is a historiography of Civil War interpretations. Pressly analyzes individual historians and also shows the changing currents of ideas concerning Civil War causation.

Rosenberg, John S. "Toward a New Civil War Revisionism." AMERICAN SCHOLAR 38 (Spring 1969): 250-72.

Rosenberg reviews historical evaluations of the Civil War, focusing on the "New Nationalists" who argue that the conflict was justified because it abolished slavery and preserved the union. He calls for a new revisionism based on the argument that preservation of the Union against the will of a large number of inhabitants did not justify sacrifices and that only limited improvement in the status of the Negro did not justify the expenditure in lives.

Saloutos, Theodore. "The Professors and the Populists." AGRICULTURAL HISTORY 40 (October 1966): 235-54.

This is a study of historical revisionism and populism. Historians have been interested in the relationship of populism with McCarthyism, socialism, and fascism.

Sellers, Charles Grier, Jr. "Andrew Jackson versus the Historians." MISSISSIPPI VALLEY HISTORICAL REVIEW 44 (March 1958): 615-34.

Jacksonian historiography has been riddled with disagreements and contradictions. Jackson and his Democracy were beneficiaries of the pro-democratic orientation that dominated historical writing in the late nineteenth and early twentieth centuries, but later writers have emphasized the paradoxical nature of the Jacksonian democratic impulse.

Sorin, Gerald. ABOLITIONISM: A NEW PERSPECTIVE. New York: Praeger, 1972. 187 p.

Sorin exposes the relevant studies of abolitionism and sums up what the authors are saying. He emphasizes the importance of the abolitionists in the coming of the Civil War.

Stampp, Kenneth M. "Rebels and Sambos: The Search for the Negro's Personality in Slavery." JOURNAL OF SOUTHERN HISTORY 37 (August 1971): 367-92.

Knowledge concerning slave life and behavior comes mainly from white observers. Stampp suggests that role conflict should be applied to slave personality since slaves were forced to wear the mask of Sambo and suffered from a conflict of roles.

Stephenson, Wendell H. "A Half Century of Southern Historical Scholarship." JOURNAL OF SOUTHERN HISTORY 11 (February 1945): 3-32.

This is a study of the evolution of scholarship concerning the South of Herbert B. Adams, William A. Dunning, Ulrich B. Phillips, and William E. Dodd. Stephenson emphasizes the interest in southern history generated by their work rather than their interpretations.

———. "A Quarter Century of American Historiography." MISSISSIPPI VAL-LEY HISTORICAL REVIEW 45 (June 1958): 3-22.

Stephenson examines "presentism" in American historiography and focuses on Civil War writing. He urges historians to integrate past-mindedness and present-mindedness, and make history less an auto-biography of the mind and more an effort to find reality.

———. SOUTHERN HISTORY IN THE MAKING: PIONEER HISTORIANS OF THE SOUTH. Baton Rouge: Louisiana State University Press, 1964. ix, 294 p.

William Garrott Brown, Herbert B. Adams, William P. Trent, John Spencer Bassett, Ulrich B. Phillips, and others are covered. These were scholars who sought answers to the broader questions of the place of the South in American history.

Stewart, James Brewer. "Politics and Belief in Abolitionism: Stanley Elkins' Concept of Antiinstitutionalism and Recent Interpretations of American Anti-slavery." SOUTH ATLANTIC QUARTERLY 75 (Winter 1976): 74-97.

The anti-institutional theme in radical abolitionism has been sup-ported by historians in the 1970s. Stewart maintains that this theme generated specific reform techniques in the 1840s and 1850s such as those of a modern public service pressure group.

Strong, Bryan. "Historians and American Socialism, 1900-1920." SCIENCE AND SOCIETY 34 (Winter 1970): 387-97.

Strong argues that consensus history was a product of the Cold War. He examines consensus interpretations of socialism and emphasizes distortions of this history.

Tager, Jack. "Progressives, Conservatives, and the Theory of Status Revolu-tion." MID-AMERICA 48 (July 1966): 162-75.

The status revolution theory of Richard Hofstadter and George Mowry as an explanation of the Progressive movement is discussed. Tager labels it a facile explanation that does not take in reform at all levels or individual motivational patterns.

Thorpe, Earl E. NEGRO HISTORIANS IN THE UNITED STATES. Baton Rouge, La.: Fraternal Press, 1958. xiv, 188 p.

Nineteenth-century black historians were justifiers of emancipation, while those in the first three decades of the twentieth century were attackers of prevailing theories of race and proponents of using history to elevate the position of their people. Since 1930, Negro historians have shown less bitterness and less inclination to use history as propaganda.

Van Tassel, David D. "The American Historical Association and the South, 1884-1913." JOURNAL OF SOUTHERN HISTORY 23 (November 1957): 465-82.

The American Historical Association was founded not only as a national organization, but as a missionary effort to promote scientific history. The South was one of the great missionary regions even though it was steeped in history.

Vitzthun, Richard C. THE AMERICAN COMPROMISE: THEME AND METHOD IN THE HISTORIES OF BANCROFT, PARKMAN, AND ADAMS. Norman: University of Oklahoma Press, 1974. ix, 236 p.

Vitzthun delineates the themes and techniques shared by the three historians. He maintains that their principal theme was the search for authority and nationhood on the part of a diverse people.

_____. "The Historian as Editor: Francis Parkman's Reconstruction of Sources in Montcalm and Wolfe." JOURNAL OF AMERICAN HISTORY 53 (December 1966): 471-86.

This study of Parkman's use of sources indicates that the historian was most accurate when using primary materials, but little more than a copyist when employing secondary works. His volumes were "scissors and paste" studies, but this is a distinguishing tool of narrative history.

Weisberger, Bernard A. "The Dark and Bloody Ground of Reconstruction Historiography." JOURNAL OF SOUTHERN HISTORY 25 (November 1959): 427-47.

Weisberger calls for a revision of the interpretation of Reconstruction history based on assumptions that carpetbaggers and white Republicans were wicked, blacks illiterate incompetents, and the restoration of white supremacy a blessing. He maintains that some useful revision has been accomplished, but no general history has been produced and textbooks deal with the period inadequately.

Welter, Rush. "The History of Ideas in America." JOURNAL OF AMERICAN HISTORY 51 (March 1965): 599-614.

Welter shows the limitations between internal and external approaches to ideas, and also discusses the problems historians have experi-

enced in dealing with pristine and popular thought. He suggests
a method based on John Dewey's psychology which he argues re-
solves methodological and other problems.

Wish, Harvey. THE AMERICAN HISTORIAN: A SOCIAL-INTELLECTUAL
HISTORY OF THE WRITING OF THE AMERICAN PAST. New York: Oxford
University Press, 1960. x, 366 p.

Social determinants are too intrusive in the writings of historians
and should inspire caution on the part of the reader. In the twentieth century, historians have been more self-critical and aware of
the subjective factors in writing history.

_____. "The New Formalism Versus the Progressive Historian." SOUTH AT-
LANTIC QUARTERLY 67 (Winter 1968): 78-93.

The formalism of abstractions, autonomous logic, and mathematics
was attacked by Progressive rebels. They emphasized that the eva-
sion of social issues throughout history and the indifference to the
psychology of conflict in historical form was a serious mistake.

Wolford, Thorp L. "Edward Eggleston: Evolution of a Historian." INDIANA
MAGAZINE OF HISTORY 63 (March 1967): 17-48.

This is a survey of Eggleston's career and his preparation for historical writing. Wolford concludes that his frontier background
and experiences in Brooklyn and London gave him an opportunity
to respond to the rich colors of life and to record these colors with
a freshness rare in historiography.

Wyatt-Brown, Bertram. "Stanley Elkins' SLAVERY: The Antislavery Interpretation Reexamined." AMERICAN QUARTERLY 25 (May 1973): 154-76.

Elkins's position on abolitionism was that Americans were unprepared
to deal with slavery since they lacked institutional means and a
proper intellectual frame of mind. Wyatt-Brown suggests that he
was not incorrect in depicting an atomistic society, but rather that
he was incomplete in not seeing the strains between folkways and
stateways that were taking place.

1915 TO THE PRESENT

Aaron, Daniel, et al. ESSAYS ON HISTORY AND LITERATURE. Edited by
Robert H. Bremner. Columbus: Ohio State University Press, 1966. xi, 190 p.

These essays cover the problems of treating recent literary history,
the assumption that American intellectual life from 1865 to 1900
was sterile, the gentry of the Revolution, and the argument that
history belongs with the arts and not with the social sciences.

Auerbach, Jerold S. "New Deal, Old Deal, or Raw Deal: Some Thoughts on New Left Historiography." JOURNAL OF SOUTHERN HISTORY 34 (February 1969): 18-30.

New Left critics have charged that the New Deal was a sad story of what might have been, that it failed to attack or solve social problems, and that it served only to recognize antagonist social groups and integrate them conservatively. These are all parts of a one-dimensional interpretation that sacrifices the past for current political protest.

Beale, Howard K. CHARLES A. BEARD: AN APPRAISAL. Lexington: University of Kentucky Press, 1954. xiv, 312 p.

This is a symposium of twelve appraisals of Beard. They portray Beard the man and discuss relativism in history and his economic interpretation.

Bell, Whitfield J., Jr. "Richard H. Shryock: Life and Work of a Historian." JOURNAL OF THE HISTORY OF MEDICINE AND ALLIED SCIENCES 29 (January 1974): 15-31.

Shryock was one of the principal figures in the professionalization of medical history in the twentieth century. He wrote and taught that medicine and public health are basic elements of every society and are influenced by most ideas and actions.

Bennett, James D. FREDERICK JACKSON TURNER. Boston: Twayne, 1975. 138 p.

This is an analysis of Turner's major writings interspersed with biographical information. Criticisms of the frontier hypothesis are highlighted.

Benson, Lee. TOWARD THE SCIENTIFIC STUDY OF HISTORY: SELECTED ESSAYS. Philadelphia: J.B. Lippincott, 1972. xi, 352 p.

Benson argues that the historian should inform the public, and that events in history should be case studies using theories in the social sciences.

_____. TURNER AND BEARD: AMERICAN HISTORICAL WRITING RECONSIDERED. Glencoe, Ill.: Free Press, 1960. xiv, 241 p.

The intellectual context of Turner's frontier theory and the methodological errors of Beard and his critics on the making of the constitution are considered. Turner's claim to originality is challenged and Beard's blurring of the distinction between economic determinism and economic interpretation is delineated.

Berkhofer, Robert F., Jr. A BEHAVIORAL APPROACH TO HISTORICAL ANALYSIS. New York: Free Press, 1969. viii, 339 p.

Berkhofer criticizes historians for only wishing to illuminate the past and also surveys writings in the social sciences. Classic historical analysis has failed from artistic and scientific viewpoints because it has not considered the variables in human behavior.

_____. "Clio and the Culture Concept: Some Impressions of a Changing Relationship in American Historiography." SOCIAL SCIENCE QUARTERLY 53 (Spring 1972): 297-320.

Consensus history is the application of the culture concept adopted by social scientists and the educated public following World War II. This concept in the social sciences and history rose and fell because of an effort to achieve greater analytical precision.

Billington, Ray Allen. AMERICA'S FRONTIER HERITAGE. New York: Holt, Rinehart and Winston, 1966. xiv, 302 p.

Billington reassesses Turner's frontier hypothesis by applying the findings of economists, anthropologists, sociologists, social psychologists, and demographers. In doing so he modifies it by discarding Turner's successive stages of settlement and arguing that the social rather than the physical environment altered cultural patterns.

Blackwood, George D. "Frederick Jackson Turner and John Rogers Commons-- Complimentary Thinkers." MISSISSIPPI VALLEY HISTORICAL REVIEW 41 (December 1954): 471-88.

Although Turner and Commons worked at a time when the social sciences were splitting apart, they shared many insights. They believed each age writes the history of the past anew; emphasized the study of institutions; argued that American political and economic growth represented a balance between conflicting forces; and exhibited a relentless spirit of inquiry.

Blakey, George T. HISTORIANS ON THE HOMEFRONT: AMERICAN PROPAGANDISTS FOR THE GREAT WAR. Lexington: University Press of Kentucky, 1970. 168 p.

During World War I, some three dozen historians, including J. Franklin Jameson, Albert Bushnell Hart, and Guy Stanton Ford, offered to help the government sell the war to the public. They were criticized by younger historians, such as Harry Elmer Barnes, for prostituting the profession and promoting a monstrous and unjust conflict.

Brauer, Jerold C., ed. REINTERPRETATION OF AMERICAN CHURCH HISTORY. Chicago: University of Chicago Press, 1968. xi, 227 p.

These essays examine the secularization of religious history and the shift of research out of seminaries and into history departments, the incorporation of black Christianity into religious history, and religious interaction among western Christians.

Burson, George S. "The Second Reconstruction: A Historiographical Essay on Recent Works." JOURNAL OF NEGRO HISTORY 59 (October 1974): 322-36.

The period between the Brown decision of 1954 and Stokeley Carmichael's call for Black Power in 1966 has been treated mainly by political scientists, sociologists, and journalists. Burson reviews historical treatments and argues that historians should begin answering significant questions that have not been addressed.

Cave, Alfred A. "Main Themes in Recent Southern History." WESTERN HUMANITIES REVIEW 20 (Spring 1966): 97-112.

Cave traces the transition in southern historical thought from justification of southern traditions to the present ambivalent attitude toward the southern heritage. He defines the main themes of southern history.

Cohen, Warren I. THE AMERICAN REVISIONISTS: THE LESSONS OF INTERVENTION IN WORLD WAR I. Chicago: University of Chicago Press, 1967. xv, 252 p.

Revisionism appeared during the wartime debates on intervention and when many intellectuals were disillusioned by the rejection of the Treaty of Versailles. It was the controversy over war guilt, however, that brought revisionism to full flower in the works of Harry Elmer Barnes, Charles A. Beard, Walter Millis, and C.C. Tansill.

Cole, Wayne S. "American Entry into World War II: A Historiographical Appraisal." MISSISSIPPI VALLEY HISTORICAL REVIEW 43 (March 1957): 595-617.

Interpretive controversies of historians have been in part an extension of the pre-Pearl Harbor debate between interventionists and noninterventionists. Interventionists find the causes of American intervention in developments in other parts of the world beyond American control, while noninterventionists contend that the Axis powers were not a threat to the United States and that President Roosevelt followed policies designed to get the country into war while promoting peace.

Coleman, William. "Science and Symbol in the Turner Frontier Hypothesis." AMERICAN HISTORICAL REVIEW 72 (October 1966): 22-49.

The metaphor of social organism provides the central theme of the frontier hypothesis. The power of the thesis derives from its poetic imagery of the American West and the premises of evolutionary human geography.

Crunden, Robert M. "Freud, Erikson, and the Historian: A Bibliographical Essay." CANADIAN REVIEW OF AMERICAN STUDIES 4 (Spring 1973): 48–64.

In recent American historiography there has been a Freudian reading of history that has been criticized for its sexual reductionism. Controversies have centered around David Donald's CHARLES SUMNER and the Georges's analysis of Woodrow Wilson.

Cuff, Robert D. "American Historians and the 'Organizational Factor,'" CANADIAN REVIEW OF AMERICAN STUDIES 4 (Spring 1973): 19–31.

There has been a resurgence of studying organization-building and associational activities in American historiography. These have been fragmented and scattered across many areas as the work of Alfred Chandler, Gabriel Kolko, Michael Katz, and Richard Hofstadter indicate.

Cunliffe, Marcus. "American Watersheds." AMERICAN QUARTERLY 13 (Winter 1961): 480–94.

Cunliffe condemns the conceptualization of American history in terms of the metaphors of watersheds and turning points as being clumsy and imprecise. He calls for a history based on the dialogues concerning contradictory ideals and desires carried on by opposing groups and within the minds of single individuals.

Cunliffe, Marcus, and Winks, Robin W., eds. PASTMASTERS: SOME ESSAYS ON AMERICAN HISTORIANS. New York: Harper and Row, 1969. xv, 492 p.

These essays concern historians who lived in the nineteenth or twentieth centuries such as Parkman, Adams, Turner, Beard, Parrington, Miller, Bemis, Boorstin, Handlin, Hofstadter, and Potter. This is an impressionistic, collective biography that shows historians not only interpret the past but also suggest courses of action concerning the problems of the world.

Curti, Merle. "The Democratic Theme in American Historical Literature." MISSISSIPPI VALLEY HISTORICAL REVIEW 39 (June 1952): 3–28.

The treatment of democracy by historians has been peripheral rather than central to their work. Current confusion and uncertainty about democracy must rest on historians' shoulders.

_____. PROBING OUR PAST. New York: Harper & Brothers, 1954. xii, 294 p.

This is a collection of Curti's essays written between 1926-53. He covers topics such as the democratic theme in American literature, the Turner thesis, and John Locke's influence on America.

Davis, David Brion. "Some Recent Directions in American Cultural History." AMERICAN HISTORICAL REVIEW 73 (February 1968): 696-707.

This a study of three levels of abstraction that characterize American cultural history. One is the description of the characteristic styles, motifs, and patterns of a given period. Another is the focusing of attention on a central problem or segment of culture. The third is searching outlines of intersection between the development of culture and individual personality.

Degler, Carl N. "The Sociologist as Historian: Riesman's THE LONELY CROWD." AMERICAN QUARTERLY 15 (Winter 1963): 483-497.

The LONELY CROWD describes the other-directed man as a new personality emerging in twentieth-century America. Degler argues that Riesman's categories of inner-directed and other-directed are useful to historians, particularly since other-directness seems to be a dominant element in American character through most of American history.

_____. "The South in Southern History Textbooks." JOURNAL OF SOUTHERN HISTORY 30 (February 1964): 48-57.

This is a study of textbooks written by Francis Butler Simkins, William B. Hesseltine, Clement Eaton, and John Ezell. There is some defensiveness in these books, but mainly the authors emphasize that the South is American and also a diverse region.

Diggins, John P. "Consciousness and Ideology in American History: The Burden of Daniel J. Boorstin." AMERICAN HISTORICAL REVIEW 76 (February 1971): 99-118.

Boorstin has adopted a cheerful vision of the American past and has seen America as always becoming. It is his intention to liberate the American past from ideology, and in doing so he makes history into philosophy.

_____. "The Perils of Naturalism: Some Reflections on Daniel J. Boorstin's Approach to History." AMERICAN QUARTERLY 23 (May 1971): 153-80.

Diggins quarrels with Boorstin's consensus history because in it democracy is a historical fact rather than an unfinished human ideal. The present thus becomes the fulfillment of the past and the past an ideal world.

Donovan, Timothy Paul. HISTORICAL THOUGHT IN AMERICA: POSTWAR PATTERNS. Norman: University of Oklahoma Press, 1973. ix, 182 p.

Post-World War II American historians have engaged in self-scrutiny, found richness in their discipline, reacted against determinism, and enlarged the role or conscience and moral judgment in the writing of history.

Genovese, Eugene D. "Race and Class in Southern History: An Appraisal of the Work of Ulrich Bonnell Phillips." AGRICULTURAL HISTORY 41 (October 1967): 345-58.

Phillips's work can be read with profit for its understanding of slavery as a social system. The Old South had to face questions of social power and responsibility because the slave system demanded it, but this was not true of the urban-industrial wage labor of the North.

Greene, John C. "Objectives and Methods in Intellectual History." MISSISSIPPI VALLEY HISTORICAL REVIEW 44 (June 1957): 58-74.

The intellectual historian should elucidate the presuppositions of thought in given epochs and explain the changes they undergo. Intellectual history must be analytical, cross-disciplinary, and devoted to the study of the long history of thought.

Hendricks, Luther V. JAMES HARVEY ROBINSON: TEACHER OF HISTORY. New York: King's Crown Press, 1946. xii, 120 p.

This is an account of the professional career of a distinguished teacher. Robinson focused on intellectual cross-currents and attempted to determine why people are chauvinistic, narrow-minded, cruel, and stupid.

Herbst, Jurgen. THE GERMAN HISTORICAL SCHOOL IN AMERICAN SCHOLARSHIP: A STUDY IN THE TRANSFER OF CULTURE. Ithaca, N.Y.: Cornell University Press, 1965. xvii, 262 p.

Herbst examines movements in Germany with their counterparts in the United States. He illuminates the historical philosophies of Herbert Baxter Adams, Carl Becker, and Charles A. Beard.

Higham, John. "American Intellectual History: A Critical Appraisal." AMERICAN QUARTERLY 13 (Summer 1961): 219-33.

Intellectual history concerns how and why particular human experiences have followed one another and it centers attention on the experiences of thought rather than external behavior. Higham discusses the scholarly environment of intellectual history and suggests that feelings and ideas rather than action and art should stand at the center of the intellectual historian's vision.

_____. "Beyond Consensus: The Historian as a Moral Critic." AMERICAN HISTORICAL REVIEW 67 (April 1962): 609-25.

The dilemma of historical scholarship is the need of historians to be responsive to questions and issues of their own age and at the same time be faithful to an age gone by. Historians should not search for patterns of conflict and consensus, but should look for the moral standards of an age.

_____. WRITING AMERICAN HISTORY: ESSAYS ON MODERN SCHOLAR-SHIP. Bloomington: Indiana University Press, 1970. x, 207 p.

In these essays, Higham discusses his changing views on conflict and consensus in American historiography, his belief that scientific history is being revived to the detriment of biography and intellectual history, and his conclusion that the ideal historian should be a moral critic. In all, he assesses shifting American ideology rather than the practical matter of gaining understanding of human behavior.

Higham, John, with Leonard Krieger and Felix Gilbert. HISTORY. Englewood Cliffs, N.J.: Prentice-Hall, 1965. xiv, 402 p.

The authors write on American history and cover the evolution of the discipline from the evolutionists of the turn of the twentieth century to the writers of the 1950s and 1960s. The Progressive historians sought a science of man, but turned increasingly nationalistic and gave way to the scholars of the post-World War II era who searched for stability.

Hofstadter, Richard. THE PROGRESSIVE HISTORIANS: TURNER, BEARD, PARRINGTON. New York: Alfred A. Knopf, 1968. xvii, 498 p.

This study is divided into three sections: a survey of American historiography until the end of the nineteenth century; essays on Turner, Beard, and Parrington; and an essay on conflict and consensus in American history. Hofstadter emphasizes the contributions to an enduring understanding of history and suggests what can best be forgotten.

Hollingsworth, J. Rogers. "Consensus and Continuity in Recent American Historical Writing." SOUTH ATLANTIC QUARTERLY 61 (Winter 1962): 40-51.

Following the Second World War, a change took place in the intellectual climate of the United States that represented a fusion of a conservative temper with a liberal frame of mind. It was taken up by historians who emphasized conservatism as the dominant force in the American past.

Jacobs, Wilbur R. THE HISTORICAL WORLD OF FREDERICK JACKSON TUR-
NER WITH SELECTIONS FROM HIS CORRESPONDENCE. New Haven, Conn.:
Yale University Press, 1968. xxii, 289 p.

> These letters show why Turner's formal publications were meager.
> He was a perfectionist who was not satisfied until he had seen
> every document, and he was an inspiring teacher who gave of him-
> self to his students.

_____. "Turner's Methodology: Multiple Working Hypotheses or Ruling
Theory?" JOURNAL OF AMERICAN HISTORY 54 (March 1968): 853-63.

> Jacobs shows that Turner was strongly influenced by the idea of
> multiple hypotheses in scientific research. In his writings, how-
> ever, he centered on two matters—frontier and section—in which
> the minutiae of history would take form and which became a rul-
> ing theory.

_____, ed. FREDERICK JACKSON TURNER'S LEGACY: UNPUBLISHED
WRITINGS IN AMERICAN HISTORY. San Marino, Calif.: Huntington Library, 1965. xiii, 217 p.

> This collection includes long essays on sectionalism and the devel-
> opment of American society. They reinforce Turner's theory of
> multiple causation in history.

Johannsen, Robert W. "David Potter, Historian and Social Critic: A Review
Essay." CIVIL WAR HISTORY 20 (March 1974): 35-44.

> Johannsen reviews Potter's Civil War historiography, writings on
> the South, and his study of American character and behavior.
> Potter viewed history as the record of past experiences applied to
> the issues and problems of the present.

Kammen, Michael, ed. "WHAT IS THE GOOD OF HISTORY?" SELECTED
LETTERS OF CARL L. BECKER, 1900-1945. Ithaca, N.Y.: Cornell University Press, 1973. xlii, 372 p.

> This collection includes three hundred pieces of correspondence
> arranged chronologically to show Becker's changing ideas and in-
> tellectual growth. Most were written to Beard and Turner.

Kelly, R. Gordon. "Literature and the Historian." AMERICAN QUARTERLY
26 (May 1974): 141-59.

> Kelly considers the use of imaginative literature as historical evi-
> dence and applies his ideas to late nineteenth-century children's
> literature. He argues in favor of the use of a theory that systems
> of reality are created and maintained by symbol systems.

Kennedy, Thomas C. CHARLES A. BEARD AND AMERICAN FOREIGN POL-
ICY. Gainesville: University of Florida Press, 1975. xi, 199 p.

This is an intellectual history of Beard's writings on foreign policy
from the IDEA OF NATIONAL INTEREST to his much criticized
revisionist interpretations of American entry into World War II. It
shows the dilemma Beard faced between being a dispassionate teacher
and a passionate public figure.

Kristol, Irving. "American Historians and the Democratic Idea." AMERICAN
SCHOLAR 39 (Winter 1969-70): 89-103.

Historians have provided only a confusing perspective concerning
the fate of the democratic idea in America. Kristol reviews the
work of Turner, Boorstin, and Hartz to make his point.

Krueger, Thomas A. "The Historians and the Edenic Myth: A Critique."
CANADIAN REVIEW OF AMERICAN STUDIES 4 (Spring 1973): 3-18.

Many authors have written about the Edenic myth or the idea that
the archetypal American cultural pattern has been the faith in
America as a New World Garden. These writers have established
the presence of the myth, but they have not delineated range or
the Importance of its influence.

Levin, David. IN DEFENSE OF HISTORICAL LITERATURE: ESSAYS ON
AMERICAN HISTORY, AUTOBIOGRAPHY, DRAMA, AND FICTION. New
York: Hill and Wang, 1967. xi, 144 p.

Historians should recognize what the discipline of literature can
offer to history. The relation of form and content, role of con-
jecture, and the use of symbols are matters important to historical
writing.

Link, Arthur S., and Patrick, Rembert W., eds. WRITING SOUTHERN HIS-
TORY: ESSAYS IN HISTORIOGRAPHY IN HONOR OF FLETCHER M. GREEN.
Baton Rouge: Louisiana State University Press, 1965. x, 502 p.

This is not a miscellany of articles but a comprehensive survey of
historical writing concerning the South. Contributors deal with
the question, "What is southern history?," a question that is difficult when applied to periods other than the nineteenth century.

Little, Lester K. "Psychology and Recent American Historical Thought."
JOURNAL OF THE HISTORY OF THE BEHAVIORAL SCIENCES 5 (April 1969):
152-72.

Early in the twentieth century, historians were deterministic, believing that what men thought and did were shaped by impersonal
forces. The growing use of psychology as a methodological tool
recently has placed the individual back into the center of history.

McCoy, Donald R. "Underdeveloped Sources of Understanding in American History." JOURNAL OF AMERICAN HISTORY 54 (September 1967): 255-70.

McCoy advocates that American historians study the United States as a nation among nations and not as a world unto itself; tap sources of attitudes and opinion that are more typical of and closer to the doers of the nation than fashionable and highly literate sources; and recognize the fact that before the twentieth century, activities and occurrences in addition to the national government were important.

McDermott, John Francis, ed. RESEARCH OPPORTUNITIES IN AMERICAN CULTURAL HISTORY. Lexington: University of Kentucky Press, 1961. x, 205 p.

This collection covers travel literature, midwestern literature, science, recreation, the immigrant, folklore, the book trade, popular education, the visual arts, and other matters.

Maddox, Robert James. THE NEW LEFT AND THE ORIGINS OF THE COLD WAR. Princeton, N.J.: Princeton University Press, 1973. ix, 169 p.

This is an attack on the uses of evidence by William Appleman Williams, D.F. Fleming, Gar Alperovitz, David Horowitz, Gabriel Kolko, Diane Shaver Clemens, and Lloyd C. Gardner. Through textual criticism, Maddox argues that these historians have quoted out of context, omitted passages, and produced polemics rather than scholarly analysis.

Maier, Charles S. "Revisionism and the Interpretation of Cold War Origins." PERSPECTIVES IN AMERICAN HISTORY 4 (1970): 313-50.

Vietnam has influenced the revisionist critique of the Cold War. For twenty years, the Soviet-American conflict was blamed on Stalin's effort to expand Soviet control, but revisionists now are arguing that the United States must bear responsibility for the Cold War's origins.

Marcell, David W. "Charles Beard: Civilization and the Revolt Against Empiricism." AMERICAN QUARTERLY 21 (Spring 1969): 65-86.

In the early 1930s Beard came to believe that the Western world was experiencing a dislocation that portended the collapse of social systems and the failure of the social philosophies on which they rested. He turned to a consensus philosophy of history based on the idea of civilization, during the last two decades of his life.

Mathews, Joseph J. "The Study of History in the South." JOURNAL OF SOUTHERN HISTORY 31 (February 1965): 3-20.

Mathews traces the development of history as an academic discipline in southern colleges and universities. Southern institutions responded slowly to the academic changes in the late nineteenth century because most were struggling to survive, but course offerings were expanded in the 1920s and the Southern Historical Association was founded in 1934 to stimulate the study of history.

May, Henry F. "The Recovery of American Religious History." AMERICAN HISTORICAL REVIEW 70 (October 1964): 79-92.

The recovery of American religious history may well be the most important achievement of the last thirty years. It has brought American history back into the great dialogue between secular and religious thought.

_____. "Shifting Perspectives on the 1920s." MISSISSIPPI VALLEY HISTORI-CAL REVIEW 43 (December 1956): 405-27.

Three contemporary pictures of the 1920s have emerged: that the decade was a new era; that social scientists contributed new know-ledge; and that the decade was a period of decline. Historians can effectively see the history of the twenties as a period of dis-integration, but they must approach this in terms of interdisciplin-ary studies.

Morton, Marian J. THE TERRORS OF IDEOLOGICAL POLITICS: LIBERAL HISTORIANS IN A CONSERVATIVE MOOD. Cleveland: Press of Case West-ern Reserve University, 1972. xi, 192 p.

Morton contends that the ideological tensions of the McCarthy era influenced liberal historiography. She argues that liberals furnished McCarthy with anticommunism and blames villains such as Arthur Schlesinger, Jr., Louis Hartz, Daniel Boorstin, Edmund Morgan, and Richard Hofstadter.

Newby, I.A. "Historians and Negroes." JOURNAL OF NEGRO HISTORY 54 (January 1969): 32-47.

Negro history encompasses what blacks have done in America and what whites have done to them. Most American history has been written from a white, middle-class perspective, ignoring the nation's failures.

Payne, Darwin. THE MAN OF ONLY YESTERDAY: FREDERICK LEWIS ALLEN: FORMER EDITOR OF HARPER'S MAGAZINE, AUTHOR, AND INTER-PRETER OF HIS TIMES. New York: Harper and Row, 1975. xi, 340 p.

This is an analysis of Allen's years with HARPER'S, during which he transformed the magazine from a literary publication to one of public arfairs. Allen's historical writing is also discussed, as his interpretations of recent events have earned a lasting place in American historiography.

Perkins, Dexter; Snell, John L.; and the Committee on Graduate Education of the American Historical Association. THE EDUCATION OF HISTORIANS IN THE UNITED STATES. New York: McGraw-Hill, 1962. xiv, 244 p.

This study presents tables on where Ph.D. recipients come from, their fields of specialty, and other matters. Recommendations are also made that Ph.D. candidates be oriented toward good teaching and that the degree be viewed as the beginning of scholarly development.

Pomeroy, Earl. "Toward a Reorientation of Western History: Continuity and Environment." MISSISSIPPI VALLEY HISTORICAL REVIEW 41 (March 1955): 579-600.

We need western history that will disregard arbitrary boundaries of time and space. Interpretive studies that gain freedom from the old radical-environmental bias in western history must replace factual treatises.

Ratner, Sidney. "The Historian's Approach to Psychology." JOURNAL OF THE HISTORY OF IDEAS 2 (January 1941): 95-109.

Ratner challenges the scientific historian to extend his critical acumen from the weighing of evidence to explaining the psychological mechanisms involved in events. He reviews Turner, Beard, and Parrington, and shows how psychology would add a dimension to their historical views.

Rodgers, Hugh I. "Charles A. Beard, the 'New Physics,' and Historical Relativity." HISTORIAN 30 (August 1968): 545-60.

Beard's historiography was as much influenced by the new physics as by the pragmatic revolt and evolution. His historical relativism that included an attack on objectivity, denial of determinism, and phrases such as "frame of reference" points to the impact of changes in the physical sciences.

Rogin, Michael Paul. THE INTELLECTUALS AND McCARTHY: THE RADICAL SPECTER. Cambridge: M.I.T. Press, 1967. xi, 366 p.

Sen. Joseph McCarthy aroused anxieties that reinforced a profound transformation in thinking concerning political problems and movements. Instead of seeing him as a brazen, conservative Republican, social scientists such as Richard Hofstadter, Seymour Martin Lipset, and Daniel Bell placed McCarthy in a pluralist context and associated him with agrarian radicalism and progressivism, which they condemned as irrational mass movements and made into a popular radical right.

Rundell, Walter, Jr. IN PURSUIT OF AMERICAN HISTORY: RESEARCH AND TRAINING IN THE UNITED STATES. Norman: University of Oklahoma Press, 1970. xv, 445 p.

Through extensive interviews and other research, Rundell has found that the great research needs of the profession are gaining improved access to materials, better communication between researchers and persons with historical vocations, and more adequate training in methodology.

_____. "Walter Prescott Webb: Product of Environment." ARIZONA AND THE WEST 5 (Spring 1963): 4-28.

This is a review of Webb's historiography. He was a Texan whose historical views and hypotheses were conditioned by environmental influences.

Skotheim, Robert Allen. AMERICAN INTELLECTUAL HISTORIES AND HISTO-RIANS. Princeton, N.J.: Princeton University Press, 1966. xi, 326 p.

This is not a study of the founding fathers of intellectual history but rather of specific historians who represent what Skotheim describes as distinctive schools. Eggleston, Robinson, Beard, Becker, Parrington, and Curti are those who ascribe intellectual changes to progressive social changes, while Tyler, Morison, Miller, and Gabriel emphasize timeless social values that have survived even in changing circumstances.

_____. "Environmental Interpretations of Ideas by Beard, Parrington, and Curti." PACIFIC HISTORICAL REVIEW 32 (February 1964): 35-44.

These historians have emphasized the environmental influences on human thought and have stimulated readers to look beyond the word for causation. They argue that ideas are creatures not creators, and that beliefs, values, and opinions do not exist alone in space.

_____. "The Writing of American Histories of Ideas: Two Traditions in the XXth Century." JOURNAL OF THE HISTORY OF IDEAS 25 (April-June 1964): 257-78.

The writings of Eggleston, Robinson, Beard, Becker, Parrington, and Curti, all of whom embraced social reform, dominated the history of ideas in the first half of the twentieth century. They were challenged, however, by Morison, Miller, and Gabriel, who emphasized the power of ideas.

Smith, Charlotte Watkins. CARL BECKER: ON HISTORY AND THE CLIMATE OF OPINION. Ithaca, N.Y.: Cornell University Press, 1956. xiv, 225 p.

This book includes a life of Becker and a study of his thoughts on history as a means of attaining truth and understanding. The section on his relativism is especially illuminating.

Snyder, Phil L., ed. DETACHMENT AND THE WRITING OF HISTORY: ESSAYS AND LETTERS OF CARL L. BECKER. Ithaca, N.Y.: Cornell University Press, 1958. xvi, 240 p.

Some of Becker's most significant observations on the writing of history are found in these essays and letters. He never tired of emphasizing the futility of achieving complete detachment in historical writing.

Sorenson, Lloyd R. "Charles A. Beard and German Historiographical Thought." MISSISSIPPI VALLEY HISTORICAL REVIEW 42 (September 1955): 274-87.

In the 1930s, Beard turned to German antipositivist history in a limited way. He caused American historians to reexamine their procedures and view assumptions as assumptions and not as self-evident truths that scientific history had thought them to be.

Stephenson, Wendell Holmes. THE SOUTH LIVES IN HISTORY: SOUTHERN HISTORIANS AND THEIR LEGACY. Baton Rouge: Louisiana State University Press, 1955. xvi, 163 p.

Stephenson describes the plight of post-Civil War historians--the lack of libraries, and parochial attitudes. He emphasizes the work of William E. Dodd, Ulrich B. Phillips, and Walter Lynwood Fleming.

Sternsher, Bernard. CONSENSUS, CONFLICT, AND AMERICAN HISTORIANS. Bloomington: Indiana University Press, 1975. ix, 432 p.

This is an intellectual history of historians' disputes in the 1950s and 1960s. It covers recent scholarship on political parties during the Jacksonian era and the histories of the last several decades.

Strout, Cushing. THE PRAGMATIC REVOLT IN AMERICAN HISTORY: CARL BECKER AND CHARLES BEARD. New Haven, Conn.: Yale University Press, 1958. xii, 182 p.

Both Becker and Beard tried to ground the study of history in a new philosophy appropriate to the development of modern thought. Becker withdrew into the type of detachment he criticized, while Beard believed the historian should draw the outlines of the past in terms of a faith in the future.

Susman, Warren I. "History and the American Intellectual: Uses of a Usable Past." AMERICAN QUARTERLY 16 (Summer 1964): 243-63.

Susman discusses treatments of the past designated as mythic and historical, and shows how American intellectuals used them in response to their own eras. Intellectuals generally have used myth to enable history to retreat from ideology.

Swierenga, Robert P. "Ethnocultural Political Analysis: A New Approach to American Ethnic Studies." JOURNAL OF AMERICAN STUDIES 5 (April 1971): 59-79.

> The historiography of American ethnic history emphasizing ethno-cultural political analysis, introduced by Samuel Lubell and taken up by Lee Benson, is examined. This approach has shown ethnic conflict rather than assimilation in the political sense.

Thorpe, Earl E. THE CENTRAL THEME OF BLACK HISTORY. Durham, N.C.: Seeman Printery, 1969. xii, 240 p.

> This is a collection of nine essays that cover Negro historiography, teaching, and race relations. Thorpe maintains that black history has served as a weapon in the struggle for racial equality.

Tobin, Gregory M. THE MAKING OF HISTORY: WALTER PRESCOTT WEBB AND THE GREAT PLAINS. Austin: University of Texas Press, 1976. xiv, 184 p.

> Webb's Great Plains concept is discussed. Tobin uses a psycho-sociological approach to trace the evolution of an environmental-ist.

Unger, Irwin. "The 'New Left' and American History: Some Recent Trends in United States Historiography." AMERICAN HISTORICAL REVIEW 72 (July 1967): 1237-63.

> New Left historians have dismissed the postwar American consensus history because they see it as history in service to an elitist and aristocratic definition of society. Unger discusses the work of Wil-liam A. Williams, Walter LaFeber, Staughton Lynd, Norman Pol-lack, Stephan Thernstrom, and others who are trying to reconstruct a leftist past.

Wallace, Michael. "The Uses of Violence in American History." AMERICAN SCHOLAR 40 (Winter 1970-71): 81-102.

> Americans suffer from historical amnesia when considering their his-tory of violent struggles between people for power. They have forgotten this history because of the Horatio Alger myth of oppor-tunity to advance and prosper peacefully and because most violence has not been directed against the state.

Welter, Rush. "The History of Ideas in America." JOURNAL OF AMERICAN HISTORY 51 (March 1965): 599-614.

> Welter shows the limitations between internal and external approaches to ideas, and also discusses the problems historians have experi-enced in dealing with pristine and popular thought. He suggests a

method based on John Dewey's psychology which, he argues, re-
solves methodological and other problems.

Wise, Gene. AMERICAN HISTORICAL EXPLANATIONS: A STRATEGY FOR
GROUNDED INQUIRY. Homewood, Ill.: Dorsey, 1973. xx, 370 p.

Historians must give up amassing useless data. Wise draws on the
suggestions of cognitive and the Gestalt psychologists and Thomas
Kuhn, and shows the dissolution of the Progressive paradigm of
Beard, Turner, and Parrington, as well as the new explanation
form of Perry Miller, R.W.B. Lewis, and Richard Hofstadter.

_____. "The Contemporary Crisis in Intellectual History Studies." CLIO 5
(Fall 1975): 55-72.

There has been a consensus in American intellectual history that
there is a relatively homogeneous American mind. Wise surveys the
objections to this consensus and suggests that intellectual historians
should view ideas as ways of negotiating or as coping strategies.

_____. "'Political Reality' in Recent American Scholarship: Progressives
versus Symbolists." AMERICAN QUARTERLY 19 (Summer 1967): 303-28.

Wise elucidates American historiography in the twentieth century
in terms of attitudes concerning political reality. Using Kenneth
Burke's PHILOSOPHY OF LITERARY FORM as a model, he con-
structs ideal Progressive and symbolist points of view.

Woodward, C. Vann. "The Age of Reinterpretation." AMERICAN HISTORI-
CAL REVIEW 66 (October 1960): 1-19.

This essay deals with reinterpretations that have been inspired by
historical events. The present generation of historians have a
special obligation and a unique opportunity because they have witnessed a scope and sweep of change.

_____. THE BURDEN OF SOUTHERN HISTORY. Baton Rouge: Louisiana
State University Press, 1960. xvi, 205 p.

In this collection, Woodward explains the effect on southern people of the knowledge that history has happened to them. He believes that history, as a collective experience, has set the South
as a region apart from the nation.

_____. "The Irony of Southern History." JOURNAL OF SOUTHERN HISTORY
19 (February 1953): 3-19.

Employing the ideas of Reinhold Niebuhr, Woodward shows the
irony in southern dreams of the antebellum period and their shat-
tering by the Civil War. He argues that this experience has pro-

vided southerners with a different point of view to understand their own history.

Wright, William D. "Richard Hofstadter: Critic of History and Progenitor of Consensus." CONNECTICUT REVIEW 8 (April 1975): 25-36.

This is an examination of Hofstadter's historical views. Wright shows how he moved from a consensus-conflict interpretation to a multiple causation structural-functional point of view.

Zagorin, Perez. "Carl Becker on History, Professor Becker's Two Histories: A Skeptical Fallacy." AMERICAN HISTORICAL REVIEW 62 (October 1956): 1-11.

The two histories are history as it actually was and history as it is known to us. Becker thinks the findings of historians are something less than knowledge and that every historical event involves the question of certainty.

Zucker, Morris. THE PHILOSOPHY OF AMERICAN HISTORY. 2 vols. Vol. 1: THE HISTORICAL FIELD THEORY. Vol. 2: PERIODS IN AMERICAN HISTORY. New York: Arnold-Howard, 1945. xxii, 694; xxxii, 1,070 p.

This is a criticism of pragmatism and economic determinism as historical methods. It is also an effort to construct a science of history based on the laws of physics.

Chapter 8
LITERATURE

COLONIAL PERIOD TO 1815

Axelrod, Jacob. PHILIP FRENEAU: CHAMPION OF DEMOCRACY. Austin: University of Texas Press, 1967. xii, 480 p.

This is an analysis of the political implications of Freneau's prose and poetry. He is depicted as a man incapable of political compromise, who was too intense for balanced judgment and too partisan for purity.

Bercovitch, Sacvan, ed. THE AMERICAN PURITAN IMAGINATION: ESSAYS IN REVALUATION. London and New York: Cambridge University Press, 1974. 265 p.

These essays cover Puritan literary forms such as the jeremiad and the spiritual biography. The works of individuals such as William Bradford, Anne Bradstreet, Edward Taylor, and Cotton Mather also are discussed.

Cantor, Milton. "The Image of the Negro in Colonial Literature." NEW ENGLAND QUARTERLY 36 (December 1963): 452-77.

The earliest settlers viewed the Negro as different and inferior. The Revolution caused colonists to admit that he was like them politically, but the movement for debasement continued.

Emerson, Everett, ed. MAJOR WRITERS OF EARLY AMERICAN LITERATURE. Madison: University of Wisconsin Press, 1972. 301 p.

In this volume, scholars have published individual essays on William Bradford, Anne Bradstreet, Cotton Mather, Jonathan Edwards, William Byrd, and others.

Granger, Bruce Ingham. POLITICAL SATIRE IN THE AMERICAN REVOLUTION, 1763-1783. Ithaca, N.Y.: Cornell University Press, 1960. xiv, 314 p.

Literature

The literary quality of revolutionary satire was not high, but authors lashed out bitterly at George III, Lord North, Tories, Parliament, Howe, Gage, and other subjects. Benjamin Franklin, Philip Freneau, John Trumbull, and Francis Hopkinson stood above other writers.

Harap, Louis. "Image of the Jew in American Drama, 1794–1823." AMERICAN JEWISH HISTORICAL QUARTERLY 60 (March 1971): 242–58.

Conventions of the stage Jew established by British writers were followed by American dramatists. Interestingly, many American plays dealt with Jews in Algiers, and they were portrayed as being good or bad depending upon the author.

Howard, Leon. THE CONNECTICUT WITS. Chicago: University of Chicago Press, 1943. xiii, 453 p.

This is the story of the writing careers of John Trumbull, Timothy Dwight, David Humphreys, and Joel Barlow. It includes a critical analysis of their styles, social environment, and human development.

Lemay, J.A. Leo. MEN OF LETTERS IN COLONIAL MARYLAND. Knoxville: University of Tennessee Press, 1972. xvi, 407 p.

Lemay emphasizes biography, literary criticism, and themes. Annapolis was the colony's literary capital, where writers kept abreast of vogues in England.

Lowance, Mason I., Jr. INCREASE MATHER. New York: Twayne, 1974. 185 p.

This a literary analysis of Mather's work. Lowance argues that Mather skillfully integrated New England's relationship with God into every aspect of his career.

Martin, John S. "Rhetoric, Society, and Literature in the Age of Jefferson." MIDCONTINENT AMERICAN STUDIES JOURNAL 9 (Spring 1961): 77–90.

Rhetoric in the age of Jefferson underwent a revolution from the use of typology to the use of experiential situations in testing the resolution of an audience to bring about desired goals. Jefferson and other writers used the persona to structure images, experiential situations, and scenes of the sublime in a way that truth would become superior to man's arguments about truth.

Parrington, Vernon Louis. MAIN CURRENTS IN AMERICAN THOUGHT: AN INTERPRETATION OF AMERICAN LITERATURE FROM THE BEGINNINGS TO 1920. Vol. 1: THE COLONIAL MIND, 1620–1800. New York: Harcourt, Brace, 1927. vii, 413 p.

In this classic study of American letters, Parrington shows how European ideas domesticated themselves in America. He is noted for his emphasis on liberalism.

Roth, George L. "Verse Satire on 'Faction,' 1790-1815." WILLIAM AND MARY QUARTERLY 17 (October 1960): 473-85.

Satirical verse was directed against education, religion, medicine, law, and fashions, but mainly against politics and politicians. Satires illustrated rather than caused the political feelings of this early period when the Federalists disappeared even as a faction.

Rovit, Earl H. "American Literature and 'The American Experience.'" AMERI-CAN QUARTERLY 13 (Summer 1961): 115-25.

American literature was born when Americans attempted to formulate in words what they were. The fiction writer invented a kind of dramatic structure in which self-definition could be narrated in time, and his protagonists became both an observing man of thought and an active participant in life.

Shea, Daniel B., Jr. SPIRITUAL AUTOBIOGRAPHY IN EARLY AMERICA. Princeton, N.J.: Princeton University Press, 1968. xvi, 280 p.

Shea discusses the spiritual autobiographies of both Quakers and Puritans. They came in many different shapes, and they failed because they subordinated personal life to public argument.

Spingarn, Lawrence P. "The Yankee in Early American Fiction." NEW ENG-LAND QUARTERLY 31 (December 1958): 484-95.

In New England, the writer interested in character and setting ignored the city and emphasized the country native. Novelists used Yankee traits with increasing realism and treated them as outgrowths of the environment.

Stoddard, Roger Eliot. "Notes on American Play Publishing, 1765-1865." PROCEEDINGS OF THE AMERICAN ANTIQUARIAN SOCIETY 81 (21 April 1971): 161-90.

The market for published plays was determined by patrons of the theater who bought the texts of plays they had seen or were about to see. British copyright was not recognized in America during this period, and the entire repertoire of the British stage was available to publishers with the result that few American plays were written.

Literature

1815-1915

Aaron, Daniel. THE UNWRITTEN WAR: AMERICAN WRITERS AND THE
CIVIL WAR. New York: Alfred A. Knopf, 1973. xix, 399 p.

> Aaron argues that America's greatest historical event did not pro-
> duce a literary masterwork. He emphasizes northern writers who
> experienced Civil War combat and wrote about it, but southern
> figures are not neglected.

Allen, Gay Wilson. WALT WHITMAN HANDBOOK. Chicago: Packard,
1946. xviii, 560 p.

> This is a review of everything Whitman has written. It is a sum-
> mary of his life, literary technique, fundamental ideas and their
> relationship to American life, and the influence of world litera-
> ture.

Appleby, Joyce. "Reconciliation and the Northern Novelist, 1865-1880."
CIVIL WAR HISTORY 10 (June 1964): 117-29.

> Sixty-four novels which show that reconciliation between the sec-
> tions as a major theme are analyzed. This body of fiction, with
> its spirit of charity toward the South, is a direct contrast to the
> idea of northern hostility in the postwar period.

Arrington, Leonard J., and Haupt, Jon. "Intolerable Zion: The Image of
Mormonism in Nineteenth Century American Literature." WESTERN HUMANI-
TIES REVIEW 22 (Summer 1968): 243-60.

> This is a study of some of the myths and symbols of early anti-
> Mormon fiction. Non-Mormon fiction writers and their myths were
> more potent in molding public opinion than the realities Mormons
> asserted, and these myths were converted into the realities of of-
> ficial policy.

Barnett, Louise K. THE IGNOBLE SAVAGE: AMERICAN LITERARY RACISM,
1790-1890. Westport, Conn.: Greenwood, 1975. 220 p.

> The frontier romance and Indian stereotypes are the focus of this
> study. The author shows that James Fenimore Cooper's "noble
> savages" were those Indians who served white interests.

_____. "Nineteenth-Century Indian Hater Fiction: A Paradigm for Racism."
SOUTH ATLANTIC QUARTERLY 74 (Spring 1975): 224-36.

> Pre-Civil War frontier fiction was concerned with Indian-white con-
> frontation within the context of a genteel love story. The subgenre
> of Indian-hater fiction, however, focused on behavior generated by
> violent and overt race hatred.

Beard, James Franklin, ed. THE LETTERS AND JOURNALS OF JAMES FENI-
MORE COOPER. 2 vols. Cambridge, Mass.: Belknap Press of Harvard University Press, 1960. xlvi, 444; viii, 420 p.

> The frame of reference in which Cooper worked as well as the ef-
> fect of the climate of opinion upon him are delinated. These two
> volumes carry Cooper through 1833.

Berthoff, Warner. THE FERMENT OF REALISM: AMERICAN LITERATURE,
1884-1919. New York: Free Press, 1965. xvi, 330 p.

> Berthoff concentrates on the best work done in the period rather
> than on careers and battles of opinion. He covers Twain, Howells,
> James, Crane, Cable, and others.

Bier, Jesse. "Weberism, Franklin, and the Transcendental Self." NEW ENG-
LAND QUARTERLY 43 (June 1970): 179-92.

> In this essay, Bier examines some of the writings of Emerson and
> Thoreau, and argues that they are the last clear literary reflex of
> the Protestant ethic as Max Weber described it. Franklin was the
> quintessential ethical capitalist in Weber's view and therefore a
> historical model for the transcendentalists.

Boller, Paul F., Jr. AMERICAN TRANSCENDENTALISM, 1830-1860: AN
INTELLECTUAL INQUIRY. New York: G.P. Putnam's Sons, 1974. xxiii,
227 p.

> Boller has selected a group of New England intellectuals and has
> constructed a transcendentalist ideal type. The book is best on
> religious and philosophical themes.

Bowron, Bernard R., Jr. HENRY B. FULLER OF CHICAGO: THE ORDEAL
OF A GENTEEL REALIST IN UNGENTEEL AMERICA. Westport, Conn.: Greenwood, 1974. xxvi, 278 p.

> Fuller was the author of the so-called Chicago novels THE CLIFF-
> DWELLERS (1893) and WITH THE PROCESSION (1895). Bowron
> argues that he was the first American novelist to use the city as
> material for his art.

Bradbury, Malcolm. "Sociology and Literary Studies II. Romance and Reality
in MAGGIE." JOURNAL OF AMERICAN STUDIES 3 (July 1969): 111-21.

> Bradbury takes Henry Nash Smith's suggestion that a method in
> American studies lies somewhere in cultural anthropology and ex-
> amines MAGGIE as a social manifestation. He argues that Crane
> does not urge social action in his novel, but presents the vigor
> and moral crudity of people.

Literature

Brown, Herbert Ross. THE SENTIMENTAL NOVEL IN AMERICA, 1789-1860. Durham, N.C.: Duke University Press, 1940. ix, 407 p.

Brown traces some manifestations of the sentimental mind in popular fiction. He is concerned with trends, forces, creeds, movements, and literary fashions, and shows that novels represent a wide area of taste.

Budd, Louis J. "The Southward Currents Under Huck Finn's Raft." MISSISSIPPI VALLEY HISTORICAL REVIEW 46 (September 1959): 222-37.

The debate over the New South was central in Huck Finn's genesis. Twain found fault with southern violence, the region's resistance to intellectual and material progress, and other matters, and infused an antebellum setting with opinions and judgments that reflected the 1880s.

Callow, James T. KINDRED SPIRITS: KNICKERBOCKER WRITERS AND AMERICAN ARTISTS, 1807-1855. Chapel Hill: University of North Carolina Press, 1967. xxii, 287 p.

Writers such as Bryant, Cooper, and Irving enjoyed much greater stature than artists such as Cole, Durand, and Morse, but they advanced the careers of artists by employing them as illustrators, gaining them government commissions, and popularizing their travels. There was a primacy of word and authorship, and artists played a dependent role.

Carter, Everett. HOWELLS AND THE AGE OF REALISM. Philadelphia: J.B. Lippincott, 1954. 307 p.

Howells is depicted as a symbol for his age. The role of the "Age of Realism" in America is evaluated.

Cohn, Jan. "The Negro Character in Northern Magazine Fiction of the 1860s." NEW ENGLAND QUARTERLY 43 (December 1970): 572-92.

The 1860s were the one decade in which northern attitudes concerning the Negro could develop without the need to propagandize. Negro characters that escaped from the northern stereotype of the noble seeker of freedom were accorded unpleasant or immoral traits.

Crozier, Alice C. THE NOVELS OF HARRIET BEECHER STOWE. New York: Oxford University Press, 1969. x, 235 p.

Crozier examines the influence of Byron on American writers of the "renaissance" and shows the relationship of religion to reform thought. Her literary analysis of the Stowe novels makes clear America's racial dilemma and the response of liberals.

Current-Garcia, Eugene. "Southern Literary Criticism and the Sectional Dilemma." JOURNAL OF SOUTHERN HISTORY 15 (August 1949): 325-41.

Until the 1850s, critics in the North and South predicted the birth of a national literature based on expression of the democratic ideal. But after that time, southerners saw the spread of the bourgeois ideal, labeled "Americanizing," that made the tone of American society grim in their minds, falsely pious, and avaricious.

Davenport, F. Garvin, Jr. "Thomas Dixon's Mythology of Southern History." JOURNAL OF SOUTHERN HISTORY 36 (August 1970): 350-67.

Davenport uses the social-historical novels of Dixon, written in the early twentieth century, to elucidate the mythology of a southern mission to save the nation from the illusions of progress and affluence. Dixon was a leading spokesman for American racism.

Davis, David Brion. HOMICIDE IN AMERICAN FICTION, 1789-1860: A STUDY IN SOCIAL VALUES. Ithaca, N.Y.: Cornell University Press, 1957. xviii, 346 p.

The sensationalism of violent fiction and the works of moral philosophers, psychiatrists, and legal theorizers are discussed. Davis depicts the psychological relationship in fiction between sex and death and rationalizations of violence.

Davis, Richard Beale. "The 'Virginia Novel' Before SWALLOW BARN." VIRGINIA MAGAZINE OF HISTORY AND BIOGRAPHY 71 (July 1963): 278-93.

The Virginia novel set either among the great scenes and events in the state's political and martial history or within the confines of the antebellum plantation is discussed. Its beginnings are usually dated with the appearance of John P. Kennedy's SWALLOW BARN in 1832, but Davis argues that there were significant Virginia novels during the thirty years before the publication of Kennedy's work.

Dowty, Alan. "Urban Slavery in Pro-Southern Fiction of the 1850s." JOURNAL OF SOUTHERN HISTORY 32 (February 1966): 25-41.

Dowty's focus is the literary battle over slavery precipitated by the publication of UNCLE TOM'S CABIN in 1852. The urban slave, who lived in more congenial surroundings than his plantation counterpart, was virtually ignored because southern writers were attacking the sweatshops and industrial jungles of the urban North.

Emmons, David M. GARDEN IN THE GRASSLANDS: BOOMER LITERATURE OF THE CENTRAL GREAT PLAINS. Lincoln: University of Nebraska Press, 1971. xi, 220 p.

This is a study of what people thought about Kansas, Nebraska, Colorado, and Wyoming based on promotional literature. Interestingly, the author shows the pioneers believed that rain followed the plows, which reveals their basic hopes and fears.

Ferguson, Alfred R. "The Abolition of Blacks in Abolitionist Fiction, 1830-1860." JOURNAL OF BLACK STUDIES 5 (December 1974): 134-57.

An unconscious racism speaks in abolitionist fiction. Ferguson argues that this writing demands the abolition of slavery, but in reality it advocates the abolition of blacks by transformation of the black man into a suitable imitation of white Christian purity.

Fiedler, Leslie A. LOVE AND DEATH IN THE AMERICAN NOVEL. Rev. ed. New York: Stein and Day, 1966. 512 p.

The American novel has a character and fate different from the novel in Europe. Fiedler engages in comparative criticism and emphasizes themes.

Fine, David M. "Attitudes Toward Acculturation in the English Fiction of the Jewish Immigrant, 1900-1917." AMERICAN JEWISH HISTORICAL QUARTERLY 63 (September 1973): 45-56.

Fine contrasts Abraham Cahan's RISE OF DAVID LEVINSKY and Sydney Nyburg's THE CHOSEN PEOPLE with other Jewish novels. A number of Jewish novels were enthusiastic affirmations of Americanization, but Cahan, for example, depicted the chasm that existed between Old World values and New World experience.

Flanagan, John T., ed. AMERICA IS WEST: AN ANTHOLOGY OF MIDDLE-WESTERN LIFE AND LITERATURE. Minneapolis: University of Minnesota Press, 1945. vii, 677 p.

This collection emphasizes that the mainsprings of American literary life have migrated from the East coast to the nation's heartland. It covers geography, folklore, towns, cities, and middle westerners who have won renown.

Floan, Howard R. THE SOUTH IN NORTHERN EYES, 1831 TO 1861. Austin: University of Texas Press, 1958. xii, 198 p.

This is a study of the opinions of New England and New York literary men concerning the South. The abolitionists among them are shown as being narrow-minded and hysterical.

Flusche, Michael. "Thomas Nelson Page: The Quandary of a Literary Gentleman." VIRGINIA MAGAZINE OF HISTORY AND BIOGRAPHY 84 (October 1976): 464-85.

Page was the best-known southern writer during the last years of the nineteenth century. He was identified as the foremost champion of the "Lost Cause," but he became trapped by a literary formula he hoped would earn him a little money and a reputation.

Foster, Charles H. THE RUNGLESS LADDER: HARRIET BEECHER STOWE AND NEW ENGLAND PURITANISM. Durham, N.C.: Duke University Press, 1954. 278 p.

This is a detailed study of all of Stowe's books. Foster maintains that the theology of Jonathan Edwards was her primary concern and the key to understanding her works.

Foster, Edward Halsey. THE CIVILIZED WILDERNESS: BACKGROUNDS TO AMERICAN ROMANTIC LITERATURE, 1817-1860. New York: Free Press, 1975. xx, 220 p.

Writings on travel and scenery and their use by literary figures such as Cooper and Bryant are examined. The literature of the American Renaissance was an attack on the ideal of a civilized wilderness.

Frederick, John T. "American Literary Nationalism: The Process of Definition, 1825-1850." REVIEW OF POLITICS 21 (January 1959): 224-38.

In the creation of a national literature it is necessary to consider the materials as well as the spirit and purpose of American writers. Between 1825-50, writers emphasized the immediacy in the treatment of American life and the idea that literature should be an active social and spiritual force.

Fussell, Edwin. FRONTIER: AMERICAN LITERATURE AND THE WEST. Princeton, N.J.: Princeton University Press, 1965. xv, 450 p.

Fussell explores ideas concerning the West in the works of Cooper, Hawthorne, Poe, Thoreau, Melville, and Whitman. He maintains that time and space were interchangeable terms with the West being a place, a direction, or an idea.

Gardner, Joseph H. "Bret Harte and the Dickensian Mode in America." CANADIAN REVIEW OF AMERICAN STUDIES 2 (Fall 1971): 89-101.

From 1868 until the end of the nineteenth century, Dickens was the most widely read novelist in America, and Harte was the most Dickensian of American writers. The Dickensian mode was seeking an exotic setting and then peopling it with eccentric people.

Literature

Goldbold, E. Stanly, Jr. "A Battleground Revisited: Reconstruction in Southern Fiction, 1895–1905." SOUTH ATLANTIC QUARTERLY 73 (Winter 1974): 99–116.

This period was one of social ferment in the South and also a renaissance in southern letters. Among the novelists who wrote about Reconstruction during this time there was no consensus on a southern view, because each writer wrestled with the social and political problems of his or her own decade.

Gottlieb, Lois C. "The Perils of Freedom: The New Woman in Three American Plays of the 1900s." CANADIAN REVIEW OF AMERICAN STUDIES 6 (Spring 1975): 84–98.

American plays in the pre–World War I years have been characterized as failing to come to grips with the grim truths of human existence. Using Eugene Walter's THE EASIEST WAY (1908), Clyde Fitch's THE CITY (1909), and William Vaughn Moody's THE FAITH HEALER (1910), all of which have been labeled as "plays of revolt," Gottlieb shows that the treatment of female characters illustrates the "sexual defensiveness" of many males concerning the women's movement.

Grimsted, David. MELODRAMA UNVEILED: AMERICAN THEATRE AND CULTURE, 1800–1850. Chicago: University of Chicago Press, 1968. xii, 285 p.

This is a social history of the theater. Grimsted describes the popularity of melodrama and attempts to place it in the context of the popular mind by looking at critics, audiences, playwrights, players, and repertoires.

Hall, Lawrence Sargent. HAWTHORNE, CRITIC OF SOCIETY. Yale Studies in English, vol. 99. New Haven, Conn.: Yale University Press, 1944. xii, 200 p.

This study demonstrates that Hawthorne was transformed in his Brook Farm days (1842), from a critic of society to a champion of democracy. He never escaped the zeal of reformers for remaking the world, but he became a chauvinist connected with young America.

Havens, Daniel F. THE COLUMBIAN MUSE OF COMEDY: THE DEVELOPMENT OF A NATIVE TRADITION IN EARLY AMERICAN SOCIAL COMEDY, 1787–1845. Carbondale: Southern Illinois University Press, 1973. vii, 181 p.

Havens emphasizes stage history rather than historical-literary history. He shows that the black was given a burlesque role and that the theater responded to foreign criticism even though the stage was dominated by foreign comedies.

Hough, Robert L. THE QUIET REBEL: WILLIAM DEAN HOWELLS AS SOCIAL COMMENTATOR. Lincoln: University of Nebraska Press, 1959. x, 137 p.

This is an analysis of social and economic ideas expressed in Howells's novels of the 1880s and 1890s and in his magazine essays published between 1900-20. In the essays, he revealed a continuing interest in reform and spoke out against imperialism, war, social Darwinism, and the penal system.

Hovet, Theodore R. "Christian Revolution: Harriet Beecher Stowe's Response to Slavery and the Civil War." NEW ENGLAND QUARTERLY 46 (December 1974): 535-49.

Stowe, like other anti-institutional radicals, saw the Civil War as the final stage in a revolutionary effort that would make individual and social perfection a reality. The alienation and despair of the 1850s was superseded by a reaffirmation of American promise.

Hubbell, Jay B. THE SOUTH IN AMERICAN LITERATURE, 1607-1900. Durham, N.C.: Duke University Press, 1954. xx, 987 p.

Hubbell traces the careers and discusses the writings of practically every southern writer of the seventeenth, eighteenth, and nineteenth centuries. He also briefly covers the twentieth century, but emphasizes O. Henry, Ellen Glasgow, and James Branch Cabell.

Jones, Howard Mumford. JEFFERSONIANISM AND THE AMERICAN NOVEL. New York: Teachers College Press, 1966. xii, 77 p.

Jones tries to determine whether the novel has been helped or hindered by the Jeffersonian view that man is rational and possessed of a moral sense, social duties, and an obligation to create and support a responsible government. The classical novel from 1789 to 1930, especially of Cooper and Howells, generally followed Jefferson, but Twain was against Jeffersonian belief.

Kaplan, Harold. DEMOCRATIC HUMANISM AND AMERICAN LITERATURE. Chicago: University of Chicago Press, 1972. xxi, 298 p.

This is a study of the major works of Emerson, Thoreau, Cooper, Poe, Hawthorne, Melville, Whitman, Twain, and Henry James from the perspective of man's commitment to society or his ability to reconcile freedom from it. While some of these writers, such as Emerson, Thoreau, and Whitman, were subversives, most had a double consciousness that allowed them self-transcendence and at the same time permitted contradictions.

Karolides, Nicholas J. THE PIONEER IN THE AMERICAN NOVEL, 1900-1950. Norman: University of Oklahoma Press, 1967. xii, 324 p.

The pioneer is the frontiersman, mountain man, ranger, miner, prairie farmer, and immigrant on the way West. Before World War I, they were big, brave, skilled, energetic, and durable natural aristocrats, but after the war they became natural heroes and plebeians with coarse language.

Kerr, Howard. MEDIUMS, AND SPIRIT-RAPPERS, AND ROARING RADICALS: SPIRITUALISM IN AMERICAN LITERATURE, 1850-1900. Urbana: University of Illinois Press, 1972. x, 261 p.

Authors were skeptical of spiritualism, but influenced by it nonetheless. This is mainly a study of the influence of the occult on the lives and work of Howells, Twain, and James, each of whom was interested in the psychological implications of spiritualist beliefs.

Knight, Grant C. THE STRENUOUS AGE IN AMERICAN LITERATURE, 1900-1910. Chapel Hill: University of North Carolina Press, 1954. xi, 270 p.

The literature of this age emphasized the strong man who battled for power and threatened to become a culture hero. The author covers Theodore Roosevelt, Jack London, Frank Norris, Theodore Dreiser, and other writers.

Krause, Sydney J. MARK TWAIN AS CRITIC. Baltimore: Johns Hopkins Press, 1967. xi, 308 p.

This is a study of Twain's observations, both serious and satirical, on books, authors, politicians, paintings, poetry, and even Sunday school stories. Of particular significance are his remarks on the art of writing.

Kwiat, Joseph J. "Stephen Crane and Frank Norris: The Magazine and the 'Revolt' in American Literature in the 1890s." WESTERN HUMANITIES REVIEW 30 (Autumn 1976): 309-21.

"Little magazines" and popular magazines spurred the literary revolt of the 1890s. Crane and Norris used these periodicals because they could reach a diversified audience, broaden their roles as unswervingly honest reporters of life, and speak freely and reflectively.

Lee, Robert Edson. FROM WEST TO EAST: STUDIES IN THE LITERATURE OF THE AMERICAN WEST. Urbana: University of Illinois Press, 1966. 172 p.

Lee selects nine writers who were "out West" but wrote about it in a blurred, misty way. Timothy Flint wrote escapist literature

in the Cooper tradition, Irving and Parkman saw the vast prairies,
but did not follow their journals in their published works, and
Twain's and Cather's writings were flawed by effete eastern influences.

THE LETTERS OF WILLIAM GILMORE SIMMS. 5 vols. Vol. 1: 1830-1844;
vol. 2: 1845-1849; vol. 3: 1850-1857; vol. 4: 1858-1866; vol. 5: 1867-
1870. Collected and edited by Mary C. Simms Oliphant, Alfred Taylor Odell,
and T.C. Duncan Reaves. Columbia: University of South Carolina Press,
1952-56.

Simms was a leading antebellum southern writer and cultural figure.
These letters are a mine of information on belles-letters, the theater, education, and other matters.

Lewis, R.W.B. THE AMERICAN ADAM: INNOCENCE, TRAGEDY, AND
TRADITION IN THE NINETEENTH CENTURY. Chicago: University of Chicago
Press, 1955. v, 200 p.

Lewis covers the period from 1820-60 and deals with the beginnings of an American mythology. The myth was that of an "authentic American as a figure of great innocence and potentialities,
poised at the start of a new history."

Lutwack, Leonard. "The New England Hierarchy." NEW ENGLAND QUAR-
TERLY 28 (June 1955): 164-85.

Nineteenth-century America acquired centers of tradition that com-
pelled the admiration of all countrymen. One of these was a
handful of New England writers, including Emerson, Hawthorne,
Longfellow, Lowell, Whittier, and Holmes, who were not subjected
to criticism and contributed to the development of a moribund tradition.

Lynn, Kenneth S. THE DREAM OF SUCCESS: A STUDY OF MODERN AMERI-
CAN IMAGINATION. Boston: Little, Brown, 1955. 269 p.

The work of Theodore Dreiser, Jack London, David Graham Phillips, Frank Norris, and others is explored. Rather than being in
opposition to the myth of success, these writers were caught up in
it and became part of it.

McWilliams, John P., Jr. POLITICAL JUSTICE IN A REPUBLIC: JAMES
FENIMORE COOPER'S AMERICA. Berkeley and Los Angeles: University of
California Press, 1972. xi, 420 p.

Cooper published thirty-two novels as well as travel accounts and
other works of nonfiction. As a social and political critic, he
prized the constitutional republic as the ideal form of government,
but after the 1830s his hopes for America dimmed.

Literature

Margolies, Edward. "The Image of the Primitive in Black Letters." AMERI-
CAN STUDIES 11 (Fall 1970): 67-77.

In accordance with popular American literary usage, "primitive"
usually connotes a dark-skinned person who will not submit himself
to the restraints of Western civilization. Black literature has portrayed the Negro as either a comic minstrel figure or as a savage
avenger.

Marx, Leo. THE MACHINE IN THE GARDEN: TECHNOLOGY AND THE
PASTORAL IDEAL IN AMERICA. New York: Oxford University Press, 1964.
392 p.

Marx focuses on the pastoral ideal which he believes defined
America ever since the age of discovery. He uses the ideal to
interpret American experience through the writers of the American
Renaissance.

_____. "'Noble Shit': The Uncivil Response of American Writers to Civil
Religion in America." MASSACHUSETTS REVIEW 14 (Autumn 1973): 709-39.

The use of obscenity in the title is a weapon in the continuing
struggle for egalitarian rights and principles. Back as far as Emerson's time, writers used uncivil language to cope with the rhetoric
of a spurious civil religion and to argue for equality as an ultimate good.

Moore, Jack B. "Images of the Negro in Early American Short Fiction."
MISSISSIPPI QUARTERLY 22 (Winter 1968-69): 45-59.

The Negro in early American short fiction was sentimentalized beyond recognition, and was sold into slavery. As a slave, he was
invariably noble, just, and possessed of heightened sensibility.

Myers, Andrew B. WASHINGTON IRVING: A TRIBUTE. Tarrytown, N.Y.:
Sleepy Hollow Restorations, 1972. x, 86 p.

This tribute to Irving celebrates the sesquicentennial of the publication of THE SKETCH BOOK OF GEOFFREY CRAYON, GENT.
Half of the essays focus on the SKETCH BOOK, while the remainder cover other aspects of Irving's life and work.

Noble, David W. "Cooper, Leatherstocking and the Death of the American
Adam." AMERICAN QUARTERLY 16 (Fall 1964): 419-31.

Noble argues that Cooper's LEATHERSTOCKING TALES destroy the
myth that the West represented a redemptive nature which would
provide spiritual salvation. The novelist takes Leatherstocking from
his youth to old age on the last frontier that was penetrated during Jefferson's administration.

_____. THE ETERNAL ADAM AND THE NEW WORLD GARDEN: THE CEN-
TRAL MYTH IN THE AMERICAN NOVEL SINCE 1830. New York: George
Braziller, 1968. xi, 226 p.

The cornerstone of the central myth of American civilization is the
conception of the American as a new Adam living in perfect harmony in the New World Eden. Cooper and Hawthorne rejected
the myth, the faith of Twain and Howells was shattered by corruption, Hemingway and Fitzgerald were unable to come to grips with
noninnocence, while Faulkner and Bellow reject both the concepts
of innocence and alienation.

Overland, Orm. THE MAKING AND MEANING OF AN AMERICAN CLAS-
SIC: JAMES FENIMORE COOPER'S THE PRAIRIE. New York: Humanities
Press, 1973. 206 p.

Cooper's activities between 1820-27, his sources for the novel
which was written in France, and contemporary attitudes concerning trappers, squatters, scientists, and savages are detailed. Overland maintains that the author's bleak description of the prairie's
barrenness harbored a hope that this land would be an impediment
to Western expansion.

Parrington, Vernon Louis. MAIN CURRENTS OF AMERICAN THOUGHT: AN
INTERPRETATION OF AMERICAN LITERATURE FROM THE BEGINNINGS TO
1920. Vol. 2: THE ROMANTIC REVOLUTION IN AMERICA, 1800-1860.
New York: Harcourt Brace, 1927. xxii, 493 p.

Parrington is interested in new growths--the forms they assumed
and why they assumed these forms. He argues that romanticism
swept away the "drab realisms of the past."

_____. MAIN CURRENTS OF AMERICAN THOUGHT: AN INTERPRETATION
OF AMERICAN LITERATURE FROM THE BEGINNINGS TO 1920. Vol. 3:
THE BEGINNINGS OF CRITICAL REALISM IN AMERICA, 1860-1920. New
York: Harcourt Brace, 1930. xxxix, 429 p.

A new culture, created by the machine and answering the needs
of capitalism, came into being. The democratic hopes of earlier
days had not been fulfilled, and Americans in fact had created a
plutocracy. This volume is completed only to 1900.

Pettit, Arthur G. MARK TWAIN AND THE SOUTH. Lexington: University
Press of Kentucky, 1974. x, 224 p.

Twain was a man of many faces, but his feelings concerning the
South evolved intelligibly. He longed for a South he realized
never existed and overcame his bigotry.

Literature

Pritchard, John Paul. CRITICISM IN AMERICA: AN ACCOUNT OF THE
DEVELOPMENT OF CRITICAL TECHNIQUES FROM THE EARLY PERIOD OF
THE REPUBLIC TO THE MIDDLE YEARS OF THE TWENTIETH CENTURY. Nor-
man: University of Oklahoma Press, 1956. 325 p.

> This is a survey of 150 years of literary criticism and the develop-
> ment of literary principles. Emphasis is on the major authors such
> as Emerson, Poe, Whitman, Howells, Henry James, and others.

Quinn, Arthur Hobson. A HISTORY OF THE AMERICAN DRAMA FROM THE
BEGINNING TO THE CIVIL WAR. New York: Harper & Brothers, 1923.
xv, 486 p.

> Drama is treated as a living thing in terms of what people enjoyed.
> American drama began with William Dunlap in 1790 and progressed
> through authors such as James M. Barker, John Howard Payne,
> and Edwin Forrest.

_____. HISTORY OF AMERICAN DRAMA FROM THE CIVIL WAR TO THE
PRESENT DAY. Rev. ed. New York: F.S. Crofts, 1936. xxv, 432 p.

> Quinn adds a chapter to his earlier edition covering the years
> 1927-36. He discusses mainly the work of Eugene O'Neill, Max-
> well Anderson, Sidney Howard, George S. Kaufmann, and Rachel
> Crothers.

Roemer, Kenneth M. "Sex Roles, Utopia and Change: The Family in Late
Nineteenth-Century Literature." AMERICAN STUDIES 13 (Fall 1972): 33-48.

> This essay covers utopian novels and tracts published between 1888
> and 1900. Roemer shows how the depiction of sex roles in these
> writings illuminated the complex mixture of radicalism and conser-
> vatism in reform movements.

Rose, Alan Henry. "The Image of the Negro in the Pre-Civil War Novels of
John Pendleton Kennedy and William Gilmore Simms." JOURNAL OF AMERI-
CAN STUDIES 4 (February 1971): 217-26.

> Pre-Civil War southern novelists had to strike a balance between
> presenting slave society favorably and depicting the powerful forces
> of racial destruction. Kennedy solved the problem by removing
> his novels from the present, while Simms first presented a Negro
> with demonic and chaotic destructiveness, and later transformed
> him into a figure from whom all danger had been removed.

Rubin, Joseph J. THE HISTORIC WHITMAN. University Park: Pennsylvania
State University Press, 1973. xv, 406 p.

> This study depicts Whitman's social milieu from his birth until the
> death of his father shortly after the publication of LEAVES OF

GRASS. It covers life in New York, politics, music, books, and plays, but not the men with whom Whitman associated.

Ruoff, John C. "Frivolity to Consumption: Or, Southern Womanhood in Antebellum Literature." CIVIL WAR HISTORY 18 (September 1972): 213-29.

The archetypal southern woman is white and a member of the planter class by birth or marriage. These women are presented as female children, who are variants of Little Eva in UNCLE TOM'S CABIN; spinsters, who provide comic relief; beautiful belles, who are mindless, sexless, and marriage happy; and the planters' wives, who have been transformed by marriage from an irresponsible belle to a plantation manager.

Salomon, Roger B. "Realism as Disinheritance: Twain, Howells, and James." AMERICAN QUARTERLY 16 (Winter 1964): 531-44.

One important aspect of the "mood" of the late nineteenth century was the feeling of psychic and spiritual disinheritance by those who felt deprived of a past by a technologically oriented present. One response was realism in literature, which had as an assumption that present and past are discontinuous.

_____. TWAIN AND THE IMAGE OF HISTORY. Yale Studies in English, vol. 150. New Haven, Conn.: Yale University Press, 1961. x, 216 p.

Twain started by accepting the Adamic idea and sharing confidence that America represented the ultimate stage in human progress. He came to see, however, that America was losing its uniqueness and that history was an endless cycle of cruelty and corruption.

Saum, Lewis O. "The Success Theme in Great Plains Realism." AMERICAN QUARTERLY 18 (Winter 1966): 579-98.

Saum surveys the literature of Ole Rolvaag, Willa Cather, Hamlin Garland, and other realistic portrayers of the farmer's struggles on the Great Plains. These writers depict the loneliness, melancholy, and brutalization of the pioneers, but they do not portray futility since their characters emerge more nearly successful than defeated.

Smith, Henry Nash. VIRGIN LAND: THE AMERICAN WEST AS SYMBOL AND MYTH. Cambridge, Mass.: Harvard University Press, 1950. xiv, 305 p.

Myths and symbols are defined as intellectual constructions that fuse concept and emotion into image. Smith integrates political, economic, and social materials with American literature.

_____. "The Western Farmer in Imaginative Literature, 1818-1891." MISSISSIPPI VALLEY HISTORICAL REVIEW 36 (December 1949): 479-90.

Literature

For purposes of fiction the western farmer had lower-class status and was depicted as a social inferior, a clown or peasant, or as a yeoman. Hamlin Garland revised the image of the farmer and freed him from major distortions.

Smith, Henry Nash, and Gibson, William M., with the assistance of Frederick Anderson, eds. MARK TWAIN-HOWELLS LETTERS: THE CORRESPONDENCE OF SAMUEL L. CLEMENS AND WILLIAM D. HOWELLS, 1872-1900. 2 vols. Cambridge, Mass.: Belknap Press of Harvard University Press, 1960. xxvi, 454; viii, 493 p.

Twain and Howells knew an impressive number of persons and kept a close watch on current events. They also commented on theology, painting, music, and Darwinism.

Stark, Cruse. "Brothers at/in War; One Phase of Post-Civil War Reconcilation." CANADIAN REVIEW OF AMERICAN STUDIES 6 (Fall 1975): 174-81.

Many men of letters were disillusioned by the Civil War because it did not purge the nation of its mindless, self-centered imperialism. Union veterans, who were writers, fostered reconciliation by bringing Confederate veterans into a brotherhood of arms based on the assumption that exsoldiers alone could see that the enervation of pleasure was not a substitute for noble action.

Thorp, Willard. "Catholic Novelists in Defense of Their Faith, 1829-1865." PROCEEDINGS OF THE AMERICAN ANTIQUARIAN SOCIETY 78 (17 April 1968): 25-118.

In early America, novels that championed causes attracted readers, and among these were books that attacked Catholics. Almost fifty pro-Catholic novels were published between 1829 and 1865 in response, and they mainly explained the doctrines and mysteries of the Catholic religion.

Turner, Darwin T. "Paul Laurence Dunbar: The Rejected Symbol." JOURNAL OF NEGRO HISTORY 52 (January 1967): 1-13.

Dunbar became a symbol of the creative and intellectual potential of the American Negro at the turn of the twentieth century, but he tarnished this symbol by publishing caricatures of his black brothers. Turner argues that critics demand too much of this writer because he recognized distinctions between Negroes and was intolerant of ridiculous behavior.

Tuttleton, James W. THE NOVEL OF MANNERS IN AMERICA. Chapel Hill: University of North Carolina Press, 1972. xv, 304 p.

Tuttleton argues that the novel of manners had an opportunity in America. In studying the works of Cooper, James, Wharton, Howells,

Fitzgerald, Lewis, Marquand, and others, he attempts to show that American culture was not too shallow for such novels to flourish.

Vanderbilt, Kermit. THE ACHIEVEMENT OF WILLIAM DEAN HOWELLS: A REINTERPRETATION. Princeton, N.J.: Princeton University Press, 1968. ix, 226 p.

Howells was one of the "truly perturbed spirits of the late nineteenth century." Vanderbilt argues that his novels reveal "dark interiors" and a vision of reality.

Vorpahl, Ben Merchant, ed. MY DEAR WISTER: THE FREDERIC REMINGTON-OWEN WISTER LETTERS. Palo Alto, Calif.: American West, 1972. xix, 343 p.

The cowboy-hero was to a great extent the work of Remington in art and Wister in literature. They met in Yellowstone Park in 1893 and agreed to collaborate in writing and illustrating western stories.

Wagenknecht, Edward. CAVALCADE OF THE AMERICAN NOVEL: FROM THE BIRTH OF THE NATION TO THE MIDDLE OF THE TWENTIETH CENTURY. New York: Henry Holt, 1952. xv, 575 p.

This is a cavalcade of novelists rather than of novels. Wagenknecht covers writers such as Elsie Singmaster, but he emphasizes the major authors.

_____. HARRIET BEECHER STOWE: THE KNOWN TO THE UNKNOWN. New York: Oxford University Press, 1965. 267 p.

This is a character study in which the author concludes that Stowe put family relationships above everything else. After this came her art, with services as a reformer a poor third.

Walker, Robert H. "The Poet and the Rise of the City." MISSISSIPPI VALLEY HISTORICAL REVIEW 49 (June 1962): 85-99.

The poetry of the Gilded Age presented an image of a new, urban America. Poets generally criticized the city for its ugliness, economic inequities, crime, drunkenness, sexual excesses, amorality, and artificiality, and produced an urban myth of this sort.

_____. "The Poet and the Robber Baron." AMERICAN QUARTERLY 13 (Winter 1961): 447-65.

Poets of the late nineteenth century who addressed themselves to economic conditions left a reasonably complete record of events, personalities, and movements. Some supported the gospel of wealth, but most objected to the inequities of the economic systems.

Literature

_____. "The Poets Interpret the Western Frontier." MISSISSIPPI VALLEY HISTORICAL REVIEW 47 (March 1961): 619-35.

This is a study of the reaction of poets to the passing of the frontier in the late nineteenth century. Poets criticized aspects of life in the West, but they also portrayed the frontier as a stage that led to the revitalization of American civilizational patterns.

Watson, Charles S. ANTEBELLUM CHARLESTON DRAMATISTS. University: University of Alabama Press, 1976. xv, 183 p.

The playwrights of Charleston honored American heroes of the Revolution, attempted to sway public opinion during the European wars, depicted the Federalist-Republican partisan controversies, and portrayed sectionalism.

Welsh, John R. "William Gilmore Simms, Critic of the South." JOURNAL OF SOUTHERN HISTORY 26 (May 1960): 201-14.

Simms has been held up as a writer who ruined his art through blind devotion to everything southern. Welch shows, however, that the South Carolinian criticized the antebellum South for being lazy intellectually, deficient agriculturally, and weak industrially.

Wilson, Edmund. PATRIOTIC GORE: STUDIES IN THE LITERATURE OF THE AMERICAN CIVIL WAR. New York: Oxford University Press, 1962. xxxii, 816 p.

Wilson begins with Stowe and covers other figures such as Lincoln, Alexander Stephens, U.S. Grant, Robert E. Lee, George W. Cable, Sidney Lanier, Ambrose Bierce, Kate Chopin, Albion Tourgee, and Mary Boykin Chesnut. He shows that apologists, North and South, were voluble rather than articulate.

Wister, Fanny Kemble, ed. OWEN WISTER OUT WEST: HIS JOURNALS AND LETTERS. Chicago: University of Chicago Press, 1958. xx, 269 p.

With the publication of the VIRGINIAN in 1902, Wister influenced the thinking of millions concerning the West. He went West for his health and kept journals in which he commented on the region and revealed his search for authentic sources.

Wittke, Carl. "The Immigrant on the American Stage." MISSISSIPPI VALLEY HISTORICAL REVIEW 39 (September 1952): 211-32.

Immigrants were characterized on the American stage for comic relief and dramatic entertainment. In the nineteenth century, Irish and Germans were the objects of comedy, while Jews were depicted in dramas and melodramas.

Zanger, Jules. "The 'Tragic Octoroon' in Pre-Civil War Fiction." AMERI-
CAN QUARTERLY 18 (Spring 1966): 63-70.

The tragic octoroon was a beautiful young maiden, seven-eights
white, raised in luxury by her white father, who discovers upon
his death that she had not been freed from slavery and is victim-
ized and usually driven to suicide. Such a tale was important
in abolitionist fiction.

1915 TO THE PRESENT

Baym, Max I. A HISTORY OF LITERARY AESTHETICS IN AMERICA. New
York: Frederick Ungar, 1973. xii, 388 p.

This is an overview of systematic aesthetic thought in American
philosophy. Santayana and Dewey are given the most attention.

Blake, Nelson Manfred. NOVELISTS' AMERICA: FICTION AS HISTORY,
1910-1940. Syracuse, N.Y.: Syracuse University Press, 1969. xiii, 279 p.

Blake tries to show historians how to use "the hot truth of fiction"
in historical studies. He detects the character of authors such as
Sinclair Lewis, F. Scott Fitzgerald, Thomas Wolfe, and John Dos
Passos and locates the locales and events of their plots.

Blotner, Joseph. THE MODERN POLITICAL NOVEL, 1900-1960. Austin:
University of Texas Press, 1966. x, 424 p.

Mythic patterns such as the young knight battling the dragon of
evil and the king of the sacred wood (political boss) are used to
illuminate the political novel. Major themes are followed chronologically in this book and various novels are described and appraised.

Bone, Robert A. THE NEGRO NOVEL IN AMERICA. New Haven, Conn.:
Yale University Press, 1958. x, 268 p.

Bone considers 139 novels and novelettes published between 1853
and 1952. He argues that the Negro novel was the product of
a distinctive minority culture colored by slavery, a bitter knowledge of caste, a folk culture, and the influence of institutions.

Cooper, Wayne. THE PASSION OF CLAUDE McKAY: SELECTED POETRY
AND PROSE, 1912-1948. New York: Schocken, 1973. xi, 363 p.

McKay, a Jamaican American, was one of the major figures of
the Harlem renaissance. He associated with radicals and was out
of step with integrationists in the NAACP and the Urban League.

Literature

Cooperman, Stanley. "Christ in Khaki: Religion and Post-World War I Literary Protest." WESTERN HUMANITIES REVIEW 18 (Autumn 1964): 361-72.

During World War I, religious rhetoric set the tone of a holy war with soldiers being the "imitators of Christ." War novelists were religious cynics, however, because the contrast between religious rhetoric and the realities of military life and combat was too great.

Corrigan, Robert A. "WHAT'S MY LINE: Bennett Cerf, Ezra Pound, and the AMERICAN POET." AMERICAN QUARTERLY 24 (March 1972): 101-13.

This is a study of the controversy in the mid-1940s when Cerf excluded the poetry of Pound from a Modern Library edition of great British and American poetry because of Pound's allegedly treasonous wartime behavior. Cerf had a great deal of support for this action, but he was stung by criticism that compared him with a Nazi book-burner.

Diggins, John P. "The American Writer, Fascism, and the Liberation of Italy." AMERICAN QUARTERLY 18 (Winter 1966): 599-614.

Diggins discusses the impact of Fascism and Mussolini's Italy on literary intelligentsia from sympathizers to novelists who depicted the impact of liberation. John Horne Burns's novel, THE GALLERY, is especially important because it shows what Americans did to Italians.

Durham, Frank. "The Southern Literary Tradition: Shadow or Substance?" SOUTH ATLANTIC QUARTERLY 67 (Summer 1968): 455-68.

The southern literary tradition grew from shadow to substance in the twentieth century. The force of belief in a tradition impelled southerners to create a body of literature that is not southern but world literature.

Fenton, Charles. "The American Academy of Arts and Letters Vs. All Comers: Literary Rags and Riches in the 1920's." SOUTH ATLANTIC QUARTERLY 58 (Autumn 1959): 572-86.

This is a study of the philanthropy of Archer M. Huntington and the efforts of members of the academy during the twenties to make themselves defenders of the English word. They were attacked by H.L. Mencken and Sinclair Lewis.

Flanagan, John T. "The Fiction of Jessamyn West." INDIANA MAGAZINE OF HISTORY 67 (December 1971): 299-316.

Flanagan depicts West as a writer influenced by her Quaker heritage. The principal merits of her fiction are in characterization and her feeling for language.

Gilbert, James Burkhart. WRITERS AND PARTISANS: A HISTORY OF LIT-
ERARY RADICALISM IN AMERICA. New York: John Wiley and Sons, 1968.

Gilbert covers literary radicalism from before World War I to the
1950s. He discusses the MASSES, SEVEN ARTS, Max Eastman,
and Randolph Bourne as well as the popular front, Howard Fast,
and the PARTISAN REVIEW.

Godbold, E. Stanly, Jr. ELLEN GLASGOW AND THE WOMAN WITHIN.
Baton Rouge: Louisiana State University Press, 1972. xiii, 322 p.

Glasgow created a series of novels that depicted the social history
of Virginia from the Civil War to World War II. Her life was
dreary and she took refuge in writing.

Griffith, Clark. "Frost and the American View of Nature." AMERICAN
QUARTERLY 20 (Spring 1968): 21-37.

Robert Frost is described as belonging to a long American tradition
which has stressed man's relationship with nature. He is a post-
Romantic poet, nearer to Melville and Emily Dickinson than Emerson, because he portrays the ambiguities and enigmas in nature
which prevent man's complete involvement.

Guttman, Allen. "Images of Value and the Sense of the Past." NEW ENG-
LAND QUARTERLY 34 (March 1962): 3-26.

This essay emphasizes the house as a symbol of tradition, permanence, mastery, and civilization. Guttman examines literature and
concludes that in the image of the house, the writer sought reconciliation between an artifact and the American landscape.

_____. THE JEWISH WRITER IN AMERICA: ASSIMILATION AND THE CRI-
SIS OF IDENTITY. New York: Oxford University Press, 1971. x, 256 p.

Jewish writers confronted America as marginal persons alienated
both from their own traditions and American society. They became
popular after World War II not because they had become assimilated but because Americans generally had become alienated as a
consequence of urbanism and industrialism.

Hassan, Ihab. CONTEMPORARY AMERICAN LITERATURE, 1945-1972: AN
INTRODUCTION. New York: Frederick Ungar, 1973. xi, 194 p.

The postwar period in American literature does not have a unified
character. Hassan surveys major novelists, poets, short story writers,
and dramatists.

_____. "The Idea of Adolescence in American Fiction." AMERICAN QUAR-
TERLY 10 (Fall 1958): 312-24.

With the end of innocence in American literature and culture
came a cult of adolescence. This cult, however, is not an accident of the mid-twentieth century, but rather a vision of youth,
hope, and the open road that goes back into our history and is
part of the American dream.

Herron, Ima Honaker. THE SMALL TOWN IN AMERICAN DRAMA. Dallas:
Southern Methodist University Press, 1969. xxiii, 564 p.

Herron emphasizes the content and staging of plays rather than
their historical context. She discusses Booth Tarkington's shift in
1918 from romanticizing to criticizing small towns and Eugene
O'Neill's indebtedness to towns intellectually.

_____. THE SMALL TOWN IN AMERICAN LITERATURE. Durham, N.C.:
Duke University Press, 1939. xvii, 477 p.

In this study, the small town serves as a thread for what is virtually
a history of American literature. The town of fancy is not distinguished from the town of reality.

Hobson, Fred C., Jr. SERPENT IN EDEN: H.L. MENCKEN AND THE SOUTH.
Chapel Hill: University of North Carolina Press, 1974. xv, 242 p.

Mencken was responsible for the development of southern literary
activity in the 1920s after publishing his critical essay on southern
literary sterility in PREJUDICES. Hobson shows the nature and
extent of this influence.

Howard, Leon. LITERATURE AND THE AMERICAN TRADITION. Garden City,
N.Y.: Doubleday, 1960. 354 p.

In this study, the author attempts to understand the attitudes of
mind that have given literary creativity a national character. He
discusses traditional literary interpretations, but also considers his
subject from the standpoint of the intellectual historian.

Huggins, Nathan Irvin. HARLEM RENAISSANCE. New York: Oxford University Press, 1971. xi, 343 p.

The idea of the renaissance was Negro self-creation, and Huggins
studies the dilemmas faced by black artists. He emphasizes the
work of Langston Hughes, Claude McKay, James Weldon Johnson,
and Countee Cullen.

Johnson, Abby Ann Arthur, and Johnson, Ronald M. "Forgotten Pages: Black
Literary Magazines in the 1920s." JOURNAL OF AMERICAN STUDIES 8
(August 1974): 363-82.

This is a study of black publications such as STYLUS, FIRE, SAT-
URDAY EVENING QUILL, and BLACK OPALS. These minor
journals provide insights into the Negro renaissance.

Jones, Alfred Haworth. ROOSEVELT'S IMAGE BROKERS: POETS, PLAY-
WRIGHTS, AND THE USE OF THE LINCOLN SYMBOL. Port Washington,
N.Y.: Kennikat, 1974. 134 p.

This book shows that a symbol of Lincoln was created by Carl
Sandburg, Stephen Vincent Benet, and Robert Sherwood, and used
as an analog for New Deal policies. Roosevelt consciously linked
himself with Lincoln to use the themes of unity, humanitarianism,
and the common touch.

Jones, Peter G. WAR AND THE NOVELIST: APPRAISING THE WAR NOVEL.
Columbia: University of Missouri Press, 1976. x, 260 p.

Jones believes that the war novel has become one of the logical
modes of writing about American life in the twentieth century,
since war is a logical culmination of technology. He examines
novelists from Norman Mailer to Joseph Heller and Kurt Vonnegut.

Joost, Nicholas. YEARS OF TRANSITION, THE DIAL, 1912-1920. Barre,
Vt.: Barre Publishers, 1967. xxvii, 321 p.

During its first years, THE DIAL maintained conservatism in belles-
lettres, vigorously attacking imagists and blank verse. In 1916,
when it came under the control of Martyn Johnson, it shifted to
political concerns and opened its pages to Randolph Bourne and
John Dewey, and added Thorstein Veblen to its editorial staff.

Lambert, Neal. "Saints, Sinners, and Scribes: A Look at the Mormons in
Fiction." UTAH HISTORICAL QUARTERLY 36 (Winter 1968): 63-76.

As subjects of significant serious fiction, Mormons and Mormonism
present difficulties. Popular notions of what a Mormon is has not
lent itself to great literature and Mormons have fallen into stereotyped subjects as comics or villains.

Lea, James. "Sinclair Lewis and the Implied America." CLIO 3 (October
1973): 21-34.

Lewis was both a social historian and social critic. His criticism
of the banal contemporary world embodied the conception that
there had been a more meaningful past.

Mangione, Jerre. THE DREAM AND THE DEAL: THE FEDERAL WRITER'S
PROJECT, 1935-1943. Boston: Little, Brown, 1972. xvi, 416 p.

Mangione was coordinating editor of the project and he argues
that the WPA's efforts to provide employment for writers was
unique. He is not clear, however, whether the project was designed to provide relief or more ambitious employment.

Marovitz, Sanford E. "The Lonely New Americans of Abraham Cahan."
AMERICAN QUARTERLY 20 (Summer 1968): 196-210.

Cahan established himself as an important American author with
the publication of THE RISE OF DAVID LEVINSKY in 1917. He
was more than a Jewish novelist writing about the sweatshop and
the ghetto, because he focused on human nature as he perceived
it as seen in economics and religion, exploitation and secularization.

Meyer, Roy W. THE MIDDLE WESTERN FARM NOVEL IN THE TWENTIETH
CENTURY. Lincoln: University of Nebraska Press, 1965. vii, 265 p.

Farm novels have taken their themes from the pioneer experience
and whether the farm is a desirable place to live. Some also
have entered the realm of social and economic criticism.

Milne, Gordon. THE AMERICAN POLITICAL NOVEL. Norman: University
of Oklahoma Press, 1966. xi, 210 p.

This is a survey of political novels from the eighteenth century to
the 1960s. The most successful examples of the genre are Robert
Penn Warren's ALL THE KING'S MEN, Edwin O'Connors's THE
LAST HURRAH, and Allen Drury's ADVISE AND CONSENT.

Nannes, Caspar H. POLITICS IN AMERICAN DRAMA. Washington, D.C.:
Catholic University of America Press, 1960. xvi, 256 p.

This study covers political drama on the Broadway stage from 1890
to 1959. The action of the plays discussed revolves around a political theme such as government corruption, colorful political figures, or political philosophies.

Rubin, Louis D., Jr. "The Historical Image of Modern Southern Writing."
JOURNAL OF SOUTHERN HISTORY 22 (May 1956): 147-66.

Writers of the southern literary renaissance such as William Faulkner, John Crowe Ransom, Katherine Ann Porter, Thomas Wolfe,
and Allen Tate are discussed. Rubin argues that these writers had
to face northward as they began their careers and they saw their
task as a challenge to defend an agrarian way of life.

Rubin, Louis D., Jr., and Moore, John Rees, eds. THE IDEA OF AN AMERI-
CAN NOVEL. New York: Thomas Y. Crowell, 1961. xxii, 394 p.

These essays are by and about novelists and their art. They cover novelists since Cooper, and include critiques of Hawthorne, Melville, Twain, Crane, Hemingway, Wolfe, Faulkner, Warren, and others.

Scott, Clifford. "Up the Congo Without a Paddle: Images of Blackest Africa in American Fiction." NORTH DAKOTA QUARTERLY 40 (Autumn 1972): 7-19.

American writers regardless of color saw Africans in the perspective of American views on race. The noble-savage image reflected the benevolent stereotype of black people, while the exotic-savage image presented unattractive racial traits.

Sellars, Richard West. "The Interrelationship of Literature, History, and Geography in Western Writing." WESTERN HISTORICAL QUARTERLY 4 (April 1973): 171-86.

The ninety-eight meridian marks the approximate beginning of the "final" West in history and geography, while the West and the frontier exist as a state or mind in literature. The final West, with its wild and strange geography, is the region where the myths, symbols, and imagery associated with frontiers come together.

Shideler, James H. "FLAPPERS AND PHILOSOPHERS, and Farmers: Rural-Urban Tensions of the Twenties." AGRICULTURAL HISTORY 47 (January 1973): 283-99.

FLAPPERS AND PHILOSOPHERS (1920) is the collection of F. Scott Fitzgerald short stories which, Shideler says, characterized the transformation of America from a rural-agrarian country to an urban-technological nation. This essay surveys the rural-urban collision in the twenties and emphasizes the feeling exhibited by many writers that much good was lost.

Sonnichsen, C.L. "The Sharecropper Novel in the Southwest." AGRICULTURAL HISTORY 43 (April 1969): 249-58.

Novelists argued that cotton does terrible things to the land and to the people on it. The sharecropper novels of the 1920s and 1930s concluded that men and women were able to defeat the cotton scourge.

Spengemann, William C., and Lundquist, L.R. "Autobiography and the American Myth." AMERICAN QUARTERLY 17 (Fall 1965): 501-19.

Autobiography presents a metaphor for raw experience and the American myth describes human history as a journey from imperfection to perfection. By examining a number of writings, the authors maintain that autobiographical form is bound up with cultural

belief, and that civilization prescribes fairly specific roles for
people portraying themselves.

Stenerson, Douglas C. H.L. MENCKEN: ICONOCLAST FROM BALTIMORE.
Chicago: University of Chicago Press, 1971. xv, 287 p.

This is a study of Mencken's intellectual development from a social
Darwinist and a staunch libertarian. Stenerson takes the AMERI-
CAN MERCURY in the 1920s at the height of its popularity and
shows that Mencken was best in criticizing the worst side of American life.

Tingley, Donald F. "The 'Robin's Egg Renaissance': Chicago and the Arts,
1910-1920." JOURNAL OF THE ILLINOIS STATE HISTORICAL SOCIETY 63
(Spring 1970): 35-54.

During the years around World War I, many young writers and artists flocked to Chicago. This is a study of the activities and attitudes of Floyd Dell, Sherwood Anderson, Vachel Lindsay, Carl
Sandburg, and others.

Van Auken, Sheldon. "The Southern Historical Novel in the Twentieth Century." JOURNAL OF SOUTHERN HISTORY 14 (May 1948): 157-91.

George Cable, James Lane Allen, Thomas Nelson Page, Ellen
Glasgow, and other historical novelists are examined. These writers
were popular and they influenced the mind of the nation by depicting
the Old South as a golden world and especially by placing the Confederacy in a romantic perspective.

Way, Brian. "Formal Experiment and Social Discontent: Joseph Heller's
CATCH-22." JOURNAL OF AMERICAN STUDIES 2 (October 1968): 253-70.

Way maintains that CATCH-22 has transformed American literature
and has reinvigorated fiction. Although literary output has been
characterized by protest, social discontent, and radicalism since
1900, CATCH-22 explicates the themes of C. Wright Mills's POWER
ELITE in its absurd portrayal of military bureaucracy, and absurdity
is the principal ingredient of the new literature.

West, Thomas Reed. FLESH OF STEEL: LITERATURE AND THE MACHINE IN
AMERICAN CULTURE. Nashville: Vanderbilt University Press, 1967. xv,
155 p.

West summarizes the response of Sherwood Anderson, Waldo Frank,
John Dos Passos, Carl Sandburg, and others concerning the mech-
anization of the environment. He indicates that the aesthetic and
moral attitudes of these writers can be summed up in the concepts
of discipline and energy.

Whisnant, David E. JAMES BOYD. New York: Twayne, 1972. 170 p.

> Whisnant maintains that historians and critics need to pay atten-
> tion to historical novels. He shows how Boyd, the author of
> DRUMS (1925), MARCHING ON (1927), and ROLL RIVER (1935),
> used historical sources and indicated how men were involved in
> events.

White, John. "The Novelist as Historian: William Styron and American
Negro Slavery." JOURNAL OF AMERICAN STUDIES 4 (February 1971):
233-45.

> This is a review of reviews of Styron's CONFESSIONS OF NAT
> TURNER which depict the novel either as "superlative history" or
> as the creation of a "vile racist imagination." White examines
> the authenticity of Styron's depiction of slave behavior and con-
> cludes that the book is a "provocative, massively informed . . .
> and comprehensive synthesis of the Southern slave system."

Zimmerman, Michael. "Literary Revivalism in America: Some Notes Toward
a Hypothesis." AMERICAN QUARTERLY 19 (Spring 1967): 71-85.

> Emily Dickinson and Herman Melville were rediscovered in the
> 1920s and they now enjoy the acclaim denied them during their
> lifetimes. Zimmerman insists that they were denied acclaim be-
> cause they were the victims of a middle-brow criticism in Ameri-
> can culture that shies away from extremes of thought and emotion,
> and shows a distaste for wide ranges of experience.

Chapter 9

POPULAR CULTURE

COLONIAL PERIOD TO 1815

Dorson, Richard M. AMERICA IN LEGEND: FOLKLORE FROM THE COLO-
NIAL PERIOD TO THE PRESENT. New York: Pantheon Books, 1973. xvi,
336 p.

Dorson argues that the vital folklore and legends of a given era
in American history reflect the main concerns and values, tensions
and anxieties, goals and drives of the period. He discusses folk
legends that presented the common man's outlook.

Isaac, Rhys. "Dramatizing the Ideology of Revolution: Popular Mobilization in
Virginia, 1774-1776." WILLIAM AND MARY QUARTERLY 33 (July1976):
357-86.

This is an essay on the oral tradition of country folk and dramati-
zations concerning the "Spirit of '76." Isaac maintains that the
county courthouse and its ceremonials caused the translation of the
country folk's literary vision into communal enthusiasm, popular
aspirations, and a new cultural orientation.

Kenney, W. Howland, ed. LAUGHTER IN THE WILDERNESS: EARLY AMERI-
CAN HUMOR TO 1783. Kent, Ohio: Kent State University Press, 1976.
ix, 236 p.

Essays and poems that depict how the colonists used laughter to
survive the wilderness are included in this anthology. New Eng-
landers used wit to reinforce moral codes, while southerners employed it to develop a sense of social superiority.

MacFadden, Fred R., Jr. "Popular Arts and the Revolt Against Patriarchism
in Colonial America." JOURNAL OF POPULAR CULTURE 8 (Fall 1974): 286-
94.

MacFadden suggests that there may be a timeless impulse that
pushes people toward submission to a male superego, conscience,
or overlord. This can be seen in the trauma Americans went
through in "killing" George III, as expressed in popular writings.

Sidwell, Robert T. "'Writers, Thinkers, and Fox Hunters'--Educational Theory in Almanacs of Eighteenth-Century Colonial America." HISTORY OF EDUCA-TION QUARTERLY 8 (Fall 1968): 275-88.

> In educational theory, eighteenth-century almanacs emphasized practical concern for commercial and personal advancement. They were the most widely read literary productions, and this was evidence that they mirrored the concerns of the people.

Slotkin, Richard. REGENERATION THROUGH VIOLENCE: THE MYTHOLOGY OF THE AMERICAN FRONTIER, 1600-1860. Middletown, Conn.: Wesleyan University Press, 1973. 670 p.

> The frontier produced violence rather than democracy. This became a trait of American character and was expressed in literary and subliterary genres such as the cult of the hunter-killer hero.

1815-1915

Albanese, Catherine. "Requiem for Memorial Day: Dissent in the Redeemer Nation." AMERICAN QUARTERLY 26 (October 1974): 386-98.

> Memorial Day rites constituted sacred collective representations and a cult of the dead. Albanese shows, however, that Memorial Day experienced a transvaluation owing to a gradually increasing apathy toward the cult of the dead, and she discusses some theoretical underpinnings for this historical phenomenon.

Baskerville, Barnet. "19th Century Burlesque of Oratory." AMERICAN QUAR-TERLY 20 (Winter 1968): 726-43.

> This is a study of nineteenth-century humorists such as Artemus Ward, Petroleum V. Nasby, and others, who burlesqued orators, particularly of the Fourth of July and great speech of Congress varieties, and diminished the orator from a hero. Their effect was to make the platform orator more sensible and also more responsible.

Benston, Kimberly W. "Tragic Aspects of the Blues." PHYLON 36 (Summer 1975): 164-76.

> The bluesman embodies the tragic encounter between the dream of success and the knowledge of guilt. As a tragic character, he is especially interesting because he is self-created.

Berkman, Brenda. "The Vanishing Race: Conflicting Images of the American Indian in Children's Literature, 1880-1930." NORTH DAKOTA QUARTERLY 44 (Spring 1976): 31-40.

This is a delineation of adult attitudes toward the Indian as portrayed in children's books. The Indian was depicted as a savage
or noble, but he was always regarded in racial terms as a vanishing race.

Betts, John Rickards. AMERICA'S SPORTING HERITAGE: 1850-1950. Reading, Mass.: Addison-Wesley, 1974. xv, 428 p.

Betts examines the transition from class sport (1850-1920) to the
rise of mass sport (1920-50). He argues that class distinctions
emerged from an agrarian society, but sport became a mass activity with the urban-industrial state.

_____. "P.T. Barnum and the Popularization of Natural History." JOURNAL
OF THE HISTORY OF IDEAS 20 (June-September 1959): 353-68.

Scholarly interest in natural history was encouraged in the nineteenth century, but Barnum exploited the scientific and commercial
aspects to the fullest. He was a museum entrepreneur, and he
made gifts of animal skeletons to the Smithsonian Institution and
the American Museum of Natural History.

_____. "Sporting Journalism in Nineteenth-Century America." AMERICAN
QUARTERLY 5 (Spring 1953): 39-56.

Sports reporting gained an important niche in journalism during the
1830s when William Trotter Porter published the SPIRIT OF THE
TIMES and the AMERICAN TURF REGISTER. He promoted horse
racing, rowing, yachting, and baseball during the mid-nineteenth
century and in a sense prepared the way for the athletic impulse
that swept the nation between 1865 and 1900.

_____. "The Technological Revolution and the Rise of Sports, 1850-1900."
MISSISSIPPI VALLEY HISTORICAL REVIEW 40 (September 1953): 231-56.

Industrialization and urbanization contributed importantly to the
rise of sports. The railroad, more than any other invention, made
intercommunity rivalry in sports possible, while the telegraph and
penny press opened sports journalism.

Blair, Walter. HORSE SENSE IN AMERICAN HUMOR, FROM BENJAMIN
FRANKLIN TO OGDEN NASH. Chicago: University of Chicago Press, 1942.
xv, 341 p.

The author argues that the influence of American humor is based
on its close relation to common sense and utilitarian philosophy.
It has been voiced by "fool characters" or humorists who appeared
as fool characters, witness Poor Richard and Will Rogers.

Blair, Walter, and Meine, Franklin J., eds. HALF HORSE, HALF ALLIGA-
TOR: THE GROWTH OF THE MIKE FINK LEGEND. Chicago: University of
Chicago Press, 1956. x, 289 p.

Mike Fink, the keelboatman, became known throughout the Mississippi Valley and Rocky Mountains as a marksman, strong man, and
trickster. This book shows how legendary characters were developed in a literate society.

Bloomfield, Maxwell. "Dixon's THE LEOPARD'S SPORTS: A Study in Popular
Racism." AMERICAN QUARTERLY 16 (Fall 1964): 387-401.

Thomas Dixon was a late nineteenth-century Baptist clergyman who
preached the social gospel, but he became caught up in the expansionism of the Spanish-American War and its justification of
control of backward peoples. His immensely popular novel represented a new gospel of the "black peril" which exalted the white
majority and prophesied a middle-class millenium.

Boatwright, Mody C. "The Beginnings of Cowboy Fiction." SOUTHWEST
REVIEW 51 (Winter 1966): 11-28.

The nineteenth-century writers who wished to present the cowboy
in a favorable light to a mass audience had to relate him to popular values. They relied on beliefs from the romantic movement
that earlier forms of social organization were superior to later forms
and that the good life was the simple life, lived close to nature.

Bode, Carl. THE ANATOMY OF AMERICAN POPULAR CULTURE, 1840-1861.
Berkeley and Los Angeles: University of California Press, 1959. xxii, 292 p.

Bode discusses literature, music, art, architecture, home furnish-
ings, how-to-do-it manuals, and other matters. He attempts to
show a connection between the "complexes" he sees in the period
and the archetypes of Jung.

_____. "Columbia's Carnal Bed." AMERICAN QUARTERLY 15 (Spring 1963):
52-64.

This is a survey of sex literature, both fiction and nonfiction, in
the nineteenth century. Sex literature was sparse, but a few
"scientific books" dealt with sex explicitly and a handful of novels
and poems could be labeled pornography.

Boles, John B. "Jacob Abbott and the Rollo Books: New England Culture for
Children." JOURNAL OF POPULAR CULTURE 6 (Spring 1973): 507-28.

Rollo was the first truly American child character in literature. If
he was the model child, the New England mother or father was the
model parent and both accepted the moral virtures and norms of a
mid-nineteenth-century society threatened by change.

Bowen, Elbert R. THEATRICAL ENTERTAINMENTS IN RURAL MISSOURI BE-
FORE THE CIVIL WAR. University of Missouri Studies, vol. 32. Columbia:
University of Missouri Press, 1959. xiv, 141 p.

Rural people enjoyed a variety of productions. They attended
local lyceum-society programs, musical offerings, and performances
of magicians, ventriloquists, and local dramatic societies.

Brake, Robert. "The Lion Act is Over: Passive/Aggressive Patterns of Communication in American Negro Humor." JOURNAL OF POPULAR CULTURE 9
(Winter 1975): 549-60.

This is a study of the Negro humorous tradition from its origin in
slave times to black power. Slaves exhibited a rollicking wit as
a psychological weapon of appeasement and appeal, but gallows
humor or the humor of one whose head is in the lion's mouth also
was a norm.

Branch, E. Douglas. THE SENTIMENTAL YEARS, 1836-1860. New York:
D. Appleton-Century, 1934. xiii, 432 p.

The first generation of the middle class is discussed from a social
standpoint. The social continuity of the period, according to the
author, is sentimentalism.

Bridges, William E. "Warm Hearth, Cold World: Social Perspectives on the
Household Poets." AMERICAN QUARTERLY 21 (Winter 1969): 764-79.

Bridges examines the popular poetry of antebellum America and
sees an emphasis on mother and home. He argues that the symbol
of the loving mother is as important as the Adamic symbol in
American culture becuase she symbolizes security, relatedness, and
caring.

Browne, Ray B. "Shakespeare in American Vaudeville and Negro Minstrelry."
AMERICAN QUARTERLY 12 (Fall 1960): 374-91.

Vaudeville and Negro minstrels used Shakespeare with complete
familiarity and lack of respect during the early part of the nineteenth century. They sometimes sang his songs straight, but they
also presented short, full-scale travesties of his works.

Bunkle, Phillida. "Sentimental Womanhood and Domestic Education, 1830-
1870." HISTORY OF EDUCATION QUARTERLY 14 (Spring 1974): 13-30.

An antifeminist position that defined women as spiritual, emotional,
and dependent dominated ideas in the nineteenth century. Spirituality was most important since the key to social salvation was the
maternal relation, and this supposedly gave women covert control
of society.

Carter, Everett. "Cultural History Written with Lightning: The Significance of 'Birth of a Nation.'" AMERICAN QUARTERLY 12 (Fall 1960): 347-57.

Carter shows that with "Birth of a Nation," significant motion picture history began. It provided the cinematic genre with images of an elemental struggle between black and white moral values.

Cawelti, John G. "Portrait of the Newsboy as a Young Man: Some Remarks on the Alger Stories." WISCONSIN MAGAZINE OF HISTORY 45 (Winter 1961-62): 79-83.

Alger was one of a number of children's writers who attempted to create a juvenile literature that was native in setting and exciting in incident, with enough didactic flavor to win the approval of parents. His stories show a virtuous young man's rise from poverty and obscurity to social respectability, but the major portion of the narrative presented adventures.

Clark, Thomas D. THE RAMPAGING FRONTIER: MANNERS AND HUMORS OF PIONEER DAYS IN THE SOUTH AND THE MIDDLE WEST. Indianapolis: Bobbs-Merrill, 1939. xiv, 350 p.

This study emphasizes frontier humor of the buckskin variety. The characters are "gouging" bears, telling tales in taverns, preaching at revivals, fiddlin', and foolin' with the gals.

Clements, William M. "Savage, Pastoral, Civilized: An Ecology Typology of American Frontier Heroes." JOURNAL OF POPULAR CULTURE 8 (Fall 1974): 254-66.

Using Richard Dorson's suggestion that along the frontier Americans experienced a heroic age, Clements divides frontier heroes according to a savage, pastoral, or civilized typology. Davy Crockett was a savage hero because he was shaped by folk attitudes; Johnny Appleseed was pastoral since he gained renown in contemporary literature; and Paul Bunyan was civilized since he was the product of twentieth-century popularizers.

Crandall, John C. "Patriotism and Humanitarian Reform in Children's Literature, 1825-1860." AMERICAN QUARTERLY 21 (Spring 1969): 3-22.

Children's literature was conservative in its depiction of the U.S. government as a perfected system and its eulogizing of Franklin, Washington, Clay, and Webster. The interpretation of reform currents was vague except for temperance, since it could be ascribed to human weakness.

Cripps, Thomas. "The Movie Jew as an Image of Assimilationism, 1903-1927." JOURNAL OF POPULAR FILM 4 (1975): 190-207.

Cripps argues that American movies depicted Jewish characters as virtuous and sentimentally likeable figures. The industry was controlled by a Jewish elite, and it provided institutional checks on pejorative stereotypes, thus contributing to a liberal environment where Jews had an accepted and unthreatening place.

_____. "The Reaction of the Negro to the Motion Picture BIRTH OF A NATION." HISTORIAN 25 (May 1963): 344-62.

Artistically, BIRTH OF A NATION was the finest motion picture yet produced. This essay surveys Negro pressure, and its failure, to have parts of the film deleted.

_____. SLOW FADE TO BLACK: THE NEGRO IN AMERICAN FILM, 1900-1912. New York: Oxford University Press, 1977. xi, 447 p.

This study provides clues to the study of black-white relationships from 1900 to 1912. Cripps details the disastrous black image on the screen and the futile struggle to establish a separate black Hollywood.

Davis, Ronald L. "Early Jazz: Another Look." SOUTHWEST REVIEW 58 (Winter 1973): 1-13.

Davis traces the origins of jazz in Louisiana, particularly in New Orleans. He shows the development of country blues in Afro-American music as well as classic ragtime and discusses the work of early jazz artists such as Buddy Bolden and Jelly Roll Morton.

_____. "Early Jazz: Another Look--II." SOUTHWEST REVIEW 58 (Spring 1973): 144-54.

This is an examination of the spread of jazz to the North and West from its southern beginnings. Davis discusses the development of both black jazz and white Dixieland before the 1920s.

_____. "They Played for Gold: Theater on the Mining Frontier." SOUTHWEST REVIEW 51 (Spring 1966): 169-83.

This is a study of mining frontier theaters and thespians. Theaters were often associated with saloons, and actors were accepted or rejected because of the degree of moral turpitude displayed in their private lives.

Dippie, Brian W. CUSTER's LAST STAND: THE ANATOMY OF AN AMERICAN MYTH. Missoula: University of Montana Press, 1976. xii, 214 p.

Dippie discusses how the popular mind viewed Custer's last stand. He discusses the depictions of poets, artists, novelists, and filmmakers.

Dorson, Richard M. BUYING THE WIND: REGIONAL FOLKLORE IN THE UNITED STATES. Chicago: University of Chicago Press, 1964. xvii, 574 p.

This is a collection of tales, anecdotes, riddles, and songs dealing with Maine Down-Easters, Pennsylvania Dutchmen, southern mountaineers, Louisiana Cajuns, Utah Mormons, and others.

Douglas, Ann. "Heaven Our Home: Consolation Literature in the Northern United States, 1830-1880." AMERICAN QUARTERLY 26 (December 1974): 496-515.

Fictionalized and factual accounts of death crowded the book stalls before and after the Civil War. Liberal clergymen and devout women were the principal authors of mourners' manuals.

Dulles, Foster Rhea. AMERICA LEARNS TO PLAY: A HISTORY OF POPULAR RECREATION, 1607-1940. New York: D. Appleton-Century, 1940. xvii, 441 p.

This is a history of entertainments as shaped by social forces, English contacts, and upper-class prestige. The one notable omission is the entertainment derived from books.

Erisman, Fred. "L. Frank Baum and the Progressive Dilemma." AMERICAN QUARTERLY 20 (Fall 1968): 616-23.

The dilemma of the Progressives was adapting rural ideals to a complex urban society. Baum was the author of fantasies for children in the land of Oz in which he suggested that if enough people realized the old ways they might practice them.

Fisher, Robert. "Film Censorship and Progressive Reform: The National Board of Censorship of Motion Pictures, 1909-1922." JOURNAL OF POPULAR FILM 4 (1975): 143-56.

The National Board of Censorship opposed censorship on civil libertarian grounds. It maintained that culture was a private affair and censorship a voluntary activity, but it also was aware of the need for the control of society's behavior.

Flusche, Michael. "Joel Chandler Harris and the Folklore of Slavery." JOURNAL OF AMERICAN STUDIES 9 (December 1975): 347-63.

Historians have given little attention to the folklore of slavery in attempting to determine slave personality. The cycle of folk tales recorded by Joel Chandler Harris showed that slavery brought about an individualistic, atomistic world view rather than a sense of community.

Foner, Philip S. AMERICAN LABOR SONGS OF THE NINETEENTH CEN-
TURY. Urbana: University of Illinois Press, 1975. xvii, 356 p.

Foner covers the best economic and social songs produced by and
associated with the labor movement and shows how events and personalities influenced them. There are separate chapters on the
Knights of Labor, the eight-hour day, the AF of L, and other
matters.

Frantz, Joe B., and Choate, Julian Ernest, Jr. THE AMERICAN COWBOY:
THE MYTH AND THE REALITY. Norman: University of Oklahoma Press, 1955.
xiv, 232 p.

This is a review of literary interpretations of the cowboy. The
cowboy entered history during an heroic period and was helped
along as a folk hero by dime novelists and other writers.

Graham, Philip. SHOWBOATS: THE HISTORY OF AN AMERICAN INSTITU-
TION. Austin: University of Texas Press, 1951. x, 224 p.

Popular culture when the river was the natural highway is reflected
in this study. Nearly all the best known actors of the early-nine-
teenth century performed on showboats.

Haar, Charles M. "E.L. Youmans: A Chapter in the Diffusion of Science in
America." JOURNAL OF THE HISTORY OF IDEAS 9 (April 1948): 193-213.

Youmans was a popularizer of science who fought for the dissemina-
tion of scientific ideas and shared the mystical belief that science
could lead to eventual perfection. Among many things, he founded the POPULAR SCIENCE MONTHLY and in many respects prepared America for the scientific awakening following publication
of the ORIGIN OF THE SPECIES.

Hall, James W. "Concepts of Liberty in American Broadside Ballads, 1850-
1870: A Study of the Mind in American Mass Culture." JOURNAL OF POP-
ULAR CULTURE 2 (Fall 1968): 252-77.

Broadsides are single sheets of paper printed on one side, while
ballads are songs that tell a story. The broadside ballads Hall
studied depicted liberty as abstract and impersonal rather than related to specific issues such as nation, history, heritage, and God.

Haller, John S., Jr. "From Maidenhood to Menopause: Sex Education for
Women in Victorian America." JOURNAL OF POPULAR CULTURE 6 (Summer
1972): 49-69.

Sex-in-life manuals of the nineteenth century were designed to
impress women with sentiments of virtue and chastity, and to show
that sex interfered with these objectives. The family was romanti-
cized as part of an effort to explain the incongruity between middle-class principles and reality.

Hart, James D. THE POPULAR BOOK: A HISTORY OF AMERICA'S LIT-
ERARY TASTE. Berkeley and Los Angeles: University of California Press, 1961.
351 p.

Hart analyzes the reading taste of Americans and depicts their attitudes as expressed in popular literature. He begins with the Puritans and continues through the Second World War.

Hay, Robert P. "Providence and the American Past." INDIANA MAGAZINE
OF HISTORY 65 (June 1969): 79-102.

Hay delineates some of the major facets of the legend of providen-
tial protection for the nation as depicted in popular thought from
1776 to 1876. Using Fourth-of-July editorials, odes, and orations,
he shows that Americans during their first century were convinced
that they were heaven's favorites.

Hofstadter, Richard, and Hofstadter, Beatrice. "Winston Churchill: A Study
in the Popular Novel." AMERICAN QUARTERLY 2 (Spring 1950): 12-28.

Between 1899 and 1917, Churchill was the most popular novelist
in the United States. He first wrote historical romances and then
turned to the political and problem novel, but he was popular because he was a moralist who saw the dichotomy between business
and human values.

Jervey, Edward D. "La Roy Sunderland: Prince of the Sons of Mesmer."
JOURNAL OF POPULAR CULTURE 9 (Spring 1976): 1010-26.

Sunderland, a reformer who turned from abolition to phrenology,
in the mid-nineteenth century, came to believe that the mind of
man exerts a great power over his body. This essay pictures him
as one of the enthusiasts who contributed to the later development
of psychosomatic medicine.

Jones, Daryl E. "Clenched Teeth and Curse Revenge and the Dime Novel
Outlaw Hero." JOURNAL OF POPULAR CULTURE 7 (Winter 1973): 652-65.

This is a study of Edward L. Wheeler's DEADWOOD DICK, the
noble outlaw and American Robin Hood, who first appeared in
1877. Jones maintains that "Dick" was embraced by the American
public because he appealed to sociopsychological needs and expressed American ambivalence toward law and the legal system.

Jordan, Philip D. SINGIN' YANKEES. Minneapolis: University of Minnesota Press, 1946. xi, 305 p.

The singing Hutchinsons--father, mother, and fourteen children--
who earned a living composing and performing ballads in the early
nineteenth century are covered in this study. They sang for money

and moral reform, and associated with people such as Henry Ward Beecher, Ralph Waldo Emerson, Abraham Lincoln, and others.

Jowett, Garth S. "The First Motion Picture Audiences." JOURNAL OF POPULAR FILM 3 (Winter 1974): 39-54.

Movies answered a deep social and cultural need of the people. The motion picture's first audience was made up of members of the middle class, who had never attended the theater because of religious beliefs, middle and upper working-class patrons of the theater and melodramas, and the large urban working class, many of whom were immigrants.

Karr, Kathleen. "The Long Square-Up: Exploitation Trends in the Silent Film." JOURNAL OF POPULAR FILM 3 (Spring 1974): 107-28.

Silent films depicted exploitable dramatic topics such as sex, drinking, and gambling. When an event of national interest appeared in the press, filmmakers picked up the story and beat the subject to a public death.

Kelly, R. Gordon. MOTHER WAS A LADY: SELF AND SOCIETY IN SELECTED AMERICAN CHILDREN'S PERIODICALS, 1865-1890. Westport, Conn.: Greenwood, 1974. xx, 233 p.

This period in children's literature in which popular, mass-circulation magazines were introduced was transitional. Kelly examines the stories in these magazines in order to understand the beliefs of the cultural elite.

Klotman, Phyllis R. "The Slave and the Western: Popular Literature of the Nineteenth Century." NORTH DAKOTA QUARTERLY 41 (Autumn 1973): 40-54.

The slave narrative is based on long and perilous journeys, an experience not unlike that of the frontiersman. Both the slave and the westerner chose to escape their condition by leaving the dominant culture.

Kramer, Frank R. VOICES IN THE VALLEY: MYTHMAKING AND FOLK BELIEF IN THE SHAPING OF THE MIDDLE WEST. Madison: University of Wisconsin Press, 1964. xvii, 300 p.

Mythmaking and folk belief emerged in the Middle West because of the migration of a folk movement to that region. Myths of one folk were fused with others and transformed into a myth of the American way.

Lamplugh, George R. "The Image of the Negro in Popular Magazine Fiction, 1875-1900." JOURNAL OF NEGRO HISTORY 57 (April 1972): 177-89.

> Lamplugh examines the image of the Negro that appeared in short stories published in ATLANTIC, HARPER'S, SCRIBNER'S MONTHLY/ THE CENTURY, and SCRIBNER'S, all middle-class magazines. Writers emphasized reconciliation between the sections, the inferiority of the Negro, and a form of "Old South" control over black people.

Leab, Daniel J. "The Gamut from A to B: The Image of the Black in Pre-1915 Movies." POLITICAL SCIENCE QUARTERLY 88 (March 1973): 53-70.

> The tenor of the period between the 1890s and 1915 did not encourage serious or dignified treatments of blacks. Racial libels abounded in all areas of life, and blacks were victimized more than any other group.

Leverette, William E., Jr. "E.L. Youman's Crusade for Scientific Autonomy and Respectability." AMERICAN QUARTERLY 17 (Spring 1965): 12-32.

> Youman's POPULAR SCIENTIFIC MONTHLY was dedicated to the ideal that the scientist's search for truth through a naturalistic frame of reference deserved autonomy and status. He wanted his readers to believe that science as a method of the mind was the most accurate knowledge obtainable of the order of nature with its laws and unity.

McLean, Albert F., Jr. AMERICAN VAUDEVILLE AS RITUAL. Lexington: University of Kentucky Press, 1965. xiii, 250 p.

> Vaudeville is discussed as a manifestation of psychic and social forces in American history. McLean contends that this popular art form was part of the belief in progress, the pursuit of happiness, and the hope for success basic to American character.

MacLeod, Anne Scott. A MORAL TALE: CHILDREN'S FICTION AND AMERICAN CULTURE, 1820-1860. Hamden, Conn.: Archon, 1975. 196 p.

> This is a study of the themes that dominated children's literature. The social purposes of Lydia Maria Child, Jacob Abbott, Catherine Sedgwick, and others are described.

Mellard, James M. "Racism, Formula, and Popular Fiction." JOURNAL OF POPULAR CULTURE 5 (Summer 1971): 10-37.

> In popular fiction, the formula is a designation of an essential idea. Mellard examines racial formulas in nineteenth-century novels where blacks are depicted as faithful, loyal, lovable, helpless, trusting, comic figures, and in twentieth-century stories where they are examples of sex and violence.

Moore, Ethel, and Moore, Chauncey O. BALLADS AND FOLKSONGS OF THE SOUTHWEST. Norman: University of Oklahoma Press, 1964. xv, 414 p.

This anthology includes 204 texts and 213 melodies collected in Oklahoma. They are mainly homesteader ballads that emphasized the well known and the commonplace rather than the vague and illusive.

Mott, Frank Luther. "The Magazine Revolution and Popular Ideas in the Nineties." PROCEEDINGS OF THE AMERICAN ANTIQUARIAN SOCIETY 64 (21 April 1954): 195-214.

The appearance of the ten-cent magazine brought the revolution. These publications were widely read because of the aggressive drive for self-improvement that characterized middle-class society in the nineties.

Murrell, William. A HISTORY OF AMERICAN GRAPHIC HUMOR, 1865-1938. New York: Macmillan Co., for the Whitney Museum of Art, 1938. xiv, 271 p.

This work contains 242 graphics, some of which are among the finest examples of the cartoonist's art in the Western world. Biographical material on obscure and prominent cartoonists, such as Charles Dana Gibson and Thomas Nast, as well as a history of the newspaper cartoon, comic strip, and animated cartoon, are included.

Nathan, Hans. DAN EMMETT AND THE RISE OF EARLY NEGRO MINSTRELSY. Norman: University of Oklahoma Press, 1962. xiv, 496 p.

Emmett was the composer of "Dixie." This is a study and an anthology of songs and lyrics that exemplify an important popular art form.

Nye, Russell B. THE UNEMBARRASSED MUSE: THE POPULAR ARTS IN AMERICA. New York: Dial Press, 1970. 497 p.

This is a comprehensive survey of popular books, poetry, children's literature, music, the theater, comics, movies, radio, and television. Nye begins with the colonial period and proceeds through the 1960s.

Parker, Gail Thain. MIND CARE IN NEW ENGLAND: FROM THE CIVIL WAR TO WORLD WAR I. Hanover, N.H.: University Press of New England, 1973. xi, 197 p.

This is a study of popular works concerning the power of right thinking to restore health and rout anxiety. The literature of mind control was torn between desires for spontaneity and obedience to authority.

Perry, Sandra. "Sex and Sentiment in America or What Was Really Going On Between the Staves of Nineteenth Century Songs of Fashion." JOURNAL OF POPULAR CULTURE 6 (Summer 1972): 32-48.

Nineteenth-century songs praised thr feminine function of home-making as well as virtue, love, self-pity, and death. The child was idealized as innocent and the mother gained a new importance.

Pinkerton, Jan. "From Yankee to Whitey: An American Stereotype." JOURNAL OF POPULAR CULTURE 3 (Spring 1970): 667-76.

Contemporary writers, black and white, have developed the stereotype that the white American is impotent, repressed, and secretly envious of the virile black man. This is the same stereotype that existed in the nineteenth century when the Yankee was described as being cold, women as being thin and pale-cheeked, intellectual and physically inferior to their Europeans counterparts.

Satterwhite, Joseph N. "The Tremulous Formula: Form and Technique in GODEY'S Fiction." AMERICAN QUARTERLY 8 (Summer 1956): 99-113.

The basic GODEY formula rested on the premise that a good story was one that made the reader cry and was shot through with moral purpose. Characters were tortured with frustrations and the laws of accident and chance operated as immutably as the law of gravity.

Saum, Lewis O. "Death in the Popular Mind of Pre-Civil War America." AMERICAN QUARTERLY 26 (December 1974): 477-95.

Saum shows that death was a fact for sober consideration, and ordinary men gave almost ceaseless advice to themselves and others to keep death firmly in mind. Happiness and triumph in death were important parts of a Christian hereafter.

Schwantes, Carlos A. "The Joy of Timetables." JOURNAL OF POPULAR CULTURE 9 (Winter 1975): 604-17.

Schwantes indicates that nineteenth-century railroad timetables emphasized time of departure rather than arrival and stressed the amenities of travel. In the twentieth century, bureaucratization meant standardization, especially in the system of keeping time, and this accompanied other innovations.

Siegel, Adrienne. "Brothels, Bets, and Bars: Popular Literature as Guidebook to the Urban Underground, 1840-1870." NORTH DAKOTA QUARTERLY 44 (Spring 1976): 5-22.

Popular books in the mid-nineteenth century saturated the market with tales of the city as a safe harbor for all sorts of immoral behavior. Country boys and city clerks could find vicarious thrills in these books, but they also served as guides to the locations of wicked spots of amusement.

_____. "When Cities Were Fun: The Image of the American City in Popular Books, 1840-1870." JOURNAL OF POPULAR CULTURE 9 (Winter 1975): 573-82.

Many students of the city have argued that America's literary heritage consists of a revulsion to metropolitan life. Siegel shows that mid-nineteenth-century popular novels depicted the city as a place of freedom, fun, and abundance.

Skinner, Maud, and Skinner, Otis. ONE MAN IN HIS TIME: THE ADVENTURES OF H. WATKINS, STROLLING PLAYER, 1845-1863, FROM HIS JOURNAL. Philadelphia: University of Pennsylvania Press, 1938. xvii, 258 p.

Harry Watkins's journal provides an intimate view of the mid-nineteenth-century American stage. He was not a star or manager, but he presents an interesting picture of theatrical life which is illuminated by the Skinners' comments on contemporary actors.

Snow, Robert E., and Wright, David E. "Coney Island: A Case Study in Popular Culture and Technical Change." JOURNAL OF POPULAR CULTURE 9 (Spring 1976): 960-75.

Coney Island is examined as America's first symbolic commitment to mechanized leisure. The park developed from a beach resort to an amusement park much to the disgust of the affluent and reform-minded, who associated mechanized leisure with moral depravity.

Soderbergh, Peter A. "Bibliographical Essay: The Negro in Juvenile Series Books, 1899-1930." JOURNAL OF NEGRO HISTORY 58 (April 1973): 179-87.

The BOBBSEY TWINS, TOM SWIFT, HARDY BOYS, and DOLLY DIMPLE were series books and they enjoyed a vast readership. Blacks were assigned names that drew existing stereotypes, with domestics being called uncle or aunt, and others being used for comic relief and other literary objectives.

Somers, Dale A. "The Leisure Revolution: Recreation in the American City, 1820-1920." JOURNAL OF POPULAR CULTURE 5 (Summer 1971): 125-47.

The leisure revolution was a product of the shift in America from a rural-agrarian to an urban-industrial society. It took place primarily in the theater and in organized sports.

_____. THE RISE OF SPORTS IN NEW ORLEANS: 1850-1900. Baton Rouge: Louisiana State University Press, 1972. xiv, 320 p.

This is a study of the role of sports in American life and their importance as a leisure outlet for an urban population. In the New Orleans context, Somers examines horse racing, baseball, bicycling, and boxing.

Steckmesser, Kent Ladd. THE WESTERN HERO IN HISTORY AND LEGEND. Norman: University of Oklahoma Press, 1965. xiii, 281 p.

Steckmesser looks at Kit Carson, Billy the Kid, Wild Bill Hickok, and George A. Custer as western types and historical figures. There is a pervading pattern in the history of the reputation of each: some original actions that provided a reputation, embroidery of this in popular culture, and the onslaught of detractors who hoped to kill the legend.

Suderman, Elmer F. "Popular American Fiction (1870-1900) Looks at the Attributes of God." JOURNAL OF POPULAR CULTURE 4 (Fall 1970): 383-97.

Popular novelists emphasized the love of God in his relation to man rather than righteousness, sovereignty, and majesty. Suderman argues that they were expressing a dominant belief of their age that man was the focus of the universe and the only important question concerning God was his relation to man.

Sweet, Leonard. "The Fourth of July and Black Americans in the Nineteenth Century: Northern Leadership Opinion Within the Context of the Black Experience." JOURNAL OF NEGRO HISTORY 61 (July 1976): 256-75.

Some blacks celebrated the Fourth of July to emphasize the primacy of American ideals over reality. Others marked August 1, West Indian Emancipation Day, as an alternative.

Toll, Robert C. BLACKING UP: THE MINSTREL SHOW IN NINETEENTH-CENTURY AMERICA. New York: Oxford University Press, 1974. 310 p.

The minstrel show, performed by white men in black face, deeply embedded caricatures of blacks into American popular culture. It also informed patrons on subjects from plantations to cities, fashions to morality, and from Indians to immigrants.

_____. ON WITH THE SHOW! THE FIRST CENTURY OF SHOW BUSINESS IN AMERICA. New York: Oxford University Press, 1976. 361 p.

This is a survey of entertainments from the theater to P.T. Barnum, clowns and comedians, minstrel shows, musical comedies, girlie shows, vaudeville, and the Ziegfield Follies. Toll argues that common people shaped show business in their own image.

Watson, Margaret G. SILVER THEATRE: AMUSEMENTS OF THE MINING FRONTIER IN EARLY NEVADA, 1850 to 1864. Glendale, Calif.: Arthur H. Clark, 1964. 387 p.

Miners enjoyed diverse offerings in Washoe County and Virginia City, Nevada. They saw minstrels, panoramas, bellringers, glassblowers, magicians, trapeze artists, and burlesques, as well as most of the plays the rest of the country saw.

Wector, Dixon. THE HERO IN AMERICA: A CHRONICLE OF HERO-WORSHIP. New York: Charles Scribner's Sons, 1941. viii, 530 p.

> Wector is trying to learn if the totalitarians are correct in arguing that democracy cannot create heroes in times of crisis. He discusses major and minor heroes in American history, and shows that women, professional men, artists, and writers have been excluded from the hero group.

Whisnant, David E. "Selling the Gospel News, or: The Strange Career of Jimmy Brown the Newsboy." JOURNAL OF SOCIAL HISTORY 5 (Spring 1972): 269-309.

> The story of the newsboy from his origin in the eighteenth century to the building of an elaborate newsboy myth after 1835 is discussed. The author indicates that the newsboy has been manipulated as a rugged individualist and as a technocratic functionary allowing antithetical ideologies to exist.

WHO BLOWED UP THE CHURCH HOUSE? AND OTHER OZARK FOLK TALES. Collected by Vance Randolph. New York: Columbia University Press, 1952. xviii, 232 p.

> These are yarns spun by Ozark hill people. Some tell of local heroes, others of wits, and more of everyday pranks. Included are notes by Herbert Halpert and illustrations by Glen Rounds.

Wilson, Daniel J. "Nature in Western Popular Literature from the Dime Novel to Zane Grey." NORTH DAKOTA QUARTERLY 44 (Spring 1976): 41-50.

> The basic attitude toward nature in the popular western novel remained largely unchanged from the 1860s to the 1930s. The dime novelists depicted nature as benign and beneficent, but Zane Grey showed an awareness that some of man's actions had had a detrimental effect.

Wood, Ann Douglas. "Mrs. Sigourney and the Sensibility of Inner Space." NEW ENGLAND QUARTERLY 45 (June 1972): 163-81.

> Lydia Huntley Sigourney was the most popular poetess in America before the Civil War. She was not a great poet, but she was important to American cultural history because she adapted herself to the patterns laid out for women of her day and also exploited them by using poetry to gain social mobility and as an advertisement for piety.

_____. "The 'Scribbling Women' amd Fanny Fern: Why Women Wrote." AMERICAN QUARTERLY 23 (Spring 1971): 3-24.

Fanny Fern's RUTH HALL is an unusual antebellum novel written by a female. In this book, and elsewhere, Fern urged women to write to portray their female experience, reproach men for male cruelty, and survive the "dead-levels" of their lives.

Wyld, Lionel D. LOW BRIDGE! FOLKLORE AND THE ERIE CANAL. Syracuse, N.Y.: Syracuse University Press, 1962. xii, 212 p.

Wyld examines the planning, building, and opening of the canal, views of tourists, folk characters along its banks, songs and ballads, tall tales, and the canal in literature.

Yates, Norris W. WILLIAM T. PORTER AND THE SPIRIT OF THE TIMES: A STUDY OF THE BIG BEAR SCHOOL OF HUMOR. Baton Rouge: Louisiana State University Press, 1957. xii, 222 p.

Porter's SPIRIT was an important outlet for antebellum southern humor. Yates explores the social types and frontier experiences that were treated in stories and develops the growth of comic narrative.

1915 TO THE PRESENT

Baker, Donald G. "Black Images: The Afro-American in Popular Novels, 1900-1945." JOURNAL OF POPULAR CULTURE 7 (Fall 1973): 327-46.

Baker shows that novels on the bestseller charts between 1900 and 1921, such as Winston Churchill's THE CRISIS, Owen Wister's LADY BALTIMORE, and Booth Tarkington's PENROD, were virulently racist. Those published between 1922 and 1930 depicted the black as inferior but were somewhat muted in tone.

Barnouw, Erik. A TOWER OF BABEL: A HISTORY OF BROADCASTING IN THE UNITED STATES. Vol. 1: TO 1933. New York: Oxford University Press, 1966. 344 p.

Barnouw traces the rise of radio from gadgetry to World War I innovations and finally to struggles for control during the twenties by RCA, Westinghouse, and other corporate giants. He looks at the emergence of major stations, the innovations of personalities, and the influence of programs.

_____. THE GOLDEN WEB: A HISTORY OF BROADCASTING IN THE UNITED STATES. Vol. 2: 1933-1953. New York: Oxford University Press, 1968. 391 p.

In this chronicle, the reader learns a great deal about radio soap operas, Edward R. Murrow's wartime broadcasts from London, and Ed Sullivan's concern for keeping his television show free of personalities whose loyalty was dubious to the McCarthyites. It is also emphasized that radio early allowed commercial use to triumph over educational purposes.

_____. THE IMAGE EMPIRE: A HISTORY OF BROADCASTING IN THE UNITED STATES. Vol. 3: FROM 1953. New York: Oxford University Press, 1970. 396 p.

This volume covers television and provides anecdotes and vignettes concerning personalities and programs from John Cameron Swayze to "The Man from U.N.C.L.E." Barnouw also gives attention to politics and to advertisers' custodianship of American cultural life.

Bell, Bernard W. "Folk Art and the Harlem Renaissance." PHYLON 36 (Summer 1975): 155-63.

Bell maintains that W.E.B. Dubois, Alain Locke, and James Weldon Johnson understood that folk art laid the base for high art. They were among the first to celebrate the virtues of spirituals.

Bode, Carl. "Lloyd Douglas: Loud Voice in the Wilderness." AMERICAN QUARTERLY 2 (Winter 1950): 340-52.

In his novels of the 1930s, Douglas's philosophy was one of doing good for the sake of improving one's personality, with material rewards following consistently if incidentally. THE ROBE and THE BIG FISHERMAN, both long-term bestsellers, represent a shift in perspective with the spiritual rewards of doing good being stressed in order to prepare for the next world.

Canary, Robert H. "The Sunday School as Popular Culture." MIDCONTINENT AMERICAN STUDIES JOURNAL 9 (Fall 1968): 5-13.

The literature of the American Sunday school movement is to the works of great theologians as the dime novel is to Hawthorne and Melville. This essay delineates changes in the Sunday school in the twentieth century and suggests further areas of research.

Capeci, Dominic J. "Al Capone: Symbol of a Ballyhoo Society." JOURNAL OF ETHNIC STUDIES 2 (Winter 1975): 33-46.

Capone is depicted as a folk hero who was the product of ballyhoo in the 1920s. Through ballyhoo he became the surrogate self of thousands of Americans who desired change but could not achieve it.

Cawelti, John G. ADVENTURE, MYSTERY, AND ROMANCE: FORMULA STORIES AS ART AND POPULAR CULTURE. Chicago: University of Chicago Press, 1976. viii, 336 p.

This is a study of popular story formulas, based mainly on American writings. Cawelti regards formulas as a literary art, and focuses on Puzo's THE GODFATHER, Sayers's THE NINE TAILORS, and Wister's THE VIRGINIAN to demonstrate his theories.

_____. "Beatles, Batman, and the New Aesthetic." MIDWAY 9 (Autumn 1968): 49-70.

Cawelti argues that the avant-garde and mass culture joined in the 1960s. This is seen in Andy Warhol's art, PLAYBOY magazine, the Beatles, Batman, and Joseph Heller's CATCH-22, for example.

_____. "The Gunfighter and the Hard-Boiled Dick: Some Ruminations on American Fantasies of Heroism." AMERICAN STUDIES 16 (Fall 1975): 49-64.

Cawelti argues that the gunfighter and the hard-boiled detective are contemporary versions of a myth of the isolated hero in a corrupt society. They underline a strain of pessimism and despair in the American tradition which has been part of the popular and intellectual culture.

_____. "Myth, Symbol, and Formula." JOURNAL OF POPULAR CULTURE 8 (Summer 1974): 1-9.

Myths and symbols are not the only means by which cultures express feelings, meanings, and other modes of perception. Formulas, as embodied in mysteries, westerns, and adventures, also depict the range and variety of people's imaginative concerns.

_____. THE SIX-GUN MYSTIQUE. Bowling Green, Ohio: Bowling Green University Popular Press, n.d. x, 138 p.

This is an essay on formula stories with particular attention on the western. Cawelti covers novels, films, and television programs.

Chenoweth, Lawrence. "The Rhetoric of Hope and Despair: A Study of the Jimi Hendrix Experience and the Jefferson Airplane." AMERICAN QUARTERLY 23 (Spring 1971): 25-45.

This essay represents an effort to understand the behavior of those youth who advocate either withdrawal from society or revolution. Chenoweth characterizes the rhetoric of the musical groups, Jimi Hendrix Experience and the Jefferson Airplane, as being a strong measure of hope and despair accompanied by a belief that life is isolation and anxiety.

Clipper, Lawrence J. "Archetypal Figures in Early Film Comedy." WESTERN HUMANITIES REVIEW 28 (Autumn 1974): 353-66.

Clipper employs Northrup Frye's main categories of literature--myth, romance, tragedy, low mimetic, and irony--to analyze film comedy. He discusses the work of Mack Sennett, Charlie Chaplin, Buster Keaton, Harold Lloyd, and W.C. Fields.

Cogswell, Robert. "Commercial Hillbilly Lyrics and the Folk Tradition." JOURNAL OF COUNTRY MUSIC 3 (Fall and Winter 1972): 65-106.

The roots of commercial hillbilly music are in the Anglo-American folk tradition. Cogswell explicates hillbilly lyrics, shows their general relationship to the folk tradition, and places them in their cultural setting.

Crepeau, Richard C. "Urban and Rural Images in Baseball." JOURNAL OF POPULAR CULTURE 9 (Fall 1975): 315-24.

Baseball is a game of rural origins that in the 1920s and 1930s became the pastime of urban America. Baseball writers perpetuated the agrarian myth and centered their antiurbanism on New York City.

Cripps, Thomas. "THE BIRTH OF A RACE Company: An Early Stride Toward a Black Cinema." JOURNAL OF NEGRO HISTORY 59 (January 1974): 28-37.

The BIRTH OF A RACE Company was a black reaction to D.W. Griffith's BIRTH OF A NATION. It represented an artistic response which was an alternative to censorship of the Griffith movie, and many hoped it would be an inspirational black statement with a plea for mutual respect between the races.

Denisoff, R. Serge. GREAT DAY COMING: FOLK MUSIC AND THE AMERICAN LEFT. Urbana: University of Illinois Press, 1971. 219 p.

Denisoff traces the use of folk music by leftists from 1930 to the late 1960s. He emphasizes the development of a folk consciousness, the idealization of the life-styles of the intellectual poor, and the work of folk entrepreneurs such as Burl Ives and Pete Seeger and popularizers such as Elvis Presley, Joan Baez, and Bob Dylan.

Dennis, Everette E. "Utopian Values in Journalistic Content and Organizational Structure." JOURNAL OF POPULAR CULTURE 8 (Spring 1975): 725-34.

Utopian publications in the twentieth century have professed utopian ideals in an effort to perfect the human condition. Dennis examines PM, an experimental daily newspaper that began publication in 1940, and other papers, and demonstrates that they maintained voluntarism on their staffs as a means of preserving their goals.

Donovan, Timothy P. "'Oh, What a Beautiful Mornin': The Musical OKLA-HOMA! and the Popular Mind in 1943." JOURNAL OF POPULAR CULTURE 8 (Winter 1974): 477-88.

OKLAHOMA suffered many pre-Broadway problems, but it became unusually popular because Americans were sure of their toughness in 1943 and they were confident they would gain the sweet and tender things that came with a beautiful morning.

Dorson, Richard M. AMERICAN FOLKLORE AND THE HISTORIAN. Chicago: University of Chicago Press, 1971. xii, 239 p.

This is a collection of essays on the values of folklore for American cultural history. They cover folklore theory and method.

_____. FOLKLORE AND FAKELORE: ESSAYS TOWARD A DISCIPLINE OF FOLK STUDIES. Cambridge, Mass.: Harvard University Press, 1976. x, 391 p.

Dorson maintains that folklorists have difficulty explaining their operations in the marketplace and elsewhere. He attempts to solve this problem through a series of essays on oral literature, comic Indian anecdotes, the career of John Henry, and other subjects.

Erisman, Fred. "Transcendentalism for American Youth: The Children's Books of Kate Douglas Wiggin." NEW ENGLAND QUARTERLY 41 (June 1968): 238-47.

Wiggin became a purveyor of transcendental ideals to American children through her association with the kindergarten movement. In REBECCA OF SUNNYBOOK FARM, and other works, she emphasizes the transcendental faith in individualism and the value of nature.

Etulain, Richard W. "The Historical Development of the Western." JOURNAL OF POPULAR CULTURE 7 (Winter 1973): 717-26.

Owen Wister in THE VIRGINIAN formulated the western, but Zane Grey and Max Brand systematized it as fiction based on action, romance, and conflict between good guys and bad guys. The genre underwent a change in the 1930s and 1940s when Ernest Haycox grounded his stories on solid historical background and Luke Short mixed the elements of the western and the detective story.

Fell, John L. FILM AND THE NARRATIVE TRADITION. Norman: University of Oklahoma Press, 1974. xx, 284 p.

Fell argues that early film narratives represented the culmination of themes that had developed for a hundred years. He finds these themes in literature, dime novels, melodrama, the comic strip, magazine illustrations, and other sources.

Ferguson, Robert C. "Americanism in Late Afternoon Radio Adventure Serials, 1940-1945." NORTH DAKOTA QUARTERLY·40 (Autumn 1972): 20-29.

Americanism generated during the war demanded that citizens become involved members of a united drive to safeguard America. National interests during the war years were served by radio, and serials specifically affected attitudinal changes.

Flink, James J. "Three Stages of American Automobile Consciousness." AMERICAN QUARTERLY 24 (October 1972): 451-73.

"Consciousness I" of the automobile began with its invention; "consciousness II" originated with mass production at the Ford Highland Park plant in 1910; while "consciousness III" was inaugurated in the late 1950s when the car was no longer viewed as a historically progressive force. By the 1960s, the transformation of American civilization by the car had been completed and motoring was no longer viewed as romance.

Hansdorff, Don. "Magazine Humor and Popular Morality, 1929-34." JOURNALISM QUARTERLY 41 (Autumn 1964): 509-16.

In this study of eight magazines, Hansdorff discusses humor centered on moral questions, especially those concerning alcohol, law enforcement, and organized religion. The country was "wet," law enforcement was corrupt, and organized religion was in league with capitalism.

Hansen, Arlen J. "Entropy and Transformation: Two Types of American Humor." AMERICAN SCHOLAR 43 (Summer 1974): 405-21.

Silent movies and radio illustrate the duality in American humor. One tendency in humor is to show someone doing some funny thing or breaking up a system (entropy), while the other is to display somebody saying something funny or exploiting the properties of language (transformation).

Hansen, Chadwick. "Jenny's Toe: Negro Shaking Dances in America." AMERICAN QUARTERLY 19 (Fall 1967): 554-63.

This essay portrays Negro shaking or erotic dances as being of African origin. They were adopted by white Americans after World

War I, disappeared in the 1930s, but came back strongly after
World War II in the form of the twist.

_____. "Social Influences on Jazz Style: Chicago, 1920-30." AMERICAN
QUARTERLY 12 (Winter 1960): 493-507.

During the great migration from the South following the First World
War, the Negro brought his music with him. He placed himself
in a new environment to escape vicious and degrading social institutions and adapted his jazz to the popular music of the white
middle class.

Harris, Charles W., and Rainey, Buck, eds. THE COWBOY: SIX-SHOOTERS,
SONGS, AND SEX. Norman: University of Oklahoma Press, 1976. viii,
167 p.

These essays cover the rise of the cowboy, the Saturday afternoon
"reel" cowboy, the cowpuncher and the handgun, sex on the
range, dude ranching, the cowboy's bawdy music, and other topics.

Hart, James D. "Platitudes of Piety: Religion and the Popular Modern Novel."
AMERICAN QUARTERLY 6 (Winter 1954): 311-22.

Hart examines novels of Elizabeth Phelps, James Lane Allen, Lloyd
Douglas, Henry M. Robinson, and others, and concludes that religious novels were a major medium for transmitting ideas. Religious novels are popular because they provide dramatic tales of spiritual struggle successfully resolved.

Higham, Charles. WARNER BROTHERS. New York: Charles Scribner's Sons,
1975. viii, 232 p.

This story of Warner Brothers Pictures is told in terms of the studio's major personalities. During Hollywood's golden age (1920-
50), the studio prospered because of Jack Warner's sense of what
audiences wanted to see.

Holder, Stephen C. "The Family Magazine and the American People." JOUR-
NAL OF POPULAR CULTURE 7 (Fall 1973): 264-79.

Popular magazines such as COLLIER'S, LOOK, LADIES HOME
JOURNAL, and the SATURDAY EVENING POST were successful
because they filled multiple public needs. They were conformist
by presenting prevailing moral standards, escapist in allowing the
reader to escape from everyday life, and the educators of con-
sumers.

Horton, Andrew S. "Ken Kesey, John Updike and the Lone Ranger." JOUR-
NAL OF POPULAR CULTURE 8 (Winter 1974): 570-78.

The Lone Ranger is the American dream as a defender of virtue and justice, a man of action, a masked man, and a white man. Both Kesey and Updike portray a similar hero in ONE FLEW OVER THE CUCKOO'S NEST and RABBIT RUN.

———. "Turning On and Tuning Out at the Drive-In: An American Phenomenon Survives and Thrives." JOURNAL OF POPULAR FILM 5 (1976): 233-45.

The drive-in theater is a blend of people, cars, food, music, and film. It has thrived on presenting soft pornography, hot car, horror, and disaster movies.

Hurley, F. Jack. PORTRAIT OF A DECADE: ROY STRYKER AND THE DEVELOPMENT OF DOCUMENTARY PHOTOGRAPHY IN THE THIRTIES. Baton Rouge: Louisiana State University Press, 1972. ix, 196 p.

Photographs were used to support New Deal farm programs. Stryker dramatized farm problems through photography and also influenced several individuals who became photo-essayists for LIFE and LOOK.

Isenberg, Michael T. "An Ambiguous Pacifism: A Retrospective on World War I Films, 1930-1938." JOURNAL OF POPULAR FILM 4 (1975): 98-115.

The dividing line between pacifist and other war films is very thin. In most of the pictures made between the two world wars, the war itself was the protagonist and plots reacted against militarism, authoritarianism, patriotism, honor, and glory.

———. "The Mirror of Democracy: Reflections of the War Films of World War I." JOURNAL OF POPULAR CULTURE 9 (Spring 1976): 878-85.

Isenberg shows that the films depicting World War I were a tribute to the American democratic faith. Films mirrored democracy as a faith and as the proper mode of political and social organizations.

———. "A Relationship of Constrained Anxiety: Historians and Film." HISTORY TEACHER 6 (August 1973): 553-68.

Intellectual historians generally have ignored the mass media. They should examine film not from aesthetic criteria but as visual and written evidence.

Jones, Robert A. "Mr. Woodworth's Tower: The Skyscraper as Popular Icon." JOURNAL OF POPULAR CULTURE 7 (Fall 1973): 408-24.

This is a study of the relationship of the five-and-dime tycoon, Frank W. Woolworth, and the architect, Cass Gilbert, in the construction of the Woolworth Building. They created a Gothic icon

that was a monument to the religion of commerce, and captured
the public imagination because Woolworth made it the world's
largest billboard.

Jowett, Garth, for the American Film Institute. FILM: THE DEMOCRATIC
ART. Boston: Little, Brown, 1976. xx, 518 p.

Jowett focuses on what takes place when a new medium of communication is introduced into a social system. He details how
motion pictures affected the lives of the American people, as well
as how social forces shaped the product seen on the screen.

Kaufmann, Donald L. "Woodstock: The Color of Sound." JOURNAL OF
ETHNIC STUDIES 2 (Fall 1974): 32-49.

The music festival, "Woodstock," symbolized the coexistence of
black music and white electronics with the result being a mulatto
sound called "rock."   This is a study of the "whitening" of black
music from the blues to jazz to soul and rock-and-roll, and its
influence in creating a biracial culture in the United States.

Kehl, James A.   "Defender of the Faith: Orphan Annie and the Conservative
Tradition." SOUTH ATLANTIC QUARTERLY 59 (Spring 1960): 192-203.

"Orphan Annie," which was launched in 1924, became an interpretation of economics and politics with the 1932 election. The
comic strip has been used to extoll the virtues of private enterprise and laissez-faire democracy.

Kelly, R. Gordon.   "Ideology in Some Modern Science Fiction Novels."
JOURNAL OF POPULAR CULTURE 2 (Fall 1968): 211-27.

Kelly reviews the works of Isaac Asimov, A.E. Van Vogt, Alfred
Bester, and others, and sees that science fiction soothes because
it shows that rational intelligence can preserve the future and
make it better. It also permits the reader to participate in the
corporate life of science and thus in bestowing progress.

Koppes, Clayton R.   "The Social Destiny of Radio: Hope and Disillusionment
in the 1920s." SOUTH ATLANTIC QUARTERLY 58 (Summer 1969): 363-76.

During the twenties, people hailed the radio as a means of auto-
matically achieving mankind's dreams. By the end of the decade,
advertising crept in and disillusionment was the outcome.

Lahne, Kalton C. CONTINUED NEXT WEEK: A HISTORY OF THE MOVING
PICTURE SERIAL. Norman: University of Oklahoma Press, 1964. xvii, 293 p.

The serial was important to the film industry between 1914 and
1930. Serials were money-makers, and many were better aesthe-
tically than feature-length films.

Leab, Daniel J. "'All Colored'--But Not Much Different: Films Made for Negro Ghetto Audiences, 1913-1928." PHYLON 36 (Fall 1975): 321-39.

This is a study of the efforts of black film companies during the silent period to counter stereotypes of the Negro. Black films, generally, were not made to uplift or enlighten, but were meant to entertain and make money for the producer.

_____. FROM SAMBO TO SUPERSPADE: THE BLACK EXPERIENCE IN MOTION PICTURES. Boston: Houghton Mifflin, 1975. viii, 301 p.

In the transition from Sambo to Superspade, blacks were treated as subhuman, simple-minded, superstitious, and submissive. Hollywood excluded blacks from the American dream by depicting them in undesirable stereotypes.

_____. "A Pale Black Imitation: ALL-COLORED FILMS, 1930-1960." JOURNAL OF POPULAR FILM 4 (1975): 56-76.

Leab characterizes ghetto-oriented, black productions as Jim Crow films. Filmmakers were interested only in exploiting the box office even though they gave black performers an opportunity to work.

Leonard, Neil. JAZZ AND THE WHITE AMERICANS: THE ACCEPTANCE OF A NEW ART FORM. Chicago: University of Chicago Press, 1962. 215 p.

This study is limited to the years before 1940 and to the white audience. The author argues that jazz was a new art form, but it was an innovation enjoyed by people who formed a cult and ignored traditional values.

Lyons, Timothy J. "Hollywood and World War I, 1914-1918." JOURNAL OF POPULAR FILM 1 (Winter 1972): 15-30.

The American film industry blossomed as competition from European films was foreclosed during World War I. It gave the public what it wanted--a clear view of both neutrality and involvement.

McClure, Arthur F. "Hollywood at War: The American Motion Picture and World War II, 1939-1945." JOURNAL OF POPULAR FILM 1 (Spring 1972): 123-35.

Motion pictures emotionalized the war situation for workers at home and soldiers in the field. They took the lead in communicating realities to the American people.

MacDonald, J. Frederick. "'Mr. Foreigner' in Juvenile Series Fiction, 1900-1945." JOURNAL OF POPULAR CULTURE 8 (Winter 1974): 534-48.

MacDonald examines Nancy Drew, Tom Swift, the Hardy Boys, and Bobbsey Twins as propounders of values and attitudes to American youth. This fiction shows the self-assurance of America as expressed in race consciousness, xenophobia, and imperialistic attitudes.

Malone, Bill C., and McCulloh, Judith, eds. STARS OF COUNTRY MUSIC: UNCLE DAVE MACON TO JOHNNY RODRIGUEZ. Urbana: University of Illinois Press, 1975. xii, 476 p.

These essays cover many country music personalities from the Carter family and Gene Autry to Chet Atkins and Charley Pride. These artists and their music have been interpreted in their historical context.

Margolies, Edward. "City, Nature, Highway: Changing Images in American Film and Theater." JOURNAL OF POPULAR CULTURE 9 (Summer 1975): 14-19.

Before the 1950s, theater and film portrayed cities as possessing the possibilities of having some of the saving graces of civilization, but since that time, they have conveyed a picture of urban deterioration and conflict. As far as nature and highways are concerned, the former has been shown as hostile and sterile, while the latter no longer represents avenues of escape.

Meyer, Donald. THE POSITIVE THINKERS: A STUDY OF THE AMERICAN QUEST FOR HEALTH, WEALTH AND PERSONAL POWER FROM MARY BAKER EDDY TO NORMAN VINCENT PEALE. Garden City, N.Y.: Doubleday, 1966. xvii, 342 p.

This is a study of popular psychologies aimed at health, wealth, and peace of mind. Meyer demonstrates how the theme of social status, rather than biological urges, has been important in popular psychology.

Mooney, H.F. "Popular Music Since the 1920s: The Significance of Shifting Taste." AMERICAN QUARTERLY 20 (Spring 1968): 67-85.

The popular music of the 1920s and 1930s was shaped by white middle-class tastes that demanded sophistication as seen in quasi-classical jazz and subtle, understated lyrics. By the 1960s, the trend changed to black music when lower-class youths joined middle-class rebels to reject prettiness, refinement, academic orchestration, and subtlety.

Mottram, Eric. "Living Mythically: The Thirties." JOURNAL OF AMERICAN STUDIES 6 (December 1972): 267-87.

Intellectuals and artists in the 1930s lived mythically both in a radical and conservative manner. Radicalism was exemplified by the artists of the NEW MASSES and the writers of the PARTISAN REVIEW, while conservatism was expressed by Chester Gould's "Dick Tracy," Dale Carnegie's HOW TO WIN FRIENDS, and the films chronicalling the life of Andy Hardy.

Osofsky, Gilbert. "Symbols of the Jazz Age: The New Negro and Harlem Discovered." AMERICAN QUARTERLY 17 (Summer 1965): 229-38.

The "New Negro" entered American thought in the 1920s and whites created a vogue in things Negro. They also constructed the stereotype that Harlem was en erotic utopia inhabited by people who danced, loved, and laughed.

Porter, Joseph C. "The End of the Trail: The American West of Dashiell Hammett and Raymond Chandler." WESTERN HISTORICAL QUARTERLY 6 (October 1975): 411-24.

Cowboys and Indians exemplified the nineteenth-century West and the private detective, the twentieth century. Fears and doubts about the urban nature of western society are mirrored in twentieth-century hard-boiled detective fiction which reveals parallels to the society that produced the cowboy-and-Indians stereotype.

Potter, Richard H. "Popular Religion of the 1930's as Reflected in the Best Sellers of Harry Emerson Fosdick." JOURNAL OF POPULAR CULTURE 3 (Spring 1970): 713-28.

Fosdick reached more Americans through his sermons, radio broadcasts, articles, and books than other preachers. He was a theological liberal who reacted against fundamentalism and neo-orthodoxy, and who defined religion as a psychological, spiritual experience.

Powers, Richard Gid. "J. Edgar Hoover and the Detective Hero." JOURNAL OF POPULAR CULTURE 9 (Fall 1975): 257-78.

Powers addresses the question, "What part does mass entertainment play in constructing the symbolic reality within which mass politics operates?" He suggests that Hoover was a master of symbolism who ritualized reality and made his agents into detective heroes.

Rathbun, John W. "God is Dead: Avante Garde Theology for the Sixties." CANADIAN REVIEW OF AMERICAN STUDIES 5 (Fall 1974): 166-80.

The "God is Dead" movement had currency in the 1960s because it was originated by theologians and taken up by the avant-garde. This essay constitutes an examination of the thought of Thomas Altizer, William Hamilton, Harvey Cox, and Paul Van Buren in an effort to delineate a world view of these thinkers.

Reuss, Richard A. "The Roots of American Left-Wing Interest in Folksong."
LABOR HISTORY 12 (Spring 1971): 259-79.

Political protest movements did not use folksongs until the 1930s.
This is a study of the origins of radical interest in folk materials
and particularly of the Communist Party.

Rodnitzky, Jerome L. MINSTRELS OF DAWN: THE FOLK-PROTEST SINGER
AS A CULTURAL HERO. Chicago: Nelson-Hall, 1976. xx, 192 p.

This is a collective biography of Phil Ochs, Joan Baez, Bob Dylan, and Woody Guthrie. By 1968, a big market no longer supported folk balladry concerning proletarians, because affluent youth
began to feel itself an oppressed class.

_____, "The New Revivalism: American Protest Songs, 1945-1968." SOUTH
ATLANTIC QUARTERLY 70 (Winter 1971): 13-21.

Folk concerns can be compared with revival meetings because they
generate shared emotions and a communal critique of society. Rodnitzky believes that the protest song movement is symptomatic of
a dramatic change in the social awareness of the younger generation.

Rollins, Peter C. "Will Rogers: Symbolic Man, Journalist, and Film Image."
JOURNAL OF POPULAR CULTURE 9 (Spring 1976): 851-77.

The 1920s were a time of fragmentation of culture and Will Rogers
provided for the psychological needs of Americans. Rollins reviews
his career and films, and concludes that Will Rogers was what
Americans thought other Americans were like.

Scheurer, Timothy E. "The Aesthetics of Form and Convention in the Movie
Musical." JOURNAL OF POPULAR FILM 3 (Fall 1974): 307-24.

The musical is a highly conventional film genre in which music
and dance are woven into a libretto. New ideas are expressed in
song and dance sequences which places them in a solid core of
conventions.

Scott, James F. "Beat Literature and the American Teen Cult." AMERICAN
QUARTERLY 14 (Summer 1962): 150-60.

Scott argues that the "Beats" failed as literary artists not because
they were depraved but because they lacked imaginative insight.
He believes their failure was a result of powerful social forces
that glorified immaturity and obscured adult creativity.

Seelye, John D. "The American Tramp: A Version of the Picaresque."
AMERICAN QUARTERLY 15 (Winter 1963): 535-53.

Americans hate the real tramp, but love the comic version. They
laugh with the clown tramp because he represents uninhibited activity, but they laugh at him because they feel superior.

Shain, Russell E. "Hollywood's Cold War." JOURNAL OF POPULAR FILM
3 (Fall 1974): 334-50.

Hollywood's enlistment in the Cold War came from coercion from
the House Un-American Activities Committee, economic uncertainty, and a national fear of communism. It responded with a
blacklist and with films that depicted Communists as faceless in-
truders in American society.

Sklar, Robert. MOVIE-MADE AMERICA. New York: Random House, 1975.
vii, 340 p.

This is the first study to develop a complex theory concerning the
historical and cultural role of movies. Sklar claims that films
have represented a cultural upsurge outside the dominant middle
class even though they appealed to middle-class tastes.

Slout, William L. "Popular Literature of the Dramatic Tent Show." NORTH
DAKOTA QUARTERLY 40 (Autumn 1972): 42-55.

The dramatic literature of tent shows that toured the United States
during the twentieth century conformed to the romantic images the
farmer and small towner envisioned of his environment and of himself. Familiar rural surroundings were made to appear remote from
the corruption of cities.

Small, Melvin. "Buffoons and Brave Hearts: Hollywood Portrays the Russians,
1939-1944." CALIFORNIA HISTORICAL QUARTERLY 52 (Winter 1973): 326-
37.

Hollywood's depiction of the Russians during the Second World War
affected the way Americans conceived their new ally and contributed to the climate of opinion in which wartime diplomacy was
formulated. Americans became increasingly friendly toward the
Soviet Union and Hollywood played a significant role in shaping
this attitude.

Smith, James Steel. "The Day of the Popularizers: The 1920's." SOUTH
ATLANTIC QUARTERLY 62 (Spring 1963): 297-309.

Between the end of World War I and the Depression, books by
H.G. Wells, James Harvey Robinson, Paul De Kruif, the Beards,
Will Durant, and Hendrik Van Loon were published and became
popular. This eruption of high popular efforts to popularize knowledge was a cultural happening of great consequence because the
writers set out to teach without cheapening their material.

Soderbergh, Peter A. "'Aux Armes!': The Rise of the Hollywood War Film, 1916-1930." SOUTH ATLANTIC QUARTERLY 65 (Autumn 1966): 509-22.

During the war film's childhood, basic plot patterns were set and little of significance has been added except technical virtuosity. The significant motion picture of the period 1916-30 was THE BIG PARADE which combined realistic battle scenes with characters who were not puppets.

_____. "The Great Book War: Edward Stratemeyer and the Boy Scouts of America, 1910-1930." NEW JERSEY HISTORY 91 (Winter 1973): 235-48.

The Stratemeyer Syndicate produced about seven hundred titles of series books between the years 1904-30. Among these were Boy Scouts' stories and these produced a lively battle between the publisher and the Boy Scouts of America.

_____. "The South in Juvenile Series Books, 1907-1917." MISSISSIPPI QUARTERLY 27 (Spring 1964): 131-40.

The series book is a given volume in a sequence of titles that feature the escapades of supranormal children. Writers of this fiction depicted the South in the form of stereotypes that made the southerner seem pompous in order to allow the books' heroes to appear superior.

_____. "The Stratemeyer Strain: Educators and the Juvenile Series Book." JOURNAL OF POPULAR CULTURE 7 (Spring 1974): 864-72.

Stratemeyer was the author of 150 juvenile titles and the founder of a literary syndicate that mass-produced seven hundred serial books. His series at first were attacked by the American Bookseller's Association, but by 1930 they were criticized by educators who did not want to leave the choice of books to children.

Spring, Joel H. "Mass Culture and School Sports." HISTORY OF EDUCATION QUARTERLY 14 (Winter 1974): 483-99.

Spring argues that the goal of the supporters of school sports was mass participation but the outcome was mass spectatorship. He suggests that mass spectatorship at athletic contests is a controlling instrument in our technological culture because it dilutes the political consciousness and diffuses feelings of rebellion in mass man.

Suderman, Elmer F. "Aspects of Popular Culture in the Jesus Revolution." NORTH DAKOTA QUARTERLY 40 (Autumn 1972): 77-83.

The "Jesus revolution" is in the tradition of popular culture because its religious products and ideas are making money. Adherents of the revolution also are distrustful of any complicated issues raised in regard to God or Jesus.

Turner, Ronny E., and Edgley, Charles K. "'The Devil Made Me Do It!' Popular Culture and Religious Vocabularies of Motive." JOURNAL OF POPULAR CULTURE 8 (Summer 1974): 28-34.

The authors use a theory of motivation in which motives are conceptualized theoretically as communications through which a social actor interprets his conduct to others. They employ the quotation in the title as a religious, fundamentalist communication symbol and show that users believe that all behavior is under the control of God.

Vacha, J.E. "Posterity Was Just Around the Corner: The Influence of the Depression on the Development of the American Musical Theater in the 1930s." SOUTH ATLANTIC QUARTERLY 67 (Autumn 1968): 573-90.

The Depression provided a shot in the arm for the arts, but the musical theater seemed less likely to profit because it could not shift into the character of social consciousness. It did gain a theme of social experience as expressed in STRIKE UP THE BAND, OF THEE I SING, PORGY AND BESS, and JOHNNY JOHNSON.

White, Stanley W. "The Burnt Cork Illusion of the 1920s in America: A Study in Nostalgia." JOURNAL OF POPULAR CULTURE 5 (Winter 1971): 530-50.

This is a study of the popularity of Al Jolson and Amos 'n Andy. White argues that in a period of disconcerting change, Americans turned to the past as a refuge, and Jolson and Freeman Gosden and Charles Correll filled that need.

Wolfe, Kary K., and Wolfe, Gary K. "Metaphors of Madness: Popular Psychological Narratives." JOURNAL OF POPULAR CULTURE 9 (Spring 1976): 895-907.

Psychological novels, memoirs, autobiographies, and case studies are a genre of this century and they function as a sub-genre of psychiatric literature. The Wolfes show how this genre achieved popularity in Joanne Greenberg's I NEVER PROMISED YOU A ROSE GARDEN, which has become one of the most significant and popular books of the era.

Yellis, Kenneth A. "Prosperity's Child: Some Thoughts on the Flapper." AMERICAN QUARTERLY 21 (Spring 1969): 44-64.

The "Flapper," a symbol of dress and behavior, represented the emergence of a new woman who broke with male-dominated civilization. She was a child of prosperity because prosperity permitted women to experiment with various life-styles, values, and roles.

Young, William H. "That Indomitable Redhead: Little Orphan Annie." JOURNAL OF POPULAR CULTURE 8 (Fall 1974): 309-19.

Young sheds light on editorializing in comic strips by examining "Little Orphan Annie" in the Depression and World War II. The strip was built to the specifications of Joseph Medill Patterson, founder of the New York DAILY NEWS, but Harold Gray editorialized to portray his own point of view.

Chapter 10
RELIGION

COLONIAL PERIOD TO 1815

Albanese, Catherine. "Newness Transcending: Civil Religion and the American Revolution." SOUTHERN QUARTERLY 14 (July 1976): 307-32.

The American Revolution became in its own time and for later generations a sacred historicized myth of origins. A religious understanding with humanity at the center came to birth in the Revolution.

Albright, Raymond W. A HISTORY OF THE PROTESTANT EPISCOPAL CHURCH. New York: Macmillan, 1964. x, 406 p.

Albright surveys Episcopal history with emphasis on the colonial period, the Revolution, and the nineteenth century. The church has enjoyed a unique unity and has tried to reach new levels of expression.

Aldridge, Alfred O. "George Whitefield's Georgia Controversies." JOURNAL OF SOUTHERN HISTORY 9 (August 1943): 357-80.

Whitefield was accused of being a defender of rum and slavery, a religious racketeer, a gambler, and a founder of orphanages to house his own illegitimate offspring. Some of these attacks resulted from his Methodism, while others were brought about by opposition to his missionary activities.

_____. JONATHAN EDWARDS. New York: Washington Square Press, 1966. 181 p.

Edwards is described as a "difficult personality," who devised a plan that was difficult to live by. His thought is related to the American Enlightenment, including his debt to Locke and Newton, and the extent to which he accepted the idea of progress.

Religion

Alexis, Gerhard T. "Jonathan Edwards and the Theocratic Ideal." CHURCH HISTORY 34 (September 1966): 328-43.

This is an examination of the thesis that after the Puritan theocracy collapsed, the Puritan vision of political order subdued to God persisted through various transformations until secularized. This conception is developed by looking at Edwards's efforts to support and transmit a theocratic ideal.

Armstrong, Maurice W. "The Dissenting Deputies and the American Colonies." CHURCH HISTORY 29 (September 1960): 298-320.

Protestant dissenting deputies originated in the struggle of Baptist, Congregationalist, and Presbyterian churches of Britain against the civil disabilities placed upon them by the Corporation and Test Acts. They were behind all legislation and judicial action for the relief of dissenters, and they corresponded with committees in the colonies.

Armstrong, Maurice W.; Loetscher, Lefferts A.; and Anderson, Charles A., eds. THE PRESBYTERIAN ENTERPRISE: SOURCES OF AMERICAN PRESBYTERIAN HISTORY. Philadelphia: Westminster Press, 1956.

This is a collection of documents, arranged chronologically, emphasizing the origins of Presbyterianism, the story from the adoption of the Constitution, and the latter-day emphasis on home and foreign missions.

Atkins, Gains Glenn, and Fagley, Frederick L. HISTORY OF AMERICAN CONGREGATIONALISM. Boston and Chicago: Pilgrim Press, 1942. 432 p.

Congregationalism was forged by two groups of English dissenters, the Pilgrims and Puritans. The denomination's expansion, contributions to national thought, place in national life, and structural organization are described in this volume.

Banner, Lois W. "Religion and Reform in the Early Republic: The Role of Youth." AMERICAN QUARTERLY 23 (December 1971): 677-95.

In attempting to explain why men took up the cause of religious benevolence in post-revolutionary America, Banner employs the theory of Kenneth Keniston in YOUNG RADICALS. She shows that the reformers were young men who had been educated to reform by their parents or were caught up in the history of the period.

Battis, Emory. SAINTS AND SECTARIES: ANNE HUTCHINSON AND THE ANTINOMIAN CONTROVERSY IN THE MASSACHUSETTS BAY COLONY. Chapel Hill: University of North Carolina Press for the Institute of Early American History and Culture, Williamsburg, Virginia, 1962. xviii, 379 p.

Hutchinson's assertive social life and compulsive hold over family are attributed to desires for masculine authority. Her rising religious commitment is related to her sexual condition, with her defiance of the Massachusetts clergy coinciding with menopause.

Beaver, R. Pierce. "American Missionary Motivation Before the Revolution." CHURCH HISTORY 31 (June 1962): 216-26.

The glory of God, not security reasons, motivated missionaries to the Indians in New England in the seventeenth century. The Great Awakening introduced the idea of a Christian's labor for the coming of the Kingdom of God as a new motivating factor.

Bellot, Leland J. "Evangelicals and the Defense of Slavery in Britain's Old Colonial Empire." JOURNAL OF SOUTHERN HISTORY 37 (February 1971): 19-40.

Historians, such as David Brion Davis, have commented on the ambivalence of eighteenth-century evangelicals concerning slavery, but they have attributed this ambivalence to materialist expediency since they owned slaves. Bellot argues that proslavery evangelicals defended bondage to show that their role in the slave system was not a moral evil, but rather part of a divine plan for converting Africans whose character and intellect they regarded negatively.

Bercovitch, Sacvan. "Typology in Puritan New England: The Williams-Cotton Controversy Reassessed." AMERICAN QUARTERLY 19 (Summer 1967): 166-91.

The controversy involving Roger Williams and John Cotton resulted from Williams's banishment from the Bay Colony in 1635. According to Bercovitch, both relied on typology, "the historiographic-theological method of relating Old Testament to the life of Christ (as "anti-type") and, through Him, to the doctrine and progress of the Christian church."

Bernhard, Virginia. "Cotton Mather and the Doing of Good: A Puritan Gospel of Wealth." NEW ENGLAND QUARTERLY 59 (June 1976): 225-41.

Mather published his ESSAYS TO DO GOOD in 1710, but it went through seventeen editions between 1800 and 1840. Bernhard believes that its popularity was based on the fact that it was a distinctively American statement concerning social mobility and class lines.

Birdsall, Richard D. "The Second Great Awakening and the New England Social Order." CHURCH HISTORY 39 (September 1970): 345-64.

The second Great Awakening brought about a significant revitalization of the New England social order. This came about in the area of individual belief and represented an effort to Christianize the hearts of men and convert the heathen.

Bliss, Robert M. "A Secular Revival: Puritanism in Connecticut, 1675-1708." JOURNAL OF AMERICAN STUDIES 6 (August 1972): 129-52.

Historians have argued that New England Puritans became Yankees, but their studies have been based on the historical process in Massachusetts. In examining the history of late seventeenth-century Connecticut, Bliss indicates that Puritanism declined there also but Connecticut Puritans did not undergo intense self-criticism that led to the rejection of Puritanism for materialism.

Boles, John B. THE GREAT REVIVAL, 1787-1805: THE ORIGINS OF THE SOUTHERN EVANGELICAL MIND. Lexington: University Press of Kentucky, 1972. xiii, 236 p.

In this study of the Cumberland revivals, Boles argues that beliefs of emigrants to the frontier rather than the environment created the religious climate. He also concludes that the religious mind of the South received its impulse from this movement.

Boller, Paul F., Jr. GEORGE WASHINGTON AND RELIGION. Dallas: Southern Methodist University Press, 1963. xii, 235 p.

Washington is depicted as an urbane and sophisticated man dedicated to religious liberty and cultural pluralism. While he was fair to all, it is difficult to say that he himself was a Christian.

Boyer, Paul, and Nissenbaum, Stephen. SALEM POSSESSED: THE SOCIAL ORIGINS OF WITCHCRAFT. Cambridge, Mass.: Harvard University Press, 1974. xxi, 231 p.

It is argued in this study that the witch episode could just as well have been a religious revival. Salem was a peasant economy invaded by merchant capitalism and the witch trials were the outcome of factional strife.

Bridenbaugh, Carl. MITRE AND SCEPTRE: TRANSLATLANTIC FAITHS, IDEAS, PERSONALITIES, AND POLITICS, 1689-1775. New York: Oxford University Press, 1962. xiv, 354 p.

Bridenbaugh examines the concerns of English dissenters, American Congregationalists, and Presbyterians over the Anglican establishment. He illuminates Anglican policy in England and America and shows that colonial fears were plausible.

Brown, Ira V. "Watchers for the Second Coming: The Millenarian Tradition in America." MISSISSIPPI VALLEY HISTORICAL REVIEW 39 (December 1952): 441-58.

Brown traces millenarianism from the colonial period and emphasizes America's cultural debt to the Old World. The last sectarian manifestation of the millenial tradition was Jehovah's Witnesses, founded in 1872.

Brown, Lawrence L. "The Americanization of the Episcopal Church." HIS-
TORICAL MAGAZINE OF THE PROTESTANT EPISCOPAL CHURCH 44 (December 1975): 33-52.

The American Revolution forced the church to think through its
purposes. It remained English in many ways, but so did American
society.

Brydon, George MacLaren. VIRGINIA'S MOTHER CHURCH AND THE POLITI-
CAL CONDITIONS UNDER WHICH IT GREW. Vol. 1: AN INTERPRETATION
OF THE RECORDS OF THE COLONY OF VIRGINIA AND THE ANGLICAN
CHURCH OF THAT COLONY, 1607-1727. Richmond: Virginia Historical
Society, 1947. xxii, 571 p.

The Anglican Church in Virginia suffered throughout the colonial
period because it existed as a group of widely separate parishes
and did not have central governance. The author traces efforts
to expand the church and the effects of religious turmoil in England from 1625 to 1689.

_____. VIRGINIA'S MOTHER CHURCH AND THE POLITICAL CONDITIONS
UNDER WHICH IT GREW. Vol. 2: THE STORY OF THE ANGLICAN CHURCH
AND THE DEVELOPMENT OF RELIGION IN VIRGINIA, 1727-1814. Phila-
delphia: Church Historical Society, 1952. x, 688 p.

This is the story of organized religion in Virginia during a time
of expansion and independence. The spread of dissenting sects
during the Great Awakening is also explored.

Bumsted, J.M. "A Caution to Erring Christians: Ecclesiastical Disorder on
Cape Cod, 1717 to 1738." WILLIAM AND MARY QUARTERLY 28 (July 1971):
413-38.

The ecclesiastical disputes on Cape Cod shed light on Puritanism
in eighteenth-century Massachusetts and show the relationship between ideas and action. These disputes involved finance, control
over individual and group behavior by institutions such as the
church, the role of the Puritan minister, and the lines of local
power.

Burr, Nelson R. THE ANGLICAN CHURCH IN NEW JERSEY. Philadelphia:
Church Historical Society, 1954. xvi, 768 p.

This study covers the history of the church from 1702 to 1789.
Burr details the religious currents that swept through New Jersey
and also surveys the progress of the church after 1800.

Butler, Jon. "'Gospel Order Improved': The Keithian Schism and the Exercise
of Quaker Ministerial Authority in Pennsylvania." WILLIAM AND MARY
QUARTERLY 31 (July 1974): 431-52.

Butler argues that the Keithian Schism of the 1690s was neither economic nor political, nor carried on by a flawed Quaker. It was rooted in religious issues concerning ministerial authority that disrupted Pennsylvania politics and ended Keith's career as a respected leader.

Buxbaum, Melvin H. BENJAMIN FRANKLIN AND THE ZEALOUS PRESBYTERIANS. University Park: Pennsylvania State University Press, 1975. x, 265 p.

This is a study of Franklin's conduct during the Great Awakening which makes him appear as hostile and motivated chiefly to make Pennsylvania a royal province. There is interesting information on Franklin and schools and colleges.

Chorley, E. Clowes. MEN AND MOVEMENTS IN THE AMERICAN EPISCOPAL CHURCH. New York: Charles Scribner's Sons, 1946. ix, 501 p.

The history of the right and the left in the Episcopal Church is traced through biographies of important leaders. The early period is emphasized.

Clifton, Denzil T. "Anglicanism and Negro Slavery in Colonial America." HISTORICAL MAGAZINE OF THE PROTESTANT EPISCOPAL CHURCH 39 (March 1970): 29-70.

Clifton reviews the historiography of slavery and concludes that evidence supports the Tannenbaum-Elkins-Klein thesis. The Church of England was not in any sense a source of influence on the slave population in the colonies.

Cohen, Ronald D. "Church and State in Seventeenth-Century Massachusetts: Another Look at the Antinomian Controversy." JOURNAL OF CHURCH AND STATE 12 (Autumn 1970): 475-94.

The Antinomian controversy was more than an effort on the part of the Massachusetts government to control ecclesiastical affairs. Cohen argues that the dispute's central ingredient was a search for civil stability, not religious uniformity.

Cowing, Cedric B. "Sex and Preaching in the Great Awakening." AMERICAN QUARTERLY 20 (Fall 1968): 624-44.

This is a study of the hypothesis that fornication and bastardy played a primary role in the Great Awakening. Cowing concludes that preachers preached crisis to attract men to the church and there was an increase in confessions of fornication.

Davidson, Edward H. JONATHAN EDWARDS: THE NARRATIVE OF A PURITAN MIND. Cambridge, Mass.: Harvard University Press, 1968. xii, 161 p.

Davidson depicts Edwards's thought as an amalgam of religious mysticism, Puritan dogma, and Lockean psychology. Edwards operated from a thorough understanding of traditional Puritan theology, but the scientific and philosophic thought of the Enlightenment caused him to attempt to answer the great questions concerning the nature of man and his place in the cosmos.

Davis, Richard Beale. "The Devil in Virginia in the Seventeenth Century." VIRGINIA MAGAZINE OF HISTORY AND BIOGRAPHY 65 (April 1957): 131-49.

This is a study of Virginians' attitudes toward the idea of black magic in the seventeenth century. At first, Indians were viewed as the followers of Satan, but as time went on attention was focused on the evil practices of transplanted Englishmen.

De Jong, Gerald F. "The Dutch Reformed Church and Negro Slavery in Colonial America." CHURCH HISTORY 40 (December 1971): 423-36.

The Dutch Reformed Church and other denominations condoned slavery during the colonial period. Religious groups tended to conform their theological tenets to secular mores rather than oppose the political and economic aspects of society.

D'Elia, Donald J. BENJAMIN RUSH: PHILOSOPHER OF THE AMERICAN REVOLUTION. Philadelphia: American Philosophical Society, 1974. 113 p.

This is a religious study of Rush, who changed from a Calvinist to a Universalist. As an intensely religious man, he pioneered in psychiatry and crusaded against alcohol, slavery, and war.

Elliott, Emory. POWER AND PULPIT IN PURITAN NEW ENGLAND. Princeton, N.J.: Princeton University Press, 1975. xi, 240 p.

Elliott argues that sermons depicted generational conflict in New England between 1670 and 1692, since it was during this period that the hold of the first settlers on the young was being broken. Imagery in the sermons symbolized the second generation's fear of the patriarchy and eventually charted a new direction.

Ellis, John Tracy. CATHOLICS IN COLONIAL AMERICA. Baltimore: Helicon Press, 1965. 486 p.

Ellis deals with the Spanish missions in Florida and the Northwest, French missions in Maine, New York, and mid-America, and the English missions of the Atlantic seaboard.

Endy, Melvin B., Jr. WILLIAM PENN AND EARLY QUAKERISM. Princeton, N.J.: Princeton University Press, 1973. viii, 410 p.

This is a study mainly of Penn's religious thought. Endy analyzes the Quaker leader's ideas concerning the Bible, church history, the inner light, the Trinity, and Christology.

Foster, Charles I. AN ERRAND OF MERCY: THE EVANGELICAL UNITED FRONT, 1790-1837. Chapel Hill: University of North Carolina Press, 1960. xii, 320 p.

Foster covers evangelicalism from its origin in England to its reception, domestication, and decline as an organized force in the United States. He shows that the British pattern of tract, Bible, and missionary societies, as well as male and female auxiliaries, were taken over by Americans.

Foster, Stephen. THEIR SOLITARY WAY: THE PURITAN SOCIAL ETHIC IN THE FIRST CENTURY OF SETTLEMENT. New Haven, Conn.: Yale University Press, 1971. xxii, 214 p.

Puritan values were founded on order and love and extended to government and political order. There was contradiction in Puritan culture although change was very gradual.

Frantz, John B. "The Awakening of Religion among the German Settlers in the Middle Colonies." WILLIAM AND MARY QUARTERLY 33 (April 1976): 266-88.

The German Awakening began with the Baptists in the 1720s and continued until the early 1750s. Religion gave the German settlers a sense of spiritual care and reconciled them to ecclesiastical pluralism.

Frost, J. William. "The Dry Bones of Quaker Theology." CHURCH HISTORY 39 (December 1970): 503-23.

Quaker theology began with and was structured by the inward light of Christ. Since the inward light was of Christ, the subjective illumination was equal to the revelation of God in the New Testament and this was an excellent weapon for attacking schooling, learning, liturgy, and a hireling ministry.

_____. THE QUAKER FAMILY IN COLONIAL AMERICA: A PORTRAIT OF THE SOCIETY OF FRIENDS. New York: St. Martin's Press, 1973. vi, 248 p.

Quaker religious beliefs are contrasted with those of more predominant colonial denominations. It is shown how religious beliefs shaped life-styles from childrearing to funerals.

Gannon, Michael V. THE CROSS OF SAND: THE EARLY CATHOLIC CHURCH IN FLORIDA, 1513-1870. Gainesville: University of Florida Press, 1965. xv, 210 p.

The Catholic Church in Florida existed under four flags--Spanish, English, United States, and Confederate--and it persisted, despite lukewarm parishioners and Know-Nothings. It was the protector of the Indian in the Spanish era, protector of slavery during the Confederacy, and protector of the Negro in Reconstruction.

Garrett, John. ROGER WILLIAMS: WITNESS BEYOND CHRISTENDOM, 1603-1783. New York: Macmillan, 1970. x, 306 p.

Garrett examines Williams's ideas on separatism, education, the structure of society, missionary activities, and other matters. His demands concerning freedom of conscience, separation of church and state, and popular participation in government were not the product of a rational political philosophy but of seventeenth-century Biblicism and his own Christological thought.

Gaustad, Edwin Scott. "A Disestablished Society: Origins of the First Amendment." JOURNAL OF CHURCH AND STATE 11 (Autumn 1969): 409-26.

Gaustad is concerned with how disestablishment came about. He examines the disestablishment sentiment from the standpoint of the principles of radical religion, the pragmatism of conservative religion, the position of natural religion, and the indifference and hostility toward religion.

_____. THE GREAT AWAKENING IN NEW ENGLAND. New York: Harper and Brothers, 1957. xiv, 173 p.

The Great Awakening is detailed from its origins in the Connecticut Valley with Jonathan Edwards to its triumph through the itinerant preaching of Whitefield and Tennant. The dissolution of the old order and the rise of the radical element, principally Baptists, also is examined.

_____. A RELIGIOUS HISTORY OF AMERICA. New York: Harper and Row, 1966. xxiii, 421 p.

Gaustad emphasizes a national rather than a denominational perspective. The relationship between religion and democracy is delineated.

_____. "Society and the Great Awakening in New England." WILLIAM AND MARY QUARTERLY 11 (October 1954): 566-77.

The Great Awakening (1740-42) was "great and general" because it knew no boundaries, social or geographical. It was not carried along by a disinherited, rural debtor class.

_____. "The Theological Effects of the Great Awakening in New England." MISSISSIPPI VALLEY HISTORICAL REVIEW 40 (March 1954): 681-706.

Any account of New England theology must be told in terms of movements appearing in the generation following the Great Awakening. In theology, the Awakening was divisive and pushed many of the normally orthodox into anti-Calvinist positions.

Goen, C.C. REVIVALISM AND SEPARATISM IN NEW ENGLAND, 1740-1800: STRICT CONGREGATIONALISTS AND SEPARATE BAPTISTS IN THE GREAT AWAKENING. New Haven, Conn.: Yale University Press, 1962. x, 370 p.

Separatists were important because they shattered Congregational uniformity in Connecticut and Massachusetts. They adhered to the free church ideal, hastened disestablishment, and operated in the name of Puritan principles.

Goodwin, Gerald J. "The Anglican Reaction to the Great Awakening." HISTORICAL MAGAZINE OF THE PROTESTANT EPISCOPAL CHURCH 34 (December 1966): 343-72.

The colonial Church of England was the one church hostile to the Great Awakening. It spurned vital impetus and kept itself from sharing one of the vibrant ingredients in American culture--evangelicalism--and sealed its fate as a minority church.

_____. "The Myth of 'Arminian-Calvinism' in Eighteenth Century New England." NEW ENGLAND QUARTERLY 41 (June 1968): 213-37.

Arminian-Calvinism is the doctrine expounded by various writers that an Arminian theology of free will and humane effort traveled in the guise of a Calvinist theology of determinism and predestination. Goodwin argues that New England Congregationalists clung to Calvinist doctrines through the Great Awakening and condemned Arminianism as heresy.

Gribben, William. "American Episcopacy and the War of 1812." HISTORICAL MAGAZINE OF THE PROTESTANT EPISCOPAL CHURCH 38 (March 1969): 25-36.

The Episcopal Church was vulnerable during the War of 1812 for doctrinal and historical reasons. During the war, however, the church was loyal, prudent, and patriotic.

_____. THE CHURCHES MILITANT: THE WAR OF 1812 AND AMERICAN RELIGION. New Haven, Conn.: Yale University Press, 1973. viii, 210 p.

Gribben allows religious spokesmen to define the issues of the times. The economic and political issues of the War of 1812 provoked a diversity of positions with Congregationalists attacking the war and evangelicals attacking the Congregationalists.

_____. "The Covenant Transformed: The Jeremiad Tradition and the War of 1812." CHURCH HISTORY 40 (September 1971): 297-305.

After the Revolution, Americans no longer viewed national crises as occasions for jeremiads, for confessing their sins and begging relief from the retribution they merited. During the War of 1812, however, jeremiads of the colonial church were observed by some people and they came out of the war expurgated and anxious for reform.

_____. "Republican Religion and the American Churches in the Early National Period." HISTORIAN 35 (November 1972): 61-74.

Churches used patriotic rhetoric in their denominational appeals but this does not prove their harmony with republican principles. At the same time, historians need to listen sympathetically to the churchmen who claimed their creed was closest to the nation's spirit.

_____. "The War of 1812 and American Presbyterianism: Religion and Politics During the Second War with Britain." JOURNAL OF PRESBYTERIAN HISTORY 47 (December 1969): 320-39.

Presbyterians were not united concerning the war. Some leaders influenced against it, some were extremely patriotic, and others deplored the bloodshed and avoided political involvement.

Griffen, Clifford S. "Religious Benevolence as Social Control, 1815-1860." MISSISSIPPI VALLEY HISTORICAL REVIEW 44 (December 1957): 423-44.

Presbyterians and Congregationalists formed benevolent organizations, such as the American Tract Society, devoted to convincing people that forsaking sin and believing in Christ would place man in an excellent position to merit mercy. Leaders of these societies were rising men with a conservative tinge and they hoped to use their organizations to control a chaotic society.

Hall, David D. THE FAITHFUL SHEPHERD: A HISTORY OF THE NEW ENGLAND MINISTRY IN THE SEVENTEENTH CENTURY. Chapel Hill: University of North Carolina Press, 1972. xvi, 301 p.

Hall limits his study to the orothodox majority of New England ministers. These shepherds of the church emphasized conversion and matters of conversion in their local communities and this marked the beginning of evangelism in American churches.

Hatch, Nathan O. "The Origins of Civil Millenialism in America: New England Clergy, War with France, and the Revolution." WILLIAM AND MARY QUARTERLY 31 (July 1974): 407-30.

The revolutionary struggle fired the millenial hopes of many American ministers. Civil millenialism of the revolutionary era grew out of the politicizing of Puritan millenial history during the two decades before the Stamp Act crisis.

Haynes, Leonard L., Jr. THE NEGRO COMMUNITY WITHIN AMERICAN PROTESTANTISM, 1619-1844. Boston: Christopher Publishing House, 1954. 264 p.

Haynes examines the caste status of American blacks, the approach and invitation of Protestant denominations, and the nature of black religion. Blacks protested their treatment by founding separate churches.

Healey, Robert M. JEFFERSON ON RELIGION IN PUBLIC EDUCATION. Yale Publications in Religion, no. 3. New Haven, Conn.: Yale University Press, 1962. xii, 294 p.

Jefferson was unalterably opposed to sectarianism, but he supported common religious principles as important to public education. These common principles could be found in a primitive Christianity based on the moral and ethical teachings of its founder.

Heimert, Alan. RELIGION AND THE AMERICAN MIND: FROM THE GREAT AWAKENING TO THE REVOLUTION. Cambridge, Mass.: Harvard University Press, 1966. x, 668 p.

The main currents of religious thought during this period were liberal or rational and Calvinist or evangelical. Heimert concentrates on New England and shows that liberals attempted to frustrate the Revolution because of its implications for social and political leveling.

Hogue, William M. "The Religious Conspiracy Theory of the American Revolution: Anglican Motive." CHURCH HISTORY 45 (September 1976): 277-92.

Hogue challenges the interpretation of Carl Bridenbaugh and others that the Church of England and the government conspired politically against non-Anglicans. He argues that there was not a politically-motivated Anglican collusion with the government but only an effort to save souls through the religion of the church.

Holified, E. Brooks. THE COVENANT SEALED: THE DEVELOPMENT OF PURITAN SACRAMENTAL THEOLOGY IN OLD AND NEW ENGLAND, 1570-1720. New Haven, Conn.: Yale University Press, 1974. xi, 248 p.

Puritans were ambivalent concerning the sacraments of baptism and the Lord's Supper. New England Puritans were concerned about the inner life rather than external form, about the presence of Christ in the heart of the believer rather than the elements of the communion.

_____. "The Renaissance of Sacramental Piety in Colonial New England."
WILLIAM AND MARY QUARTERLY 29 (January 1972): 33-48.

Sacramental meditations were important to New England religious
sensibility in the late seventeenth and early eighteenth centuries.
They showed the emergence of an evangelistic sacramental piety
oriented toward pastoral concerns that was designed to bring about
conversions.

Hood, Fred J. "Revolution and Religious Liberty: The Conservation of the
Theocratic Concept in Virginia." CHURCH HISTORY 40 (June 1971): 170-81.

Presbyterians in Virginia viewed religious liberty as a dogma compatible with an established religion. Every man had the right to
interpret the Bible for himself and affirm the authority of the scrip-
ture for the common life of the nation.

Hudson, Winthrop S. RELIGION IN AMERICA. AN HISTORICAL ACCOUNT
OF THE DEVELOPMENT OF AME RI CAN RELIGIOUS LIFE. 2d ed. New
York: Charles Scribner's Sons, 1973. xiii, 463 p.

This is an attempt to depict religious life by way of showing its
unity and particularities. The major diversity in American religion
has been ecclesiastical, a variety of forms in a common religious
faith.

Isaac, Rhys. "Evangelical Revolt: The Nature of the Baptists' Challenge to
the Traditional Order in Virginia, 1765 to 1775." WILLIAM AND MAR Y
QUARTERLY 31 (July 1974): 345-68.

Virginians defended their community religious corporateness against
the Baptists, but the Revolution enshrined religious pluralism.
Baptist evangelicals created a crisis of self-confidence on the part
of the gentry and an intense conflict for allegiance among people.

_____. "Religion and Authority: Problems of the Anglican Establishment in
Virginia in the Era of the Great Awakening and the Parson's Cause." WILLIAM
AND MARY QUARTERLY 30 (January 1973): 3-36.

The established church was an important part of the fabric of Virginia society and the system of authority. Yet it could not cope
with the crisis of the Great Awakening or the Parson's Cause and
this caused resentment and recrimination.

James, Sydney V. "The Impact of the American Revolution on Quakers' Ideas
about Their Sect." WILLIAM AND MARY QUARTERLY 19 (July 1962): 360-82.

The Revolution challenged Quakers to find a new role in American
society or accept isolation from it. The hostility of outsiders was
reduced, and the Friends were challenged to become a holy army
to fight for the good of the whole civil community.

_____. A PEOPLE AMONG PEOPLES: QUAKER BENEVOLENCE IN EIGH-TEENTH-CENTURY AMERICA. Cambridge, Mass.: Harvard University Press, 1963. xviii, 405 p.

This is a study of the degree, nature, and rationale of Quaker involvement in eighteenth-century American life. James elucidates Quaker social concerns such as relations with the Indians, manumission, amelioration of the Negro's condition, and peace.

Johnson, James T. "The Covenant Idea and the Puritan View of Marriage." JOURNAL OF THE HISTORY OF IDEAS 33 (January-March 1971): 107-18.

Puritan marriage was a covenant between man and wife to live together in such a way as to insure mutual happiness and prepare for salvation. Having children was not part of this conception.

Jones, James W. THE SHATTERED SYNTHESIS: NEW ENGLAND PURITANISM BEFORE THE GREAT AWAKENING. New Haven, Conn.: Yale University Press, 1973. xi, 207 p.

In this study, the early conflict between Calvinist determinism and free will is discussed in terms of short intellectual biographies of seventeenth- and eighteenth-century Puritans.

Jones, Jerome W. "The Established Virginia Church and the Conversion of Negroes and Indians, 1620-1760." JOURNAL OF NEGRO HISTORY 46 (January 1961): 12-23.

The Church of England never devised an effective policy for the integration of Negroes and Indians. This damaged the prestige of Anglicanism in Virginia, facilitated the Great Awakening, and resulted in the first serious slave revolts.

Kellaway, William. THE NEW ENGLAND COMPANY, 1649-1776: MISSIONARY SOCIETY TO THE AMERICAN INDIANS. New York: Barnes and Noble, 1962. viii, 303 p.

The company sent tools, clothes, hardware and Bibles to New England and ministered to the region's dying and drunken tribes. Missionaries tried to establish towns of praying Indians, mixed communities of Indians and whites, and other measures, but they were unsuccessful in Christianizing.

Kenney, William Howland III. "George Whitefield, Dissenter Priest in the Great Awakening, 1739-1741." WILLIAM AND MARY QUARTERLY 26 (January 1969): 75-93.

Whitefield's evangelistic power derived from his unique position as an antiestablishment Anglican. He exploited a widespread colonial resentment of Anglican influence and his revivals extended directly to the American Revolution.

Klingberg, Frank J. ANGLICAN HUMANITARIANISM IN COLONIAL NEW YORK. Publication no. 2. Philadelphia: Church Historical Society, 1940. x, 295 p.

This is a study of the efforts of missionaries, teachers, and rectors of the Society for the Propagation of the Gospel to civilize and Christianize Indians and Negro slaves, and to establish libraries, schools, and churches for white settlers. The quiet work of these people with the slaves led to abolition in England in 1833.

Kobrin, David. "The Expansion of the Visible Church in New England, 1629-1650." CHURCH HISTORY 36 (June 1967): 189-209.

Kobrin argues that the Puritan Church was not principally a fellow-ship of the saved. Since salvation was a long process and since it was difficult to determine who were in the first stages of the process, the church performed important services for the elect and for hypocrites.

Koehler, Lyle. "The Case of the American Jezebels: Anne Hutchinson and Female Agitation during the Years of Antinomian Turmoil, 1636-1640." WILLIAM AND MARY QUARTERLY 31 (January 1974): 55-78.

Instead of characterizing Hutchinson as a "Joan of Arc" or con-fused rebel, Koehler suggests that she should be perceived in terms of women's history. She was attacked by male leaders because she challenged the female role definition by promoting Antinomian theology.

Levy, Babette M. "Early Puritanism in the Southern and Island Colonies." PROCEEDINGS OF THE AMERICAN ANTIQUARIAN SOCIETY 70 (April 20, 1960): 69-348.

Puritanism was a strong factor in the southern and island colonies although its numerical strength is difficult to determine. It also lacked literary expression in terms of the printing of sermons, be-cause authorities in the various plantations saw no reason for allow-ing the establishment of printing presses.

Lodge, Martin E. "The Crisis of the Churches in the Middle Colonies, 1720-1750." PENNSYLVANIA MAGAZINE OF HISTORY AND BIOGRAPHY 95 (April 1971): 195-220.

The Great Awakening in the middle colonies was almost exclu-sively a movement of church people. The churches failed to es-tablish institutions capable of fulfilling the religious needs of an expanding population and organized religion was on the verge of collapse when the Awakening rescued the floundering churches.

Lowrie, Ernest Benson. THE SHAPE OF THE PURITAN MIND: THE THOUGHT OF SAMUEL WILLARD. New Haven, Conn.: Yale University Press, 1974. xiii, 253 p.

> Willard, more than any other Puritan divine, prepared a systematic theology in his COMPLEAT BODY OF DIVINITY (1726). This study is faithful to Willard's work and also pictures him as a patient, tolerant Puritan who believed that human beings would not support damnation for the glory of God.

Lucas, Paul R. "'An Appeal to the Learned': The Mind of Solomon Stoddard." WILLIAM AND MARY QUARTERLY 30 (April 1970): 257-92.

> Stoddard was a leading clergyman in western Massachusetts from 1669 to 1729 who preached against church discipline. He believed interest in religion was waning in all areas because of an obsession with discipline and he rejected all forms of church government.

_____. VALLEY OF DISCORD: CHURCH AND SOCIETY ALONG THE CONNECTICUT RIVER, 1636-1725. Hanover, N.H.: University Press of New England, 1976. 275 p.

> Conflict between church and society was endemic in the Connecticut River valley during the seventeenth century. This was accompanied by the rise of the laity to power and the growth of Presbyterianism.

Luebke, Fred C. "The Origins of Thomas Jefferson's Anti-Clericalism." CHURCH HISTORY 32 (September 1963): 344-56.

> Clerical attacks, beginning with his campaign for the presidency, made Jefferson anticlerical. He regarded these attacks as being slanderous and penned many letters on religion.

McGiffert, Michael, ed. GOD'S PLOT: THE PARADOXES OF PURITAN PIETY BEING THE AUTOBIOGRAPHY AND JOURNAL OF THOMAS SHEPARD. Amherst: University of Massachusetts Press, 1972. vii, 252 p.

> This autobiography is an introduction to the generation of Puritan clergymen who crossed the Atlantic for the sake of conscience. The journal covers the years 1640 to 1644 and is largely a spiritual self-examination.

Maclear, James Fulton. "'The Heart of New England Rent': The Mystical Element in Early Puritan History." MISSISSIPPI VALLEY HISTORICAL REVIEW 42 (March 1956): 621-52.

> From the earliest beginnings, Puritans emphasized immediacy in religious experience. This took on a drive toward experimental

knowledge of God which became disruptive to unity and was given permanence in the Quaker movement.

_____. "New England and the Fifth Monarchy: The Quest for the Millenium in Early American Puritanism." WILLIAM AND MARY QUARTERLY 32 (April 1975): 223-60.

Puritan apocalyptic history had an impact on thought and institutions. It prophesied the coming of the fifth monarchy (Christ's monarchy) between the 1630s and 1660s and Puritan clergy worked to construct a Christian commonwealth.

_____. "'The True American Union' of Church and State: The Reconstruction of the Theocratic Tradition." CHURCH HISTORY 28 (March 1959): 41-62.

This is a study of America's last disestablishment contest that existed in New England until the 1820s. After disestablishment, New England retained the ideal of a Christian commonwealth and a theocratic tradition was maintained in American intellectual history.

McLoughlin, William G. "Isaac Backus and the Separation of Church and State in America." AMERICAN HISTORICAL REVIEW 73 (June 1968): 1392-1413.

The role of Backus (1724-1806) and the Separate Baptists in the development of the American tradition of separation of church and state is examined. They opposed the concept of a general assessment tax that supported one state church and required conformity of conscience and uniform worship.

_____. NEW ENGLAND DISSENT 1630-1833: THE BAPTISTS AND THE SEPARATION OF CHURCH AND STATE. 2 vols. Cambridge, Mass.: Harvard University Press, 1971. xxiii, 693; vii, 697-1324 p.

McLoughlin traces Baptist growth from lowly seventeenth-century origins through the Great Awakening to the final separation of church and state in New England in 1833. Of special importance is his portrayal of Calvinistic Baptists who carried on the implications of Puritan theology in a rigorous manner.

Marietta, Jack D. "Wealth, War and Religion: The Perfection of Quaker Asceticism, 1740-1783." CHURCH HISTORY 43 (June 1974): 230-41.

Anthony Benezet and John Woolman focused their attention on the spiritually corrosive effect of wealth. This criticism of wealth coincided with war, because war made Friends worry over saving their property and wonder whether history was providentially ordered.

Marsden, George M. "Perry Miller's Rehabilitation of the Puritans: A Critique." CHURCH HISTORY 39 (March 1970): 91-105.

> Miller has rehabilitated the Puritans, but he has restored their image at the expense of important aspects of theology. They were tough-minded men of the Renaissance, but they were also uncompromising Christians and bigoted Calvinists.

Marty, Martin E. RIGHTEOUS EMPIRE: THE PROTESTANT EXPERIENCE IN AMERICA. New York: Dial Press, 1970. 295 p.

> In the colonial period and nineteenth century, Protestants characterized themselves as evangelical and set out to create an empire. More recently, this old empire has been threatened by non-Protestant people and forces.

Middlekauff, Robert. THE MATHERS: THREE GENERATIONS OF PURITAN INTELLECTUALS, 1596-1728. New York: Oxford University Press, 1971. xii, 440 p.

> As Massachusetts Bay colonists generally relaxed their concern for the spiritual character of their colony, the Mathers intensified theirs. All three Mathers emphasized millenial promise and passionate piety with Cotton laying an emotional basis for the revival of religion and the reform of morals that took place in the awakening that followed his death.

_____. "Piety and Intellect in Puritanism." WILLIAM AND MARY QUARTERLY 22 (July 1965): 457-70.

> The traditional conception of the mind as a duality has obscured the relation between piety and intellect among Puritans. Passions made the Puritan what he was, but intellect controlled that passion and was pre-eminent in the Puritan mind and character.

Miller, Glenn T. "God's Light and Man's Enlightenment: A Study in the Theology of Colonial Presbyterianism." JOURNAL OF PRESBYTERIAN HISTORY 51 (Summer 1973): 97-115.

> Miller discusses the theology of Presbyterian Evangelical Calvinists. He shows that they advocated a learned ministry and argued that the true faith was involved with true belief as an intellectual conviction.

Miller, Perry. ERRAND INTO THE WILDERNESS. Cambridge, Mass.: Belknap Press of Harvard University Press, 1956. xii, 244 p.

> This is a collection of essays written between 1931 and 1955. Miller covers the second and third generations of Puritans' fulfillment of the terms of the original covenant, Thomas Hooker and

democracy in Connecticut, the marrow of Puritan divinity, religion and society in the early literature of Virginia, and other subjects.

_____. THE NEW ENGLAND MIND: FROM COLONY TO PROVINCE. Cambridge, Mass.: Harvard University Press, 1953. xiv, 513 p.

Miller delineates the ideological process that changed Puritanism between the Cambridge Platform of 1648 and the death of Cotton Mather in 1728. Those Puritans who guarded the Covenant were faced by men who lived by trade and chafed under the restrictions of theology.

_____. THE NEW ENGLAND MIND: THE SEVENTEENTH CENTURY. New York: Macmillan, 1939. xi, 528 p.

This volume defines the New England mind to 1660. Miller shows that all the intellectual resources of the Puritans were devoted to buttressing their faith and their church establishment.

_____. ORTHODOXY IN MASSACHUSETTS, 1630-1650: A GENETIC STUDY. Cambridge, Mass.: Harvard University Press, 1933. xvi, 353 p.

This is a study of the origins of the "New England Way." Its principles were elaborated before migration as part of a controversy concerning the correct interpretation of the scriptures.

_____. "'Preparation for Salvation' in Seventeenth-Century New England." JOURNAL OF THE HISTORY OF IDEAS 4 (June 1943): 253-86.

During the second half of the seventeenth century, Puritan clerics and political leaders believed their society was degenerating, and they launched a vigorous campaign against the menace. Respecting salvation, this campaign took the form of making over their universe from one in which men labored for the glory of God to one in which men could trust themselves, even to the extent of beginning their own conversions.

Mills, Frederick V., Sr. "The Internal Anglican Controversy Over an American Episcopate, 1763-1775." HISTORICAL MAGAZINE OF THE PROTESTANT EPISCOPAL CHURCH 44 (September 1975): 257-76.

Mills argues that British ministries emphasized imperial rather than ecclesiastical problems and were not responsive to schemes for a colonial bishop. Local leaders in the colonies also were opposed, because they were afraid local vestries would lose power.

_____. "Mitre Without Sceptre: An Eighteenth Century Ecclesiastical Revolution." CHURCH HISTORY 39 (September 1970): 365-71.

Anglican churches in America separated from the Church of England as a result of the Revolution. They accomplished a revolution themselves by electing their bishop and separating this bishop from the state.

Monk, Robert C. "Unity and Diversity Among Eighteenth Century Colonial Anglicans and Methodists." HISTORICAL MAGAZINE OF THE PROTESTANT EPISCOPAL CHURCH 38 (March 1969): 51-70.

Methodists expressed allegiance to the Church of England as a practical necessity. This allegiance steadily eroded during the eighteenth century, but a spirit of cooperation was not completely lost.

Morgan, Edmund S. "New England Puritanism: Another Approach." WILLIAM AND MARY QUARTERLY 18 (April 1961): 236-42.

Instead of treating Puritanism as a monolithic system, historians should acknowledge its diversity. Morgan urges the study of the history of localities to discover this diversity.

_____. "The Puritan Ethic and the American Revolution." WILLIAM AND MARY QUARTERLY 24 (January 1967): 3-43.

The Revolution in all its phases from the resistance to Parliamentary taxation in the 1760s to the establishment of a national government in the 1790s was guided by values inherited from Puritanism. These values were clustered around the idea of "calling" which meant that every man served God by serving society.

_____. THE PURITAN FAMILY: ESSAYS ON RELIGION AND DOMESTIC RELATIONS IN SEVENTEENTH CENTURY NEW ENGLAND. Boston: Trustees of the Public Library, 1944. 118 p.

This study deals with love and marriage, parenthood, education of children, dealings with servants, and the family in the social structure among the Puritans.

_____. ROGER WILLIAMS: THE CHURCH AND THE STATE. New York: Harcourt, Brace and World, 1967. 170 p.

Morgan contends that the central concern of Williams's writings was for the institutions of men, namely, church and state. Williams not only freed religion from the state but also freed the state from religion so that it could pursue its own human ends.

_____. VISIBLE SAINTS: THE HISTORY OF A PURITAN IDEA. New York: New York University Press, 1963. xiv, 159 p.

This is a study of the halfway convenant which, Morgan argues, was not an abandonment of the Puritan ideal. The crux of the halfway covenant and of Puritan thought on the church was achieving and maintaining a church free of human corruption through making conversion a qualification for church membership.

Morison, Samuel Eliot. THE PURITAN PRONAOS: STUDIES IN THE INTELLECTUAL LIFE OF NEW ENGLAND IN THE SEVENTEENTH CENTURY. New York: New York University Press, 1936. 281 p.

The author sketches the English and religious background of intellectual life and discusses education, printing and bookselling, libraries, theology, historical and political literature, and science. He argues that the religious aspect of education has been overstressed.

Nash, Gary B. "The American Clergy and the French Revolution." WILLIAM AND MARY QUARTERLY 22 (July 1965): 392-412.

Clergymen warmly applauded the early stages of the French Revolution but they changed their minds by the late 1790s. They used the Revolution to fight religious stagnation at home and aligned themselves with the Federalist Party.

Nuesse, Celestine Joseph. THE SOCIAL THOUGHT OF AMERICAN CATHOLICS, 1634-1829. The Catholic University of American Studies in Sociology, vol. 10. Westminster, Md.: Newman Book Shop, 1945. x, 315 p.

The author defines social thought as all things concerning human associations. He finds that during the colonial and early national periods Catholics were conformist since they desired to get along with their Protestant neighbors.

Oberholzer, Emil, Jr. DELINQUENT SAINTS: DISCIPLINARY ACTION IN THE EARLY CONGREGATIONAL CHURCHES OF MASSACHUSETTS. New York: Columbia University Press, 1956. xii, 379 p.

Oberholzer covers moral offenses such as extramarital relations, drunkenness, false witness, and similar topics. He shows the systematic watchfulness over the lives of church members in Puritan Massachusetts.

O'Neill, Charles Edward. CHURCH AND STATE IN FRENCH COLONIAL LOUISIANA: POLICY AND POLITICS TO 1732. New Haven, Conn.: Yale University Press, 1966. xii, 315 p.

This study traces the complexities, diversities, and problems of church and state from the founding of the Louisiana colony in 1699 to its retrocession to the king of France in 1732. It depicts the collaboration and conflict between church and state officials which did not produce a monolithic union.

Pearce, Roy Harvey. "The 'Ruines of Mankind': The Indian and the Puritan Mind." JOURNAL OF THE HISTORY OF IDEAS 13 (April 1952): 200-217.

> The Puritan became obsessed with the Indian because he believed he had a divine right to Indian lands. He intended to convert the Indian which was the expression of a hope to save the Indian not for civilization but for God.

Perry, Ralph Barton. PURITANISM AND DEMOCRACY. New York: Vanguard Press, 1944. xvi, 688 p.

> Perry attempts to discover Americanism and identify the American cause in World War II with the American tradition. The American tradition is based on Puritanism and democracy, whose ideals overlap and form the two main strands in American history.

Pettit, Norman. THE HEART PREPARED: GRACE AND CONVERSION IN PURITAN SPIRITUAL LIFE. New Haven, Conn.: Yale University Press, 1966. ix, 252 p.

> This is a study of how theologians from Zwingli and Calvin to Cotton Mather dealt with the conversion experience and prepared for the reception of God's grace. The Antinomian Crisis of 1636-37 is examined in terms of the forces released by John Cotton.

Pope, Robert G. THE HALF-WAY COVENANT: CHURCH MEMBERSHIP IN PURITAN NEW ENGLAND. Princeton, N.J.: Princeton University Press, 1969. xi, 321 p.

> Puritans did not anticipate the dilemma that baptism would pose for them in the seventeenth century. This is a study of partial membership in the church based on the baptismal covenant but not requiring conversion.

_____. "New England Versus the New England Mind: The Myth of Declension." JOURNAL OF SOCIAL HISTORY 3 (Winter 1969-70): 95-108.

> Historians agree that Puritanism fell on bad times after the new charter of 1691, and they have either hailed or lamented this change. Pope argues that change was an effort of the church to develop new functions to fulfill the needs of a community they wished to preserve.

Posey, Walter B. "The Protestant Episcopal Church: An American Adaptation." JOURNAL OF SOUTHERN HISTORY 24 (February 1959): 3-30.

> This essay covers the adaptation of the Anglican Church following independence. The author focuses on the South, but he shows that the church avoided schism because it was characterized by class solidarity.

Robbins, Roy M. "Crusade in the Wilderness, 1750-1830." INDIANA MAGA-ZINE OF HISTORY 46 (June 1950): 121-32.

Robbins argues that the West was civilized by religious forces. Frontier lawlessness offered a challenge to civilization, but morality and religion triumphed to a greater degree than expected.

Rosenmeier, Jesper. "New England's Perfection: The Image of Adam and the Image of Christ in the Antinomian Crisis, 1634 to 1638." WILLIAM AND MARY QUARTERLY 27 (July 1970): 435-59.

Puritan elders came from England to regain the paradise Adam had lost. In the Antimomian Crisis, conflict evolved around the restorations of Adam's innocence or a new and richer holiness embracing faith, repentance, and the indwelling power of the Holy Spirit as expressed in the image of Christ in the royal seat of Eden.

_____. "The Teacher and the Witness: John Cotton and Roger Williams." WILLIAM AND MARY QUARTERLY 24 (July 1968): 408-31.

In historical debate, Williams has been priased as the first advocate of freedom of conscience and genuine political democracy while Cotton has been scorned as an apologizer for New England. An examination of their sermons indicates that the central issue in the 1630s and 1640s was the meaning of Christ's incarnation.

Rosenthal, Bernard. "Puritan Conscience and New England Slavery." NEW ENGLAND QUARTERLY 46 (March 1973): 62-81.

Puritan New England supported slavery, but the principal intellectual opposition to it came from Puritans. A coalition of the clergy and the white working class ended the institution in the region.

Rutman, Darrett B. AMERICAN PURITANISM: FAITH AND PRACTICE. Philadelphia: J.B. Lippincott, 1970. xii, 139 p.

This study represents an attempt to bridge Puritan ideas and social reality. Rutman argues that New England tried to develop an interdependent community under the conservative guidance of ministers, but the institutional church swallowed up the unleashing of the Holy Spirit.

Salisbury, Neal. "Red Puritans: The 'Praying Indians' of Massachusetts Bay and John Eliot." WILLIAM AND MARY QUARTERLY 31 (January 1974): 27-54.

Salisbury questions the assumption that missionaries alone among whites were neither aggressive nor violent toward Indians. He demonstrates that John Eliot sought to transform Indians into "civilized" saints to make them no longer Indians.

Religion

Scholz, Robert F. "Clerical Consociation in Massachusetts Bay: Reassessing the New England Way and Its Origins." WILLIAM AND MARY QUARTERLY 29 (July 1972): 391-414.

Clerical consociation, a form of ministers' conferences, was brought to Massachusetts Bay from England and Europe. Although resisted, clerical consociation became essential to the conduct of church business and illustrative of the "middle way" in congregational church polity.

Seiler, William H. "The Anglican Parish Vestry in Colonial Virginia." JOURNAL OF SOUTHERN HISTORY 22 (August 1956): 310-37.

Although the Anglican Church was the established church in Virginia during the colonial period, Virginians created their own organizational arrangements. The parish became an effective administrative unit and the vestries exercised considerable authority.

Sernett, Milton C. BLACK RELIGION AND AMERICAN EVANGELICALISM: WHITE PROTESTANTS, PLANTATION MISSIONS, AND THE FLOWERING OF NEGRO CHRISTIANITY, 1787-1865. Metuchen, N.J.: Scarecrow Press and the American Theological Library Association, 1975. 320 p.

This is a study of the evangelical conversion of southern slaves. Slaves received a religion from Methodists, Baptists, and Presbyterians that permitted them to endure and oppose oppression.

Simmons, Richard C. "Godliness, Property, and the Franchise in Puritan Massachusetts: An Interpretation." JOURNAL OF AMERICAN HISTORY 55 (December 1968): 485-511.

Simmons sees the seventeenth-century Massachusetts political system as being unique, since freemanship was based on religious status rather than property. After 1664, however, when church membership began to decline, the franchise was given not only to church members but also to propertied men.

Simpson, Alan. PURITANISM IN OLD AND NEW ENGLAND. Chicago: University of Chicago Press, 1955. x, 126 p.

Puritanism was a religious revival. The author maintains that Puritans shaped our society by contributing to limited government, self-government, education, and morality.

Slotkin, Richard. "Narratives of Negro Crime in New England, 1675-1800." AMERICAN QUARTERLY 25 (March 1973): 3-31.

In this essay, the author shows that execution sermons and crime narratives reflected the universal concern in Puritan life for conversion. At the same time, the image of the black in these writ-

ings was that of an oversexed brute, who had a proclivity for
crime and was ungrateful for the blessings of white masters.

Smith, George L. RELIGION AND TRADE IN NEW NETHERLAND: DUTCH
ORIGINS AND AMERICAN DEVELOPMENT. Ithaca, N.Y.: Cornell University Press, 1973. xiii, 266 p.

> Smith maintains that New Netherland became secular very early.
> The spirit of commerce was prevalent and led to a de facto
> religious pluralism.

Smith, James Ward, and Jamison, A. Leland, eds. RELIGION IN AMERICAN
LIFE. Vol. 1: THE SHAPING OF AMERICAN RELIGION. Vol. 2: RELIGIOUS PERSPECTIVES IN AMERICAN CULTURE. Vol. 4, in 2 vols.: A
CRITICAL BIBLIOGRAPHY OF RELIGION IN AMERICA, by Nelson R. Burr.
Princeton Studies in American Civilization, no. 5. Princeton, N.J.: Princeton University Press, 1961. 514; 427; 1219 p.

> This is a collection of interpretive essays that emphasize the role
> of Protestantism but also give attention to the development of
> Catholicism and the contributions of Judaism. Volume 1 covers
> the impact of the American scene on religion, while volume 2 includes essays on the interaction of religion and culture in American education, politics, and the arts.

Smith, Peter H. "Politics and Sainthood: Biography by Cotton Mather."
WILLIAM AND MARY QUARTERLY 20 (April 1963): 186-206.

> The purpose of Puritan biography was to establish a spiritual guide
> for the wayward descendants of New England's seventeenth-century
> orthodoxy. Mather's biographies followed this formula, but he
> also used them to respond to problems that faced the Mathers.

Smith, Timothy L. "Congregation, State and Denomination: The Forming of
the American Religious Structure." WILLIAM AND MARY QUARTERLY 25
(April 1968): 155-76.

> Denominations emerged out of the needs of congregations in a society where mobility made voluntary association the rule of religious life. Colonists departed from the life of the village and
> kin group they had known in Europe, and the quest for community
> became a dominant experience which they gained by forming congregations and denominations.

Smylie, James H. "Presbyterian Clergy and the Problems of 'Dominion' in the
Revolutionary Generation." JOURNAL OF PRESBYTERIAN HISTORY 48 (Fall
1970): 161-75.

> Dominion was not an anthropological problem for Presbyterian clergy,
> as has been argued, but a theological consideration having to do

with God's dominion. Presbyterian ministers confessed that God will have the last word about the way men exercise power over others.

Stannard, David E. "Death and Dying in Puritan New England." AMERICAN HISTORICAL REVIEW 78 (December 1973): 1305-30.

The vision of death and the act of dying were profoundly religious matters to the Puritans. They feared death, but they also tried to display "the sweetness of that unspeakable peace" when death approached.

Stearns, Raymond Phineas, and Brawner, David Holmes. "New England Church 'Relations' and Continuity in Early Congregational History." PROCEEDINGS OF THE AMERICAN ANTIQUARIAN SOCIETY 75 (21 April 1965): 13-46.

Early Congregational polity embodied in theory and practice a conception of purity by which New England church membership requirements were consistent and continuous. This was true of both nonseparating and separating Congregationalists and did not produce schism as has been suggested.

Steiner, Bruce E. SAMUEL SEABURY, 1729-1796: A STUDY IN THE HIGH CHURCH TRADITION. Athens: Ohio University Press, 1971. xiii, 508 p.

Seabury was a leader in the colonial Church of England, a loyalist in the Revolution, and the first American bishop who helped to transform the Church into the Protestant Episcopal Church. The author indicates that emphasis on the authority of the episcopacy and the importance of the sacraments shaped Seabury's religious thought and career.

Stoever, William K.B. "Nature, Grace and John Cotton: The Theological Dimension of the New England Antinomian Controversy." CHURCH HISTORY 44 (March 1975): 22-33.

On the theological level, the Antinomian Controversy of 1636-38 concerned the relationship between created nature and divine activity in the process of regeneration. Puritan elders believed that God, in accomplishing regeneration, used means that belonged to the created order, while dissenters maintained that God acted directly on men and transformed them apart from any other activity.

Sweet, Douglas H. "Church Vitality and the American Revolution: Historiographical Consensus and Thoughts Towards a New Perspective." CHURCH HISTORY 45 (September 1976): 341-57.

Historiographical consensus concerning church vitality and the Revolution paints a picture of churches decimated by war and of a decrease in piety. Sweet suggests a new view that church life did not recede following the Revolution and that religion did not lose its central position in the institutional life of communities.

Sweet, William Warren. RELIGION IN COLONIAL AMERICA. New York: Charles Scribner's Sons, 1942. xiii, 367 p.

Sweet's thesis is that, until 1660, colonial religious groups were transplanted bodies representing the conservative wing of the Protestant Reformation, but, thereafter, liberalizing influences began to operate. He delineates the Great Awakening and religious liberty.

_____. RELIGION IN THE DEVELOPMENT OF AMERICAN CULTURE, 1765-1840. New York: Charles Scribner's Sons, 1952. xiv, 338 p.

The spread of religion westward is emphasized. The author argues that the West would have reverted to barbarism if frontier life had not been tempered by religious values.

Tanis, James. DUTCH CALVINISTIC PIETISM IN THE MIDDLE COLONIES: A STUDY IN THE LIFE AND THEOLOGY OF THEODORUS JACOBUS FRELING-HUYSEN. The Hague: Martinus Nijhoff, 1967. ix, 203 p.

Frelinghuysen was a seventeenth-century New Jersey evangelist whose conversions foreshadowed the Great Awakening. His pietism came from the Reformed tradition rather than Lutheranism, a pietism that represented a struggle against apathy and indifference.

Teunnisen, John J., and Hinz, Evelyn J. "Roger Williams, St. Paul, and American Primitivism." CANADIAN REVIEW OF AMERICAN STUDIES 4 (Fall 1973): 121-36.

Primitivism refers either to a nostalgic belief in the remote past as a Golden Age or to the idea that natural man is better than civilized man. Because of his banishment from the Bay Colony, Williams likened himself to St. Paul and this became the basis for his primitivism.

Thomas, G.E. "Puritans, Indians, and the Concept of Race." NEW ENGLAND QUARTERLY 48 (March 1976): 3-27.

The interpretation of Indian-white relations in early New England that the Puritans were humane and did not destroy the Indian way of life is culturally biased. The record of Puritan attitudes, goals, and behavior concerning the Indians reveals harshness, brutality, ethnocentrism, and even racial overtones.

Thompson, J. Earl, Jr. "Slavery and Presbyterianism in the Revolutionary Era." JOURNAL OF PRESBYTERIAN HISTORY 54 (Spring 1976): 121-41.

Some Presbyterians made contributions to antislavery thought by favoring gradual abolition. They tried to build an antislavery platform that would unify rather than disrupt their religious community.

Tichi, Cecelia. "Spiritual Biography and the 'Lord's Remembrancers.'" WILLIAM AND MARY QUARTERLY 18 (January 1971): 64-85.

The "lord's remembrancers" were Puritan historians who recorded God's mercifulness for the New England people. By studying the spiritual biography in Puritan histories it is possible to discover new thematic and rhetorical grounds on which to evaluate these works.

Tolles, Frederick B. "'Of the Best Sort but Plain': The Quaker Esthetic." AMERICAN QUARTERLY 11 (Winter 1959): 484-502.

The Quaker esthetic came from the experience of the inner light which gave believers knowledge of God's will for guidance and led them toward purity. In the arts, as in living, Quakers strived for simplicity and developed a tradition of soundness of workmanship and sureness of line.

_____. QUAKERS AND THE ATLANTIC CULTURE. New York: Macmillan, 1960. xvi, 160 p.

Tolles is particularly interested in the Quaker role in the Atlantic culture of the seventeenth century. He also discusses Quakerism and politics, science, esthetics, and other matters.

Tucker, Louis Leonard. "The Church of England and Religious Liberty at Pre-Revolutionary Yale." WILLIAM AND MARY QUARTERLY 17 (July 1960): 314-28.

In the middle years of the eighteenth century, colleges generally were moving toward religious liberty because of the proliferation of sects and the multiplication of sectarian colleges. Yale University is often viewed as an exception, but only for a short period during the presidency of Thomas Clap was this institution a defender of Congregational orthodoxy and an opponent of the Anglican Church.

Van Til, L. John. LIBERTY OF CONSCIENCE: THE HISTORY OF A PURITAN IDEA. Philadelphia: Craig, 1972. vi, 192 p.

Van Til shows that Puritanism was not monolithic and authoritarian. The Puritans believed that freedom of conscience was imparted to man by God.

Wallace, Paul A.W. THIRTY THOUSAND MILES WITH JOHN HECKEWELDER. Pittsburgh: University of Pittsburgh Press, 1958. xviii, 474 p.

Heckewelder (1743-1823) was a pioneer Moravian missionary to the Indians west of the Appalachians. These journals are of travels from Bethlehem, Pennsylvania, to Vincennes, Indiana, and southern Ontario.

Walton, John. "Tradition of the Middle Way: The Anglican Contribution to American Character." HISTORICAL MAGAZINE OF THE PROTESTANT EPIS-COPAL CHURCH 44 (December 1975): 7-32.

Anglican influences on American history have been as central as Puritanism. Of utmost importance has been a pragmatic mode of thought.

1815-1915

Abell, Aaron I. AMERICAN CATHOLICISM AND SOCIAL ACTION: A SEARCH FOR SOCIAL JUSTICE, 1865-1950. Garden City, N.Y.: Hanover House, 1960. 306 p.

Catholics did not play a significant role in social reform movements in the nineteenth and early twentieth centuries because they were conservative and tended to live apart from the mainstream. Their social action came in the support of schools, orphanages, hospitals, and other social institutions.

_____. THE URBAN IMPACT ON AMERICAN PROTESTANTISM, 1865-1900. Harvard Historical Studies, vol. 54. Cambridge, Mass.: Harvard University Press, 1943. x, 275 p.

This book covers the efforts of Protestant churches to meet the new conditions created by urbanization. It deals with the Salvation Army, city missions, social service auxiliaries, and the beginnings of the teaching of social ethics in Protestant seminaries.

Ahlstrom, Sydney E. A RELIGIOUS HISTORY OF THE AMERICAN PEOPLE. New Haven: Yale University Press, 1972. xvi, 1,158 p.

This study represents an attempt to interpret the sources, development, and interrelationships of all the important aspects of Amerrican religion from Anne Hutchinson to Timothy Leary. Ahlstrom argues that the United States was settled by a special form of radical Protestantism, the Puritan impulse, and this impulse did not die until the period between 1920 and 1960.

Aiken, John R., and McDonnell, James R. "Walter Rauschenbusch and Labor Reform: A Social Gospeler's Approach." LABOR HISTORY 11 (Spring 1970): 131-50.

Labor generally rejected social gospellers, and Rauschenbusch was no exception. Labor rejected their claim to leadership and criticized the inadequacy of their tactics for improving labor conditions.

Akin, William E. "The War of the Bishops: Catholic Controversy on the School Question in New York State in 1894." NEW-YORK HISTORICAL SOCIETY QUARTERLY 50 (January 1966): 41-62.

This is a study of how interaction with American conditions split the Catholic hierarchy late in the nineteenth century. Catholic attitudes on the school issue centered on the education of immigrants, with liberals favoring Americanization and conservatives backing an education that would keep the immigrants in the flock.

Allen, James B., and Alexander, Thomas G., eds. MANCHESTER MORMONS: THE JOURNAL OF WILLIAM CLAYTON, 1840 TO 1842. Santa Barbara, Calif.: Peregrine Smith, 1974. 248 p.

Clayton, an English convert to the Mormon gospel, served as Joseph Smith's private secretary. This journal is an essential work on Mormon missionary outreach.

Anderson, Charles H. WHITE PROTESTANT AMERICANS: FROM NATIONAL ORIGINS TO RELIGIOUS GROUP. Englewood Cliffs, N.J.: Prentice-Hall, 1970. xx, 188 p.

Anderson, a sociologist, sees white Protestants as a distinctive group formed by the mingling of colonial stock and ethnic groups. Protestant faith thus has replaced national origins as the basis of ethnic identity even though in-marriage rates suggest otherwise.

Andrew, John A. III. REBUILDING THE CHRISTIAN COMMONWEALTH: NEW ENGLAND CONGREGATIONALIST AND FOREIGN MISSIONS, 1800-1830. Lexington: University Press of Kentucky, 1976. 232 p.

This is a study of the motives and methods held and used by the missionaries who invaded the Sandwich Islands (Hawaii). They wanted to convert the natives and provide a continued life for the Congregational Church.

Arden, G. Everett. AUGUSTANA HERITAGE: A HISTORY OF THE AUGUSTANA LUTHERAN CHURCH. Rock Island, Ill.: Augustana Press, 1963. xii, 424 p.

The interplay between the American environment and the church of Swedish immigrants is emphasized. This interplay shaped accomodation and identification for these people.

Argersinger, Peter H. "The Divines and the Destitute." NEBRASKA HISTORY 51 (Fall 1970): 303-18.

Churches accepted the idea that they must help those who suffer. Their work in the Plains states fluctuated with economic conditions in the late nineteenth century, but they gradually saw that their ministrations were not dependent on the prosperity and wealth of those they proposed to help.

_____. "Pentecostal Politics in Kansas: Religion, the Farmers Alliance, and the Gospel of Populism." KANSAS QUARTERLY 1 (Fall 1969): 24-35.

Populist politics was a religio-political movement that involved major demands for reform and also offered an alternative to missing religious activity. Kansas populism was a response to the perceived role of organized religion in a crisis of depression and drought.

Bailey, Kenneth K. "Protestantism and Afro-Americans in the Old South: Another Look." JOURNAL OF SOUTHERN HISTORY 41 (November 1975): 451-72.

Bailey suggests another look at the scholarship whose main concern has been to detail the involvement of southern churches in racial discrimination. His own reading of the record indicates that denominations did not totally exclude free blacks from positions of distinction, nor were rank and file blacks denied participation in worship.

_____. "Southern White Protestantism at the Turn of the Century." AMERICAN HISTORICAL REVIEW 68 (April 1963): 618-35.

Forty years after Appomattox most white church members in the South belonged to explicitly southern denominations. Southern church members were not given to skepticism and the South remained a land of piety and tradition.

Banner, Lois. "Religious Benevolence as Social Control: A Critique of an Interpretation." JOURNAL OF AMERICAN HISTORY 60 (June 1973): 23-41.

It has become standard to interpret post-revolutionary religious humanitarians as conservative and self-serving individuals who originated Bible and tract societies, formed temperance organizations, and aided the urban poor to gain power over society rather than promote social improvement. Banner argues, on the contrary, that these leaders worked to attain a stable democratic order and challenge the devotion to wealth and materialism.

Barry, Colman J. THE CATHOLIC CHURCH AND GERMAN AMERICANS. Milwaukee: Bruce Publishing Co., 1953. xii, 348 p.

This is a study of factional struggles within the Roman Catholic hierarchy following the Civil War. Of importance is the Papacy's repudiation of liberalist and nationalist attitudes in the American church and the restoration of unity.

Beaver, R. Pierce. CHURCH, STATE, AND THE AMERICAN INDIANS: TWO AND A HALF CENTURIES OF PARTNERSHIP BETWEEN PROTESTANT CHURCHES AND GOVERNMENT. St. Louis: Concordia, 1966. 230 p.

Until the 1890s, Protestants carried on a campaign against government aid to parochial schools, but federal support for missionary activities among the Indians was not questioned. Both the government and missionaries believed education and Christianization were essential in civilizing the aborigines, and missionaries became agents of governmental policy.

Bednarowski, Mary Farrell. "Spiritualism in Wisconsin in the Nineteenth Century." WISCONSIN MAGAZINE OF HISTORY 59 (Autumn 1975): 3-19.

Bednarowski argues that spiritualism stood in the context of nineteenth-century attempts to reconcile science and religion, and advanced the belief that science might free religion from the strictures of dogma and authoritarianism. Wisconsin was a fertile ground for this set of beliefs that emphasized the existence of life after death and the survival of human personality.

Bell, John L., Jr. "The Presbyterian Church and the Negro in North Carolina During Reconstruction." NORTH CAROLINA HISTORICAL REVIEW 40 (January 1963): 15-36.

The separation of Negroes from white congregations and the formation of separate Negro churches were the most significant developments between 1865 and 1875. They represented a reaction against the civil and political freedom of the Negro, missionary activities of the Northern Presbyterian Church, and Negro demands for religious equality.

Bellah, Robert N. THE BROKEN COVENANT: AMERICAN CIVIL RELIGION IN TIME OF TRIAL. New York: Seabury, 1975. xvi, 172 p.

Bellah depicts an early American society based on individualism and communalism. Americans transformed individual experience into group commitment until the Industrial Revolution, when self-interest without communal concern became the way of life and caused civil religion to decline.

Benjamin, Philip S. THE PHILADELPHIA QUAKERS IN THE INDUSTRIAL AGE, 1865-1920. Philadelphia: Temple University Press, 1976. 301 p.

Factionalism had a debilitating effect on Quakerism during this period. At the same time, however, the sect made positive responses to industrialism, women's rights, and war.

Benkart, Paula K. "Changing Attitudes of Presbyterians Toward Southern and Eastern European Immigrants, 1880-1914." JOURNAL OF PRESBYTERIAN HISTORY 49 (Fall 1971): 222-45.

The first response of Presbyterians toward immigrants was an identification of Americanism with Protestant Christianity. In time, they saw the immigrant as their brother and as a target of social uplift.

Berkhofer, Robert F., Jr. "Model Zions for the American Indian." AMERICAN QUARTERLY 15 (Summer 1963): 176-90.

Model Zions were manual-labor boarding schools that were used as agencies for missionary activity. These institutions were pursued in the nineteenth century by reformers who believed that Protestantism embraced the highest evolution of morals and that Indians could be persuaded to adopt the white man's religion and other modes of behavior if he were brought into model communities.

_____. SALVATION AND THE SAVAGE: AN ANALYSIS OF PROTESTANT MISSIONS AND AMERICAN INDIAN RESPONSE, 1787-1862. Lexington: University of Kentucky Press, 1965. xiv, 186 p.

Berkhofer argues that seventy-five years of missionary efforts failed to achieve objectives. The work was tremendous and it takes more than one generation to bring a transition from savagery to civilization.

Betts, John Rickards. "Darwinism, Evolution, and American Catholic Thought, 1860-1900." CATHOLIC HISTORICAL REVIEW 45 (July 1959): 161-85.

Many liberal Protestants silenced others who wanted to do battle with science, because they believed that science, historical criticism, and the comparative method would be significant weapons in assaulting the Catholic Church. Catholic churchmen and theologians, although more concerned with liberalism in Europe, attacked Darwinian evolution.

Bicha, Karel D. "Prairie Radicals: A Common Pietism." JOURNAL OF CHURCH AND STATE 18 (Winter 1976): 79-94.

This is a study of selected "prairie radicals" who were associated with third-party movements such as the populists. They all shared a common religious experience in pietistic or sectarian Protestantism which was social rather than theological.

Blanks, W.D. "Corrective Church Discipline in the Presbyterian Churches of the Nineteenth-Century South." JOURNAL OF PRESBYTERIAN HISTORY 44 (June 1966): 89-105.

> Membership standards of southern churches were very strict. Members were required to attend church services, support the church, and live moral lives within the standard set by the Word of God.

Bode, Frederick A. PROTESTANTISM AND THE NEW SOUTH: NORTH CAROLINA BAPTISTS AND METHODISTS IN POLITICAL CRISIS, 1894-1903. Charlottesville: University Press of Virginia, 1975. 171 p.

> This is a study of the adjustments Baptists and Methodists made in response to Populism and other movements. These denominations supported industrialism since they saw that it was replacing the agrarian way.

_____. "Religion and Class Hegemony: A Populist Critique in North Carolina." JOURNAL OF SOUTHERN HISTORY 37 (August 1971): 417-38.

> It is Bode's view that southern white Protestantism adhered to the doctrine that churches should only devote their activity to life in the world to come and not to life on earth. This had immense social implications since it became a mechanism of ruling-class hegemony, and it was attacked by populists in North Carolina for this reason.

Bodo, John R. THE PROTESTANT CLERGY AND PUBLIC ISSUES, 1812-1848. Princeton, N.J.: Princeton University Press, 1954. xiv, 291 p.

> American clergy were a self-conscious group that formed an American theocracy. They held a pessimistic view of man, argued that the nation should be Christian, but not Catholic, supported the Indians and Negro colonization, and favored temperance.

Boles, John B. RELIGION IN ANTEBELLUM KENTUCKY. Lexington: University Press of Kentucky, 1976. x, 148 p.

> Boles covers the establishment of Presbyterian, Baptist and Methodist churches; the disruptions of revivalism; the splintering of the Presbyterians; and the appeal of Shakerism. He devotes additional chapters to Catholicism and black Christianity.

Boren, Carter E. RELIGION ON THE TEXAS FRONTIER. San Antonio, Tex.: Naylor Co., 1968. xv, 375 p.

> This is a study of the Disciples of Christ, their evangelistic program, and missionary activity. They played an important role in the development of higher education by founding Texas Christian University.

Brauer, Jerald C. "Images of Religion in America." CHURCH HISTORY 30 (March 1961): 3-18.

The images of religion that nonclerical European visitors to America during the nineteenth century presented to their people are delineated. The author emphasizes Francis Grund and Tocqueville.

Brown, C.G. "Christocratic Liberalism in the Episcopal Church." HISTORICAL MAGAZINE OF THE PROTESTANT EPISCOPAL CHURCH 37 (March 1968): 5-38.

Christocratic liberalism was a response to evolution and Biblical criticism in the nineteenth century. Brown concludes that American Broad Churchmen, who espoused freedom in thought and action, made a response to the new science and new criticism from within orthodoxy that was liberal.

Brown, Ira V. LYMAN ABBOTT, CHRISTIAN EVOLUTIONIST: A STUDY IN RELIGIOUS LIBERALISM. Cambridge, Mass.: Harvard University Press, 1953. ix, 303 p.

Abbott, as editor of the OUTLOOK, reflected reaction to new ideas in the late nineteenth and early twentieth centuries. He changed from a believer in God the Creator, in 1870, to the belief in God as an immanent force and in the Bible as a record of ethical development.

Bruce, Dickson D., Jr. AND THEY ALL SANG HALLELUJAH: PLAIN-FOLK CAMP-MEETING RELIGION, 1800-1845. Knoxville: University of Tennessee Press, 1974. xii, 155 p.

Bruce argues that camp-meeting religion supplied the plain folk with a method of dealing with the world and that conversion gave them new values. The camp meeting was not a sideshow, but a serious institution.

_____. "Religion, Society and Culture in the Old South." AMERICAN QUARTERLY 26 (October 1974): 399-416.

Although both plain folk and slaves drew on evangelical Protestantism in formulating their religious traditions, each developed distinctive patterns. Bruce examines the morphology of conversion experiences to elucidate differences.

Buell, Lawrence I. "Unitarian Aesthetics and Emerson's Poet-Priest." AMERICAN QUARTERLY 20 (Spring 1968): 3-20.

Buell explores the connection between the Unitarian movement and the literary renaissance. He argues that Unitarians made religion a matter of moral and spiritual improvement, and, with this, religion and art became increasingly related.

_____. "The Unitarian Movement and the Art of Preaching in 19th Century America." AMERICAN QUARTERLY 24 (May 1972): 166-90.

This is an essay in the history of homiletics in which Buell contends that Unitarian preachers emphasized preaching as an art in which they attempted to raise literary standards. This spirit of innovation faded with the rise of evangelicalism in the 1830s and liberalization in the ranks of the orthodox.

Cannon, M. Hamlin. "Migration of English Mormons to America." AMERICAN HISTORICAL REVIEW 52 (April 1946): 436-55.

During its formative years, the Mormon Church drew most of its converts from the poor and downtrodden of England. Joseph Smith blessed twelve apostles in 1835 and sent them forth to preach to all nations and in all tongues, an undertaking continued by Brigham Young.

Carwardine, Richard. "The Second Great Awakening in the Urban Centers: An Examination of Methodism and the 'New Measures.'" JOURNAL OF AMERICAN HISTORY 59 (September 1972): 327-40.

Carwardine challenges the interpretation that Charles G. Finney invented the "New Measures" in revivalism, such as the mourners' bench, and carried revivals to the cities. He shows that Methodists preceded Finney both in using the "New Measures" and in introducing revivals in eastern urban centers.

Casper, Henry W. HISTORY OF THE CATHOLIC CHURCH IN NEBRASKA. Vol. 1: THE CHURCH ON THE NORTHERN PLAINS, 1838-1874. Milwaukee: Bruce Publishing Co., 1960. xx, 344 p.

The church in Nebraska is presented as regional history. The author shows the beginnings of Catholicism in the region and its development through the Civil War period.

_____. HISTORY OF THE CATHOLIC CHURCH IN NEBRASKA. Vol. 2: THE CHURCH ON THE FADING FRONTIER, 1864-1910. Vol. 3: CATHOLIC CHAPTERS IN NEBRASKA IMMIGRATION, 1870-1900. Milwaukee: Bruce Publishing Co., 1966. xvi, 388, xii, 201 p.

Many of the Nebraska settlers following the Civil War were Catholics and they made an indelible mark on the state. These volumes emphasize the conflicts surrounding the founding of Catholic communities, churches, and schools; financial problems; the labors of James O'Connor, first bishop of Omaha; and organized Catholic emigration.

Clark, Clifford E., Jr. "The Changing Nature of Protestantism in Mid-Nineteenth Century America: Henry Ward Beecher's SEVEN LECTURES TO YOUNG MEN." JOURNAL OF AMERICAN HISTORY 57 (March 1971): 832-46.

American Protestantism changed from an other-worldly perspective to an uncritical acceptance of the status quo. Beecher's popular SEVEN LECTURES was an expression of the status quo with a decidely middle-class orientation.

Clebsh, William A. AMERICAN RELIGIOUS THOUGHT: A HISTORY. Chicago: University of Chicago Press, 1973. xxi, 212 p.

The central theme of this study is that religious thought focused on the idea that the universe is hospitable to man, an aesthetic theme. Clebsh emphasizes Jonathan Edwards, Ralph Waldo Emerson, and William James in developing this thesis.

_____. "Christian Interpretations of the Civil War." CHURCH HISTORY 30 (June 1961): 212-22.

Theologians viewed the Civil War, regardless of the side they were on, as an act of God. In this essay, the ideas of Horace Bushnell and Philip Schaff are illuminated.

Cole, Charles C., Jr. THE SOCIAL IDEAS OF NORTHERN EVANGELISTS, 1826-1860. New York: Columbia University Press, 1954. 268 p.

The period 1826 to 1860 was one of uplift and reformation of American society, and many uplift organizations were the product of Congregational, Presbyterian, Methodist, and Baptist evangelists. Cole also discusses specific evangelists and their wealthy lay supporters.

Cross, Robert D. THE EMERGENCE OF LIBERAL CATHOLICISM IN AMERICA. Cambridge, Mass.: Harvard University Press, 1958. xiv, 328 p.

During the last third of the nineteenth century, there were conflicts within the Catholic Church over the tempo of Americanization and parochial and public education. Liberals felt at home in American culture, sought accomodation to facilitate conversions, and attempted to infuse American initiative into the church.

Cross, Whitney R. THE BURNED-OVER DISTRICT: THE SOCIAL AND INTELLECTUAL HISTORY OF ENTHUSIASTIC RELIGION IN WESTERN NEW YORK. Ithaca, N.Y.: Cornell University Press, 1950. xiii, 383 p.

Enthusiasts in western New York were inspired by an interest in evangelism, politics, and social reform. Cross covers Charles G. Finney, the anti-Masons, temperance advocates, the Mormons, John Humphrey Noyes, and others.

Crowe, Charles. "Christian Socialism and the First Church of Humanity."
CHURCH HISTORY 35 (March 1966): 93-106.

During the 1840s, a number of critics attacked the Christian status
quo and called for a visible communion of men. They demanded
a church of humanity and attempted to forge a Christian socialism
through various communitarian settlements.

Cuddy, Edward. "Pro-Germanism and American Catholicism." CATHOLIC
HISTORICAL REVIEW 54 (October 1968): 427-54.

Pro-German tendencies during World War I among Germans and
Irish within the church sprang from immigrant nationalism. The
church itself stood for peace, neutrality, and patriotism.

Cunningham, Raymond J. "From Holiness to Healing: The Faith Cure in
America, 1872-1892." CHURCH HISTORY 43 (December 1974): 499-513.

Perfectionists before the Civil War believed that all Christians
should seek a second blessing that would bring complete and in-
stantaneous purification from sin and perfect holiness toward God.
Such thinking was characteristic of religious thought following the
war, but the earliest sign of a new departure was in healing by
faith and this brought a transformation of perfectionism from denomination to sect.

_____. "The Impact of Christian Science on the American Churches, 1880-
1910." AMERICAN HISTORICAL REVIEW 72 (April 1967): 885-905.

Clerical reaction to Christian Science covered a broad spectrum of
opinion, from utter rejection to cautious approval. More clergymen attacked the cult because of its relation to historic Christianity, moral tendencies, bearing on Christian social ethics, and the
hygienic implications of its therapy.

Dabbs, James McBride. HAUNTED BY GOD. Richmond, Va.: John Knox
Press, 1972. 255 p.

In explaining the uniqueness of southern history, Dabbs argues that
the South professed to be Christian, but could not reconcile social
institutions with beliefs. The southern Protestant churches did not
meet the needs of southern people.

Daniel, W. Harrison. "The Southern Baptists in the Confederacy." CIVIL
WAR HISTORY 6 (December 1960): 389-401.

Southern Baptists blamed the North for forcing war on a peace-
loving people. They ministered to the needs of Confederate soldiers, and they provided Bibles, New Testaments, and religious
tracts for the people of the Confederacy.

_____. "Southern Presbyterians and the Negro in the Early National Period." JOURNAL OF NEGRO HISTORY 58 (July 1973): 291-312.

Presbyterians in the early national period did not advocate emancipation, but they did not believe that slaveholding possessed divine favor. They presented numerous arguments to justify why the ideals of the Declaration of Independence were not applicable to blacks.

_____. "Southern Presbyterians in the Confederacy." NORTH CAROLINA HISTORICAL REVIEW 44 (July 1967): 231-55.

Presbyterian leaders were outspoken and articulate in their pro-secession sentiments, but they did not influence the course of secession. They made valiant efforts to minister to the soldiers during the war and their churches suffered as a result of the conflict.

_____. "Southern Protestantism and Secession." HISTORIAN 29 (May 1967): 391-408.

Churchmen of the South counseled peace in the election of 1860, but they supported secession after Lincoln's victory. They advanced arguments already made familiar by politicians and failed to exert forceful leadership.

_____. "Southern Protestantism and the Negro, 1860-1865." NORTH CAROLINA HISTORICAL REVIEW 41 (July 1964): 338-59.

By 1861, Protestantism was making its greatest effort to Christianize the Negro. During the war, this work suffered, but interest was high because many Protestants viewed the war as Divine judgment for inadequately performing the mission to the Negro.

_____. "Virginia Baptists, 1861-1865." VIRGINIA MAGAZINE OF HISTORY AND BIOGRAPHY 72 (January 1964): 94-114.

Virginia Baptists were troubled by sectional tensions before 1860, but they did not oppose secession after Lincoln ordered troops. They were patriots during the war, although they exhibited little bitterness toward the North or federal authorities.

_____. "Virginia Baptists and the Myth of the Southern Mind, 1865-1900." SOUTH ATLANTIC QUARTERLY 73 (Winter 1974): 85-98.

The southern mind has been described as provincial or parochial, narrow and bigoted, and outside the mainstream of American thought and attitudes. Daniel examines the thought of Virginia Baptists and finds that their opinions constituted a part of the mainstream of American social and intellectual development.

_____. "Virginia Baptists and the Negro, 1865-1902." VIRGINIA MAGA-
ZINE OF HISTORY AND BIOGRAPHY 76 (July 1968): 340-63.

The collapse of the Confederacy did not change the views of Virginia Baptists concerning the propriety of slavery or alter their
concept of the Negro. During the late nineteenth century, they
expressed concern for the spiritual and educational welfare of
blacks but their determination to maintain white supremacy made
their concern virtually useless.

_____. "Virginia Baptists and the Negro in the Antebellum Era." JOURNAL
OF NEGRO HISTORY 56 (January 1971): 1-16.

Baptist churches acknowledged that hereditary slavery was not a
religious or moral issue and that discussion of it should be left to
politicians. Throughout the antebellum period, Negroes were members of Baptist churches in Virginia, subject to the same rules of
discipline as whites, but when slavery was attacked, Baptists entered into a spirited defense.

Davis, Lawrence B. IMMIGRANTS, BAPTISTS, AND THE PROTESTANT MIND
IN AMERICA. Urbana: University of Illinois Press, 1973. 230 p.

This study deals with the response of Baptists to immigration between 1880 and 1925. Baptists were supportive of most immigrant
groups, including the Chinese.

Davis, Moshe. THE EMERGENCE OF CONSERVATIVE JUDAISM: THE HIS-
TORICAL SCHOOL IN NINETEENTH CENTURY AMERICA. Philadelphia:
Jewish Publication Society of America, 1963. xiv, 527 p.

Judasim was in a state of flux in the nineteenth century with reform, orthodox, and conservative viewpoints emerging concerning
Jewish life and thought. The conservative or historical school
struggled with its counterparts over education and the handling of
immigrants.

Dawley, Powel Mills. THE STORY OF THE GENERAL THEOLOGICAL SEMI-
NARY: A SESQUICENTENNIAL HISTORY, 1817-1867. New York: Oxford
University Press, 1969. xvii, 390 p.

This is a study of theological education in the Anglican tradition.
The seminary was caught in the conflicts between the Evangelical
and High Church branches of the denomination and did not achieve
a sound financial and scholastic footing until well into the nineteenth century.

Delp, Robert W. "Andrew Jackson Davis: Prophet of American Spiritualism."
JOURNAL OF AMERICAN HISTORY 54 (June 1967): 43-56.

Davis became noted for his ability to diagnose disease clairvoy-
antly and for his conversations with the spirits of the Swedenborg
brothers. His fame spread beyond central New York when his
psychic discourses were published in the 1840s, and he gave spiritualism respectability through the publication of more than thirty
works.

Des Champs, Margaret Burr. "Union or Division? South Atlantic Presbyterians
and Southern Nationalism, 1820-1861." JOURNAL OF SOUTHERN HISTORY
20 (November 1954): 484-98.

Des Champs shows that southern Presbyterians tried to stem the tide
of southern nationalism before the Civil War. They believed that
both the Union and the Presbyterian General Assembly were di-
vinely ordained and they did not support nationalism until it was
evident that the fireeaters had won control of public opinion.

Doherty, Robert W. THE HICKSITE SEPARATION: A SOCIOLOGICAL ANAL-
YSIS OF RELIGIOUS SCHISM IN EARLY NINETEENTH CENTURY AMERICA.
New Brunswick, N.J.: Rutgers University Press, 1967. vii, 157 p.

This is an examination of the years 1827-28 in the Society of
Friends in Pennsylvania. Urban orthodox Friends, who had prospered from business, wanted their economic materialism and attempted to modify the Friends' individualistic faith, but they were
opposed by liberal Hicksites who opposed orthodoxy.

_____. "Religion and Society: The Hicksite Separation of 1827." AMERICAN
QUARTERLY 17 (Spring 1965): 63-80.

Doherty explores the influence of society on religion in terms of
the Quaker schism of 1827. He argues that the schism resulted
from churchly and sectarian tendencies with orthodox Friends seeking to create a church-oriented society and the Hicksites attempting to preserve and restore the sectarian tendencies in which activity rather than belief was the key to salvation.

_____. "Social Bases of the Presbyterian Schism of 1837-1838: The Phila-
delphia Case." JOURNAL OF SOCIAL HISTORY 2 (Fall 1968): 69-79.

Presbyterians split into Old School and New School groups, and
historians have shown that the New Schoolers prospered where the
socioeconomically disinherited were adherents. In Philadelphia,
however, New School converts were wealthier than members of the
Old School faction, which suggests that social bases perhaps more
than environment were responsible for the schism.

Dolan, Jay P. "A Critical Period in American Catholicism." REVIEW OF
POLITICS 35 (October 1973): 523-36.

The middle decades of the nineteenth century were a critical period in American Catholicism, during which the church acquired a more settled form. The rise of the city and industrialization changed the shape of religion and conditioned the pattern of the future.

_____. THE IMMIGRANT CHURCH: NEW YORK'S IRISH AND GERMAN CATHOLICS, 1815-1865. Baltimore: Johns Hopkins University Press, 1975. xiv, 221 p.

Irish and German immigrants made the important decision that gave the Catholic community its shape today. The Catholic Church withdrew into its own community with a national parish and parochial schools in response to nativism and social concern.

_____. "Immigrants in the City: New York's Irish and German Catholics." CHURCH HISTORY 41 (September 1972): 354-68.

Irish and German Catholics were New York's most significant ethnic groups in the antebellum period. The ethnic parish gave them an opportunity to worship in the way of their ancestors and this enabled the Catholic Church to survive in a new environment.

Drury, Clifford M. MARCUS AND NARCISSA WHITMAN AND THE OPENING OF OLD OREGON. 2 vols. Glendale, Calif.: Arthur H. Clark, 1973. 476; 435 p.

These volumes are a refinement of Drury's previous eight books on the missionaries of the American Board of Commissioners of Foreign Missions. They cover the Whitmans from 1830 to 1847.

_____. PRESBYTERIAN PANORAMA: ONE HUNDRED FIFTY YEARS OF NATIONAL MISSIONS HISTORY. Philadelphia: Board of Christian Education, Presbyterian Church in the United States of America, 1952. xvi, 458 p.

Drury emphasizes the period from 1802 to 1952. He discusses the expansion of missions, the schism of 1837, the challenge of slavery, role of women, and the work in Alaska.

Durnbaugh, Donald F. "Work and Hope: The Spirituality of Radical Pietist Communitarians." CHURCH HISTORY 39 (March 1970): 72-90.

This is a sketch of pietist communities such as the Woman in the Wilderness, Ephrata, the Harmony Society, Separatists of Zoar, and the Community of True Inspiration or the Amana Society. The characteristics of these societies were an advocacy of celibacy, a millenial expectation, and an emphasis on active work rather than contemplation.

Eames, S. Morris. THE PHILOSOPHY OF ALEXANDER CAMPBELL. Bethany, W.Va.: Bethany College, 1966. 110 p.

Campbell, the founder of the Disciples of Christ, was influenced by Locke and the Scottish common-sense realists. This explains the curious combination of reason and sense perception with revelation and faith that forms the basis of his thought.

Edgell, David P. WILLIAM ELLERY CHANNING: AN INTELLECTUAL PORTRAIT. Boston: Beacon Press, 1955. xvi, 264 p.

Channing's life is covered briefly, but his Unitarian theology, place in the transcendentalist movement, and political theory are emphasized. He is depicted as a publicist more than a creative thinker and as a moralist rather than a critic.

Eighmy, John Lee. CHURCHES IN CULTURAL CAPTIVITY: A HISTORY OF THE SOCIAL ATTITUDES OF SOUTHERN BAPTISTS. Knoxville: University of Tennessee Press, 1972. xviii, 249 p.

In this study of social thought from the Southern Baptist Convention of 1845, Eighmy shows that Southern Baptists were leading spokesmen of the southern social mind. They were influenced by the social gospel, and preoccupied by the church's responsibility for social reform.

_____. "Religious Liberalism in the South During the Progressive Era." CHURCH HISTORY 38 (September 1969): 359-72.

Social Christianity has been treated as the Protestant response to industrialization in the North. Religious elements in southern progressivism indicate that the region's church life was not in the grip of fundamentalism and that the Social Gospel broke the conservative solidarity of southern religion.

Ellis, John Tracy. PERSPECTIVES IN AMERICAN CATHOLICISM. Benedictine Studies, no. 5. Baltimore: Helicon Press, 1963. xvi, 313 p.

This is a collection of addresses, sermons, and other pieces of occasional writing that illuminate Catholic history. They cover the position of Catholic leaders on the church-state question, role of the laity, Catholic personalities, and other matters.

_____, ed. DOCUMENTS OF AMERICAN CATHOLIC HISTORY. Milwaukee: Bruce Publishing Co., 1956. xxvi, 667 p.

This collection begins with the Papal Bull of 1493 and ends with the founding of the CATHOLIC WORKER of 1933 and Pope Pius XII's encyclical of 1939. Reports on missions, landmarks of religion, and the efforts of the hierarchy to protect labor are covered.

Elsmere, Jane Shaffer. HENRY WARD BEECHER, THE INDIANA YEARS, 1837-1847. Indianapolis: Indiana Historical Society, 1973. xiii, 317 p.

> This is an account of Beecher's Indiana ministry that details his daily life, the people he encountered, and his challenges, responsibilities, disappointments, and successes. The author, however, omits an account of Beecher's ministry in the context of revivalism.

Endy, Melvin B., Jr. "Abraham Lincoln and American Civil Religion: a Reinterpretation." CHURCH HISTORY 44 (June 1975): 229-41.

> Lincoln has been characterized as the leading theologian of the religion of the Republic. Endy sees him, however, as a compromiser concerning the Negro and slavery who was not a consistent spokesman for the equality of men or democracy.

Ericksen, Ephraim Edward. THE PSYCHOLOGICAL AND ETHICAL ASPECTS OF MORMON GROUP LIFE. Chicago: University of Chicago Press, 1922. Reprint. Salt Lake City: University of Utah Press, 1975. xxii, 101 p.

> Mormon history is explained through the use of social psychology. Ericksen saw Mormonism as the response of a people to specific crises and needs rather than as the product of Divine Revelation.

Esslinger, Dean R. "American German and Irish Attitudes Toward Neutrality, 1914-1917: A Study of Catholic Minorities." CATHOLIC HISTORICAL REVIEW 53 (July 1967): 194-216.

> Many Catholics considered neutrality in terms of the national interest of the United States, but a greater percentage of them than the rest of the population were sympathetic to the Central Powers. Many Catholic publications openly or subtly rejected the allied cause.

Farley, Ena L. "Methodists and Baptists on the Issue of Black Equality in New York, 1865 to 1868." JOURNAL OF NEGRO HISTORY 61 (October 1976): 374-92.

> Most clergymen decided that the Thirteenth Amendment settled the moral question of freedom and that the churches should not meddle in moral questions. Only a small minority believed that blacks should be admitted to political and social equality, but they were overwhelmed, and the Methodists and Baptists lost their chance to exert their immense moral influence.

Feingold, Henry L. ZION IN AMERICA: THE JEWISH EXPERIENCE FROM COLONIAL TIMES TO THE PRESENT. New York: Twayne, 1974. xii, 357 p.

> This study develops the story of the Jews in the context of American history. Feingold avoids cataloging prominent Jews and instead emphasizes integration, adaptation, and intragroup relations.

Feldman, Egal. "The Social Gospel and the Jews." AMERICAN JEWISH
HISTORICAL QUARTERLY 58 (March 1969): 308-22.

The new theology accomplished little in improving the relations
between Christian and Jew. If social reform and human betterment
were objectives of the Social Gospelers, there is little evidence
that the elimination of bigotry and prejudice against the Jew was
a significant part of their goals.

Findlay, James. "Moody, 'Gapmen,' and the Gospel: The Early Days of
Moody Bible Institute." CHURCH HISTORY 31 (September 1962): 322-35.

This is a study of Dwight L. Moody's campaign in urban evangelism in the 1880s. The "Gapmen" were graduates of his Bible institute who were trained in the message and how to deliver it in
the workaday world.

Fish, John O. "Southern Methodism and Accommodation of the Negro, 1902-
1915." JOURNAL OF NEGRO HISTORY 60 (July 1970): 200-214.

Southern Methodist's contribution to Negro work during the Progressive era was not predicated upon notions of Christian brotherhood and love. They were afraid he would be replaced by the
Roman Catholic Italian immigrant, but many were convinced the
Negro was inferior and uneducable.

Flynt, Wayne. "Dissent in Zion: Alabama Baptists and Social Issues, 1900-
1914." JOURNAL OF SOUTHERN HISTORY 35 (November 1969): 523-42.

Between 1900 and 1914, Alabama Baptists, mostly in the cities,
devoted themselves to social concerns and proposed ameliorative
solutions not unlike those voiced by proponents of the Social Gospel in the northeast. These social critics remained fundamentalists
and devoted to a literal interpretation of the scriptures, but they
became social activists because of the existence of poverty and
the need for prohibition.

Fordham, Monroe. MAJOR THEMES IN NORTHERN BLACK RELIGIOUS
THOUGHT, 1800-1860. Hicksville, N.Y.: Exposition, 1975. xii, 172 p.

Northern blacks adopted the religious doctrines of whites associated
with evangelism and used them to criticize northern society. The
idea of universal equality was such a doctrine.

Frederick, Peter J. KNIGHTS OF THE GOLDEN RULE: THE INTELLECTUAL
AS CHRISTIAN SOCIAL REFORMER IN THE 1890s. Lexington: University
Press of Kentucky, 1976. xvi, 323 p.

This is a critical revisionist view of the Social Gospelers. Frederick was an active participant in the free speech movement at
Berkeley in 1964 and he examines the Social Gospel crusade in
terms of its effectiveness based on the standards of more recent traditions.

Gabriel, Ralph Henry. RELIGION AND LEARNING AT YALE: THE CHURCH OF CHRIST IN THE COLLEGE AND UNIVERSITY, 1757-1957. New Haven, Conn.: Yale University Press, 1958. xii, 271 p.

The Church of Christ is a parish church within an institution of higher learning. This is a study of two centuries of Western religious ideas, with glimpses of the church and Yale College.

Gaustad, Edwin Scott. DISSENT IN AMERICAN RELIGION. Chicago History of American Religion Series. Chicago: University of Chicago Press, 1973. xii, 184 p.

In this volume, Gaustad shows that schismatics in American religion have spurned national ideals. He emphasizes that authority should hear what dissenters have to say.

_____. HISTORICAL ATLAS OF RELIGION IN AMERICA. New York: Harper and Row, 1962. xii, 179 p.

Nearly 150 maps, graphs, and statistical tables reveal denominational growth in several periods as well as the geographical concentrations of major religious bodies. Religious regionalism is shown.

_____, ed. THE RISE OF ADVENTISM: RELIGION AND SOCIETY IN MID-NINETEENTH CENTURY AMERICA. New York: Harper and Row, 1974. xx, 329 p.

Many believe millenialism is an exotic belief. These essays by historians, such as Winthrop Hudson, Timothy Smith, William McLoughlin, and others, show it was not.

Gleason, Philip. THE CONSERVATIVE REFORMERS: GERMAN-AMERICAN CATHOLICS AND THE SOCIAL ORDER. Notre Dame, Ind.: University of Notre Dame Press, 1968. x, 272 p.

This is a study of the Roman Catholic Central-Verein begun by German Catholics in 1855. It began propagandizing on social questions after 1900 and played a part in awakening a social consciousness on the part of Catholics generally.

Goldstein, Doris S. TRIAL OF FAITH: RELIGION AND POLITICS IN TOCQUEVILLE'S THOUGHT. New York: Elsevier, 1975. xi, 144 p.

Goldstein shows Tocqueville's efforts to reconcile the liberal spirit and religion. His visit to America convinced him that republicanism and religious faith were not incompatible, although he failed to understand Protestant revivalism.

Gottschalk, Stephen. THE EMERGENCE OF CHRISTIAN SCIENCE IN AMERICAN RELIGIOUS LIFE. Berkeley and Los Angeles: University of California Press, 1973. xxix, 305 p.

Gottschalk covers the period from 1885 to 1910 and examines the religious situation of the Gilded Age, Mary Baker Eddy's teachings, schisms and conflicts in the young denomination, development of institutional authority, and the impact of Christian Science on the lives of individuals.

Gravely, William. GILBERT HAVEN, METHODIST ABOLITIONIST: A STUDY IN RACE, RELIGION, AND REFORM, 1850-1880. Edited by the Commission on Archives and History of the United Methodist Church. Nashville: Abingdon, 1973. 272 p.

Haven was an anti-Garrisonian abolitionist who became an outspoken racial egalitarian during the Civil War and Reconstruction. He became a bishop in Atlanta in 1872, and his excoriations of those who opposed equality and amalgamation brought about the end of his administration.

Green, Fletcher M. "Northern Missionary Activities in the South, 1846-1861." JOURNAL OF SOUTHERN HISTORY 21 (May 1955): 147-72.

Resentment in New England against the American Home Missionary Society and the American Board of Commissioners for Foreign Missions for tacitly recognizing slavery prompted the formation of the American Home Missionary Association. At first, missionaries of this new antislavery organization worked effectively in the upper South, but eventually, in the minds of many, it became an instrument of sectionalism.

Griffen, Clyde C. "Rich Laymen and Early Social Christianity." CHURCH HISTORY 36 (March 1967): 45-65.

This is a study of the reaction of rich laymen to social Christianity in New York City. Clerical social reformers encountered a great deal of tolerance from wealthy parishioners, especially within the Episcopal Church, and this made social reform more respectable and gained it a wider audience.

Griffin, Clifford S. "Converting the Catholics: American Benevolent Societies and the Ante-Bellum Crusade against the Church." CATHOLIC HISTORICAL REVIEW 47 (October 1961): 325-43.

Organizations such as the American Bible Society, American Tract Society, and the American Home Missionary Society mounted a crusade against the Catholic Church. This was part of their struggle to establish a Protestant Kingdom of God on earth and bring about the moral regeneration of the nation.

Gutman, Herbert G. "Protestantism and the American Labor Movement: The Christian Spirit in the Gilded Age." AMERICAN HISTORICAL REVIEW 72 (October 1966): 74-101.

Protestantism in the Gilded Age permeated the social structure and value system of the nation. There were specific connections between the religious mode of expression of trade unionists and Protestant workers.

Guttman, Allen. "From Brownson to Eliot: The Conservative Theory of Church and State." AMERICAN QUARTERLY 17 (Fall 1965): 483-500.

American conservatives for the most part have ignored the necessity of a church establishment preached by Edmund Burke and Pope Leo XIII, the important nineteenth-century formulator of church-state theory. Only Orestes Brownson and T.S. Eliot called eloquently for establishment, and they were out of step with American attitudes.

Hanchett, William. "The Blue Law Gospel in Gold Rush California." PACIFIC HISTORICAL REVIEW 24 (November 1955): 361-68.

The Blue Law Gospel proclaimed belief in the sinfulness of alcohol, gambling, swearing, smoking, theater-going, dancing, cards, and the desecration of the Sabbath. This essay surveys the success of Sabbatarianism in gold-rush California.

Handy, Robert T. A CHRISTIAN AMERICA: PROTESTANT HOPE AND HISTORICAL REALITIES. New York: Oxford University Press, 1971. x, 282 p.

Handy argues that Protestants have hoped that ultimately America would be fully Christian. By the end of the nineteenth century, however, Protestant priorities had been reversed by the progress of secular civilization and the churches had become the captives of American culture.

_____. A HISTORY OF THE CHURCHES IN THE UNITED STATES AND CANADA. New York: Oxford University Press, 1977. xiii, 471 p.

The histories of North American churches seem parallel and oddly detached from one another. Church history is emphasized in this study and theological developments mostly are downplayed.

Hansen, Klaus J. QUEST FOR EMPIRE: THE POLITICAL KINGDOM OF GOD AND THE COUNCIL OF FIFTY IN MORMON HISTORY. East Lansing: Michigan State University Press, 1967. 237 p.

The Kingdom of God was a vital element in Mormon thought and it occupied Mormon leaders for more than half a century. The Council of Fifty was an outgrowth of Joseph Smith's millenial thought and it served as a political organization that helped to insure the success of the Mormon experiment.

Harrell, David Edwin, Jr. QUEST FOR A CHRISTIAN AMERICA: THE
DISCIPLES OF CHRIST AND AMERICAN SOCIETY TO 1866. Nashville: Disciples of Christ Historical Society, 1966. xvi, 256 p.

> This is an analysis of the mind of the Disciples. The author treats
> the denomination's stands on slavery and sectionalism, pacifism and
> patriotism, the American economic gospel, and other social issues.

_____. "The Sectional Origins of the Churches of Christ." JOURNAL OF
SOUTHERN HISTORY 30 (August 1964): 261-77.

> The Disciples of Christ emerged as a denomination in the 1830s but
> it was soon rent by dissension along sectional lines, a fact that was
> acknowledged in 1906 when the southern-offshoot Churches of Christ
> was recognized. This split was the product of urban and rural prej-
> udices, as well as agricultural and middle-class economic views.

_____. "Sin and Sectionalism: A Case Study of Morality in the Nineteenth-
Century South." MISSISSIPPI QUARTERLY 19 (Fall 1966): 157-70.

> Harrell uses the Disciples of Christ as a case study of southern
> moral codes. They adopted a puritanical moral code, but this
> code was promulgated in pulpits all over the section well into the
> twentieth century.

_____. A SOCIAL HISTORY OF THE DISCIPLES OF CHRIST. Vol. 2: THE
SOCIAL SOURCES OF DIVISION IN THE DISCIPLES OF CHRIST, 1865-1900.
Atlanta: Publishing Systems, 1973. xi, 458 p.

> An important indigenous denomination, the Disciples were plagued
> by diversity in social thought and by organizational formlessness.
> This study emphasizes its grassroots dynamics.

Harwood, Thomas F. "British Evangelical Abolitionism and American Churches
in the 1830s." JOURNAL OF SOUTHERN HISTORY 28 (August 1962): 287-
306.

> This is a study of the impact of British antislavery religious groups
> on American churches. British Baptists and Methodists exerted pres-
> sure first and were followed by Presbyterians and Quakers, and
> these pressures helped to produce schisms in these denominations.

Hatch, Carl E. THE CHARLES A. BRIGGS HERESY TRIAL: PROLOGUE TO
TWENTIETH-CENTURY LIBERAL PROTESTANTISM. New York: Exposition
Press, 1969. 139 p.

> The trial of Briggs, a professor of Biblical theology at Union Theo-
> logical Seminary in New York, took place in 1891. His accep-
> tance of German Biblical criticism made him a target of conserva-
> tive Presbyterians, whose actions led the seminary to disaffiliate
> from the Presbyterian Church.

Hennesey, James. "Papacy and Episcopacy in Eighteenth and Nineteenth Century America." RECORDS OF THE AMERICAN CATHOLIC HISTORICAL SOCIETY OF PHILADELPHIA 77 (September 1966): 175-89.

> The Roman Catholic Church in the United States cannot be understood in terms of European experience. American bishops were devoted to the pope, but this was a spiritual loyalty, not mixed with political considerations.

Henry, Stuart C. "The Lane Rebels: A Twentieth Century Look." JOURNAL OF PRESBYTERIAN HISTORY 49 (Spring 1971): 1-14.

> Henry compares the protesting students of the Lane Theological Seminary of the 1830s with the New Left. He finds that the Lane dissenters went out not knowing whither they were going, while the new radicals know where they are bound.

Hinckley, Ted C. "American Anti-Catholicism during the Mexican War." PACIFIC HISTORICAL REVIEW 31 (May 1962): 121-37.

> The 1830s and 1840s were characterized partly by instances of anti-Catholicism, but Protestants did not make the Mexican War an anti-Catholic conflict. This was the case because there was no unified anti-Catholic base to launch a campaign.

_____. "The Presbyterian Leadership in Pioneer Alaska." JOURNAL OF AMERICAN HISTORY 52 (March 1966): 742-56.

> When Protestantism was at its nadir late in the nineteenth century, Presbyterians in frontier Alaska, under the leadership of Sheldon Jackson, exercised strong leadership. They called for territory-wide ecumenical planning, racial equality, and the use of public money to reinforce private investment.

Hopkins, Charles Howard. THE RISE OF THE SOCIAL GOSPEL IN AMERICAN PROTESTANTISM, 1865-1915. Yale Studies in Religious Education. New Haven, Conn.: Yale University Press, 1940. xii, 352 p.

> The Social Gospel arose as reaction against the Industrial Revolution. This is an uncritical study that ignores the movement's connection with socialism and its failure to attack war as a social evil.

Howard, Victor B. "Presbyterians, the Kansas-Nebraska Act, and the Election of 1856." JOURNAL OF PRESBYTERIAN HISTORY 49 (Summer 1971): 133-56.

> New School Presbyterians were committed to the new political movement engendered by the Kansas-Nebraska Act, while those of the Old School were neutral. The election campaign contributed to the final phase of the New School controversy over slavery.

_____. "The Southern Aid Society and the Slavery Controversy." CHURCH HISTORY 41 (June 1972): 208-24.

The Southern Aid Society was formed in 1853 to spread gospel truth in the South and counter the American Home Missionary Society. The rise of this organization served as an excuse for liberals, especially in the West, to work for an end to Home Missionary Society efforts in the South.

Howe, Daniel Walker. THE UNITARIAN CONSCIENCE: HARVARD MORAL PHILOSOPHY, 1805-1861. Cambridge, Mass.: Harvard University Press, 1970. viii, 398 p.

Unitarians were important in American intellectual history because they were at Harvard when it and a few other institutions dominated cultural life and represented the establishment. They became significant when humanitarian and reform movements were on the rise, but their humanism was too genteel and cautious.

Hudson, Winthrop S. THE GREAT TRADITION OF THE AMERICAN CHURCHES. New York: Harper and Brothers, 1953. 282 p.

Churches have flourished and become strong when they have been subjected to coercion of a voluntary sort. At the same time, however, churches must feel a compulsion to fulfill a distinctive vocation in society.

_____. "Protestant Clergy Debate the Nation's Vocation, 1898-1899." CHURCH HISTORY 42 (March 1973): 110-118.

Why did the United States embark on a colonial career in 1898 and then suddenly cease imperial expansion eighteen months later? Hudson argues that the coalescence of opinion leaders among Protestant clergy against imperialism is at least a partial answer to this question.

Huggins, Nathan Irvin. PROTESTANTS AGAINST POVERTY: BOSTON'S CHARITIES, 1870-1900. Westport, Conn.: Greenwood, 1971. xiv, 225 p.

In response to what they believed was a decline of community in the late nineteenth century, Boston's civic leaders and reformers urged right conduct, self-reliance, thrift, industriousness, and temperance on the poor. If poverty-stricken workers accepted Protestant, middle-class values, social fragmentation would be overcome.

Hughes, Richard B. "Old School Presbyterians: Eastern Invaders of Texas, 1830-1865." SOUTHWESTERN HISTORICAL QUARTERLY 74 (January 1971): 324-36.

Old School Presbyterians were influenced by their eastern orientation but this assisted them in giving divine sanction to the slavoc-
racy. They lost the masses to revivalists but they left an important legacy in education.

Hutchison, William R. "Disapproval of Chicago: The Symbolic Trial of
David Swing." JOURNAL OF AMERICAN HISTORY 59 (June 1972): 30-47.

The intellectual history of American religion before 1900 has emphasized the Northeast and Congregationalism, and has depicted
change as having moved from New England to the West. The
Presbyterian hersey trial in 1874 of David Swing for preaching a
liberal gospel indicates that forces of liberalism were operating in
the Midwest before the East caught up with this theology.

_____. "Liberal Protestantism and the 'End of Innocence.'" AMERICAN
QUARTERLY 15 (Summer 1963): 126-39.

Theologians and church historians place the "end of American innocence" at the beginning of the Depression decade. Hutchinson
shows that liberal realism in religion was seen on the popular level
before the 1920s, and on a more serious level from the 1880s.

_____. THE TRANSCENDENTALIST MINISTERS: CHURCH REFORM IN THE
NEW ENGLAND RENAISSANCE. New Haven, Conn.: Yale University Press,
1959. Reprint. Boston: Beacon Press, 1965. xiv, 240 p.

Transcendentalism took form as a protest against the theological
and social assumptions of Boston Unitarians. This is a reassessment
of the theological controversy and of the Concord group's activities as Christian ministers.

Jick, Leon A. THE AMERICANIZATION OF THE SYNAGOGUE, 1820-1870.
Hanover, N.H.: University Press of New England, 1976. xi, 247 p.

American Reform Judaism was the handiwork of central European
Jews who came to the United States during the nineteenth century.
The humble immigrant synagogue was transformed into a reform
temple through enterprising laymen who adapted their church to
the new environment.

Johnson, Charles A. "The Frontier Camp Meeting: Contemporary and Historical Appraisals, 1805-1840." MISSISSIPPI VALLEY HISTORICAL REVIEW 37
(June 1950): 91-110.

The camp meeting has been depicted historically as an orgy of excitement. Johnson sees it as an answer to the spiritual poverty
of the backwoodsman, a civilizing influence, and a means of
awakening communities to religious and humanitarian fervor.

_____. THE FRONTIER CAMP MEETING: RELIGION'S HARVEST TIME.
Dallas: Southern Methodist University Press, 1955. xiv, 325 p.

The camp meeting in the West was begun under the leadership of
the Presbyterians, but the Methodists made it an almost exclusive
operation. The arrangements of the meetings, preachers, sermons,
hymns, and other matters are discussed in this study.

Johnson, Clifton H. "Abolitionist Missionary Activities in North Carolina."
NORTH CAROLINA HISTORICAL REVIEW 40 (July 1963): 295-320.

This is a study of the strife within the ranks of northern and southern Methodism. Abolitionists were sent to North Carolina to labor
among the Wesleyan churches, and southerners were willing to deny
freedom of speech and thought in order to protect the institution of
slavery.

Johnson, James E. "Charles G. Finney and a Theology of Revivalism."
CHURCH HISTORY 38 (September 1969): 338-58.

Finney was a revivalist first and foremost, and his theology was
patterned to fit this career. He moved from Old School to New
School and eventually to perfectionism, which was progress according to the optimism of his time.

Jones, Charles Edwin. PERFECTIONIST PERSUASION: THE HOLINESS MOVE-
MENT AND METHODISM, 1867-1936. Metuchen, N.J.: Scarecrow, 1974.
xix, 242 p.

Jones argues that the holiness movement derived from John Wesley's
conception of Christian perfection. It was developed in response
to worldliness in the Methodist Church after 1865, and included
the Pentecostal Church of the Nazarene and the Pilgrim Holiness
Church.

Keller, Ralph A. "Methodist Newspapers and the Fugitive Slave Law: A New
Perspective for the Slavery Crisis in the North." CHURCH HISTORY 43 (September 1974): 319-39.

Methodist newspapers emphasized the Fugitive Slave Law as a mo-
mentous blunder but there was wide disagreement as to how to proceed against it. Some editors thought that involvement in a political question would damage church unity, while others viewed the
question of morality as a matter the church could not avoid.

Larson, Gustive O. THE "AMERICANIZATION" OF UTAH FOR STATEHOOD.
San Marino, Calif.: Huntington Library, 1971. x, 328 p.

This is a study of the Mormon's retreat from polygamy in the late
nineteenth century. After renouncing this practice in 1890, the

church urged affiliation with the Republican Party as the best
means of gaining self-rule under statehood.

Levesque, George A. "Inherent Reformers–Inherited Orthodoxy: Black Baptists
in Boston, 1800–1873." JOURNAL OF NEGRO HISTORY 60 (October 1975):
491–525.

The black church was a school, forum, political arena, social
club, art gallery, conservatory of music, lyceum, gymnasium, and
religious center. Of the two Baptist churches in Boston, one was
reformist in the abolitionist tradition, while the other was conservative and a weapon against the moral and psychological aggres-
sion of racism.

Lewit, Robert T. "Indian Missions and Antislavery Sentiment: A Conflict of
Evangelical and Humanitarian Ideals." MISSISSIPPI VALLEY HISTORICAL RE-
VIEW 50 (June 1963): 39–55.

The American Board of Commissioners for Foreign Missions became
involved with the slavery issue in their efforts to Christianize the
Cherokees and Choctaws. They angered northern supporters when
they used slaves to maintain the missions and were accused by
southerners of being abolitionists.

Loetscher, Lefferts A. "The Problem of Christian Unity in Early Nineteenth-
Century America." CHURCH HISTORY 32 (March 1963): 3–16.

American churches were divided according to denominations and
also by revivalism. Unity was promoted, however, by religious
liberty, disestablishment, the new religious press, church history,
voluntary societies, and other means.

Loveland, Anne C. "Evangelicalism and 'Immediate Emancipation' in American
Antislavery Thought." JOURNAL OF SOUTHERN HISTORY 32 (May 1966):
172–88.

Loveland argues that historians have misinterpreted the abolitionists'
immediatist slogan as a temporal rather than a moral requirement.
Immediatism reflected changes in evangelicalism where "instanta-
neous" conversion was emphasized and a remaking of the world in
the image of the millenium was demanded.

Lyon, T. Edgar. "Religious Activities and Development in Utah, 1847–1910."
UTAH HISTORICAL QUARTERLY 35 (Fall 1967): 292–306.

This essay covers the missionary and anti-Mormon activities mainly
of the Presbyterians, Methodists, Congregationalists, Baptists, Luth-
erans, and the Church of Christ. They distrusted Mormonism and
attempted to raise public opinion against Utah statehood unless conditions were met.

McAllister, Lester G., and Tucker, William E. JOURNEY IN FAITH: A HISTORY OF THE CHRISTIAN CHURCH (DISCIPLES OF CHRIST). St. Louis: Bethany, 1975. 505 p.

> This is a study of the Disciples from Alexander and Thomas Campbell in the late eighteenth and early nineteenth centuries to the schisms in the denomination in the twentieth. It treats the church as a part of American Christianity and American history.

McAvoy, Thomas T. A HISTORY OF THE CATHOLIC CHURCH IN THE UNITED STATES. Notre Dame, Ind.: University of Notre Dame Press, 1969. v, 504 p.

> Catholic history from the founding of Maryland in 1634 to the close of Vatican Council II in 1965 is covered. McAvoy examines the position of the Catholic minority concerning the flood of immigrants after 1840, the anti-Catholic movement brought about by the immigrants, the church's activities concerning the heresy of Americanism, the lack of a Catholic intellectual tradition, and other topics.

McLoughlin, William C. THE MEANING OF HENRY WARD BEECHER: AN ESSAY ON THE SHIFTING VALUES OF MID-VICTORIAN AMERICA, 1840-1870. New York: Alfred A. Knopf, 1970. xiii, 275 p.

> McLoughlin uses Beecher's writings as an index to popular values and shows the shifts from revivalism to romantic Christianity, transcendentalism to social Darwinism, egalitarianism to conspicuous consumption. Beecher espoused a romantic Christianity that attempted to resolve the conflict between science and religion and moderated exploitive individualism.

McLoughlin, William G., Jr. MODERN REVIVALISM: CHARLES GRANDISON FINNEY TO BILLY GRAHAM. New York: Ronald Press, 1959. viii, 551 p.

> The methods used by evangelists are examined. The author argues that periods of mass enthusiasm were caused by theological reorientation in the churches, a feeling of cleavage between the churches and the world, and the growth of public interest in religion.

_____. "Pietism and the American Character." AMERICAN QUARTERLY 17 (Summer 1965): 163-86.

> Pietism-perfectionism offers as many useful insights into the nature of the American experience as pragmatism, democratic liberalism, or the frontier. Americans historically feel perpetually guilty because they do not live up to their own ideals.

Maddex, Jack P. "From Theocracy to Spirituality: The Southern Presbyterian Reversal on Church and State." JOURNAL OF PRESBYTERIAN HISTORY 54 (Winter 1976): 438-58.

Maddex argues that antebellum southern Presbyterians did not teach absolute separation of religion and politics. Most were proslavery activists who worked through the church to defend slavery.

Marsden, George M. THE EVANGELICAL MIND AND THE NEW SCHOOL PRESBYTERIAN EXPERIENCE: A CASE STUDY OF THOUGHT AND THEOLOGY IN NINETEENTH-CENTURY AMERICA. New Haven: Conn.: Yale University Press, 1970. xiii, 278 p.

Marsden argues that the principal weakness of the church was a willingness to embrace American nationalism and middle-class values. He attempts to show that the source of these tendencies was the nineteenth-century evangelical Protestant establishment.

_____. "Kingdom and Nation: New School Presbyterian Millenialism in the Civil War Era." JOURNAL OF PRESBYTERIAN HISTORY 46 (December 1968): 254-73.

New School Presbyterians played a conspicuous role in identifying the cause of the Union with Christ's approaching millenial kingdom. As the Civil War progressed to its end, they gave increasing attention to millenial themes, and expressed optimism with the victory of the North.

Marty, Martin E. "Living with Establishment and Disestablishment in Nineteenth-Century Anglo-America." JOURNAL OF CHURCH AND STATE 18 (Winter 1976): 61-78.

This is a comparative study of England and America. In the former, the religious establishment continued to receive support from spokesmen who wanted to be tolerant, while in the latter disestablishment was carried out by people who wanted religion to be favored in habits and ideas.

Mathews, Donald G. "Charles Colcock Jones and the Southern Evangelical Crusade to Form a Biracial Community." JOURNAL OF SOUTHERN HISTORY 41 (August 1975): 299-320.

Jones and William L. Garrison had much in common since both were evangelicals and moral elitists who wanted a perfect society. A graduate of Princeton Seminary in 1830, who believed everyone should be raised in the scale of moral excellence, Jones went home to Georgia and spent the rest of his life preaching for Christian education for blacks as a means of bringing blacks and whites together in a biracial community.

_____. "The Methodist Mission to the Slaves, 1829-1844." JOURNAL OF AMERICAN HISTORY 51 (March 1965): 615-31.

The mission to the slaves was the South's conscientious alternative to antislavery activity. Missionaries believed that piety was more important than emancipation, and claimed that their mission gave

slaves a Christian life, stabliized conditions between master and
slave, and extended moral concern to the Negro.

_____. "The Methodist Schism of 1844 and the Popularization of Antislavery
Sentiment." MID-AMERICA 51 (January 1968): 3-23.

Churches were the major social institutions in antebellum America.
Mathews maintains that the Methodist schism over slavery ideologi-
cally transformed the Civil War from a means to nationalize power
into a crusade against slavery.

_____. "Religion in the Old South: Speculation on Methodology." SOUTH
ATLANTIC QUARTERLY 73 (Winter 1974): 34-52.

Southern self-consciousness has been partially attributed to religion,
but this identification has not been explained. Students of religious history should relate religious symbols and institutions to the
social context, general idea system, and political events of the
past.

_____. "The Second Great Awakening as an Organizing Process, 1780-1830:
An Hypothesis." AMERICAN QUARTERLY 21 (Spring 1969): 23-43.

The second Great Awakening should be characterized by unity,
organization, and movement. It began after the Revolution in a
period of social and intellectual turmoil to provide unity theologi-
cally, adopted the Methodist organizational conception of the
church as a missionary movement, and served as a nationalizing
force by creating a common world of experience for Americans.

_____. SLAVERY AND METHODISM: A CHAPTER IN AMERICAN MORALITY.
1780-1845. Princeton, N.J.: Princeton University Press, 1965. xi, 329 p.

In 1780, a conference of Methodist ministers declared slavery as
being contrary to the laws of God, man, and nature, as well as
hurtful of society, but conferences between 1784 and 1844 made
concessions to slaveholders. The 1830s brought attacks on these
positions by proslavery southerners and antislavery northerners, and
in 1845 this most tightly organized Protestant church divided.

May, Henry F. PROTESTANT CHURCHES AND INDUSTRIAL AMERICA. New
York: Harper and Brothers, 1949. x, 297 p.

May covers Protestant social thought during the last three quarters
of the nineteenth century. Of importance is his study of the conservative element in American evangelicalism.

Mead, Sidney E. THE LIVELY EXPERIMENT: THE SHAPING OF CHRISTIANITY
IN AMERICA. New York: Harper and Row, 1963. xiii, 220 p.

Mead argues that American Christianity is wholly new. It is a
motley sampler of all church history.

Religion

Melton, Julius. PRESBYTERIAN WORSHIP IN AMERICA: CHANGING PAT-
TERNS SINCE 1787. Richmond, Va.: John Knox Press, 1967. 173 p.

Presbyterian worship evolved from a very austere pattern devoid of
liturgy to a form with greater congregational participation with the
use of choirs and organs, and even robes. This change took place
because of a rising standard of living, advances in educational
levels, and also because of changing attitudes concerning the relationship between God and man.

Merideth, Robert. THE POLITICS OF THE UNIVERSE: EDWARD BEECHER,
ABOLITION, AND ORTHODOXY. Nashville: Vanderbilt University Press,
1968. xi, 274 p.

Beecher was a conservative abolitionist who rejected perfectionism,
anti-institutionalism, and anti-clericalism. He also believed that
politics was a problem of theology, and his theology influenced
Harriet Beecher Stowe's UNCLE TOM'S CABIN.

Merwick, Donna. BOSTON PRIESTS, 1848-1910: A STUDY OF SOCIAL AND
INTELLECTUAL CHANGE. Cambridge, Mass.: Harvard University Press,
1973. xiii, 276 p.

This study deals with Archbishop William H. O'Connell, who reversed Catholic policy that called for cooperation with Protestant
luminaries. O'Connell imposed a Catholicism on Boston that was
both Roman and Irish and rejected pluralism.

Messbarger, Paul R. FICTION WITH A PAROCHIAL PURPOSE: SOCIAL USES
OF AMERICAN CATHOLIC LITERATURE, 1884-1900. Notre Dame, Ind.:
University of Notre Dame Press, 1971. xviii, 179 p.

This study covers Catholic literature during a period identified by
cultural historians as an "Americanist era." Messbarger shows the
development of a distinctive Catholic literary-publishing world
which hoped Catholic-non-Catholic separation would dissolve but
which actually created more separation.

Miyakawa, T. Scott. PROTESTANTS AND PIONEERS: INDIVIDUALISM AND
CONFORMITY ON THE AMERICAN FRONTIER. Chicago: University of
Chicago Press, 1964. 306 p.

Miyakawa, a sociologist, argues that the Methodist and Baptist
denominations in the Old Northwest were powerful socializing
agencies and that the pioneers in these churches tended to operate
by group-approved norms. Churchgoing frontiersmen accepted a
high degree of group control over habits and became the founders
of a new orthodoxy.

Monroe, Haskell. "Southern Presbyterians and the Secession Crisis." CIVIL WAR HISTORY 6 (December 1960): 351-60.

Presbyterians hesitated to mix politics and religion, but they exerted a great deal of influence. At times they tried to postpone action on secession, but when the final choice seemed necessary they were among the first to assist the Confederate effort.

Moore, Le Roy, Jr. "The Spiritual: Soul of Black Religion." AMERICAN QUARTERLY 23 (December 1971): 658-76.

Spirituals represent the fusion between Christian piety and the slave experience. The religion of the spiritual was a religion of presence, where man is present to himself and others, and of a freedom that includes rejoicing, laughing, and dancing.

Morrow, Ralph E. NORTHERN METHODISM AND RECONSTRUCTION. East Lansing: Michigan State University Press, 1956. x, 269 p.

The federal government allowed all sorts of southerners to worship as they pleased and did not attempt to impose beliefs. The group most energetic in attempting to redefine religion in the defeated South was the Northern Methodists, who believed the end of political division would end religious division.

_____. "Northern Methodism in the South during Reconstruction." MISSISSIPPI VALLEY HISTORICAL REVIEW 51 (September 1954): 197-218.

Methodists had buttressed the Civil War effort in the North and during Reconstruction they set out to retrieve the South from political and social errors. They failed in this endeavor because they were highly political and preached a Christian patriotism.

Murray, Andrew E. PRESBYTERIANS AND THE NEGRO--A HISTORY. Philadelphia: Presbyterian Historical Society, 1966. xiv, 270 p.

In every period of American history, the Negro Presbyterian was considered a black man and only secondarily a Christian. The church was shaped by prevailing racial attitudes and did not take the lead in shaping them.

Norman, E.R. THE CONSCIENCE OF THE STATE IN NORTH AMERICA. New York: Cambridge University Press, 1968. 199 p.

This is a comparative history of the relations of church and state in the United States, Canada, and the British Isles. The fact that the American experience in redefining religious and governmental spheres was not unique is emphasized.

Norton, Herman. "Revivalism in the Confederate Armies." CIVIL WAR HISTORY 6 (December 1960): 410-24.

The "Great Revival" was the most publicized aspect of religion in the Confederate armies. It had a permanent effect on many soldiers and enabled them to exercise patience in enduring the hardships of the postwar period.

Numbers, Ronald L. PROPHETESS OF HEALTH: A STUDY OF ELLEN G. WHITE. New York: Harper and Row, 1976. xiv, 271 p.

This is a study of the health theories and practices of the founder of the Seventh Day Adventists. White had visions of the path the church should follow, but her writings were very similar to those of health reformers.

O'Dea, Thomas F. THE MORMONS. Chicago: University of Chicago Press, 1957. xii, 289 p.

O'Dea, a Catholic scholar, covers the evolution of Mormonism and examines its impact on frontier development. He sees Joseph Smith as a normal person, who lived in an atmosphere of religious excitement, and became a prophet and leader of an important religious movement.

Opie, John. "Finney's Failure of Nerve: The Untimely Demise of Evangelical Theology." JOURNAL OF PRESBYTERIAN HISTORY 51 (Summer 1973): 155-73.

Evangelism was more than procedure, it included "right doctrine." Charles G. Finney failed in his charge to bring Evangelicalism to fruition and it became irrelevant.

Pearson, Samuel C., Jr. "From Church to Denomination: American Congregationalism in the Nineteenth Century." CHURCH HISTORY 38 (March 1969): 67-87.

Following the Revolution, American religious groups organized themselves into national churches or denominations united in a common purpose rather than in terms of a precise theology. The Congregationalists held themselves aloof from this rush to create a denomination and did not hold a national convention until 1852 or form a national council until 1871.

Peel, Robert. MARY BAKER EDDY: THE YEARS OF DISCOVERY. New York: Holt, Rinehart and Winston, 1966. xi, 372 p.

Peel, a committed Christian Scientist, had access to inaccessible materials and paints a sympathetic portrait of Eddy. He ends this study in 1875 and emphasizes that Eddy went far beyond Phineas Quimby, whom she has been accused of copying.

Persons, Stow. FREE RELIGION: AN AMERICAN FAITH. New Haven, Conn.: Yale University Press, 1947. v, 168 p.

This is a study of radical movements stemming from Unitarianism. The Free Religious Association of 1867 was the radicals' answer to the conservatives and preached a gospel of faith in man.

Posey, Walter Brownlow. THE BAPTIST CHURCH IN THE LOWER MISSISSIPPI VALLEY, 1776-1845. Lexington: University of Kentucky Press, 1957. x, 166 p.

Posey discusses Baptist preachers, the churches as disciplinary forces, camp meetings, work among the Indians and slaves, and education. He emphasizes the period of rapid Baptist expansion from 1812 to 1845.

_____. FRONTIER MISSION: A HISTORY OF RELIGION WEST OF THE SOUTHERN APPALACHIANS TO 1861. Lexington: University of Kentucky Press, 1966. viii, 436 p.

The Methodists, Presbyterians, Baptists, Roman Catholics, Episcopalians, Cumberland Presbyterians, and Disciples of Christ in the Old Southwest are discussed. The author covers church polity, Indians, Negroes, education, and church discipline.

_____. THE PRESBYTERIAN CHURCH IN THE OLD SOUTHWEST, 1778-1838. Richmond, Va.: John Knox Press, 1952. 192 p.

The men who were responsible for expanding the denomination and formulating its positions on religious and secular matters are emphasized. The development of beliefs and practices, as well as the role of the minister, are covered.

_____. RELIGIOUS STRIFE ON THE SOUTHERN FRONTIER. Baton Rouge: Louisiana State University Press, 1965. x, 112 p.

These lectures cover religious strife in three stages. In the first, Protestants fought one another until the camp meeting brought cooperation; in the second, older denominations fought new sects such as the Campbellites; while the third was identified by Protestant-Catholic conflict.

_____. "The Slavery Question in the Presbyterian Church in the Old Southwest." JOURNAL OF SOUTHERN HISTORY 15 (August 1949): 311-24.

Posey traces the slavery question from 1787 to 1837 when the church divided into Old and New Schools. Presbyterians in the Old Southwest moved from antislavery to colonization to rigid support.

Pratt, John Webb. RELIGION, POLITICS, AND DIVERSITY: THE CHURCH-STATE THEME IN NEW YORK HISTORY. Ithaca, N.Y.: Cornell University Press, 1967. xi, 327 p.

The church-state issue was a state rather than a national problem. In New York, materialism, a polyglot population, secularism, and the Protestant insistence that each individual mold his own religious life brought religious liberty.

Purifoy, Lewis M. "The Southern Methodist Church and the Proslavery Argument." JOURNAL OF SOUTHERN HISTORY 32 (August 1966): 325-41.

Following the schism of 1844 in the Methodist Church that was produced by antislavery agitation, southern Methodists attempted to argue that slavery was strictly a matter of civil regulation, but they could not ignore the moral question. Their proslavery argument was at first based on the attitude that Christians must subject themselves to the state unless the laws of the state contravene God's laws, but eventually they became immersed in the South's cause.

Quandt, Jean B. "Religion and Social Thought: The Secularization of Postmillenialism." AMERICAN QUARTERLY 25 (October 1973): 390-409.

Quandt shows the relationship between the ideas of religious leaders such as Washington Gladden, Josiah Strong, and Lyman Abbott, and intellectuals such as Richard Ely, John Dewey, and John R. Commons. These individuals depicted a teleological model of historical change that predicted attainment of peace, justice, and love.

Quinn, D. Michael. "The Mormon Church and the Spanish-American War: An End to Selective Pacifism." PACIFIC HISTORICAL REVIEW 43 (August 1974): 342-66.

For half a century the Mormon Church had maintained a right to participate in any given conflict, with this power resting with the current prophet. When the church gave up polygamy in 1890 and gained statehood, Mormons also capitulated to federal authority which meant they had to give up selective pacifism.

Rice, Madeleine Hooke. AMERICAN CATHOLIC OPINION IN THE SLAVERY CONTROVERSY. Studies in History, Economics, and Public Law, no. 508. New York: Columbia University Press, 1944. 177 p.

The Catholic Church interpreted slavery as being legitimate and scripture-sanctioned, and Catholic laymen were loyal to the pro-southern Democratic Party, feared the competition of freed slaves, and hated the ultra-Protestant abolitionists. Southern bishops defended the institution.

Rosenberg, Carol Smith. RELIGION AND THE RISE OF THE AMERICAN CITY: THE NEW YORK CITY MISSION MOVEMENT, 1812-1870. Ithaca, N.Y.: Cornell University Press, 1971. x, 300 p.

This is a study of religious benevolence toward the poor in New York from the second Great Awakening to the Social Gospel years. The author describes the work of the New York City Tract Society and the New York Female Moral Reform Society.

Rudolph, L.C. HOOSIER ZION: THE PRESBYTERIANS IN EARLY INDIANA. Yale Publications in Religion, no. 5. Presbyterian Historical Society Publications, no. 4. New Haven, Conn.: Yale University Press, 1963. xiv, 218 p.

Presbyterianism advanced slowly in Indiana even though most settlers were not church members. This can be attributed partly to the Old School-New School controversy that dismembered the Indiana synod soon after its founding.

Saeger, Robert II. "Some Denominational Reactions to Chinese Immigration to California, 1856-1892." PACIFIC HISTORICAL REVIEW 28 (February 1959): 49-66.

Protestant clergymen believed that God Himself had brought the Chinese to California to be Christianized. Some argued for the assimilation of the Chinese in terms of a vigorous and sustained attack on Roman Catholicism.

Sandeen, Ernest R. THE ROOTS OF FUNDAMENTALISM: BRITISH AND AMERICAN MILLENARIANISM, 1830-1930. Chicago: University of Chicago Press, 1970. xix, 328 p.

Fundamentalism was neither parochially American nor rurally based. The roots of fundamentalism were in nineteenth-century millenarianism, the Biblical literalism of the Princeton Theological Seminary, and the prophesies of William Miller, all of which influenced Dwight L. Moody and others.

_____. "Towards a Historical Interpretation of the Origins of Fundamentalism." CHURCH HISTORY 36 (March 1967): 66-83.

Fundamentalism resulted from an alliance between two nineteenth-century theologies, dispensationalism and the Princeton theology. Dispensationalism stemmed from a small British sect called the Plymouth Brethren while the Princeton theology was born with the founding of Princeton Seminary in 1812.

Sernett, Milton C. "Behold the American Cleric: The Protestant Minister as 'Pattern Man,' 1850-1900." WINTERTHUR PORTFOLIO 8 (1973): 1-18.

This is a study of the image of ministers presented in pastoral theology textbooks. This pattern represented something older, the reactionary, and made for professional tension and, ultimately, transition.

Sewrey, Charles L. "Infallibility, the American Way, and Catholic Apologetics." JOURNAL OF CHURCH AND STATE 15 (Spring 1973): 293-302.

The efforts of Catholic spokesmen to explain papal infallibility following the Vatican Council of 1870 are delineated. The secular and religious press saw infallibility as a threat to American institutions, and Catholics did not want the doctrine to become a new anti-Catholic weapon.

Sharrow, Walter G. "John Hughes and a Catholic Response to Slavery in Antebellum America." JOURNAL OF NEGRO HISTORY 57 (July 1972): 254-69.

The prominence of Archbishop Hughes of New York rendered his voice important in molding the institutional response of the Catholic Church to slavery. His thoughts on the institution were ambiguous, sometimes contradictory, and always filled with the tension that characterized northern intellectuals who tried to reconcile slavery with human equality.

_____. "Northern Catholic Intellectuals and the Coming of the Civil War." NEW-YORK HISTORICAL SOCIETY QUARTERLY 58 (January 1974). 35-56.

Catholic thinking on the causes of the Civil War was not monolithic, but dominant members of the northern Catholic intellectual community developed a conservative pattern of ideas. Probably the dominant position voiced by these thinkers was that the war was part of a divine plan to renovate American religious life.

Silver, James W. CONFEDERATE MORALE AND CHURCH PROPAGANDA. Confederate Centennial Studies, no. 3. Tuscaloosa, Ala.: Confederate Publishing Co., 1957. 120 p.

The people of the South acknowledged the hand of God in every event, believed in personal salvation, and viewed slavery as part of God's plan. Southern clergymen were in the vanguard of the secession movement and taught their people to fight without moral reservation and as a religious duty.

Smith, Elwyn A. "The Forming of a Modern American Denomination." CHURCH HISTORY 31 (March 1962): 74-99.

Modern denominations began after the Revolution with an upsurge of new groupings of local churches in which the missionary impulse was inherent or dominant. They possessed a purposive system of executive and promotional agencies, the association of this structure with a specific religious tradition, and a conservative determination to maintain a distinctive identity in the face of change.

_____. "The Fundamental Church-State Tradition of the Catholic Church in the United States." CHURCH HISTORY 38 (December 1969): 486-505.

> The American Catholic tradition has never opposed church-state separation. The separation of church and state has been regarded as a safeguard of religious freedom which has been a deep commitment and practical necessity of American Catholicism.

_____. RELIGIOUS LIBERTY IN THE UNITED STATES: THE DEVELOPMENT OF CHURCH THOUGHT SINCE THE REVOLUTIONARY ERA. Philadelphia: Fortress, 1972. xiv, 386 p.

> This study is divided into three sections--the Protestant tradition, Catholic tradition, and legal tradition. The author shows that the Protestant tradition was essentially a nativistic tradition opposed to Catholicism and that secularist separation means that religion is a bad thing.

_____. "The Role of the South in the Presbyterian Schism of 1837-38." CHURCH HISTORY 29 (March 1960): 44-63.

> The Presbyterian schism cannot be attributed to a dispute over slavery. It evolved because of disputes between Old School (South) and New School (North) Presbyterians over doctrine and church discipline.

Smith, H. Sheldon. IN HIS IMAGE, BUT . . . : RACISM IN SOUTHERN RELIGION, 1780-1910. Durham, N.C.: Duke University Press, 1972. x, 318 p.

> Smith describes the capitulation of southern churches to slavery and then to segregation and racial orthodoxy. Southerners supported slavery before abolition, committed themselves to secession, resisted missionary work with the freedmen, and encouraged the formation of separate black congregations within their denominations.

Smith, John Abernathy. "Ecclesiastical Politics and the Founding of the Federal Council of Churches." CHURCH HISTORY 43 (September 1974): 350-65.

> The Federal Council of Churches, founded in 1908, was not a stage in the flowering of social Christianity. It was the product of a movement for Christian unity that swept through denominational assemblies during the 1880s and 1890s.

Smith, Timothy L. REVIVALISM AND SOCIAL REFORM IN MID-NINETEENTH-CENTURY AMERICA. Nashville: Abingdon Press, 1957. 253 p.

> Smith believes that the revivalism and perfectionism of the pre-Civil War period contributed as much to the development of the Social Gospel as did industrialization and urbanization. He covers

the revivals between 1830 and 1858, and emphasizes their impact on reform and American nationalism.

_____. "Slavery and Theology: The Emergence of Black Christian Consciousness in Nineteenth-Century America." CHURCH HISTORY 41 (December 1972): 497-512.

What was unique in black Christianity in the nineteenth century was the acceptance of the radical view of man's duty and destiny that characterized primitive Christian thought. The Christian beliefs slaves adopted enabled them to endure slavery because these beliefs supported their moral revulsion to the institution.

Smylie, James H. "American Protestants Interpret Vatican Council I." CHURCH HISTORY 38 (December 1969): 459-74.

Protestant intellectuals were concerned with the Vatican Council of 1869-70. They discussed the background and the ecclesiastical procedures employed in arriving at the dogmatic formulation of papal infallibility and primacy.

Sontag, Frederick, and Roth, John K. THE AMERICAN RELIGIOUS EXPERIENCE: THE ROOTS, TRENDS, AND FUTURE OF AMERICAN THEOLOGY. New York: Harper and Row, 1972. xiii, 401 p.

Puritanism, Edwardsean thought, romantic religion, the Social Gospel, radical theology, and black theology are the principal themes of this book. The authors argue that American aspirations became monolithic and materialistic in the nineteenth century, but religious pluralism holds hope for the future.

Spain, Rufus B. AT EASE IN ZION: SOCIAL HISTORY OF SOUTHERN BAPTISTS, 1865-1900. Nashville: Vanderbilt University Press, 1967. xii, 247 p.

The Southern Baptist Convention helped shape southern attitudes following the Civil War. The Baptists were sensitive to problems affecting personal morality such as temperance and dancing, but they were ineffective in dealing with racial and economic injustice.

Staiger, C. Bruce. "Abolitionism and the Presbyterian Schism of 1837-1838." MISSISSIPPI VALLEY HISTORICAL REVIEW 36 (December 1949): 391-414.

Slavery played an important role in the division of the Presbyterian Church. Opposition to the New School came from those concerned with the purity of their faith, conservatives, and those whose fortunes were affected by antislavery agitation.

Stewart, James Brewer. "Evangelicalism and the Radical Strain in Southern Antislavery Thought During the 1820s." JOURNAL OF SOUTHERN HISTORY 39 (August 1973): 379-96.

Stewart challenges the notion that there was not a genuine anti-slavery tradition in the ante-bellum South. A concerted, ongoing movement never existed, but during the 1820s some southern evangelicals developed an antislavery ideology based on the moral errors of slaveholders.

Strout, Cushing. THE NEW HEAVENS AND EARTH: POLITICAL RELIGION IN AMERICA. New York: Harper and Row, 1974. xv, 400 p.

Political religion, according to Strout, is making politics out of religion. He employs Tocqueville's observation that in America great political consequences flowed from religious beliefs, and he shows the transition from Puritanism to republicanism in the nineteenth century.

Suderman, Elmer F. "The Social-Gospel Novelists' Criticisms of American Society." MIDCONTINENT AMERICAN STUDIES JOURNAL 7 (Spring 1966): 45-58.

The message of social-gospel novelists was that the Kingdom of God could not be served by converting individuals and leaving the institutions of society unregenerate. Although they emphasized the application of the teachings of Jesus for the salvation of society, they did not insist on thoroughgoing change.

Sweet, Leonard I. "The View of Man Inherent in New Measures Revivalism." CHURCH HISTORY 45 (June 1976): 206-21.

Charles G. Finney's new-measures revivalism has been viewed as the religious counterpart of the Jacksonian faith in the worth and dignity of man. Sweet argues that Finney's evangelism, instead of expressing confidence in man, was conservative, status-conscious, and pessimistic about human nature.

Sweet, William Warren. AMERICAN CULTURE AND RELIGION: SIX ESSAYS. Dallas: Southern Methodist University Press, 1951. 114 p.

Sweet includes essays on cultural pluralism in the American tradition; the church, sect, and the cult in America; natural religion and religious liberty; and Protestantism and democracy. He views Protestantism as being individualistic.

Szasz, Ferenc M. "The Progressive Clergy and the Kingdom of God." MID-AMERICA 55 (January 1973): 3-20.

Conservative ministers saw a kingdom of converted Christians that would help usher in the millenium, while liberals envisioned a reaching out of Christianity to the world. Szasz maintains that these ministers gave progressivism its moral dimension and when they became disillusioned as a result of the First World War, the movement simply became liberalism.

Tomasi, Silvano M. PIETY AND POWER: THE ROLE OF THE ITALIAN PARISHES IN THE NEW YORK METROPOLITAN AREA, 1880-1930. Staten Island, N.Y.: Center for Migration Studies, 1975. xi, 201 p.

Tomasi analyzes the assimilation of Italians and the role played by the church. The Catholic Church was a creative force in the lives of immigrants.

Tucker, David M. BLACK PASTORS AND LEADERS: MEMPHIS, 1819-1972. Memphis: Memphis State University Press, 1975. xi, 158 p.

This is a series of biographical essays on black clergymen in Memphis. The book does not have a unifying theme, but the author shows the change in theology resulting from the black power movement.

Tucker, William E. J.H. GARRISON AND DISCIPLES OF CHRIST. St. Louis: Bethany Press, 1964. 270 p.

Garrison was a church leader between the Civil War and 1930. For more than sixty years, he edited or contributed to the CHRISTIAN-EVANGELIST and advanced a moderate position that permitted his denomination to preserve its historic position and at the same time adopt programs for liberalization.

Warnock, Henry Y. "Andrew Sledd, Southern Methodists, and the Negro: A Case History." JOURNAL OF SOUTHERN HISTORY 31 (August 1965): 251-71.

Sledd was a Methodist minister and a professor of classics who was drummed out of Emory College, Georgia, in 1902 for publishing an article condemning the denial of rights to blacks and excoriating lynching as the core of the South's race problem. Warnock maintains that Sledd was a moderate Methodist calling for a freer system of racial adjustment, a position held by others that eventually helped to bring about the reunification of the Methodist Church in 1939.

_____. "Prophets of Change: Some Southern Baptist Leaders and the Problem of Race, 1900-1921." BAPTIST HISTORY AND HERITAGE 7 (July 1972): 172-83.

Some leaders exhibited impressive evidence of moderate racial thought, attitudes, and concerns, and played an important role in the movement for social awareness. They believed in racial inferiority, but they were not proponents of a static society.

Weisberger, Bernard A. THEY GATHERED AT THE RIVER: THE STORY OF THE GREAT REVIVALISTS AND THEIR IMPACT UPON RELIGION IN AMERICA. Boston: Little, Brown, 1958. xii, 345 p.

Weisberger covers revivals and revivalists, and not just popular preachers. He interprets revivals in secular terms, focusing mainly on the nineteenth century.

Weisenburger, Francis P. ORDEAL OF FAITH: THE CRISIS OF CHURCH-GOING AMERICA, 1865-1900. New York: Philosophical Library, 1959. xii, 380 p.

Protestants, Catholics, Jews, Mormons, and free-thinkers are discussed. The author seeks the meaning of religion to clerics and laymen in their nonchurchgoing moments.

_____. TRIUMPH OF FAITH: CONTRIBUTIONS OF THE CHURCH TO AMERICAN LIFE, 1865-1900. [Richmond, Va.]: The Author, 1962. x, 221 p.

Weisenburger attempts to delineate the basic trends of religious belief and determine the effect of faith on American life. He argues that there has been little relationship between membership in a church and personal morality, but churches have set standards of behavior and most Americans have been influenced by religion.

White, Dana F. "A Summons for the Kingdom of God on Earth: The Early Social-Gospel Novel." SOUTH ATLANTIC QUARTERLY 67 (Summer 1968): 469-85.

Protestant America in the late nineteenth and early twentieth centuries attempted to reform industrial society through the converted individual. The Social Gospel novel was a distinct literary form that emphasized stewardship, the dedication of the individual and his resources to social betterment, and a new exhibition of discipleship.

Wight, Willard E. "The Churches and the Confederate Cause." CIVIL WAR HISTORY 6 (December 1960): 361-73.

Southern Christians believed that slavery was sanctioned by God and that disruption of the Union was necessary to preserve slavery, God's work on earth. The Confederate states were the creation of Providence and it was the duty of Christians to support the government with unfaltering loyalty.

Wilson, Major L. "Paradox Lost: Order and Progress in Evangelical Thought of Mid-Nineteenth-Century America." CHURCH HISTORY 44 (September 1975): 352-66.

The paradox in the mid-nineteenth-century liberal outlook was an optimistic embrace of the future blended with a nostalgia for the past. Evangelicals believed in the essential perfection of the republican system, but they also argued that daily life and the relations of freemen be constantly shaped by God's will.

Wolf, William J. THE ALMOST CHOSEN PEOPLE: A STUDY OF THE RELIGION OF ABRAHAM LINCOLN. Garden City, N.Y.: Doubleday, 1959. 215 p.

Wolf depicts Lincoln as a universalist and a predestinarian. He also emphasizes the piety of Lincoln's politics and social conscience.

Wright, Conrad. THE BEGINNINGS OF UNITARIANISM IN AMERICA. Boston: Beacon Press, 1955. 305 p.

Unitarianism began with Arminianism in the 1750s. The discovery of a benevolent diety and opposition to Trinitarianism led eventually to the Unitarian belief in the dignity of human nature.

_____. THE LIBERAL CHRISTIANS: ESSAYS ON AMERICAN UNITARIAN HISTORY. Boston: Beacon Press, 1970. x, 147 p.

Wright focuses on those Unitarians who did not disengage themselves from Christianity, but who disliked its illiberal versions. In one essay, he directs attention to William Ellery Channing, whom, he emphasizes, developed a form of supernatural rationalism.

_____. A STREAM OF LIGHT: A SESQUICENTENNIAL HISTORY OF AMERICAN UNITARIANISM. Boston: Unitarian Universalist Association, 1975. xiv, 178 p.

These essays depict the growth of Unitarianism from the scholarly study of the scriptures in the early nineteenth century to the merger with the Universalists and the development of Beacon Press in the 1950s.

1915 TO THE PRESENT

Ahlstrom, Sydney E. "The Problem of the History of Religion in America." CHURCH HISTORY 39 (June 1970): 224-35.

The first and special problem of American church history is its multifariousness and complexity. In addition, in the 1960s, a new present has created a new past, because religion has become a part of world history and it is much more than church history.

Aiken, John R. "Walter Rauschenbusch and Education for Reform." CHURCH HISTORY 36 (December 1967): 456–69.

Rauschenbusch's road to social reform was education, but his elitism committed him to the existing educational system. His Christianized education was not suited to evolving a Christian socialistic society.

Bailey, Kenneth K. "The Enactment of Tennessee's Antievolution Law." JOURNAL OF SOUTHERN HISTORY 16 (November 1950): 472–90.

Bailey argues that Tennessee's antievolution law was not atypical, because in all parts of the country, particularly the South, efforts were made during the 1920s to curb the teaching of evolution. This was part of the fundamentalist–modernist controversy and the law was based on the tenet that the schools should not be permitted to undermine the orthodox religious beliefs of children.

_____. SOUTHERN WHITE PROTESTANTISM IN THE TWENTIETH CENTURY. New York: Harper and Row, 1964. x, 180 p.

Methodists, Presbyterians, Baptists and regional interaction are stressed. Southern religion in this century has been characterized by Biblical literalism, segregated churches, the gospel of individual regeneration, and moral privatism.

Betten, Neil. CATHOLIC ACTIVISM AND THE INDUSTRIAL WORKER. Gainesville: University Presses of Florida, 1976. x, 191 p.

This is a study of the impact of the Catholic Church of unionism. Fear of Marx, rather than Christian radicalism, guided many church leaders in approaching the labor question, although a minority supported unions and strikes as compatible with Catholic social thought.

_____. "Catholic Periodicals in Response to Two Divergent Decades." JOURNALISM QUARTERLY 47 (Summer 1970): 303–8.

Catholic journalism during the 1920s and 1930s indicates that Catholicism was responsive to the times. Major Catholic periodicals did not follow the party line of a monolith nor were they static in their views.

Billington, Monroe. "Roosevelt, the New Deal, and the Clergy." MID-AMERICA 54 (January 1972): 20–33.

In September 1935, Franklin Roosevelt requested that clergymen write him about conditions in their communities and tell him how the government could better serve the people. This is a survey of responses that Billington argues was an accurate barometer of the opinion that the people favored the New Deal but saw shortcomings in the administration of it.

Bridges, Hal. AMERICAN MYSTICISM: FROM WILLIAM JAMES TO ZEN.
New York: Harper and Row, 1970. xi, 208 p.

American mysticism has not been isolated from mystical thought
throughout the world. Bridges begins with the philosophic idealism
of James, moves to Quakers such as Rufus Jones and other intellectuals including Thomas Merton, and ends with Vedanta, Zen,
and the psychedelic experience.

Brown, Michael Gary. "All, All Alone: The Hebrew Press in America from
1914 to 1924." AMERICAN JEWISH HISTORICAL QUARTERLY 59 (December
1969): 139-78.

The first World War cut off American Jews from their former European sources and they had to create their own spiritual and intellectual life. A number of Jewish periodicals came into existence
after the war, not to serve a community that did not read English,
but because it was believed that Jewish people should read Hebrew.

Burr, Nelson. "The American Church Historian and the Biblical View of History." HISTORICAL MAGAZINE OF THE PROTESTANT EPISCOPAL CHURCH
39 (December 1970): 347-60.

The Biblical view differs from the nineteenth-century positivist
view that history is strictly determined by circumstances, uninflu-
enced by supernatural intelligence. It finds meaning in the dia-
lect of time and eternity, and sees history as being ruled through
a Divine Providence.

Carter, Paul A. THE DECLINE OF THE SOCIAL GOSPEL: SOCIAL AND
POLITICAL LIBERALISM IN AMERICAN PROTESTANT CHURCHES, 1920-1940.
Ithaca, N.Y.: Cornell University Press, 1956. x, 265 p.

Editorials in the religious press on public issues are emphasized.
In the 1920s, overconcern with Prohibition, the rise of fundamentalism, and the prestige of business were unfavorable to religious
criticism, but in the next decade the breakdown of international
law and order called attention to the need for Christianizing the
social order.

_____. "The Idea of Progress in Most Recent American Protestant Thought,
1930-1960." CHURCH HISTORY 32 (March 1963): 75-89.

The idea of progress is the belief that civilization has moved, is
moving, and will continue to move in a desirable direction. Protestants were not only progressive in their outlook but also continued in this manner in spite of war and the bomb.

Cohen, Naomi W. AMERICAN JEWS AND THE ZIONIST IDEA. New York: KTAV, 1975. xvi, 172 p.

American Jews were not friendly to Zionism until the outbreak of World War II because they did not suffer the anti-Semitism rampant in Europe. The war gave Zionism a fresh start and brought to leadership Louis Brandeis, who made the movement purposeful.

Crimmins, Timothy J. "Commonweal Catholics." SOUTH ATLANTIC QUARTERLY 71 (Spring 1972): 189-204.

THE COMMONWEAL, a journal of opinion edited by Catholic laymen, gained autonomy from control by the Catholic Church in 1939 with its stand on the Spanish Civil War. It has articulated a philosophy of lay autonomy and helped to create a freer and more open church as a result.

Cross, Robert D. "The Changing Image of the City Among American Catholics." CATHOLIC HISTORICAL REVIEW 48 (April 1962): 33-52.

Cross surveys a century of Catholic opinion and finds that the urban impact elicited alarm from Catholic spokesmen. Churchmen tended to concentrate on resisting the city's impact on the church instead of on developing the church's impact on the city in promoting general welfare.

Cunningham, Raymond J. "The Emmanuel Movement: A Variety of American Religious Experience." AMERICAN QUARTERLY 14 (Spring 1962): 48-63.

The Emmanuel movement, an endeavor of Episcopal clergymen and physicians, directed its efforts toward stemming the popularity of mental healing cults, such as Christian Science. Its founder was Elwood Worcester, rector of Emmanuel Church in Boston from 1904 to 1929, and its techniques of treating functional illnesses included religious casuistry, scientific psychiatry, and secular ethics.

De Santis, Vincent P. "American Catholics and McCarthyism." CATHOLIC HISTORICAL REVIEW 51 (April 1965): 1-30.

Even though Sen. Joseph McCarthy was a Catholic, the church could not take a position on McCarthyism as a social issue. Catholic laymen were split, but a majority, many of whom were isolationists, favored the senator.

Ellis, John Tracy, ed. THE CATHOLIC PRIEST IN THE UNITED STATES: HISTORICAL INVESTIGATIONS. Collegeville, Minn.: St. John's University Press, 1971. xvii, 488 p.

This collection deals with issues raised by Vatican II. The essays present a liberal but loyal image and cover contemporary ecclesiastical turmoil.

Ernst, Eldon G. "The Interchurch World Movement and the Great Steel Strike of 1919-1920." CHURCH HISTORY 39 (June 1970): 212-23.

The Interchurch World movement represented not only the optimism that followed the First World War, but also the disillusionment and retreat of Protestant activity in the 1920s. The movement's report on the steel strike was a high point in social Christianity but it failed to stem the decline of the Social Gospel.

Feldblum, Esther. "On the Eve of a Jewish State: American-Catholic Responses." AMERICAN JEWISH HISTORICAL QUARTERLY 64 (December 1974): 99-119.

The idea is prevalent that the Holocaust stirred Christian sympathy for Jews and increased the acceptance of a Jewish state. This was not true so far as the Catholic press was concerned since Catholic periodicals expressed outright hostility to Israel.

Fishman, Hertzel. AMERICAN PROTESTANTISM AND A JEWISH STATE. Detroit: Wayne State University Press, 1973. 249 p.

The author discusses Protestant thought concerning Israel and political Zionism from 1937 to 1967, as typified by the CHRISTIAN CENTURY and CHRISTIANITY AND CRISIS. Liberal Protestants had a positive view of individual Jews but opposed statehood.

Flynn, George Q. AMERICAN CATHOLICS AND THE ROOSEVELT PRESIDENCY, 1932-1936. Lexington: University of Kentucky Press, 1968. xv, 272 p.

Franklin Roosevelt was free of doctrinal intolerance and also a canny politician who understood Catholic political strength. He gave Catholics recognition through appointments to high office (James Farley and Joseph Kennedy), and Catholic clergymen, such as Father John A. Ryan and George Cardinal Mundelein) enlisted the sympathy of Catholic laymen for New Deal programs.

_____. ROOSEVELT AND ROMANISM: CATHOLICS AND AMERICAN DIPLOMACY, 1937-1945. Westport, Conn.: Greenwood, 1976. xx, 268 p.

This is a study of Catholic attitudes and influence concerning the Neutrality Acts, the peace movement, the Spanish Civil War, lend-lease, aid to Russia, the peacetime draft, and other matters. Roosevelt was interested in keeping Catholic support and he consulted Catholic leaders on policy matters.

Furniss, Norman F. THE FUNDAMENTALIST CONTROVERSY, 1918-1931. New Haven, Conn.: Yale University Press, 1954. x, 199 p.

The fundamentalist movement was a serious threat to intellectual freedom and a part of the repressive temper of the 1920s. The characteristics of fundamentalists, their organizations, and their impact on Baptists, Presbyterians, Methodists, Episcopalians, and Disciples of Christ are covered in this study.

Gatewood, Willard B., Jr. "Politics and Piety in North Carolina: The Fundamentalist Crusade at High Tide, 1925-1937." NORTH CAROLINA HISTORICAL REVIEW 42 (July 1965): 275-90.

Many North Carolinians experienced profound uneasiness in the presence of "new day" realities of the 1920s. They fought evolution to prevent the loosening of restraints that would jeopardize their state's status as a "Christian Commonwealth."

Glazer, Nathan. AMERICAN JUDAISM. Chicago History of American Civilization series. Edited by Daniel J. Boorstin. Chicago: University of Chicago Press, 1957. xii, 176 p.

Glazer, a sociologist, is not optimistic about the future of the Jewish religion in the United States. He assesses the superficiality of much contemporary Jewish thinking.

Gleason, Philip. "Catholicism and Cultural Change in the 60s." REVIEW OF POLITICS 34 (October 1972): 91-107.

American Catholics were disposed to respond actively to the "aggiornamento" set in motion by Pope John XXIII. They also were the recipients of cultural change in the United States, because they had made it as members of the middle class and had lost identity as outsiders, which caused crises in the 1960s.

_____. "Coming to Terms with American Catholic History." SOCIETAS 3 (Autumn 1973): 283-312.

This is an examination of the uses of the terms Americanism and Americanization in the context of Catholic history. Gleason concludes that usage went through stages based on attitudes concerning cultural assimilation and its effect on Catholic values.

_____. "Mass and Maypole Revisited: American Catholics and the Middle Ages." CATHOLIC HISTORICAL REVIEW 57 (July 1971): 249-74.

Gleason traces the change in the Catholic Church regarding the Middle Ages. He shows that thirty years ago Catholics took pride in the medieval connection, but today they regard the Middle Ages as authoritarian.

Graebner, Alan. UNCERTAIN SAINTS: THE LAITY IN THE LUTHERAN CHURCH--MISSOURI SYNOD, 1900-1970. Westport, Conn.: Greenwood, 1975. xiii, 274 p.

This is one of the first books on the laity of a church, rather than the clergy. Graebner emphasizes the emergence of the laity as immigrant Germans became Americanized and the search for a meaningful role in the church for these people.

Handy, Robert T. "The American Religious Depression, 1925-35." CHURCH HISTORY 29 (March 1960): 3-16.

Handy distinguishes between the religious depression and the economic depression. The religious depression was exemplified by a decline in the vitality of missionary programs, a slump in church attendance, the absence of a religious revival, mushrooming of newer and smaller sects, and a decline in evangelical liberal theology.

Harrell, David Edwin, Jr. WHITE SECTS AND BLACK MEN IN THE RECENT SOUTH. Nashville: Vanderbilt University Press, 1971. xvii, 161 p.

This is a study of the sects of lower-class whites, such as the Assemblies of God, Churches of Christ, and Pentecostal Holiness Churches, that have had little opportunity for public expression. These groups, because of status concerns, supported segregation and Negro inferiority.

Hefley, J. Theodore. "Freedom Upheld: The Civil Liberties Stance of THE CHRISTIAN CENTURY Between the Wars." CHURCH HISTORY 37 (June 1968): 174-94.

The CHRISTIAN CENTURY ranks with the NATION and NEW RE-PUBLIC during the interwar years as a standard-bearer of social change through the Bill of Rights. It was critical of America in terms of potential unfulfilled but it was optimistic in terms of the country's vitality.

Hitchcock, James. "The Evolution of the Catholic Left." AMERICAN SCHOL-AR 43 (Winter 1973-74): 66-84.

This is a study of the clerical Catholic Left from John Courtney Murray in the 1950s through the Berrigan brothers. Hitchcock argues that the Left has broadened the acceptable limits of thought and action, and has made Catholicism more pluralistic.

Hutchison, William R. "Cultural Strain and Protestant Liberalism." AMERI-CAN HISTORICAL REVIEW 76 (April 1971): 386-411.

Cultural strain is defined as an upsetting of patterns on which men construct their lives. This is a study of status theory and of the shape, sources, and consequences of religion as an ideology.

Lankford, John. "The Contemporary Revolution in Historiography." HISTORI-
CAL MAGAZINE OF THE PROTESTANT EPISCOPAL CHURCH 36 (March 1967):
11-34.

> The history of religion has improved qualitatively through narrative
> syntheses and specialized monographs. Lankford reviews Episcopal
> historiography and finds it largely out of touch with these new di-
> rections.

_____. "The Impact of the Religious Depression upon Protestant Benevolence,
1925-1935." JOURNAL OF PRESBYTERIAN HISTORY 42 (June 1964): 104-
23.

> There was a spirit of religious lethargy in the 1920s and 1930s.
> This was expressed in a decline of financial support for the bene-
> volent work of churches, but there was also an increase in non-
> benevolent giving for church construction between 1920 and 1929.

Linkh, Richard M. AMERICAN CATHOLICISM AND EUROPEAN IMMIGRANTS
(1900-1924). Staten Island, N.Y.: Center for Migration Studies, 1975. x,
200 p.

> This is a study of the relationship of the Catholic hierarchy to im-
> migrant religious organizations. The church moved by way of
> policy from Americanization to cultural pluralism.

Littell, Franklin Hamlin. FROM STATE CHURCH TO PLURALISM: A PROTES-
TANT INTERPRETATION OF RELIGION IN AMERICAN HISTORY. Garden
City, N.Y.: Doubleday, 1962. xxii, 174 p.

> The history of American churches from established Protestantism to
> the post-Protestant era of Protestant-Catholic-Jewish trialogue is
> covered. The author believes that Protestants have not accepted
> the present religious situation and that this has been the worst
> enemy of ecumenical understanding.

McAvoy, Thomas T., ed. ROMAN CATHOLICISM AND THE AMERICAN WAY
OF LIFE. Notre Dame, Ind.: University of Notre Dame Press, 1960. viii, 248 p.

> These eighteen essays cover the present situation of Catholics and
> the Catholic immigrant. Protestant and Jewish contributors argue
> that the United States has become a pluralistic society, while
> Catholics are skeptical and indecisive about this position.

McBeth, Leon. "Southern Baptists and Race Since 1947." BAPTIST HISTORY
AND HERITAGE 7 (July 1972): 155-68.

> Attitudes of southern Baptists concerning blacks have changed in
> the last quarter century. Southern Baptists seem less convinced of
> white supremacy and more willing to accept the personhood and
> dignity of all people.

Marty, Martin E. "Ethnicity: The Skeleton of Religion in America." CHURCH HISTORY 41 (March 1972): 5-21.

> Historians of the 1960s concentrated on the regrouping of citizens along radical, ethnic, and religious lines and this has served as an occasion for reexamining American religion. Marty argues that racial and ethnic themes should be reintroduced into religious historiography because denominationalism may not be the theme and civil religion the soul of American religion.

_____. A NATION OF BEHAVERS. Chicago: University of Chicago Press, 1976. xi, 239 p.

> Marty is interested in the visible loyalties of people as evidenced in their beliefs and social behavior. He covers mainline religion, evangelism-fundamentalism, pentecostal, new religion, and ethnic religion.

Mead, Sidney E. THE NATION WITH THE SOUL OF A CHURCH. New York: Harper and Row, 1975. x, 158 p.

> Mead argues that there is an unresolved tension between the theology that legitimates the constitutional structure of the United States and that professed in the major religious denominations. This is a collection of individual essays.

_____. "The Nation with the Soul of a Church." CHURCH HISTORY 36 (September 1967): 262-83.

> The United States is not a nation with the soul of a church in the sense that it is a single, organic society. It is a pluralistic society in which no religious sect must aspire to anything more than equality with all others.

Meyer, Donald B. THE PROTESTANT SEARCH FOR POLITICAL REALISM, 1919-1941. Berkeley and Los Angeles: University of California Press, 1960. x, 482 p.

> This is a study of the Social Gospel movement during its years of decline. As capital, labor, and the churches failed to transform America, anxiety replaced hope and led Reinhold Niebuhr to devise a theology of Christian realism which emphasized grace and a sacramental role for the churches.

Miller, Douglas T. "Popular Religion of the 1950s: Norman Vincent Peale and Billy Graham." JOURNAL OF POPULAR CULTURE 9 (Summer 1975): 66-76.

> Americans turned to religion in large numbers during the 1950s to find hope in an anxious world and achieve a sense of well-being.

This explains the popularity of Peale and his cult of reassurance and Graham's crusades for conversion.

Miller, Robert Moats. AMERICAN PROTESTANTISM AND SOCIAL ISSUES, 1919-1939. Chapel Hill: University of North Carolina Press, 1958. xiv, 385 p.

The role of selected Protestant churches concerning the social order is delineated. These churches had deep social concerns and implemented them through public expression.

_____. "The Attitudes of Major Protestant Churches in America Toward War and Peace, 1919-1929." HISTORIAN 19 (November 1956): 13-38.

Most Protestant clergymen supported the war in 1917-18. But in the decade that followed most became antiwar and declared for peace through American cooperation with the other nations of the world.

_____. "The Protestant Churches and Lynching, 1919-1939." JOURNAL OF NEGRO HISTORY 42 (April 1957): 118-31.

Devout Protestants were participants in mob violence, but churches were concerned with lynching. The religious press spoke out against the practice and helped to banish the evil from the land.

Morgan, Richard E. THE SUPREME COURT AND RELIGION. New York: Free Press, 1972. viii, 216 p.

Morgan favors judicial restriction of publicly sponsored religious exercises, including school prayer, but criticizes the separation of church and state. He believes public support of parochial schools would encourage diversity and individualism.

Morrison, John L. "American Catholics and the Crusade Against Evolution." RECORDS OF THE AMERICAN CATHOLIC HISTORICAL SOCIETY OF PHILADELPHIA 64 (June 1953): 59-71.

In the evolution controversy of the 1920s, many Catholics who opposed evolution were viewed as fundamentalists. There were actually three schools of thought: one argued that evolution was an indisputable fact; another took the position that science had not proved its point; while the third occupied a middle ground and urged Catholics to wait and see on the subject.

Murphey, Murray G. "The Relation between Science and Religion." AMERICAN QUARTERLY 20 (Summer 1968): 275-95.

Murphey argues that science and religion as belief systems are not fundamentally different. The science-religion typology is misleading because it is based on the assumption that there are no gods and therefore theories concerning gods are noncognitive and lack explanatory power.

Nelson, E. Clifford. LUTHERANISM IN NORTH AMERICA, 1914-1970. Minneapolis: Augsburg, 1972. xvi, 315 p.

World War I confronted all churches with a new situation, and the Lutheran response was to form the National Lutheran Council that included all groups but the Missouri Synod. The council, however, became the seedbed of theological conflict that led to the formation of the American Lutheran Church and the Lutheran Church in America.

Nicholl, Grier. "The Image of the Protestant Minister in the Christian Social Novel." CHURCH HISTORY 37 (September 1968): 319-34.

The image of the Protestant minister in the novel of the late nineteenth and early twentieth centuries has been a negative one. In the Social Gospel novel, however, the clergyman was depicted as a new kind of preacher--physically rugged, intelligent, deeply religious, compassionate, and deeply committed to the application of the gospel to social problems.

O'Brien, David J. "American Catholic Historiography: A Post-Conciliar Evaluation." CHURCH HISTORY 37 (March 1968): 80-94.

Catholic history has been based on the assumptions that there is no incompatibility between Americanism and Catholicism and that Catholics are a minority. With Vatican Council II, modern Catholic historians should not be spokesmen of a self-conscious and defensive church.

_____. "American Catholics and Organized Labor in the 1930s." CATHOLIC HISTORICAL REVIEW 52 (October 1966): 323-49.

Catholics argued that unionization was necessary to fulfill the recovery program of Franklin Roosevelt and to begin construction of the new social order described by Pius XI. They differed sharply, however, in their assessments of the methods and objectives of existing unions and other matters.

_____. AMERICAN CATHOLICS AND SOCIAL REFORM: THE NEW DEAL YEARS. New York: Oxford University Press, 1968. xi, 287 p.

Until 1930, Catholics concentrated on parish social work and endeavored to defend their independence from a hostile Protestant majority. The Depression, however, produced Catholic positions on social issues, but Catholic thinkers did not evolve a consistent social philosophy because of disagreements over a powerful federal government.

Orser, W. Edward. "Racial Attitudes in Wartime: The Protestant Churches During the Second World War." CHURCH HISTORY 41 (September 1972): 337-53.

In March 1946, the Federal Council of Churches adopted a report committing the council to work for a nonsegregated society. Before 1939, denominations paid little attention to the race issue, but by 1945 race was a frequent subject of pronouncements and editorials in the church press.

_____. "World War II and the Pacifist Controversy in the Major Protestant Churches." AMERICAN STUDIES 14 (Fall 1973): 5-24.

The Baptists, Congregational Christians, Episcopalians, Methodists, and Presbyterians exhibited a strong pacifist strain between the wars. This essay covers the pacifist controversy that produced cleavages and anguish in these mainstream churches during American involvement in World War II.

Osborne, William A. THE SEGREGATED COVENANT: RACE RELATIONS AND AMERICAN CATHOLICS. New York: Herder and Herder, 1967. 252 p.

Osborne shows the historic prejudice of Catholics toward blacks, the slowness of church leaders to move toward social justice, and the abuse of individual bishops and priests who tried to hasten the process by members of the laity. Prejudice had many versions as practiced by the Irish and the Slavs.

Paul, Rodman W. "The Mormons as a Theme in Western Historical Writing." JOURNAL OF AMERICAN HISTORY 54 (December 1967): 511-23.

Historical writing concerning the West has been criticized for lacking analysis and interpretation, and Paul suggests that this be met by subjecting some of the major topics to "reflective examination." He emphasizes that Mormon history is one such topic since these people not only control a large cultural area, but started out as innovators only to become conservatives who appear to be incapable of adjusting to modern life.

Philp, Kenneth. "John Collier and the Crusade to Protect Indian Religious Freedom, 1920-1926." JOURNAL OF ETHNIC STUDIES 1 (Spring 1973): 22-38.

The 1920s was a period in which Indian land was being confiscated and Indian culture was being attacked in an effort to destroy. John Collier served as executive secretary of the American Indian Defense Association, and successfully fought Indian cultural annihilation because he was convinced that tribal life offered an alternative to the excessive materialism and shallow individualism of American society.

Rathbun, John W. "Martin Luther King: The Theology of Social Action."
AMERICAN QUARTERLY 20 (Spring 1968): 38-53.

King's theology of social action is based on the Social Gospel,
Protestant neo-orthodoxy, personalism, and the nonviolent philosophy of love of Ghandhi. This theology produced a revolution in
King's mind, a revolution that involved the overthrow of segregation and a better distribution of wealth.

Reimers, David M. "The Race Problem and Presbyterian Union." CHURCH
HISTORY 31 (June 1962): 203-15.

This essay concerns the failure of union in 1954-55 between the
northern and southern Presbyterian churches. The author maintains
that while race was not the only problem, it contributed to the
decisive nature of the merger's defeat.

Schneider, Herbert Wallace. RELIGION IN 20TH CENTURY AMERICA. Cambridge, Mass.: Harvard University Press, 1952. x, 244 p.

The twentieth century has been a revolutionary age that promoted
religious reconstruction. It brought new theological thought, notably modernism and liberalism, as well as the realization of the
social dimension of religious experience.

Smith, Timothy L. "Religious Denominations as Ethnic Communities: A Regional
Case Study." CHURCH HISTORY 35 (June 1966): 207-26.

This is a study of the religious life of the Lake Superior copper
and iron mining region. Smith suggests that congregations and denominations be studied in terms of social and institutional necessity
and that ethnic communities in religious history be looked at in
terms of social psychology.

Smith, Willard H. "William Jennings Bryan and the Social Gospel." JOUR-
NAL OF AMERICAN HISTORY 53 (June 1966): 41-60.

Bryan was always a fundamentalist as well as a progressive social
Christian with an evangelical base. He became more orthodox in
religion as he grew older, but he was not an ultraconservative nor
a reactionary in the 1920s.

Smylie, James H. "American Religious Bodies, Just War, and Vietnam."
JOURNAL OF CHURCH AND STATE 11 (Autumn 1969): 383-408.

The Americanization of the Vietnam war raised a critical problem
within the churches and synagogues concerning how America should
deal with worldwide responsibilities in a just way. Smylie surveys
religious debate on the war and argues that it helped produce a
reevaluation of national direction.

_____. "The Roman Catholic Church, the State, and Al Smith." CHURCH HISTORY 29 (September 1960): 321-43.

The presidential candidacy of Al Smith in 1928 gave people who knew the literature of Roman Catholicism an opportunity to raise questions concerning Catholic teaching on church and state. This assumed the status of a national political debate in which Catholics were accused of being a threat to American liberties.

Szasz, Ferenc M. "William Jennings Bryan, Evolution, and the Fundamentalist-Modernist Controversy." NEBRASKA HISTORY 56 (Summer 1975): 259-78.

Bryan was not the main leader of the fundamentalist movement in the 1920s. He supported fundamentalism on evolution, but differed on theology, tactics, and the nature of American society.

Thompson, Dennis C. "The Basic Doctrines and Concepts of Reinhold Niebuhr's Political Thought." JOURNAL OF CHURCH AND STATE 17 (Spring 1975): 275-300.

Niebuhr occupies a seminal position in political thought, but he often changed his positions. He called himself a "realist" who recognized the effects of power in society as well as the corruption imposed on the Christian norm.

Toy, E.V., Jr. "The National Lay Committee and the National Council of Churches: A Case Study of Protestants in Conflict." AMERICAN QUARTERLY 21 (Summer 1969): 190-209.

This is a study of the clash between social activists in the National Council and ultraconservatives among the council's lay sponsors during the 1950s. Political conservatives allied themselves with fundamentalists since both opposed church participation in economic and social issues and equated free enterprise with spiritual freedom.

_____. "Spiritual Mobilization: The Failure of an Ultraconservative Ideal in the 1950s." PACIFIC NORTHWEST QUARTERLY 61 (April 1970): 77-86.

Spiritual mobilization was an effort to make religion an instrument for alleviating social conflict and promoting anticommunism. It died because it did not have a dynamic program and had only vague principles in support of capitalism.

Urofsky, Melvin I. AMERICAN ZIONISM FROM HERZL TO THE HOLOCAUST. Garden City, N.Y.: Doubleday, 1975. xi, 538 p.

Urofsky shows that Zionism in the United States took root as a philanthropic movement dedicated to the needs of oppressed Jews elsewhere. He emphasizes the period from 1914 to 1930, when Louis Brandeis was working to fuse Zionism with Americanism.

_____. "Zionism: An American Experience." AMERICAN JEWISH HISTORI-
CAL QUARTERLY 63 (March 1974): 215-29.

Zionism in the United States was not the product of anti-Semitism.
Louis Brandeis and others argued that Zionism was not incompatible
with American ideals, that both were dedicated to democracy and
social justice, and American Jews could have a spiritual association with a Jewish state without becoming disloyal Americans.

Valaik, J. David. "American Catholic Dissenters and the Spanish Civil War."
CATHOLIC HISTORICAL REVIEW 53 (January 1968): 537-55.

This essay portrays the efforts of COMMONWEAL and the CATHO-
LIC WORKER to support the republican cause in the Spanish Civil
War. The WORKER urged peace, while COMMONWEAL called
for neutrality.

_____. "Catholics, Neutrality, and the Spanish Embargo, 1937-1939."
JOURNAL OF AMERICAN HISTORY 54 (June 1967): 73-85.

Franklin Roosevelt's embargo on arms shipments to either side in
the Spanish Civil War angered liberals but pleased many Catholics
who supported Franco. These Catholics and others organized the
Keep the Spanish Embargo Committee and the leaders of the Catholic Church made every effort to convince the faithful of the recti-
tude of Franco's cause.

_____. "In the Days Before Ecumenism: American Catholics, Anti-Semitism,
and the Spanish Civil War." JOURNAL OF CHURCH AND STATE 13 (Autumn
1971): 465-78.

During times when the followers of Catholicism and Judaism should
have been united in facing depression and a worsening international order, they were fighting each other over the Spanish
Civil War. Many Catholics supported the Franco faction and virulently opposed Jews who supported the Loyalists.

Varg, Paul A. MISSIONARIES, CHINESE, AND DIPLOMATS: THE AMERI-
CAN PROTESTANT MISSIONARY MOVEMENT IN CHINA, 1890-1952. Princeton, N.J.: Princeton University Press, 1958. xii, 335 p.

Varg stresses the missionaries' attitudes toward imperialism, education, the early political awakening of China, and the development
of Chinese nationalism. He concludes that they had very little
impact on day-to-day decision making in China.

Vinca, Robert H. "The American Catholic Reaction to the Persecution of the
Church in Mexico, 1926-1936." RECORDS OF THE AMERICAN CATHOLIC
HISTORICAL SOCIETY OF PHILADELPHIA 79 (March 1968): 3-38.

American Catholics viewed the persecution of the church in Mexico as a negative phase in the modern Mexican Revolution. The introduction of socialist education caused a commotion in Catholic circles, and pressure was exerted on the United States government to conduct investigations.

Vinz, Warren L. "The Politics of Protestant Fundamentalism in the 1950s and 1960s." JOURNAL OF CHURCH AND STATE 14 (Spring 1972): 235–60.

The views of fundamentalist leaders, which constituted the radical Right, were taken seriously by the rank and file. These political attitudes, furthermore, were compatible with theological convictions.

Warnock, Henry Y. "Southern Methodists, the Negro, and Unification: The First Phase." JOURNAL OF NEGRO HISTORY 52 (October 1967): 287–324.

When northern and southern Methodists merged in 1939, the presence of more than three hundred thousand Negro communicants in the northern church provoked heated debate. The argument, however, was never over segregation per se but whether segregation should be within the church or outside it.

Wentz, F.K. "American Catholic Periodicals React to Nazism." CHURCH HISTORY 31 (December 1962): 400–420.

This is a study of reactions to Nazism in AMERICA, the BROOKLYN TABLET, and COMMONWEAL. These periodicals viewed Hitler as an obstreperous ally against communism until 1935, when it became evident that Nazis were attacking the Roman Catholic Church.

White, Edward A. SCIENCE AND RELIGION IN AMERICAN THOUGHT: THE IMPACT OF NATURALISM. Stanford, Calif.: Stanford University Press, 1952. viii, 117 p.

White discusses spokesmen for evolution such as Andrew D. White and John Fiske, William James, David Starr Jordan, John Dewey, and others. He attempts to revive a Christian interpretation of history.

White, Ronald C., Jr., and Hopkins, C. Howard. THE SOCIAL GOSPEL: RELIGION AND REFORM IN CHANGING AMERICA. Philadelphia: Temple University Press, 1976. xix, 306 p.

This is a collection of essays that begins with the origins of the Social Gospel and continues until the 1960s. The authors define religious movements in terms of a sense of social consciousness and mission, but they do not show how they were influenced by the Social Gospel.

Williams, J.D. "Separation of Church and State in Mormon Theory and Practice." JOURNAL OF CHURCH AND STATE 9 (Spring 1967): 238–62.

The Mormon Church's record in politics has been pragmatic, ranging from near theocracy in the early days to more recent endorsement of candidates. This is based on ambivalence in Mormon theory which permits the church to find precedents either for or against involvement in politics.

Wilson, E. Raymond. UPHILL FOR PEACE: QUAKER IMPACT ON CONGRESS. Richmond, Ind.: Friends United Press, 1975. xx, 432 p.

The Friends Committee on National Legislation, organized in 1943, attempted to get the U.S. government to distribute food surpluses to the hungry of Europe, give justice to minorities, support the poor, launch the Peace Corps, and end universal military training, among many things. The organization achieved only a few victories as this study shows.

Chapter 11

SCIENCE AND MEDICINE

COLONIAL PERIOD TO 1815

Beall, Otho T., Jr., and Shryock, Richard H. COTTON MATHER, FIRST SIGNIFICANT FIGURE IN AMERICAN MEDICINE. Baltimore: Johns Hopkins University Press, 1954. x, 241 p.

Mather studied medicine because he thought a speech impediment would prevent him from becoming a theologian. He wanted to ameliorate the health conditions of the poor and he played a leading role in the inoculation movement.

Bedini, Silvio A. THINKERS AND TINKERS: EARLY AMERICAN MEN OF SCIENCE. New York: Charles Scribner's Sons, 1975. xix, 520 p.

This study is designed to correct earlier ones that focused on major personalities and the scientific elite. Bedini discusses the "little men" with practical skills who applied practical science and devices.

Bell, Whitfield J., Jr. EARLY AMERICAN SCIENCE: NEEDS AND OPPORTUNITIES FOR STUDY. Williamsburg, Va.: Institute for Early American History and Culture, 1955. x, 85 p.

Bell surveys early American science and delineates its international aspects. The field needs historians trained in the technical knowledge of the field.

Binger, Carl. REVOLUTIONARY DOCTOR: BENJAMIN RUSH, 1746-1813. New York: W.W. Norton and Co., 1966. 326 p.

Binger is a psychiatrist who explains Rush's contribution to psychiatry with empathy, but without psychoanalyzing his subject. Rush was opinionated and stubborn, but he was also tolerant to minorities and farsighted with respect to the mentally ill.

Brown, Ira V., ed. JOSEPH PRIESTLEY: SELECTIONS FROM HIS WRITINGS. University Park: Pennsylvania State University Press, 1962. 343 p.

Priestley was a leading eighteenth-century scientist, teacher, minister, and writer. This sampling of his work includes his memoirs and selections from his writings on education, political theory, science, and religion.

Burchell, Howard B. "Coincidental Bicentennials: United States and Foxgloves Therapy." JOURNAL OF THE HISTORY OF MEDICINE AND ALLIED SCIENCES 31 (July 1976): 292-306.

Burchell credits William Withering of Boston with originating foxglove therapy for the treatment of dropsy in 1775. The foxglove plant is a wildflower and a source of digitalis that is still being studied today.

Butterfield, L.H., ed. LETTERS OF BENJAMIN RUSH. 2 vols. Memoirs of the American Philosophical Society, vol. 3, pts. 1-2. Princeton, N.J.: Princeton University Press, 1951. lxxxvii, 1,295 p.

Rush was a leading figure in medicine, literature, and civic life. These letters record his interest in religion, politics, medicine, morality, welfare, and humanism as well as his many crusades and campaigns.

Cash, Philip. MEDICAL MEN AT THE SIEGE OF BOSTON, APRIL, 1775-APRIL, 1776. Philadelphia: American Philosophical Society, 1973. xi, 185 p.

This is an evaluation of the medical personalities and problems of British and colonial physicians in the early years of the Revolution, particularly of those who headed the Continental army medical service. Most of the physicians had experience beyond medical apprenticeship.

Cassedy, James H. "Meteorology and Medicine in Colonial America: Beginnings of an Experimental Approach." JOURNAL OF THE HISTORY OF MEDICINE AND ALLIED SCIENCES 24 (April 1969): 193-204.

Among medical investigations in early America was the study of the relationship between diseases and the environment. A few physicians carried out experiments concerning the effects of the weather on disease.

Cutright, Paul Russell. LEWIS AND CLARK: PIONEERING NATURALISTS. Urbana: University of Illinois Press, 1969. xiii, 506 p.

This study, written by a biologist, emphasizes that Lewis trained himself as a naturalist in President Jefferson's library and acquired field work on the expedition. Both he and Clark recorded scien-

tific data, including information on diseases, that was detailed
and accurate enough for later classification.

D'Elia, Donald J. "Benjamin Rush, David Hartley, and the Revolutionary Uses
of Psychology." PROCEEDINGS OF THE AMERICAN PHILOSOPHICAL SOCIETY
114 (13 April 1970): 109-18.

> Rush regarded Hartley's Christian system of physiological psychology
> as a great philosophical discovery. He argued, in using Hartley,
> that the life of man was the effect of God's sovereign will realiz-
> ing His loving purposes directly in the natural world and that re-
> publican governments were the agents of moral reformation.

_____. "Dr. Benjamin Rush and the American Medical Revolution." PRO-
CEEDINGS OF THE AMERICAN PHILOSOPHICAL SOCIETY 110 (23 August
1966): 227-34.

> The unifying principle in Rush's medical system was the oneness of
> all disease. He believed that disease was in the nature of fever,
> had its origin in the distension of the arteries and blood vessels,
> and that purging and blood-letting were demanded as cures.

_____. "Jefferson, Rush, and the Limits of Philosophical Friendship." PRO-
CEEDINGS OF THE AMERICAN PHILOSOPHICAL SOCIETY 117 (25 October
1973): 333-43.

> Jefferson and Rush were brought together by their faith in Enlight-
> enment liberalism. They fell out because of Rush's conception of
> modern science as being complementary to religious faith.

Duffy, John. EPIDEMICS IN COLONIAL AMERICA. Baton Rouge: Louisiana
State University Press, 1953. xi, 274 p.

> Medical training and practice, science, the terror and panics of
> epidemics, and the despair of parents who lost children are de-
> scribed. Only strong religious convictions could steady a community
> in the terror of an epidemic, and clergymen were often physicians
> also.

Earnest, Ernest. JOHN AND WILLIAM BARTRAM, BOTANISTS AND EX-
PLORERS, 1699-1777, 1739-1823. Pennsylvania Lives. Philadelphia: University of Pennsylvania Press, 1940. vi, 187 p.

> The Bartrams, father and son, were not only distinguished scientists,
> but also important writers of prose. Earnest portrays their lives,
> but does not treat the underlying forces that made the Bartrams
> great.

Ewan, Joseph, and Ewan, Nesta. JOHN BANISTER AND HIS NATURAL HIS-
TORY OF VIRGINIA, 1678-1692. Urbana: University of Illinois Press, 1970.
xxx, 485 p.

Banister was a clergyman-botanist who contributed to the systematic study of the natural history of America. His descriptions, sketches, and specimens contributed importantly to pre- and post-Linnean science in England.

Fox, Sanford J. SCIENCE AND JUSTICE: THE MASSACHUSETTS WITCH-CRAFT TRIALS. Baltimore: Johns Hopkins Press, 1968. xix, 121 p.

Seventeenth-century science accommodated itself to religion and did not contradict a belief in witches. At the same time, science provided a proof of harm done by witches by indicating that illnesses that lay beyond diagnostic skills and did not respond to treatment might be evidence of their work.

Frick, George Frederick, and Stearns, Raymond Phineas. MARK CATESBY: THE COLONIAL AUDUBON. Urbana: University of Illinois Press, 1961. x, 137 p.

Supported by English sponsors, Catesby carried out investigations during the early eighteenth century in the Carolinas, Florida, and the Bahamas that earned him election to the Royal Society. This study shows that western science from its beginnings was an international undertaking.

Greene, John C. "American Science Comes of Age, 1780-1820." JOURNAL OF AMERICAN HISTORY 55 (June 1968): 22-41.

Greene traces the relationships between American and British scientists but also shows that independence fostered a patriotism expressed in the desire that the discovery and description of the scientific treasures of the New World should be carried out by Americans. After 1820, American science no longer depended on European benefactions and began to work out its own destiny.

Harper, Francis, ed. THE TRAVELS OF WILLIAM BARTRAM: NATURALIST'S EDITION. New Haven, Conn.: Yale University Press, 1958. lxii, 727 p.

Bartram traveled through Georgia, Florida, and west to the Mississippi between 1773 and 1777. This book is an important source on the flora, fauna, topography, and human inhabitants of the area.

Hawke, David Freeman. BENJAMIN RUSH: REVOLUTIONARY GADFLY. Indianapolis: Bobbs-Merrill, 1971. x, 790 p.

Rush is portrayed as a secondary thinker who derived his medical ideas and political thoughts from others. He advocated his thinking with persistence even though his opinions were often incorrect or rejected.

Hindle, Brooke. "Cadwallader Colden's Extension of the Newtonian Principles."
WILLIAM AND MARY QUARTERLY 13 (October 1956): 459-75.

> Colden attempted to explain the properties of gravity. In doing
> this, he was a follower of Sir Isaac Newton and not a scientist
> who wanted to overthrow his theory.

_____. THE PURSUIT OF SCIENCE IN REVOLUTIONARY AMERICA, 1753-
1789. Chapel Hill: University of North Carolina Press for the Institute of
Early American History and Culture, Williamsburg, Virginia, 1956. xii, 410 p.

> Hindle emphasizes the organization of scientific works from Peter
> Collinson to the American Philosophical Society, the American
> Academy, and other organizations. He discusses the cultural na-
> tionalism of the revolutionary generation and its capacity to sustain
> scientific endeavors.

_____. TECHNOLOGY IN EARLY AMERICA: NEEDS AND OPPORTUNITIES
FOR STUDY. With the "Directory of Artifact Collections" by Lucius F. Ells-
worth. Chapel Hill: University of North Carolina Press for the Institute of
Early American History and Culture, Williamsburg, Virginia, 1966. xix, 145 p.

> This is a guide and reference for scholars. In an introduction,
> Hindle compares the history of technology with the history of sci-
> ence and emphasizes the effect of science on technology.

Hornberger, Theodore. SCIENTIFIC THOUGHT IN THE AMERICAN COLLEGES,
1638-1800. University Research Institute, project no. 67. Austin: University
of Texas Press, 1945. 108 p.

> The development of scientific thought in Harvard, Yale, William
> and Mary, and the younger colleges progressed from elementary
> mathematics to physics, astronomy, botany, zoology, chemistry,
> and geography. Few professors or students made original contribu-
> tions since they depended largely on outdated European texts.

Jaffe, Bernard. MEN OF SCIENCE IN AMERICA: THE ROLE OF SCIENCE
IN THE GROWTH OF OUR COUNTRY. New York: Simon and Schuster, 1944.
xi, 600 p.

> Using the biographical approach, beginning with the Virginia natural-
> ist and mathematician Thomas Herriot (1560-1621) and ending with
> the early career of nuclear physicist Ernest O. Lawrence (1901-58),
> the author attempts to explain the internal development of his sub-
> jects as well as the irrelationship with social and economic condi-
> tions. The synthesis is comprehensive, includes both biological
> and physical scientists, and covers a long period of time.

Jellison, Richard M. "Scientific Enquiry in Eighteenth-Century Virginia."
HISTORIAN 25 (May 1963): 292-311.

Virginia has been overlooked as a focal point for science in the eighteenth century. The colony and state was the scene of much and varied scientific activity, and its scientists were not lesser men.

Jones, Gordon W. "Medicine in Virginia in Revolutionary Times." JOURNAL OF THE HISTORY OF MEDICINE AND ALLIED SCIENCES 31 (July 1976): 250-70.

Virginia was a disease-ridden society in revolutionary times. There were about five hundred physicians, but medical practice was primitive and people were infected with smallpox, typhus, diphtheria, pneumonia, intestinal worms, and other diseases.

Kerber, Linda K. "Science in the Early Republic: The Society for the Study of Natural Philosophy." WILLIAM AND MARY QUARTERLY 29 (April 1972): 263-80.

The Society for the Study of Natural Philosophy was an experiment in postgraduate education in Boston during the opening years of the nineteenth century. Members set up a laboratory and conducted experiments at a time when amateur scientific groups elsewhere were playing roles in the diffusion of knowledge and the self-education of their members.

Leventhal, Herbert. IN THE SHADOW OF ENLIGHTENMENT: OCCULTISM AND RENAISSANCE SCIENCE IN EIGHTEENTH-CENTURY AMERICA. New York: New York University Press, 1976. 330 p.

Renaissance science emphasized the relationship between the animal, vegetable, and mineral, as well as beliefs in witchcraft, astrology, and alchemy. Leventhal depicts the vitality of these assumptions in eighteenth-century science.

McKeehan, Louis W. YALE SCIENCE: THE FIRST HUNDRED YEARS, 1701-1801. Yale University School of Medicine, Historial Library, publication no. 18. New York: Henry Schuman, 1947. ix, 82 p.

Yale received a collection of books rich in scientific thought in 1714 but did not establish a professorship in mathematics and science until 1770. This study deals with professors and students and their work.

Miller, Genevieve. "Smallpox Inoculation in England and America: A Reappraisal." WILLIAM AND MARY QUARTERLY 13 (October 1956): 476-92.

Historians have believed that the permanent establishment of smallpox inoculation in England was a consequence of its successful employment in the American colonies. Miller argues that its use in the colonies had little influence, because English physicians already were favorably disposed.

Shryock, Richard H. "Empiricism versus Rationalism in American Medicine, 1650-1950." PROCEEDINGS OF THE AMERICAN ANTIQUARIAN SOCIETY 79 (15 April 1969): 99-150.

An empirical approach to medicine was taking little interest in theories or even cumulative knowledge, while rational procedures concerned evidence or formulating theories. Shryock explores the medical settings in which discussions of these two differences of opinion took place.

_____. MEDICAL LICENSING IN AMERICA, 1650-1965. Baltimore: Johns Hopkins Press, 1967. xi, 124 p.

Licensing of physicians is designed to protect the public from quacks and also to protect reputable physicians against competition from the poorly trained. From the late eighteenth century through the nineteenth, licensing was the province of medical societies and schools, but because of commercialism in medical schools national examinations under professional control were adopted.

_____. "The Medical Reputation of Benjamin Rush: Contrasts over Two Centuries." BULLETIN OF THE HISTORY OF MEDICINE 45 (November-December 1971): 507-53.

Shryock discusses historical and other assessments of the eighteenth-century physician. He characterizes Rush as miscast as a medical thinker or scientist.

_____. MEDICINE AND SOCIETY IN AMERICA, 1660-1860. New York: New York University Press, 1960. x, 182 p.

This volume consists of four lectures on the origins of the medical profession, medical thought and practice to 1820, health and disease to 1820, and medicine and society from 1820 to 1860. Shryock shows that modernization in medical theory evoked little response among practitioners, but life expectancy increased after 1800 as a result of smallpox vaccination and improvements in sanitation.

Stearns, Raymond Phineas. SCIENCE IN THE BRITISH COLONIES OF AMERICA. Urbana: University of Illinoss Press, 1970. xx, 760 p.

Stearns covers American science to 1770. He begins with the Royal Society and the work in America stimulated by its fellows, turns to biographies and the formation of American scientific organizations after 1740, and in this manner discusses natural history, medicine, agriculture, and technology.

Van de Wetering, John E. "God, Science, and the Puritan Dilemma." NEW ENGLAND QUARTERLY 38 (December 1965): 494-507.

The self-sufficient, mechanical universe of Newton offered the church a dilemma because there was little room for God to exert an influence. This is a study of Thomas Prince (1687-1758), a clergyman who sought God in natural law and found God as the force behind all motion in the physical world.

Williams, William H. "The 'Industrious Poor' and the Founding of the Pennsylvania Hospital." PENNSYLVANIA MAGAZINE OF HISTORY AND BIOGRAPHY 97 (October 1973): 431-43.

This is a study of the founding of Pennsylvania Hospital. It was a copy of the British voluntary hospital that was supported by voluntary subscribers, attended by consulting physicians free of charge, and designed for the poor to keep down rates and render these people more content with their lot.

1815-1915

Anderson, Oscar E., Jr. THE HEALTH OF A NATION: HARVEY W. WILEY AND THE FIGHT FOR PURE FOOD. Chicago: University of Chicago Press for the University of Cincinnati, 1958. x, 333 p.

This is a study of what happened to the idea that people should know what they were eating and drinking when it became entangled with the political process. Efforts to give legislative shape to this belief brought scientific experiments, bureaucratic inertia, budgets, special interests, public opinion, and the whim of Congress into play.

Bates, Ralph S. SCIENTIFIC SOCIETIES IN THE UNITED STATES. New York: John Wiley and Sons for the Technology Press, Massachusetts Institute of Technology, 1945. vii, 246 p.

Five hundred national, state, and local institutions are mentioned in this book. Bates tries to deal with the development of science and technology not only in America but throughout the world.

Baur, John E. "The Health Seeker in the Westward Movement, 1830-1900." MISSISSIPPI VALLEY HISTORICAL REVIEW 46 (June 1959): 91-110.

Almost every caravan westward carried rheumatics, dyspeptics, and refugees from the recurring epidemics of yellow fever, smallpox, and cholera to the dry plains. After the Civil War, with the railroads, health seekers came to Colorado, California, Arizona, New Mexico, and Nevada to achieve cures for tuberculosis and other ailments.

_____. THE HEALTH SEEKERS OF SOUTHERN CALIFORNIA, 1870-1900. San Marino, Calif.: Huntington Library, 1959. xviii, 202 p.

Health seekers were important in the settlement and development of California. Indeed, they became the dynamic in development, founded communities such as Pasadena, Palm Springs, and Santa Monica, and contributed vitally to the beekeeping and citrus industries.

Beardsley, Edward H. "The American Scientist as Social Activist: Franz Boas, Burt G. Wilder, and the Fight for Racial Justice, 1900-1915." ISIS 64 (March 1973): 50-66.

Boas and Wilder, contrary to the traditional interpretation that most scientists in the early twentieth century favored discrimination, were deeply committed to racial justice for the Negro. They influenced colleagues in anthropology and anatomy to proceed with caution in applying their research to contemporary racial problems.

Betts, John R. "Mind and Body in Early American Thought." JOURNAL OF AMERICAN HISTORY 54 (March 1968): 787-805.

The origins of American thought about mind and body can be traced to the Enlightenment, the romantic spirit of the early republic, and the appeals of physicians, educators, health advocates, and sports enthusiasts of the middle period. Physicians emphasized health and educators alerted Americans to the threat against their physical and mental powers that came from the confinements of home and school and of life in the city.

Boccaccio, Mary. "Ground Itch and Dew Poison: The Rockefeller Sanitary Commission, 1909-14." JOURNAL OF THE HISTORY OF MEDICINE AND ALLIED SCIENCES 27 (January 1972): 30-53.

This is a study of the efforts of the Rockefeller Sanitary Commission to eradicate hookworm disease in the South. This disease was known as ground itch or dew poison because it resulted from soil pollution and the parasite entered the body through the skin.

Bonner, Thomas Neville. AMERICAN DOCTORS AND GERMAN UNIVERSITIES: A CHAPTER IN INTERNATIONAL INTELLECTUAL RELATIONS, 1870-1914. Lincoln: University of Nebraska Press, 1963. x, 210 p.

The activities of American medical students in German universities following the Civil War are discussed. Most studied in Vienna where they monopolized medical courses, demanded that courses be taught in English, and even gained official control over enrollments.

_____. THE KANSAS DOCTOR: A CENTURY OF PIONEERING. Lawrence: University of Kansas Press, 1959. xiv, 334 p.

Bonner describes the role of the pioneer physician in Kansas's turbulent history. He also shows that Kansas later pioneered in public and mental health and produced leaders such as Arthur Hertzler, Samuel Crumbine, Karl Menninger, and Logan Clendening.

_____. MEDICINE IN CHICAGO, 1850-1950: A CHAPTER IN THE SOCIAL AND SCIENTIFIC DEVELOPMENT OF A CITY. Madison, Wis.: American Historical Research Center, 1957. xviii, 302 p.

The medical profession in Chicago did not enjoy a position of confidence in the last half of the nineteenth century. In the twentieth, the Chicago Medical Society opposed contract care, health insurance, and state medicine.

Bordley, James III, and Harvey, A. McGehee. TWO CENTURIES OF AMERICAN MEDICINE, 1776-1976. Philadelphia: Saunders, 1976. xv, 844 p.

Most of this book covers the period since 1876 and especially the post-World War II years. The authors use the hypothesis that medical science advanced in a series of "explosion phenomena"--the bacteriology explosion of the 1880s, vitamins in 1910, and so forth.

Bozeman, Theodore Dwight. "Joseph LeConte: Organic Science and a 'Sociology for the South.'" JOURNAL OF SOUTHERN HISTORY 39 (November 1973): 565-82.

Bozeman argues that southern intellectuals of the antebellum period resorted to organic images in expressing themselves concerning social and political ideas. LeConte, a geologist and professor who emphasized the dignity of organic life in his scientific writings and argued for the fundamentally organic nature of society and social development, was an example of this trend.

Breedon, James O. "Body Snatchers and Anatomy Professors: Medical Education in Nineteenth-Century Virginia." VIRGINIA MAGAZINE OF HISTORY AND BIOGRAPHY 83 (July 1975): 321-45.

Improvement of instruction in anatomy called for more cadavers and Virginia did not have legal provisions for dissection material. This is a study of John Staige Davis, demonstrator in practical anatomy in the University of Virginia, and his efforts to secure classroom material in the 1850s.

_____. "Thomsonianism in Virginia." VIRGINIA MAGAZINE OF HISTORY AND BIOGRAPHY 82 (April 1974): 150-80.

Thomsonian medical practice based on sweating and enemas challenged traditional medicine during the early years of the nineteenth century. This is a study of its rise and fall in Virginia.

Buerki, Robert A. "Medical Views of Narcotics and Their Effects in the Mid-1890s." PHARMACY IN HISTORY 17 (1975): 3-12.

> Physicians viewed opium and morphine as habit forming, freely available to the public, and subject to intentional and unintentional abuse. Treatment for addiction was becoming less harsh by 1895, but moral overtones still existed.

Bullough, Vern L., and Voght, Martha. "Homosexuality and Its Confusion with the 'Secret Sin' in Pre-Freudian America." JOURNAL OF THE HISTORY OF MEDICINE AND ALLIED SCIENCES 28 (April 1973): 143-55.

> This paper is concerned with American medical conceptions of masturbation and homosexuality in the nineteenth century, and the effect the confusion of the two had in creating a general fear of sex. It was believed that excessive sexual activity caused insanity, a view that came from the observation that large numbers of patients in mental institutions masturbated.

_____. "Women, Menstruation, and Nineteenth-Century Medicine." BULLETIN OF THE HISTORY OF MEDICINE 47 (January-February 1973): 66-82.

> A recurrent theme in the history of medicine is the reluctance of physicians to accept new scientific findings. This is a study of the arguments and research concerning menstruation and women's health.

Burnham, John C. "The Progressive Era Revolution in American Attitudes toward Sex." JOURNAL OF AMERICAN HISTORY 59 (March 1973): 885-908.

> Reformers in the social hygiene movement directed their efforts against two tenets of Victorian morality: the conspiracy of silence that prevented public discussion of sex, and the double standard that demanded women be pure and allowed men considerable freedom in sex both before and outside marriage. Physicians who fought these beliefs did so to control gonorrhea and syphilis through education.

_____. "Psychiatry, Psychology and the Progressive Movement." AMERICAN QUARTERLY 12 (Winter 1960): 457-65.

> Reformers in psychiatry and psychology shared a set of social assumptions with reformers in politics and economics. Psychotherapists tried to decide how the world should be run and behaviorists attempted to predict and control behavior.

_____. PSYCHOANALYSIS AND AMERICAN MEDICINE: 1894-1918. MEDICINE, SCIENCE, AND CULTURE. New York: International Universities Press, 1967. 249 p.

The cultural and scientific environment into which psychoanalytic ideas were introduced as well as the Americanization of Freudian concepts are emphasized. American empiricism, social environmentalism, and progressive reformism influenced the development of the new psychology and caused it to become a subspecialty in medicine by 1918.

Burns, Chester R. "Malpractice Suits in American Medicine before the Civil War." BULLETIN OF AMERICAN MEDICINE 43 (January-February 1969): 41-56.

Medical practitioners were held legally responsible for what they professed they were able to do and for the attainment of necessary skills. They were also expected to use reasonable care and exercise good judgment.

Calhoun, Daniel Hovey. THE AMERICAN CIVIL ENGINEER: ORIGINS AND CONFLICT. Cambridge, Mass.: Harvard University Press, 1960. xvi, 295 p.

Early civil engineers gained their training mainly through experience, notably the Canal School in New York and the engineering departments of railroads. They collaborated with entrepreneurs to insure the correct fulfillment of contracts and eventually became organization men.

Calvert, Monte A. THE MECHANICAL ENGINEER IN AMERICA, 1830-1910: PROFESSIONAL CULTURES IN CONFLICT. Baltimore: Johns Hopkins Press, 1967. xviii, 296 p.

The life-styles and professional concerns of mechanical engineers from the introduction of textile and railroad machinery to the time of electrical and newer types of machinery are detailed. Conflict developed between shop culture carried on by patrician engineers and school culture identified by those with schooling who had specific professional goals.

Camfield, Thomas M. "The Professionalization of American Psychology, 1870-1917." JOURNAL OF THE HISTORY OF THE BEHAVIORAL SCIENCES 9 (January 1973): 66-75.

G. Stanley Hall launched the new psychology during the 1880s. Psychology was divorced from natural philosophy and it was subsidized by the academic establishment and professionalized during the early years of the twentieth century.

Carrigan, Jo Ann. "Privilege, Prejudice, and the Strangers' Disease in Nineteenth-Century New Orleans." JOURNAL OF SOUTHERN HISTORY 36 (November 1970): 568-78.

An examination of the mystery concerning the origin and transmission of yellow fever showed a close relationship between medical theories and social attitudes in New Orleans. Although the wealthy and native born were just as susceptible to the disease as others, they tended to dismiss yellow fever as a sickness of immigrants and the lower classes.

Cassedy, James H. "An Early American Hangover: The Medical Profession and Intemperance, 1800-1860." BULLETIN OF THE HISTORY OF MEDICINE 50 (Fall 1976): 405-13.

Physicians did not identify alcoholism as a disease in the antebellum period, but they associated the use of alcohol with other diseases. Many of them helped to further the work of temperance socities.

_____. "The 'Germ of Laziness' in the South, 1900-1915: Charles Wardell Stiles and the Progressive Paradox." BULLETIN OF THE HISTORY OF MEDICINE 45 (March-April 1971): 159-69.

Cassedy examines the growth of public health concerning hookworm disease. Stiles became something of a folk hero for his work, and he was successful because he harmonized state control with the laissez-faire sensibilities of the public.

_____. "The Microscope in American Medical Science, 1840-1860." ISIS 67 (March 1976): 76-97.

American medical students of the 1830s and early 1840s found that their texts treated the microscope with distrust and contempt. This is a study of the evolution of microscopy to a position of importance in biomedical science rather than a plaything.

Dain, Norman. CONCEPTS OF INSANITY IN THE UNITED STATES, 1789-1865. New Brunswick, N.J.: Rutgers University Press, 1964. xv, 304 p.

The thought of clergymen, lawyers, general practitioners, and psychiatrists concerning insanity is discussed. Such ideas as mental illness were cyclical, with some being advanced and then discarded only to reappear again.

Daniels, George H. "An American Defense of Bacon: A Study in the Relations of Scientific Thought, 1840-1845." HUNTINGTON LIBRARY QUARTERLY 28 (August 1965): 321-40.

In the nineteenth century, the method of Bacon and Newton meant studying facts as opposed to idle speculation. This is a study of a fundamental Protestant defense of Baconian philosophy because it could be used with ease to sustain what Protestantism explains.

_____. AMERICAN SCIENCE IN THE AGE OF JACKSON. New York: Columbia University Press, 1968. viii, 282 p.

> Jacksonian science emphasized the observation and classification of facts and the harmony of science and religion. Using a quantitative approach, Daniels reviews the works of fifty-six writers and demonstrates that natural history did not dominate scholarship and that Jacksonian emphasis on the "practical" did not penetrate research.

Davies, John D. PHRENOLOGY: FAD AND SCIENCE; A 19TH CENTURY AMERICAN CRUSADE. New Haven, Conn.: Yale University Press, 1955. xvi, 203 p.

> Phrenology held that mental behavior and moral character were products of the anatomy of the brain. In the brain there were "organs" that controlled human faculties, and size and configuration of the skull revealed the degree of development of these organs.

Davis, Robert C. "Social Research in America before the Civil War." JOURNAL OF THE HISTORY OF THE BEHAVIORAL SCIENCES 8 (January 1972): 69-85.

> This is a study of statisticians who concerned themselves with social matters and worked with physical, biological, and economic phenomena. Early social statisticians were motivated by national pride, scientific curiosity, economic calculation, and reformist humanitarianism.

Duffy, John. A HISTORY OF PUBLIC HEALTH IN NEW YORK CITY, 1866-1966. New York: Russell Sage Foundation, 1974. xxi, 690 p.

> The year 1866 marked the modern era of public health in New York City when a movement was launched that led the state legislature to create a metropolitan board of health. This study is not set in a broad social context nor does it emphasize the impact of public health on the control of social life.

_____. "Medical Practice in the Ante Bellum South." JOURNAL OF SOUTHERN HISTORY 24 (February 1959): 53-72.

> Medical practice, except surgery, had not developed far beyond the medieval period. Most physicians treated disease, regardless of its nature, by bleeding, blistering, purging, vomiting, sweating, and using calomel, although change to homeopathic treatment was being practiced, as was hydropathy.

_____. "A Note on Ante-Bellum Southern Nationalism and Medical Practice." JOURNAL OF SOUTHERN HISTORY 34 (May 1968): 266-76.

Nineteenth-century American medicine was preoccupied with disease and climate. Medical exponents of southern nationalism such as Samuel A. Cartwright argued that southern disease and southern medical practice were distinctive, assumptions that led to the establishment of southern medical schools.

_____. "Sectional Conflict and Medical Education in Louisiana." JOURNAL OF SOUTHERN HISTORY 23 (August 1957): 289-306.

In the 1850s, New Orleans was not only a center for commerce but also the leading medical center of the South. The Civil War had disastrous effects on medical education and the late nineteenth century was spent achieving prewar levels.

_____, ed. THE RUDOLPH MATAS HISTORY OF MEDICINE IN LOUISIANA. 2 vols. Baton Rouge: Louisiana State University Press for the Rudolph Matas Trust Fund, 1958, 1962. xviii, 522; xiv, 599 p.

Volume one covers the period from 1699 to 1825 and describes the change from superstition and callous individualism to empiricism and social conscience. Volume two follows the story of Louisiana medicine from 1825 to the early twentieth century. Duffy illuminates the practice of medicine and surgery, regulations governing practice, epidemics, public health, hospitals, medical education, medical writings, and medical societies.

Dupree, A. Hunter. SCIENCE IN THE FEDERAL GOVERNMENT: A HISTORY OF POLICIES AND ACTIVITIES TO 1940. Cambridge, Mass.: Belknap Press of Harvard University Press, 1957. xii, 460 p.

Science in the federal government had its origins in the constitution but it did not begin to record substantial accomplishments until the three decades before the Civil War when professional scientists began to man the scientific agencies. The post-Civil War period saw the establishment of the Department of Agriculture, Geological Survey, and the National Bureau of Standards.

Etheridge, Elizabeth W. THE BUTTERFLY CASTE: A SOCIAL HISTORY OF PELLAGRA IN THE SOUTH. Westport, Conn.: Greenwood, 1972. ix, 278 p.

Pellagra was known as the disease of the four D's in the South--diarrhea, dermatitis, dementia, and death. This is a medical detective story covering its cause and cure.

Flexner, Simon, and Flexner, James Thomas. WILLIAM HENRY WELCH AND THE HEROIC AGE OF AMERICAN MEDICINE. New York: Viking Press, 1941. x, 539 p.

Welch studied in Europe and brought the promise of pathology, physiology, and bacteriology to America in the 1870s. He recorded a number of firsts--the first laboratory course in pathology, first professor of pathology at Johns Hopkins, and first dean of the medical school--and he raised medicine to university stature during a career that lasted until 1934.

Fullenwider, S.P. "Insanity as the Loss of Self: The Moral Insanity Controversy Revisited." BULLETIN OF THE HISTORY OF MEDICINE 49 (Spring 1975): 87-101.

During the middle part of the nineteenth century, there was a dispute involving superintendents of mental hospitals over "moral insanity." This is a study of the debate over whether one's moral sense could be deranged without an accompanying intellectual derangement.

_____. "Neurasthenia: The Genteel Caste's Journey Inward." ROCKY MOUNTAIN SOCIAL SCIENCE JOURNAL 11 (April 1974): 1-10.

Neurology emerged during the Gilded Age in response to the genteel caste's demand for a scientific approach to mental illness. Young neurologists developed perceptions of the mentally ill that were scientifically up-to-date and conditioned by social class attitudes.

Galishoff, Stuart. SAFEGUARDING THE PUBLIC HEALTH: NEWARK, 1895-1918. Westport, Conn.: Greenwood, 1975. xv, 191 p.

The U.S. Census of 1890 showed that Newark had the highest death rate of any city in the nation. Galishoff discusses the acquisition of a safe source of drinking water, an adequate sewer system, reforms in tenement housing, and other matters that made Newark a safer place to live.

Gerstner, Patsy A. "A Dynamic Theory of Mountain Building: Henry Darwin Rogers, 1842." ISIS 66 (March 1975): 26-37.

Roger's mountain elevation theory was one of the most important contributions to theoretical science before 1850. He believed that mountains were built during upheavals of the land brought about by molten matter beneath the earth's crust.

Gish, Lowell. REFORM AT OSAWATOMIE STATE HOSPITAL: TREATMENT OF THE MENTALLY ILL, 1866-1970. Lawrence: University Press of Kansas, 1972. xi, 289 p.

This hospital was established in 1863. The author describes the social pressures that influenced institutional growth and focuses on the aspirations and frustrations of physicians who worked in a failing system.

Gobar, Ash. "The Phenomenology of William James." PROCEEDINGS OF THE AMERICAN PHILOSOPHICAL SOCIETY 114 (20 August 1970): 294-311.

Gobar argues that phenomenology in contemporary philosophy and the life sciences was not a foreign importation to America. James was influenced by German phenomenologists and, in turn, profoundly influenced them.

Goetzmann, William H. EXPLORATION AND EMPIRE: THE EXPLORER AND THE SCIENTIST IN THE WINNING OF THE AMERICAN WEST. New York: Alfred A. Knopf, 1966. xxii, 656 p.

Goetzmann looks at the West as it was discovered over and over again by many men, including fur traders, government explorers, geologists, paleontologists, artists, and others. Discovery was not an isolated event but a process with cultural significance.

Graustein, Jeannette E. THOMAS NUTTAL, NATURALIST: EXPLORATIONS IN AMERICA, 1808-1841. Cambridge, Mass.: Harvard University Press, 1967. xiii, 481 p.

Nuttall was a significant collector and naturalist whose major concern was botany, but who also wrote on geology, mineralogy, and ornithology. His travels with the Astoria expedition of 1811 and the second Wyeth expedition of 1834 are emphasized.

Grob, Gerald N. "Class, Ethnicity, and Race in American Mental Hospitals, 1830-75." JOURNAL OF THE HISTORY OF MEDICINE AND ALLIED SCIENCES 28 (July 1973): 207-29.

In theory, the public mental hospital was a beneficent institution that served all groups, but in practice the quality of care was dependent on class, ethnic origin, and color. Since mental hospitals served predominantly lower-class minorities, their reputation, funding, and quality of care declined.

_____. "Edward Jarvis and the Federal Census: A Chapter in the History of Nineteenth-Century American Medicine." BULLETIN OF THE HISTORY OF MEDICINE 50 (Spring 1976): 4-27.

This is a study of the role played by Jarvis, the psychiatrist, in using the census to confirm or deny existing theories concerning the etiology, nature, and incidence of mental illness. He was exemplary of the commitment of mid-nineteenth-century science to quantification and the assemblage of facts.

Guralnik, Stanley M. "Geology and Religion before Darwin: The Case of Edward Hitchcock, Theologian and Geologists (1793-1864)." ISIS 63 (December 1972): 529-43.

Hitchcock, an early leader in the development of the American Association for the Advancement of Science, and a Congregational minister, articulated his twin faiths in science and religion throughout his career. His efforts demonstrate little originality, but they show the adjustments scientists were making before the Darwinian controversy broke full force.

_____. SCIENCE AND THE ANTE-BELLUM AMERICAN COLLEGE. Philadelphia: American Philosophical Society, 1975. xiv, 227 p.

Guralnick emphasizes fifteen northeastern colleges. He demonstrates that by 1850 science had an almost dominant position in the supposedly hidebound classical curriculum.

_____. "Sources of Misconception on the Role of Science in the Nineteenth-Century American College." ISIS 65 (September 1974): 352-66.

Science and the antebellum college enjoyed an amicable and profitable relationship. Instead of emphasizing the graduate school, historians should look to the colleges where scientific priorities were assessed and scientific endeavors grew.

Hale, Nathan G., Jr. FREUD AND THE AMERICANS: THE BEGINNINGS OF PSYCHOANALYSIS IN THE UNITED STATES, 1876-1917. New York: Oxford University Press, 1971. xvi, 574 p.

Hale argues that during the last quarter of the nineteenth century Americans developed civilized morality or a code that disciplined sexuality by a premium on prudery, purity of thought and behavior. He shows how Freud and scholars in various disciplines challenged this morality and helped promote a revolution in moral and ethical codes.

Haller, John S. "Civil War Anthropometry: The Making of a Racial Ideology." CIVIL WAR HISTORY 16 (December 1970): 309-24.

Body measurements taken during the Civil War years identified the various races or species of men. Conclusions were not new, but Civil War anthropometry served as the basis of attitudes concerning racial inferiority in the late nineteenth century.

_____. OUTCASTS FROM EVOLUTION: SCIENTIFIC ATTITUDES OF RACIAL INFERIORITY, 1859-1900. Urbana: University of Illinois Press, 1971. xv, 228 p.

Haller examines late nineteenth-century social ideas and shows that anthropometric studies produced a vocabulary that placed the idea of racial inferiority in American thought. Physicians, anthropologists, and others decreed that Negroes were permanently inferior and should be condemned to extinction.

_____. "The Physician versus the Negro: Medical and Anthropological Concepts of Race in the Late Nineteenth Century." BULLETIN OF THE HISTORY OF MEDICINE 44 (March-April 1970): 154-67.

Throughout the nineteenth century, the physician was the principal source for comparative race analysis. These scientists, in the late nineteenth century, saw the Negro race working in harmony with the laws of nature and gradually succumbing to competition.

_____. "Samson of Materia Medica: Medical Theory and the Use and Abuse of Calomel in the Nineteenth Century." PHARMACY IN HISTORY 13 (1971): 27-34, 67-76.

Calomel (mercurous chloride) enjoyed great popularity in the nineteenth century. Physicians administered it with almost scholastic devotion, and medical journals were replete with communications concerning the latest uses of the drug.

Haller, John S., Jr., and Haller, Robin M. THE PHYSICIAN AND SEXUALITY IN VICTORIAN AMERICA. Urbana: University of Illinois Press, 1974. xv, 331 p.

Victorian physicians saw their mission as exposing quackery. They approached sex in a positivistic and moralistic manner, and exposed men who squandered their force in sexual enterprise.

Haller, Mark H. EUGENICS: HEREDITARIAN ATTITUDES IN AMERICAN THOUGHT. New Brunswick, N.J.: Rutgers University Press, 1963. viii, 264 p.

Haller examines the science devoted to the improvement of man through better breeding as well as the social consequences of hereditarian thinking. He indicates that eugenics reached its zenith between 1905 and 1930 when thirty states passed eugenics legislation.

Hill, Forest G. "Formative Relations of American Enterprise, Government and Science." POLITICAL SCIENCE QUARTERLY 85 (September 1960): 400-419.

This is a survey of the developing role played by the federal government in the early advancement of science and private enterprise. The government's scientific endeavors to the 1860s were extremely important for territorial and industrial expansion.

Jahns, Patricia. MATTHEW FONTAINE MAURY AND JOSEPH HENRY: SCIENTISTS OF THE CIVIL WAR. New York: Hastings House, 1961. xii, 308 p.

This is not a study of wartime research and discovery. Maury is depicted as a practical scientist who worked in the navy's charts and instruments depot and compiled weather and currents data from

logbooks, while Henry is described as the inventor of the electro-
magnet and founder of the Smithsonian Institution.

JAMES JACKSON PUTNAM AND PSYCHOANALYSIS: LETTERS BETWEEN
PUTNAM AND SIGMUND FREUD, ERNEST JONES, WILLIAM JAMES, SAN-
DOR FERENCZI, AND WILLIAM PRINCE, 1877-1917. Edited by Nathan G.
Hale, Jr. Translated by Judith Bernays Heller. Cambridge, Mass.: Harvard
University Press, 1971. xiv, 384 p.

> Putnam was a Harvard neurologist who promoted psychoanalysis.
> These letters show how Americans learned to comprehend Freud's
> theory.

Hendrickson, Walter B. "Science and Culture in the American Middle West."
ISIS 64 (September 1973): 326-40.

> Hendrickson surveys the development of scientific academies. He
> argues that they were an urban phenomenon and that they lost their
> influence as centers for research as science became interested in
> matters other than taxonomy.

Hudson, Robert P. "Abraham Flexner in Perspective: American Medical Education, 1865-1910." BULLETIN OF THE HISTORY OF MEDICINE 46 (November-December 1972): 545-61.

> Medical education in the years before the Flexner report is discuss-
> ed. The tide of reform was running heavily before 1910, and
> Flexner's contribution to educational reform was catalytic rather
> than revolutionary.

Joncich, Geraldine. "Scientists and the Schools of the Nineteenth Century:
The Case of American Physicists." AMERICAN QUARTERLY 18 (Winter 1966):
667-75.

> After 1957, the little red schoolhouse reappeared as a standard of
> education in the attacks on public education that followed the
> launching of Sputnik. Joncich examines the autobiographies of
> one hundred physicists born before 1900 and concludes that educa-
> tion below college was both haphazard and ineffective.

Jones, Billy M. HEALTH SEEKERS IN THE SOUTHWEST, 1817-1900. Norman:
University of Oklahoma Press, 1967. xiii, 254 p.

> In the nineteenth century, the afflicted moved West to live in
> health-restoring environments in the great American desert and the
> Rocky Mountains. Reputable physicians made studies of climate to
> guide easterners to helpful areas, and promoters advertised the de-
> sirability of their regions until this health frontier gradually dis-
> appeared in the twentieth century.

THE JOURNALS OF JOSEPH N. NICOLLET: A SCIENTIST ON THE MISSIS-
SIPPI HEADWATERS WITH NOTES ON INDIAN LIFE, 1836-37. Edited by
Martha Coleman Bray. Translated by Andre Fertey. St. Paul: Minnesota His-
torical Society, 1970. xviii, 288 p.

> Nicollet, a French explorer, was a deeply religious man as well
> as a scientist. His journals catalog Minnesota flora and fauna,
> and detail the culture of the Chippewa Indians before they had ex-
> tensive contact with western civilization.

Kaufman, Martin. "The American Anti-Vaccinationists and Their Arguments."
BULLETIN OF THE HISTORY OF MEDICINE 41 (September-October 1967):
463-78.

> Anti-vaccinationists were convinced that vaccinations had proved
> unsuccessful in the prevention of smallpox or that they were unsafe.
> Some even went so far as to argue that smallpox was not a serious
> illness and could easily be treated.

_____. AMERICAN MEDICAL EDUCATION: THE FORMATIVE YEARS, 1765-
1910. Westport, Conn.: Greenwood, 1976. x, 208 p.

> From the founding of the colonies to the early years of the twen-
> tieth century, medical education was skimpy. Kaufman examines
> the apprentice system of the colonial years, the establishment of
> medical schools, burgeoning of weaker schools in opposition to
> aristocratic medicine, broad scale reform, state licensing require-
> ments, and other matters.

_____. HOMEOPATHY IN AMERICA: THE RISE AND FALL OF A MEDICAL
HERESY. Baltimore: Johns Hopkins University Press, 1971. x, 205 p.

> Homeopathy was introduced during the 1830s and 1840s and its re-
> liance on small doses and the curative powers of nature competed
> with massive doses of drugs and bleeding as preferred medical
> treatments. This study concentrates on its relationship with ortho-
> dox medicine and its absorption by orthodox practitioners.

Kett, Joseph F. THE FORMATION OF THE AMERICAN MEDICAL PROFESSION.
THE ROLE OF INSTITUTIONS, 1780-1860. New Haven, Conn.: Yale University Press, 1968. xi, 217 p.

> Kett maintains that the formation of proprietary medical schools in
> the nineteenth century lowered educational standards, but they
> gave the profession an identity. Physicians could not understand
> epidemics or endemic disorders and they were divided philosophically
> concerning the treatment of disease.

King, John Owen. "Labors of an Estranged Personality: Josiah Royce on 'The
Case of John Bunyan.'" PROCEEDINGS OF THE AMERICAN PHILOSOPHICAL
SOCIETY 120 (5 February 1976): 46-58.

Royce explored abnormal experiences of the mind especially obsessional or obsessive-compulsive neurosis. An obsessional himself, Royce studied Bunyan with whom he developed a dialogue on the malaise and developed it into a model of self-alienation.

Kobrin, Frances E. "The American Midwife Controversy: A Crisis of Professionalization." BULLETIN OF THE HISTORY OF MEDICINE 40 (July-August 1966): 350-63.

Obstetrics as a specialty was sensitive to conditions and attitudes. Early in the twentieth century, a virulent debate ensued that brought the defeat of the midwife and the triumph of single standard obstetrics.

Kohlstedt, Sally Gregory. THE FORMATION OF THE AMERICAN SCIENTIFIC COMMUNITY: THE AMERICAN ASSOCIATION FOR THE ADVANCEMENT OF SCIENCE, 1848-1860. Urbana: University of Illinois Press, 1976. lxxix, 264 p.

The AAAS was begun by antebellum scientists to separate themselves from amateurs and establish a secure professional image. The beginning of this organization was a struggle because scientists lacked role definitions and institutional connections.

_____. "The Geologists' Model for National Science, 1840-1847." PROCEEDINGS OF THE AMERICAN PHILOSOPHICAL SOCIETY 118 (19 April 1974): 179-95.

Geologists were among the first American scientists to organize science on a national level. The Association of American Geologists and Naturalists was a precursor of the American Association for the Advancement of Science and attempted to increase the exchange of ideas through regular research-oriented meetings.

Kuna, David P. "The Concept of Suggestion in the Early History of Advertising Psychology." JOURNAL OF THE HISTORY OF THE BEHAVIORAL SCIENCES 12 (October 1976): 347-53.

The psychology of advertising began in the United States in 1896, but it gained prominence after 1901 through the work of Walter Dill Scott of Northwestern University. He called for the use of involuntary attention, mental imagery, the association of ideas, and the concept of suggestion in advertising.

Lange, Charles H., and Riley, Carroll L., eds. THE SOUTHWESTERN JOURNALS OF ADOLPH F. BANDELIER, 1880-1882. Albuquerque: University of New Mexico Press, 1966. xvi, 462 p.

Bandelier, born in Switzerland, was a pioneer investigator of the Indians of the American Southwest. These journals cover his first field studies of Pueblo Indian society.

Lawrence, Philip J. "Edward Hitchcock: The Christian Geologist." PRO-
CEEDINGS OF THE AMERICAN PHILOSOPHICAL SOCIETY 116 (15 February
1972): 21-34.

The nineteenth century was a time of tension in geology between
science and its link with religion through natural theology. Hitchcock was a major figure in geology and his career represented a
continuous attempt to reconcile the Bible with the evidence of the
strata.

Legan, Marshall Scott. "Hydropathy in America: A Nineteenth-Century Panacea." BULLETIN OF THE HISTORY OF MEDICINE 45 (May-June 1971):
267-80.

Legan associates hydropathy with the triumph of the common man
in the age of Jackson. It was based on taking cold water inter-
nally and inducing perspiration, and it was a widely-used remedy
although sometimes labeled as medical quackery.

Loewenberg, Bert James. "The Reaction of American Scientists to Darwinism."
AMERICAN HISTORICAL REVIEW 38 (July 1933): 687-701.

This is a study of the reaction of Louis Agassiz, Asa Gray, and
James Dwight Dana to Darwinism. Agassiz opposed the theory of
evolution, while Gray and Dana, although critical, supported it.

Longton, William Henry. "The Carolina Ideal World: Natural Science and
Social Thought in Ante Bellum South Carolina." CIVIL WAR HISTORY 20
(June 1974): 118-34.

Nineteenth-century writers placed great emphasis on the harmoni-
zation of theology, science, and social theories. The ideal world
signified that living beings developed under God's control and that
they possessed changeless characters which gave them their definitions.

Ludmerer, Kenneth M. "American Geneticists and the Eugenics Movement:
1905-1935." JOURNAL OF THE HISTORY OF BIOLOGY 2 (Fall 1969): 337-
62.

Between 1905 and 1935, many geneticists argued the issue as to
whether genetic principles should form the basis of social legislation. Between 1905 and 1915, many supported the eugenics movement and gave it popularity, but in the 1930s, they renounced the
movement and helped doom it to extinction.

_____. GENETICS AND AMERICAN SOCIETY: A HISTORICAL APPROACH.
Baltimore: Johns Hopkins University Press, 1972. x, 222 p.

After Mendel's work was rediscovered, genetics developed in the
United States. For a generation enculturated with the idea of perfection and Darwinism, genetics became the scientific way to
genius.

McMahon, A. Michael. "An American Courtship: Psychologists and Advertising Theory in the Progressive Era." AMERICAN STUDIES 13 (Fall 1972): 5-18.

> During the Progressive era, advertisers, urged on by academic psychologists, turned to experimental psychology with the hope of making consumption a central function in the life of the individual. The basis of this new theory of advertising was social control or seeing man as nonrational and capable of having his desires and aspirations manipulated in the interest of economic stability.

McVaugh, Rogers. EDWARD PALMER: PLANT EXPLORER OF THE AMERICAN WEST. Norman: University of Oklahoma Press, 1956. xviii, 430 p.

> Palmer was a British-born field collector in the southwestern United States and northern Mexico. He worked between 1859 and 1911 and also served as collector of archaeological and other materials for the United States Bureau of Ethnology.

Malin, James C. DOCTORS DEVILS AND THE WOMAN: FORT SCOTT, KANSAS 1870-1890. Lawrence, Kans.: Coronado, 1975. 122 p.

> Dr. Sarah C. Hall is the woman in this study and the devils are male physicians who obstructed her efforts to gain professional status and enlarge the rights of women. Hall gained membership in the Kansas State Medical Society but she was prevented from establishing a charitable hospital in Fort Scott.

Manning, Thomas G. GOVERNMENT IN SCIENCE: THE U.S. GEOLOGICAL SURVEY, 1867-1894. Lexington: University of Kentucky Press, 1967. xiv, 257 p.

> The U.S. Geological Survey represented the interrelationships of government, social utility, science, and private enterprise. Manning discusses geographical and geological exploration of the trans-Mississippi West, the spending of tax dollars on scientific research, and the views of geologists on ore deposits, geological strata, and the causes of physical changes in the earth's surface.

Markowitz, Gerald E., and Rosner, David Karl. "Doctors in Crisis: A Study of the Use of Medical Education Reform to Establish Modern Professional Elitism in Medicine." AMERICAN QUARTERLY 24 (March 1973): 83-107.

> The authors maintain that modern elitism in medicine can be traced to the early years of the twentieth century. Doctors attempted to reform medical education to assure financial security, as well as status and power in the community.

Matthews, F.H. "The Americanization of Sigmund Freud: Adaptations of Psychoanalysis before 1917." JOURNAL OF AMERICAN STUDIES 1 (April 1967): 39-62.

This is a study in the Americanization of foreign ideas. Before 1917, reaction to psychoanalysis took the form of outright rejection, but also of assimilation, especially in becoming an element in positivist and determinist psychology.

Meier, Hugo A. "Technology and Democracy, 1800-1860." MISSISSIPPI VALLEY HISTORICAL REVIEW 43 (March 1957): 618-40.

Applied science was viewed as a means of achieving the objectives of political, social, and economic democracy. Between 1800 and 1860, popular needs tended to determine the goals of engineers, inventors, and mechanics, although there were criticisms of American materialism.

Miller, Howard S. DOLLARS FOR RESEARCH: SCIENCE AND ITS PATRONS IN NINETEENTH-CENTURY AMERICA. Seattle: University of Washington Press, 1970. xi, 258 p.

As the intellectual content of science grew beyond the understanding of laymen, scientists found themselves increasingly dependent on laymen for support. This is a study of the means scientists employed to surmount this difficulty and it focuses on the disposition of the Smithson bequest, endowment of the Sheffield School in New Haven, the establishment of the University of Chicago, and other matters.

Mitchell, Martha Carolyn. "Health and the Medical Profession in the Lower South, 1845-1860." JOURNAL OF SOUTHERN HISTORY 10 (November 1944): 424-46.

Between 1845 and 1860, when states of the lower South were passing through a frontier stage, people suffered from epidemics of malaria and yellow fever. Before 1850, most physicians believed that all fevers were caused by a miasma created by decaying vegetable and animal matter, but some began looking at insect and germ theories.

Moore, R. Laurence. "Spiritualism and Science: Reflections on the First Decade of Spirit Rappings." AMERICAN QUARTERLY 24 (October 1972): 474-500.

Spiritualism became popular in the 1850s. It was accepted by a population that liked marvels and it was believable just as electrical phenomena were believable.

Moyers, David M. "From Quackery to Qualification: Arkansas Medical and Drug Legislation, 1881-1909." ARKANSAS HISTORICAL QUARTERLY 35 (Spring 1976): 3-26.

Arkansas began its movement for the regulation of patent and proprietary medicine in the late nineteenth century. The establishment of local medical societies made physicians and pharmacists more sensitive toward those who entered their professions and this paved the way for state medical legislation.

Nash, Gerald D. "The Conflict Between Pure and Applied Science in Nineteenth-Century Public Policy: The California State Geological Survey." ISIS 54 (June 1963): 217-28.

Differing objectives in the nineteenth century almost undermined the rate of scientific progress. The California Geological Survey is an example of the conflict between applied and pure science with mining and agricultural interests demanding goals that would lead to direct economic benefits.

Oliver, John W. HISTORY OF AMERICAN TECHNOLOGY. New York: Ronald Press, 1956. x, 676 p.

Oliver believes that American civilization is fundamentally technology based on man's conquest of the environment. He reviews the basic technologies such as agriculture, clothing, building, metals, transportation, and the military.

THE PAPERS OF JOSEPH HENRY. Vol. 1: DECEMBER 1797-OCTOBER 1832: THE ALBANY YEARS. Edited by Nathan Reingold et al. Washington: Smithsonian Institution Press, 1972. xxxix, 496 p.

The spotlight does not shift to Henry in this volume until 1824. The first part deals with Albany Academy, a school for boys who were not destined for college, where Henry was educated, while the remainder covers Henry's work in electromagnetism.

Paul, Rodman Wilson. "Colorado as a Pioneer of Science in the Mining West." MISSISSIPPI VALLEY HISTORICAL REVIEW 47 (June 1960): 34-50.

In Colorado, narrow, steep canyons offered only a limited field for placer mining, and ores one hundred feet below the surface created problems in ore treatment. To solve these and other problems, Colorado made contributions in science to western mining.

Persons, Stow, ed. EVOLUTIONARY THOUGHT IN AMERICA. New Haven, Conn.: Yale University Press, 1950. x, 462 p.

This is a collection of essays on evolution. It contains sections on the theory of evolution and the relationship of evolution to sociology.

Pfeifer, Edward J. "The Genesis of American Neo-Lamarckism." ISIS 56 (Summer 1965): 156-67.

Neo-Lamarckian evolutionists made important contributions to biology, geology, paleontology, and evolutionary theory. Their work represented an attack on natural selection as the primary factor in evolution.

Ponko, Vincent, Jr. SHIPS, SEAS, AND SCIENTISTS: U.S. NAVAL EXPLORATION AND DISCOVERY IN THE NINETEENTH CENTURY. Annapolis, Md.: Naval Institute Press, 1974. xii, 283 p.

This is a series of narratives of surveying and exploring expeditions to the Antarctic, Pacific, Dead Sea, Amazon, Rio de la Plata, and other places. It emphasizes the research that needs to be done in the future.

Richmond, Phyllis Allen. "American Attitudes Toward the Germ Theory of Disease (1860-1880)." JOURNAL OF THE HISTORY OF MEDICINE AND ALLIED SCIENCES 9 (October 1954): 428-54.

The American medical profession displayed a lack of interest concerning the germ theory of disease. Interestingly, after the Civil War, attention was drawn to the theory by popular magazines such as SCIENTIFIC AMERICAN and POPULAR SCIENCE MONTHLY.

Riznick, Barnes. "The Professional Lives of Early Nineteenth-Century New England Doctors." JOURNAL OF THE HISTORY OF MEDICINE AND ALLIED SCIENCES 19 (January 1964): 1-16.

New England families had a faith in medicine to cope with sickness, but not in regular physicians. They were not all prejudiced against doctors, however, and medical practitioners as a self-conscious class came into existence.

Rodgers, Andrew Denny III. AMERICAN BOTANY, 1873-1892: DECADES OF TRANSITION. Princeton, N.J.: Princeton University Press, 1944. 340 p.

Botanists contributed not only to scientific knowledge but to practical knowledge as well. The decades of transition in this book were ones when botany moved away from description and taxonomy to experimental work.

Rosenberg, Charles E. "The Bitter Fruit: Heredity, Disease, and Social Thought in Nineteenth-Century America." PERSPECTIVES IN AMERICAN HISTORY 8 (1974): 189-238.

Rosenberg shows how hereditarian ideas were shaped to support social action. Social hereditarianism was a response to emotional needs created by modernization and was a means of ensuring a continuity of social norms.

_____. THE CHOLERA YEARS: THE UNITED STATES IN 1832, 1849, AND 1866. Chicago: University of Chicago Press, 1962. x, 257 p.

Cholera was a classic epidemic disease in the nineteenth century. The author emphasizes social ideas concerning the disease and attitudes on public health.

_____. "Factors in the Development of Genetics in the United States: Some Suggestions." JOURNAL OF THE HISTORY OF MEDICINE AND ALLIED SCIENCES 22 (January 1967): 27-46.

Americans played an extraordinarily important role in the formative period of modern genetics. Rosenberg suggests that this took place in medicine, plant and animal breeding, and university departments before 1900, the year Mendel's laws were rediscovered.

_____. NO OTHER GODS: ON SCIENCE AND AMERICAN SOCIAL THOUGHT. Baltimore: Johns Hopkins University Press, 1976. xiii, 273 p.

Essays on Victorian sexology, hereditarianism, biological views of women in the nineteenth century, eugenics, the discovery of neurasthenia, and other matters are included in this volume.

_____. "Science, Technology, and Economic Growth: The Case of the Agricultural Experiment Station Scientists, 1875-1914." AGRICULTURAL HISTORY 45 (January 1971): 1-20.

This is a study of the behavior of scientists and scientist-administrators within an institutional context defined by social and economic factors. Interest group politics created the experiment stations and scientists in them became an interest group on their own.

_____. "Social Class and Medical Care in Nineteenth-Century America: The Rise and Fall of the Dispensary." JOURNAL OF THE HISTORY OF MEDICINE AND ALLIED SCIENCES 29 (January 1974): 32-54.

The dispensary in the nineteenth century was a primary means of caring for the urban poor and a vital link in the prevailing system of medical education. It rose in the eighteenth century and fell in the twentieth not because it lost its social function, but because it became marginal to the needs of the medical profession.

_____. THE TRIAL OF THE ASSASSIN GUITEAU: PSYCHIATRY AND LAW IN THE GILDED AGE. Chicago: University of Chicago Press, 1968. xvii, 289 p.

This book deals mainly with the trial of Garfield's assassin and the moral, legal, and medical issues involved. The problem was defining criminal responsibility or whether an "insane" person could be held responsible for his acts.

Rosencrantz, Barbara G. "Cart before Horse: Theory, Practice and Professional Image in American Public Health, 1870-1920." JOURNAL OF THE HISTORY OF MEDICINE AND ALLIED SCIENCES 29 (January 1974): 55-73.

In the late nineteenth century, public hygiene exemplified a happy marriage of engineers, physicians, and public spirited citizens. Health authorities were not able to maintain this happy image in the twentieth, because they had to justify impersonal and standardized controls in order to assure their authority to act.

_____. PUBLIC HEALTH AND THE STATE: CHANGING VIEWS IN MASSACHUSETTS, 1842-1936. Cambridge, Mass.: Harvard University Press, 1972. xiv, 259 p.

In the nineteenth century, public health was regarded as part of the state's moral responsibility for its citizens. In time, however, public health came to be conceived as the destruction of germs rather than how people should live.

Rossiter, Margaret W. "Benjamin Silliman and the Lowell Institute: The Popularization of Science in Nineteenth-Century America." NEW ENGLAND QUARTERLY 44 (December 1971): 602-26.

The popularity of Silliman's lectures in the Lowell Institute shows that Americans of the 1840s were capable of supporting science of a high order. The Lowell Institute attracted scientists with its high fees and the lecturers were required to provide solid instruction.

Rothstein, William G. AMERICAN PHYSICIANS IN THE NINETEENTH CENTURY: FROM SECTS TO SCIENCE. Baltimore: Johns Hopkins University Press, 1972. xv, 362 p.

Rothstein combines sociological analysis and historical research in this study of institutional changes in medicine. He describes the growth of Thomsonianism and homeopathy as medical sects and shows how bacteriological developments converted medicine into a science.

Russett, Cynthia Eagle. DARWIN IN AMERICA: THE INTELLECTUAL RESPONSE, 1865-1912. San Francisco: Freeman, 1976. ix, 228 p.

The impact of Darwinism on representative thinkers such as John Fiske, Chauncey Wright, William James, W.G. Sumner, Henry Adams, Jack London, and Theodore Dreiser is discussed. The author argues that Darwinism became both a symbol of and a mechanism for intellectual change.

Shapiro, Henry D., and Miller, Zane L. PHYSICIAN TO THE WEST: SELECTED WRITINGS OF DANIEL DRAKE ON SCIENCE AND SOCIETY. Lexington: University Press of Kentucky, 1970. xxxviii, 419 p.

Drake was an author and medical professor who founded medical schools and other cultural institutions. As a scientist, he believed that nature's purposes could be discovered through observation, classification, and inductive generalization, and he spent his life founding schools to teach this method.

Shryock, Richard H. AMERICAN MEDICAL RESEARCH: PAST AND PRESENT. New York: Commonwealth Fund, 1947. xiv, 350 p.

Shryock explains the impact of German medical research on William H. Welch in the 1870s, and then devotes most of his essay to research in the twentieth century. He relates the history of medical institutes and clinics to developments in science, technology, and education.

_____. THE DEVELOPMENT OF MODERN MEDICINE: AN INTERPRETATION OF THE SOCIAL AND SCIENTIFIC FACTORS INVOLVED. Rev. ed. New York: Hafner Publishing Co., 1969. xv, 457 p.

From the beginning of the eighteenth century until the 1930s, the physician has been a philosopher, healer, scientist, and businessman. The character of society is conditioned by the diseases common to it.

_____. MEDICINE IN AMERICA: HISTORICAL ESSAYS. Baltimore: Johns Hopkins Press, 1966. xviii, 346 p.

This is a collection of fifteen articles published between 1930 and 1962. They concentrate on the nineteenth century and include discussions of medicine's scientific and social concerns.

Sicherman, Barbara. "The Paradox of Prudence: Mental Health in the Gilded Age." JOURNAL OF AMERICAN HISTORY 62 (March 1976): 890-912.

Physicians of the late nineteenth century believed they could conquer insanity through mental hygiene. Sicherman argues that beliefs of mental hygenists showed their own values and fears and exemplified the culture of the time.

Sinclair, Bruce. PHILADELPHIA'S PHILOSOPHER MECHANICS: A HISTORY OF FRANKLIN INSTITUTE, 1824-1865. Baltimore: Johns Hopkins University Press, 1974. 353 p.

The Franklin Institute was established to promote the intellectual interests of skilled workers. Eventually, heavy industrial interest emerged in the institute.

Smith, Dale C. "Quinine and Fever: The Development of the Effective Dosage." JOURNAL OF THE HISTORY OF MEDICINE AND ALLIED SCIENCES 34 (July 1976): 343-67.

Physicians struggled in early medicine to reconcile theory and practice. Smith traces the development of the use of quinine in the treatment of malarial fevers and shows that by the end of the Civil War physicians had found an effective dosage.

Smith-Rosenberg, Carol, and Rosenberg, Charles. "The Female Animal: Medical and Biological Views of Woman and Her Role in Nineteenth-Century America." JOURNAL OF AMERICAN HISTORY 60 (September 1973): 332-56.

This is a study of the debate concerning woman's domestic and childbearing roles. Nineteenth-century medical orthodoxy depicted the female as the prisoner of her reproductive system, and this influenced education and social questions such as birth control and abortion.

Stanton, William. THE GREAT UNITED STATES EXPLORING EXPEDITION OF 1838-1842. Berkeley and Los Angeles: University of California Press, 1975. x, 433 p.

This is a narrative of the Wilkes expedition based on the reports and notes of the participants, both sailors and scientists. The most important part of the study deals with the disposition of the scientific collections after the voyage and the compilation of the reports.

_____. THE LEOPARD'S SPOTS: SCIENTIFIC ATTITUDES TOWARD RACE IN AMERICA, 1815-59. Chicago: University of Chicago Press, 1960. x, 245 p.

The American school of anthropologists that included Samuel G. Norton, Josiah Nott, Ephraim George Squier, and George Gliddon is discussed. The author focuses on the tension that existed between polygenism and Jeffersonian equalitarianism.

Sterling, Keir B. LAST OF THE NATURALISTS: THE CAREER OF C. HART MERRIAM. New York: Arno, 1974. xv, 478 p.

This is a study of a nineteenth-century scientist and scientific administrator who made contributions to mammalogy and directed the U.S. Department of Agriculture's biological survey between 1885 and 1910.

Stocking, George W., Jr. "Lamarckism in American Social Science: 1890-1915." JOURNAL OF THE HISTORY OF IDEAS 23 (April-June 1962): 239-56.

Stocking argues that the Lamarckian doctrine of inherited acquired characteristics was the last link between biological and social theory as social Darwinism declined. This was well suited to the social sciences since they explain the behavior of man in terms of interaction with his environment.

_____. RACE, CULTURE, AND EVOLUTION: ESSAYS IN THE HISTORY OF ANTHROPOLOGY. New York: Free Press, 1968. xvii, 380 p.

The work of Franz Boas, E.B. Tylor and others, as well as the professionalization of anthropology are discussed. The author argues that professionalism can be just as culture-bound as earlier dogmas even though it is moving under the banner of social science.

Taylor, Lloyd C., Jr. THE MEDICAL PROFESSION AND SOCIAL REFORM, 1885-1945. New York: St. Martin's Press, 1974. 168 p.

With the attitude of social service at Johns Hopkins Medical School and Massachusetts General Hospital at the beginning of the twentieth century, some physicians tried to involve their colleagues in reforming American society. Efforts were killed off in the long run by the American Medical Association's fear of "socialized medicine."

Torchia, Marion M. "The Tuberculosis Movement and the Race Question, 1890-1950." BULLETIN OF THE HISTORY OF MEDICINE 49 (Summer 1975): 152-68.

The mortality rate of blacks from tuberculosis was several times larger than the rate of whites. This fact was debated in the tuberculosis movement, but integration came very late and segregation hindered the cure of blacks.

Van Tassel, David D., and Hall, Michael G., eds. SCIENCE AND SOCIETY IN THE UNITED STATES. Homewood, Ill.: Dorsey Press, 1966. vi, 360 p.

This collection includes essays tracing science from its beginnings, science and industry, agriculture, and medicine, science and social thought, and the support of science in higher education, private agencies, and the government.

Waserman, Manfred. "The Quest for a National Health Department in the Progressive Era." BULLETIN OF THE HISTORY OF MEDICINE 49 (Fall 1975): 353-80.

The quest for a national health department failed in the Progressive era, but improved public health succeeded. During this time, communicable diseases were increasingly brought under control.

White, George W. "The History of Geology and Mineralogy as Seen by American Writers, 1803-1835: A Bibliographic Essay." ISIS 64 (June 1973): 197-214.

This is a study of the writings of Samuel Miller, DeWitt Clinton, Jeremiah van Rensselaer, G.W. Featherstonhaugh, William Gibbons, and N.F. Moore. Their histories of geology show the change in

America from belief in catastrophism and a short duration of geological time to actualism and a longer span of geological time.

White, Leslie A., ed. LEWIS HENRY MORGAN: THE INDIAN JOURNALS, 1859-1862. Ann Arbor: University of Michigan Press, 1959. xii, 233 p.

Morgan created the science of kinship. These journals cover his field research among the Kaw, Ottawa, Shawnee, Omaha, and other tribes and include comments on life in western towns. Illustrations are selected and edited by Clyde Walton.

Whitnah, Donald R. A HISTORY OF THE UNITED STATES WEATHER BUREAU. Urbana: University of Illinois Press, 1961. xii, 267 p.

Whitnah traces the history of the U.S. Weather Bureau from its establishment in 1870 to the launching of the first weather satellite in 1960. He emphasizes that pressures to satisfy public demands and stretch a meager budget caused the bureau to focus on the application of meteorology rather than research.

Wirtschafter, Jonathan Dine. "The Genesis and Impact of the Medical Lobby: 1898-1906." JOURNAL OF THE HISTORY OF MEDICINE AND ALLIED SCIENCES 13 (January 1958): 15-49.

This is a study of the American Medical Association's committee on national legislation through its first half-decade of activity. The committee was established not only as a negative force to oppose antivivisection bills and higher postal rates for medical journals, but also to propose national sanitary laws, better medical care in the armed services, and higher standards of medical education.

Wood, Ann Douglas. "'The Fashionable Diseases': Women's Complaints and their Treatment in Nineteenth-Century America." JOURNAL OF INTERDISCIPLINARY HISTORY 4 (Summer 1973): 25-52.

Books written between 1840 and 1900 consistently asserted that a large number of middle-class women were ill. Medical explanations of female illness were directed toward the womb, while cultural conclusions portrayed sick ladies as sexually aggressive, intellectually ambitious, and defective in submissiveness.

Wrobel, Arthur. "Orthodoxy and Respectability in Nineteenth Century Phrenology." JOURNAL OF POPULAR CULTURE 9 (Summer 1975): 38-50.

Phrenologists attempted to give their "science" respectability by arguing that they had assimilated Baconian science and Scottish philosophy. Baconian inductive reasoning was based on observation to induce laws, while Scottish philosophy argued that man was endowed with senses to understand and admire God's works as well as substantiate His existence.

Yates, Wilson. "Birth Control Literature and the Medical Profession in Nineteenth Century America." JOURNAL OF THE HISTORY OF MEDICINE AND ALLIED SCIENCES 31 (January 1976): 42–54.

> Yates criticizes the assumption that the medical profession provided little printed information on birth control between 1830 and 1860. There was a continual, extensive and increasing flow of information during this period and throughout the nineteenth century even though the Comstock Law of 1873 rendered as obscene any materials on contraception.

Young, James Harvey. "American Medical Quackery in the Age of the Common Man." MISSISSIPPI VALLEY HISTORICAL REVIEW 47 (March 1961): 579–93.

> The appeal of the medical quack during the Jacksonian era was a response to heroic therapy of medical practitioners such as bleeding and purging, as well as an aspect of anti-intellectualism. Voters favored medical democracy, and ignored criticism of nostrum makers by physicians.

_____. THE TOADSTOOL MILLIONAIRES: A SOCIAL HISTORY OF PATENT MEDICINES IN AMERICA BEFORE FEDERAL REGULATION. Princeton, N.J.: Princeton University Press, 1961. xii, 282 p.

> Young traces quackery from its English beginnings to the present day and emphasizes that not all practitioners were unscrupulous. Producers of patent medicines were among the first producers to feel the impact of competitive selling and they made their names and trademarks visible everywhere through advertising.

Zochert, Donald. "Science and the Common Man in Ante-Bellum America." ISIS 65 (December 1974): 448–74.

> Democracy in the 1830s and 1840s brought about the rapid diffusion of science. Science came to the common people through newspapers, and they approved science because of social utility and a desire for order.

1915 TO THE PRESENT

Akin, William E. TECHNOCRACY AND THE AMERICAN DREAM: THE TECHNOCRAT MOVEMENT, 1900–1941. Berkeley and Los Angeles: University of California Press, 1977. xv, 227 p.

> Technocracy had its roots in the ideas of Thorstein Veblen and flowed in the thought of James Burnham. It was based on the proposition that how to best produce and distribute man's products is an engineering problem for which there is always a right answer.

Antler, Joyce, and Fox, Daniel M. "The Movement Toward a Safe Maternity: Physician Accountability in New York City, 1915-1940." BULLETIN OF THE HISTORY OF MEDICINE 50 (Winter 1976): 569-95.

This is a study of the development of medical interest in maternal health. The New York Academy of Medicine, between 1915 and 1940, developed a mechanism for reform and regulation of obstetrics which played an important part in advancing a technological focus for childbirth.

Bakan, David. "Behaviorism and American Urbanization." JOURNAL OF THE HISTORY OF THE BEHAVIORAL SCIENCES 2 (January 1966): 5-28.

Bakan argues that the development of behaviorism was related to the transformation of the United States from a rural to an urban-industrial society. John B. Watson, the father of the movement, characterized behaviorism as a psychology appropriate to urban life.

Baxter, James Phinney III. SCIENTISTS AGAINST TIME. Boston: Little, Brown, 1946. xv, 473 p.

This is the official history of the U.S. Office of Scientific Research and Development during World War II. It is the record of the application of science to the destruction of humans on a wholesale scale.

Benison, Saul. "Poliomyelitis and the Rockefeller Institute: Social Effects and Institutional Response." JOURNAL OF THE HISTORY OF MEDICINE AND ALLIED SCIENCES 29 (January 1974): 74-92.

In this essay, Benison discusses the roles of Dr. Simon Flexner and Dr. Rufus Cole of the Rockefeller Institute in clinical polio research. He also treats the social problems caused by ignorance of this disease.

Berger, Michael L. "Influence of the Automobile on Rural Health Care, 1900-29." JOURNAL OF THE HISTORY OF MEDICINE AND ALLIED SCIENCES 28 (October 1973): 319-35.

The automobile brought improvement in the quality of medical care for rural people, increased the complexities of practice, and introduced impersonalization. Rural people were no longer part of the doctor's social life, but rather persons seen on a professional basis.

Birnbaum, Lucille C. "Behaviorism in the 1920's." AMERICAN QUARTERLY 7 (Spring 1955): 15-30.

Birnbaum traces John B. Watson's crusade to put behaviorism across to the people. He was attacked by theologians and philosophers, but was approved by educators and studied by middle-class mothers who read his articles in PARENT'S COSMOPOLITAN, COLLIER'S, and HARPER'S magazines.

Burnham, John Chynoweth. "The New Psychology: From Narcissism to Social Control." In CHANGE AND CONTINUITY IN TWENTIETH CENTURY AMERICA: THE 1920'S edited by John Braemann, Robert H. Bremner, and David Brody, pp. 351-98. Columbus: Ohio State University Press, 1968.

Early in the 1920s, the new psychology of instincts, drives, and wants of men produced self-indulgent behavior. Later it suggested ways of controlling the minds of men.

_____. "The Struggle between Physicians and Paramedical Personnel in American Psychiatry, 1917-41." JOURNAL OF THE HISTORY OF MEDICINE AND ALLIED SCIENCES 29 (January 1974): 93-107.

Burnham discusses the mental hygiene movement and especially the endeavors of mental hygenists to set up a team approach for care. They brought neurologists, endocrinologists, psychologists, social workers, educational specialists, nurses, dietitians, and others together, because they realized their limitations when they went into a community.

Carter, Paul A. "Science and the Common Man." AMERICAN SCHOLAR 45 (Winter 1975/76): 778-94.

This is an essay concerning efforts to disseminate science to the common man. Carter focuses on the efforts of the Science Service, founded in 1921, to serve as a scientific news syndicate modeled on the Associated Press.

Coben, Stanley. "The Scientific Establishment and the Transmission of Quantum Mechanics to the United States, 1919-32." AMERICAN HISTORICAL REVIEW 76 (April 1971): 442-66.

Improvement in American theoretical physics is delineated. Money came from various sources to bring quantum mechanics from Europe to institutions such as the California Institute of Technology, University of Chicago, University of Michigan, and Princeton University.

Cravens, Hamilton, and Burnham, John C. "Psychology and Evolutionary Naturalism in American Thought, 1890-1940." AMERICAN QUARTERLY 23 (December 1971): 635-57.

Psychologists changed evolutionary naturalism in the twentieth century by portraying man both as a civilized being and an animal. This work in the nurture and nature of man produced a science of personality in the 1930s in which the person was studied as a whole.

Christy, Teresa E. CORNERSTONE FOR NURSING EDUCATION: A HISTORY OF THE DIVISION OF NURSING EDUCATION OF TEACHERS COLLEGE, COLUMBIA UNIVERSITY, 1899-1947. New York: Teachers College Press, 1969. xii, 123 p.

Christy discusses the impact of professionalization on nursing. The Teachers College program was the first advanced training offered at any university.

Creelan, Paul G. "Watsonian Behaviorism and the Calvinist Conscience." JOURNAL OF THE HISTORY OF THE BEHAVIORAL SCIENCES 10 (January 1974): 95-118.

The behaviorist John B. Watson has been viewed as a rebel against traditional Christian religion. Creelan examines Watson's life and thought, and concludes that he remained in bondage to the fundamentalist Calvinist ideas he had encountered in rural South Carolina.

Dupree, A. Hunter. "The History of American Science--A Field Finds Itself." AMERICAN HISTORICAL REVIEW 71 (April 1966): 863-74.

Science is a thread woven into the fabric of American civilization from the beginning. The object of study in the history of science is man in a social context, thus making the history social history.

Fleming, Donald. "Emigré Physicists and the Biological Revolution." PERSPECTIVES IN AMERICAN HISTORY 11 (1968): 152-89.

Fleming examines the contributions of Erwin Schrodinger, Leo Szilard, Max Delbrück, and Salvador Luria. He specifically discusses their work with DNA.

Gifford, James F., Jr. THE EVOLUTION OF A MEDICAL CENTER: A HISTORY OF MEDICINE AT DUKE UNIVERSITY TO 1941. Durham, N.C.: Duke University Press, 1972. viii, 249 p.

The Duke Medical School was not founded until 1931, but Gifford fleshes out his study by tracing the story of the Duke family. The Duke Foundation wanted to improve medical care in North Carolina, and the medical school improved medical education by promoting and improving hospitals.

Hewlett, Richard G., and Anderson, Oscar E., Jr. A HISTORY OF THE UNITED STATES ATOMIC ENERGY COMMISSION. Vol. 1: THE NEW WORLD 1939/46. University Park: Pennsylvania State University Press, 1962. xv, 766 p.

The effect of technological developments on policy decisions are explored. The authors cover the evolution of Oak Ridge, the bombing of Japan, and various efforts to control the atom.

Hewlett, Richard G., and Duncan, Francis. A HISTORY OF THE UNITED STATES ATOMIC ENERGY COMMISSION. Vol. 2: ATOMIC SHIELD, 1947-1952. University Park: Pennsylvania State University Press, 1969. xviii, 718 p.

When the AEC inherited the nation's atomic energy program from the Manhattan Project in 1947, it was isolated by security barriers and protected by unprecedented legislation. Commission chairman David Lilienthal tried to end this by substituting declassified research on the peaceful uses of atomic energy, but it became evident that the atom would bear the image of war.

Jackson, Charles O. "The Amphetamine Democracy: Medicinal Abuse in the Popular Culture." SOUTH ATLANTIC QUARTERLY 74 (Summer 1975): 308-23.

Amphetamine was introduced in the American market by Smith, Kline, and French through the benzedrine inhaler in 1932. In the 1950s, the federal government made amphetamine abuse a major concern, but they were unsuccessful because of apathy on the part of the public and the claim that the drug had many legitimate uses.

_____. "The Amphetamine Inhaler: A Case Study of Medicinal Abuse." JOURNAL OF THE HISTORY OF MEDICINE AND ALLIED SCIENCES 26 (April 1971): 187-96.

The employment of amphetamines was regulated by the federal government in the 1930s, but not the Smith, Kline, and French benzedrine inhaler. This is a study of how the use of the contents of this inhaler became a major element in drug abuse.

Jones, Bartlett C. "A Prohibition Problem: Liquor as Medicine, 1920-1933." JOURNAL OF THE HISTORY OF MEDICINE AND ALLIED SCIENCES 18 (October 1963): 353-69.

The disagreement between "wets" and "drys" was whether alcohol should be severely restricted to protect both individuals and society from possible ill effects. "Drys" campaigned to make alcohol therapeutically unfashionable, while "wets" called the limited value of alcohol in medical practice sufficient reason for doctors to administer it as they saw fit.

Kennedy, David M. BIRTH CONTROL IN AMERICA: THE CAREER OF MARGARET SANGER. New Haven, Conn.: Yale University Press, 1970. xi, 320 p.

Sanger invented the term "birth control" and made it a public issue. Kennedy describes her active career (1915-40), depicts her as a woman who sought fulfillment in reform rather than in social climbing, and relates her birth control movement to the intellectual and social climate of the times.

Kevles, Daniel J. "'Into Hostile Political Camps': The Reorganization of International Science in World War I." ISIS 62 (Spring 1971): 47-60.

This is a study of the effort mainly of George Ellery Hale, astrophysicist and director of the Mount Wilson Observatory in Pasadena, California, to form an international research council during and after World War I. The hostile camps came from those nations joined to the allies and neutrals friendly to the central powers.

_____. "Testing the Army's Intelligence: Psychologists and the Military in World War I." JOURNAL OF AMERICAN HISTORY 55 (December 1968): 565-81.

Robert M. Yerkes, president of the American Psychological Association in 1917, campaigned for the introduction of intelligence testing in the army's personnel procedures. The introduction of testing changed the army, because recruiting officers began using instruments to determine literacy, and the foundations for a scientific personnel system were laid.

Lasby, Clarence G. PROJECT PAPERCLIP: GERMAN SCIENTISTS AND THE COLD WAR. New York: Atheneum, 1971. x, 338 p.

The United States government imported 642 alien scientists between May 1945 and December 1952. This Project Paperclip was first designed to gain the benefits of advanced research and development, but soon became an effort to deny German scientists to the Russians.

Layton, Edwin T., Jr. THE REVOLT OF THE ENGINEERS: SOCIAL RESPONSIBILITY AND THE AMERICAN ENGINEERING PROFESSION. Cleveland: Press of Case Western Reserve University, 1971. xiv, 286 p.

Layton focuses on the first quarter of the twentieth century when a group of engineer-reformers attempted to unify their profession and use it to bring about social reform. This effort to free engineering from business control failed because of business opposition, and engineers drifted back into apathy.

Lillie, Frank R. THE WOODS HOLE MARINE BIOLOGICAL LABORATORY. Chicago: University of Chicago Press, 1944. ix, 284 p.

This is a study of the evolution of one type of cooperative research. While cooperative endeavor is characteristic of the United States, this laboratory received opposition and succeeded only because of Charles O. Whitman, the Rockefeller Foundation, and the Carnegie Corporation.

McNeil, Donald R. THE FIGHT FOR FLUORIDATION. New York: Oxford University Press, 1957. xii, 241 p.

In 1930-31, fluorine was identified as the agent in the water of
Colorado Springs that was retarding tooth decay. The fight over
fluoridation raged in the 1940s and 1950s until today it is endorsed by virtually every professional group concerned with dentistry,
medicine, and public health.

McVaugh, Michael, and Mauskopf, Seymour H. "J.B. Rhine's EXTRA-SEN-
SORY PERCEPTION and Its Background in Psychical Research." ISIS 67 (June
1976): 161-89.

This is a study of Rhine's 1934 book on the internal history of
parapsychology. The authors argue that it is a paradigmatic work
in that it brings together the conclusions of a great number of researchers and presents them as a single model for experimentation.

Mandler, Jean Matter, and Mandler, George. "The Diaspora of Experimental
Psychology: The Gestaltists and Others." PERSPECTIVES IN AMERICAN HIS-
TORY 2 (1968): 371-419.

The emigration of the Gestaltists, Kurt Lewin and others, to the
United States is discussed. The Mandlers argue that these German
immigrants played a major role in pushing a young science to
greater maturity.

Nieburg, H.L. IN THE NAME OF SCIENCE. Chicago: Quadrangle, 1966.
xi, 431 p.

This is a study of federal scientific policy, government contracts,
and politics. Nieburg exposes the cancerous growth afflicting
free enterprise that government contracting and the military-indus-
trial complex brought to bear.

Olch, Peter D. "Evarts A. Graham, the American College of Surgeons, and
the American Board of Surgery." JOURNAL OF THE HISTORY OF MEDI-
CINE AND ALLIED SCIENCES 27 (July 1972): 247-61.

The purpose of this paper is to describe the central role of Graham
in the reform of the American College of Surgeons and the establishment of the American Board of Surgery. He fought to have
young surgeons appointed to the board of the college and he was
instrumental in forming the American Board of Surgery to upgrade
training.

Roberts, Mary M. AMERICAN NURSING: HISTORY AND INTERPRETATION.
New York: Macmillan, 1954. xvi, 688 p.

The development of nursing from the turn of the twentieth century
is covered. Nursing, by 1900, was private, but as medicine advanced, nurses became members of health teams.

Robinson, Paul. THE MODERNIZATION OF SEX: HAVELOCK ELLIS, ALFRED KINSEY, WILLIAM MASTERS AND VIRGINIA JOHNSON. New York: Harper & Row, 1976. 200 p.

Robinson argues that Ellis, Kinsey, and Masters and Johnson made sexual thought a part of intellectual history. These sexologists challenged cultural orthodoxy.

Skolnikoff, Eugene B. SCIENCE, TECHNOLOGY, AND FOREIGN POLICY. Cambridge: M.I.T. Press, 1967. xvi, 330 p.

Policymakers need to cultivate a science-affairs competence or the ability to recognize the political intangibles implied by scientific uncertainties. The history of science-policy since 1945 is surveyed, and this shows that few agencies of the federal government have achieved a relatively advanced stage of scientific integration.

Spring, Joel H. "Psychologists and the War: The Meaning of Intelligence in the Alpha and Beta Tests." HISTORY OF EDUCATION QUARTERLY 12 (Spring 1972): 3-15.

The great experiment of the First World War in psychology and the schools was the standardization of the alpha and beta group intelligence tests to differentiate men within disciplined and highly stratified social organizations. The tests were based on a particular conception of a good society, a particular attitude toward intelligence, and the assumption that the army was a beehive in which everyone performed a task suitable to his capabilities.

Sulman, A. Michael. "The Humanization of the American Child: Benjamin Spock as a Popularizer of Psychoanalytic Thought." JOURNAL OF THE HISTORY OF THE BEHAVIORAL SCIENCES 9 (July 1973): 258-65.

Psychoanalytic thought was not popularized in the United States during the 1920s and 1930s. Through the use of content analysis, Sulman argues that psychoanalysis penetrated the mass media only after the Second World War when Spock's BABY AND CHILD CARE achieved popularity.

Tobey, Ronald C. THE AMERICAN IDEOLOGY OF NATIONAL SCIENCE, 1919-1930. Pittsburgh: University of Pittsburgh Press, 1971. xiii, 263 p.

This is a study of attempts by some physical scientists to popularize their work and thus gain support for research. They failed to build national institutions in support of basic research, and they also were unable to convince many of their colleagues that popular support was worthwhile.

Turner, Thomas B. HERITAGE OF EXCELLENCE: THE JOHNS HOPKINS MEDICAL INSTITUTIONS, 1914-1947. Baltimore: Johns Hopkins University Press, 1974. viii, 648 p.

A year-by-year chronicle, this book charts the development of the Johns Hopkins Medical School and Hospital. Turner describes the establishment of the School of Hygiene and the introduction of a full-time system of clinicians.

Wright, Helen; Warnow, Joan N.; and Weiner, Charles, eds. THE LEGACY OF GEORGE ELLERY HALE: EVOLUTION OF ASTRONOMY AND SCIENTIFIC INSTITUTIONS IN PICTURES AND DOCUMENTS. Cambridge: M.I.T. Press, 1972. vii, 293 p.

Hale was a founder of American astrophysics and was noted for his solar work at the University of Chicago and Mount Wilson Observatory. This book includes almost two hundred photographs.

Young, James Harvey. AMERICAN SELF-DOSAGE MEDICINES: AN HISTORICAL PERSPECTIVE. Lawrence, Kans.: Coronado, 1974. xiv, 75 p.

This is a series of lectures on the emergence from quackery of American proprietary medicines. Young believes the 1970s will be a period of criticism of proprietary medicines because of consumerism.

_____. "Botulism and the Ripe Olive Scare of 1919-1920." BULLETIN OF THE HISTORY OF MEDICINE 50 (Fall 1976): 372-91.

Young describes the development of research concerning botulism, particularly in the ripe olive industry. The ripe olive scare of 1919-20 gave impetus to improved food processing technology.

_____. THE MEDICAL MESSIAHS: A SOCIAL HISTORY OF HEALTH QUACKERY IN TWENTIETH-CENTURY AMERICA. Princeton, N.J.: Princeton University Press, 1967. xiv, 460 p.

The expectations of the reformers who passed the Pure Food and Drug Act of 1906 have not been realized. Quackery has persisted because of social forces such as advertising and man's cupidity and gullibility, and it has flourished in areas of medical uncertainty.

AUTHOR INDEX

In addition to authors, this index includes all editors, compilers, and other contributors to works cited in the text. References are to page numbers, and alphabetization is letter by letter.

A

Aaron, Daniel 255, 276
Abbott, Richard H. 23
Abell, Aaron I. 365
Abzug, Robert B. 134
Adair, Douglas 132
Adams, Richard P. 69
Adams, W. Paul 123
Adams, William Howard 65
Ahlstrom, Sydney E. 365, 406
Aiken, John R. 365, 407
Akers, Charles W. 91
Akin, William E. 366, 456
Albanese, Catherine 304, 337
Albright, Raymond W. 337
Aldridge, Alfred Owen 13, 337
Alexander, Charles C. 176
Alexander, Robert L. 70
Alexander, Thomas G. 366
Alexis, Gerhard T. 338
Allen, Frederick S. 204
Allen, Gay W. 94, 276
Allen, James B. 366
Allen, William Francis 70
Allmendinger, David F., Jr. 204
Altbach, Philip G. 230
American Theological Library
    Association 10
Ames, William E. 23
Anderson, Charles A. 338

Anderson, Charles H. 366
Anderson, Clifford B. 176
Anderson, Frederick 290
Anderson, Oscar E., Jr. 430, 459
Andrew, John A. III 366
Andrews, J. Cutler 23
Andrews, Wayne 65
Angle, Paul M. 23
Antler, Joyce 457
Appleby, Joyce 123, 276
Appleton, Le Roy H. 70
Archer, John 65
Arden, G. Everett 366
Argersinger, Peter H. 367
Arieli, Yehoshua 123
Armstrong, Maurice W. 338
Arrington, Leonard J. 276
Atherton, Lewis A. 24
Atkins, Gains Glenn 338
Auerbach, Jerold S. 256
Auerbach, M. Morton 176
Autican, Chester J. 123
Axelrod, Jacob 273
Axtell, James 197

B

Bacciocco, Edward T. 177
Baer, Helene G. 94
Baigell, Matthew 70
Bailey, Hugh C. 94

465

Author Index

Author Index

Author Index

Author Index

Author Index

Author Index

Author Index

Author Index

Author Index

Author Index

TITLE INDEX

This index includes all books cited in the text; in some cases, titles have been shortened. References are to page numbers, and alphabetization is letter by letter.

Title Index

Title Index

Title Index

H

Title Index

Title Index

O

Title Index

Title Index

SUBJECT INDEX

This index includes topics covered in the text. Underlined numbers refer to main areas of emphasis. Alphabetization is letter by letter.

Subject Index

Subject Index

Subject Index

Subject Index

Subject Index

Subject Index

religion in 326
slavery in 301
social comment in 297
the South in 299
about war 294, 297
See also Dime novels; Historical
novels; Science fiction
Field, Stephen J., as a conservative
158
Fields, James T. 113-14
Fields, W.C. 323
Fight for Freedom Committee 178
Films. See Motion pictures
Fine arts
colonial period to 1830 19
1815-1915 79-80
philanthropy in 37
Fink, Mike 306
Finney, Charles G. 214, 372, 389,
391, 403
Fisk University 238
Fiske, John 421
impact of Darwinism on 451
on progress 159-60
Fitch, Clyde, portrayal of women by
282
Fitzgerald, F. Scott 287, 293, 299
novel of manners of 290
Fitzhugh, George 115
economic thought of 153
patriarchal thought of 139
Fleming, D.F. 265
Fleming, Walter Lynwood 269
Flexner, Abraham 182, 234, 442
Flexner, Simon 457
Flexner Report 224
Flint, Timothy 284
Florida
Catholic missions of 343
early Catholic Church of 344
Florida Agricultural and Mechanical
University 238
Fluoridation of water 461-62
Flynn, John 192
Folk art 321
Folklore and legends 324
as cultural history 265
1815-1915 306, 310
of the Erie Canal 320
of the Midwest 313

of the Ozarks 319
of slavery 310
history of 303
value of to cultural history 324
Folk music and songs 34, 332
left wing interest in 332
of Oklahoma 315
Folk painting 70
Folk singers, biography of 332
Folkways, of small towns 24
Food
colonial period to 1830 19
Nineteenth century struggle for
legislation concerning
430
Ford, Edsel, philanthropy of 57
Ford, Guy Stanton 257
Ford, Henry 182
philanthropy of 57
Foreigners, in Twentieth century
children's literature
330. See also Immi-
grants
Foreign policy
of C. Beard 264
criticism of the radical left for
attitudes on 195
of F.D. Roosevelt 176
influence of Washington's Farewell Address on 128
science and 463
use of the Navy in (1776-1882)
33
See also Cold War; Diplomatic
history; Isolationism
Formalism, revolt against 189, 196
Forrest, Edwin 84, 288
Fort Scott, Kansas, medical practice
at 446
Fortune, Timothy Thomas 48, 142
Fosdick, Harry Emerson 331
Foster, William Z., on industrialization 182
Foundation for Economic Education
190
Foundations and charitable trusts 61
in education 236
See also Charities

532

Subject Index

Subject Index

Hooker, Thomas 354
Hookworm, eradication of in the
        South 431
Hoover, Herbert 182
Hoover, J. Edgar 331
Hopkins, Mary 223
Hopkinson, Francis, as a political
        satirist 274
Horkheimer, Max 186
Horowitz, David 265
Hospitals
    in colonial Pennsylvania 430
    1815-1915
        in Louisiana 437
        voluntary 37
    See also Dispensaries; Mental
        hospitals
Houghton Mifflin Co., history of to
        1920 24
Houses, as symbols of tradition 295
Howard, Sidney 288
Howard University 238
Howe, Frederic C. 178
    concept of community of 166
Howe, Samuel Gridley 111
Howells, William Dean 114, 277,
        278, 287, 291
    influence of spiritualism on 284
    the Jeffersonian view of 283
    letters of 290
    novel of manners of 290
    realism in the writings of 289
    as a social critic 283
Hudson River School
    relationship to poetry 72, 81
    use of the Catskill Mountain region
        by 83
Hudson River Valley, painters of the
        colonial 68
Hughes, John 400
Hughes, Langston 296
Hull House 221. See also Addams,
    Jane
Humanism, the Enlightenment and 18
Humanities 58
Human nature 30, 56
    Jefferson's ideas on 133
Humphreys, David 274
Huneker, James Gibbons 81

Huntington, Archer M. 294
Huntington (Henry E.) Library and
        Art Gallery, history of
        61
Hutchins, Robert Maynard 234
Hutchinson, Anne 338-39, 351,
        365
Hutchinson family (singers) 312-13
Hydropathy 445
Hymns, camp meeting 389. See
        also Spirituals

I

Idealism
    criticism of Jeffersonian 107
    in early sociological thought 153
    of J. Marsh 32
    of W. Torrey 105
    See also Emersonians
Illinois, University of 215, 216,
        226
ILLINOIS MONTHLY MAGAZINE
        102
Immigrants
    as antisemitists 248
    as depicted in minstrel shows 318
    education of 216-17, 220-21,
        225-26, 231, 366
    influence on California archi-
        tecture 86
    stage characterizations of 292
    vocational education as a means of
        thwarting mobility of
        207
Immigration
    Baptist Church and 376
    Bostonian attitudes toward 170
    Cardinal Gibbons and 101
    Catholic Church and 372, 391,
        413
    cultural history of 265
    Jane Addams on 30
    Jewish views on 376
    of Mormons 372
    Presbyterian attitudes toward 369
    prostitution and 145
    restrictions on 150, 152, 170
    Southern attitudes toward 135
    in understanding the Progressive
        era 245

Subject Index

Subject Index

McKay, Claude 293, 296
Mackenzie, Alexander, as a liberal-
    democrat 155
Macon, Dave 330
Madison, James 16, 130
Mailer, Norman, war fiction of 297
Maine
    Catholic missions of 343
    folklore of 310
Makemie, Francis 93
Malaria 447
    treatment of 452–53
Malpractice, medical. See Medicine
Malthus, Thomas Robert, criticism of
    107
Management, scientific. See
    Scientific management
Manifest Destiny. See Territorial
    expansion
Mann, Horace 108, 145
Manners
    colonial 19
    Nineteenth century novels of 290
    pre–World War I women and 41
Manuscripts and archives 40
    guides to 7
    See also Historical societies
Marcuse, Herbert 179, 186, 187
    idea of freedom of 177
Marquand, John P., novels of
    manners of 290
Marriage
    Nineteenth century 36, 139
    Puritan idea of 350, 356
    See also Divorce
Marsh, George Perkins 105
Marsh, James 32
Marshall, John 145, 242, 244
Marshall, Louis 120
Martin, Francois-Xavier 242
Marxism 31, 166
    American disciples of 152
    in the face of science and
        technology 173
    failure of the ideas of in America
        150
    in interpreting American history
        118, 249
    rejection of by independent liberals
        188

trade-unions and 407
use of in explaining human
    nature 56
Maryland
    architecture of (1634–1865) 67
    buildings, gardens, and furniture
        of 75
    writers of colonial 274
Mason, Lowell 81
Masons. See Freemasons
Massachusetts, Nineteenth century
    educational reform in 215–16,
        217
    public health in 451
    See also Boston; Cambridge,
        Mass.; Quincy, Mass.
Massachusetts Bay Colony
    church and state in 342
    clerical consociation in 360
    education in 202
    the franchise in 360
    missions to the Indians in 359
    the Puritan oligarchy of 22
    religion in 355
    settlement of 13
    See also Boston; Cape Cod,
        Mass.; Salem, Mass.
Massachusetts General Hospital 454
Massachusetts Peace Society 140
MASSES, THE (periodical) 52,
    164, 295
Masters, William 462
Masturbation, Nineteenth century
    concepts of 433
Matas, Rudolph 437
Materialism
    colonial period to 1815 340
        decline of classicism and 18
    1815–1915 114
        religious liberty and 398
        in sociological thought 153
    Twentieth century conservative
        critique of 189
Mather, Cotton 273, 339, 358
    biographies by 361
    as a historian 240
    medical career of 423
Mather, Increase 274
Mather, John 358
Mather family 354

Subject Index

Subject Index

Subject Index

Subject Index

of the Puritans 126, 344
of the Quakers 350
of W. Penn 124
1815 to 1915 34, 136-37, 150,
154, 157, 170, 307
in abolition disputes 156
of blacks 139
British influences on 159
Darwinism and 136
of the Disciples of Christ 385
in education 208, 227
in evangelicalism 373, 405-6
hereditarian ideas in 449
of J. Strong 162
in literature 277, 279, 282,
283
in McGuffey's Readers 162
in medicine 452
natural science and 445
of the Progressives 174
of Protestantism 393
of R. Bourne 161
of R.S. Baker 134
in religion 398
of S.N. Patten 147
science and 450
of the South 142
of Southern Baptists 379, 402
of the Vrooman family 164
1915 to the present 180, 191,
196
in education 232
of F.D. Roosevelt 185
in literature 297, 300
migration of from fascist
countries 186
of R. Niebuhr 189
radical 187
in religion 415, 418
See also Social Reform
Social welfare
F.D. Roosevelt's ideas on 184
growth of private organizations for
(1920s) 179
Protestantism and 365
See also Welfare state
Social work
1815-1915 137
professionalization of 149, 158
1915 to the present 178

Social workers, in the peace movement 160
Society for the Propagation of the
Gospel 351
Society for the Study of Natural
Philosophy 428
Society of Friends. See Quakers
Sociological jurisprudence. See
Jurisprudence, sociologi-
cal
Sociology
of colonial witchcraft 340
1815-1915 112, 152-53, 174
relationship to evolution 448
relationship to literary study
37-38
social Darwinism and 140
Spencer's influence on 138
history of 260
Songs, Nineteenth century 316
of American labor groups 311
regional 310
slave 70
See also Hymns; Spirituals
Soule, George 188
South Carolina
defense of slavery in colonial
128
natural science in Nineteenth
century 445
South Dakota, University of 233
Southern Aid Society 387
Southern California, University of
225
Southern Historical Association 266
Southern states
bibliography of the literature of
9
colonial period to 1815 23
architecture of 67
colleges in 202
Puritanism and 22, 351
revivals in 340
wit and humor in 303
1815-1915 27, 32-33, 135,
148
abolition in 403
American Historical Association and 254
architecture of 67, 71

Subject Index

Subject Index

Subject Index